BIRDS OF
SOUTH-EAST ASIA

BIRDS OF
SOUTH-EAST ASIA

Text and Illustrations by Norman Arlott

WILLIAM
COLLINS

DEDICATION

I dedicate this book to my wife Marie, in thanks for all her love and support.

This edition published in 2017 by William Collins,
An imprint of HarperCollins Publishers

1 London Bridge Street
London SE1 9GF

WilliamCollinsBooks.com

First published in 2017

A catalogue record for this book is available from the British Library.

ISBN 978-0-00-742954-7

William Collins uses papers that are natural, renewable and recyclable products made
from wood grown in sustainable forests. The manufacturing processes conform to the
environmental regulations of the country of origin.

Edited and designed by D & N Publishing, Baydon, Wiltshire
Cartography by Martin Brown

Printed and bound in Hong Kong by Printing Express Ltd

CONTENTS

ACKNOWLEDGEMENTS

Bird books take a relatively short time to paint and write, but the knowledge that enables them to be completed is gained over many, many years. I well remember that my passion started as a very young boy collecting bird's eggs (now, quite rightly, frowned upon) with my father. That passion has since been enhanced by being fortunate enough to be in the field with, and be inspired by some well known and not so well known 'birders'. I must mention the following who have encouraged me and allowed me to pick their brains over the years: the late John G. Williams; the late Eric Hosking; the late Crispin Fisher; Robert Gillmor; the late Basil Parsons, Brian Leflay and Moss Taylor.

This book could not have gone ahead without the help of the staff at the British Museum at Tring, especially Mark Adams and Robert Prys-Jones. David Price-Goodfellow and Sherry Valentine deserve special praise for their skill, and patience, in putting together the various component parts of this book.

Without publishers there would not be a book, so it gives me great pleasure to thank everyone at Harper Collins, particularly Myles Archibald and Julia Koppitz.

Last, but definitely not least, I must thank friends and family who have had to put up with my various mood changes whilst trying to sort out some of the more difficult aspects of putting this book together; my wife Marie probably endured more than most.

INTRODUCTION

The format of this book follows that of my Palearctic, West Indies, North American and Indian volumes.

Although my brief was, predominantly, to produce an illustrated checklist (space would not allow me to produce a 'full' field guide) it is hoped that within these pages I have given a helpful nudge towards what to look for when searching for new birds as well as being a reminder of birds seen.

Most of the text in this book is based on the type of notes I make before embarking on a field trip to a new area. Hopefully the text, along with the illustrations, will help to identify most birds encountered in South-East Asia. Obviously the use of more in-depth tomes will be required for some of the trickier species (see Further Reading).

I can only hope that with this work I have been able to add to the pleasure of anticipation or memory, and perhaps even added some extra piece of knowledge about the birds of this vast region.

AREA AND SPECIES COVERED

This book covers China (south of the line used to define the Palearctic in my previous books; this being a line drawn roughly NE from the mountains in NE Myanmar and N Yunnan through the mountains W of the Red Basin in Sichuan and the Qinling mountains in S Shaanxi then eastwards along the 34 degree latitude to the Yellow sea); Hainan (treated separately from SE China); Taiwan; Myanmar; Thailand; Laos; Cambodia; Vietnam; Peninsular Malaysia; Singapore and the Coco Islands.

I have endeavoured to include every species recorded in the region, apart from non-established introductions, and also as many of the major subspecies as possible. Each has been depicted in breeding plumage, and non-breeding plumage when it differs significantly. To keep the book to a manageable size, no juvenile plumages have been illustrated, although, when thought necessary and room permits, a short passage in 'Field notes' has been included.

The family order of the book follows closely the order used in my previous Indian guide. This will conflict with much of the 'modern' order used by the International Ornithological Congress (IOC), whose nomenclature I have used in the main. I have, as usual, tweaked much of the species order as a means to better plate composition. In many cases this is because I prefer to have similar-looking species next to, or close to, each other as an aid to identification – after all that is the main purpose of the book; hopefully this will not cause too much aggravation.

PLATES

The abbreviations and symbols used on the plates are as follows:
♂ = male, ♀ = female, br = breeding, n-br = non-breeding.

NOMENCLATURE

I have headlined the English names that I believe are those used by most birders in the field, which means I have, in many cases reverted to 'old school' names rather than some of the more modern interpretations. (Most of these 'new', along with other well-used names, are included in parenthesis.)

IDENTIFICATION

The illustrations should be all you need to identify a specific bird, but with some of the trickier species, more information is needed, hence the need for Field Notes, Voice and Habitat.

FIELD NOTES: Because of the need to keep text to a minimum this section rarely mentions those aspects of a bird that should be obvious from the illustrations, e.g. wing-bars, bill shape and so on. It is used mainly to point to a bird's habits or to mention facets of identification that are hidden in a standing or perched bird.

VOICE: Probably the first sign of a bird's presence. The descriptions are shown in *italics*. Where space has allowed I have included different interpretations of the same song. Although it is difficult to produce an accurate reproduction of bird songs or calls in the written word, this section is worth studying to get a feel for what is often the most important area of bird identification.

HABITAT: The main habitat preferences mentioned are those in which a species breeds, wintering habitats are included if appropriate.

DISTRIBUTION: Mainly general so should be read in conjunction with the maps.

Note: When mentioning Chinese areas, e.g. N, NE, NW, etc., these refer only to the parts of China in SE Asia and not the country as a whole.

DISTRIBUTION MAPS

Distribution maps (*see* pp.369–408) are shown for all species except vagrants and those seen rarely, those with a very limited distribution, species that have been recently introduced and those that spend most of their time at sea or only occur on offshore islands. They should only be used as a rough guide to where a species can be found at different times of the year. Red █ areas indicate where a species may be found in the summer on its breeding grounds; blue █ shows where it is found in winter when not breeding; and purple █ areas are where a species is a year-round resident.

MAP OF THE REGION

BIRD TOPOGRAPHY

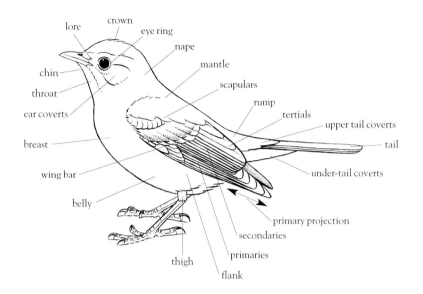

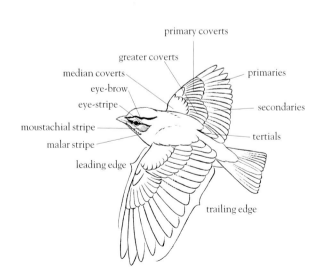

1 GEESE

1 SWAN GOOSE *Anser cygnoides* 81–94cm FIELD NOTES: Juvenile slightly duller and lacks white at the base of the bill. VOICE: Various honking and cackling calls, much like those of a domestic goose, usually uttered in flight. HABITAT: Lowland marshes and wet cultivation. DISTRIBUTION: Winter visitor to C and E China and Taiwan, vagrant elsewhere.

2 GREYLAG GOOSE *Anser anser* 75–90cm FIELD NOTES: Gregarious. In flight shows a distinctive pale grey forewing. Juvenile much as adult but more scaly with a duller bill. VOICE: In flight utters a deep, honking *aahng-ahng-ung*. HABITAT: Wet grassland, agricultural land, lakes, rivers and estuaries. DISTRIBUTION: Winters mainly in S China and Taiwan, vagrant elsewhere.

3 BEAN GOOSE *Anser fabalis* 66–84cm FIELD NOTES: Gregarious, often mixes with other geese. Juvenile more scaly on back, otherwise similar to adult. VOICE: Various cackling calls, a *wink-wink* and a deep nasal *hank-hank*. HABITAT: Marshes and wet agricultural land near lakes and rivers. DISTRIBUTION: Winters in C and E China, vagrant elsewhere.

4 WHITE-FRONTED GOOSE (GREATER WHITE-FRONTED GOOSE) *Anser albifrons* 64–78cm FIELD NOTES: In flight shows a uniform grey upperwing. Juvenile lacks white at base of the bill and has unmarked belly. VOICE: Typical goose cackling and a musical *lyo-lyok* flight call. HABITAT: Wet grassland, stubble fields, lakes and rivers. DISTRIBUTION: Winters in C and E China and Taiwan, vagrant elsewhere.

5 LESSER WHITE-FRONTED GOOSE *Anser erythropus* 53–66cm FIELD NOTES: Agile and quick moving compared to White-fronted Goose. Juvenile lacks white at the base of the bill and has unmarked belly. Differs from juvenile White-fronted Goose by having a yellow eye-ring, usually only visible at close range. VOICE: In flight utters a repeated, squeaky *kyu-yu-yu*. HABITAT: Wet grassland, agricultural land and around rivers and lakes. DISTRIBUTION: Winters in C and E China, vagrant elsewhere.

6 BAR-HEADED GOOSE *Anser indicus* 71–76cm FIELD NOTES: Usually occurs in small flocks. Juvenile has dark grey hind-neck and lacks black nape bars. VOICE: In flight utters a low, nasal honking. HABITAT: Freshwater rivers and lakes, fields and grassy areas. DISTRIBUTION: Winters in C China, rare in Myanmar and vagrant elsewhere.

7 SNOW GOOSE *Chen caerulescens* 65–84cm FIELD NOTES: In white phase, juvenile has grey crown, hind-neck, back and wings, the latter with white fringes. Juvenile blue phase is mainly dark slaty-brown. VOICE: In flight gives a nasal, cackling *la-luk*, said to resemble the barking of a small dog. HABITAT: Arable land in coastal areas. DISTRIBUTION: Rare winter visitor to E China.

8 BRENT GOOSE (BRANT or BLACK BRANT) *Branta bernicla* 55–66cm FIELD NOTES: Juvenile lacks white neck markings. Race occurring in the region is dark-bellied *B. b. nigricans* (Black Brant). VOICE: A rolling, gargling *raunk-raunk-raunk*. HABITAT: Coastal grasslands and bays. DISTRIBUTION: Scarce winter visitor to E China.

9 RED-BREASTED GOOSE *Branta ruficollis* 53–55cm FIELD NOTES: Unmistakeable; juvenile a dull version of adult. VOICE: In flight utters a squeaky, repeated *kik-yoik kik-yik*. HABITAT: Lakes, lagoons and on agricultural pastures. DISTRIBUTION: Rare winter vagrant to C China.

white phase

blue phase

2 SWANS; DUCKS

1 WHOOPER SWAN *Cygnus cygnus* 140–165cm FIELD NOTES: Longer-necked than Tundra Swan. Juvenile greyish-brown, slightly darker than juvenile Tundra Swan; base of bill pink. VOICE: Various honking and bugling calls. In flight utters a deep *hoop-hoop-hoop.* HABITAT: Wet pastures, lakes and large rivers. DISTRIBUTION: Winter visitor to E China.

2 TUNDRA SWAN (BEWICK'S SWAN) *Cygnus columbianus* 115–140cm FIELD NOTES: Shorter-necked than Whooper Swan. Juvenile greyish-brown, paler than juvenile Whooper Swan; base of bill pink. VOICE: Various honking and yapping calls. In flight gives a low *hoo-hoo.* HABITAT: Flooded grassland, rivers, lakes and sheltered coastal waters. DISTRIBUTION: Winters in C and E China and Taiwan.

3 MUTE SWAN *Cygnus olor* 125–155cm FIELD NOTES: Neck usually held more curved than previous two swans. In flight wings make a distinctive pulsating, throbbing sound. Juvenile dull brownish-grey; bill dull pinkish-grey lacking frontal knob. VOICE: Utters various hisses, grunts and snorts. HABITAT: Lakes, rivers and nearby grassy areas. DISTRIBUTION: Occasional winter visitor to S China.

4 RUDDY SHELDUCK *Tadorna ferruginea* 61–67cm FIELD NOTES: In flight shows extensive white forewing, above and below. Juvenile much as adult female, although slightly duller with an overall greyish-brown tone. VOICE: Utters a honking *aakh* or *ah-onk* also a repeated, trumpet-like *pok-pok-pok-pok.* HABITAT: Large rivers and lakes. DISTRIBUTION: Winter visitor to S, E China and Myanmar, vagrant elsewhere.

5 SHELDUCK (COMMON SHELDUCK) *Tadorna tadorna* 58–67cm FIELD NOTES: Appears black and white in flight due to extensive white forewing. Juvenile has white forehead, foreneck, chin and underparts, greyish scapulars and grey-brown hind-neck and face. VOICE: Male utters a thin, whistling *sliss-sliss-sliss-sliss;* female gives a rapid, nasal *gag-ag-ag-ag-ag-ak.* HABITAT: Large rivers, lakes, coastal mudflats and inland wetlands. DISTRIBUTION: Widespread winter visitor to S China, vagrant elsewhere.

6 KNOB-BILLED DUCK *Sarkidiornis melanotos* 56–76cm FIELD NOTES: In flight shows all-dark wings. Juvenile has back scaled with buff fringes; hindneck, crown and eye-stripe brownish-black, supercillium is pale buff; underparts, foreneck and face generally pale buff. VOICE: Usually silent. During breeding season may utter grunts, hisses and whistles. HABITAT: Lakes, rivers and swamps in sparsely wooded country. DISTRIBUTION: Resident from Myanmar, N Thailand and N Cambodia to Laos and extreme S China.

7 WHITE-WINGED DUCK *Asarcornis scutulata* 66–81cm FIELD NOTES: Shy and chiefly nocturnal. In flight shows extensive white forewing. Female as male but duller. VOICE: Generally silent; in flight may utter a wailing honk, ending in a nasal whistle. HABITAT: Streams and pools in tropical forest, also in nearby open swamp areas. DISTRIBUTION: Very rare local resident in Myanmar, Thailand, Cambodia, Laos and Vietnam.

white-headed phase

3 DUCKS

1 WIGEON (EURASIAN WIGEON) *Anas penelope* 45–50cm FIELD NOTES: In flight male shows large white patch on upperwing; underwing grey. Grazes more often than other ducks. VOICE: Male utters a clear, whistling *wheeooo*, female a growling *krrr*. HABITAT: Wet grasslands, marshes, lakes, rivers, coastal creeks and estuaries. DISTRIBUTION: Locally common winter visitor to China and Taiwan, less common further south.

2 AMERICAN WIGEON (BALDPATE) *Anas americana* 45–50cm FIELD NOTES: Male upperwing pattern very similar to Wigeon; grey underwing has white central area. VOICE: Male gives a distinct throaty, whistled *wiw-weew*, female a growling *rred*. HABITAT: Freshwater marshes. DISTRIBUTION: Rare vagrant to SE China.

3 FALCATED DUCK (FALCATED TEAL) *Anas falcata* 48–54cm FIELD NOTES: Often found in large numbers. Eclipse male similar to female but with blacker crown. VOICE: Male gives a low whistle followed by a wavering *uit-trr*, female a throaty *quack*. HABITAT: Freshwater lowland lakes, large rivers and marshes. Less commonly on coastal lagoons and estuaries. DISTRIBUTION: Winter visitor to S and E China and Taiwan, less common or rare further south.

4 GADWALL *Anas strepera* 46–55cm FIELD NOTES: In flight both sexes show a distinct white secondary patch on upperwing. Usually associates in small groups; can be quite wary. VOICE: Male gives a sharp *ahrk*, also a low whistle; female a mechanical-sounding *quack*. HABITAT: Freshwater lakes and marshes; less common on coastal lagoons and estuaries. DISTRIBUTION: Winter visitor to much of S China and Taiwan much more scarce further south.

5 MALLARD *Anas platyrhynchos* 50–65cm FIELD NOTES: Often found in large flocks. Eclipse male like female but bill dull yellow. VOICE: Male utters a rasped *kreep*, female a *quack-quack-quack*. HABITAT: Lakes, ponds, rivers and estuaries. DISTRIBUTION: Locally common winter visitor to S China and Taiwan, less common or rare further south.

6 ANDAMAN TEAL (SUNDA TEAL) *Anas gibberifrons* 37–47cm FIELD NOTES: White facial markings variable, two extremes shown. In flight upperwing shows broad white wing-bar; underwing shows white axillaries. VOICE: Male utters a clear, low *preep*, female a series of loud, laughing *quacks*. HABITAT: Freshwater marshes and pools, paddyfields, mangrove swamps, coastal lagoons and estuaries. DISTRIBUTION: Vagrant to S Myanmar.

7 SPOT-BILLED DUCK (INDIAN or WESTERN SPOT-BILLED DUCK) *Anas poecilorhyncha* 58–63cm FIELD NOTES: In flight, from above, shows large white patch on tertials and green speculum; from below wing shows dark primaries and secondaries contrasting with white coverts. VOICE: Calls very similar to those of Mallard. HABITAT: Well-vegetated lakes, pools and marshes. DISTRIBUTION: Widespread resident over much of southernmost China, Myanmar, Thailand, Laos, Cambodia and northern Vietnam.

8 CHINESE SPOT-BILLED DUCK (EASTERN SPOT-BILLED DUCK) *Anas zonorhyncha* 53cm FIELD NOTES: In flight looks plain, with blue speculum. VOICE: Calls similar to Mallard. HABITAT: Well-vegetated lakes, pools and marshes. DISTRIBUTION: Breeds over much of China. Northern populations move south to join resident populations in SE China, southernmost China and northern areas of Myanmar, Laos and Vietnam.

9 PHILIPPINE DUCK *Anas luzonica* 48–58cm FIELD NOTES: In flight, from below, shows whitish coverts and dark grey primaries and secondaries. Juvenile like adult but duller. VOICE: Similar to Mallard, but slightly harsher. HABITAT: Lakes, rivers, marshes and tidal creeks. DISTRIBUTION: Rare vagrant.

10 SHOVELER (NORTHERN or EUROPEAN SHOVELER) *Anas clypeata* 44–52cm FIELD NOTES: Due to large bill, birds in flight look 'front heavy'. Male upperwing shows pale blue forewing and green speculum separated by a white wing-bar, female wing duller with thinner white wing-bar. VOICE: Generally silent. Female has a quacking *gak-gak-gak-ga-ga*. HABITAT: Open freshwater areas, less often on coastal lagoons and estuaries. DISTRIBUTION: Widespread winter visitor to China, less common further south.

white-faced form

n-br

br

4 DUCKS

1 PINTAIL (NORTHERN PINTAIL) *Anas acuta* 51–56cm (Male with tail 61–66cm) FIELD NOTES: Gregarious. Long neck and tail make for an elongated look in flight. VOICE: Generally silent, but male may give a mellow *proop-proop;* female utters a series of weak *quacks* and a low croak if flushed. HABITAT: Lakes, marshes, coastal lagoons and estuaries. DISTRIBUTION: Widespread winter visitor, vagrant in the far south.

2 GARGANEY *Anas querquedula* 37–41cm FIELD NOTES: Gregarious, often in large flocks. In flight, from above, male shows pale grey forewing separated from green speculum by white wing-bar; at a distance can look very pale winged. VOICE: Generally silent but male may utter a rattling *knerek* and the female a high nasal *quack.* HABITAT: Freshwater lakes, marshes and coastal lagoons. DISTRIBUTION: Widespread winter visitor.

3 BAIKAL TEAL (FORMOSA TEAL) *Anas formosa* 39–43cm FIELD NOTES: Gregarious, often forms large flocks. Eclipse male shows a 'shadow' of distinctive breeding facial pattern. Female similar to female Teal; note pale loral spot. VOICE: Male utters a clucking *wot-wot-wot* and female a low *quack.* HABITAT: Fresh and brackish water areas. DISTRIBUTION: Widespread in SE China and Taiwan, vagrant elsewhere.

4 TEAL (COMMON or EURASIAN TEAL) *Anas crecca* 34–38cm FIELD NOTES: Flight is rapid with much twisting and turning. In flight, from above, male shows dark grey forewing separated from green speculum by a white wing-bar. VOICE: Male utters a soft, high-pitched *preep-preep.* Females generally silent although may give a nasal *quack* when alarmed. HABITAT: Lakes, pools, marshes and estuaries. DISTRIBUTION: Widespread winter visitor.

5 GREEN-WINGED TEAL *Anas carolinensis* 34–38cm FIELD NOTES: Compared to Teal has a white breast stripe and lacks yellow lining on facial pattern. Female very similar to female Teal. VOICE: As Teal. HABITAT: As Teal DISTRIBUTION: Rare vagrant.

6 PINK-HEADED DUCK *Rhodonessa caryophyllacea* 60cm FIELD NOTES: Secretive. Feeds by both dabbling and diving. May perch in trees. VOICE: Male gives a low, weak, wheezy whistle; female a low *quack.* HABITAT: Secluded marshes and pools in elephant-grass jungle. DISTRIBUTION: Resident in Myanmar, although almost certainly now extinct.

7 RED-CRESTED POCHARD *Netta rufina* 53–57cm FIELD NOTES: Upperwing of both sexes show very pale grey flight feathers with a narrow blackish trailing edge. Male in eclipse has a red bill, otherwise similar to female. VOICE: Generally silent. HABITAT: Freshwater lakes, rivers and sometimes coastal waters. DISTRIBUTION: Winter visitor to Myanmar and scattered locations in S China.

8 WHITE-HEADED DUCK (WHITE-HEADED STIFFTAIL) *Oxyura leucocephala* 43–48cm FIELD NOTES: Usually in small parties. Juvenile a duller version of adult female, some may show a complete brownish-black head. VOICE: Usually silent. HABITAT: Lakes and brackish lagoons with fringing vegetation. DISTRIBUTION: Rare vagrant.

9 COTTON PYGMY GOOSE (COTTON TEAL) *Nettapus coromandelianus* 30–37cm FIELD NOTES: Occurs in pairs or small parties. Regularly perches in trees. Male in flight shows white primaries with black tips and a white trailing edge to secondaries; female primaries all black. VOICE: Male utters a sharp *car-car-carawak,* female gives a weak *quack.* HABITAT: Vegetated freshwater ponds, lakes and marshes. DISTRIBUTION: Widespread breeder, Chinese birds move south during the winter.

10 MANDARIN (MANDARIN DUCK) *Aix galericulata* 41–49cm FIELD NOTES: Unmistakeable. Eclipse male has pink bill, otherwise much like female. VOICE: Male may utter a whistled *hwick* in flight or short whistles during display, otherwise generally silent. Female makes low clucking notes, usually only given when tending young or in display. HABITAT: Lakes and rivers with surrounding trees and shrubs. In winter may be on more open waters. DISTRIBUTION: Breeds in Taiwan, winter visitor to S China, vagrant elsewhere.

5 DUCKS

1 POCHARD (COMMON or EUROPEAN POCHARD) *Aythya ferina* 42–49cm
FIELD NOTES: Gregarious, often in very large flocks. In flight shows pale grey flight feathers and darker forewing. VOICE: Generally silent. HABITAT: Large open lakes. Occasionally seen on rivers and coastal waters. DISTRIBUTION: Widespread winter visitor in S China, Taiwan, N Myanmar, N Thailand, N Laos and N Vietnam.

2 CANVASBACK *Aythya valisineria* 48–61cm FIELD NOTES: Sloping forehead. In flight upperwing of male very pale. VOICE: Generally silent away from breeding grounds. HABITAT: Winters on open lakes, estuaries and sheltered coastal waters. DISTRIBUTION: Rare vagrant.

3 REDHEAD *Aythya americana* 45–56cm FIELD NOTES: Steep forehead. Male has black-tipped blue bill. In flight upperwing of both sexes show pale grey secondaries. VOICE: Generally silent away from breeding sites. HABITAT: Freshwater lakes, marshes and coastal waters. DISTRIBUTION: Rare vagrant.

4 FERRUGINOUS DUCK (COMMON WHITE-EYE, WHITE-EYED POCHARD)
Aythya nyroca 38–42cm FIELD NOTES: Rather secretive, usually in pairs or small groups. In flight upperwing of both sexes has distinct wide white bar across all flight feathers. Underwing and large oval belly spot white. VOICE: Generally silent away from breeding sites. HABITAT: Marshes, lakes, coastal lagoons and estuaries. DISTRIBUTION: Winter visitor to SW and C China, much of Myanmar, N Thailand and N Vietnam.

5 BAER'S POCHARD (BAER'S or SIBERIAN WHITE-EYE) *Aythya baeri* 41–46cm
FIELD NOTES: Usually in pairs or small parties. In flight upperwing of both sexes shows a prominent white bar on all flight feathers. VOICE: Generally silent. HABITAT: Ponds, lakes, rivers and marshes. DISTRIBUTION: Winter visitor to S China, Taiwan, W Myanmar, N Thailand, N Laos and N Vietnam.

6 TUFTED DUCK *Aythya fuligula* 40–47cm FIELD NOTES: Gregarious, often in large numbers. In flight upperwing of both sexes shows a prominent white wing-bar on all flight feathers. VOICE: Usually silent, may give a low growl when flushed. HABITAT: Lakes, large rivers and sheltered coastal waters. DISTRIBUTION: Widespread in winter in S China and Taiwan, less common in Myanmar, NW and C Thailand and N Vietnam; vagrant elsewhere.

7 SCAUP (GREATER SCAUP) *Aythya marila* 40–51cm FIELD NOTES: Gregarious. In flight upperwing of both sexes shows a prominent white wing-bar across all flight feathers; male has a grey forewing. VOICE: Generally silent. HABITAT: Coastal waters, estuaries and inland freshwater lakes and reservoirs. DISTRIBUTION: Winter visitor to S and SE China and Taiwan; vagrant elsewhere.

8 WHITE-WINGED SCOTER *Melanitta deglandi* 51–58cm FIELD NOTES: Gregarious, often in large flocks. In flight both sexes show distinctive white secondaries. VOICE: Generally silent. HABITAT: Coastal waters, may resort to freshwater lakes during migration. DISTRIBUTION: Winter visitor to coast of SE China.

9 BLACK SCOTER *Melanitta americana* 44–54cm FIELD NOTES: Gregarious, often forms large flocks. Regularly seen flying low over sea in long undulating lines.VOICE: Generally silent. HABITAT: Coastal waters. Migrating birds may occasionally stop over on freshwater lakes. DISTRIBUTION: Uncommon winter visitor to SE China coast.

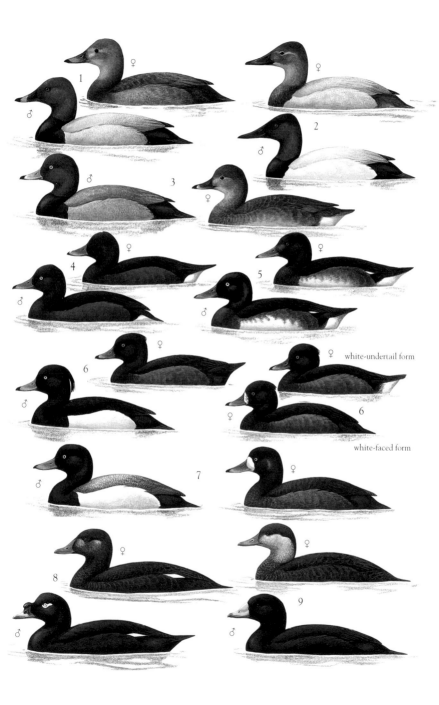

white-undertail form

white-faced form

6 DUCKS

1 LONG-TAILED DUCK (OLDSQUAW) *Clangula hyemalis* 36–47cm (male with tail 48–60cm) FIELD NOTES: Often winters in sexually segregated groups. In winter, facial patches sometimes very weakly coloured, which can make birds appear white headed. Both sexes show all-dark wings in flight, contrasting with mainly white body. VOICE: Male utters a yodelling *ow-ow-owlee…caloocaloo*. Female renders various weak *quacks*. HABITAT: Mainly shallow coastal waters, but will use inland freshwater lakes. DISTRIBUTION: Rare winter visitor in SE China.

2 GOLDENEYE (COMMON GOLDENEYE) *Bucephala clangula* 42–50cm FIELD NOTES: Gregarious, often encountered in large flocks. In flight upperwing of male shows large white patch on inner wing, female's white patch crossed by two black bars. VOICE: Usually silent. HABITAT: Lakes and coastal waters. DISTRIBUTION: Winter visitor over much of S China and Taiwan, vagrant elsewhere.

3 SMEW *Mergellus albellus* 38–44cm FIELD NOTES: In winter often found in sexually segregated flocks. Upperwing of both sexes shows white patch on forewing. VOICE: Generally silent. HABITAT: Freshwater lakes, large rivers, estuaries and sheltered coastal bays. DISTRIBUTION: Uncommon winter visitor over much of S China, vagrant elsewhere.

4 RED-BREASTED MERGANSER *Mergus serrator* 52–58cm FIELD NOTES: In flight both sexes show much white on the inner part of upperwing. VOICE: Generally silent. HABITAT: Inshore and coastal waters. DISTRIBUTION: Winter visitor to coastal areas of S and SE China and Taiwan.

5 GOOSANDER (COMMON MERGANSER) *Mergus merganser* 58–72cm FIELD NOTES: Inner part of male upperwing shows extensive white patch, female similar but forewing greyer. VOICE: Generally silent away from breeding sites. HABITAT: Lakes, rivers and coastal bays. DISTRIBUTION: Common winter visitor over much of S China and N Myanmar, vagrant elsewhere.

6 SCALY-SIDED MERGANSER (CHINESE MERGANSER) *Mergus squamatus* 52–62cm FIELD NOTES: Both sexes show much white on upperwing, similar to Red-breasted Merganser. Usually in pairs or small parties. VOICE: Generally silent away from breeding areas. HABITAT: Large rivers and lakes. DISTRIBUTION: Winters mainly in SE China, vagrant elsewhere.

7 FULVOUS WHISTLING DUCK (FULVOUS TREE DUCK) *Dendrocygna bicolor* 45–53cm FIELD NOTES: Usually occurs in small flocks. In flight, wings all dark brown. Juvenile paler and duller. VOICE: Very vocal. In flight, when feeding and at rest utters a wader-like, whistled *k-weeoo k-weeoo*. Also gives a harsh *kee kee kee* during disputes. HABITAT: Freshwater lakes and marshes with fringing vegetation. DISTRIBUTION: Rare resident in W and SW Myanmar.

8 LESSER WHISTLING DUCK (LESSER TREE DUCK) *Dendrocygna javanica* 38–42cm FIELD NOTES: Usually occurs in small flocks of around a dozen birds, occasionally in much larger groups. In flight shows chestnut forewing. At close range note yellow eye-ring. VOICE: In flight utters a constant thin, whistled *whi-whee*. HABITAT: Mainly freshwater pools, lakes and swamps with fringing vegetation; also noted on paddyfields and mangroves. DISTRIBUTION: Widespread resident from SE China south to Peninsular Malaysia; SE China birds move south after breeding.

9 WANDERING WHISTLING DUCK (WANDERING TREE DUCK) *Dendrocygna arcuata* 40–45cm FIELD NOTES: Gregarious, often in large flocks. Note white outer uppertail coverts. VOICE: A high-pitched, twittering *pwit-wit-ti-t-t…* Also utters high-pitched whistles, usually when in flight. HABITAT: Various wetlands including freshwater lakes and marshes. DISTRIBUTION: Scarce introduced resident in Singapore.

7 SCRUBFOWL; SNOWCOCK; SNOW PARTRIDGE; MONAL PARTRIDGES; FRANCOLIN; PARTRIDGES

1 NICOBAR SCRUBFOWL (NICOBAR MEGAPODE) *Megapodius nicobariensis* 43cm FIELD NOTES: Usually in pairs or family groups. A ground forager, takes to trees when alarmed. VOICE: A cackling *kuk-a-kuk-kuk* and bullfrog-like *kiouk-kiouk-kok-kok-kok-kok...* HABITAT: Coastal forest. DISTRIBUTION: May be resident on Coco Island, but probably extinct due to natural disasters and/or human disturbance.

2 TIBETAN SNOWCOCK *Tetraogallus tibetanus* 50–56cm FIELD NOTES: Shy and wary. Occurs in pairs or small parties. Often walks with tail raised and undertail-coverts fluffed out. VOICE: A croaking *gu-gu-gu-gu*, also a chuckling *chuck-aa-chuck-aa-chuck-chuck-chee-da-da-da*. HABITAT: High alpine pastures, bare or grassy mountain slopes. DISTRIBUTION: Possibly occurs in the mountainous regions in the NW of South-East Asia.

3 SNOW PARTRIDGE *Lerwa lerwa* 38–40cm FIELD NOTES: Occurs in pairs or small groups. If flushed flies rapidly downhill on whirring and clapping wings. VOICE: A clear *jiju jiju jiju* that gradually quickens and rises in pitch. HABITAT: High-altitude grassy, shrubby mountain slopes. DISTRIBUTION: Mountainous regions in NW China.

4 SZÉCHENYI'S MONAL PARTRIDGE (BUFF-THROATED PARTRIDGE) *Tetraophasis szechenyii* 50cm FIELD NOTES: Occurs in small parties, larger parties recorded post breeding. When disturbed tends to 'freeze' or fly into nearby forest cover. VOICE: Loud 2–4 note cackling interspersed with grating notes. HABITAT: Rocky ravines in mountain forests. DISTRIBUTION: Resident in the mountainous regions of NW China.

5 VERREAUX'S MONAL PARTRIDGE (CHESTNUT-THROATED PARTRIDGE) *Tetraophasis obscurus* 48cm FIELD NOTES: Little recorded. When disturbed tends to walk off with tail cocked. VOICE: Similar to Széchenyi's Monal Partridge apart from a loud 'cry' when flushed. HABITAT: Alpine meadows and scree near treeline, also in rhododendron scrub. DISTRIBUTION: Possibly resident in the mountainous regions of NW China.

6 CHINESE FRANCOLIN *Francolinus pintadeanus* 31–34cm FIELD NOTES: Wary, although often sings from a prominent perch. VOICE: A harsh, metallic *kak-kak-kuich ka-ka* or *wi-ta-tak-takaa*, normally repeated after lengthy pauses. HABITAT: Dry, open forest and scrub-covered hills. DISTRIBUTION: Resident in S and SE China, Myanmar, much of Vietnam, Laos, Cambodia and Thailand, although absent from the peninsular.

7 TIBETAN PARTRIDGE *Perdix hodgsoniae* 28–31cm FIELD NOTES: Often encountered in groups of 10–15 birds. Usually runs for cover rather than taking wing. VOICE: A rattling *scherrrrreck-scherrrrrreck*. HABITAT: Rocky mountain slopes, scrubby alpine meadows. DISTRIBUTION: Possible resident in the mountainous regions in NW China.

8 DAURIAN PARTRIDGE (MONGOLIAN or BEARDED PARTRIDGE) *Perdix dauurica* 28–30cm FIELD NOTES: Usually occurs in parties of 15–30 birds, with larger groups in winter. VOICE: Various creaking calls. HABITAT: Variable; occurring on plains, montane foothills, riverine scrub and rocky hills, prefers light wooded areas with nearby grassland. DISTRIBUTION: May occur in the far north region of the region.

9 CHUKAR (CHUKAR PARTRIDGE) *Alectoris chukar* 32–34cm FIELD NOTES: Usually in small parties. VOICE: Typically a *chuck chuck chuck* or *chuck chuck chuck chuckARR chuckARR chuckARR*. HABITAT: Mountain slopes, semi-arid hills and grassy slopes. DISTRIBUTION: May occur in the mountainous regions of N China.

10 LONG-BILLED PARTRIDGE *Rhizothera longirostris* 36–41cm FIELD NOTES: When flushed flies to rest in trees, little else recorded. VOICE: A dueted, bell-like *ti-ooah-whee*, repeated over long periods. HABITAT: Lowland and montane forest, also bamboo. DISTRIBUTION: Resident in extreme S Myanmar, peninsular areas of Thailand and Malaysia.

11 BLACK PARTRIDGE *Melanoperdix niger* 24–27cm FIELD NOTES: Shy. Generally in pairs, but little else recorded. VOICE: A low, creaking contact call. HABITAT: Evergreen forest. DISTRIBUTION: Scarce resident on Peninsular Malaysia.

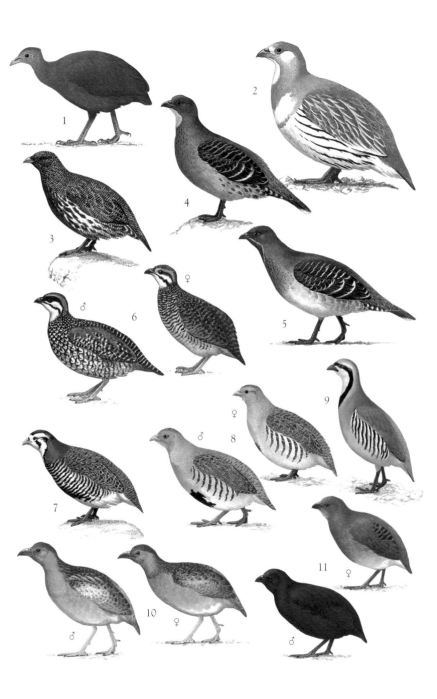

8 PARTRIDGES

1 HILL PARTRIDGE (COMMON or NECKLACED HILL PARTRIDGE)
Arborophila torqueola 28–30cm FIELD NOTES: Forages in forest litter in small parties. Roosts in trees. VOICE: A mournful, repeated *pooo* or *pheaw* followed by a rising, whistled *do-eat do-eat do-eat do-eat*. Also duets, female uttering a *kwikwikwikwikwik* while male joins in with a series of *do-eat* calls. HABITAT: Montane oak forest mixed with laurel and rhododendron. DISTRIBUTION: Resident in N, W Myanmar, N Vietnam and SW China.

2 RUFOUS-THROATED PARTRIDGE *Arborophila rufogularis* 26–29cm FIELD
NOTES: Actions similar to Hill Partridge. Dark throated race *A. r. intermedia* (2b) occurs in N Myanmar and SE China; race *A. r. guttata* (2c) occurs in Laos and Vietnam, *A. r. annamensis* (2d) occurs in S Annam region of Vietnam. VOICE: A far-carrying, mournful *wheeea-whu*, occasionally given in a repeated series, ascending and ending abruptly. HABITAT: Montane oak forest mixed with laurel and rhododendron with thick undergrowth. DISTRIBUTION: Resident in N Myanmar, N Thailand, N Laos, Vietnam and SE China.

3 WHITE-CHEEKED PARTRIDGE *Arborophila atrogularis* 25–27cm FIELD NOTES:
Actions and habits similar to Hill Partridge. VOICE: A far-carrying, quavering *prrrer prrrer prrrer prrrer…* ascending, accelerating and ending abruptly. Often followed by a number of *wi-chu* notes. HABITAT: Bamboo and damp undergrowth in broadleaved evergreen forest. DISTRIBUTION: Resident in N Myanmar and SW China.

4 TAIWAN PARTRIDGE *Arborophila crudigularis* 27–28cm FIELD NOTES: Forages on the ground in small parties. Roosts in trees. VOICE: A soft whistle, presumably used as a territorial call. HABITAT: Thickets and damp undergrowth in broadleaved evergreen forest. DISTRIBUTION: Resident in Taiwan.

5 BAR-BACKED PARTRIDGE (BROWN-BREASTED HILL PARTRIDGE)
Arborophila brunneopectus 26–29cm FIELD NOTES: Actions much as Hill Partridge. White-throated race *A. b. albigula* (5b) occurs in SC Vietnam. VOICE: Call is a whistled *ti-hu ti-hu ti-hu* preceded by a series of throaty *brr* notes. Often duets, partner answering with a repeated *kew-kew-kew*. HABITAT: Broadleaved evergreen forest. DISTRIBUTION: Resident in SW China, E Myanmar, N, W Thailand and N, SC Vietnam.

6 SICHUAN PARTRIDGE *Arborophila rufipectus* 29–31cm FIELD NOTES: Actions and habits similar to Hill Partridge. VOICE: A slow *ho-wo ho-wo*, also a complex whistle. HABITAT: Broadleaved forest with an understorey of bamboo and other shrubs. DISTRIBUTION: Probably resident in SW China (extreme NW Yunnan and SE Sichuan).

7 MALAYSIAN PARTRIDGE *Arborophila campbelli* 28cm FIELD NOTES: Habits unrecorded, presumably similar to others of the genus. VOICE: A series of loud, whistled *pi-hor* notes preceded by a soft whistled *oii oii oii…* HABITAT: Undergrowth in broadleaved evergreen forest. DISTRIBUTION: Resident in the central highlands of Peninsular Malaysia.

8 WHITE-NECKLACED PARTRIDGE (COLLARED HILL PARTRIDGE)
Arborophila gingica 30cm FIELD NOTES: Actions and habits presumed to be similar to others of the genus. VOICE: A far-carrying, mournful, repeated *wooop* or a quickly repeated *co-qwee*. HABITAT: Dense, moist forest in foothills and mountains. DISTRIBUTION: Resident in SE China.

9 ORANGE-NECKED PARTRIDGE *Arborophila davidi* 27cm FIELD NOTES: Forages among forest leaf litter in forest undergrowth. VOICE: A repeated *prruu* accelerating and becoming higher pitched. Also a faster series of plaintive piping *tu* notes – up to 60. Often duets, partner responding with a repeated *tchew-tchew-tchew*. HABITAT: Broadleaved evergreen and semi-evergreen forests in low hills, preferring non-thorny bamboo forest with sparse undergrowth. DISTRIBUTION: Resident in E Cochinchina region of S Vietnam.

10 CHESTNUT-HEADED PARTRIDGE (CAMBODIAN HILL PARTRIDGE)
Arborophila cambodiana 28cm FIELD NOTES: Actions similar to Hill Partridge, although said to be easier to approach than others of the genus. VOICE: Unknown. HABITAT: Broadleaved evergreen forest. DISTRIBUTION: Resident in SW Cambodia.

intermedia 2b

guttata 2c

annamensis 2d

1 ♀ ♂

2 ♀ ♂

albigula 5b

3

4 ♀

5

6 ♀ ♂

7

8

9

10

9 PARTRIDGES; WOOD PARTRIDGES; BAMBOO PARTRIDGES; GROUSE

1 SIAMESE PARTRIDGE *Arborophila diversa* 28cm FIELD NOTES: No details recorded, actions as Hill Partridge? VOICE: A whistled *tu-u---hu tu-u---hu.* HABITAT: Tropical evergreen forest. DISTRIBUTION: Resident in the Khao Sabap Mountains in SE Thailand.

2 HAINAN PARTRIDGE *Arborophila ardens* 26–28cm FIELD NOTES: Forages among leaf litter, usually singly, in pairs or small parties. VOICE: A repeated whistled *kwe-ho kwe-ho kwe-ho,* sometimes accelerating and rising in pitch. HABITAT: Broadleaved evergreen tropical forest understorey, also monsoon evergreen forest. DISTRIBUTION: Resident on Hainan.

3 GREEN-LEGGED PARTRIDGE *Arborophila chloropus* 26–31cm FIELD NOTES: Actions similar to others of the genus. Race *A. c. cognacqi* (3b) occurs in the Cochinchina region of S Vietnam. VOICE: A plaintive *tu-tu…tu-tu…tu-tu…tu tu tu tu tututututututu CHIRRA-CHEW-CHIRRA-CHEW-CHIRRA-CHEW* that ascends then descends. HABITAT: Dense evergreen and mixed deciduous primary forest with bamboo thickets. DISTRIBUTION: Resident in SW China, Myanmar, N and W Thailand, Cambodia, Laos and S Vietnam.

4 ANNAM PARTRIDGE *Arborophila merlini* 29cm FIELD NOTES: Actions similar to Hill Partridge. VOICE: Very similar to Green-legged Partridge. HABITAT: Lowland broadleaved evergreen and secondary growth. DISTRIBUTION: Resident in NC Annam in Vietnam.

5 CHESTNUT-NECKLACED PARTRIDGE *Arborophila charltoni* 26–32cm FIELD NOTES: Shy, forages on the ground at forest edge; usually in small parties. Race *A. c. tonkinensis* (5b) occurs in N Vietnam. VOICE: Similar to Green-legged Partridge. HABITAT: Dense lowland jungle and foothills with dense evergreen forest. DISTRIBUTION: Resident in S Thailand, Peninsular Malaysia and N Vietnam. Some authors place N Vietnamese subspecies with Green-legged Partridge.

6 FERRUGINOUS PARTRIDGE *Caloperdix oculeus* 23–27cm FIELD NOTES: Forages on the forest floor, singly, in pairs or sometimes larger parties. VOICE: A rising *pi-pi-pi-pipipipipipi,* repeated 8–9 times, followed by a clanging *dit-duit dit-duit.* HABITAT: Broadleaved evergreen forest, bamboo and freshwater swamp forest. DISTRIBUTION: Resident in S Myanmar and peninsular Thailand and Malaysia.

7 CRESTED PARTRIDGE *Rollulus rouloul* 25cm FIELD NOTES: Forages on the ground among leaf litter, usually singly or in pairs. With a brisk gait. VOICE: A long series of mournful *si-ul* whistles, second note higher-pitched. HABITAT: Lowland rainforest. DISTRIBUTION: Resident in S Myanmar and peninsular Thailand and Malaysia.

8 MOUNTAIN BAMBOO PARTRIDGE *Bambusicola fytchii* 25–30cm FIELD NOTES: Usually in family parties of 5–6. Wary, feeds early morning and late evening. VOICE: A rapidly repeated, cackling. HABITAT: Various open and scrubby areas, including tall grassland in damp areas, bamboo patches and woodland. DISTRIBUTION: Resident in SW China, W, N and E Myanmar, NW Thailand, N Laos and N Vietnam.

9 CHINESE BAMBOO PARTRIDGE *Bambusicola thoracicus* 30–32cm FIELD NOTES: Occurs in pairs or groups of up to 20, with larger groups recorded in winter. VOICE: A loud *gi-gi-gi-gi-gi-gigeroi-gigeroi* also a dueted *killy-killy e-put-kwai.* In non-breeding season utters a *sih-mo-kuai sih-mo-kuai* often transcribed as *people pray people pray.* HABITAT: Bamboo, shrubs and grassy areas. DISTRIBUTION: Widespread resident over C, E and SE China.

10 TAIWAN BAMBOO PARTRIDGE *Bambusicola sonorivox* 30–32cm FIELD NOTES: Forages on the ground in pairs or small groups. VOICE: Similar to Chinese Bamboo Partridge. HABITAT: Bamboo and grassy areas. DISTRIBUTION: Taiwan.

11 SEVERTSOV'S GROUSE (CHINESE GROUSE) *Tetrastes sewerzowi* 34cm FIELD NOTES: Forages for buds, shoots, seeds, flowers and berries on ground and in trees and bushes. Winters in small- to medium-sized flocks (c12) in valley bottoms. VOICE: During confrontations male utters a hoarse *en er en er en…* HABITAT: Montane conifer forests with thickets of birch or willow. DISTRIBUTION: Possibly resident in NW Yunnan region of SW China.

cognacqi

tonkinensis

10 TRAGOPANS; MONALS; PHEASANTS; JUNGLEFOWL

1 TEMMINCK'S TRAGOPAN *Tragopan temminckii* male 64cm, female 58cm FIELD NOTES: Wary. Often feeds in trees. During spectacular display inflates bare skin of throat, showing off a dark blue oval, spotted paler blue and surrounded by a pale blue rim with red patches. VOICE: During breeding season gives an *eerie woh – woah – woah – woah – waah – waah – waah – waah - griiiik.*HABITAT: Temperate and subalpine forests with dense undergrowth. DISTRIBUTION: Resident in SW, C China, N Myanmar and N Vietnam.

2 BLYTH'S TRAGOPAN *Tragopan blythii* male 65–70cm, female 58cm FIELD NOTES: Little known, actions and habits probably similar to other Tragopans. VOICE: Male utters a loud, moaning *ohh ohhah – ohaah ohaaah – ohaaaha – ohaaaha ohaaaha.* Also a resounding *gock gock gock* or *wak wak wak* given during display. HABITAT: Lush broadleaved forest with dense understorey. DISTRIBUTION: Resident in W, N Myanmar.

3 CABOT'S TRAGOPAN *Tragopan caboti* male 61cm, female 50cm FIELD NOTES: Forages on the ground and in trees in small groups usually in early morning or late afternoon. VOICE: Territorial call resembles babies' cry, *wa-r* followed by a few *gua* notes. When alarmed utters a loud *gua-gua-gua,* often continuing for several minutes. During the breeding season a fast, continuous *chi-chi-chi chi-chi-chi chi-chi-chi…* sound is made by rapid beating of the wings. HABITAT: Evergreen and mixed forest, also recorded in open country above the tree line during summer. DISTRIBUTION: Resident in SE China.

4 HIMALAYAN MONAL *Lophophorus impejanus* 64–72cm FIELD NOTES: Plumage variable both in colour of gloss on breast, from green to purple, and amount of white on back; some have no white. A little less wary than others of the genus, usually occurring singly or in small, loose parties. VOICE: A ringing *kur-lieu* or *kleeh-wick.* HABITAT: Coniferous and broadleaved forest with thick understorey, venturing onto alpine meadows in summer. DISTRIBUTION: Rare resident in extreme N Myanmar.

5 SCLATER'S MONAL *Lophophorus sclateri* 64–68cm FIELD NOTES: Little known, actions said to be similar to the previous species. VOICE: A loud, whistled *go-li,* said to sound like part owl and part curlew. HABITAT: Open broadleaved, mixed broadleaved and coniferous forest, forest edge, scrub and alpine meadows. DISTRIBUTION: Resident in eastern N Myanmar, possibly also in NW region of Yunnan in SW China.

6 CHINESE MONAL *Lophophorus lhuysii* 72–80cm FIELD NOTES: Occurs in parties of 2–8 individuals. Forages on the ground feeding on bulbs, tubers, mosses, flowers and leaves. VOICE: A repeated *guli* and a whistled *guo-guo-guo* uttered every few minutes, starting high then dropping before fading at the end. HABITAT: High-elevation coniferous and rhododendron forests and adjacent alpine and subalpine rocky meadows. DISTRIBUTION: Possibly resident in the NW region of Yunnan in SW China.

7 BLOOD PHEASANT *Ithaginis cruentus* 44–48cm FIELD NOTES: Usually encountered in small groups, often quite tame, rarely flies. Race *L. c. clarkei* (7b) occurs in SW China. VOICE: A repeated *chuck* or *chic,* a high-pitched, repetitive *see* and when maintaining contact utters a loud *sree-cheeu-cheeu* or a high trill. HABITAT: Forest or scrub at mid to high altitudes, resorts to lower forests during bad winters. DISTRIBUTION: Resident in N Myanmar and in NW Yunnan region of SW China.

8 KOKLASS PHEASANT *Pucrasia macrolopha* male 56–64cm, female 52–56cm FIELD NOTES: Wary. Small groups forage early and late in the day. Roosts socially, in trees. VOICE: Early morning call is a loud *kok-kok-kok-kok ko-kras.* HABITAT: Coniferous and mixed forest with thick understorey. DISTRIBUTION: Widespread over much of C and SE China.

9 RED JUNGLEFOWL *Gallus gallus* male 65–78cm, female 41–46cm FIELD NOTES: Generally in small groups: a male and several females. Race *G. g. spadicus* (9b) occurs over much of the area away from central SE Asia. VOICE: *Cock-a-doodle-do,* similar to farmyard cockerel, although with a more shrill and strangulated finish. HABITAT: Forest undergrowth and scrub. DISTRIBUTION: Resident over most of the region from S China southward.

clarkei

7b

spadiceus

9b

11 PHEASANTS

1 KALIJ PHEASANT *Lophura leucomelanos* male 63–74cm, female 50–60cm FIELD NOTES: Wary. Usually occurs in small groups, forages early or late. Variable; main portrait *L. l. lathami* occurs in SW China, *L. l. williamsi* (1b) from NW Myanmar and *L. l. crawfordi* (1c) from SE Myanmar and SW Thailand. The latter is often considered a race of Silver Pheasant. VOICE: At dawn or dusk gives a loud whistling chuckle or chirrup. When alarmed utters a rapid *koorchi koorchi* or *whoop-keet-keet.* HABITAT: Forests with dense undergrowth. DISTRIBUTION: Resident over much of the northern areas of Myanmar and in NW Yunnan in SW China.

2 SILVER PHEASANT *Lophura nycthemera* male 80–125cm, female 56–70cm FIELD NOTES: Encountered in small groups; forages on the ground. Tends to run when disturbed. Distinctive female of race *L. n. whiteheadi* (2b) occurs on Hainan, the male has bolder dark markings. Race *L. n. lewisi* (2c) occurs in SW Cambodia and SE Thailand. VOICE: Contact calls include a throaty *wutch-wutch-wutch* and a short *UWH* or *ORH*. When alarmed utters a grunting *WWERK* and *WWICK* that runs into a *WWERK wuk-uk-uk-uk-uk* combined with a sharp *SSSiik* or *HSSiik* also a rising *swiiieeik* and or *hwiiieeik.* HABITAT: Broadleaved evergreen and mixed deciduous forests. DISTRIBUTION: Resident in S China, NE and S Myanmar, W N and C Thailand, E Laos and N Vietnam; isolated populations also occur in Hainan, the Thai-Cambodia border, S Laos and S Vietnam.

3 EDWARD'S PHEASANT *Lophura edwardsi* 58–65cm FIELD NOTES: Little known. Said to be wary, keeping to dense cover. Race *L. e. hatinhensis* (3b) occurs on the border of N Annam and C Annam region of Vietnam; considered by some authors to be a full species. VOICE: A low, guttural *uk uk uk uk uk…* Males also indulge in wing-whirring. HABITAT: Lowland evergreen forest with dense understorey. DISTRIBUTION: Resident in C Vietnam.

4 IMPERIAL PHEASANT *Lophura imperialis* male 75cm, female 60cm FIELD NOTES: Little recorded, sometimes considered to be a hybrid of Silver and Edward's Pheasant. VOICE: No records, although wing-whirring is reported. HABITAT: Lowland broadleaved secondary forest. DISTRIBUTION: Resident in the N Annam region of Vietnam.

5 SWINHOE'S PHEASANT *Lophura swinhoii* male 79cm, female 50cm FIELD NOTES: Shy. Forages, early morning or late afternoon, in open areas of forest floor and among cover at road edges. Usually seen singly, although pairs and small groups have been recorded. VOICE: Generally silent. Soft murmurings reported as birds forage. HABITAT: Hardwood forest with dense undergrowth. DISTRIBUTION: Resident in the central mountains of Taiwan.

6 CRESTLESS FIREBACK *Lophura erythrophthalma* male 47–50cm, female 42–44cm FIELD NOTES: Wary. Forages on the forest floor, in pairs or small groups. VOICE: A vibrating, throaty *purr* and a repeated, croaking *tak-takuru* or *tooktaroo*. When alarmed utters a loud *kak.* Wing-whirring takes place during display. HABITAT: Secondary forest. DISTRIBUTION: Resident in Peninsular Malaysia.

7 CRESTED FIREBACK *Lophura ignita* male 65–70cm, female 56–57cm FIELD NOTES: Wary. Usually encountered in small groups. Presence often given away by contact calls or males wing-whirring sounds. VOICE: Male utters a subdued *woonk-k woonk-k* often accompanied by loud wing-whirring. When alarmed gives a sharp *chukun chukun*. HABITAT: Lowland forest. DISTRIBUTION: Resident in peninsular Thailand and Malaysia.

8 SIAMESE FIREBACK *Lophura diardi* male 70–80cm, female 53–60cm FIELD NOTES: Forages early mornings and late afternoon, singly or in small groups, in cover. Also recorded by forest tracks and roads. VOICE: Utters a loud whistling. Also a continual *pee-yu pee-yu.* Male produces wing-whirring sounds. HABITAT: Lowland evergreen, semi-evergreen and bamboo forests. DISTRIBUTION: Resident in E Myanmar, NE and SE Thailand, Laos, C and S Vietnam and Cambodia.

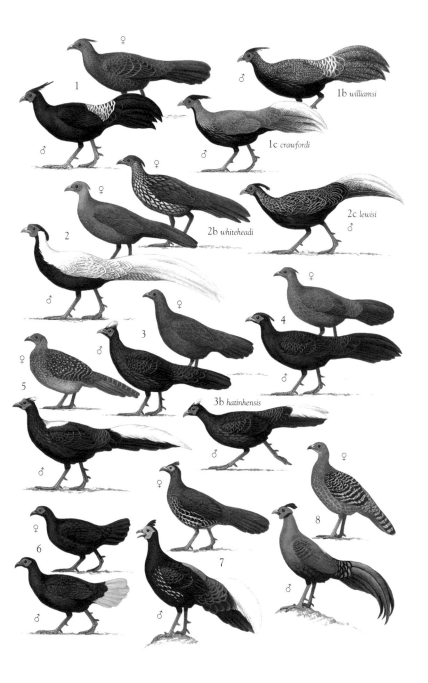

12 PHEASANTS

1 WHITE EARED PHEASANT *Crossoptilon crossoptilon* 86–96cm FIELD NOTES: Forages, early and late, in small groups; larger groups are formed in winter. VOICE: A far-carrying, grating *gag gag gagerah gagerah gagerah gagerah*. HABITAT: Subalpine birch and rhododendron scrub, above the tree-line; in winter occurs in coniferous and mixed forests. DISTRIBUTION: Possibly resident in NE Myanmar and SW China.

2 BLUE EARED PHEASANT *Crossoptilon auritum* 96cm FIELD NOTES: Feeds, early and late, in small groups, with much larger groups occurring in winter. VOICE: A loud, hoarse *ka ka…la krip kraah kraah* or *wu wu wu*. When alarmed utters a *ziwo-ge ziwo-ge*. HABITAT: Coniferous and mixed forests, juniper scrub and alpine meadows. DISTRIBUTION: Possibly occurs in the mountainous areas in the NW of the region.

3 ELLIOT'S PHEASANT *Syrmaticus ellioti* male 80cm, female 50cm FIELD NOTES: Forages mainly in morning and late afternoon in shy, small groups. VOICE: Simple low clucks and chuckles. Indulges in wing-whirring usually followed by a repeated, low-pitched *ge-ge-ge-ge-ge-ge*. HABITAT: Evergreen broadleaved and conifer forests, also bamboo and other dense scrub in mountains. DISTRIBUTION: Resident in SE China.

4 MRS HUME'S PHEASANT *Syrmaticus humiae* male 90cm, female 60cm FIELD NOTES: Generally forages in small groups, keeping to the cover of dense vegetation at forest edge. VOICE: Contact calls are a loud *chuck* and a low, muttering *buk-buk-buk-buk*. Similar calls, even louder, and a noisy screech, are given when alarmed. HABITAT: Evergreen broadleaved and mixed forest with patches of grass and bracken on steep rocky hillsides, oak-pine forest with scattered clearings, also conifer plantations and scrubby areas. DISTRIBUTION: Resident in N, W, C and E Myanmar, NW Thailand and SW China.

5 MIKADO PHEASANT *Syrmaticus mikado* male 87cm, female 53cm FIELD NOTES: Shy and elusive. Usually forages at dawn and dusk; tends to show more during light rain or after heavy rain. Regularly takes to trees during heavy rain. VOICE: Mostly silent. During breeding season utters a short, rising squeal, preceded by a mellow *chup chup*. Gives a quiet, high-pitched *wok wok wok* when alarmed. HABITAT: Primary forest with dense undergrowth of rhododendron and bamboo. DISTRIBUTION: Resident in central mountains of Taiwan.

6 REEVE'S PHEASANT *Syrmaticus reevesii* male 150–210cm, female 70–80cm FIELD NOTES: Forages at forest edge or on farmland, early mornings or late afternoons, otherwise keeps to forests. VOICE: A series of high chirps accompanied by wing-whirring. Contact call is a soft *pu pu pu*. HABITAT: Forests and areas of tall grass and bushes. DISTRIBUTION: Resident in much of C China.

7 PHEASANT (COMMON or RING-NECKED PHEASANT) *Phasianus colchicus* male 66–89cm, female 53–63cm FIELD NOTES: Forages both in cover and open areas. Very variable plumage; depicted are a green-necked form *P. c. elegans* from SW China and N Myanmar and a ring-necked form *P.c. formosanus* (7b) from Taiwan. VOICE: A harsh *korkk korkk KO OK korkk-kok*, often followed by wing-whirring. When alarmed utters a rapid *kut-UK kut-UK kut-UK*. HABITAT: Varied, including open woodland, woodland edge, open country and riverine scrub. DISTRIBUTION: Resident in China, N, E Myanmar and N Vietnam.

8 LADY AMHERST'S PHEASANT *Chrysolophus amherstiae* male 105cm, female 60–70cm FIELD NOTES: Skulking, usually keeps to thick cover. Forms large groups in winter. VOICE: A loud *cheek ker-chek* or *su-ik-ik*. HABITAT: Forests, bamboo and thick scrub on hills and mountains. DISTRIBUTION: Resident in SW China and N, E Myanmar.

9 GOLDEN PHEASANT *Chrysolophus pictus* male 100–115cm, female 61–70cm FIELD NOTES: Forages early and late on tracks and clearings, otherwise keeps to thick cover. VOICE: A loud *ka-cheek* or *cha-chak*. HABITAT: Bamboo and scrub on rocky hills. DISTRIBUTION: Resident in much of C China.

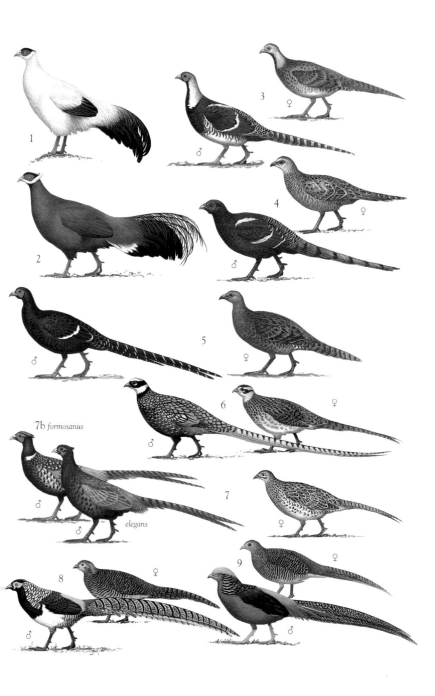

7b *formosanus*

elegans

13 PEAFOWL; PEACOCK PHEASANTS; ARGUS PHEASANTS

1 GREEN PEAFOWL *Pavo muticus* male 180–300cm, female 100–110cm FIELD NOTES: Unmistakeable. Timid and secretive. Best located when calling from roost sites. Tends to forage near watercourses. VOICE: A repeated, trumpeting *ki-wao* or *yee-ow*. Female utters a loud *AOW-aa AOW-aa*. When agitated gives a repeated *tak tak ker-r-r-r oo oo ker-r-r-roo*. HABITAT: Riverine forest and nearby open country. DISTRIBUTION: Resident in SW China, C, S Myanmar, W, NW Thailand, Cambodia, N, S Laos and C, S Vietnam.

2 MOUNTAIN PEACOCK-PHEASANT *Polyplectron inopinatum* male 65cm, female 46cm FIELD NOTES: Frequently encountered on tracks or close to ridges, in small parties. Wary; if disturbed, quietly disappears into undergrowth. VOICE: Utters a burbling, descending whistle, also 1–4 loud, harsh clucks or squawks, repeated every few seconds. When alarmed gives a chicken-like *cluck*. HABITAT: Rugged mountain forest. DISTRIBUTION: Resident in mountains of central Peninsular Malaysia.

3 GERMAIN'S PEACOCK-PHEASANT *Polyplectron germaini* male 56–60cm, female 48cm FIELD NOTES: Wary and difficult to observe, best located by calls. Usually runs if alarmed; flight is fast and low. VOICE: Gives a chuckling or low purring, which becomes more rapid when responding to a rival. HABITAT: Lowland and sub-montane evergreen and semi-evergreen forest, also recorded in secondary, swamp and bamboo forest. DISTRIBUTION: Resident in S Vietnam.

4 GREY PEACOCK-PHEASANT *Polyplectron bicalcaratum* male 56–76cm, female 48–55cm FIELD NOTES: Extremely wary, creeps away through undergrowth at the first sign of alarm. During display male crouches and fans wings and tail, showing off ocelli. VOICE: Male utters a shrill, whistled *trew-tree*, *phee-hoi* or *taa-pwi* and a guttural, raucous *qua qua qua* or *wak wak wak*, the latter also given when alarmed. HABITAT: Verdant broadleaved evergreen and semi-evergreen forest with dense undergrowth. DISTRIBUTION: Resident in SW China, Myanmar, N Thailand, Laos and C N Vietnam.

5 HAINAN PEACOCK-PHEASANT *Polyplectron katsumatae* male 53–65cm, female 40–45cm FIELD NOTES: Presumably habits as Grey Peacock-Pheasant, with which it is often thought to be conspecific. VOICE: Male utters a loud, melodious *guang-gui guang-gui*; female a more rapid *ga ga ga*. HABITAT: Evergreen and semi-evergreen forests. DISTRIBUTION: Resident in SW Hainan.

6 MALAYAN PEACOCK-PHEASANT *Polyplectron malacense* male 50–53cm, female 40–45cm FIELD NOTES: Very wary, disappears into undergrowth at the slightest disturbance. Best located by calls or by cleared areas of leaf litter 'scrapes' that are used as display sites. VOICE: Male territorial call is a loud, clear, melancholy *PUU PWORR*; also utters a harsh cackle that runs into a series of throaty clucks. HABITAT: Broadleaved evergreen forest with a rich understorey, preferably containing small palms. DISTRIBUTION: Resident in the lowland forests of Peninsular Malaysia.

7 CRESTED ARGUS *Rheinardia ocellata* male 190–235cm, female 64–75cm FIELD NOTES: Wary, slinks into undergrowth at the slightest alarm. Best located by calls or the presence of display 'scrapes'. Long-crested race *R. o. nigrescens* (7b) occurs in Peninsular Malaysia. VOICE: Utters a series, up to eight, loud *oowaaa* or *oowaaau* notes that vary in volume and length. Male gives a loud, resonant *WOO-KIA WAU* during 'dancing' display. HABITAT: Various forests, including damp forest in Laos, primary and secondary evergreen forest in Vietnam and Montane forest in Peninsular Malaysia. DISTRIBUTION: Resident in Peninsular Malaysia, C, S Laos and C Vietnam.

8 GREAT ARGUS *Argusianus argus* male 160–200cm, female 72–76cm FIELD NOTES: Wary, moves into undergrowth at the least disturbance. Best located by calls or display 'scrapes'. VOICE: A distinctive, repeated *kwoow-wow* and musical *wow* that is repeated up to 70 times or more, getting higher and higher pitched. HABITAT: Broadleaved evergreen forest. DISTRIBUTION: Resident in S Myanmar, S Thailand and Peninsular Malaysia.

14 QUAILS; BUTTONQUAILS

1 QUAIL (COMMON or EUROPEAN QUAIL) *Coturnix coturnix* 16–18cm FIELD NOTES: Shy and furtive, more often heard than seen. Usually encountered in pairs but may be found in larger numbers where food is plentiful. If flushed, rises rapidly. Long pointed wings distinguish them from other small gamebirds and buttonquails. VOICE: Male utters a rapid *quip quip-ip* often interpreted as *wet-my-lips* and a shrill *tree-tree* when flushed. Female gives a low *bree-bree*. HABITAT: Open grasslands, pastures, paddy stubbles and weedy waste areas. DISTRIBUTION: Rare winter visitor or vagrant to W and S Myanmar.

2 JAPANESE QUAIL (ASIAN MIGRATORY QUAIL) *Coturnix japonica* 17–19cm FIELD NOTES: Actions and habits similar to Quail, probably best distinguished by voice. In non-breeding dress the rufous face is often obscured by pale feathering. VOICE: A chattering *chrr-chuerrk-churr*. Flushed call similar to Quail. HABITAT: Rolling grasslands, agricultural land, montane foothills and forest clearings. DISTRIBUTION: Winter visitor C and S China, Myanmar, NW Thailand, N Laos and N Vietnam; vagrant elsewhere. Possibly breeds in N Myanmar and E Tonkin area of N Vietnam.

3 RAIN QUAIL (BLACK-BREASTED QUAIL) *Coturnix coromandelica* 16–18cm FIELD NOTES: Shy and furtive. Female distinguished from Quail and female Japanese Quail by fairly distinctive spotted flanks and unbarred primaries. VOICE: Male advertising call is a high-pitched *whit-whit-whit-whit-whit-whit-whit-whit*. Flushed call is similar to Quail. HABITAT: Open grassland, cultivated fields, dry rice stubbles and dry grassland mixed with scrub. DISTRIBUTION: Resident in much of Myanmar, away from the south, N and C Thailand, Cambodia and S Vietnam.

4 KING QUAIL (BLUE-BREASTED QUAIL) *Excalfactoria chinensis* 12–15cm FIELD NOTES: Shy and furtive, difficult to flush, preferring to squat or run for cover. Most often observed when running or dust bathing. Usually encountered in pairs or small parties running, mouse-like, through rank grass pausing to feed before running on again. VOICE: A piping *ti-yu ti-yu ti-yu ti-yu ti-yu* or *ti-ti-yu*, the last note being lower pitched. When flushed utters a weak *tir-tir-tir* or a sequence of sharp *cheeps*. HABITAT: Shrubby and swampy grassland, cultivated land and scrubby wetland edges with rank vegetation. DISTRIBUTION: Resident, fairly widespread from Taiwan, S China and Hainan southwards.

5 SMALL BUTTONQUAIL (LITTLE or COMMON BUTTONQUAIL) *Turnix sylvaticus* 15–16cm FIELD NOTES: Secretive, when alarmed prefers to run rather than fly. Usually adopts a crouched posture while feeding but can be quite upright when crossing open ground. In flight shows short blunt wings with buff upperwing coverts contrasting with dark flight feathers. VOICE: A low, droning *hoooo hoooo hoooo*, reminiscent of a distant foghorn or the lowing of cattle; also a low *cree cree cree*, the latter probably used as a contact call. HABITAT: Grassland, scrub and grassy areas at the edges of cultivation. DISTRIBUTION: Resident in S China, Taiwan, C, S, E Myanmar, C Thailand, Cambodia, N and C Laos and much of Vietnam.

6 YELLOW-LEGGED BUTTONQUAIL *Turnix tanki* 15–18cm FIELD NOTES: Actions and habits similar to Small Buttonquail. VOICE: A human-like, moaning hoot and a far-carrying *off-off-off*. Also recorded is a *pook-pook*. HABITAT: Scrub, grassland, slightly marshy areas and cultivated land. DISTRIBUTION: Resident, widespread over the region apart from Peninsular Malaysia, W, N Myanmar and S Vietnam.

7 BARRED BUTTONQUAIL *Turnix suscitator* 15–17cm FIELD NOTES: Secretive. Actions and habits similar to Small Buttonquail. If flushed only flies a short distance before dropping back into cover. VOICE: A *groo groo groo drr-r-r-r-r-r*, said to sound like a distant motorbike, also a far-carrying *hoon-hoon-hoon*. HABITAT: Dry grasslands, cultivated land, scrub and secondary growth. DISTRIBUTION: Widespread resident from Taiwan and S China southwards.

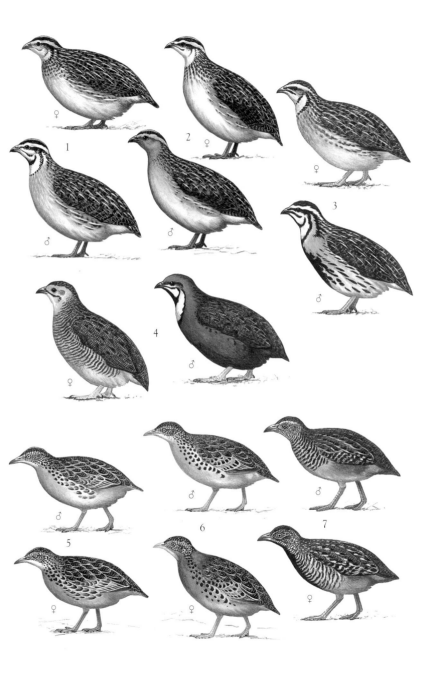

15 DIVERS; GREBES

1 RED-THROATED DIVER (RED-THROATED LOON) *Gavia stellata* 53–69cm
FIELD NOTES: Upturned bill, usually holds head and bill noticeably upwards. Juvenile as
non-breeding adult but with greyish face and neck. VOICE: Male utters a rolling, growling
oorroo-uh oorroo-uh also various barking and mewing sounds; female gives a slightly
longer, higher-pitched *aarroo aarroo aarroo*. In flight gives a goose-like *kah kah kah kah kah*.
HABITAT: Shallow coastal waters. DISTRIBUTION: Winters off E and SE China.

2 BLACK-THROATED DIVER (BLACK-THROATED or ARCTIC LOON) *Gavia
arctica* 58–73cm FIELD NOTES: Tends to hold bill horizontally. Note white flank patch.
Juvenile very similar to non-breeding adult but with slight scaling on upperparts. VOICE: A
loud, mournful *clowee-col-clowee-cok-clowee* a snoring *knarr-knorr-knarr-knorr* and a gull-like
aaah-owww. HABITAT: Coastal waters. DISTRIBUTION: Winters off E China.

3 YELLOW-BILLED DIVER (WHITE-BILLED DIVER, YELLOW-BILLED LOON)
Gavia adamsii 76–91cm FIELD NOTES: Distinctive angled-up tip to lower mandible. Juvenile
as winter adult but with pale scaly fringes on back. VOICE: A loud, haunting yodelling and a
tremulous scream. HABITAT: Coastal waters. DISTRIBUTION: Vagrant off SE China.

4 LITTLE GREBE (DABCHICK) *Tachybaptus ruficollis* 25–29cm FIELD NOTES: Usually
encountered in pairs or small parties. In flight shows whitish secondaries. Juvenile as non-
breeding adult but with blackish streaks on face. VOICE: A high-pitched whinnying trill
with various twitterings. When alarmed utters a metallic *whit whit*. HABITAT: Vegetated
lakes, ponds and rivers; occurs on more open waters, including sheltered coastal waters post
breeding. DISTRIBUTION: Widespread throughout the area.

5 GREAT CRESTED GREBE *Podiceps cristatus* 46–51cm FIELD NOTES: In flight
shows white secondaries and white forewing. Juvenile much like non-breeding adult but
with dark streaks on face. VOICE: A barking *rah-rah-rah*, also various croaks, growls and
a slow nasal moaning. HABITAT: Lakes, reservoirs, rivers and sheltered coastal waters.
DISTRIBUTION: Winter visitor to Southern China and Northern Myanmar; vagrant
elsewhere.

6 RED-NECKED GREBE *Podiceps grisegena* 40–50cm FIELD NOTES: Generally
encountered singly or in pairs. In flight upperwing shows a white forewing and white
secondaries. Juvenile like a 'shadowy' version of adult but with dark face streaks. VOICE:
Wailing, braying and squeaking noises, also a grating *cherk-cherk-cherk*. HABITAT: Lakes,
estuaries and sheltered coastal waters. DISTRIBUTION: Winter visitor to E China.

7 SLAVONIAN GREBE (HORNED GREBE) *Podiceps auritus* 31–38cm FIELD NOTES:
Often found in small flocks. Non-breeding birds show clear white cheeks compared to dusky
face of Black-necked Grebe. Juvenile much as non-breeding adult but with darkish marks
on cheek. In flight looks like a miniature Great-crested Grebe. VOICE: A far-carrying, rattled
joarrh, also an accelerating trill, quite similar to that of Little Grebe. HABITAT: Lakes and
coastal waters. DISTRIBUTION: Winter visitor to E China.

8 BLACK-NECKED GREBE (EARED GREBE) *Podiceps nigricollis* 28–34cm FIELD
NOTES: Steep forehead. Non breeding adult shows blackish cheeks compared to the clear
white of Slavonian Grebe. In flight shows black forewing and white secondaries. Juvenile
a dull version of non-breeding adult with a buff wash to head and neck. VOICE: A flute-like
poo-eeet and a vibrant, trilled *tssrrrrrooooeep*. HABITAT: Inland lakes and shallow coastal
waters. DISTRIBUTION: Winter visitor to SW and SE China; vagrant elsewhere.

16 ALBATROSSES; PETRELS

1 SHORT-TAILED ALBATROSS (STELLER'S ALBATROSS) *Phoebastria albatrus*
84–94cm FIELD NOTES: Largest Albatross occurring in the North Pacific. Tends not
to follow ships. Juvenile generally dark brown with a pink bill. VOICE: Usually silent.
HABITAT: Maritime. DISTRIBUTION: Occurs of the E coast of China.

2 BLACK-FOOTED ALBATROSS *Phoebastria nigripes* 68–74cm FIELD NOTES: Often
encountered around fishing boats and ships. Some adults show pale greyish head and
underparts. Juvenile sooty-brown with a narrow whitish area at base of bill. VOICE: Usually
silent. HABITAT: Maritime. DISTRIBUTION: Occurs of the E coast of China.

3 LAYSAN ALBATROSS *Phoebastria immutabilis* 79–81cm FIELD NOTES: Sometimes
follows ships. Juvenile similar to adult but with greyish bill. VOICE: Usually silent.
HABITAT: Maritime. DISTRIBUTION: Possibly occurs off the E coast of China.

4 BULWER'S PETREL *Bulweria bulwerii* 26–28cm FIELD NOTES: Usually flies low over
water in an erratic buoyant manner, much like a large storm petrel. Tail wedge-shaped
when fanned. VOICE: Usually silent; at breeding sites utters a hoarse *hroo-hroo-hroo…*
HABITAT: Mainly maritime. Breeds in burrows, holes, cracks, or under vegetation on island
slopes or cliffs. DISTRIBUTION: Resident in seas off E China; breeds on islands off SE China
and Taiwan, offshore vagrant elsewhere.

5 BONIN PETREL *Pterodroma hypoleuca* 30cm FIELD NOTES: Typical fast, bounding
'gadfly' flight – beating wings to gain height followed by long glides and wide banking arcs.
Tends not to follow ships. VOICE: Generally silent. HABITAT: Maritime. DISTRIBUTION:
Vagrant off the coast of E China and Taiwan.

6 TAHITI PETREL *Pseudobulweria rostrata* 39cm FIELD NOTES: Stout bill, long bodied.
Flight usually low over water with loose wing-beats. Solitary, rarely follows ships or fishing
boats. VOICE: Generally silent. HABITAT: Maritime. DISTRIBUTION: Vagrant, recorded from
NE Taiwan.

17 SHEARWATERS; STORM PETRELS

1 STREAKED SHEARWATER (WHITE-FACED SHEARWATER) *Calonectris leucomelas* 48cm FIELD NOTES: Occurs in large flocks. Sometimes shows a pale crescent at base of tail. Flight can appear lazy although is actually quite fast, with dynamic small albatross-like soaring in strong winds. Follows fishing boats. VOICE: Generally silent. HABITAT: Mainly maritime; breeds in burrows on forested hills. DISTRIBUTION: Breeds on offshore islands of E China; migrant or vagrant elsewhere.

2 WEDGE-TAILED SHEARWATER *Puffinus pacificus* 41–46cm FIELD NOTES: Slow wing-flaps followed by short glides; more bounding flight in strong winds. Often found around fishing boats. VOICE: Generally silent. HABITAT: Maritime. DISTRIBUTION: Vagrant off the coasts of E China, W Peninsular Malaysia and Singapore.

3 FLESH-FOOTED SHEARWATER (PALE-FOOTED SHEARWATER) *Puffinus carneipes* 40–45cm FIELD NOTES: Gregarious. Flight consists of lazy wing-flaps followed by long glides on stiff wings. VOICE: Generally silent. HABITAT: Maritime. DISTRIBUTION: Vagrant off the coast of E China.

4 SOOTY SHEARWATER *Puffinus griseus* 40–46cm FIELD NOTES: Flight consists of quick wing-flaps followed by long glides. Often scavenges around fishing vessels. VOICE: Generally silent. HABITAT: Maritime. DISTRIBUTION: Vagrant off coasts of E China and Taiwan.

5 SHORT-TAILED SHEARWATER (SLENDER-BILLED SHEARWATER) *Puffinus tenuirostris* 41–43cm FIELD NOTES: Gregarious. Flight consists of quick flaps followed by glides, often appears hurried and jerky. VOICE: Generally silent. HABITAT: Maritime. DISTRIBUTION: Vagrant off the coasts of Taiwan and Thailand; the inland record from Singapore was probably due to high winds.

6 WILSON'S STORM PETREL *Oceanites oceanicus* 15–19cm FIELD NOTES: Yellow webs between toes, visible only at close range. Often dangles feet and 'dances' on sea surface while feeding. Attracted to fishing vessels. VOICE: A rapid 'chattering' occasionally uttered while feeding. HABITAT: Maritime. DISTRIBUTION: Coastal migrant or vagrant recorded from S Myanmar, Peninsular Malaysia and SE China.

7 SWINHOE'S STORM PETREL (SWINHOE'S PETREL) *Oceanodroma monorhis* 19–20cm FIELD NOTES: Feeds erratically with bounding flight and hovers with shallow wing-beats to pick prey from sea surface. Tends not to follow ships. VOICE: A trilling chatter at breeding sites, usually silent at sea. HABITAT: Breeds in burrows, otherwise maritime. DISTRIBUTION: Breeds on islands off E China and Taiwan; winter visitor or migrant off Peninsular Malaysia, Singapore, S Thailand and S and E China.

8 MATSUDAIRA'S STORM PETREL (SOOTY STORM PETREL) *Oceanodroma matsudairae* 24–25cm FIELD NOTES: Feeds on the wing, holding wings in a shallow V while dipping down to pick food from sea surface; also feeds by landing on water. Often follows ships. VOICE: Generally silent. HABITAT: Maritime. DISTRIBUTION: Vagrant off the E China coast.

18 FRIGATEBIRDS; BOOBIES; TROPICBIRDS

All young frigatebirds undergo a complicated series of plumage changes before gaining adult plumage; see *Seabirds: An Identification Guide* (P. Harrison) for details.

1 GREAT FRIGATEBIRD *Fregata minor* 86–100cm FIELD NOTES: During breeding season, male inflates red skin of throat. Pursues other seabirds, forcing them to regurgitate food. Scavenges around boats. Juvenile has a pale head and white belly separated by a black breast band, the latter tends to fade as bird ages. VOICE: Braying, clapping and rattling calls at breeding sites, otherwise generally silent. HABITAT: Mainly maritime. Nests are built on trees or flat ground. DISTRIBUTION: Breeds on islets off Hainan, regular visitor off S and E China and S Thailand; vagrant elsewhere.

2 LESSER FRIGATEBIRD *Fregata ariel* 71–81cm FIELD NOTES: Habits similar to Great Frigatebird. Juvenile has a pale head, white belly and axillaries separated by a thin, darkish breast band, the latter fades as the head darkens. VOICE: Generally silent. HABITAT: Maritime. DISTRIBUTION: Regular visitor off E China, Taiwan, S Thailand and Peninsular Malaysia; vagrant elsewhere.

3 CHRISTMAS ISLAND FRIGATEBIRD *Fregata andrewsi* 90–100cm FIELD NOTES: Habits similar to Great Frigatebird. Juvenile much like Lesser Frigatebird but with a broader black breast band. VOICE: Generally silent. HABITAT: Coastal waters, occasionally inland. DISTRIBUTION: Regular visitor off S Thailand and Peninsular Malaysia; vagrant elsewhere.

4 BROWN BOOBY *Sula leucogaster* 64–74cm FIELD NOTES: Feeds by angled plunge-diving. Juvenile has white parts tinged brownish, bill greyish. Often attracted to ships. Gregarious. VOICE: At breeding sites males give high-pitched whistles; female utters grunts and honks. HABITAT: Mainly maritime. Usually breeds on the ground, often amongst vegetation. DISTRIBUTION: Breeds on islets off Taiwan; regular visitor off E China and W Peninsular Malaysia; vagrant elsewhere.

5 MASKED BOOBY (WHITE or BLUE-FACED BOOBY) *Sula dactylatra* 81–92cm FIELD NOTES: Feeds by plunge-diving, usually at a more vertical angle than other boobies. Juvenile very similar to adult Brown Booby but with a paler mantle and white collar on hindneck, brown of the head does not extend to the upper breast. VOICE: At nest sites male utters a wheezy or piping whistle; female gives a loud honking or braying. Generally silent at sea. HABITAT: Maritime. DISTRIBUTION: Rare off Peninsular Malaysia, vagrant elsewhere. May breed on Con Dao Island off S Vietnam.

6 RED-FOOTED BOOBY *Sula sula* 66–77cm FIELD NOTES: Actions similar to Brown Booby. Variations on the brown morph include a white tailed form and a white headed, white tailed form. VOICE: Silent at sea; at nest sites utters a harsh squawk and a guttural *ga-ga-ga-ga...* HABITAT: Maritime away from breeding sites. DISTRIBUTION: Regular visitor to coastal waters off SE China and Taiwan, vagrant elsewhere. Breeds on islands off SE China.

7 RED-BILLED TROPICBIRD *Phaethon aethereus* 90–105cm FIELD NOTES: Flight consists of fluttering *wing-beats* followed by long glides. Feeds by hovering then plunge-diving on half-closed wings. Juvenile has a yellow bill, black nape collar and lacks elongated tail streamers. VOICE: A shrill, rasping *kee-arrr.* HABITAT: Maritime; breeds in crevices or scrape on ground. DISTRIBUTION: Breeds on islands off SE China; regular visitor to coastal waters of SE China and Taiwan, vagrant elsewhere.

8 RED-TAILED TROPICBIRD *Phaethon rubricauda* 78–81cm FIELD NOTES: Actions as Red-billed Tropicbird. Juvenile like juvenile red-billed Tropicbird but with less black on primaries, black bill and no black nape collar. VOICE: A harsh, rapid *keek-keek-keek...* HABITAT: Maritime. DISTRIBUTION: Vagrant off coasts of S Thailand and Taiwan.

9 WHITE-TAILED TROPICBIRD *Phaethon lepturus* 70–82cm FIELD NOTES: Actions similar to Red-billed Tropicbird. Juvenile similar to juvenile Red-billed Tropicbird but lacks the black nape collar. VOICE: A squeaky *chip-chip-chip...* HABITAT: Maritime. DISTRIBUTION: Vagrant, recorded off Taiwan, S Thailand and Myanmar.

19 PELICANS; DARTER; CORMORANTS

1 DALMATIAN PELICAN *Pelecanus crispus* 160–180cm FIELD NOTES: In non-breeding plumage crest is smaller and bill pouch dull yellow. Juvenile brownish-grey, especially on wings. Occurs singly or in small groups, sometimes fishes cooperatively like White Pelican. VOICE: Generally silent. HABITAT: Lakes, rivers and sheltered coastal waters. DISTRIBUTION: Winter visitor to E China.

2 SPOT-BILLED PELICAN *Pelecanus philippensis* 140cm FIELD NOTES: Rare. Non-breeding adult greyer with paler bill and facial skin. Sociable, often feeds cooperatively like White Pelican. VOICE: At breeding sites utters squeaking, barking and bleating sounds. Fishing groups may utter a deep bleating noise. HABITAT: Large lakes, lagoons, large rivers and estuaries. Breeds colonially, preferring tall dead or bare trees within range of feeding waters. DISTRIBUTION: Resident in Cambodia, possibly S Vietnam and S Myanmar; non-breeding visitor or migrant to Thailand, Laos, N Vietnam and Myanmar, vagrant elsewhere.

3 WHITE PELICAN (GREAT WHITE PELICAN) *Pelecanus onocrotalus* 140–175cm FIELD NOTES: Bill pouch pale yellow in non-breeding plumage. Juvenile brownish on wings and neck. Often fishes cooperatively; forms a semi-circle to push fish into shallows enabling each bird to scoop up a pouchful of fish. VOICE: In flight may utter a deep croak. HABITAT: Lakes, rivers and sheltered coastal waters. DISTRIBUTION: Winter visitor to S Myanmar; vagrant elsewhere.

4 INDIAN DARTER (ORIENTAL DARTER or SNAKEBIRD) *Anhinga melanogaster* 85–97cm FIELD NOTES: In flight holds neck in a distinct kink. Often sits on an exposed perch with wings outstretched. Non-breeding plumage is duller. Often swims with only head and neck visible. VOICE: Breeding birds utter a loud *chigi chigi chigi chigi* and various grunts and croaks, otherwise silent. HABITAT: Lakes, marshes and large rivers. DISTRIBUTION: Rare resident over much of area south of China; vagrant in S China and W Peninsular Malaysia.

5 CORMORANT (GREAT CORMORANT) *Phalacrocorax carbo* 80–100cm FIELD NOTES: In flight outstretched neck shows a slight kink. Regularly sits with wings held open. Juvenile dark brown above, dirty white below, greyer on neck and breast. VOICE: At breeding sites utters various deep, guttural calls; otherwise generally silent. HABITAT: Lakes, rivers, reservoirs and coastal waters. DISTRIBUTION: Resident in SE China, Cambodia and possibly Myanmar, Thailand and S Vietnam; winter visitor elsewhere in south of the region.

6 JAPANESE CORMORANT (TEMMINCK'S CORMORANT) *Phalacrocorax capillatus* 92cm FIELD NOTES: In flight outstretched neck shows a slight kink. Juvenile dark brown above, whitish below. VOICE: Usually silent. HABITAT: Mainly maritime, otherwise rocky cliffs. DISTRIBUTION: Winter visitor to coasts and offshore waters of E China and Taiwan.

7 PELAGIC CORMORANT *Phalacrocorax pelagicus* 63–73cm FIELD NOTES: Flies with neck held straight. Juvenile dark brown. VOICE: Generally silent. HABITAT: Maritime. DISTRIBUTION: Winter visitor off coast of E China.

8 INDIAN CORMORANT (INDIAN SHAG) *Phalacrocorax fuscicollis* 63cm FIELD NOTES: Flies with neck outstretched and held in a slight kink. Regularly perches with wings held open. Juvenile scaly brown above, greyish-white below with flanks mottled with black. VOICE: A breeding sites utters a sharp *kit-kit-kit-kit…* HABITAT: Various fresh and salt water wetlands. DISTRIBUTION: Resident in S Myanmar, C and SE Thailand, Cambodia and S Vietnam.

9 LITTLE CORMORANT *Microcarbo niger* 51cm FIELD NOTES: Flies with neck outstretched with a slight kink. Regularly sits with wings held open. Juvenile has brown upperparts with slight scaling, paler below with white throat and centre of abdomen. VOICE: At breeding sites utters various grunts, groans and roaring sounds; also a low-pitched *ah-ah-ah* and *kok-kok-kok*. HABITAT: Fresh water wetlands, mangroves and estuaries. DISTRIBUTION: Resident over much of the area south from SW China; winter visitor or vagrant to peninsular region.

20 HERONS

1 CHINESE POND HERON *Ardeola bacchus* 42–45cm FIELD NOTES: In flight shows white wings and tail. Breeds in small colonies. VOICE: Generally silent; when alarmed or in flight may utter a harsh croak. HABITAT: Various wetlands, including marshes, ponds, paddyfields, ditches and coastal waters. DISTRIBUTION: Widespread summer visitor to China. Northern birds move south to join resident populations in SE China and N Vietnam; winter visitor elsewhere.

2 INDIAN POND HERON (PADDYBIRD) *Ardeola grayii* 42–47cm FIELD NOTES: In flight shows white wings and tail, the former with a pale buff wash on secondaries. Non-breeding adult probably indistinguishable from non-breeding Chinese Pond Heron. VOICE: Utters a harsh squawk when flushed or in flight. HABITAT: Various freshwater wetlands, such as marshes, ponds and paddyfields; also coastal pools. DISTRIBUTION: Resident in Myanmar; migrant or vagrant to coastal and C Thailand and NW Peninsular Malaysia.

3 JAVAN POND HERON *Ardeola speciosa* 45cm FIELD NOTES: In flight shows white wings and tail. Tends to feed around dusk. Non-breeding adult probably indistinguishable from other non-breeding pond herons. VOICE: When flushed may give a harsh *kaa kaa*; in flight utters a squawk. HABITAT: Various inland and coastal wetlands. DISTRIBUTION: Resident in C Thailand, Cambodia and S Vietnam; vagrant elsewhere.

4 HERON (GREY HERON) *Ardea cinerea* 90–98cm FIELD NOTES: Generally forages alone. Often stands motionless at water's edge or on a branch. Flies with arched wings and neck drawn back. Grey underwing-coverts contrast with dark flight feathers. Juvenile has a grey neck and a dull black crown. VOICE: At breeding sites utters harsh croaks; in flight gives a harsh *frahnk*. HABITAT: Variety of wetlands, including lakes, marshes, rivers, mangroves and tidal creeks. DISTRIBUTION: Widespread resident in China, W Peninsular Malaysia, Singapore, Cambodia and S Vietnam. Possible resident in C Myanmar and C Thailand; winter visitor elsewhere.

5 PURPLE HERON *Ardea purpurea* 78–90cm FIELD NOTES: More secretive than others of the genus, tending to prefer the cover of aquatic vegetation. Flies with arched wings and neck drawn back. Has a more pronounced neck bulge than Heron. Underwing appears all dark. Juvenile browner than adult, showing less dark streaks on head and neck. VOICE: At breeding sites gives various harsh utterances. Flight call like Heron but higher-pitched. HABITAT: Marshes and lakes with dense aquatic vegetation; post breeding often visits more open waters. DISTRIBUTION: Breeds over much of China, Thailand, Cambodia, S Vietnam, S Laos and possibly S Myanmar; winter visitor elsewhere. Birds from northern and central China move south post breeding.

6 GOLIATH HERON *Ardea goliath* 135–150cm FIELD NOTES: Large, much larger than superficially similar Purple Heron. Typically forages alone, in the open. Flies with arched wings and neck drawn back. Underwing-coverts extensively purple. Juvenile a dull version of adult. VOICE: In flight gives a deep, loud *kowoorrk-kowoorrk-woorrk-work-worrk*. HABITAT: Lakes, rivers, marshes and coastal mudflats. DISTRIBUTION: Vagrant, disputed record from S Myanmar.

7 GREAT-BILLED HERON (SUMATRAN HERON) *Ardea sumatrana* 115cm FIELD NOTES: Generally shy and wary, forages alone or in pairs. Flies with arched wings and neck drawn back; underwing-coverts grey contrasting little with flight feathers. VOICE: Occasional loud, harsh croaks. HABITAT: Mangroves, islets, undisturbed beaches and large rivers near coasts. DISTRIBUTION: Resident mainly on the coasts of SW Myanmar, S Thailand, Peninsular Malaysia, Singapore and Cambodia.

8 WHITE-BELLIED HERON (IMPERIAL HERON) *Ardea insignis* 127cm FIELD NOTES: Forages alone or in pairs. Flies with arched wings and neck drawn back; white underwing-coverts contrasting with darker flight feathers. VOICE: A braying, croaking *ock ock ock ock urrrrr*; when disturbed utters a deep croak. HABITAT: Large rivers and adjacent wetlands. DISTRIBUTION: Rare resident in N Myanmar and possibly W Myanmar.

n-br

n-br

1

br

2

n-br

3

br

br

4

5

6

7

8

21 HERONS

1 GREAT WHITE EGRET (GREAT EGRET) *Ardea alba* 85–102cm FIELD NOTES: Regularly walks stealthily with neck erect. For a short while prior to breeding bill becomes darker, lores bluish and tibia pink-red. Non-breeding birds loose long back plumes. Breeds and roosts colonially. VOICE: Generally silent although my give a throaty croak. HABITAT: Fresh and salt water wetlands. DISTRIBUTION: Widespread resident or winter visitor.

2 LITTLE EGRET *Egretta garzetta* 55–65cm FIELD NOTES: At the onset of breeding, lores become yellow, yellow-orange or reddish. Often feeds by dashing to and fro with wings held open. Non-breeding adults and juveniles lack head, breast and back plumes. Breeds and roosts colonially. VOICE: Utters a harsh *aaah* or *kgarrk* during feeding disputes or when alarmed. HABITAT: Lakes, rivers, marshes, paddyfields, tidal creeks and estuaries. DISTRIBUTION: Widespread resident or winter visitor, northern breeders move south post breeding.

3 INTERMEDIATE EGRET (YELLOW-BILLED or PLUMED EGRET) *Egretta intermedia* 65–72cm FIELD NOTES: Bill becomes black for a short time during breeding. Non-breeding adults lack the breast and back plumes. Breeds and roosts colonially. VOICE: Utters a harsh *kwark* or *kuwark* when disturbed. HABITAT: Freshwater lakes, rivers and marshes; also tidal creeks and mangrove swamps. DISTRIBUTION: Widespread resident, northern breeders move south post breeding.

4 CHINESE EGRET (SWINHOE'S EGRET) *Egretta eulophotes* 65–68cm FIELD NOTES: Non-breeding birds lack the head and back plumes. Often feeds by dashing to and fro with wings held open and flapped. VOICE: Generally silent. HABITAT: Tidal mudflats, coastal bays and mangroves. DISTRIBUTION: Non-breeding visitor to N and S Vietnam, W Peninsular Malaysia and Singapore; passage migrant elsewhere.

5 PIED HERON *Egretta picata* 50cm FIELD NOTES: Agile forager, even seen to feed by 'hovering' before dropping onto prey. Juvenile is brownish-grey with head wholly white. VOICE: In flight utters a loud *awk* or *ohrk*. HABITAT: Various wetlands, including lakes, mudflats and estuaries. DISTRIBUTION: Vagrant, possible record from Taiwan.

6 PACIFIC REEF EGRET (EASTERN REEF EGRET or HERON) *Egretta sacra* 58–66cm FIELD NOTES: Breeding birds have a short inconspicuous nape crest. Usual feeding action is lethargic with a more rapid pursuit when potential prey is spotted. VOICE: A hoarse croak and when alarmed a harsh *arrk*. HABITAT: Rocky shores, beaches and mudflats. DISTRIBUTION: Widespread coastal resident north to E China and Taiwan.

7 CATTLE EGRET *Bubulcus ibis* 48–53cm FIELD NOTES: Sociable, regularly seen feeding on insects disturbed by grazing animals. VOICE: At breeding sites utters a low croak, in flight may give a harsh, croaking *ruk* or *Rik-rak*, otherwise usually silent. HABITAT: Various wetlands and grasslands. DISTRIBUTION: Resident in S Myanmar, C Thailand, Cambodia and S Vietnam, more widespread in winter or on passage.

8 STRIATED HERON (GREEN-BACKED or LITTLE HERON) *Butorides striata* 40–48cm FIELD NOTES: Often forages alone and in the same location for many days, usually among thick vegetation on the banks of rivers and ponds. Mainly crepuscular or nocturnal. Juvenile brown with pale spots on wings and dark streaking on neck and underparts. A darker race *B. s. spodiogaster* (8b) occurs on the Coco Islands off S Myanmar. VOICE: When disturbed utters a harsh *kyah*. HABITAT: Mangroves, rivers and streams in or near forests, tidal mudflats and lakes. DISTRIBUTION: Summer visitor to most of China, but resident in Taiwan, Hainan and S, W China. Widespread resident and winter visitor further south.

dark morph

light morph

5

6

n-br

br

7

8

8b *spodiogaster*

22 HERONS; BITTERNS

1 NIGHT HERON (BLACK-CROWNED NIGHT HERON) *Nycticorax nycticorax*
58–65cm FIELD NOTES: Adult unmistakeable. Mainly crepuscular or nocturnal. Usually
forages alone. Juvenile upperparts dark brown spotted buff-white; head, neck and underparts
pale streaked brown. VOICE: Various croaks given at breeding colonies. In flight utters a frog-
like croak. HABITAT: Various watery areas including marshes, lakes and rivers with extensive
border vegetation. Also paddyfields and mangroves. DISTRIBUTION: Widespread resident.
Winter visitor in the far south; central China breeders move south after breeding.

2 WHITE-EARED NIGHT HERON *Gorsachius magnificus* 54–56cm FIELD NOTES:
Crepuscular or nocturnal. Secretive. Female face pattern less distinct with some white mottling
on back and wings; juvenile similar but with bolder white mottling. VOICE: A repeated, raspy
whoa, said to sound like a large owl. HABITAT: Dense undergrowth in marshy areas around
forest streams. DISTRIBUTION: Scarce resident in S China, Hainan and N Vietnam.

3 JAPANESE NIGHT HERON (JAPANESE BITTERN) *Gorsachius goisagi* 49cm
FIELD NOTES: Skulking. Primaries have extensive rufous tips. Juvenile has darker crown
and streaking and spotting on neck. VOICE: A deep *buo-buo* usually uttered at night. May
emit a croak while feeding. HABITAT: Dense undergrowth in forests, usually near water.
DISTRIBUTION: Rare non-breeding visitor to SE China and Taiwan.

4 MALAYAN NIGHT HERON (TIGER BITTERN) *Gorsachius melanolophus* 49cm
FIELD NOTES: Shy. Generally crepuscular or nocturnal. In flight shows white-tipped
primaries. Juvenile has greyish upperparts densely spotted and vermiculated with white and
buff, underparts vermiculated and barred brown. VOICE: A deep *oo oo oo oo…* also croaks and
a rasping *arh-arh-arh*. HABITAT: Marshes and streams in dense forest. DISTRIBUTION: Resident
in Taiwan, Hainan, SW and SE China, Thailand, Laos and N, C Vietnam; passage migrant
or winter visitor elsewhere.

5 YELLOW BITTERN (CHINESE LITTLE or LONG-NOSED BITTERN)
Ixobrychus sinensis 30–40cm FIELD NOTES: Skulking, mainly crepuscular or nocturnal.
In flight shows black flight feathers and tail. Juvenile buff above with dark streaking,
whitish below with brownish streaks on foreneck and breast. VOICE: In flight utters a sharp
kakak kakak. HABITAT: Vegetation surrounding marshes, lakes and flooded paddyfields.
DISTRIBUTION: Widespread breeder over much of the region; northern most birds move
south post breeding.

6 SCHRENCK'S BITTERN (VON SCHRENCK'S BITTERN) *Ixobrychus eurhythmus*
33–39cm FIELD NOTES: Skulking, usually solitary. Juvenile similar to adult female. VOICE: A
low, repeated *gup*; in flight utters a low squawk. HABITAT: Marshes, pools and paddyfields
near forest and open well-vegetated wetlands. DISTRIBUTION: Summer visitor to China;
winter visitor to Hainan, and rarely to N Vietnam and Laos; passage migrant elsewhere.

7 CINNAMON BITTERN (CHESTNUT BITTERN) *Ixobrychus cinnamomeus* 40–
41cm FIELD NOTES: Secretive. Generally forages alone, usually crepuscular. Juvenile dark
brown above with pale mottling, buff-white below heavily streaked dark brown. VOICE: A
low *kwok-kwok-kwok…* sometimes ends with two or three quieter notes. HABITAT: Various
wetland areas including, flooded paddyfields, swamps and reedbeds. DISTRIBUTION: Resident
over much of the region, Central China birds retreat south post breeding.

8 BLACK BITTERN (YELLOW-NECKED or MANGROVE BITTERN) *Dupetor
flavicollis* 54–66cm FIELD NOTES: Secretive, skulks in dense cover; mainly crepuscular.
VOICE: In flight utters a hoarse croak. HABITAT: Freshwater wetlands, swamp forest and
mangroves. DISTRIBUTION: Breeds over much of the area apart from Peninsular Malaysia;
many of those breeding in S and C China move south post breeding.

9 BITTERN (GREAT or EURASIAN BITTERN) *Botaurus stellaris* 70–80cm FIELD
NOTES: Secretive, more often seen in flight. Juvenile less distinctly marked. VOICE: In flight
utters a harsh *kau*. HABITAT: Freshwater and brackish reedbeds. DISTRIBUTION: Winter
visitor mainly to E China and southernmost Myanmar; vagrant elsewhere.

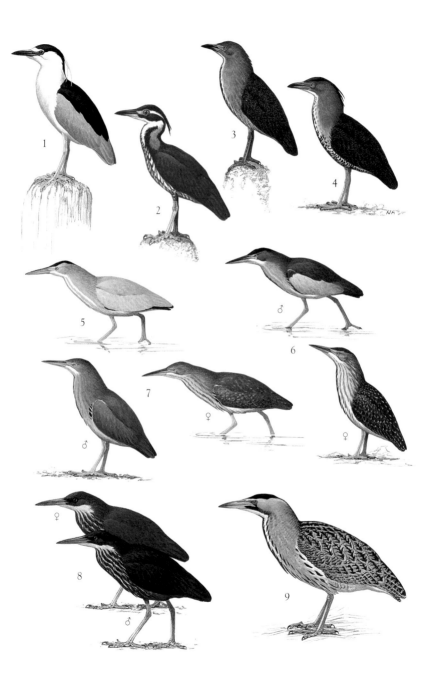

23 FLAMINGOES; STORKS

1 GREATER FLAMINGO *Phoenicopterus roseus* 120–145cm FIELD NOTES: Unmistakeable. Juvenile dingy grey-brown. VOICE: In flight utters a honking *kla-ha*. HABITAT: Salt lakes and sea bays; less so on freshwater lakes. DISTRIBUTION: Recorded from Tonle Sap Lake in Cambodia, probably no longer occurring. Old records may refer to vagrants rather than breeders.

2 PAINTED STORK *Mycteria leucocephala* 93–100cm FIELD NOTES: In flight shows a dark underwing. Juvenile greyer, facial skin yellowish. VOICE: Generally silent. HABITAT: Lakes, marshes, swamp forest and paddyfields. DISTRIBUTION: Decreasing resident in S Cambodia, S Vietnam and possibly C Myanmar. Non-breeding visitor to Thailand, Laos, N, C Vietnam and N, W, E Myanmar; vagrant elsewhere.

3 MILKY STORK *Mycteria cinerea* 92–97cm FIELD NOTES: Non-breeding birds have a pinkish-yellow bill. Juvenile is dingy grey-brown, head and neck browner; facial skin and bill pale yellow. VOICE: Generally silent. During breeding utters screaming-hissing sounds along with bill-clapping. HABITAT: Tidal mudflats, mangroves and flooded forests in Cambodia. DISTRIBUTION: Resident in Cambodia (Tonle Sap Lake, dispersing post breeding, possibly to coastal areas) and W Peninsular Malaysia; vagrant elsewhere.

4 ASIAN OPENBILL (ASIAN OPENBILL STORK) *Anastomus oscitans* 68–81cm FIELD NOTES: Gregarious. Non-breeding adult has blacks more brownish, neck and head greyish and grey bill. In flight underwing shows white coverts and black flight feathers with black tail. Juvenile brownish-grey with darker mantle. VOICE: During display utters a series of hollow, nasal *hoo-hoo* calls. HABITAT: Freshwater marshes, shallow lakes and paddyfields. DISTRIBUTION: Resident in C Thailand, Cambodia and S Vietnam. Non-breeding visitor to Myanmar, much of Thailand and S Laos; passage migrant or vagrant elsewhere.

5 BLACK STORK *Ciconia nigra* 95–105cm FIELD NOTES: Usually encountered alone or in pairs. In flight underwing is black with a white triangle formed by the inner wing-coverts and axillaries; tail is black. VOICE: Generally silent. HABITAT: Marshes, shallow lakes, rivers and grasslands. DISTRIBUTION: Winter visitor to S China, N Myanmar, N, W Thailand, N, C Laos and N Vietnam.

6 WOOLLY-NECKED STORK *Ciconia episcopus* 75–92cm FIELD NOTES: Usually encountered singly or small flocks. Underwing black in flight, with black tail often obscured by white undertail-coverts. VOICE: Generally silent except for whistling greeting calls and bill-clapping at nest site. HABITAT: Marshes, streams or ponds in open forest and freshwater swamp forest. DISTRIBUTION: Resident in much of Myanmar, S, W Thailand, Cambodia, S Laos, S Vietnam and N Peninsular Malaysia.

7 STORM'S STORK *Ciconia stormi* 75–91cm FIELD NOTES: Usually forages alone or in pairs. In flight shows black underwing and tail, the latter often covered by white undertail-coverts. VOICE: A short series of sibilant whistles and a *karau*. Bill-clapping occurs at the nest site. HABITAT: Freshwater peat-swamp forest, rivers, streams and pools in forests. DISTRIBUTION: Resident in S Thailand and Peninsular Malaysia.

8 WHITE STORK *Ciconia ciconia* 100–115cm FIELD NOTES: In flight underwing shows white coverts and black flight feathers, tail white. VOICE: Generally silent. HABITAT: Dry or damp grassland. DISTRIBUTION: Vagrant.

9 ORIENTAL STORK (EASTERN WHITE STORK) *Ciconia boyciana* 110–150cm FIELD NOTES: In flight underwing similar to White Stork. Generally in small flocks. VOICE: Generally silent. May bill-clap while gliding. HABITAT: Marshes, wet meadows, lakes and coastal intertidal areas. DISTRIBUTION: Winter visitor to SE China and Taiwan.

10 BLACK-NECKED STORK *Ephippiorhynchus asiaticus* 129–150cm FIELD NOTES: In flight both upperwing and underwing white with wide black band on coverts, tail black. VOICE: Generally silent. HABITAT: Freshwater swamps, wet areas in open forest. DISTRIBUTION: Resident in S Thailand, Cambodia, S Laos; possibly Myanmar and N, C Laos.

24 STORKS; IBISES; SPOONBILLS

1 LESSER ADJUTANT *Leptoptilos javanicus* 110–120cm FIELD NOTES: Usually encountered singly or in small flocks. In flight blackish underwing shows a small white triangle in axillary area. Flies with neck drawn back. VOICE: During display utters a series of high-pitched squeaks and cow-like *moos*. HABITAT: Marshes, forest pools, freshwater swamp forest, mangroves and mudflats. DISTRIBUTION: Resident in S Myanmar (Tenasserim), S Thailand, Cambodia, S Laos, S Vietnam and Peninsular Malaysia.

2 GREATER ADJUTANT *Leptoptilos dubius* 120–150cm FIELD NOTES: Non-breeding adults have wings more uniform slate black. In flight underwing paler grey than Lesser Adjutant, but retains small white triangle in axillary area. VOICE: At breeding sites utters squealing and mooing sounds along with much bill-clapping. HABITAT: Marshes and pools in or near open dry forests, swamp forest, paddyfields and various open areas. DISTRIBUTION: Rare resident in Cambodia and possibly S Myanmar; non-breeding visitor to Thailand, S Laos and S Vietnam, vagrant elsewhere.

3 BLACK-HEADED IBIS (ORIENTAL or BLACK-NECKED IBIS) *Threskiornis melanocephalus* 65–75cm FIELD NOTES: Usually seen in small groups. Breeds in colonies, often with herons, storks and cormorants. Juvenile has bare skin restricted to face. VOICE: Generally silent; makes strange grunts at breeding sites. HABITAT: Marshes, mudflats, saltmarshes and coastal mudflats. DISTRIBUTION: Resident in Cambodia and S Vietnam. Non-breeding resident in Myanmar, Thailand, N Vietnam, SE China and Taiwan; vagrant elsewhere.

4 GLOSSY IBIS *Plegadis falcinellus* 55–65cm FIELD NOTES: Usually found in small groups. Flies with neck extended and legs protruding beyond tail. VOICE: A grunting *grru* or *graa*; at breeding sites utters grunting and croaking sounds. HABITAT: Various wetlands, including marshes, lakes and coastal lagoons. DISTRIBUTION: Resident in Cambodia, S Vietnam and possibly C Myanmar. Non-breeding visitor to SW, S, E Myanmar, vagrant elsewhere.

5 RED-NAPED IBIS (BLACK IBIS) *Pseudibis papillosa* 68cm FIELD NOTES: Usually in small groups. White covert patch often concealed when perched or walking, but very obvious in flight. Juvenile lacks the bare skin of crown and nape. VOICE: Male utters a trumpet-like call when advertising or on the wing. HABITAT: Grasslands, cultivations, lakesides and marshes. DISTRIBUTION: Scarce resident in SW Myanmar.

6 WHITE-SHOULDERED IBIS *Pseudibis davisoni* 75–85cm FIELD NOTES: In flight shows a white patch on inner forewing. Juvenile browner with dirty white collar. VOICE: Utters a hoarse, screaming *ERRRRRRRROH* alongside a subdued *ohhaaa ohhaaa* and *errr-ah*; also other screams and honking sounds. HABITAT: Streams, ponds and marshy areas in open lowland forests. DISTRIBUTION: Rare in Cambodia, S Laos, S Vietnam and possibly Myanmar and C Vietnam.

7 GIANT IBIS *Pseudibis gigantea* 102–106cm FIELD NOTES: Shy, probably best located by calls given at dawn or dusk; usually encountered in pairs or small groups. In flight upperwing greyish with black primaries, underwing all dark. VOICE: A repeated, loud and ringing *a-leurk a-leurk*. HABITAT: Marshy areas, ponds and streams in open lowland forest. Also around lakes, marshes and on open plains. DISTRIBUTION: Rare resident in Cambodia, S Laos and possibly S Vietnam.

8 SPOONBILL (EURASIAN or WHITE SPOONBILL) *Platalea leucorodia* 80–90cm FIELD NOTES: Sociable. Non-breeding birds lack the yellow tinge to crest and breast. Juvenile has pinkish bill and legs and black tips to primaries. VOICE: Generally silent. HABITAT: Freshwater lakes, swamps, coastal lagoons and mudflats. DISTRIBUTION: Non-breeding visitor to Taiwan, SW, E China and Vietnam; vagrant elsewhere.

9 BLACK-FACED SPOONBILL (LESSER SPOONBILL) *Platalea minor* 60–84cm FIELD NOTES: Usually found in groups. Non-breeding birds lose the yellow tinge to crest and breast. Juvenile has black tips to primaries. VOICE: Generally silent. HABITAT: Tidal mudflats, saltmarshes, estuaries and inland lakes. DISTRIBUTION: Non-breeding visitor to parts of C China, SE China, Taiwan and Vietnam; vagrant elsewhere.

25 OSPREY; VULTURES

1 OSPREY *Pandion haliaetus* 55–63cm FIELD NOTES: Feeds on fish, by hovering then plunging feet-first to grab prey. Juvenile as adult, but mantle and wing feathers fringed pale buff. VOICE: When alarmed gives a hoarse, sharp *kew-kew-kew-kew*. HABITAT: Lakes, rivers, coastal lagoons and estuaries. DISTRIBUTION: Resident in SE China and Taiwan; fairly widespread non-breeding visitor from S China southwards.

2 EGYPTIAN VULTURE *Neophron percnopterus* 60–70cm FIELD NOTES: Flight consists of deep wing-beats with more flaps than larger vultures. Juvenile generally dark brownish-black; some show pale fringes to wing feathers. VOICE: Usually silent. HABITAT: Mountains, open areas and around rubbish dumps. DISTRIBUTION: Vagrant.

3 LAMMERGEIER (BEARDED VULTURE) *Gypaetus barbatus* 100–115cm FIELD NOTES: Spends much time soaring, sometimes at a great height; glides with wings slightly bowed. Juvenile generally dark brownish-black with a whitish patch on mantle; ash grey below from breast to undertail-coverts. VOICE: Generally silent apart from a shrill *feeeee* uttered during aerial display. HABITAT: Mountains with sheer crags. Hunts over plains, slopes and valleys. During winter resorts to lower areas. DISTRIBUTION: Possibly occurs in mountainous areas of SW China.

4 SLENDER-BILLED VULTURE *Gyps tenuirostris* 93–100cm FIELD NOTES: Note pale thighs, which often show well in flight. Glides with wings flat, soars with wings held in a shallow V. VOICE: May utter hissing and cackling sounds, otherwise generally silent. HABITAT: Open country. DISTRIBUTION: Resident in S Laos, Cambodia and possibly Myanmar and C Vietnam (C Annam).

5 HIMALAYAN GRIFFON VULTURE (HIMALAYAN GRIFFON) *Gyps himalayensis* 115–125cm FIELD NOTES: Glides with wings flat, soars with wings held in a shallow V. Juvenile generally dark with pale shaft streaks, head and neck whitish; underwing shows pale lines on coverts. VOICE: Occasionally utters whistling and clucking noises. HABITAT: Open country and high mountain areas. DISTRIBUTION: Vagrant recorded from Thailand, Peninsular Malaysia and Singapore.

6 INDIAN WHITE-BACKED VULTURE (WHITE-RUMPED VULTURE) *Gyps bengalensis* 75–85cm FIELD NOTES: Adult in flight from above shows prominent white rump. Soars with wings held in a shallow V. Juvenile is dark brown with pale streaking on underparts and pale fringes above; lacks white rump. VOICE: At roosts or when feeding utters a strident, creaky *kakakaka*; also various grunts, hisses and squeals. HABITAT: Open country, cliffs and around abattoirs. DISTRIBUTION: Massive population decline since the late 20th century has seen populations plummet to zero across much of its range. Possibly extinct in China; small populations remain in Myanmar and Cambodia. Rare in Thailand, Laos and S Vietnam.

7 RED-HEADED VULTURE (KING VULTURE) *Sarcogyps calvus* 85cm FIELD NOTES: Soars with wings held in a shallow V. Juvenile generally dull brown with white down on head; in flight shows dull grey-white belly and white undertail-coverts. VOICE: Hoarse croaks and screams, usually given during feeding disputes. HABITAT: Open country and wooded hills. DISTRIBUTION: Resident in SW China, W Thailand, S Laos, NE Cambodia, C Vietnam and possibly Myanmar.

8 CINEREOUS VULTURE (EURASIAN BLACK or MONK VULTURE) *Aegypius monachus* 100–110cm FIELD NOTES: Glides and soars with wings held flat. Juvenile generally all black, including head feathering; cere whitish. VOICE: Usually silent. HABITAT: Grasslands, open forest and mountains. DISTRIBUTION: Winter visitor to Myanmar and Laos, otherwise widespread recordings of vagrancy.

26 HARRIERS

1 MARSH HARRIER (WESTERN or EURASIAN MARSH HARRIER) *Circus aeruginosus* 48–56cm FIELD NOTES: Generally flies close to the ground, quartering reedbeds or open grassland using a series of flaps followed by a glide with wings held in a shallow V. When prey is sighted, stops quickly and drops feet-first to capture victim. Juvenile similar to adult female but usually lacks buff forewing and sometimes buff head markings. Dark morph male, all brownish-black with tail, secondaries and inner primaries greyish. VOICE: Generally silent but when alarmed may give a cackling *chek-ek-ek-ek-ek*. HABITAT: Reedbeds, grasslands, cultivated fields and saltmarsh. DISTRIBUTION: Winter visitor to Myanmar and C Thailand; vagrant elsewhere.

2 EASTERN MARSH HARRIER (SPOTTED MARSH HARRIER) *Circus spilonotus* 47–55cm FIELD NOTES: Actions and habits similar to Marsh Harrier, which is often thought to be conspecific. Sometimes forms large flocks especially near roosting sites. Intensity of head markings variable, often leading to a blackish face or blackish head. Juvenile like adult male Marsh Harrier but with darker secondaries, face and tail, the latter barred black. VOICE: Generally silent, may utter a mewing *keeau* at roost sites. HABITAT: Marshes, grasslands and paddyfields. DISTRIBUTION: Widespread winter visitor.

3 HEN HARRIER *Circus cyaneus* 44–52cm FIELD NOTES: Glides with wings held level or in a shallow V. Feeding technique similar to Marsh Harrier but with quicker wing-beats and shorter glides. Juvenile similar to adult female but with rufous tinge to underparts and underwing-coverts; there is a pronounced dark crescent on ear-coverts. VOICE: When alarmed male gives a *chek-ek-ek-ek* and female a twittering *chit-it-it-it-it-et-it-et-it-et*. HABITAT: Open grasslands, marshes and coastal marshes. DISTRIBUTION: Winter visitor to S, SE China, N Myanmar, NW Thailand and N Laos; vagrant elsewhere.

4 PALLID HARRIER *Circus macrourus* 40–48cm FIELD NOTES: Compared to Hen Harrier has a slimmer build and a more buoyant, tern-like flight, with wings held in a shallow V. Hunting technique similar to Hen Harrier. Juvenile upperparts similar to adult female, underparts and underwing-coverts plain rufous; dark ear-coverts and neck are accentuated by a pale collar. VOICE: When alarmed gives a rapid *chit-er chit-er chit-it-it*. HABITAT: Open grasslands, cultivations and marshes. DISTRIBUTION: Winter visitor to Myanmar; vagrant elsewhere.

5 MONTAGU'S HARRIER *Circus pygargus* 43–47cm FIELD NOTES: Flight more buoyant than Hen Harrier, wings held in a shallow V. Hunting actions as Hen Harrier. Juvenile similar to juvenile Pallid Harrier but with less noticeable pale collar, which if showing is usually more rufous. VOICE: When alarmed utters a shrill *chekk-ekk-ekk-ekk…* HABITAT: Open country, including grasslands, scrubby plains, cultivations and marshes. DISTRIBUTION: Vagrant.

6 PIED HARRIER *Circus melanoleucos* 41–49cm FIELD NOTES: Usually appears heavier in flapping flight than either Pallid or Montagu's Harrier. Glides with wings held in a shallow V. Juvenile dark brown above with white band on uppertail-coverts; underparts, including underwing-coverts, rufous; streaked darker, face pattern much as adult female. VOICE: Generally silent; female utters a *chak-chak-chak-chak-chak* when alarmed. HABITAT: Open grasslands, marshes, paddyfields and stubble fields. DISTRIBUTION: Widespread winter visitor.

27 KITES; EAGLES

1 BLACK-SHOULDERED KITE (BLACK-WINGED KITE) *Elanus caeruleus* 31–35cm
FIELD NOTES: Often hovers when searching for prey. In flight shows large black patch on
upperwing-coverts. Upperwing of juvenile tinged brownish with pale fringes, breast and
crown washed rusty. VOICE: Various calls noted including a harsh *w-eeyah*, a sharp *kree-ak* and a piping *pii-uu*. HABITAT: Grassland mixed with scattered trees and cultivations.
DISTRIBUTION: Widespread resident from S China southwards.

2 BLACK KITE *Milvus migrans* 55–60cm FIELD NOTES: Gregarious. Scavenger. Flight
action 'loose' with much twisting of tail; fork of tail often disappears when tail spread.
Juvenile grey-buff below streaked dark, pale fringes to mantle and wings; dark eye surround.
M. m. lineatus (Black-eared Kite) (2b) a resident in China and a winter visitor elsewhere is
often regarded as a separate species. VOICE: A whinnying *pee-errrr*. HABITAT: Open areas,
wetlands and urban areas. DISTRIBUTION: Widespread summer and winter resident.

3 BRAHMINY KITE (RED-BACKED KITE) *Haliastur indus* 45–51cm FIELD NOTES:
Glides on raised wings, soars with wings held in a flat V. Juvenile generally rusty-brown,
mantle and wings fringed rusty-buff, underparts and head streaked rusty-buff. Juvenile
underwing dark with large pale patch formed by inner primaries and base of outer primaries.
VOICE: A wheezy squeal. HABITAT: Lakes, rivers, flooded paddyfields, coastal lagoons,
estuaries and fishing harbours. DISTRIBUTION: Resident in Taiwan, E, SE China, Vietnam,
Cambodia, Peninsular Malaysia, S Thailand, Myanmar and possibly Laos.

4 WHITE-BELLIED SEA EAGLE *Haliaeetus leucogaster* 66–71cm FIELD NOTES: Glides
and soars with wings held in a stiff V. Juvenile has brown mantle and wings with pale
fringes, head and underparts greyish white, the latter with a brownish tinge, mainly on
the breast; tail whitish with a dark subterminal band. VOICE: A loud, honking *kank kank
kank kank...* also a faster *ken-ken-ken-ken* and *ka ka-kaaa*. HABITAT: Rocky coasts, islets and
sometimes on large lakes. DISTRIBUTION: Resident, mainly in coastal areas of SE China,
Vietnam, Cambodia, Thailand, Peninsular Malaysia, Myanmar and the Coco Islands.

5 WHITE-TAILED EAGLE (WHITE-TAILED SEA EAGLE) *Haliaeetus albicilla* 69–
92cm FIELD NOTES: Glides or soars on flat or slightly bowed wings. Juvenile generally
dark brown, tail feathers dark with pale grey-white centres; bill grey; underwing shows
pale axillaries and pale tips to greater-coverts, which forms a pale bar. VOICE: A shrill *klee
klee klee klee*, when alarmed gives a lower *klek klek klek*. HABITAT: Coasts, lakes, marshes
and rivers. DISTRIBUTION: Winter visitor to SW China, coastal SE China, Taiwan and N
Myanmar; vagrant elsewhere.

6 PALLAS'S FISH EAGLE *Haliaeetus leucoryphus* 76–84cm FIELD NOTES: Glides and
soars with wings held level. Juvenile generally dark brown; underwing shows a wide whitish
bar on greater-coverts and a large white patch on base of inner primaries; tail dark brown.
VOICE: A hoarse, barking *kvok kvok kvok*. HABITAT: Lakes, rivers, marshes and coastal
waters. DISTRIBUTION: Resident in S Myanmar; vagrant elsewhere.

7 LESSER FISH EAGLE *Haliaeetus humilis* 53–68cm FIELD NOTES: Soars and glides on
flattish wings. Spends much time perched on waterside trees. Juvenile generally greyish-brown with faint barring on flight feathers; tail grey with slightly paler base. VOICE: A
plaintive, gull-like *pheeow-pheeoow-pheeow...* also a repeated *pheeo-pheeo* given during
breeding. HABITAT: Large rivers in forests. DISTRIBUTION: Resident in Hainan, N, E, S
Myanmar, N, NW, S Thailand, Peninsular Malaysia, Laos and N, S Vietnam.

8 GREY-HEADED FISH EAGLE *Haliaeetus ichthyaetus* 69–74cm FIELD NOTES: Glides
and soars on flattish wings. Juvenile upperparts brown with head, neck and breast heavily
streaked whitish, undertail whitish; underwing pale buff-brown with darker trailing edge;
tail greyish-white, barred darker. VOICE: A squawking *kwok*, harsh screams and, during
display, a far-carrying *tiu-weeeu*. HABITAT: Rivers and lakes in wooded areas, coastal lagoons
and estuaries. DISTRIBUTION: Resident in Myanmar, Peninsular Malaysia, Singapore, SW
Thailand, Cambodia, N, S Laos, Vietnam and Hainan.

lineatus

28 SPARROWHAWKS

1 CRESTED GOSHAWK *Accipiter trivirgatus* 30–46cm FIELD NOTES: Usual flight consists of stiff wing-beats followed by short glides; often soars high above forest canopy. Female is browner than male, especially on head. Juvenile has dark mantle and wings with pale fringes and head pale rusty with dark streaks. Juvenile has underparts white tinged rusty with dark spots or streaks on breast, wide brownish bars on flanks and narrow brownish bars on thighs. VOICE: A shrill, prolonged scream, *he he hehehehe*; also loud screams and deep croaks. HABITAT: Broadleaved evergreen, deciduous and mixed broadleaved and coniferous forest. DISTRIBUTION: Resident over much of the region south from S China. Also occurs on Taiwan.

2 SHIKRA (LITTLE BANDED GOSHAWK) *Accipiter badius* 30–36cm FIELD NOTES: Usually hunts from hidden, leafy perch, taking prey from trees or the ground. Juvenile generally brown above, pale buff below with dark streaks on breast and dark bars on flanks; black line down centre of throat. VOICE: A piping *keeu-keeu-keeu* and a shrill *kewick*. HABITAT: Open woodland, forest edge and wooded cultivations. DISTRIBUTION: Widespread resident south from S China.

3 CHINESE SPARROWHAWK (HORSFIELD'S SPARROWHAWK, GREY FROG HAWK) *Accipiter soloensis* 27–35cm FIELD NOTES: Generally catches frogs, lizards and insects on the ground. Female larger with faint barring below. Juvenile generally dark brown, head with pale streaks; underparts whitish, heavily streaked dark on breast, rusty bars on flanks; underwing shows barring on flight feathers and faintly barred buff coverts. VOICE: A rapid, accelerating piping that descends in pitch. HABITAT: Woodland, often near wetlands. DISTRIBUTION: Widespread summer visitor to China, passage migrant elsewhere.

4 JAPANESE SPARROWHAWK (JAPANESE LESSER or ASIATIC SPARROWHAWK) *Accipiter gularis* 29–34cm FIELD NOTES: Often migrates in large flocks. Perches inconspicuously before dashing out after avian prey. Juvenile similar to adult female but breast streaked not barred. VOICE: When alarmed utters a shrill *kek-kek-kek*. HABITAT: Lightly wooded areas, forest edge and open country. DISTRIBUTION: Winter visitor to SE China, Taiwan, C Thailand, Peninsular Malaysia and Singapore, passage migrant elsewhere.

5 BESRA *Accipiter virgatus* 29–36cm FIELD NOTES: Hunting technique as Japanese Sparrowhawk. Juveniles lack rufous flanks and upperparts are fringed rusty, otherwise much like adult female. VOICE: A rapid *tchew-tchew-tchew*. HABITAT: Dense forests; uses more open woodland post breeding. DISTRIBUTION: Resident in S, SE China, Taiwan, Hainan, C Vietnam, Laos, Myanmar and N Thailand; vagrant elsewhere.

6 SPARROWHAWK (EURASIAN or NORTHERN SPARROWHAWK) *Accipiter nisus* 28–38cm FIELD NOTES: Surprises avian prey by dashing from a hidden perch or chasing after prey using a stealthy, twisting flight. Juvenile like adult female but with browner upperparts. VOICE: When alarmed utters a rapid *kew-kew-kew-kew-kew*. HABITAT: Forests, scrub forest, open woodlands and wooded cultivations. DISTRIBUTION: Winter visitor to C, S, E China, Hainan, Myanmar, N Thailand, N, C Laos and N Vietnam.

7 GOSHAWK (NORTHERN GOSHAWK) *Accipiter gentilis* 48–62cm FIELD NOTES: Hunting method similar to Sparrowhawk. Female larger and browner-grey. Juvenile generally brown above, pale buff-white below with dark streaking. VOICE: When alarmed utters a loud *kyee-kyee-kyee*. HABITAT: Wooded areas and sometimes more open areas. DISTRIBUTION: Resident in SW China and N Myanmar; winter visitor to SE China, Taiwan, NW Thailand and N Vietnam; vagrant elsewhere.

29 BUZZARDS

1 CRESTED SERPENT EAGLE *Spilornis cheela* 56–74cm FIELD NOTES: Often seen soaring and calling high over forests. Juvenile has underparts white with fine dark streaking, upperparts grey-brown with pale fringes; in flight from below appears white, with dark barred tail. Various races occur in the region including the paler *S. c. ricketti* from N Vietnam and SE China and the darker *S. c. malayensis* south from S Myanmar (neither depicted). VOICE: In flight utters a shrill *kwee-kwee-kwee-kwee-kwee-kwee-kwee*. HABITAT: Well-wooded areas. DISTRIBUTION: Resident southwards from S China. Also occurs on Taiwan.

2 WHITE-EYED BUZZARD *Butastur teesa* 36–43cm FIELD NOTES: Sits for long periods on a prominent perch from where it drops onto ground-based prey. Juvenile buffish below with dark streaks on breast, head paler with facial and throat stripes narrower or lacking. VOICE: A melancholic *pit-weer pit-weer*. HABITAT: Dry open country with scattered trees and scrub. DISTRIBUTION: Resident in Myanmar.

3 GREY-FACED BUZZARD *Butastur indicus* 46cm FIELD NOTES: Often forms flocks during migration. Hunts frogs, lizards and rodents, using a dead tree as a lookout site. Juvenile paler below with dark streaking on breast and pale supercillium. VOICE: A tremulous *chit-kwee*. HABITAT: Wooded country with nearby open areas. DISTRIBUTION: Widespread winter visitor south of China, also occurs on Hainan and Taiwan; passage migrant elsewhere.

4 RUFOUS-WINGED BUZZARD *Butastur liventer* 35–41cm FIELD NOTES: Solitary. Not shy. Regularly uses low-level perch. Glides and soars with wings held flat. Juvenile like adult but darker with a pale supercillium. VOICE: A shrill *pit-piu*. HABITAT: Dry deciduous forest, secondary growth, savannah and paddyfields. DISTRIBUTION: Resident in SW China, S Myanmar, N Thailand, Cambodia, C, S Laos and S Vietnam.

5 BUZZARD (COMMON BUZZARD) *Buteo buteo* 51–57cm FIELD NOTES: Regularly perches in the open on posts or trees. Glides with wings held flat, soars with wings in a shallow V, may hover. Plumage very variable; *B. b. vulpinus* (5b) possibly occurs in mountainous areas in north of region. Juveniles lack dark subterminal band on tail. VOICE: A mewing *peeeeooo*. HABITAT: Open country with scattered trees, open forest and forest edge. DISTRIBUTION: Widespread winter visitor.

6 LONG-LEGGED BUZZARD *Buteo rufinus* 50–65cm FIELD NOTES: Often encountered perched on a prominent post. More 'flexible' wing-beats than Buzzard; soars and glides with wings held in a shallow V. Plumage variable, some very pale cream-buff. Juvenile has tail finely barred. VOICE: A mellow *aaah*. HABITAT: Open country. DISTRIBUTION: Vagrant.

7 UPLAND BUZZARD (MONGOLIAN BUZZARD) *Buteo hemilasius* 66–71cm FIELD NOTES: Plumage variable. Deep flexible wing-beats, soars with wings held in a shallow V. Often hovers. Juvenile like adult but more streaked below, tail more barred. VOICE: A prolonged mewing. HABITAT: Open areas in hills and mountains. DISTRIBUTION: Winter visitor to E China.

8 ROUGH-LEGGED BUZZARD (ROUGH-LEGGED HAWK) *Buteo lagopus* 45–62cm FIELD NOTES: Plumage variable, some much paler especially on head and breast. Slow 'loose' wing-beats, flight sometimes recalls a large harrier. Regularly hovers, with deep wing-beats. VOICE: A low-pitched, cat-like *peeeooo*. HABITAT: Open country. DISTRIBUTION: Rare winter visitor to E China.

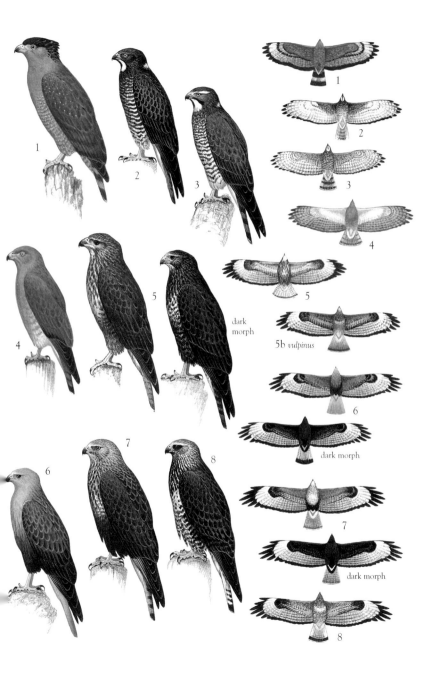

30 EAGLES

1 BLACK EAGLE (INDIAN or ASIAN BLACK EAGLE) *Ictinaetus malaiensis* 69–81cm FIELD NOTES: Often seen soaring low over forest canopy, with wings held in a shallow V, searching for nests. Preys on eggs and nestlings. Juvenile has head, underparts and underwing-coverts pale streaked dark brown. VOICE: A plaintive *kleeee-kee* or *hee-lee-leeuw.* HABITAT: Broadleaved evergreen forest and nearby open areas. DISTRIBUTION: Widespread resident south from southern China; also occurs in Taiwan.

2 INDIAN SPOTTED EAGLE *Clanga hastata* 59–67cm FIELD NOTES: Solitary. Glides on slightly arched wings. Gape extends to back or slightly beyond eye. Juvenile has pale tips to feathers of mantle and wings, less pronounced than on juvenile Spotted Eagle. VOICE: A high-pitched laughing cackle. HABITAT: Wooded areas interspersed with cultivation and open country. DISTRIBUTION: Small population in N Cambodia; possibly resident in S, SW Myanmar.

3 SPOTTED EAGLE (GREATER SPOTTED EAGLE) *Clanga clanga* 59–69cm FIELD NOTES: Often encountered perched on a riverside tree, bush or bank. Solitary or in small groups during migration. Glides on arched wings Juvenile usually has pronounced white tips to mantle and wing feathers. VOICE: A yelping *kyak, kluck-kluck or tyuck-tyuck.* HABITAT: Wetlands and open country. DISTRIBUTION: Winter visitor to Taiwan, E China, S Myanmar, Thailand, Cambodia, N, C Laos, S Vietnam and Peninsular Malaysia; scarce passage migrant or vagrant elsewhere.

4 TAWNY EAGLE *Aquila rapax* 65–75cm FIELD NOTES: Gape extends to middle of eye. Plumage variable; can often look scruffy. Scavenges, often gregariously. Soars on flat or slightly raised wings, glides with wings arched. VOICE: May utter a barking *kowk,* otherwise usually silent. HABITAT: Open country. DISTRIBUTION: Vagrant.

5 STEPPE EAGLE *Aquila nipalensis* 67–87cm FIELD NOTES: Gape extends to rear of eye. Glides with wings arched, although may be flatter than both Indian Spotted and Spotted Eagles. VOICE: May utter deep barking *ow,* otherwise usually silent. HABITAT: Open country DISTRIBUTION: Winter visitor or vagrant to SE China, Myanmar, S Thailand, Peninsular Malaysia, Singapore and N Vietnam.

6 IMPERIAL EAGLE (EASTERN IMPERIAL EAGLE) *Aquila heliaca* 72–84cm FIELD NOTES: Usually solitary. Often seeks a prominent perch, on tree or the ground, to survey surrounding area. In soaring and gliding flight wings usually held level. Juvenile pale greyish-buff with pronounced white tips to head. Mantle and wing feathers, underparts grey-buff streaked with dark brown. VOICE: A deep, barking *owk-owk-owk.* HABITAT: Open country, cultivation and around large wetlands. DISTRIBUTION: Winter visitor to S, E China, vagrant further south.

7 GOLDEN EAGLE *Aquila chrysaetos* 76–93cm FIELD NOTES: Spends long periods soaring around mountain crags with wings held in a shallow V. Hunts by both in low flight and from stoops from height. In flight juvenile shows large white patches at base of primaries, outer secondaries and on base of tail. VOICE: Generally silent, although in flight may give a fluty whistle. HABITAT: Mountains, rocky hills and open country. DISTRIBUTION: May occur in the mountains of China bordering the region, otherwise a vagrant.

31 EAGLES

1 BONELLI'S EAGLE *Aquila fasciata* 65–72cm FIELD NOTES: Usually in pairs. Glides with wings held level. Juvenile pale rufous, or whitish below; in flight shows pale rufous underwing-coverts, tail pale grey barred darker. VOICE: Generally silent, during display utters a fluting *klu-klu-klu-kluee*, a melodious *iuh* and a long *eeeoo*. HABITAT: Wooded areas, often near cliffs or wetlands. DISTRIBUTION: Resident in China, C, E Myanmar, possibly also NW Thailand and Laos.

2 BOOTED EAGLE *Hieraaetus pennatus* 50–57cm FIELD NOTES: Glides on arched wings. Some plumage variation occurs in both morphs, especially on underwing-coverts, which can be more rufous tinged. In head-on flight shows white 'headlights' at joint of neck and wing. VOICE: A shrill, chattering *ki-ki-ki...* also a buzzard-like *hiyaah*. HABITAT: Forested areas with nearby open land. DISTRIBUTION: Vagrant, mainly to Myanmar, Thailand, S Laos, Peninsular Malaysia and Singapore.

3 SHORT-TOED EAGLE (SHORT-TOED SNAKE-EAGLE) *Circaetus gallicus* 62–67cm FIELD NOTES: Plumage variable, head and upper breast pale grey-white to blackish, underparts virtually plain or barred black and white in the darker-headed forms. Often hovers when searching for prey. VOICE: A plaintive *weeo* or *weeooo*, also a gull-like *woh-woh-woh*. HABITAT: Varied, including wooded open country and scrub. DISTRIBUTION: Vagrant, recorded from many parts south of China.

4 RUFOUS-BELLIED EAGLE (RUFOUS-BELLIED HAWK EAGLE) *Lophotriorchis kienerii* 53–61cm FIELD NOTES: Soars high above forest canopy from where it makes spectacular falcon-like stoops to capture prey; also makes attacks on prey using a hidden perch. Juvenile white below, including underwing-coverts. VOICE: A low-pitched series *whi-whi-whi-whi* ending with a thin *yii*. HABITAT: Broadleaved evergreen forest. DISTRIBUTION: Resident in S Myanmar, Thailand, Peninsular Malaysia, C, S Laos and Vietnam; non-breeding visitor to Singapore.

5 MOUNTAIN HAWK EAGLE *Nisaetus nipalensis* 67–86cm FIELD NOTES: May soar above forest canopy but more often concealed among foliage. Juvenile has plain buff underparts, including underwing-coverts. VOICE: Mountain and hill forests. HABITAT: A shrill whistled *tlueet-weet-weet* and a repeated *kee-kikik*. DISTRIBUTION: Resident in Taiwan, Hainan, S, E China, W, N Myanmar, NE Thailand, Laos and Vietnam.

6 CHANGEABLE HAWK EAGLE (DIMORPHIC HAWK EAGLE) *Nisaetus cirrhatus limnaeetus* 58–77cm FIELD NOTES: Uses a concealed forest perch from where it makes a short dash to capture prey. Juvenile has buff-white underparts and underwing-coverts. The race concerned in this region is considered by some authors to be a full species. VOICE: A series of shrill whistles. HABITAT: Broadleaved evergreen and deciduous forest. DISTRIBUTION: Widespread resident south of China, apart from C Thailand and Vietnam.

7 BLYTH'S HAWK EAGLE *Nisaetus alboniger* 50–58cm FIELD NOTES: Soars with wings held level. Hunts in the upper storey with an agile accipiter-like flight through trees. Juvenile generally pale rufous-buff on head, underparts and underwing, mantle and wings brown. VOICE: A screaming *yhu yhu yip-yip-yip* a shrill *pik-wuee* and a fast *wiii-hi*. HABITAT: Broadleaved evergreen upland forest. DISTRIBUTION: Resident in S Thailand and Peninsular Malaysia; vagrant elsewhere.

8 WALLACE'S HAWK EAGLE *Nisaetus nanus* 45–49cm FIELD NOTES: Actions and habits probably much as Blyth's Hawk Eagle. Juvenile like juvenile Blyth's Hawk Eagle but paler creamy below. VOICE: A shrill, high-pitched *yik-yee* or *kliit-kleeik*. HABITAT: Broadleaved evergreen forest. DISTRIBUTION: Resident in S Myanmar (Tenasserim), S Thailand and Peninsular Malaysia.

pale morph

dark morph

1

pale
morph

2

dark
morph

3

4

5

6

7

8

32 BAZAS; HONEY BUZZARD; BATHAWK; FALCONS

1 JERDON'S BAZA *Aviceda jerdoni* 41–48cm FIELD NOTES: Hunts from a perch, making short sorties to grab prey, usually insects, lizards or frogs. Juvenile similar to adult but with dark streaks on breast and neck. VOICE: A plaintive *pee-ow*. During display utters an excited, mewing *kip-kip-kip* or *kikiya kikiya*. HABITAT: Broadleaved evergreen forest and freshwater swamp forest. DISTRIBUTION: Resident in Hainan, SW China, S Myanmar (Tenasserim), Thailand, Peninsular Malaysia, Vietnam and Cambodia; may wander further afield post breeding.

2 BLACK BAZA *Aviceda leuphotes* 30–35cm FIELD NOTES: Flies much like a crow interspersed with level-winged glides. Regularly hovers or hangs from foliage to capture prey. Juvenile browner with more white markings on mantle and white streaks on throat. *A. i. syama* (2b) resident in S China and Hainan, also winters throughout the south of the region. VOICE: A soft, quavering squeal or whistle, *tcheeoua*. HABITAT: Glades or streams in broadleaved evergreen forest, deciduous forest and freshwater swamp forest. DISTRIBUTION: Summer visitor to S China; resident in Hainan, northern areas of Myanmar, N, NW Thailand, Cambodia, Laos and C, S Vietnam. Winter visitor or passage migrant elsewhere.

3 ORIENTAL HONEY BUZZARD (CRESTED HONEY BUZZARD) *Pernis ptilorhynchus* 52–68cm FIELD NOTES: Very variable, especially underparts, which range from pale with reddish bars, rufous with slightly darker bars to almost solid black. Juvenile paler below with flight feathers more closely barred; tail has thinner, fainter large bars. Dark race *P. p. torquatus* (3b) is resident in S Myanmar (Tenasserim) and SW Thailand southward. VOICE: A high-pitched *wee-way-who* or *weehey-weehey*. HABITAT: Wooded areas. DISTRIBUTION: Widespread summer and winter visitor from S, SE China southward.

4 BAT HAWK *Macheiramphus alcinus* 41–51cm FIELD NOTES: Crepuscular or nocturnal hunter of bats. Flight is rapid with shallow stiff wing-beats. Juvenile brown above, white below with variable blackish blotches. VOICE: A high, yelping *kwik kwik kwik kwik…* HABITAT: Open areas near broadleaved evergreen forest, near bat caves and around human habitations. DISTRIBUTION: Resident in S Myanmar (Tenasserim) and Peninsular Malaysia; vagrant elsewhere.

5 WHITE-RUMPED FALCON (WHITE-RUMPED PYGMY FALCON) *Polihierax insignis* 24–27cm FIELD NOTES: Shrike-like actions: sits on high, bare branches and dives to the ground to take prey, which includes insects and frogs. Breeds in tree holes or nests of other birds. Juveniles like adults but with more streaking on head and breast. VOICE: A long, descending whistle. HABITAT: Open deciduous woodland, clearings and forest edge. DISTRIBUTION: Resident in SW, C, S Myanmar, Thailand, Cambodia, Laos and S Vietnam.

6 COLLARED FALCONET (RED-THIGHED, RED-LEGGED or RED-BREASTED FALCONET) *Microhierax caerulescens* 15–18cm FIELD NOTES: Seeks prominent exposed perch from where to make short shrike-like sorties to capture prey. Slowly pumps tail and nods head while perched. Breeds in old woodpecker or barbet holes. Juvenile has forehead and supercillium pale rufous and a whitish throat. VOICE: A high-pitched *kli-kli-kli* or *killi-killi-killi*. HABITAT: Edges and clearings in broadleaved evergreen and mixed forest. DISTRIBUTION: Resident in Myanmar, northern Thailand, Cambodia, Laos and S Vietnam.

7 BLACK-THIGHED FALCONET (BLACK-LEGGED FALCONET) *Microhierax fringillarius* 15–17cm FIELD NOTES: Actions and habits similar to Collared Falconet. Juvenile like adult but supercillium tinged rufous. VOICE: A shrill, squealing *kweer*. HABITAT: Broadleaved evergreen forest clearings, forest edge, wooded cultivations and parkland. DISTRIBUTION: Resident in S Myanmar (Tenasserim), S Thailand, Peninsular Malaysia and Singapore.

8 PIED FALCONET (WHITE-LEGGED FALCONET) *Microhierax melanoleucos* 18–20cm FIELD NOTES: Habits and actions much as other falconets. Juvenile similar to adult but with a yellowish bill and orbital skin. VOICE: A shrill whistle, a low chattering and hissing sounds when agitated. HABITAT: Broadleaved evergreen forest edge and clearings. DISTRIBUTION: Resident in SW, S, E China, N, C Laos and N Vietnam.

2b *syama*

torquatus

3b

dark

normal

♀

♂

♂

♀

33 FALCONS

1 LESSER KESTREL *Falco naumanni* 29–32cm FIELD NOTES: A social bird, migrates in flocks. Typically hovers less than Kestrel and, in level flight, wing-beats appear faster and shallower. White claws. VOICE: A rasping *chay-chay-chay*. When agitated utters a trilling *keerrrl* or *kikikik* HABITAT: Open areas including cultivations. DISTRIBUTION: Possible winter visitor to Myanmar and Laos.

2 KESTREL (COMMON or EURASIAN KESTREL) *Falco tinnunculus* 31–37cm FIELD NOTES: Frequently hovers when searching for food; also sits on a prominent post or other perch, from which to drop onto prey. Usually seen alone or in pairs. Black claws. VOICE: A shrill *kee-kee-kee-kee* and a trilling *vriii*. HABITAT: Open areas, including cultivations, cliffs and around human habitations. DISTRIBUTION: Resident in Taiwan and China; winter visitor and passage migrant elsewhere.

3 AMUR FALCON (EASTERN or MANCHURIAN RED-FOOTED FALCON) *Falco amurensis* 28–30cm FIELD NOTES: Highly manoeuvrable flight when pursuing flying insects; also hovers. Gregarious. Juvenile like adult female, but head, mantle and wings brownish-grey with rufous fringes. VOICE: A shrill *kew-kew-kew* given at roost sites. HABITAT: Open country and wooded areas. DISTRIBUTION: Passage migrant or vagrant.

4 MERLIN *Falco columbarius* 25–30cm FIELD NOTES: Pursuit flight is often dashing and slightly undulating, with twists and turns, usually at low level. Juvenile like adult female but browner without greyish cast, underparts streaks darker. VOICE: Generally silent away from breeding sites. HABITAT: Open country. DISTRIBUTION: Rare winter visitor to China, vagrant elsewhere.

5 HOBBY (EURASIAN or NORTHERN HOBBY) *Falco subbuteo* 30–36cm FIELD NOTES: Fast acrobatic flier; catches prey, mainly insects and small birds, in flight. Regularly perches on isolated trees. Juvenile like adult but browner above and on head, underparts generally buff, heavily streaked dark brown. VOICE: A rapid *kew-kew-kew-kew…* HABITAT: Open and wooded areas. DISTRIBUTION: Summer visitor to north of region; resident S, SE China; winter visitor, passage migrant or vagrant elsewhere.

6 ORIENTAL HOBBY (INDIAN HOBBY) *Falco severus* 27–30cm FIELD NOTES: Actions and habits much as Hobby. Juvenile very similar to juvenile Hobby, but underparts pale rufous-buff and upperparts darker. VOICE: A rapid *ki-ki-ki-ki*. HABITAT: Open glades in forests, secondary growth, cultivations, mangroves and near limestone cliffs. DISTRIBUTION: Resident in Hainan, SW, S China, Myanmar, Vietnam, Thailand, N Laos and E Cambodia.

7 SAKER (SAKER FALCON) *Falco cherrug* 45–55cm FIELD NOTES: Often encountered sitting on rocks. Usually hunts at low level. Most prey, predominantly rodents, taken on the ground. Occasionally hovers or makes aerial stoops to catch birds. Juvenile is darker above and has heavier spotting below. VOICE: A harsh *kek-kek-kek…* HABITAT: Open grasslands and wetlands. DISTRIBUTION: Possible winter visitor to the northern borders of the region.

8 LAGGAR (LAGGAR FALCON) *Falco jugger* FIELD NOTES: Waits on an exposed perch. When prey is sighted, makes a swift, low-level attack; victim taken on the ground or in the air. Juvenile like adult but crown browner and underparts heavily dark streaked, throat whitish. VOICE: A shrill *whi-ee-ee*. HABITAT: Semi-arid open country and dry cultivations. DISTRIBUTION: Scarce resident in northern Myanmar.

9 PEREGRINE (PEREGRINE FALCON) *Falco peregrinus* 36–48cm FIELD NOTES: Prey captured and killed in mid-air following a fast pursuit and high-speed stoop on closed wings. Juvenile brown above, pale below with dark streaking, head pattern as adult but browner. The bright race *P. p. perigrinator* (9b), which is sometimes more barred below than depicted, is resident in China and Myanmar. VOICE: A loud *ka-yak ka-yak ka-yak…* or when alarmed a shrill *kek-kek-kek…* HABITAT: Variable, including open areas, wetlands and cliffs (coastal and inland). DISTRIBUTION: Resident in China, S, E Myanmar, W, NE, S Thailand and Peninsular Malaysia; widespread winter visitor.

peregrinator

peregrinator

34 CRANES

1 COMMON CRANE (EURASIAN CRANE) *Grus grus* 110–120cm FIELD NOTES: Gregarious, often forms large flocks post breeding. Flies with neck outstretched and legs protruding well beyond tail. In flight, from below, shows black primaries and secondaries. Juvenile more-brownish-grey on upperparts, neck and head; lacks adult head pattern. VOICE: A far-carrying *krooh* and a repeated, harsh *kraah*. HABITAT: Marshes, open and cultivated areas. DISTRIBUTION: Winter visitor to China, N, E Myanmar and N Vietnam.

2 BLACK-NECKED CRANE *Grus nigricollis* 115cm FIELD NOTES: Flies with neck outstretched and legs protruding well beyond tail. In flight, from below, shows black flight feathers and tail. Juvenile has a brownish head and upper neck; upperparts greyish-ochre. VOICE: A series of loud, trumpeting honks. HABITAT: Marshes and agricultural valleys. DISTRIBUTION: Winter visitor to SW China.

3 HOODED CRANE *Grus monacha* 100cm FIELD NOTES: Often migrates alongside Common Cranes. Flies with neck outstretched and legs protruding well beyond tail. In flight, from below, shows black flight feathers. Juvenile has head and neck buffish-white with a dark eye-patch. VOICE: A loud *krurrk*. HABITAT: Open wetlands, grasslands, agricultural fields, lake and river shores. DISTRIBUTION: Winter visitor to E China.

4 SARUS CRANE *Grus antigone* 156–176cm FIELD NOTES: Flies with neck outstretched and legs protruding well beyond tail. In flight, from below, shows black primaries. Juvenile has rusty head and upper neck, upperparts tinged rufous. Grey race *G. a. sharpii* (4b) is the chief race found in the area, nominate race has been recorded from Myanmar. VOICE: A loud trumpeting. HABITAT: Watery areas such as marshes, paddyfields, lakes and rivers. DISTRIBUTION: Rare resident in E Myanmar, Cambodia, S Laos and S Vietnam; formally more widespread.

5 SANDHILL CRANE *Grus canadensis* 100–120cm FIELD NOTES: Older birds often stained rusty. In flight, from below, shows black primaries and secondaries. Juvenile generally sandy-brown, lacking the red on head. VOICE: A loud bugle-like rattle, *gar-oo-oo*. HABITAT: Marshes, agricultural land and coastal wetlands. DISTRIBUTION: Vagrant from N America to E China.

6 WHITE-NAPED CRANE *Grus vipio* 125–150cm FIELD NOTES: Gregarious; large flocks occur in some wintering areas. In flight, from below, shows black primaries and secondaries, with a wide white bar on greater underwing-coverts that contrasts with the grey lesser underwing-coverts and body. Juvenile has a brown head with a pale throat. VOICE: A high-pitched bugling. HABITAT: Lakes and river banks. DISTRIBUTION: Winter visitor to E China; vagrant elsewhere.

7 JAPANESE CRANE (RED-CROWNED CRANE) *Grus japonensis* 150cm FIELD NOTES: Gregarious. In flight, from below, shows white primaries and black secondaries. Juvenile has rusty head and neck, body mainly white tinged rusty on wings and mantle; elongated tertials brownish-black. VOICE: A penetrating, high-pitched trumpeting. HABITAT: Freshwater wetlands, saltmarshes and mudflats. DISTRIBUTION: Winter visitor to far NE of the region; vagrant elsewhere.

8 SIBERIAN CRANE *Grus leucogeranus* 140cm FIELD NOTES: Normally the most aquatic of all cranes. Flies with neck outstretched and legs protruding well beyond tail. In flight shows black primaries. Juvenile generally rusty-buff on upperparts, neck and hind-neck; underparts white. VOICE: A hollow, honking *koonk koonk* and a musical *ahooya* that is usually given in flight on the way to roosts. HABITAT: Freshwater lakes and marshes. DISTRIBUTION: Winter visitor to E China (mainly on Poyang and nearby lakes).

9 DEMOISELLE CRANE *Grus virgo* 90–100cm FIELD NOTES: In flight, from below, shows blackish primaries and secondaries; flies with neck outstretched and legs protruding well beyond tail. Juvenile has head and neck pale grey, tertials much shorter than those of adult. VOICE: Like Common Crane but drier and higher-pitched. HABITAT: River or lake sandbanks and cultivations. DISTRIBUTION: Vagrant recorded from Myanmar.

35 FINFOOT; RAILS; CRAKES

1 MASKED FINFOOT (ASIAN FINFOOT) *Heliopais personatus* 43–55cm FIELD NOTES: Very elusive, although can be quite confiding. Most active at dawn or dusk. VOICE: A high-pitched bubbling, a grunting *quack* and when alarmed a *keek-keek-keek*. HABITAT: Fresh or brackish water in dense forest and mangroves, sometimes water away from forests. DISTRIBUTION: Scarce resident in S Myanmar; winter visitor and passage migrant in S Thailand and Peninsular Malaysia, vagrant in Singapore. Possibly more widespread.

2 SWINHOE'S RAIL (SWINHOE'S CRAKE, SIBERIAN YELLOW RAIL) *Coturnicops exquisitus* 13cm FIELD NOTES: Very secretive. In weak, butterfly-like flight shows white secondaries. VOICE: A *tick-tick-tick-tick*. HABITAT: Wet fields, grassy marshes and swamps. DISTRIBUTION: Winter visitor to SE China.

3 RED-LEGGED CRAKE (MALAYSIAN BANDED CRAKE) *Rallina fasciata* 23–25cm FIELD NOTES: Skulker, difficult to observe or flush. Juvenile duller than adult with less pronounced barring on underparts and wings; legs brownish-yellow. VOICE: A loud *gogogogok*, a *girrr* and a nasal *pek pek pek…* also a slow, descending trill. HABITAT: Wet areas in forest and secondary growth, reedy swamps, marshes and paddyfields. DISTRIBUTION: Resident in S Thailand and Singapore. Summer visitor or resident in S Laos and S Vietnam; winter visitor in Peninsular Malaysia (possibly breeds) and Singapore. Passage migrant elsewhere.

4 SLATY-LEGGED CRAKE (BANDED CRAKE) *Rallina eurizonoides* 27cm FIELD NOTES: Shy, often flies into trees when flushed. Juvenile olive-brown above, head and neck dull ochre-brown. VOICE: A persistent *kek-kek-kek-kek…* or *ow-ow-ow-ow…* HABITAT: Forest and forest edge with marshes or wet areas. DISTRIBUTION: Resident in Taiwan, Hainan and S China; breeding visitor to N Vietnam. Winter visitor to S Thailand and Peninsular Malaysia; passage migrant or vagrant elsewhere.

5 SLATY-BREASTED RAIL *Gallirallus striatus* 29cm FIELD NOTES: Very secretive. Juvenile generally more pale ochre-grey below, dark bars on flanks; paler brown above. VOICE: A sharp *terrik*, which may be strung together as a 'song'; also a noisy *ka-ka-ka*. HABITAT: Marshes, reedbeds, paddyfields and mangroves. DISTRIBUTION: Widespread resident.

6 INDIAN WATER RAIL (BROWN-CHEEKED RAIL) *Rallus indicus* 23–28cm FIELD NOTES: Secretive, but feeds in the open when undisturbed. VOICE: A long, clear, piping *kyu*, also a repeated, metallic, slurred *shrink shrink*. HABITAT: Marshes. DISTRIBUTION: Winter visitor to S, E China, Taiwan, Myanmar, coastal Thailand, N Laos and N Vietnam.

7 WATER RAIL *Rallus aquaticus* 29cm FIELD NOTES: Secretive, more often seen than heard, although will feed in the open if undisturbed. Juvenile like adult but grey underparts replaced with buff-grey, breast area mottled brownish. VOICE: Various pig-like squeals and grunts. HABITAT: Dense reedbeds, marshes and overgrown ditches. DISTRIBUTION: Possibly wanders to E China.

8 CORNCRAKE *Crex crex* 27–30cm FIELD NOTES: Most active early and late and more often heard than seen. VOICE: A monotonous, dry *krek-krek-krek-krek*. HABITAT: Grasslands and cultivated areas. DISTRIBUTION: Vagrant.

9 BROWN CRAKE *Amaurornis akool* 26–28cm FIELD NOTES: Usually skulking, feeds more in the open at dawn or dusk, but runs into cover at the slightest alarm. VOICE: A long vibrating trill. HABITAT: Swamps, paddyfields and overgrown water-courses. DISTRIBUTION: Resident S, E China, SW Myanmar and N Vietnam.

10 WHITE-BREASTED WATERHEN *Amaurornis phoenicurus* 28–33cm FIELD NOTES: Often seen in the open, also climbs about in bushes and trees. Juvenile is a dull grey-brown version of adult; rear of ear-coverts, lores and forehead also grey-brown. VOICE: Loud grunts, croaks and chuckles, transcribed as *kru-ak kru-ak kru-ak-wak-wak* or *krr-kwaak-kwaak krr-kwaak-kraak…* contact call is a *pwik pwik pwik…* HABITAT: Various wet areas, including damp scrub, thick waterside vegetation, open forest streams, mangroves and adjacent open areas. DISTRIBUTION: Widespread resident in Taiwan and southwards from S, E China.

36 CRAKES; SWAMP-HEN; MOORHEN; COOT

1 BLACK-TAILED CRAKE (ELWES'S or RUFOUS-BACKED CRAKE) *Porzana bicolor* 20–22cm FIELD NOTES: Secretive. Will feed in the open at dawn or dusk, but retreats into cover at the slightest disturbance. Juvenile duller than adult with brownish legs. VOICE: A rasping *waak-waak* followed by a descending trill. HABITAT: Swamp areas, overgrown streams in or near forests. DISTRIBUTION: Resident in SW China, northern Myanmar, NW Thailand, N Laos and N Vietnam.

2 BAILLON'S CRAKE *Porzana pusilla* 17–19cm FIELD NOTES: Forages at dawn or dusk, close to or in dense cover. Juvenile like adult above, below whitish barred brown-grey. VOICE: A dry frog-like rattle. HABITAT: Marshes, paddyfields and vegetation surrounding lakes and ponds. DISTRIBUTION: Winter visitor or passage migrant to SE China and southwards from China.

3 SPOTTED CRAKE *Porzana porzana* 22–24cm FIELD NOTES: Secretive; will forage in the open if undisturbed. VOICE: A high-pitched, whiplash-like *whit*, also a ticking *tik-tak* and croaking *qwe-qwe-qwe*. HABITAT: Marshes, wet meadows, reedy edges of watercourses and paddyfields. DISTRIBUTION: Vagrant; records from Myanmar and C Thailand.

4 RUDDY-BREASTED CRAKE (RUDDY CRAKE) *Porzana fusca* 21–23cm FIELD NOTES: Secretive, although often feeds at the edge of reedbeds. VOICE: A harsh *tewk* that often speeds up and ends with a descending trill. HABITAT: Marshes, reedy marshes, paddyfields and vegetation by watercourses. DISTRIBUTION: Widespread resident.

5 BAND-BELLIED CRAKE *Porzana paykullii* 20–22cm FIELD NOTES: Secretive, heard more than seen. VOICE: Said to sound like a wooden rattle. HABITAT: Marshes, wet meadows, damp woodlands and paddyfields. DISTRIBUTION: Winter visitor to N, S Vietnam, C Thailand and Peninsular Malaysia; passage migrant elsewhere.

6 WHITE-BROWED CRAKE *Porzana cinerea* 19–22cm FIELD NOTES: Forages early and late, regularly in the open, runs for cover at the slightest disturbance; more often seen than heard. VOICE: A loud, nasal chattering *chika*, repeated 10–12 times; also recorded is a repeated, nasal *hee* note. While feeding utters a sharp, loud *kek-kro*. HABITAT: Well-vegetated lakes, marshes, overgrown ditches and paddyfields. DISTRIBUTION: Resident C, S Thailand, Cambodia, Peninsular Malaysia and Singapore.

7 WATERCOCK *Gallicrex cinerea* 42–43cm FIELD NOTES: Mainly crepuscular, skulking; readily swims. VOICE: A long series of *kok* notes followed by a series of hollow *utumb* notes ending with a short series of *kluck* notes. HABITAT: Swamps, marshes, paddyfields and mangroves on passage. DISTRIBUTION: Widespread breeding visitor to China, NE Myanmar and northern Thailand; resident in C Myanmar, southern Thailand, Cambodia, S Laos and C, S Vietnam. Winter visitor and passage migrant elsewhere.

8 PURPLE SWAMPHEN (PURPLE GALLINULE) *Porphyrio porphyrio* 45–50cm FIELD NOTES: Readily forages in the open, although stays close to cover. Walks on floating water-plants and clambers among reeds and bushes. VOICE: Various, including a series of plaintive, nasal rattles ending in a crescendo, a low *chuk-chuk* and a trumpeting *toot*. HABITAT: Dense reedbeds and fringing vegetation by lakes, ponds and rivers. DISTRIBUTION: Widespread resident from SW China southwards (apart from W Myanmar, SW Thailand and N Vietnam).

9 MOORHEN (COMMON MOORHEN or GALLINULE) *Gallinula chloropus* 32–35cm FIELD NOTES: Usually keeps to the edge of cover. Swims, with a jerky action. Juvenile dull brownish with a whitish throat and faint buff flank stripe. VOICE: A bubbling *krrrruk* or *kurr-ik*. When alarmed utters a *kik-kik-kik*. HABITAT: Marshes, lakes and watercourses with surrounding emergent vegetation. DISTRIBUTION: Widespread resident over most of the region.

10 COOT (COMMON or EURASIAN COOT) *Fulica atra* 36–38cm FIELD NOTES: Usually seen swimming, although regularly grazes on lakeside banks. VOICE: Various metallic notes. HABITAT: Open water with fringing vegetation. DISTRIBUTION: Widespread winter visitor to much of region; vagrant to S Thailand, Peninsular Malaysia and Singapore.

37 BUSTARDS; THICK-KNEES; JACANAS

1 GREAT BUSTARD *Otis tarda* male 105cm, female 75cm FIELD NOTES: Large and weighty. In flight upperwing appears mainly greyish-white with darker tips to primaries and black secondaries; forewing as mantle. Flies with neck outstretched. VOICE: A low bark given during disputes or when alarmed. HABITAT: Open grassland and agricultural land. DISTRIBUTION: Vagrant, recorded from E China and N Myanmar.

2 BENGAL FLORICAN *Houbaropsis bengalensis* 64–68cm FIELD NOTES: Rare. In flight upperwing of male is predominantly white; female has brownish flight feathers barred darker, and pale buffish wing-coverts. Flies with neck outstretched. During display male leaps into the air and hovers momentarily at the top of the jumps before gliding back to earth. VOICE: While displaying the male emits a deep hum; when alarmed utters a shrill, metallic *chik-chik-chik*. HABITAT: Grassland with nearby cultivation. DISTRIBUTION: Resident NW, SE Cambodia and S Vietnam.

3 GREAT THICK-KNEE (GREAT STONE-PLOVER, GREAT STONE CURLEW) *Esacus recurvirostris* 49–54cm FIELD NOTES: Shy, mainly crepuscular or nocturnal. In flight upperwing shows black secondaries, white inner primaries with black sub-terminal bar and black outer primaries with white sub-terminal spots on three outer feathers. Centre of wing grey with a black bar separating it from brownish-grey forewing. VOICE: A wailing whistled *see* or *see-ey*, also a harsh *see-eek* given in alarm. HABITAT: Shingle and sandbanks on large rivers, dry lake shores, estuaries and coastal sandflats. DISTRIBUTION: Resident in SW China, much of Myanmar, northern Thailand, Cambodia, Laos and C Vietnam.

4 BEACH THICK-KNEE (BEACH STONE-CURLEW) *Esacus magnirostris* 53–57cm FIELD NOTES: Mainly crepuscular or nocturnal; spends the day resting in shade. In flight upperwing shows grey secondaries and secondary-coverts and white inner primaries. Forewing and primaries black, the latter with large white sub-terminal spots on three outer feathers. VOICE: A harsh, wailing *wee-loo*. When alarmed utters a weak, yapping *quip*, *peep* or a rising *quip-ip-ip*. HABITAT: Coastal shores, often near mangroves. DISTRIBUTION: Resident on Coco Islands, S Myanmar (Tenasserim), S Thailand, Peninsular Malaysia and Singapore.

5 INDIAN STONE CURLEW (THICK-KNEE) *Burhinus indicus* 36–39cm FIELD NOTES: Timid. Mainly crepuscular; during the day often stands motionless in shade. Can be hard to see against scrub or dry stony background. VOICE: A *cur-lee* or *churrreee*, usually given at night. HABITAT: Open stony or scrubby barren areas, sand-dunes and river sandbanks. DISTRIBUTION: Resident in Myanmar (except W, E), SE Thailand and Cambodia; vagrant elsewhere.

6 BRONZE-WINGED JACANA *Metopidius indicus* 28–31cm FIELD NOTES: Forages by walking on floating vegetation or wading in shallow water. Juvenile brown above, whitish below with pinkish-buff wash on neck and breast. Also has russet cap and line through eye split in front of eye by short supercillium, with blackish lores. VOICE: A harsh grunt; when alarmed utters a wheezy, piping *seek-seek-seek*. HABITAT: Lakes and ponds with floating and emergent vegetation. DISTRIBUTION: Resident in SW China, Myanmar (except W), Thailand (except SE), Laos, Cambodia and S Vietnam.

7 PHEASANT-TAILED JACANA (WATER-PHEASANT) *Hydrophasianus chirurgus* 31–58cm FIELD NOTES: Often gregarious. Forages by walking on floating vegetation, wading in shallow water or swimming. In flight shows strikingly white wings. Juvenile similar to non-breeding adult, feathers of upperparts have pale fringes and the black necklace is less distinct. VOICE: In breeding season has a far-carrying, mewing *me-e-ou* or *me-onp*, post-breeding flocks utter a nasal *tewn*. HABITAT: Well-vegetated lakes, ponds and marshes. On migration frequents rivers and mangroves. DISTRIBUTION: Breeds in mainland China (moves south post breeding), Taiwan, Hainan, Myanmar (except W), C, NE Thailand and Cambodia. Winter visitor or passage migrant elsewhere; vagrant in Singapore.

38 PLOVERS

1 PACIFIC GOLDEN PLOVER (ASIAN or EASTERN GOLDEN PLOVER)
Pluvialis fulva 23–26cm FIELD NOTES: Gregarious. At rest wing tips project beyond tail, tertials and legs longer than those of American Golden Plover. VOICE: A rapid *chu-wit* and a drawn-out *klu-ee*. HABITAT: Coastal lagoons, mudflats, lake and river margins; also grasslands and fields. DISTRIBUTION: Widespread winter visitor to Taiwan and southward from S China.

2 AMERICAN GOLDEN PLOVER (LESSER GOLDEN PLOVER) *Pluvialis dominica* 24–28cm FIELD NOTES: Non-breeding birds tend to be slightly 'greyer' than Pacific Golden Plover, with shorter tertials and legs. VOICE: A sharp *klu-eet, kleep* or *kluee-uh*. HABITAT: Grassland and coastal mudflats. DISTRIBUTION: Vagrant, record from SE China; probably overlooked.

3 GREY PLOVER (BLACK-BELLIED PLOVER) *Pluvialis squatarola* 27–30cm FIELD NOTES: Occurs in pairs or small parties. In flight from above shows white lower rump and white wing-bar. Underwing white with prominent black axillaries. VOICE: A mournful *tlee-oo-ee*. HABITAT: Mainly coastal mudflats and beaches. DISTRIBUTION: Widespread winter visitor and passage migrant.

4 LAPWING (NORTHERN LAPWING, GREEN PLOVER, PEEWIT) *Vanellus vanellus* 28–31cm FIELD NOTES: Generally encountered in pairs or small flocks. In flight from above looks black apart from white on lower rump and on the tips of outer primaries. Juvenile like adult non-breeding, but with more prominent pale fringes on upperparts. VOICE: A plaintive *wee-ip* or *pee-wit*. HABITAT: Grasslands, margins of lakes and rivers; also on estuaries. DISTRIBUTION: Widespread winter visitor to China, N, C Myanmar, NW, NE, C Thailand and N Vietnam; uncommon in N Laos.

5 YELLOW-WATTLED LAPWING *Vanellus malabaricus* 26–28cm FIELD NOTES: Generally occurs in pairs but may form small flocks after breeding. In flight upperwing shows a prominent white bar on secondary coverts, contrasting with black flight feathers and brown forewing; lower rump white, tail black with white sides. Juvenile like adult, but crown brown and upperparts have pale fringes. VOICE: A plaintive *tchee-it*, when alarmed gives a *chit-oo-eet* or a sharp *whit-whit-whit*. HABITAT: Dry grasslands, open dry country and fringes of wetlands. DISTRIBUTION: Vagrant, recorded from S Myanmar and Peninsular Malaysia.

6 RIVER LAPWING (ASIAN SPUR-WINGED PLOVER) *Vanellus duvaucelii* 29–32cm FIELD NOTES: Occurs singly, in pairs or small flocks. In flight upperwing shows a broad white wing-bar contrasting with black flight feathers and grey-brown forewing; rump is white and tail black. VOICE: A sharp *tip-tip* and a longer *dip-dip-to-weet*. HABITAT: Sand and shingle areas by rivers. DISTRIBUTION: Resident, over most of the region, southward from S China.

7 GREY-HEADED LAPWING *Vanellus cinereus* 34–37cm FIELD NOTES: Normally occurs in small flocks. In flight upperwing shows white secondaries and secondary-coverts; primaries and primary-coverts black, rest of wing grey-brown. Rump shows white, tail black with white sides. Non-breeding birds have whitish throat, neck tinged brown and partly obscured black breast-band. VOICE: A plaintive *chee-it*. When disturbed gives a rasping *cha-ha-eet* or a sharp *pink*. HABITAT: Marshland, swampy grassland, paddyfields and river margins. DISTRIBUTION: Winter visitor or passage migrant over much of the region.

8 RED-WATTLED LAPWING (RED-WATTLED PLOVER) *Vanellus indicus* 32–35cm FIELD NOTES: Occurs in pairs or small flocks. In flight upperwing appears dark with white bar on secondary-coverts; rump white, tail black with white tip. VOICE: A shrill *did-he-do-it* or *kree-dee-der*. When alarmed gives a sharp *trint trint trint trint*. HABITAT: Open areas, farmland, river, marsh and lake margins. DISTRIBUTION: Resident southward from Hainan and S China.

39 PLOVERS

1 RINGED PLOVER (COMMON or GREAT RINGED PLOVER) *Charadrius hiaticula* 18–20cm FIELD NOTES: In flight upperwing shows bold white wing-bar. Juvenile like dull non-breeding adult, upperparts with pale fringes. VOICE: A mellow, rising *too-lee* and a soft *too-weep* when alarmed. HABITAT: Shores of coasts, lakes and rivers. DISTRIBUTION: Winter visitor to SE China, vagrant elsewhere.

2 LONG-BILLED PLOVER (LONG-BILLED RINGED PLOVER) *Charadrius placidus* 19–21cm FIELD NOTES: Yellowish base to lower mandible, dark eye-ring. In flight upperwing shows inconspicuous white wing-bar. VOICE: A clear *pewee*, also a pleasant *tudulu*. HABITAT: Lakes, rivers, marshes, coastal pools and paddyfields. DISTRIBUTION: Winter visitor to China (except C), N, C Myanmar, NW, C Thailand, N, C Laos and Vietnam (E Tonkin and C Annam); vagrant elsewhere.

3 LITTLE RINGED PLOVER *Charadrius dubius* 14–17cm FIELD NOTES: Yellowish base to lower mandible, yellow eye-ring. In flight upperwing shows inconspicuous white wing-bar. VOICE: A descending *pee-oo*. When alarmed utters a *pip-pip-pip*. HABITAT: Margins of lakes and rivers, marshes, mudflats and estuaries. DISTRIBUTION: Widespread summer visitor to China. Resident in SW, SE China, Myanmar, NW, NE Thailand, Cambodia, Laos and S Vietnam. Winter visitor to E China, Taiwan and southward over most of the region.

4 KENTISH PLOVER *Charadrius alexandrinus* 15–17cm FIELD NOTES: Incomplete black breast-band. In flight upperwing has white wing-bar; white sides to lower rump and tail. White-faced race *C. a. dealbatus*, which breeds on the Chinese coast and winters south to Peninsular Malaysia, is sometimes considered a full species. VOICE: A soft, clear *pit* or *pit-pit-pit*. When alarmed gives a hard *prrr*, *too-eet* or *pweep*. HABITAT: Sandy shores of coasts, lakes, lagoons and saltpans. DISTRIBUTION: Summer visitor and resident in C, E China, Taiwan, Hainan, S Myanmar and S Vietnam; widespread winter visitor south from China, passage migrant elsewhere.

5 MALAYSIAN PLOVER (MALAYSIAN SAND PLOVER) *Charadrius peronii* 14–16cm FIELD NOTES: Usually encountered in pairs or small flocks. In flight upperwing shows prominent white wing-bar, especially at base of primaries; outer-tail feathers white. VOICE: A soft *whit* or *twik*. HABITAT: Undisturbed sandy, coral and shell beaches, also adjacent mudflats. DISTRIBUTION: Coastal resident in Thailand, Cambodia, S Vietnam, Peninsular Malaysia and Singapore.

6 LESSER SAND PLOVER (MONGOLIAN SAND PLOVER) *Charadrius mongolus* 19–21cm FIELD NOTES: Usually shows narrow white bar on upperwing. Two distinct types occur in the region the 'mongolus type' with a white forehead, wintering mainly in Taiwan and the black forehead 'atrifrons type' (6b), wintering in the rest of the region. VOICE: A short *drrit*, also a sharp *chitik* or *chiktik*. HABITAT: Mainly coastal mud- and sandflats. DISTRIBUTION: Winter visitor to Taiwan and southwards from S China. Passage migrant through E China southwards.

7 GREATER SAND PLOVER (LARGE SAND PLOVER, GEOFFROY'S PLOVER) *Charadrius leschenaultii* 22–25cm FIELD NOTES: In flight upperwing shows prominent white wing-bar; toes project beyond end of tail. VOICE: A soft *trrri* and a melodious *pipruirr*. HABITAT: Mainly coastal wetlands. DISTRIBUTION: Winter visitor to Taiwan; widespread coastal winter visitor south from China.

8 ORIENTAL PLOVER (ORIENTAL DOTTEREL or EASTERN SAND PLOVER) *Charadrius veredus* 22–25cm FIELD NOTES: Powerful flight, often with erratic turns; upperwing uniform brown, although juvenile may show a slight white wing-bar; toes project beyond end of tail. VOICE: Trilling calls and a short, piping *klink*; in flight gives a sharp, whistled *chip-chip-chip*. HABITAT: Dry grasslands, dry areas near wetlands also coastal mud- and sandflats. DISTRIBUTION: Widespread passage migrant in China, vagrant elsewhere.

40 PRATINCOLES; PAINTED SNIPE; IBISBILL; CRAB PLOVER; OYSTERCATCHER; AVOCET; STILT

1 COLLARED PRATINCOLE (COMMON or RED-WINGED PRATINCOLE) *Glareola pratincola* 23–26cm FIELD NOTES: Gregarious. In flight shows white trailing edge to secondaries, white rump and deeply forked tail. Underwing shows chestnut coverts. VOICE: A harsh *kik* or *kirrik*, also a rolling *kikik-krrik-irrik*. HABITAT: Open dry areas, lake and swamp surrounds and coastal creeks. DISTRIBUTION: Vagrant to E China.

2 ORIENTAL PRATINCOLE (EASTERN, EASTERN COLLARED or LARGE INDIAN PRATINCOLE) *Glareola maldivarum* 23–24cm FIELD NOTES: Gregarious. In flight from above, wings brown, rump white and tail forked. Underwing-coverts chestnut. VOICE: A sharp *kyik*, *chik-chik* or *chet*, also a rising *trooeet* and a *ter-ack*. HABITAT: Bare flats, dry paddyfields, marshes, lake and river margins and coastal pools. DISTRIBUTION: Summer resident to Hainan, E China, Myanmar, Thailand, Cambodia and C, S Vietnam. Resident in Taiwan and possibly parts of Myanmar, otherwise passage migrant over most of the area.

3 SMALL PRATINCOLE (LITTLE, SMALL INDIAN or MILKY PRATINCOLE) *Glareola lactea* 17cm FIELD NOTES: Gregarious. In flight from below shows mainly white secondaries and inner primaries, the former with a black trailing edge; upperwing similar but all primaries black; tail square-ended. VOICE: A *tuck-tuck-tuck*. In flight utters a high-pitched, rolling *prrip* or *tiririt*. HABITAT: Margins of large rivers, lakes and dry marshes, occasionally coastal areas. DISTRIBUTION: Resident in SW China, Myanmar, Thailand, Cambodia and Laos; vagrant elsewhere.

4 PAINTED SNIPE (GREATER PAINTED SNIPE) *Rostratula benghalensis* 23–28cm FIELD NOTES: Mainly crepuscular. Secretive. Flies with legs dangling. VOICE: In display female utters a soft *koh koh koh*, likened to blowing across the top of an empty bottle. Also uses various hisses and growls. When flushed utters a sharp *kek*. HABITAT: Marshes, swamps and overgrown paddyfields. DISTRIBUTION: Resident over most of the region (except C China and C Vietnam).

5 IBISBILL *Ibidorhyncha struthersii* 39–41cm FIELD NOTES: Forages among stones and rocks of riverbeds, often wades up to belly. In flight upperwing shows white bar on primaries that forms into a patch on inner feathers. Juveniles lack dark face. VOICE: A ringing *klew-klew* and a loud, rapid *tee-tee-tee-tee*. HABITAT: Mountain streams and rivers with shingle beds. DISTRIBUTION: Winter visitor to N Myanmar.

6 CRAB-PLOVER *Dromas ardeola* 38–41cm FIELD NOTES: Wary, crepuscular. Juveniles have a greyish mantle; can look gull-like, especially when they rest on their tarsi. VOICE: A barking *ka-how-ka-how*. In flight utters a nasal, yapping *kirruc*. HABITAT: Sandy coasts, estuaries and lagoons. DISTRIBUTION: Non-breeding visitor to S Myanmar and S Thailand.

7 OYSTERCATCHER (EURASIAN OYSTERCATCHER) *Haematopus ostralegus* 40–46cm FIELD NOTES: In flight upperwing shows broad white wing-bar, white rump and uppertail-coverts; tail black. Juvenile upperparts brown with pale fringes. VOICE: A sharp *kleep* or *kle-eap* and a quiet *weep*. HABITAT: Rocky coasts and mudflats. DISTRIBUTION: Winter visitor to E China and Taiwan; vagrant elsewhere.

8 AVOCET (PIED AVOCET) *Recurvirostra avosetta* 42–45cm FIELD NOTES: Gregarious. Readily swims, upending to feed like a dabbling duck. VOICE: A melodious *kluit-kluit-kluit*, when alarmed utters a harsh *kloo-eet u*. HABITAT: Mainly shallow saline or brackish lakes, lagoons, saltpans and estuaries. DISTRIBUTION: Winter visitor to C, S Myanmar, E China and Taiwan; vagrant elsewhere.

9 BLACK-WINGED STILT *Himantopus himantopus* 35–40cm FIELD NOTES: Gregarious. Crown and hindneck pattern varies from white to slate-grey. VOICE: A sharp *kek*, a high-pitched *kikikikik* and a yelping *kee-ack*. HABITAT: Various wetlands, including saltmarsh, saltpans, lakes and marshes. DISTRIBUTION: Scarce resident in C, S Myanmar, coastal Thailand, Cambodia, N, C Laos and S Vietnam. Winter visitor to SE China, Taiwan, Thailand, Cambodia, Peninsular Malaysia and Singapore.

41 SNIPE; WOODCOCK

1 JACK SNIPE *Lymnocryptes minimus* 17–19cm FIELD NOTES: Secretive, tends to wait until nearly trodden on before being flushed; flies away with less erratic movements than Snipe. VOICE: May utter a weak *gah* when disturbed. HABITAT: Marshes, flooded land and wet grassy areas surrounding lakes, ponds and rivers. DISTRIBUTION: Winter visitor to SE China, much of Myanmar, NW, C Thailand and N Vietnam; vagrant elsewhere.

2 SNIPE (COMMON SNIPE) *Gallinago gallinago* 25–27cm FIELD NOTES: Usually feeds close to cover. When flushed flies off in a rapid, erratic zigzagging manner. In flight shows white trailing edge and pale banding on underwing-coverts. VOICE: When alarmed utters a harsh *scaap*. HABITAT: Various wet areas, including marshes, swampy ground, lake and riversides. DISTRIBUTION: Widespread winter visitor.

3 GREAT SNIPE *Gallinago media* 27–29cm FIELD NOTES: Actions usually more sluggish than Snipe. Spread tail shows extensive white on outer feathers. Underwing uniformly dark barred, upperwing shows white wing-bars. VOICE: Utters a weak *aitch-aitch-aitch* when flushed. HABITAT: Marshes, swamp edges and wet grassy areas. DISTRIBUTION: Vagrant, recorded from Myanmar.

4 SWINHOE'S SNIPE (CHINESE SNIPE) *Gallinago megala* 27–29cm FIELD NOTES: At rest primaries extend beyond tertials. In flight toes project slightly beyond tail and underwing is uniformly barred. Flight is not so dynamic as Snipe, more sluggish. VOICE: Sometimes utters a gruff *scaap* when flushed. HABITAT: Marshes, flooded grasslands, paddyfields and sometimes in dryer areas such as rice stubbles. DISTRIBUTION: Winter visitor to Hainan, SE China, N, C, S Myanmar, C Thailand, Laos, Peninsular Malaysia and Singapore.

5 PIN-TAILED SNIPE (PINTAIL SNIPE) *Gallinago stenura* 25–27cm FIELD NOTES: At rest tertials overlap primaries, tail short. In flight toes project well beyond tail and underwing is uniformly barred. Flushed flight is usually short and less towering than Snipe. Supercillium wider at base of bill than Snipe. VOICE: When flushed may utter a low-pitched, weak *scaap, squik* or *etch*. HABITAT: Marshes, paddyfields and wet grasslands, often in drier areas than Snipe. DISTRIBUTION: Winter visitor from Hainan and SE China southwards.

6 SOLITARY SNIPE *Gallinago solitaria* 29–31cm FIELD NOTES: In flight toes do not project beyond tail. When flushed zigzags away with a heavier flight than Snipe and drops into cover quite quickly. VOICE: When flushed utters a harsh *kensh*. HABITAT: Marshes, bogs and *watercourses*. DISTRIBUTION: Winter visitor to SW, SE, E, C China and W, N E Myanmar.

7 LATHAM'S SNIPE (JAPANESE SNIPE) *Gallinago hardwickii* 28–30cm FIELD NOTES: When flushed flight is fairly heavy with few zigzags before bird drops quite quickly back into cover. Underwing uniformly dark barred. Tertials overlap primaries. Longer-tailed than Pin-tailed Snipe. VOICE: When flushed utters a short *chak*. HABITAT: Freshwater margins. DISTRIBUTION: Passage migrant in Taiwan.

8 WOOD SNIPE (HIMALAYAN SNIPE) *Gallinago nemoricola* 28–32cm FIELD NOTES: Flight is direct and heavy; when flushed rarely flies far. VOICE: When flushed gives a low, croaking *chok-chok*. HABITAT: Wet areas in or near forests. DISTRIBUTION: Winter visitor to SW China, much of Myanmar, NW Thailand, N, C Laos and N Vietnam.

9 WOODCOCK (EURASIAN WOODCOCK) *Scolopax rusticola* 33–35cm FIELD NOTES: Usually encountered when flushed or during display flight (roding) when flies above territory with slow wing-beats giving squeaks and grunts. When flushed zigzags away through trees and then drops out of sight. VOICE: Generally silent when flushed but occasionally utters a snipe-like *schaap* or *schaap schaap*. HABITAT: Woodland and plantations with dry areas for nesting and nearby wetter areas for feeding. DISTRIBUTION: Resident in N Myanmar; winter visitor to Myanmar, Thailand (except S), Laos and Vietnam (except S). Vagrant to S Thailand, Peninsular Malaysia and Singapore.

42 DOWITCHERS; GODWITS; CURLEWS

1 LONG-BILLED DOWITCHER *Limnodromus scolopaceus* 27–30cm FIELD NOTES: Shorter yellow-green legs compared to Asian Dowitcher. In flight shows white oval on lower back, white trailing edge to flight feathers and distinctly black and white barred tail. Juvenile like non-breeding adult but neck and breast pale rufous-buff and mantle feathers edged rufous. VOICE: A sharp *kik* or *kik-kik-kik-kik*. When alarmed utters a *kreeek*. HABITAT: Various wetlands both inland and coastal. DISTRIBUTION: Vagrant, recorded from SE China, C, W Thailand, N Vietnam and Singapore.

2 ASIAN DOWITCHER (ASIATIC or SNIPE-BILLED DOWITCHER) *Limnodromus semipalmatus* 33–36cm FIELD NOTES: Often associates with godwits. In flight shows whitish lower back barred and streaked dark grey; tail whitish barred darker grey. Juvenile darkish-brown with buff fringes above; neck, breast and flanks are tinged warm buff with dark streaks. VOICE: A yelping *chep-chep* or *chowp*, also a soft, human-like *kiaow*. HABITAT: Coastal wetlands. DISTRIBUTION: Rare coastal passage migrant; occasionally winters in Peninsular Malaysia.

3 BLACK-TAILED GODWIT *Limosa limosa* 40–44cm FIELD NOTES: Gregarious. In flight shows bold white wing-bar on upperwing, white rump and black tail. Juvenile similar to breeding adult but neck more buff and mantle feathers fringed pale buff; underparts lack barring. VOICE: A *kek, tuk* or *kip*, usually repeated. HABITAT: Mudflats, coastal pools, marshes and lake shores. DISTRIBUTION: Widespread coastal winter visitor and passage migrant southwards from S China; also winters on Taiwan.

4 BAR-TAILED GODWIT *Limosa lapponica* 37–41cm FIELD NOTES: Gregarious, often in large flocks mixed with Black-tailed Godwits and other waders. In flight shows white from rump to mid back; tail barred black and white. Juvenile similar to adult breeding female but with wider mantle fringes. VOICE: Contact and alarm call is a barking *kak-kak*, a deep *kirruc* or variations of these. HABITAT: Estuaries, muddy or sandy shores and coastal pools. DISTRIBUTION: Winter visitor to Taiwan, Hainan, coastal areas of SE China, Thailand, Cambodia, Vietnam, Peninsular Malaysia and Singapore.

5 LITTLE CURLEW (LITTLE WHIMBREL) *Numenius minutus* 29–32cm FIELD NOTES: Slightly decurved bill. No white rump. In flight underwing-coverts buff with black bars. VOICE: In flight utters a whistled *te-te-te* or a rougher *tchew-tchew-tchew*. When alarmed gives a harsh *kweek-ek*. HABITAT: Short grasslands, margins of various wetlands. DISTRIBUTION: Passage migrant to E China; vagrant with records from C Thailand and Singapore.

6 WHIMBREL *Numenius phaeopus* 40–46cm FIELD NOTES: Usually found in small parties. In flight shows white rump and lower back. Eastern race *L. p. variegatus*, which is widespread but scarce, is darker with whitish rump strongly barred dark, often showing little contrast with rest of mantle (not shown). VOICE: A tittering, flat-toned *tetti-tetti-tetti-tet, bibibibibiibi* or similar. HABITAT: Coastal wetlands and nearby grassland, marshes, mangroves and by large rivers. DISTRIBUTION: Widespread, mainly coastal winter visitor southwards from Hainan and SE China; also occurs in Taiwan.

7 CURLEW (EURASIAN, WESTERN or COMMON CURLEW) *Numenius arquata* 50–60cm FIELD NOTES: Usually found in small parties. In flight shows white rump and lower back. Females slightly larger and longer billed than males. VOICE: A far-carrying *cour-lee*, a low *whaup* and a stammering *tutututu* or *tyuyuyuyu* when disturbed. HABITAT: Mudflats, sandflats, lake margins and flooded and dry grasslands. DISTRIBUTION: Widespread, mainly coastal, winter visitor.

8 EASTERN CURLEW (FAR-EASTERN or AUSTRALIAN CURLEW) *Numenius madagascariensis* 60–66 cm FIELD NOTES: Shy, may mix with flocks of Curlews. In flight lacks white rump and lower back. Female slightly larger and longer billed than male. VOICE: A far-carrying *cour-lee*, flatter toned than Curlew; when disturbed utters a strident *ker-ker-ee-ker-ee*. HABITAT: Mudflats, sandflats and estuaries. DISTRIBUTION: Rare winter visitor to Taiwan and S China, otherwise a widespread passage migrant (except in Myanmar).

43 SHANKS; SANDPIPERS

1 SPOTTED REDSHANK (DUSKY REDSHANK) *Tringa erythropus* 29–32cm FIELD NOTES: Moulting birds have a non-breeding type plumage blotched with black. In flight shows white oval in centre of back. Often wades up to belly when foraging. Juvenile like non-breeding adult but with fine barring on underparts. VOICE: In flight gives a distinctive *chu-it;* when alarmed utters a short *chip.* HABITAT: Upper reaches of estuaries, coastal lagoons, lakes and marshes. DISTRIBUTION: Winter visitor to Taiwan, E, S China, widespread further south (except parts of Myanmar, Thailand and Vietnam).

2 REDSHANK (COMMON REDSHANK) *Tringa totanus* 27–29cm FIELD NOTES: Wary, takes noisily to flight at the slightest disturbance, usually the first in a group of waders to take to the air. In flight shows white oval in centre of back and striking white secondaries and inner primaries. Juvenile like adult breeding, but mantle and wing feathers fringed and notched with ochre-buff. VOICE: A piping *teu-hu teu-hu-hu* or similar. When alarmed utters a loud *tli-tli-tli-tli.* HABITAT: Wide variety of coastal and inland waters. DISTRIBUTION: Widespread winter visitor, apart from central S China.

3 SPOTTED GREENSHANK (NORDMANN'S GREENSHANK) *Tringa guttifer* 30–35cm FIELD NOTES: Wary. Often wades up to belly. In flight shows white rump and back; tail pale grey. Legs do not protrude beyond tail. Juvenile like non-breeding adult but upperparts browner with buff spots. VOICE: A piercing *keyew* and a harsh *gwark.* HABITAT: Mainly coastal wetlands. DISTRIBUTION: Widespread winter visitor south from S China (except W, N Myanmar, SE, E Thailand and N, S Vietnam); passage migrant in Taiwan and SE China.

4 GREENSHANK (COMMON or GREATER GREENSHANK) *Tringa nebularia* 30–35cm FIELD NOTES: Wary. Usually seen singly but sometimes in larger flocks at roost. In flight shows white rump and back. Feet project slightly beyond tail. VOICE: A ringing *chew-chew-chew;* when alarmed gives a *kiu-kiu-kiu.* HABITAT: Wide variety of coastal and inland wetlands. DISTRIBUTION: Widespread winter visitor (except central S China).

5 MARSH SANDPIPER *Tringa stagnatilis* 22–25cm FIELD NOTES: Wary. Usually seen singly or in scattered parties. In flight looks like a small Greenshank but feet project well beyond tail. Juvenile like-non-breeding adult but upperparts browner with pale fringes. VOICE: A plaintive *keeuw* or *kyu-kyu-kyu;* when flushed utters a loud *yip.* HABITAT: Marshes, ponds, lakes and coastal waters. DISTRIBUTION: Widespread, mainly coastal, winter visitor south from C China (except W Myanmar, NW Thailand, S Laos and parts of N Vietnam). Summer records from S Vietnam and Peninsular Malaysia.

6 LESSER YELLOWLEGS *Tringa flavipes* 23–25cm FIELD NOTES: Active feeder, often runs through water. In flight shows square white rump; toes project well beyond tail. VOICE: A flat, harsh *tew-tew* or *tew.* HABITAT: Wide variety of coastal and inland wetlands. DISTRIBUTION: Vagrant to SE China.

7 WOOD SANDPIPER *Tringa glareola* 19–21cm FIELD NOTES: Often found in scattered groups. In flight shows white rump and white tail with narrow black bars. Juvenile has upperparts as adult breeding but shows extensive buff spots and fringes. VOICE: A high-pitched *chiff-iff-iff* and, when alarmed, a *chip* or *chip-chip-chip.* HABITAT: Lakes, pools and marshes, less often on coastal wetlands. DISTRIBUTION: Widespread winter visitor and passage migrant.

8 GREEN SANDPIPER *Tringa ochropus* 21–24cm FIELD NOTES: Usually seen singly. In flight shows white rump and tail, the latter with broad black bars. VOICE: A musical *tlueet-wit-wit* and, when alarmed, a sharp *wit-wit-wit.* HABITAT: Lake, pool, river and stream edges. DISTRIBUTION: Widespread winter visitor.

44 SANDPIPERS; *CALIDRIS* SANDPIPERS

1 GREY-TAILED TATTLER (POLYNESIAN, SIBERIAN or GREY-RUMPED TATTLER, GREY-RUMPED SANDPIPER) *Tringa brevipes* 24–27cm FIELD NOTES: Generally occurs singly or in loose parties. Walks with a bobbing rear end. In flight slate-grey underwing contrasts with white belly. VOICE: In flight utters an upslurred *tu-whip* and when alarmed a *klee, klee-klee* or *weet-weet*. HABITAT: Rocky, sandy or muddy shores. DISTRIBUTION: Winter visitor to Taiwan and Hainan; coastal passage migrant elsewhere.

2 WANDERING TATTLER *Tringa incana* 26–29cm FIELD NOTES: In non-breeding plumage only safely distinguished from Grey-tailed Tattler by voice. VOICE: In flight gives a ringing *pewtu-tu-tu-tu-tu-tu*. HABITAT: Rocky coasts and adjoining beaches. DISTRIBUTION: Vagrant or winter visitor to Taiwan and E China.

3 TEREK SANDPIPER *Xenus cinereus* 22–25cm FIELD NOTES: Usually encountered singly or in small scattered groups, may be larger groups at roosts. Often feeds in an active, dashing manner. In flight upperwing shows wide white trailing edge. VOICE: In flight utters a rippling *du-du-du-du-du* or a mellow *chu-du-du*. HABITAT: Mainly coastal wetlands. DISTRIBUTION: Passage migrant in E China; widespread coastal winter visitor to the south of the region.

4 COMMON SANDPIPER *Actitis hypoleucos* 19–21cm FIELD NOTES: Bobs rear end when walking. Flies, often low, with stiff, flicking wing-beats; shows a white bar on upperwing. VOICE: Gives a piping *tswee-wee-wee* in flight and a *sweet-eet* when alarmed. HABITAT: Various fresh and saltwater wetlands. DISTRIBUTION: Widespread winter visitor (except in central S China).

5 GREAT KNOT (GREATER or EASTERN KNOT, GREAT SANDPIPER) *Calidris tenuirostris* 26–28cm FIELD NOTES: Usually met with in flocks, often in the company of other waders. In flight upperwing shows narrow white wing-bar. Lower rump is white sparsely marked with dark specks (appears white) and tail dark grey. Juvenile like adult non-breeding but with mantle and wing feathers fringed pale. VOICE: A low *nyut-nyut*, also noted is a harsh *chuker-chuker-chuker* and a soft *prrt*. HABITAT: Mainly sandy or muddy coastal shores. DISTRIBUTION: Coastal winter visitor to Hainan, SE China, S Thailand, W Peninsular Malaysia and N Vietnam (E Tonkin); coastal passage migrant elsewhere.

6 KNOT (RED or LESSER KNOT) *Calidris canutus* 23–25cm FIELD NOTES: Usually in small parties. In flight upperwing shows a narrow white wing-bar; lower rump is white barred blackish (appears grey). VOICE: A soft, nasal *knut, wutt* or *whet;* when alarmed utters a *kikkiik*. HABITAT: Sandy or muddy coastal shores. DISTRIBUTION: Winter visitor to Taiwan, Hainan, SE China and occasionally C, W Thailand and N Vietnam (E Tonkin). Coastal passage migrant in S Myanmar, C, W, S Thailand, N Vietnam, Peninsular Malaysia and Singapore.

7 SANDERLING *Calidris alba* 20–21cm FIELD NOTES: Usually in small parties feeding along the water's edge. Typically makes rapid runs interspersed with quick dips to pick up prey. In non-breeding plumage upperwing shows broad white wing-bar and dark leading edge. Juvenile like adult non-breeding but darker above with pronounced pale fringes, giving a chequered effect. VOICE: In flight utters a *twick* or *kip*, often repeated or forming a quick trill. HABITAT: Sandy or muddy coastal shores. DISTRIBUTION: Winter visitor to Taiwan and SE China; further south a winter visitor or passage migrant (except in SW Myanmar and Tenasserim, SE Thailand, Cambodia and C Vietnam).

45 *CALIDRIS* SANDPIPERS AND STINTS

1 WESTERN SANDPIPER *Calidris mauri* 14–17cm FIELD NOTES: Often forages in water. Slightly down-curved bill, thick at base. VOICE: A thin high-pitched *jeet.* HABITAT: Coastal and inland wetlands. DISTRIBUTION: Vagrant, recorded in Taiwan and E China.

2 LITTLE STINT *Calidris minuta* 12–14cm FIELD NOTES: Has a quick 'running around' foraging action. Thin, short bill. Sometimes shows a split supercillium, although more noticeable in juvenile plumage when also shows distinct pale 'braces' on mantle. VOICE: A short *stit-tit.* HABITAT: Fresh- and saltwater wetlands. DISTRIBUTION: Winter visitor or passage migrant to Myanmar and SE China; vagrant elsewhere.

3 RED-NECKED STINT (RUFOUS-NECKED STINT) *Calidris ruficollis* 13–16cm FIELD NOTES: Actions much as Little Stint. In non-breeding plumage very similar to Little Stint, although rear end appears more attenuated and bill is slightly blunter and shorter. VOICE: A coarse *chit, kreep, creek* or *chritt.* HABITAT: Salt- and freshwater wetlands. DISTRIBUTION: Winter visitor and passage migrant over most of the region.

4 TEMMINCK'S STINT *Calidris temminckii* 13–15cm FIELD NOTES: Has a slow, deliberate foraging action, often among waterside vegetation; if alarmed flees with a towering, jinking flight. At rest white-sided tail projects beyond wing-tips. Greenish-yellow legs. VOICE: A rapid *tiririririr* or trilled *trirr.* HABITAT: Marshes, lake and pond edges, paddyfields, saltpans and estuaries. DISTRIBUTION: Coastal winter visitor throughout (except E, S China, Hainan, W Myanmar and N, C Vietnam); passage migrant in China, C Myanmar and N Vietnam.

5 LONG-TOED STINT *Calidris subminuta* 13–16cm FIELD NOTES: Regularly forages among vegetation at water's edge. When alarmed often stands upright with neck extended, if flushed flees with a towering flight with weak, fluttery wing-beats. Juvenile like juvenile Little Stint, but darker with more pronounced white 'braces'. VOICE: A soft *prrt, chrrup* or *chulip,* also a sharp *tik-tik-tik.* HABITAT: Marshes, edges of lakes and pools, coastal pools and estuaries. DISTRIBUTION: Coastal winter visitor throughout (except E China, W, N Myanmar, C Laos and N Vietnam); passage migrant elsewhere.

6 STILT SANDPIPER *Calidris himantopus* 18–23cm FIELD NOTES: In flight shows white rump and plain upperwing; feet project well beyond tail. Often wades up to belly. VOICE: A soft *kirr* or *drr,* also a low *dlew* or *toof.* HABITAT: Inland and coastal wetlands. DISTRIBUTION: Vagrant, recorded from Taiwan and Singapore.

7 DUNLIN (RED-BACKED SANDPIPER) *Calidris alpina* 16–22cm FIELD NOTES: Walks quickly, interspersed with short runs, probing and pecking vigorously. In flight upperwing shows a prominent white wing-bar and white sides to rump and uppertail-coverts. Juvenile like non-breeding adult but mantle darker brown and all feathers fringed rufous-buff; breast and face tinged warm-buff with dark streaks that continue onto belly and flanks. VOICE: A rasping *kreeeep,* also a low *beep.* HABITAT: Coastal mudflats, seashore, marshes, also lake and river sides. DISTRIBUTION: Winter visitor to Taiwan, Hainan, SE, E and northern C China, NW, NE Thailand, N Laos and N Vietnam (E Tonkin); vagrant elsewhere.

8 SHARP-TAILED SANDPIPER (SIBERIAN PECTORAL SANDPIPER) *Calidris acuminata* 17–21cm FIELD NOTES: Usually very confiding. In flight looks similar to Pectoral Sandpiper; if seen very well, white sides to rump and uppertail-coverts show dark shaft streaks. Juvenile similar to breeding adult, but fringes of upperparts brighter rufous and breast washed rufous-buff. VOICE: A soft *wheep, pleep* or *trrt,* also a twittering *prrt-wheep-wheep.* HABITAT: Freshwater and coastal wetlands. DISTRIBUTION: May winter in Taiwan, otherwise passage migrant or vagrant.

9 PECTORAL SANDPIPER *Calidris melanotos* 19–23cm FIELD NOTES: Generally confiding; if alarmed often stands upright with neck erect. In flight upperwing shows small white wing-bar and white sides to lower rump and uppertail-coverts. VOICE: A reedy *churk* or *trrit.* HABITAT: Fresh and saltwater wetlands. DISTRIBUTION: Vagrant, recorded from S, E China, Peninsular Malaysia and Singapore.

46 SANDPIPERS; RUFF; TURNSTONE; PHALAROPES

1 CURLEW SANDPIPER *Calidris ferruginea* 18–23cm FIELD NOTES: Regularly wades, often up to belly, in shallow water. In flight upperwing has a prominent white wing-bar and a white lower rump and uppertail-coverts. Juvenile similar to non-breeding adult but with buff fringes on upperparts and a buffish wash to breast and face. VOICE: A rippling *chirrup*. HABITAT: Coastal mudflats, lagoons, saltmarshes and estuaries; less so on inland wetlands. DISTRIBUTION: Mainly coastal winter visitor or passage migrant from SE China, Hainan southwards (except C Vietnam).

2 SPOON-BILLED SANDPIPER (SPOONBILL SANDPIPER) *Eurynorhynchus pygmeus* 14–16cm FIELD NOTES: Sweeps bill from side to side while foraging in shallow water. In flight shows a prominent white bar on upperwing, sides of rump white. VOICE: A rolling *preep* or a shrill *wheet*. HABITAT: Coastal lagoons and muddy shores. DISTRIBUTION: Scarce winter visitor to SE China, N Vietnam (E Tonkin) and possibly SW, S Myanmar; vagrant elsewhere.

3 BROAD-BILLED SANDPIPER *Limicola falcinellus* 16–18cm FIELD NOTES: Often forages among stint flocks. In flight upperwing shows a narrow white wing-bar; in non-breeding plumage shows a dark leading edge. VOICE: A buzzing *chrrreet* or *trreet*. HABITAT: Coastal creeks, lagoons and mudflats. DISTRIBUTION: Fairly widespread coastal winter visitor.

4 RUFF (REEVE: Female) *Philomachus pugnax* 26–32cm FIELD NOTES: Breeding male plumage unmistakeable and very variable. In moult males often have a non-breeding type plumage splattered with dark blotches on the breast. In flight upperwing shows a narrows white wing-bar and prominent white sides to uppertail-coverts. Has been noted swimming and pecking surface of water like a phalarope. VOICE: Normally silent but a shrill *hoo-ee* may be given by migrating flocks. HABITAT: Lake, pool and river margins, marshes, wet grassland and coastal mudflats. DISTRIBUTION: Winter visitor to Taiwan, E China, SW, S Myanmar, NE C, W Thailand, Peninsular Malaysia, Singapore, Cambodia and S Vietnam.

5 BUFF-BREASTED SANDPIPER *Tryngites subruficollis* 18–20cm FIELD NOTES: Can be very confiding. White underwing with dark tips to flight feathers and primary coverts, the latter forming a pronounced crescent. VOICE: Sometimes utters a low growling *pr-r-r-reet* in flight. HABITAT: Grasslands or dry mud surrounds or lakes and rivers. DISTRIBUTION: Vagrant, recorded from Taiwan and E China.

6 TURNSTONE (RUDDY TURNSTONE) *Arenaria interpres* 21–26cm FIELD NOTES: Typically forages by flicking over small stones, shells or seaweed in search of small invertebrates. In flight upperwing shows a white wing-bar and a white triangle on innerwing-coverts; centre of back and lower rump white split by a black band on upper rump. VOICE: A rapid, staccato *trik-tuk-tuk-tuk, tuk-e-tuk* or *chit-uk* and when alarmed a sharp *chick-ik, kuu* or *teu*. HABITAT: Stony, rocky and sandy shores, also mudflats. DISTRIBUTION: Widespread coastal winter visitor; except S Myanmar (Tenasserim) and Vietnam (E Tonkin and N Annam).

7 GREY PHALAROPE (RED PHALAROPE) *Phalaropus fulicarius* 20–22cm FIELD NOTES: Forages mainly by swimming. Short thick bill with yellowish base. In flight upperwing shows a wide white wing-bar. VOICE: In flight utters a sharp *pik*. HABITAT: Generally pelagic, sometimes found on coastal pools or lakes. DISTRIBUTION: Vagrant to SE, E China.

8 RED-NECKED PHALAROPE (NORTHERN PHALAROPE) *Phalaropus lobatus* 18–19cm FIELD NOTES: Forages while swimming. Short, thin black bill. In flight upperwing shows a white wing-bar. Juvenile has upperparts much like breeding adult with a pink-buff tinge, neck and breast also tinged pink-buff. VOICE: In flight gives a short *twick*, *clip* or *kip*. HABITAT: At sea, coastal waters and mudflats, sometimes inland. DISTRIBUTION: Winter visitor to Taiwan and Hainan; passage migrant elsewhere.

1

br

n-br

2

n-br

3

n-br

br

br

br

♂ n-br

4

♀ br

5

br

♂

♂ breeding
varieties

6

n-br

br

♂ br

n-br

n-br

7

8

♂ br

♀ br

♀ br

47 SKUAS

1 POMARINE SKUA (POMARINE JAEGER) *Stercorarius pomarinus* 46–51cm FIELD NOTES: In flight the bulkiest of the 'smaller' skuas; wings show a distinct white flash at base of primaries. Aggressive pursuer of seabirds in order to steal their food, even going so far as to kill the victim of these chases. Non-breeding plumage similar to breeding but with pale scalloping. Juvenile has upperparts variable from mid-brown to dark brown, barred paler; underparts paler brown barred dark. VOICE: Generally silent. HABITAT: Coastal waters. DISTRIBUTION: Winter visitor off the coasts of Taiwan, E China, S Myanmar (Tenasserim), C, SE, S Thailand, Peninsular Malaysia and Singapore.

2 ARCTIC SKUA (PARASITIC JAEGER) *Stercorarius parasiticus* 41–46cm FIELD NOTES: In flight wings show a distinct white flash at base of primaries. Aerobatically chases and harries seabirds in an attempt to make them disgorge food. Non-breeding plumage as breeding but with pale scalloping. Juvenile very variable, from all-dark brown to brown above with paler brown underparts and a whitish head; whichever form, all dark areas have pale barring and a shorter central tail feathers. VOICE: Generally silent although in flight may utter a nasal *gi-ooo*. HABITAT: Coastal waters. DISTRIBUTION: Winter visitor off the coasts of Taiwan and E China; vagrant elsewhere.

3 LONG-TAILED SKUA (LONG-TAILED JAEGER) *Stercorarius longicaudus* 48–53cm FIELD NOTES: In flight shows no, or indistinct, white flash at base of primaries. In flight often gives the impression of being heavy chested. Less piratical than other skuas; when indulging in harassment tends to pick on terns. Juvenile very variable and similar in plumage to juvenile Arctic Skua, best told by lack of extensive white flash at base of primaries and general lighter structure. VOICE: Generally silent. HABITAT: Coastal waters. DISTRIBUTION: Vagrant, recorded off the coasts of Hainan, SE China, S Thailand and Peninsular Malaysia.

4 SOUTHERN SKUA (BROWN SKUA) *Stercorarius antarcticus* 61–66cm FIELD NOTES: In flight shows a prominent white flash at base of primaries. Very aggressive to seabirds, recorded killing victims when attempting to rob them of food. Juvenile has upperparts grey-brown with pale rufous spots and fringes; underparts uniform rufous, head grey-brown. VOICE: Generally silent. HABITAT: Coastal waters. DISTRIBUTION: Vagrant off the coast of Taiwan.

5 SOUTH POLAR SKUA (MACCORMICK'S SKUA) *Stercorarius maccormicki* 50–55cm FIELD NOTES: In flight shows a prominent white flash at base of primaries. Various morphs occur, grading from pale to dark; all tend to lack any rufous. Juveniles similar in plumage to the respective adult morphs but with pale fringes to upperparts and bill blue with a blackish tip. VOICE: Generally silent. HABITAT: Coastal waters. DISTRIBUTION: Vagrant off the coast of E China.

pale morph

dark morph

dark morph

1

pale morph

1

pale morph

2

dark morph

dark morph

2

pale morph

pale morph

3

dark morph

intermediate morph

pale morph

3

4

pale morph

dark morph

dark morph

4

5

pale morph

5

48 GULLS

Due to the complex plumage of young gulls (often a four-year process to get from brown juvenile to adult white-grey) and the difficulty in explaining such within a limited text, it was thought better to refer the reader to books that cover this area more fully (*see* Further Reading).

1 COMMON GULL (MEW GULL) *Larus canus* 40–46cm FIELD NOTES: Often associates with other gull species. In flight upperwing shows black outer primaries with prominent white subterminal spots on two outermost feathers. VOICE: A high-pitched, laughing *ke ke ke kleeh-a…kleeeh-a…kay-a-kay-a-kay-a-kay-a ke ke*, also a yelping *keea keea*. HABITAT: Coasts, lakes and large rivers. DISTRIBUTION: Winter visitor to China (except central S); vagrant elsewhere.

2 GLAUCOUS GULL *Larus hyperboreus* 64–77cm FIELD NOTES: Aggressive scavenger. Flight lumbering, on broad wings with white flight feathers. VOICE: Generally silent, may give a hoarse, laughing *keeah-keeah-keeah-keah-kau-kau…* HABITAT: Mainly coasts. DISTRIBUTION: Uncommon winter visitor to coastal SE China.

3 GLAUCOUS-WINGED GULL *Larus glaucescens* 61–68cm FIELD NOTES: Aggressive predator with slow powerful flight. Upperwing pattern resembles American Herring Gull, but outer primaries grey, not black. VOICE: A low *klook-klook-klook* and a screamed *ka-ka-ako*. HABITAT: Primarily coastal. DISTRIBUTION: Vagrant, recorded off the coast of E China.

4 SLATY-BACKED GULL *Larus schistisagus* 55–67cm FIELD NOTES: In flight shows a broad white trailing edge and often has an indistinct white band dividing the slaty upperwing from the black outer primaries; the latter with a white subterminal spot on outer feather. VOICE: Similar to Glaucous-winged Gull. HABITAT: Coastal. DISTRIBUTION: Winter visitor to Taiwan and SW, SE China.

5 VEGA GULL *Larus vegae* 57–64cm FIELD NOTES: In flight upperwing shows black-tipped outer primaries with white subterminal spots on two outermost feathers. Paler backed race *L. v. mongolicus* (5b) possibly occurs in SE China. VOICE: A laughing *keeah-keeah-keeah-keah-kau-kau…* HABITAT: Coastal and along large rivers. DISTRIBUTION: Winter visitor to Taiwan and coastal SW, SE China.

6 AMERICAN HERRING GULL *Larus smithsonianus* FIELD NOTES: In flight shows black primaries with distinct white subterminal spot on outer pair of feathers. VOICE: A loud, laughing, similar to Vega Gull. HABITAT: Mainly coastal. DISTRIBUTION: Rare winter visitor to coastal E China.

7 HEUGLIN'S GULL *Larus heuglini* 58–65cm FIELD NOTES: Upperwing has a white trailing edge; black outer primaries have a white subterminal spot on two outermost feathers. VOICE: A deep nasal *gagaga*. HABITAT: Coasts and inland waters. DISTRIBUTION: Winter visitor to coastal SE China, C, W Thailand, N Vietnam and probably further south.

8 CASPIAN GULL *Larus cachinnans* 52–58cm FIELD NOTES: Upperwing shows black outer primaries with large white tip to outer feather and white subterminal spot on next feather. There is still confusion as to which species of the Caspian, Herring and Vega Gull complex actually occur in the region. VOICE: A deep, nasal *keeah-keeah-keeah-keeah-kau-kau…* HABITAT: Mainly coastal. DISTRIBUTION: Rare winter visitor to SE China.

9 BLACK-TAILED GULL (JAPANESE or TEMMINCK'S GULL) *Larus crassirostris* 44–47cm FIELD NOTES: Upperwing primaries black with small white tips, outermost feather may have a small white subterminal spot. VOICE: A plaintive mewing. HABITAT: Rocky islands, cliffs and seashores; in winter also on rivers and lakes. DISTRIBUTION: Breeds in E China (Fujian coast), in winter spreads to northern C, SW, SE, E China and Taiwan; vagrant further south.

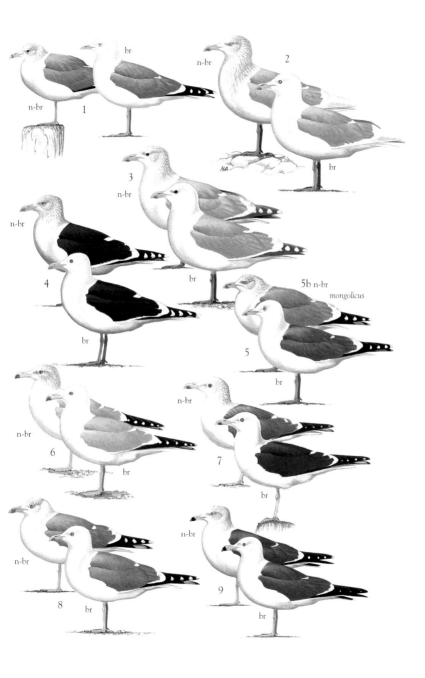

49 GULLS

See note on plate 48 referring to young gulls.

1 GREAT BLACK-HEADED GULL (PALLAS'S GULL) *Ichthyaetus ichthyaetus* 57–61cm FIELD NOTES: In flight upperwing shows a black subterminal band on white outer primaries; flight action ponderous with a prominent projecting head. VOICE: A low *kyow-kyow* and a nasal *kraagh*. HABITAT: Coasts, lakes and large rivers. DISTRIBUTION: Rare winter visitor off coasts of SE China, S Myanmar, C, W Thailand and N Vietnam; vagrant elsewhere.

2 RELICT GULL (MONGOLIAN GULL) *Ichthyaetus relictus* 44cm FIELD NOTES: Upperwing pattern similar to Great Black-headed Gull. VOICE: A laughing *ka-ka-ka-ka kee-aa*. HABITAT: Estuaries and mudflats. DISTRIBUTION: Vagrant, recorded from SE China and N Vietnam.

3 LAUGHING GULL *Leucophaeus atricilla* 36–41cm FIELD NOTES: Upperwing shows a white trailing edge and black outer primaries. VOICE: A high-pitched, laughing *ka-ka-ka-ka-ka-kaa-kaa-kaaa-kaaa*; also a shorter *kahwi*. HABITAT: Coastal areas. DISTRIBUTION: Vagrant.

4 SAUNDER'S GULL (CHINESE BLACK-HEADED GULL) *Chroicocephalus saundersi* 29–32cm FIELD NOTES: Buoyant tern-like flight. Inner primaries form a black wedge, making underwing pattern diagnostic. Upperwing grey with black subterminal tips on white primaries. VOICE: A shrill *eek eek*. HABITAT: Coastal areas. DISTRIBUTION: Coastal winter visitor to Taiwan, Hainan, SE, E China and N Vietnam (E Tonkin).

5 BLACK-HEADED GULL (COMMON BLACK-HEADED GULL) *Chroicocephalus ridibundus* 37–43cm FIELD NOTES: In flight upperwing pale grey, outer primaries white, tipped black; underwing pale grey, inner primaries darker grey, outer primaries white, tipped black. VOICE: A high-pitched *karr* or *krreearr* and a sharp *kek-kek*. HABITAT: Coasts, lakes and rivers. DISTRIBUTION: Winter visitor over much of the region.

6 BROWN-HEADED GULL (INDIAN BLACK-HEADED GULL) *Chroicocephalus brunnicephalus* 41–45cm FIELD NOTES: Outermost primaries of upperwing white with broad black tips broken by subterminal white spots on outermost feathers; underwing pattern similar. VOICE: A harsh *gek gek* or *grarhh* a wailing *ko-yek ko-yek* and a raucous *kreeak*. HABITAT: Coastal waters, lakes and large rivers. DISTRIBUTION: Winter visitor to SE China, much of Myanmar, Thailand, Peninsular Malaysia, Cambodia, Laos and S, N Vietnam.

7 SLENDER-BILLED GULL *Chroicocephalus genei* 42–44cm FIELD NOTES: Upperwing pale grey, outer primaries white, tipped black; underwing pale grey, inner primaries darker grey, outer primaries white tipped black. VOICE: A harsh rolling *krerr*. Other notes similar to Black-headed Gull but lower-pitched. HABITAT: Coastal waters. DISTRIBUTION: Occasional winter visitor or vagrant to coastal S, E China and Thailand.

8 LITTLE GULL *Hydrocoloeus minutus* 25–30cm FIELD NOTES: Buoyant tern-like flight. Underwing dark grey, upperwing silver-grey. VOICE: A short nasal *keck* or *keck-keck-keck*. HABITAT: Coasts or nearby lagoons. DISTRIBUTION: Vagrant, recorded from SE China.

9 KITTIWAKE (BLACK-LEGGED KITTIWAKE) *Rissa tridactyla* 38–40cm FIELD NOTES: In flight upperwing and underwing show black-tipped primaries; underwing white. Slightly forked tail. VOICE: A nasal wailing *kitt-i-waak kitt-i-waak*. HABITAT: At sea, unless blown inland. DISTRIBUTION: Rare winter visitor to the coast of E China.

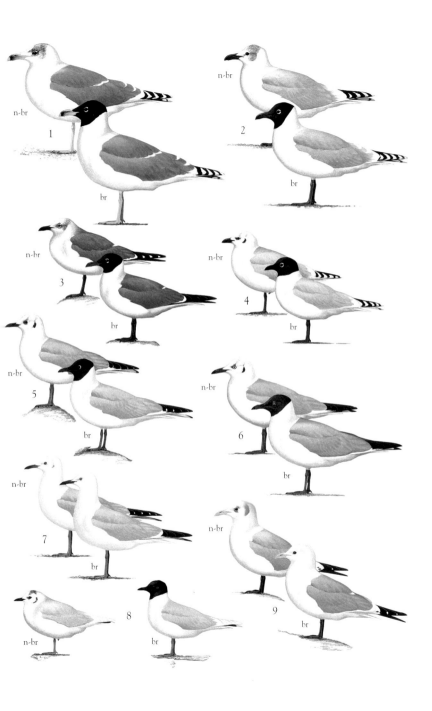

50 SKIMMER; TERNS

1 INDIAN SKIMMER (SCISSORBILL) *Rhynchops albicollis* 38–43cm FIELD
NOTES: Feeds by 'ploughing' water with lower mandible whilst in skimming flight.
In flight upperwing shows a broad white trailing edge and white underwing with
dark greyish primaries. Tail white with a black central streak; forked. VOICE: A nasal,
yapping *kap kap kap*. HABITAT: Sandbanks on large rivers, occasionally coastal mudflats.
DISTRIBUTION: Scarce resident over much of northern Myanmar; vagrant elsewhere.

2 GULL-BILLED TERN *Gelochelidon nilotica* 33–43cm FIELD NOTES: Feeds by
hawking insects or dipping to pick prey from the surface of water or ground. Flight gull-like
with outer to mid-primaries showing a dark trailing edge; rump and tail same colour as
upperparts. VOICE: A nasal *kay-did, kay-tih-did, gur-WICK, ger-erk or kay-vek*, also a metallic
kak-kak and when alarmed a *kvay-kvay*. HABITAT: Coasts, saltmarsh, brackish and freshwater
lakes, pools and rivers. DISTRIBUTION: Resident in Taiwan and SE China, otherwise mainly
a coastal winter visitor to Myanmar, Thailand, Cambodia, N, S Vietnam, Peninsular
Malaysia and Singapore.

3 CASPIAN TERN *Hydroprogne caspia* 47–54cm FIELD NOTES: Feeds mainly by
hovering then plunge-diving, also picks from surface of water; sometimes harasses foods
from other terns and gulls. Upperwing shows grey outer primaries with darker tips;
underwing shows dark outer primaries; tail shallowly forked. VOICE: A loud, croaking *kraah,
krah-krah or kree-ahk*. HABITAT: Coastal waters, mudflats, inland lakes, rivers and marshes.
DISTRIBUTION: Breeds in E China and Hainan (northern birds move south post breeding).
Resident in SE China; winter visitor, mainly coastal, to Taiwan, S Myanmar, Thailand,
Cambodia, N, S Vietnam, Peninsular Malaysia and Singapore.

4 GREATER CRESTED TERN (SWIFT TERN) *Thalasseus bergii* 43–53cm FIELD
NOTES: Feeds mainly by plunge-diving but also picks from surface of water. Underwing
shows dark greyish tips to outer primaries; rump and tail same colour as upperparts.
Tail deeply forked. VOICE: A grating *krrik or kee-rit*, also a high-pitched *kree-kree*.
HABITAT: Coastal waters. DISTRIBUTION: Resident, mainly coastal to Taiwan, Hainan, S, E
China, S, SW Myanmar, Cambodia and S Vietnam.

5 CHINESE CRESTED TERN *Thalasseus bernsteini* 42cm FIELD NOTES: Upperwing has
outer webs of outer primaries blackish; underwing white. VOICE: Harsh high-pitched cries.
HABITAT: Coastal. DISTRIBUTION: Recent breeding records on the E China coast (Zhejiang
and Fujian), otherwise a rare non-breeding visitor or passage migrant in SE China, Taiwan
and S Thailand.

6 LESSER CRESTED TERN *Thalasseus bengalensis* 36–41cm FIELD NOTES: Feeds
mainly by hovering and then plunge-diving. Inner webs of outer primaries form an
indistinct silver-grey wedge on upperwing; outer primaries on underwing show dusky tips.
Rump and tail pale grey the latter deeply forked. VOICE: A harsh *krrrik-krrrik or kerrick*.
HABITAT: Coastal waters. DISTRIBUTION: Non-breeding coastal visitor to S, SW Myanmar, S
Thailand, W Peninsular Malaysia and Singapore; vagrant elsewhere.

7 RIVER TERN (INDIAN RIVER TERN) *Sterna aurantia* 38–46cm FIELD
NOTES: Usually feeds by plunge-diving. In flight whitish upperwing primaries form a
conspicuous flash on outer-wing. Tail deeply forked with long outer-tail feathers. VOICE: In
flight utters a shrill, staccato *kiuk-kiuk*. HABITAT: Large rivers and lakes, rare on coasts.
DISTRIBUTION: Resident in SW China, Myanmar, Cambodia, S, C Laos and NW, NE
Thailand; vagrant elsewhere.

1

n-br 2

3 n-br

br N br

br

4 n-br

n-br

5 br

br

6 n-br

br

br 7

n-br

51 TERNS

1 COMMON TERN *Sterna hirundo* 32–39cm FIELD NOTES: Feeds mainly by plunge-diving. In flight, from below inner primaries appear translucent. Tail deeply forked with long outer-tail feathers. Dark-billed race *S. h. longipennis* (1b) occurs as a passage migrant in S, SE China, Taiwan and Hainan and probably further south. VOICE: A rapid *kye-kye-kye-kye…* also a *kirri-kirri-kirri*; when alarmed utters a screeching *kreeearh* or *kreee-eer* and a sharp *kik*. HABITAT: Coasts and large inland waters. DISTRIBUTION: Widespread, mainly coastal winter visitor to the region, except Myanmar and N Vietnam (N Annam).

2 BLACK-NAPED TERN *Sterna sumatrana* 34–35cm FIELD NOTES: Feeds mainly by plunge-diving, but also by skimming low over water picking food from the surface. Outer web of outermost primary blackish; tail deeply forked with long outer-tail feathers. VOICE: A sharp *tsii-chee-chi-chip* and a *chit-chit-chit-er* uttered when excited or alarmed. HABITAT: Rocky islets, coastal bays and lagoons. DISTRIBUTION: Resident in Taiwan, Hainan, S, E China, SE, S Thailand, Cambodia, S Vietnam, Peninsular Malaysia and Singapore. Non-breeding visitor elsewhere, except SW Myanmar, C Thailand and N Vietnam.

3 ROSEATE TERN *Sterna dougallii* 33–38cm FIELD NOTES: Feeds mainly by plunge-diving, usually from a greater height than Common Tern. Also picks food from surface of water. Tail deeply forked with very long outer-tail feathers. VOICE: A rasping *kraak* or *zraaach*, also a short, soft *cher-vik*. HABITAT: Offshore islets and coastal waters. DISTRIBUTION: Coastal resident in Taiwan, Hainan, S, E China, S Vietnam, Peninsular Malaysia and possibly S Myanmar (Tenasserim); more widespread post breeding, except SW Myanmar, Cambodia and C, N Vietnam.

4 BLACK-BELLIED TERN *Sterna acuticauda* 33cm FIELD NOTES: Feeds by plunge-diving and also by picking food off water surface or ground. In flight whitish primaries of upperwing contrast with grey of the rest of the wing; tail deeply forked with long outer-tail feathers. VOICE: A clear, piping *peuo*, also a shrill *krek-krek*. HABITAT: Large rivers and lakes. DISTRIBUTION: Resident in SW China, Myanmar and possibly NW Thailand, Cambodia and Laos; vagrant elsewhere.

5 ALEUTIAN TERN (KAMCHATKA TERN) *Onychoprion aleuticus* 32–34cm FIELD NOTES: Feeds by dipping to take food from water surface. Underwing white with dark trailing edge to secondaries and dusky outer primaries; white rump and tail, the latter deeply forked. VOICE: A soft wader-like *twee-ee-ee*. HABITAT: Mainly maritime. DISTRIBUTION: Scarce winter visitor off the coasts of SE China, SE Peninsular Malaysia and Singapore.

6 BRIDLED TERN (BROWN-WINGED TERN) *Onychoprion anaethetus* 34–36cm FIELD NOTES: Flight very buoyant. Feeds by plunge-diving and by dipping to pick from water surface. Underwing mainly white with dusky tips to primaries and secondaries; rump and tail dark grey, the latter deeply forked with white outer-tail feathers. VOICE: A yapping *wep-wep* or *wup-wup*. HABITAT: Mainly maritime. DISTRIBUTION: Offshore resident or non-breeding visitor to Taiwan, Hainan, E China, Thailand, Cambodia, C, S Vietnam, Peninsular Malaysia and Singapore.

7 SOOTY TERN (WIDEAWAKE TERN) *Onychoprion fuscatus* 36–45cm FIELD NOTES: Feeds mainly by dipping and picking from the surface of water, occasionally plunge-dives. Underwing white with dusky primaries and dusky tips to secondaries. Rump and tail blackish, the latter deeply forked with white outer-tail feathers. VOICE: A distinctive *ker-wacki-wah, ker-wacki-wack* or *wide-awake*, also utters a short *kraark*. HABITAT: Mainly maritime. DISTRIBUTION: Vagrant, recorded from Taiwan, SE China, S Myanmar, C, S Thailand and Peninsular Malaysia.

1b *longipennis*

br

1

n-br

br

2

n-br

br

3

n-br

br

4

5

6

7

52 TERNS; NODDIES

1 LITTLE TERN *Sternula albifrons* 22–28cm FIELD NOTES: Very active forager, feeds by plunge-diving, which is preceded by prolonged hovering. In flight upperwing shows a dark pair of outer primaries. Tail deeply forked. VOICE: A rapid *kirrikikki kirrikiki*, a sharp *kik-kik* and a rasping *zr-e-e-e-p*. HABITAT: Sand bars and shingle banks on coasts, lakes and rivers. DISTRIBUTION: Breeds in China, moves to coasts post breeding. Mainly coastal resident in Myanmar, Thailand, Cambodia, C Vietnam, E Peninsular Malaysia and Singapore. Widespread coastal non-breeding visitor. (Breeds inland in Myanmar, Cambodia and Laos.)

2 SAUNDER'S TERN (BLACK-SHAFTED TERN) *Sternula saundersi* 20–28cm FIELD NOTES: Actions and habits as Little Tern. Compared to Little Tern upperwing has three outer primaries blackish, slightly darker grey upperparts and lacks the short white supercillium. VOICE: Like Little Tern, but a little less chattering. HABITAT: Coastal waters. DISTRIBUTION: Probably occurs on the coasts of the west of the region.

3 WHISKERED TERN *Chlidonias hybrida* 23–29cm FIELD NOTES: Buoyant foraging flight, regularly dipping to pick prey from water's surface, may also plunge-dive. Rump grey, paler in non-breeding plumage. Tail shallowly forked. VOICE: A rasping *cherk* also a *kek* or *kek-kek*. HABITAT: Vegetated lakes, marshes, paddyfields, coastal pools and mudflats. DISTRIBUTION: Breeds in Taiwan and S, E, north C China, moving to coasts post breeding. Widespread winter resident to E China, Hainan and further south, except W, N Myanmar, SE Thailand, Laos and N Vietnam (W Tonkin); passage migrant elsewhere.

4 BLACK TERN *Chlidonias niger* 22–24cm FIELD NOTES: Foraging flight is buoyant with regular dips to pick up prey from water's surface. Underwing pale grey. Tail, rump and upperparts all same colour. Tail shallowly forked. In non-breeding plumage shows a black smudge at the side of breast. VOICE: A weak *kik* or *kik-kik*, also a shrill, nasal *kyeh*, *kreek* or *ki ki ki* when alarmed. HABITAT: Vegetated lakes, marshes and estuaries. DISTRIBUTION: Vagrant, recorded from SE China and Singapore.

5 WHITE-WINGED TERN (WHITE-WINGED BLACK TERN) *Chlidonias leucopterus* 23–27cm FIELD NOTES: Actions similar to Black Tern. Underwing-coverts black, rump white, tail pale grey and very shallowly forked. In non-breeding plumage underwing whitish with grey primaries and secondaries; many birds have vestiges of black coverts in the form of lines or patches. VOICE: A harsh, high-pitched *kreek*, a soft *kek* and a rasping *kesch* or *chr-re re*. HABITAT: Coastal lagoons, estuaries, marshes, paddyfields, lakes, pools and large rivers. DISTRIBUTION: Winter visitor to E, S China, Hainan, Taiwan, C, S Thailand, Peninsular Malaysia and Singapore. Fairly widespread passage migrant; summer records from S Thailand, Peninsular Malaysia and Singapore.

6 WHITE TERN (FAIRY TERN) *Gygis alba* 25–30cm FIELD NOTES: Dives to the water's surface to catch small fish as they leap out. Forked tail. Juvenile has tips of mantle and wing feathers tinged brownish. VOICE: A guttural *heech heech*. HABITAT: Maritime. DISTRIBUTION: Coastal vagrant, recorded from S Vietnam and SE China.

7 BLACK NODDY (WHITE-CAPPED NODDY) *Anous minutus* 35–39cm FIELD NOTES: Feeds by hovering and dipping to pick prey from water's surface, also foot patters on the surface of water. Underwing-coverts brownish-black contiguous with flight feathers. Tail wedge-shaped, may looked forked during moult of central feathers. VOICE: A distinctive *tik-tikoree* and a staccato rattle. HABITAT: Maritime. DISTRIBUTION: Vagrant off the coast of SW Peninsular Malaysia.

8 BROWN NODDY (COMMON NODDY) *Anous stolidus* 38–45cm FIELD NOTES: Feeding actions similar to Black Noddy. Underwing-coverts slightly paler than flight feathers. Tail wedge-shaped, may look forked during moult of central tail feathers. VOICE: A crow-like *kwok-kwok*, *karruuk* or *krao*. HABITAT: Maritime. DISTRIBUTION: Coastal offshore vagrant and non-breeding visitor to W Peninsular Malaysia (may breed), E China and Taiwan.

53 PIGEONS

1 ROCK DOVE (ROCK or COMMON PIGEON) *Columba livia* 31–34cm FIELD NOTES: The ancestor of the well-known town and city pigeon. Feral birds can be extremely variable. VOICE: A moaning *gootr-goo gootr-goo, oorh* or *oh-oo-oor*; also a hurried *oo-roo-coo t coo* given during display. HABITAT: Cliffs and ruins, cultivations and around human habitations, including villages, towns and cities. DISTRIBUTION: Common throughout the region, pure stock probably only occurring in Myanmar.

2 HILL PIGEON (EASTERN ROCK PIGEON) *Columba rupestris* 33–35cm FIELD NOTES: Usually encountered in small flocks. Looks like a very pale version of Rock Dove, with white rump and a whitish band on tail. VOICE: A high-pitched, rolling *gut-gut-gut-gut*. HABITAT: Cliffs, gorges and caves in open rugged country. DISTRIBUTION: Resident in E China, S to Shanghai. Possibly breeds in SW China.

3 SNOW PIGEON (TIBETAN PIGEON) *Columba leuconota* 31–34cm FIELD NOTES: In flight shows a white patch on upper rump; lower rump and tail black, the latter with a white mid-band. Post breeding may occur in large flocks. VOICE: A *hic hic cuck-cuck hic,* also a prolonged *coo-ooo-ooo.* HABITAT: High-altitude rocky cliffs, steep gorges and high-level cultivations. DISTRIBUTION: Resident in SW China and N Myanmar.

4 SPECKLED WOOD PIGEON (HODGSON'S PIGEON) *Columba hodgsonii* 38–40cm FIELD NOTES: Mainly arboreal. In flight appears uniformly dark grey-brown; usually seen in pairs or small flocks. VOICE: A deep *whock-whrroo-whrrooo*. HABITAT: Broadleaved evergreen forest. DISTRIBUTION: Resident in SW China and northern Myanmar; winter visitor to NW Thailand and N Laos.

5 PALE-CAPPED PIGEON (PURPLE WOOD PIGEON) *Columba punicea* 36–41cm FIELD NOTES: Generally encountered in pairs or small groups. Juvenile duller, with crown, mantle and wings dull brown, the latter with rusty fringes. VOICE: A soft mew. HABITAT: Broadleaved evergreen forest, secondary growth, mangroves and island forest; more open areas during local nomadic wanderings. DISTRIBUTION: Resident in Myanmar (except W, N), C, S Laos and C, S Vietnam.

6 ASHY WOOD PIGEON (BUFF-COLLARED PIGEON) *Columba pulchricollis* 31–36cm FIELD NOTES: Mainly arboreal, usually occurs in pairs or small flocks. In flight appears darkish grey with a paler head. VOICE: A deep *whuoo whuoo whuoo* or *coo coo coo*. HABITAT: Broadleaved evergreen forest. DISTRIBUTION: Resident in Taiwan, SW China and northern parts of Myanmar, NW Thailand and N Laos.

7 GREEN IMPERIAL PIGEON *Ducula aenea* 43–47cm FIELD NOTES: Usually seen in pairs or small parties, although may be in larger flocks at fruiting trees. Juvenile duller with less pronounced pink tinge to head and underparts. VOICE: A deep, hollow *currr-whoo*. HABITAT: Broadleaved evergreen, semi-evergreen, mixed deciduous and island forest, also mangroves. DISTRIBUTION: Resident from Hainan, SE, SW China southwards (except C Thailand). Scarce non-breeding visitor to Singapore.

8 MOUNTAIN IMPERIAL PIGEON (MAROON-BACKED IMPERIAL PIGEON) *Ducula badia* 43–51cm FIELD NOTES: Usually seen in pairs or small parties. Juvenile duller, mantle and wings with rusty fringes and pale terminal band less distinct. VOICE: A clicking or clucking sound followed by a deep, resonant, double-booming note. HABITAT: Broadleaved evergreen forest. DISTRIBUTION: Resident in SW China, Hainan, much of Myanmar, Thailand, Peninsular Malaysia, Cambodia, Laos and Vietnam (except S).

9 PIED IMPERIAL PIGEON *Ducula bicolor* 35–42cm FIELD NOTES: Unmistakeable. In flight shows black primaries and secondaries and a black terminal band on tail. Usually encountered in small parties. Juvenile has white parts tinged greyish and buffish fringes to most feathers. VOICE: A deep purring, also a chuckling *hu-hu-hu* and a *cru-croo*. HABITAT: Island forest, coastal mainland forests and mangroves. DISTRIBUTION: Coastal resident in S, SW Myanmar, S, SE Thailand, Cambodia, S Vietnam and Peninsular Malaysia; scarce non-breeding visitor to coastal W Thailand and Singapore.

feral varieties

54 DOVES; CUCKOO DOVES

1 COLLARED DOVE (EUROPEAN or EURASIAN COLLARED DOVE)
Streptopelia decaocto 31–33cm FIELD NOTES: Feeds mainly on the ground. In flight shows white corners to tail. Juvenile lacks neck collar. Yellow eye-ring race *S. d. xanthocyclus* (1b) occurs in Myanmar and SW China. VOICE: A low-pitched *koo-KOO-kook* or *koo-kooo-koo*. On landing often gives a harsh *kreair* or *whaaa*. HABITAT: Open country with scattered trees, cultivations, groves and villages. DISTRIBUTION: Resident in northern parts of China, SW China and northern areas of Myanmar.

2 RED TURTLE DOVE (RED COLLARED DOVE) *Streptopelia tranquebarica* 31–33cm FIELD NOTES: Feeds mainly on the ground. In flight tail shows white sides and greyish-white corners. Juvenile duller, mantle and wings with buff fringes, no black collar. VOICE: A deep *cru-u-u-u-u* or *groo-gurr-goo*. HABITAT: Dry open country, scrub and cultivations. DISTRIBUTION: Widespread resident, except S Thailand, N Vietnam (W Tonkin), Peninsular Malaysia and Singapore. A feral population occurs in Peninsular Malaysia and Singapore.

3 ORIENTAL TURTLE DOVE (RUFOUS TURTLE DOVE) *Streptopelia orientalis* 30–35cm FIELD NOTES: Usually singly or in pairs. May occur in small flocks at rich feeding sites. In flight tail shows grey sides and terminal band contrasting with blackish subterminal bar. Juvenile much duller grey-brown with pale fringes on scapulars and mantle, and lacks black and white neck pattern. VOICE: A mournful *coo-cooroo-coocoo* or *gur-grugroo*. HABITAT: Open forest, secondary growth, scrub and cultivations. DISTRIBUTION: Resident in China, Myanmar and E, NE, NW Thailand; winter visitor to N Myanmar, NW, NE Thailand, Cambodia, Laos and Vietnam.

4 SPOTTED DOVE (NECKLACE DOVE) *Spilopelia chinensis* 30cm FIELD NOTES: In flight shows white corners to dark tail. Juvenile generally sandy-brown, slightly darker above with pale fringes, no neck pattern. Race *S. tigrina* (4b) occurs in the south of the region. VOICE: A melodious *coo croo-oo croo-oo* or *coocoo croor-croor*. HABITAT: Cultivated areas, open forests and around human habitations. DISTRIBUTION: Resident throughout the region.

5 ZEBRA DOVE *Geopelia striata* 21–22cm FIELD NOTES: Feeds mainly on the ground. During display bows with tail raised and fanned. VOICE: A high-pitched soft trilling that leads to a series of rapid *coo* notes. HABITAT: Open country with scrub, cultivations, parks and gardens. DISTRIBUTION: Resident in S Myanmar (Tenasserim), S Thailand, Peninsular Malaysia and Singapore; feral populations occur in Thailand and N Laos.

6 BARRED CUCKOO-DOVE (BAR-TAILED CUCKOO-DOVE) *Macropygia unchall* 37–41cm FIELD NOTES: Usually seen in pairs or small flocks. Acrobatically clambers around tree branches foraging for small fruits. On the ground carries tail slightly raised. Juvenile generally dark with darker barring. VOICE: A booming *croo-oom*. HABITAT: Broadleaved evergreen and semi-evergreen forest. DISTRIBUTION: Resident from S, E China and Hainan southwards, except SW Myanmar, C, S Thailand and Singapore.

7 PHILIPPINE CUCKOO-DOVE *Macropygia tenuirostris* 38cm FIELD NOTES: Actions and habits similar to Barred Cuckoo-Dove. VOICE: A deep *wua wu*. HABITAT: Heavy wooded areas and ravines. DISTRIBUTION: Resident on Lanyu Islet off Taiwan.

8 LITTLE CUCKOO-DOVE *Macropygia ruficeps* 30cm FIELD NOTES: Usually occurs in pairs or small parties. Feeds on the ground and in trees, generally in the middle storey or lower canopy. VOICE: A soft, monotonous *wup-wup-wup-wup-wup-wup...* also a rapidly repeated *croo-wuck croo-wuck croo-wuck*. HABITAT: Broadleaved evergreen forest and forest edge. DISTRIBUTION: Resident in SW China, SE Myanmar, W, NE, NW, S Thailand, N Laos, N Vietnam and Peninsular Malaysia.

1b *xanthocyclus*

♀

1

2

♂

4b *tigrina*

3

4

♀

♂

6

5

♀

8

♂

♀

♂

7

55 DOVES; PIGEONS

1 JAMBU FRUIT DOVE (CRIMSON-HEADED FRUIT DOVE) *Ptilinopus jambu*
22–28cm FIELD NOTES: Feeds in trees, although recorded feeding on the ground on
fallen fruit. VOICE: A soft, repeated *hooo*, although generally silent. HABITAT: Broadleaved
evergreen forest and occasionally mangroves. DISTRIBUTION: Scarce or uncommon resident
in S Thailand and Peninsular Malaysia.

2 BLACK-CHINNED FRUIT DOVE (BLACK-THROATED FRUIT DOVE)
Ptilinopus leclancheri 26–28cm FIELD NOTES: Feeds in fruiting trees. Juvenile similar to
adult female but lacks the pectoral band. VOICE: A well spaced *whoo - whoo - whoo...*
HABITAT: Lowland rain forest. DISTRIBUTION: Resident on Taiwan.

3 EMERALD DOVE (COMMON EMERALD or GREEN-WINGED DOVE)
Chalcophaps indica 23–27cm FIELD NOTES: Usually encountered singly, in pairs or small
groups, feeding on the ground; often uses forest tracks. In flight shows two white bars on
black lower back. VOICE: A soft, drawn-out *tuk-hoop, hoo hoo* or *tk-hoon*. HABITAT: Broadleaved,
semi-evergreen and mixed deciduous forest. DISTRIBUTION: Resident in Taiwan, Hainan and
southward from SE, SW China.

4 NICOBAR PIGEON (HACKLED, WHITE-TAILED or VULTURINE PIGEON)
Caloenas nicobarica 40cm FIELD NOTES: Usually forages at dusk or dawn, mainly on
the ground, feeding on fallen fruit. Female has a smaller cere, shorter hackles and
browner upperparts. Juvenile lacks hackles and is generally brownish-black, including
tail. VOICE: Usually silent, although recorded as uttering a short, soft cooing and
pig-like grunting during disputes. HABITAT: Wooded islands, bushes and mangroves.
DISTRIBUTION: Resident on islands off S Myanmar (Tenasserim), S Thailand, Peninsular
Malaysia, S Vietnam and on the Coco Islands.

5 LITTLE GREEN PIGEON *Treron olax* 21–27cm FIELD NOTES: Arboreal, feeds from
the middle storey to the canopy, usually in groups of up to eight birds. VOICE: A high-
pitched *wiiiiii-iiu-iiu-iiu-iiu iiui-iiuwu*, repeated after short intervals. HABITAT: Broadleaved
evergreen forest, freshwater swamp forest and secondary growth. DISTRIBUTION: Resident in
S Thailand and Peninsular Malaysia; non-breeding visitor to Singapore.

6 ORANGE-BREASTED GREEN PIGEON *Treron bicinctus* 29cm FIELD NOTES:
Usually arboreal, feeds on fruit and berries in small flocks, although at rich food sites may be
in large flocks. VOICE: A modulated, mellow whistle; also a croaking note and a chuckling
call. HABITAT: Deciduous and semi-evergreen forest, secondary growth, occasionally
broadleaved evergreen forest and mangroves. DISTRIBUTION: Resident in Hainan,
widespread in the south, except C Thailand, N, C Laos, N Vietnam and Singapore.

**7 CINNAMON-HEADED GREEN PIGEON (CHESTNUT-HEADED GREEN
PIGEON)** *Treron fulvicollis* 25–27cm FIELD NOTES: Said to feed mainly in small trees on
fruit. VOICE: Similar to Little Green Pigeon, but less whining. HABITAT: Freshwater Swamp
Forest, coastal forest, secondary growth and mangroves. DISTRIBUTION: Resident in S
Myanmar (S Tenasserim), S Thailand and Peninsular Malaysia; rare non-breeding visitor to
Singapore.

8 PINK-NECKED GREEN PIGEON *Treron vernans* 26–32cm FIELD NOTES: Feeds from
middle storey to canopy, usually in small flocks, larger flocks occur at rich feeding sites.
VOICE: Foraging groups utter a hoarse, rasping *krrak krrak...* HABITAT: Freshwater swamp
forest, mangroves, scrub and cultivations. DISTRIBUTION: Coastal resident in S Myanmar
(Tenasserim), Thailand (except NE), Cambodia, S Vietnam, Peninsular Malaysia and
Singapore.

9 ASHY-HEADED GREEN PIGEON *Treron phayrei* 27–28cm FIELD NOTES: Actions
and habits similar to Orange-breasted Green Pigeon. VOICE: Low-pitched mellow whistles.
HABITAT: Broadleaved evergreen and semi-evergreen forest. DISTRIBUTION: Resident in SW
China, Myanmar, Thailand (except C, S), Cambodia, Laos and S Vietnam.

56 PIGEONS

1 THICK-BILLED GREEN PIGEON *Treron curvirostra* 24–31cm FIELD NOTES: Usually arboreal, feeds on fruit and berries in small flocks, but at rich food sites may occur in larger numbers. VOICE: Low-pitched, throaty whistles, also a hoarse *goo-goo* when feeding. HABITAT: Various woodland, including broadleaved evergreen, semi-evergreen, mixed deciduous, mangroves and secondary growth. DISTRIBUTION: Widespread resident southwards from SW China and Hainan, except C Thailand and N Vietnam (W Tonkin), non-breeding visitor to Singapore.

2 LARGE GREEN PIGEON *Treron capellei* 35–36cm FIELD NOTES: Forages in small groups of up to a dozen birds, often in fruiting figs. VOICE: A variable, deep nasal creaking *oo-oo-aah oo-oo-aah aa-aa-aah*; also *oooOOah oo-aah…* HABITAT: Broadleaved evergreen and freshwater water swamp forest, forest edge and clearings. DISTRIBUTION: Resident in S Myanmar (S Tenasserim), S Thailand and Peninsular Malaysia.

3 YELLOW-FOOTED GREEN PIGEON (COMMON GREEN PIGEON) *Treron phoenicopterus* 33cm FIELD NOTES: Acrobatic forager in fruiting trees; will venture to the ground to visit salt-licks. Usually seen in small flocks with larger flocks at rick food sites. Darker race *T. p. annamensis* (3b) occurs in E Thailand, S Laos and S Vietnam. VOICE: Melodious whistling notes. HABITAT: Mixed deciduous forest and secondary growth. DISTRIBUTION: Resident in SW China, Myanmar, northern Thailand, Cambodia, C, S Laos and C, S Vietnam.

4 PIN-TAILED GREEN PIGEON (LONG-TAILED GREEN PIGEON) *Treron apicauda* 28–32cm FIELD NOTES: Acrobatic, parakeet-like, feeding actions; often found in flocks of 10 to 30 birds foraging on small and large fruits; goes to the ground to feed at salt-licks. VOICE: A deep musical *oou ou-ruu oo-ru ou-rooou*; also a mellow, whistled *ko-kla-oi-oi-oi-oilli-illio-kla.* HABITAT: Broadleaved evergreen forest. DISTRIBUTION: Resident in SW China, Myanmar, W, NW, NE Thailand, E Cambodia, Laos and C, N Vietnam.

5 YELLOW-VENTED GREEN PIGEON *Treron seimundi* 26–28cm FIELD NOTES: Feeds on fruit in tree canopy; also recorded flying across valleys at a great height. VOICE: A high-pitched *pooaah po-yo-yo-pooaah.* HABITAT: Broadleaved evergreen forest and forest edge. DISTRIBUTION: Resident in W, NW, SE Thailand, C, S Laos, Vietnam (except W Tonkin) and Peninsular Malaysia.

6 WEDGE-TAILED GREEN PIGEON (SINGING GREEN PIGEON) *Treron sphenurus* 30–33cm FIELD NOTES: Acrobatic forager in fruiting trees; occurs singly, in pairs or in small flocks. VOICE: A series of musical whistling or fluting notes; also a curious grunting. HABITAT: Broadleaved evergreen forest and forest edge; post breeding sometimes occurs on plains in N Laos and C Vietnam. DISTRIBUTION: Resident from SW China southwards, except C, S Thailand, Vietnam (E Tonkin and Cochinchina) and Singapore.

7 WHISTLING GREEN PIGEON (FORMOSAN GREEN PIGEON) *Treron formosae* 35cm FIELD NOTES: Feeds on small fruits in tree canopy, actions much as other green pigeons. VOICE: A *po-po-peh.* HABITAT: Tropical forests. DISTRIBUTION: Resident in Taiwan and Lanyu Islet.

8 WHITE-BELLIED GREEN PIGEON *Treron sieboldii* 33cm FIELD NOTES: Feeds mainly in fruiting trees, although also recorded feeding on the ground. Usually encountered in small parties. VOICE: A mournful *oaooh oaooh* or *o-vuuo-vuuo-vuuo-vououo-oo.* HABITAT: Broadleaved evergreen forest, forest edge and clearings. DISTRIBUTION: Resident in Taiwan, Hainan, most of China, W, NE Thailand, C Laos and C, N Vietnam.

3b
annamensis

57 PARROTS

1 YELLOW-CRESTED COCKATOO *Cacatua sulphurea* 33–35cm FIELD NOTES: Mainly arboreal, occurring in small groups. VOICE: A raucous screeching and a variety of whistles and squeaks. HABITAT: Open forest, plantations, parks and gardens. DISTRIBUTION: Feral resident in Singapore and Hong Kong.

2 TANIMBAR CORELLA *Cacatua goffiniana* 30–32cm FIELD NOTES: In flight underwing and undertail tinged yellow. VOICE: Loud, harsh screeches. HABITAT: Open forests and cultivations. DISTRIBUTION: Feral resident in Singapore.

3 VERNAL HANGING PARROT *Loriculus vernalis* 14cm FIELD NOTES: Sleeps hanging upside-down, like a bat. Usually encountered in pairs or small parties, presence generally indicated by squeaking calls. VOICE: A squeaking *chi-chi-chee chi-chi-chee chi-chi-chee*. HABITAT: Broadleaved evergreen and deciduous woodlands. DISTRIBUTION: Resident in SW China, Myanmar (except W, N), Thailand (except C), N Peninsular Malaysia, Cambodia, Laos and Vietnam (except Tonkin and N Annam).

4 BLUE-CROWNED HANGING PARROT *Loriculus galgulus* 12–14cm FIELD NOTES: Actions similar to Vernal Hanging Parrot. VOICE: A shrill *tsi, tsrri* or *tsi-tsi-tsi…* HABITAT: Broadleaved evergreen forest, plantations, wooded gardens and mangroves. DISTRIBUTION: Resident in S Thailand, Peninsular Malaysia and Singapore.

5 BLUE-RUMPED PARROT *Psittinus cyanurus* 18–19cm FIELD NOTES: Pairs or small parties are often seen flying above trees and foraging in the upper branches. VOICE: A sharp *chi-chi-chi* and *chew-ee*; also a high-pitched *peep*. HABITAT: Open broadleaved evergreen forest, clearings, plantations and mangroves. DISTRIBUTION: Resident in S Myanmar (S Tenasserim), W, S Thailand, Peninsular Malaysia and Singapore.

6 ALEXANDRINE PARAKEET *Psittacula eupatria* 53–58cm FIELD NOTES: Occurs in small flocks, with larger concentrations at rich food sources and roosts. VOICE: A hoarse screaming *kii-e-rick, keeak* or *keeah*. HABITAT: Well-wooded areas. DISTRIBUTION: Resident in Myanmar (except S Tenasserim), C Thailand, Cambodia, S Laos and C, S Vietnam.

7 RING-NECKED PARAKEET (ROSE-RINGED PARAKEET) *Psittacula krameri* 37–43cm FIELD NOTES: Usually in flocks. Flight fast and direct. VOICE: A screeching *kee-a* or *kee-ak*. HABITAT: Open woodland, plantations, parks and gardens. DISTRIBUTION: Resident in Myanmar (except N and Tenasserim); feral resident in Singapore and Hong Kong.

8 GREY-HEADED PARAKEET *Psittacula finschii* 36–40cm FIELD NOTES: Flight swift and agile, especially when flying among trees. Female lacks the maroon shoulder patch. VOICE: A loud, shrill *sweet sweet swit*. HABITAT: Broadleaved evergreen, mixed deciduous and pine forests; also cultivations. DISTRIBUTION: Resident in SE China, Myanmar, W, NW, NE Thailand, Cambodia, Laos and C, N Vietnam.

9 BLOSSOM-HEADED PARAKEET *Psittacula roseata* 30–36cm FIELD NOTES: Generally in small parties, but where food is plentiful found in much bigger flocks. VOICE: A high-pitched *tooi-tooi*. HABITAT: Open broadleaved and mixed deciduous forest; visits cultivations. DISTRIBUTION: Resident in SE China, Myanmar (except N), northern Thailand, Cambodia, Laos (except N) and Vietnam (except Tonkin).

10 ROSE-BREASTED PARAKEET (RED-BREASTED PARAKEET) *Psittacula alexandri* 33–38cm FIELD NOTES: Usually in small parties, larger flocks where food is plentiful. VOICE: A short nasal *kaink* often repeated. HABITAT: Open forests, groves and cultivations. DISTRIBUTION: Resident in S, SW, SE China, Hainan, Myanmar, Thailand (except S), Cambodia, Laos, Vietnam and possibly N Peninsular Malaysia; feral resident in Singapore.

11 LONG-TAILED PARAKEET *Psittacula longicauda* 40–48cm FIELD NOTES: Usually in small flocks with larger flocks occurring at rich food sources. *P. l. tytleri* (11b) occurs on the Coco Islands. VOICE: A high-pitched *pee-yo pee-yo pee-yo* and a nasal quavering *graak graak graak*. HABITAT: Open broadleaved evergreen forest, Freshwater swamp forest, plantations and mangroves. DISTRIBUTION: Resident in Peninsular Malaysia, Singapore and the Coco Islands.

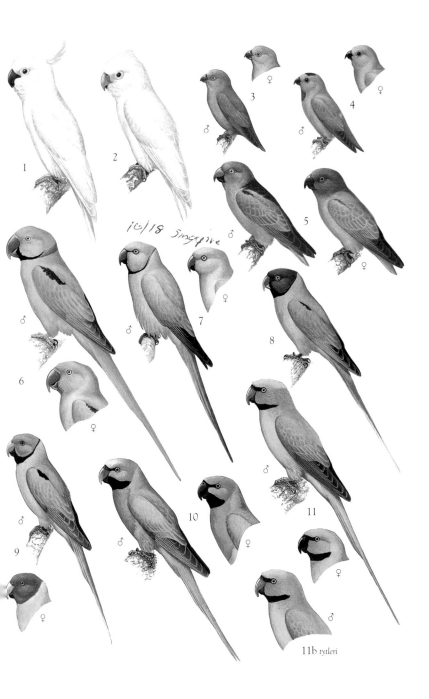

1

2

3 ♂ ♀

4 ♂ ♀

5 ♀

i☺/18 Singapore ♂

6 ♂ ♀

7 ♂ ♀

8

9 ♂ ♀

10 ♂ ♀

11 ♂

11b *tytleri* ♀ ♂

58 CUCKOOS

1 LARGE HAWK-CUCKOO *Hierococcyx sparverioides* 38–40cm FIELD NOTES: Keeps to the foliage of trees. VOICE: A screaming *pi-pee-ha…pi-pee-ha* that leads to a frenetic climax. HABITAT: Open forests and open areas. DISTRIBUTION: Breeds in China (moves south post breeding); resident in SW China, Hainan, Myanmar (except S), W, NE, NW Thailand, Cambodia, Laos and N Vietnam. Winters in Thailand, Peninsular Malaysia and S Vietnam.

2 COMMON HAWK-CUCKOO *Hierococcyx varius* 33cm FIELD NOTES: Arboreal secretive forager. VOICE: A monotonous, high-pitched *wee-piwhit…wee-pwhit…* becomes shriller and frenetic before stopping abruptly. HABITAT: Open deciduous forest and secondary growth. DISTRIBUTION: Resident in SW Myanmar; vagrant in W Thailand.

3 MOUSTACHED HAWK-CUCKOO *Hierococcyx vagans* 28–30cm FIELD NOTES: Best located by call. VOICE: A loud, monotonous *peu-peu*; also an ascending sequence of mellow notes that accelerate to fever-pitch then ends abruptly. HABITAT: Broadleaved evergreen forest and secondary growth. DISTRIBUTION: Uncommon resident in S Myanmar (Tenasserim), SE, S Thailand, S Laos and Peninsular Malaysia.

4 MALAYSIAN HAWK-CUCKOO *Hierococcyx fugax* 28–30cm FIELD NOTES: Arboreal, skulking, usually low down, moves higher when calling. VOICE: A shrill, insistent *gee-whizz… gee-whizz…* often followed by rapid *ti-tu-tu* phases. Accelerates to a shrill crescendo and ends with a slower *tu-tu-tu*. HABITAT: Broadleaved evergreen and mixed deciduous forests. DISTRIBUTION: Resident in S Myanmar (Tenasserim), S Thailand and Peninsular Malaysia.

5 HODGSON'S HAWK-CUCKOO *Hierococcyx nisicolor* 28–30cm FIELD NOTES: Actions as Malaysian Hawk-cuckoo. VOICE: Much as Malaysian Hawk-cuckoo but with a rapid *trrrrr-titititititrrrtrrr* at the end. HABITAT: Broadleaved evergreen and mixed deciduous forests. DISTRIBUTION: Breeds in E Myanmar, Thailand, N, C Laos, C, N Vietnam and Hainan.

6 RUFOUS HAWK-CUCKOO *Hierococcyx hyperythrus* 28–30cm FIELD NOTES: Actions similar to Malaysian Hawk Cuckoo. VOICE: A shrieking *joo-ichi joo-ichi*. HABITAT: Tropical and sub-tropical forests. DISTRIBUTION: Breeds in NE and SE China, wintering in SE.

7 INDIAN CUCKOO *Cuculus micropterus* 33cm FIELD NOTES: Usually forages in the tree canopy. VOICE: A loud, persistent whistle; transcribed as *'one more bottle'*. HABITAT: Broadleaved evergreen and deciduous forest and secondary growth. DISTRIBUTION: Breeds in China, moving south post breeding; resident over most of the region south of China.

8 CUCKOO (COMMON or EURASIAN CUCKOO) *Cuculus canorus* 32–34cm FIELD NOTES: Often perches horizontally with tail cocked and wings drooped. VOICE: Male gives a far-carrying *cuck-oo*. Female delivers a bubbling call. HABITAT: Open broadleaved forest, secondary growth, reedbeds and more open areas on migration. DISTRIBUTION: Breeding visitor to China, W, N, C, E Myanmar, N Laos and N Vietnam; scarce passage migrant elsewhere.

9 HIMALAYAN CUCKOO *Cuculus saturatus* 30–32 cm FIELD NOTES: Best separated from Cuckoo by voice; also underparts are more buff tinged with slightly broader and darker barring. VOICE: A *hoop hoop-hoop* or *tun-tadun*. HABITAT: Broadleaved evergreen forest and open wooded country. DISTRIBUTION: Breeding visitor to Taiwan, Hainan, China, W, N Myanmar, N, C Laos and N Vietnam (W Tonkin); passage migrant elsewhere.

10 ORIENTAL CUCKOO *Cuculus optatus* 30–33cm FIELD NOTES: Forages in tree canopy. VOICE: A low *hoop hoop hoop hoop*; also a harsh *gaak-gaak gak-ak-ak-ak*. HABITAT: Evergreen, mixed forests and thickets. DISTRIBUTION: Winter visitor to the far south of the region.

11 LESSER CUCKOO *Cuculus poliocephalus* 26cm FIELD NOTES: Actions much as Indian Cuckoo. VOICE: A loud, cheery *pretty-peel-lay-ka-beet*. HABITAT: Broadleaved evergreen forest and secondary growth. DISTRIBUTION: Summer visitor to C China, non-breeding visitor or passage migrant elsewhere.

12 SUNDA LESSER CUCKOO *Cuculus lepidus* 26–29cm FIELD NOTES: Secretive, best located by call. VOICE: A loud *kuk hoo hoo hoo*. HABITAT: Broadleaved evergreen forest and open wooded country. DISTRIBUTION: Resident in Peninsular Malaysia.

1

2

3

4

5

6

♀ ♂

7

8 ♂

9 ♂

rufous morph ♀

normal morph ♀ rufous morph ♀

10

11 ♀

12

♂

59 CUCKOOS

1 BANDED BAY CUCKOO *Cacomantis sonneratii* 24cm FIELD NOTES: Frequents bare treetop branches. Calls with tail depressed. VOICE: A shrill *pi-pi-pew-pew*. HABITAT: Broadleaved evergreen forest, deciduous forest and secondary growth. DISTRIBUTION: Widespread resident south from SW China, except SW Myanmar, C Thailand and N Vietnam (W Tonkin).

2 RUSTY-BREASTED CUCKOO *Cacomantis sepulcralis* 21–25cm FIELD NOTES: Forages among foliage of trees and bushes. VOICE: A melancholy, descending *whi whi whi whi whi…* also an accelerating series of *whi-wibu* notes. HABITAT: Broadleaved evergreen forest, forest edge, secondary growth, mangroves and gardens. DISTRIBUTION: Uncommon resident W, S Thailand, Peninsular Malaysia and Singapore.

3 PLAINTIVE CUCKOO *Cacomantis merulinus* 23cm FIELD NOTES: Mainly arboreal, restless forager among foliage at the top of trees, sometimes makes sallies after flying insects or drops to the ground to collect prey. VOICE: A repeated *tay…ta…tee…* also a descending, accelerating trilled *pwee pwee pwee pee-pee-pee-pee*. HABITAT: Open woodlands, secondary growth, scrub, cultivations, grasslands, parks and gardens. DISTRIBUTION: Summer visitor to southern parts of China; resident in Hainan and the rest of the south of the region.

4 GREY-BELLIED CUCKOO *Cacomantis passerinus* 23cm FIELD NOTES: Actions and habits similar to Plaintive Cuckoo. VOICE: A clear *pee-pipee-pee…pipee-pee*. HABITAT: Open woodland, secondary growth, bush, scrub and cultivations. DISTRIBUTION: Dubious record from N Myanmar.

5 FORK-TAILED DRONGO-CUCKOO *Surniculus dicruroides* 24–25cm FIELD NOTES: Arboreal, sluggish movements while searching in the foliage of the tree canopy. When calling, uses a bare treetop branch and posture becomes more horizontal with wings drooped. Juvenile black with whitish spots on all feather tips. VOICE: A rising *pip-pip-pip-pip-pip-pip*; also a shrill, accelerating *phew phew phewphewphewphew* that falls away at the finish. HABITAT: Broadleaved evergreen and deciduous forests, secondary growth, plantations and occasionally mangroves, parks and gardens. DISTRIBUTION: Widespread, birds in China move south post breeding.

6 SQUARE-TAILED DRONGO-CUCKOO *Surniculus lugubris* 24–25cm FIELD NOTES: Actions similar to Fork-tailed Drongo-cuckoo, which is sometimes considered con-specific. VOICE: Loud, clear, mellow whistles rising up the scale. HABITAT: Broadleaved evergreen and deciduous forests, secondary growth, plantations and sometimes parks, gardens and mangroves. DISTRIBUTION: Resident in S Thailand and Peninsular Malaysia.

7 PIED CUCKOO (JACOBIN CUCKOO) *Clamator jacobinus* 34cm FIELD NOTES: Mainly arboreal, often perches in the open. In flight shows a white patch at base of the primaries. VOICE: A loud fluting *piu piu pee-pee piu pee-pee-piu;* when alarmed utters a harsh *chu-chu-chu-chu*. HABITAT: Open deciduous woodland, scrub and groves. DISTRIBUTION: Summer visitor to C, S Myanmar; vagrant recorded in Thailand.

8 CHESTNUT-WINGED CUCKOO (RED-WINGED CRESTED CUCKOO) *Clamator coromandus* 41–47cm FIELD NOTES: Shy, usually hidden among foliage in tree canopy, although regularly forages in low vegetation in search of insects. Juvenile duller with rufous fringes on mantle feathers. VOICE: A metallic whistled *thu-thu thu-thu thu-thu…* also a harsh *chee-ke-kek* or *critititititit*. HABITAT: Broadleaved evergreen forest, secondary growth, scrub, bamboo thickets and mangroves. DISTRIBUTION: Summer visitor to Taiwan, Hainan, China, Myanmar (except S), Thailand (except S, SE), Laos and N, C Vietnam; non-breeding visitor or passage migrant to S Thailand, Peninsular Malaysia and Singapore.

9 KOEL (COMMON, ASIAN or INDIAN KOEL) *Eudynamys scolopaceus* 40–43cm FIELD NOTES: Unobtrusive, usually keeps to dense foliage; first sign is often of a bird flying silently from tree to tree. Juvenile blackish with white tips to mantle and wing feathers and variable white barring below. VOICE: A shrill *ko-el ko-el ko-el ko-el* that increases in scale and pitch before ending abruptly; also a descending, bubbling *wreep-wreep-wreep-wreep-wreepwreepwreep…* HABITAT: Open woodland, forest edge, scrub, cultivations, parks and gardens. DISTRIBUTION: Summer visitor to China, widespread resident further south.

60 CUCKOOS; COUCALS

1 LITTLE BRONZE CUCKOO *Chrysococcyx minutillus* 15–16cm FIELD NOTES: Unobtrusive, tends to forage in dense foliage. VOICE: A descending *rhew rhew rhew rhew…* or *teu teu teu teu teu…* sometimes includes a rising, screeching *wireg-reeg-reeg*; also utters a high-pitched, drawn-out trill. HABITAT: Coastal scrub, mangroves, secondary growth, forest edge, parks and gardens. DISTRIBUTION: Resident in S Thailand, Cambodia, S Vietnam, Peninsular Malaysia and Singapore.

2 VIOLET CUCKOO *Chrysococcyx xanthorhynchus* 17cm FIELD NOTES: Secretive, creeps among foliage in search of insects; often perches at the top of a tall tree when calling. Juvenile similar to juvenile Asian Emerald Cuckoo but upperparts more barred and fringed rufous-buff. VOICE: A loud, sharp, repeated *tee-wit*, often uttered in flight; also a descending trilled *seer-se-seer seeseeseesee*. HABITAT: Broadleaved evergreen, semi-evergreen and deciduous forests, cultivations and occasionally parks and gardens. DISTRIBUTION: Resident SW China, W, S, E Myanmar, Thailand (except C), Cambodia, S Laos, S Vietnam, Peninsular Malaysia and Singapore.

3 HORSFIELD'S BRONZE CUCKOO *Chrysococcyx basalis* 16cm FIELD NOTES: Forages in foliage and on the ground. Flight swift and direct. VOICE: A descending high-pitched whistled *peeer* or *tseeeuw*, incessantly repeated. HABITAT: Open woodland, coastal scrub, mangroves and secondary growth. DISTRIBUTION: Vagrant, recorded from Singapore.

4 ASIAN EMERALD CUCKOO (ORIENTAL EMERALD CUCKOO) *Chrysococcyx maculatus* 18cm FIELD NOTES: Favours the branches and foliage of the tree canopy. Active forager, often making aerial sallies to capture flying insects. Flight is fast and direct. Juvenile like adult female but with rufous-buff fringes on the feathers of wings and mantle. VOICE: A loud, descending *kee-kee-kee*; also a *chweek* given in flight. HABITAT: Broadleaved evergreen forest, secondary growth, freshwater swamp forest, plantations and gardens. DISTRIBUTION: Summers in SW China, moves south post breeding. Resident in Hainan, Myanmar, W, NW Thailand and C Vietnam; winter visitor to Thailand, Cambodia, C, S Laos and S Vietnam; vagrant in Peninsular Malaysia and Singapore.

5 GREATER COUCAL *Centropus sinensis* 48cm FIELD NOTES: Skulks in vegetation; when searching for food often walks with tail held horizontally. Underwing-coverts black. Flight weak and clumsy. Juvenile has brownish-black head and underparts narrowly barred white; upperparts rufous barred dark brown; tail black with narrow white bars. VOICE: A deep, descending then rising *hoop-hoop-hoop-hoop-hoop-hoop*. HABITAT: Open woodland, forest edge, scrub, grassland and mangroves. DISTRIBUTION: Resident south from southern China.

6 LESSER COUCAL *Centropus bengalensis* 31–33cm FIELD NOTES: Chestnut underwing-coverts. Actions and habits similar to Greater Coucal. Juvenile is a duller version of non-breeding adult. VOICE: A deep *whoop whoop whoop whoop kurook kurook kurook…* that increases in tempo and descends in pitch. HABITAT: Tall grassland, reedbeds and thickets. DISTRIBUTION: Resident in Taiwan, Hainan, E, S China and a widespread resident in the south of the region.

7 SHORT-TOED COUCAL *Centropus rectunguis* 37cm FIELD NOTES: Shy and skulking, looks very similar to Greater Coucal but much smaller and shorter tailed. Black underwing-coverts. VOICE: Four or five resonant booming notes, *buup buup buup buup*, descending towards the end and repeated every few seconds. HABITAT: Broadleaved evergreen forest. DISTRIBUTION: Resident in extreme S Thailand and Peninsular Malaysia.

8 BROWN COUCAL (ANDAMAN COUCAL) *Centropus andamanensis* 45–48cm FIELD NOTES: Actions and habits much as Greater Coucal. Juvenile like adult but finely barred above and below. VOICE: A rapid, deep *hoop-hoop-hoop-hoop-hoop* that starts weakly then slowly increases in intensity before ending abruptly. When alarmed utters a scolding cat-like *skaaah*. HABITAT: Forest edge, cultivations, mangroves and gardens. DISTRIBUTION: Resident on Coco Islands.

61 MALKOHAS; GROUND CUCKOO

1 BLACK-BELLIED MALKOHA *Phaenicophaeus diardi* 38cm FIELD NOTES: Forages amidst dense undergrowth and creepers. VOICE: A gruff *gwuap*, a hurried *gwagaup* and a loud *pauk*. HABITAT: Broadleaved evergreen forest, forest edge, secondary growth and plantations. DISTRIBUTION: Resident in S Myanmar (S Tenasserim), S Thailand and Peninsular Malaysia.

2 CHESTNUT-BELLIED MALKOHA *Phaenicophaeus sumatranus* 40–41cm FIELD NOTES: Quiet, creeps through trees and thickets. VOICE: A low *tok tok…* also a thin, high-pitched mewing. HABITAT: Broadleaved evergreen forest, mangroves, secondary growth and plantations. DISTRIBUTION: Uncommon resident in S Myanmar (S Tenasserim), S Thailand, Peninsular Malaysia and Singapore.

3 GREEN-BILLED MALKOHA *Phaenicophaeus tristis* 38cm FIELD NOTES: Skulking, forages in dense thickets; best located when flying weakly from one thicket to another. VOICE: A mellow, nasal *oh – oh – oh – oh*, a frog-like *ko ko ko ko ko* and a peculiar chuckle when flushed. HABITAT: Broadleaved evergreen, deciduous, freshwater and peat swamp forest, secondary growth, coastal scrub, bamboo and occasionally plantations. DISTRIBUTION: Common resident southward from Hainan and S China (except S Peninsular Malaysia and Singapore).

4 CHESTNUT-BREASTED MALKOHA *Phaenicophaeus curvirostris* 42–49cm FIELD NOTES: Often sits motionless in tree canopy watching for prey; moves around waving tail like a squirrel. VOICE: A low, clucking *kuk kuk kuk* and a faster *kok-kok-kok…* when agitated utters a cat-like *miaou*. HABITAT: Broadleaved evergreen forest, secondary growth, occasionally mangroves, plantations and gardens. DISTRIBUTION: Resident S Myanmar (S Tenasserim), W, S Thailand and Peninsular Malaysia.

5 RED-BILLED MALKOHA *Zanclostomus javanicus* 42cm FIELD NOTES: Actions much as other Malkohas. VOICE: A frog-like *uc uc uc uc uc…* occasionally ends in a quick *uc-uc-uc*; also a whistled *who-oo*, repeated every ten seconds. HABITAT: Broadleaved evergreen forest, forest edge and secondary growth. DISTRIBUTION: Resident S Myanmar (S Tenasserim), southern W, S Thailand and Peninsular Malaysia.

6 RAFFLES'S MALKOHA *Rhinortha chlorophaea* 32–35cm FIELD NOTES: Moves steadily among middle-storey foliage and creepers. VOICE: A series of descending mewing notes, a hoarse, strained heeah and harsh croaking sounds. HABITAT: Broadleaved evergreen forest, forest edge and occasionally plantations. DISTRIBUTION: Resident in S Myanmar (S Tenasserim), W, S Thailand and Peninsular Malaysia.

7 CORAL-BILLED GROUND CUCKOO *Carpococcyx renauldi* 65cm FIELD NOTES: Terrestrial, but roosts in trees. Shy, runs when disturbed but when takes to the wing, flight is strong and rapid. Juvenile browner on head and neck, upperparts dark grey with rusty bars and fringes; underparts grey-white tinged rusty. VOICE: A repeated, loud, mellow, moaning *woaaaah, wooaa* or *wohaaau;* also a short *pohh-poaaah*, a vibrant, rolling *wh ohh-whaaaaohu* and a grumbling *grrro grrro…* HABITAT: Broadleaved evergreen forest and secondary forest. DISTRIBUTION: Resident in NW, NE, SE Thailand, Cambodia, N, C, S Laos, C, N Vietnam.

62 OWLS

1 BARN OWL *Tyto alba* 33–35cm FIELD NOTES: Appears strikingly white in flight. Nocturnal, although often hunts during daylight. Hunts close to the ground in an undulating flight with much hovering; drops onto prey with talons extended. VOICE: A shrill, hoarse *shrrreeeeee*, also various chuckling, snoring and hissing sounds. HABITAT: Cultivations, open country, marsh and urban areas. DISTRIBUTION: Widespread resident over most of the region south from SW China.

2 GRASS OWL (EASTERN GRASS OWL) *Tyto longimembris* 32–38cm FIELD NOTES: Crepuscular and nocturnal. When quartering an area, searching for prey, flight is low, with frequent gliding and hovering. Normally perches on or near the ground. VOICE: Similar to Barn Owl. HABITAT: Grassland. DISTRIBUTION: Resident in Taiwan, SW, SE, E China, C, S, E Myanmar and Vietnam.

3 ORIENTAL BAY OWL *Phodilus badius* 29cm FIELD NOTES: Nocturnal, usually hunts under the forest canopy with a rapid flight, twisting through vertical tree stems. Hides in tree hollows during the day. VOICE: A series of eerie whistles, with an upward inflection, that rise and then fade away. HABITAT: Broadleaved evergreen forest and landside mangrove edge. DISTRIBUTION: Resident southward from SW China and Hainan, except W, C Myanmar, C Thailand, C, N Vietnam (W Tonkin and C, S Annam) and Singapore.

4 EAGLE OWL (EURASIAN EAGLE OWL) *Bubo bubo* 56–66cm FIELD NOTES: Nocturnal or crepuscular. Rests during the day in tree or rock fissure. Race *B. b. bengalensis* (Indian Eagle Owl) (4b), recorded from SW Myanmar, is often considered a full species. VOICE: A deep *whooh-tu* or *woo-hoooo*, the latter is uttered by *B. b. bengalensis*. HABITAT: Cliffs, rocky areas and woodlands. DISTRIBUTION: Resident in China and possibly SW Myanmar.

5 DUSKY EAGLE OWL *Bubo coromandus* 53–66cm FIELD NOTES: Usually encountered in pairs. Said to be quite active during the day especially in dull weather. VOICE: An accelerating *wo wo wo wo wo wowowowo*, also a deep, rumbling *woo-woo-woo*. HABITAT: Woodland, usually near water. DISTRIBUTION: Resident in E China, S, SW, C Myanmar and Peninsular Malaysia.

6 SPOT-BELLIED EAGLE OWL (FOREST EAGLE OWL) *Bubo nipalensis* 63cm FIELD NOTES: Usually nocturnal, during the day hides in the shady parts of forest trees. Juvenile generally white with dark barring on crown, neck, mantle, wings and underparts. VOICE: A deep *hoo…hoo* and a rising and falling mournful scream. HABITAT: Broadleaved evergreen, semi evergreen and deciduous forests. DISTRIBUTION: Resident in SW China, S, E Myanmar, Thailand (except C, S), Cambodia, N, S Laos and Vietnam (except E Tonkin and S Annam).

7 BARRED EAGLE OWL *Bubo sumatranus* 40–46cm FIELD NOTES: Nocturnal and crepuscular, hunts from a perch from where it drops on to small mammals and insects. Hops on the ground. VOICE: A loud *whooa-who whooa-who*, also a quacking *gagagagogogo*. HABITAT: Broadleaved evergreen forest, forest edge and clearings, also mature plantations. DISTRIBUTION: Resident in S Myanmar (S Tenasserim), W, S Thailand, Peninsular Malaysia and Singapore.

8 SNOWY OWL *Bubo scandiacus* 53–65cm FIELD NOTES: Usually crepuscular, although may forage during daylight. Flight rapid and agile when chasing prey. VOICE: A booming *goo goo*, when alarmed male gives a cackling *kre-kre-kre*, the female a loud mewing or whistling. HABITAT: In winter occurs in open country. DISTRIBUTION: Possibly a vagrant to the north of the region.

4b *bengalensis*

63 OWLS

1 BROWN FISH OWL *Ketupa zeylonensis* 50–57cm FIELD NOTES: Crepuscular and nocturnal. Hunts from a perch, swoops to catch fish in talons. VOICE: A deep *boom boom* or *boo-o-boom*, a subdued *hu-who-hu* and a harsh *we-aaah*. HABITAT: Forests and well-wooded areas near water. DISTRIBUTION: Resident in S, SW, SE China, Hainan, Myanmar, Thailand (except C, SE), Cambodia, Laos, Vietnam (except W Tonkin and S Annam) and NW Peninsular Malaysia.

2 TAWNY FISH OWL *Ketupa flavipes* 58–61cm FIELD NOTES: Crepuscular and nocturnal. Captures fish in talons by swooping from a waterside perch. VOICE: A deep *whoo-hoo* and a cat-like mewing. HABITAT: Broadleaved evergreen forest by rivers and streams. DISTRIBUTION: Resident in Taiwan, China, N Myanmar, N, C Laos and Vietnam (W Tonkin and Cochinchina).

3 BUFFY FISH OWL *Ketupa ketupu* 38–44cm FIELD NOTES: Mainly nocturnal. Captures fish in talons by swooping from a perch, walking along river shore or wading in shallow water. VOICE: A loud monotonous *kootookookootook…* a ringing *pof pof pof*, a musical *to-whee to-whee* and various hisses, mews and shrieks. HABITAT: Forested watercourses, mangroves, plantations and wooded gardens. DISTRIBUTION: Resident in SW, S Myanmar, NE, SE, S Thailand, Cambodia, C, S, Vietnam, Peninsular Malaysia and Singapore.

4 BROWN WOOD OWL *Strix leptogrammica* 47–53cm FIELD NOTES: Nocturnal. Very shy, rests during the day in dense tree foliage. Variable, the white-faced race *S. l. newarensis* (main illustration) occurs in N, C Myanmar, buff-faced *S. l. ticehursti* (4b) in S, SE China, S, E Myanmar, S, N, W Thailand, N Laos and N Vietnam and the russet-faced *S. l. maingayi* (4c) southwards from S Thailand. VOICE: A low hollow *tok tu-hoo tok-tu-hoo*, also eerie shrieks and chuckles. HABITAT: Dense forests. DISTRIBUTION: Resident in Taiwan, Hainan and southwards from S and E China, except SW Myanmar, C Thailand, Vietnam (W Tonkin and Cochinchina) and Singapore.

5 MOTTLED WOOD OWL *Strix ocellata* 40–48cm FIELD NOTES: Mainly nocturnal; during the day rests in the thick foliage of trees. VOICE: An eerie, quavering *whaa-aa-aa-aa-ah*, also a mellow hoot and occasionally a harsh screech. HABITAT: Open woodland, cultivations and wooded gardens. DISTRIBUTION: Resident in SW Myanmar.

6 SPOTTED WOOD OWL *Strix seloputo* 45–47cm FIELD NOTES: Hunts from a perch, preying mainly on small rodents, small birds and insects. VOICE: A deep *who*, usually preceded by a rolling *huhuhuwhuwhu*; also a resonant, rising *hoop-hoong* and a deep growling. HABITAT: Broadleaved evergreen forest edge, logged forests, plantations, wooded parks and occasionally mangroves. DISTRIBUTION: Resident in S, E Myanmar, NE, C, S Thailand, Cambodia, S Laos, S Vietnam, Peninsular Malaysia and Singapore.

7 HIMALAYAN OWL (HIMALAYAN WOOD OWL) *Strix nivicolum* 37–39cm FIELD NOTES: Nocturnal, during the day rests among the foliage on a branch near a tree trunk. Hunts mainly from a perch, dropping onto small mammals, rodents, birds, amphibians, insects and worms. VOICE: A haunting *HU-HU* and a shrill *kewick*. HABITAT: Broadleaved evergreen and coniferous forests. DISTRIBUTION: Resident in China, W, E Myanmar and N Vietnam (W Tonkin).

4b *ticehursti*

4c *maingayi*

64 OWLS

1 LONG-EARED OWL *Asio otus* 35–37cm FIELD NOTES: Generally nocturnal. During the day rests on a shady branch close to a tree trunk or on the ground under a bush or grass tussock. In flight, outer primaries show four or five dark bars. VOICE: A drawn-out *hoo hoo hoo hoo hoo hoo…* when alarmed utters a barking *ooack ooack ooack.* HABITAT: Woodland, wooded cultivations and tall grasslands. DISTRIBUTION: Winter visitor to S, SE China and Taiwan; vagrant further south.

2 SHORT-EARED OWL *Asio flammeus* 37cm FIELD NOTES: Generally active during daytime. Hunts by quartering low over vegetation; often hovers before pouncing on prey. In flight outer primaries appear dark-tipped compared to Long-eared Owl. VOICE: Generally silent although may give various barking notes. HABITAT: Open country with scattered bush, scrubby hillsides and marshland. DISTRIBUTION: Winter visitor to Taiwan, Hainan, SW, SE, E China, N, C, S Myanmar, NW Thailand, N Laos and C, N Vietnam; vagrants recorded from C Thailand, Peninsular Malaysia and Singapore.

3 BROWN HAWK OWL *Ninox scutulata* 27–33cm FIELD NOTES: Crepuscular and nocturnal, shortly before dusk recorded as hunting insects in the manner of a nightjar. Tends to frequent the same perch over a prolonged period. VOICE: A haunting *whu-up whu-up whu-up.* HABITAT: Open forests, mangroves, wooded parks and gardens. DISTRIBUTION: Summer visitor to northern parts of the region, moving south post breeding. Resident in Taiwan, Hainan, S China and south of the region, except C Thailand and Vietnam (W Tonkin and S Annam). Winter visitor to C, S Thailand, Cambodia, Peninsular Malaysia and Singapore.

4 ASIAN BARRED OWLET *Glaucidium cuculoides* 22–25cm FIELD NOTES: Mainly diurnal. Often seen in the open, perched on a bare branch or stump. Variable plumage: those depicted are *G. c. whitely* (main illustration) from China, E Myanmar and N Vietnam; *G. c. bruegeli* (4b), which occurs in S Myanmar and S Thailand and *G. c. deignani* (4c), which is found in SE Thailand, Cambodia, Laos and Vietnam. VOICE: A bubbling, whistled *wowowowowowowowowo* and a loud *hooloo hooloo hooloo kok kok* ending in a shrill *chiurr.* HABITAT: Broadleaved evergreen forest. DISTRIBUTION: Resident in China, Hainan, Myanmar, Thailand, Cambodia, Laos and Vietnam.

5 JUNGLE OWLET *Glaucidium radiatum* 20cm FIELD NOTES: Mainly crepuscular, although also recorded hunting during the day. Roosts amid leafy branches or in tree hollows. VOICE: A loud *kao…kao…kao kao-kuk kao-kuk kao-kuk…* that quickens then fades at the end; also a monotonous *cur-cur-cur-cur-cur-ur.* HABITAT: Mixed deciduous forest and secondary growth. DISTRIBUTION: Resident in SW, S Myanmar.

6 COLLARED OWLET (COLLARED PYGMY OWL) *Glaucidium brodiei* 16–17cm FIELD NOTES: Crepuscular and diurnal. Bold, fierce hunter taking birds as large as itself. Has eye-like markings on the rear of head. VOICE: A mellow, bell-like *hoo hoo-hoo hooo* or *toot-tootoot-toot.* HABITAT: Broadleaved evergreen hill forest. DISTRIBUTION: Resident in Taiwan, Hainan, China and south of the region, except SW Myanmar, C Thailand, S Vietnam and Singapore.

7 SPOTTED LITTLE OWL (SPOTTED OWLET) *Athene brama* 19–21cm FIELD NOTES: Nocturnal and crepuscular, although often seen abroad in daylight. Generally roosts within hollows or foliage of trees. VOICE: A harsh, screeching *chirurrr chirurrr chirurrr* interspersed with, or followed by a *cheevak cheevak cheevak;* also utters a rapid *kuerk-kuerk-kuerk* that is said to sound like fighting cats. HABITAT: Open woodland, cultivations and around human habitations. DISTRIBUTION: Resident in SW China, SW, W, C, S, E Myanmar, Thailand (except S), Cambodia, C, S Laos and C, S Vietnam.

bruegeli

deignani

rufous
morph

65 SCOPS OWLS

1 WHITE-FRONTED SCOPS OWL *Otus sagittatus* 25–28cm FIELD NOTES: Little known; actions probably much like other scops owls. VOICE: A hollow, whistled *hooo,* much like the call of Reddish Scops Owl but more abrupt. HABITAT: Broadleaved evergreen forest. DISTRIBUTION: Rare resident in S Myanmar (Tenasserim), W, S Thailand and Peninsular Malaysia.

2 REDDISH SCOPS OWL *Otus rufescens* 20cm FIELD NOTES: Actions presumably much as other scops owls. VOICE: A hollow, whistled *hoooo* that fades at the end. HABITAT: Broadleaved evergreen forest. DISTRIBUTION: Resident in S Thailand and Peninsular Malaysia.

3 MOUNTAIN SCOPS OWL *Otus spilocephalus* 17–21cm FIELD NOTES: Nocturnal. Hunts beneath the tree canopy, reported as keeping close to the ground. Roosts by day in a tree hollow. VOICE: A far-carrying *plew-plew, too-too* or *tunk-tunk.* HABITAT: Broadleaved evergreen forest and montane forest. DISTRIBUTION: Resident in Taiwan, Hainan and south from S, E China (except C Thailand and Singapore).

4 ORIENTAL SCOPS OWL (EASTERN or ASIAN SCOPS OWL) *Otus sunia* 18–21cm FIELD NOTES: Nocturnal. Hunts from a perch or in flight usually along forest edges. VOICE: A toad-like *wuk-tuk-tah, wut-chu-chraaii* or similar. HABITAT: Broadleaved evergreen forest and mixed deciduous forest; forest edge and clearings on migration. Also occurs in mangroves, island forests and plantations. DISTRIBUTION: Resident in Taiwan, Hainan, China, N, S Myanmar, W, NW, NE Thailand, Cambodia, S Laos and C Vietnam; winter visitor or passage migrant elsewhere.

5 RYUKU SCOPS OWL (ELEGANT SCOPS OWL) *Otus elegans* 20cm FIELD NOTES: Actions similar to Oriental Scops Owl. VOICE: A hoarse, cough-like *uhu, kuru* or *u-kuruk,* repeated at 2–4 second intervals. HABITAT: Dense evergreen forest. DISTRIBUTION: Resident on Lanyu Islet off Taiwan.

6 COLLARED SCOPS OWL *Otus lettia* 23–25cm FIELD NOTES: Nocturnal. Daytime roost is on a branch close to the tree trunk or in a tree hollow. VOICE: A soft downward-inflected *buuo,* repeated every 12–20 seconds; also utters a chattering when alarmed. HABITAT: DISTRIBUTION: Resident in Taiwan, Hainan and southwards from China, except S Thailand, Peninsula Malaysia and Singapore.

7 SUNDA SCOPS OWL *Otus lempiji* 20cm FIELD NOTES: Hunts from a perch, dropping onto insects and occasionally small birds. VOICE: A soft upward-inflected *wooup;* birds from the far south are said to lack the inflection. HABITAT: Second growth evergreen and deciduous forest and forest edge. Also open areas with scattered trees, parks, well-wooded gardens and tree-lined urban areas. DISTRIBUTION: Resident in S Thailand and Peninsular Malaysia.

1

2

3

4

grey
morph

rufous
morph

5

grey morph

rufous morph

6

grey
morph

rufous morph

7

grey morph

rufous morph

66 FROGMOUTHS; NIGHTJARS

1 LARGE FROGMOUTH *Batrachostomus auritus* 40–43cm FIELD NOTES: Nocturnal. During daylight stays motionless in the tree canopy. Makes sallies from a perch to take insects. VOICE: A tremulous *prrrrooh prrrrooh prrrrooh…* HABITAT: Broadleaved evergreen forest. DISTRIBUTION: Resident in S Thailand and Peninsular Malaysia.

2 GOULD'S FROGMOUTH *Batrachostomus stellatus* 21–25cm FIELD NOTES: Nocturnal. Sits motionless during daylight, little other information. VOICE: Male utters an eerie, weak *woah-weeo*, sometimes just *weeo*; female gives a growling and a rapid, high-pitched yapping. HABITAT: Broadleaved evergreen forest. DISTRIBUTION: Resident in S Thailand and Peninsular Malaysia.

3 BLYTH'S FROGMOUTH *Batrachostomus affinis* 23–24cm FIELD NOTES: During the day sits very upright with beak pointing skywards, usually close to the ground. *B. a. continentalis* (3b) occurs in SE Myanmar, Thailand, S Laos and Vietnam. VOICE: Male gives a plaintive whistle; female utters a maniacal laughing. HABITAT: Broadleaved evergreen and mixed deciduous forest, forest edge and secondary growth. DISTRIBUTION: Resident in S Myanmar (Tenasserim), Thailand (except C), N, S Laos, S Vietnam and Peninsular Malaysia.

4 HODGSON'S FROGMOUTH *Batrachostomus hodgsoni* 22–27cm FIELD NOTES: Nocturnal. Little recorded on actions and habits. VOICE: A soft *gwaa gwaa gwaa…* also a long, rising, then descending whistle. HABITAT: Broadleaved evergreen, mixed coniferous and evergreen forest and secondary growth. DISTRIBUTION: Resident in SW China, W, N, E Myanmar, NW Thailand, Laos and C Vietnam.

5 MALAYSIAN EARED NIGHTJAR *Lyncornis temminckii* 25–28cm FIELD NOTES: Forages, in flight, over open areas. VOICE: A repeated *tut-wee-ow.* HABITAT: Clearings in or near broadleaved evergreen forest. DISTRIBUTION: Resident in S Thailand, Peninsular Malaysia and Singapore.

6 GREAT EARED NIGHTJAR *Lyncornis macrotis* 40cm FIELD NOTES: Crepuscular and nocturnal. Hunts above forest clearings, flying with leisurely wing-beats, much like a small harrier. VOICE: A wailing *pee-wheeoo wheeoo wheeoo.* HABITAT: Open areas in or near broadleaved evergreen and deciduous forest. DISTRIBUTION: Resident in Myanmar, Thailand (except C), Cambodia, Laos, Vietnam (except Tonkin and N, S Annam) and Peninsular Malaysia; vagrant in SW China.

7 GREY NIGHTJAR *Caprimulgus jotaka* 28–32cm FIELD NOTES: Nocturnal. In flight male shows white spots on outer primaries and on tips of outer-tail feathers; female wing and tail spots tawny-buff. VOICE: A rapid *tuk tuk tuk tuk…* HABITAT: Open broadleaved evergreen and coniferous forest, secondary growth and open areas. DISTRIBUTION: Summer visitor to China; resident W, N, E Myanmar and NW, W Thailand: widespread winter visitor in the south, except SW, C, S Myanmar, SE Thailand and possibly Singapore.

8 LARGE-TAILED NIGHTJAR *Caprimulgus macrurus* 33cm FIELD NOTES: Nocturnal. In flight male shows white patch on outer primaries and on outer-tail feathers. VOICE: A resonant *tok tok tok…* HABITAT: Open forest, forest edge, secondary growth and cultivations. DISTRIBUTION: Widespread resident southwards from Hainan and SW China.

9 INDIAN NIGHTJAR *Caprimulgus asiaticus* 24cm FIELD NOTES: Crepuscular and nocturnal. In flight male shows white spots on outer-primaries and white tips to outer-tail feathers. VOICE: A far-carrying *chuck-chuck-chuck-chuck-k-k-roo*; in flight gives a *quit-quit.* HABITAT: Open dry forest, semi-desert and dry scrub. DISTRIBUTION: Resident over much of Myanmar, Thailand, Cambodia, N, S Laos and C Vietnam.

10 SAVANNA NIGHTJAR *Caprimulgus affinis* 23cm FIELD NOTES: Crepuscular and nocturnal. In flight, male shows white patch on outer primaries and white tail sides. VOICE: A repeated *chweep.* HABITAT: Pine, broadleaved evergreen and open dry forest. DISTRIBUTION: Resident in Taiwan, SE, E China (summer in SW China), Myanmar (except SW, E), Thailand (except S), Cambodia, Laos, C, S Vietnam, S Peninsular Malaysia and Singapore.

dark
form

2

normal

♂
3

♀

3b
continentalis

♂

1

5

4

♀

6

♂

7

8

9

10

67 SWIFTS

1 WHITE-THROATED NEEDLETAIL (NEEDLE-TAILED SWIFT) *Hirundapus caudacutus* 21–22cm FIELD NOTES: Flight is fast and powerful. In flight, from below underparts show a white throat and a white horseshoe-shaped area from undertail to flanks. Juvenile has less clear-cut white throat, black streaking on white flanks and dark fringes on white undertail-coverts. Race with black forehead and lores, *H. c. nudipes* (not shown) occurs in NW Thailand and Cambodia. VOICE: A weak, high-pitched twittering. HABITAT: Forested and open areas. DISTRIBUTION: Resident in Taiwan and SW China. Passage migrant to NE, NW, SE Thailand, Cambodia, N, C Laos, Vietnam (E Tonkin and S Annam) and Peninsular Malaysia; vagrant elsewhere.

2 SILVER-BACKED NEEDLETAIL *Hirundapus cochinchinensis* 20–22cm FIELD NOTES: Usually encountered over forests, in small groups. Fast and powerful flight. Note darker throat compared to White-throated Needletail. Juvenile has dark fringes on white undertail-coverts. VOICE: A soft, rippling *trp-trp-trp-trp-trp*. HABITAT: Forested and open areas, rivers near or in forests. DISTRIBUTION: Summer visitor to Taiwan and Hainan; resident in N Myanmar, Thailand (except W, S), Cambodia, Laos and S, C, N Vietnam. Winter visitor and passage migrant to Peninsular Malaysia; passage migrant in Singapore.

3 BROWN-BACKED NEEDLETAIL (BROWN-THROATED SPINETAILED SWIFT) *Hirundapus giganteus* 23–25cm FIELD NOTES: *H. g. indicus* (3b) has white lores and a slightly paler throat. Typical powerful flight; wings make whooshing sound when overhead. Hawks insects over forests and grasslands. Drinks at pools or rivers in evenings, scooping up water in flight. VOICE: In flight utters a slow, rippling trill; also a squeaky, repeated *cirrwiet* and a thin *chiek*. Juvenile has dark fringes on white undertail-coverts. HABITAT: Forested and open areas. DISTRIBUTION: Widespread resident south from China.

4 FORK-TAILED SWIFT (PACIFIC SWIFT) *Apus pacificus* 17–18cm FIELD NOTES: Forages over forests and open hilltops. Pale fringes below, especially on belly and undertail-coverts. VOICE: A high-pitched *skree-ee-ee*. HABITAT: Mountain forests, forested areas and open areas. DISTRIBUTION: Resident in China, Taiwan, E Myanmar, NW Thailand, N, C Laos and N, C Vietnam (W Tonkin and C Annam). Winter visitor Thailand (except C), Cambodia and Peninsular Malaysia; common passage migrant elsewhere.

5 DARK-RUMPED SWIFT (DARK-BACKED SWIFT) *Apus acuticauda* FIELD NOTES: Does not appear to forage far from breeding cliffs, although recorded feeding above nearby forests. Belly can look very pale in strong light, contrasting with darker undertail-coverts. VOICE: A high-pitched *tsee-tsee*. HABITAT: Rocky cliffs, gorges and forested areas. DISTRIBUTION: Possibly breeds in W, N Myanmar; winter visitor or vagrant to NW Thailand.

6 HOUSE SWIFT *Apus nipalensis* 15cm FIELD NOTES: Slightly forked tail. Fluttering bat-like flight combined with short glides. VOICE: A shrill whickering scream. HABITAT: Urban, open, mountain and occasionally forested areas. DISTRIBUTION: Resident in S, E China, Hainan, Taiwan and throughout the south of the region except SW, W Myanmar.

7 SILVER-RUMPED SPINETAIL *Rhaphidura leucopygialis* 11cm FIELD NOTES: Flight is fluttery and erratic. Forages around forest clearings and rocky outcrops in high-level forests. VOICE: A high-pitched *tirrr-tirrr* and a rapid chattering. HABITAT: Broadleaved evergreen forests, clearings and secondary growth. DISTRIBUTION: Resident in S Myanmar (S Tenasserim), S Thailand and Peninsular Malaysia.

8 ASIAN PALM SWIFT *Cypsiurus balasiensis* 13cm FIELD NOTES: Slim. Often in small active groups. Flight agile and rapid, with fluttering wing-beats and short glides. VOICE: A trilling *te-he-he-he-he* or *tititee*. HABITAT: Open country, cultivation and urban areas, usually with nearby palms. DISTRIBUTION: Widespread resident in Hainan, SW China and throughout the south of the region, except N Vietnam (W Tonkin).

144

3b *indicus*

68 SWIFTS; TREESWIFTS

1 WATERFALL SWIFT (GIANT SWIFTLET) *Hydrochous gigas* 16cm FIELD NOTES: Gregarious, often encountered in the company of other swifts. VOICE: Sharp *wicker* notes and a loud twittering. HABITAT: High forests with nearby waterfalls. DISTRIBUTION: Recorded from Peninsular Malaysia.

2 GLOSSY SWIFTLET (WHITE-BELLIED SWIFTLET) *Collocalia esculenta* 10cm FIELD NOTES: Gregarious. Banking and gliding flight interspersed with fluttering, bat-like wing-beats. VOICE: A sharp twitter. HABITAT: Open and forested areas. DISTRIBUTION: Resident in S Myanmar (S Tenasserim), S Thailand and Peninsular Malaysia; non-breeding visitor to Singapore.

3 HIMALAYAN SWIFTLET *Aerodramus brevirostris* 13–14cm FIELD NOTES: Regularly occurs in flocks flying over forests; flight similar to Glossy Swiftlet. VOICE: A twittering *chit-chit*; also a low rattle. HABITAT: Forested and open areas. DISTRIBUTION: Breeds in China (west of the region); resident in SW China, W, E Myanmar, W, NW Thailand. Winter visitor to Thailand (except SE), Vietnam (except W Tonkin), Peninsular Malaysia and Singapore; passage migrant elsewhere.

4 BLACK-NEST SWIFTLET *Aerodramus maximus* 12–13cm FIELD NOTES: Most active in crepuscular period; gregarious, often in the company of other swifts. VOICE: Similar to Himalayan Swiftlet. HABITAT: Open areas, offshore islets, urban areas and occasionally over forests. DISTRIBUTION: Resident in S Myanmar (Tenasserim), S Thailand, Peninsular Malaysia and Singapore.

5 EDIBLE-NEST SWIFTLET *Aerodramus fuciphagus* 12cm FIELD NOTES: Gregarious, often found in the company of other swifts and swallows. Flight actions similar to Glossy Swiftlet. Grey rump is sometimes indistinct. VOICE: A loud, metallic *zwing*. HABITAT: Open areas, offshore islets and over forests and mangroves. DISTRIBUTION: Vagrant or offshore breeder to S Myanmar (Tenasserim).

6 GERMAIN'S SWIFTLET *Aerodramus germani* 11–12cm FIELD NOTES: Gregarious, often found alongside other swifts and swallows. Colonial, breeds on cliff faces and sometimes on buildings. VOICE: Similar to Edible-nest Swiftlet; also utters a various *chip* notes, used as echo location. HABITAT: Open areas, offshore islets, urban areas and occasionally over forests. DISTRIBUTION: Mainly coastal resident in S Myanmar, C, S Thailand, Vietnam (except N Annam and W Tonkin), Peninsular Malaysia and Singapore.

7 CRESTED TREESWIFT (CRESTED SWIFT) *Hemiprocne coronata* 23–25cm FIELD NOTES: Readily perches on branches and occasionally on wires. In flight tail often held in a 'spike', which can make it appear like a larger version of the Asian Palm Swift. At rest, tail extends past folded wings. Juvenile whitish below scalloped with dark grey; upperparts and wings with white fringes. VOICE: In flight utters a harsh *whit-tuck whit-tuck* or *ti-chuck ti-chuck*. HABITAT: Open deciduous forests and open areas. DISTRIBUTION: Resident in SW China, Myanmar, northern Thailand, Cambodia, Laos and C, S Vietnam.

8 GREY-RUMPED TREESWIFT *Hemiprocne longipennis* 21–25cm FIELD NOTES: Makes long sorties from a favourite bare branch that is often located in tree canopy. At rest tail does not extend beyond folded wings. VOICE: A harsh, piercing *ki ki-ki-kew*, a staccato *chi-chi-chi-chew* and a *too-it*. HABITAT: Well-exposed bare branches in forest and open wooded areas. DISTRIBUTION: Resident in S Myanmar (S Tenasserim), W, S Thailand, Peninsular Malaysia and Singapore.

9 WHISKERED TREESWIFT *Hemiprocne comata* 15–17cm FIELD NOTES: In flight, from below shows a dark underwing, white trailing edge and white undertail-coverts. Spends much time perched, making only short flights to capture insect prey below tree canopy. VOICE: A high-pitched, chattering *she-she-she-she-shoo-shee*; also a plaintive *chew*, given when perched. HABITAT: Clearings and edges of broadleaved evergreen forest. DISTRIBUTION: Resident in S Myanmar (S Tenasserim), S Thailand and Peninsular Malaysia; non-breeding visitor to Singapore.

69 TROGONS; HOOPOE

1 RED-NAPED TROGON *Harpactes kasumba* 31–35cm FIELD NOTES: Sits motionless for long periods, typical trogon behaviour. Tends to frequent the middle to upper storey. VOICE: A subdued, harsh *kau kau kau kau kau*; female utters a quiet whirring rattle. HABITAT: Broadleaved evergreen and freshwater swamp forest and in bamboo. DISTRIBUTION: Resident in S Thailand, Peninsular Malaysia and Singapore.

2 DIARD'S TROGON *Harpactes diardii* 32–35cm FIELD NOTES: Very unobtrusive, usually found in the middle storey; sitting still for long periods. VOICE: A descending *kau kau kau kau kau…* HABITAT: Broadleaved evergreen forest. DISTRIBUTION: Resident in S Thailand and Peninsular Malaysia.

3 ORANGE-BREASTED TROGON *Harpactes oreskios* 25–26cm FIELD NOTES: Frequents the middle to upper storey. Recorded following mixed species flocks. VOICE: A subdued, rapid *tu tu tau-tau-tau*. HABITAT: Broadleaved evergreen, semi-evergreen and mixed deciduous forests; also bamboo. DISTRIBUTION: Resident in SW China and over much of the south, except W, N, C Myanmar, C Thailand, N Vietnam and Singapore.

4 CINNAMON-RUMPED TROGON *Harpactes orrhophaeus* 25cm FIELD NOTES: Very shy, frequents the lower to middle storey. Noted in mixed-species feeding flocks. VOICE: A weak, descending *ta-aup ta-aup ta-aup*; also an explosive *purr*. HABITAT: Broadleaved evergreen forest. DISTRIBUTION: Resident in S Thailand and Peninsular Malaysia.

5 SCARLET-RUMPED TROGON *Harpactes duvaucelii* 23–26cm FIELD NOTES: Frequents the lower to middle storey and occasionally forest borders. Often a member of mixed-species feeding flocks. VOICE: Male utters a rapid, accelerating, descending *yau-yau-yau-yau-yau-yau…* When alarmed gives a quiet whirring *kir-r-r-r*. HABITAT: Broadleaved evergreen forest. DISTRIBUTION: Resident in S Myanmar (S Tenasserim), S Thailand and Peninsular Malaysia.

6 RED-HEADED TROGON *Harpactes erythrocephalus* 31–35cm FIELD NOTES: Unobtrusive, sits motionless for long periods in the middle to upper storey. Pink-bellied race *H. e. yamakanensis* (6b) occurs in S, SE, E China. VOICE: A mellow, descending *tyaup tyaup tyaup tyaup tyaup*; when alarmed utters a chattering croak, *tewirr*. HABITAT: Broadleaved evergreen forests. DISTRIBUTION: Resident in southern China, Hainan and throughout the south of the region, except from C Thailand and Singapore.

7 WARD'S TROGON *Harpactes wardi* 35–38cm FIELD NOTES: Typical trogon actions, sitting motionless in cover of foliage and making occasional sallies to catch winged insects. Frequents lower storey, undergrowth and bamboo. VOICE: A mellow *klew klew klew klew klew…* that often slightly accelerates and drops in pitch. HABITAT: Montane broadleaved evergreen forest. DISTRIBUTION: Resident in SW China, N Myanmar and N Vietnam (W Tonkin).

8 HOOPOE (COMMON or EURASIAN HOOPOE) *Upupa epops* 26–32cm FIELD NOTES: Unmistakeable, even in flight where it gives the impression of a giant butterfly. When agitated, or alighting, crest is often fanned. Forages mainly on the ground, usually in pairs. VOICE: A low *hoop-hoop-hoop or poop-poop-poop*; when alarmed gives a harsh *schaahr*. HABITAT: Open country with scattered trees, cultivations, parks and gardens. DISTRIBUTION: Resident in China and the south of the region, except Peninsular Malaysia and Singapore; winter visitor to N, S Myanmar and NW, C, S Thailand.

70 ROLLERS; BEE-EATERS

1 INDIAN ROLLER *Coracias benghalensis* 30–32cm FIELD NOTES: Generally uses a prominent perch, such as a post, bare branch or overhead wires, from where it pounces on prey. During display indulges in an acrobatic rolling and diving performance. VOICE: A short *rack*, a chattering *rack rack rack rackrak-ak* and a screeching *aaaarrr* given in warning. During display utters a loud rattling *ra-ra-ra-ra-raa-raa-aaaaaa-aaaaar.* HABITAT: Open country with trees and bushes, coastal scrub, cultivations, parkland and gardens. DISTRIBUTION: Resident in SW China and southwards, except N Vietnam (E Tonkin).

2 DOLLARBIRD (ORIENTAL DOLLARBIRD, RED-BILLED or BROAD-BILLED ROLLER) *Eurystomus orientalis* 25–28cm FIELD NOTES: Often perches on the top-most branches of tall dead trees, from where acrobatic sallies are made after flying insects. In flight shows a large pale blue patch on base of primaries. Juvenile duller with dusky pink bill. VOICE: A fast *krak-kak-kak-kak-kak* and a hoarse *chak.* HABITAT: Open broadleaved evergreen, semi-evergreen and deciduous forests, forest clearings and edge, plantations, mangroves and island forest. DISTRIBUTION: Summer visitor over most of China, N, C Laos and N Vietnam. Resident in SE China, Myanmar, Thailand (except C), Cambodia, S Laos, C, S Vietnam, Peninsular Malaysia and Singapore. Winter visitor in the far south.

3 BLUE-BEARDED BEE-EATER *Nyctyornis athertoni* 31–34cm FIELD NOTES: Catches insects in flight, but also recorded foraging by clambering about in trees in search of insects. VOICE: A gruff *gga gga ggr* a *kir-r-r kir-r-r* and a purring *grrew-grrew-grrew.* HABITAT: Edges and clearings in dense broadleaved evergreen forest. DISTRIBUTION: Resident in SW China, Hainan and throughout the south, apart from S Myanmar (S Tenasserim), C, S Thailand, Peninsular Malaysia and Singapore.

4 RED-BEARDED BEE-EATER *Nyctyornis amictus* 27–31cm FIELD NOTES: Often frequents the lower canopy. Sits quietly, partly hidden, before making short flying sorties to catch winged insects. VOICE: A loud, hoarse *chachachacha...quo-qua-qua-qua* or a descending *kak kak-ka-ka-ka-ka*; also utters a deep *kwow* or *kwok.* HABITAT: Broadleaved evergreen forest and occasionally well-wooded gardens. DISTRIBUTION: Resident in S Myanmar (Tenasserim), W, S Thailand and Peninsular Malaysia.

5 LITTLE GREEN BEE-EATER (GREEN BEE-EATER) *Merops orientalis* 22–25cm FIELD NOTES: Makes darting flights from a branch or wire to capture flying insects. Roosts communally. VOICE: A quiet, trilling *trrr trrr trrr*, also a sharp *ti-ic* or *ti-ti-ti* given when alarmed. HABITAT: Open country with scattered trees, cultivations, semi-desert and coastal scrub. DISTRIBUTION: Resident from SW China southwards, except S Myanmar (S Tenasserim), S Thailand, N Vietnam, Peninsular Malaysia and Singapore.

6 BLUE-THROATED BEE-EATER *Merops viridis* 22–24cm FIELD NOTES: Often in flocks, especially at roosts. Makes flying sorties from tall trees or power-lines. VOICE: A fast, short, trilled *brk brk.* In flight utters a loud *prrrp prrrp prrrp...* When alarmed gives a sharp *chip.* HABITAT: Open country, river margins, forest edge, forest clearings, cultivations, parks and gardens. DISTRIBUTION: Summer visitor to S, E China, Hainan, N Vietnam and N Laos; winter visitor or passage migrant further south.

7 BLUE-TAILED BEE-EATER *Merops philippinus* 23–26cm FIELD NOTES: Gregarious. Actions typical of *Merops* bee-eaters. VOICE: A rolling *diririp* or similar. HABITAT: Open country, coastal scrub, river margins and mangroves. DISTRIBUTION: Resident in southern China, Hainan, Myanmar, Thailand, Cambodia, S Laos and Vietnam; winter visitor or passage migrant elsewhere.

8 CHESTNUT-HEADED BEE-EATER (BAY-HEADED BEE-EATER) *Merops leschenaulti* 18–20cm FIELD NOTES: Actions as other *Merops* bee-eaters. VOICE: A *pruik* or *churit.* HABITAT: Forests, often along watercourses, forest edge, coastal scrub, cultivations, mangroves and island forest. DISTRIBUTION: Resident in SW China and the south, except C Thailand and N Vietnam (E Tonkin and N Annam). Moves south post breeding; winter visitor to C Thailand and S Peninsular Malaysia.

71 KINGFISHERS

1 BLYTH'S KINGFISHER (GREAT BLUE KINGFISHER) *Alcedo hercules* 22cm
FIELD NOTES: Dives after fish from a low concealed perch. Female has orange-red base
to lower mandible. VOICE: In flight gives a loud *pseet*. HABITAT: Streams and rivers in
broadleaved evergreen forest and secondary growth. DISTRIBUTION: Resident in SW China,
Hainan, W, N, S Myanmar, Laos, NW Thailand and C, N Vietnam.

2 KINGFISHER (COMMON or RIVER KINGFISHER) *Alcedo atthis* 16–17cm FIELD
NOTES: First sight is often just a blue flash flying low along a river giving a high-pitched
call. Regularly uses a prominent perch from where it plunge-dives after small fish. Female
has orange-red base to lower mandible. VOICE: A penetrating, high-pitched *tseee* or *tseee
ti-ee ti-ee ti-ee*; when disturbed utters a harsh *shrit-it-it*. HABITAT: Rivers, streams and ponds
in open wooded areas, occasionally mangroves or estuaries; tends to avoid denser forests.
DISTRIBUTION: Resident in China, Taiwan, Hainan, Myanmar, NW, NE, W Thailand, N
Laos, N Vietnam (N Annam) and Peninsular Malaysia; more widespread post breeding.

3 BLUE-EARED KINGFISHER *Alcedo meninting* 17cm FIELD NOTES: Tends to fish
from a low, shady perch overhanging a forest stream. Juvenile has orange ear-coverts, dusky
tips to breast feathers and a black bill with a whitish tip. VOICE: A high-pitched, shrill *seet*;
also thin, shrill contact calls. HABITAT: Streams, small rivers and pools in dense forest; also
creeks and channels in mangroves. DISTRIBUTION: Resident in SW China and throughout
the south, except SW, E Myanmar, C Thailand and N Vietnam.

4 BLUE-BANDED KINGFISHER *Alcedo euryzona* 17cm FIELD NOTES: Hunts from
a low perch near forest streams; active, always moving from perch to perch. VOICE: A
high-pitched *cheep*, usually given in flight. HABITAT: Streams in broadleaved evergreen
forests. DISTRIBUTION: Resident in S Myanmar (Tenasserim), W, S Thailand and Peninsular
Malaysia.

5 ORIENTAL DWARF KINGFISHER *Ceyx erithaca* 14cm FIELD NOTES: Perches low,
in vegetation or on rocks, from where fish or insects are taken. Rufous form '*rufidorsa*' (5b)
occurs in S Thailand and Peninsular Malaysia; some authorities have considered it a full
species, but the two forms hybridise widely. VOICE: A high-pitched shrill *tsriet-tsriet* or a
soft *tjie-tjie-tjlie*. HABITAT: Shady streams or ponds in damp broadleaved evergreen forests;
occasionally in mangroves. DISTRIBUTION: Resident in SW, S China, Hainan, Myanmar
(except W, E), Thailand (except C), Laos and Vietnam; winter visitor to Singapore.

6 BANDED KINGFISHER *Lacedo pulchella* 21–25cm FIELD NOTES: Often sits
motionless for long periods. Hunts insects from a forest perch, sometimes hawks insects in
the tree canopy. Males of race *L. p. amabilis* (not shown) that lack the rufous hind collar are
found in S Myanmar, Laos, Cambodia, C, S Vietnam and N Peninsular Malaysia. VOICE: A
long whistled *wheeeoo* followed by up to fifteen short *chi-wiu* whistles that gradually fade
away. Calls include a sharp *wiak* or *wiak wiak*. HABITAT: Broadleaved evergreen forest,
mixed deciduous forest and bamboo. DISTRIBUTION: Resident in S, E Myanmar, Thailand
(except C), Cambodia, Laos, C, S Vietnam and Peninsular Malaysia.

7 BROWN-WINGED KINGFISHER *Pelargopsis amauroptera* 35cm FIELD NOTES:
Usually perches high in mangroves; feeds on fish and crabs. Azure rump conspicuous in
flight. VOICE: A harsh *chak-chak-chak-chak-chak*, a mournful and a descending *tree treew-
treew* HABITAT: Mangroves. DISTRIBUTION: Coastal resident in SW Myanmar, S Thailand
and islands off NW Peninsular Malaysia.

8 STORK-BILLED KINGFISHER *Pelargopsis capensis* 35cm FIELD NOTES: Sits quietly,
fairly well concealed, on a waterside branch. VOICE: Calls include a shrieking *ke-ke-ke-ke*,
also a pleasant *peer peer peer* and a descending *trew-trew* or *kwee-kwau*. HABITAT: Shady
waters in well-wooded country, also in mangroves. DISTRIBUTION: Resident throughout the
south from China, except Vietnam (W, E Tonkin and N, S Annam).

5b *rufidorsa*

72 KINGFISHERS

1 RUDDY KINGFISHER *Halcyon coromanda* 25cm FIELD NOTES: Shy and secretive. Hunts from a perch, catching insects or diving for fish. Juvenile duller with a dark bill. VOICE: A high-pitched, descending *titititititititi*, also a tremulous *pyorr pyorr pyorr…* HABITAT: Watercourses in dense evergreen forests, mangroves and island forests. DISTRIBUTION: Resident in Taiwan, W, E, S Thailand, Peninsular Malaysia and Singapore; summer visitor to SW China and C Vietnam; winter visitor or passage migrant elsewhere.

2 WHITE-BREASTED KINGFISHER (WHITE-THROATED or SMYRNA KINGFISHER) *Halcyon smyrnensis* 27–28cm FIELD NOTES: Often encountered far from water. In flight shows a large pale blue patch at base of primaries. VOICE: A rapid, trilling *kilililili…* also a cackling *chake ake ake-ake-ake-ake*, usually given as bird takes flight. HABITAT: Open areas, secondary growth, plantations and coastal wetlands. DISTRIBUTION: Resident throughout the region, except the far north.

3 BLACK-CAPPED KINGFISHER *Halcyon pileata* 28cm FIELD NOTES: Shy, but will perch on exposed branches or overhead wires. In flight shows prominent white patches at base of primaries. VOICE: A ringing, cackling *kikikikikiki*, higher pitched than White-breasted Kingfisher. HABITAT: Coastal and inland wetlands, also in cultivations and gardens. DISTRIBUTION: Summer visitor in the north; resident in southern China, Hainan, Taiwan, SW, N Myanmar and N Laos. Winter visitor throughout the south.

4 COLLARED KINGFISHER (MANGROVE or WHITE-COLLARED KINGFISHER) *Todiramphus chloris* 23–25cm FIELD NOTES: Conspicuous, bold and noisy, especially early in the day. Buff-bellied, darker-eared race *T. c. davisoni* (4b) occurs in the Coco Islands. VOICE: A harsh *krerk-krerk-krerk-krerk* that often ends with *jew-jaw* notes, also a shrieking *kick kyew kick kyew…* HABITAT: Coastal wetlands, mangroves, cultivations, gardens and parks; occasionally large rivers and marshes. DISTRIBUTION: Coastal resident throughout the south, except N Vietnam (E Tonkin and N Annam); inland in NE Thailand, S Vietnam, Peninsular Malaysia and along the Mekong river in Cambodia.

5 SACRED KINGFISHER *Todiramphus sanctus* 18–23cm FIELD NOTES: Usually encountered in pairs, sitting on an exposed perch. Most prey is taken from the ground, although will dive for fish. VOICE: A rapid, high-pitched *kik-kik-kik-kik*; also a rasping *schssk schssk*. HABITAT: Mangroves, open country, cultivations and gardens. DISTRIBUTION: Vagrant, recorded from Singapore.

6 RUFOUS-COLLARED KINGFISHER *Actenoides concretus* 24–25cm FIELD NOTES: Perches in the lower storey, keeping still apart from a slow wagging tail and alert head movements as the ground is scanned for prey. VOICE: A rising, whistled *kwee-i*, repeated every second for about 10 seconds. HABITAT: Broadleaved evergreen forest, generally close to water. DISTRIBUTION: Resident in S Myanmar (S Tenasserim), S Thailand and Peninsular Malaysia.

7 CRESTED KINGFISHER *Megaceryle lugubris* 41–43cm FIELD NOTES: Unmistakeable. Shy; usually in pairs perched on rocks or branches in or by a river pool. VOICE: A loud *ping*. Also deep croaks and raucous grating notes. When disturbed utters a loud *kek*. HABITAT: Fast-flowing rivers and streams in high-level forests. DISTRIBUTION: Resident in China, Myanmar, W, NW Thailand, Laos and Vietnam (except Cochinchina).

8 PIED KINGFISHER *Ceryle rudis* 25cm FIELD NOTES: Usually encountered in pairs or small parties. Regularly hovers and dives to catch fish. VOICE: A noisy *kwik-kwik* or *chirruk-chirruk*; also a high-pitched *TREEtiti TREEtiti*. HABITAT: Lakes, rivers, estuaries, tidal creeks, coastal lagoons and mangroves. DISTRIBUTION: Resident throughout, except W China, NE, S Thailand, Peninsular Malaysia and Singapore.

4b *davisoni*

73 HORNBILLS

1 ORIENTAL PIED HORNBILL (ASIAN or NORTHERN PIED HORNBILL)
Anthracoceros albirostris 55–60cm FIELD NOTES: Usually encountered in small groups, bigger flocks may form post breeding. Mainly arboreal, forages in tree foliage, but may descend to the ground to feed. In flight shows prominent white tips to flight feathers and large white tips to outer-tail feathers; race *A. a. convexus* from extreme S Thailand and Peninsular Malaysia has white outer-tail feathers (not depicted). VOICE: Various loud squeals and raucous cackles. HABITAT: Broadleaved evergreen forest, mixed deciduous forest, island forest and secondary growth. Occasionally coastal scrub, plantations and gardens. DISTRIBUTION: Resident southwards from SW China, except C Thailand.

2 BLACK HORNBILL *Anthracoceros malayanus* 76cm FIELD NOTES: Usually found in pairs or small flocks, occasionally in much larger flocks. Forages in tangles in the lower to middle levels of forest; recorded catching bats emerging from caves at dusk. VOICE: Harsh grating growls and retching noises. HABITAT: Broadleaved evergreen forest. DISTRIBUTION: Resident in S Thailand and Peninsular Malaysia.

3 RHINOCEROS HORNBILL *Buceros rhinoceros* 91–122cm FIELD NOTES: Arboreal. Usually in pairs or small flocks post breeding. VOICE: Male utters deep *hok* notes, female gives a *hak*, often given in duet, *hok-hak hok-hak…* Both give a loud throaty *ger-ronk* during flight. Juveniles lack the casque. HABITAT: Broadleaved evergreen forest. DISTRIBUTION: Resident in S Thailand and Peninsular Malaysia.

4 GREAT HORNBILL (GREAT PIED HORNBILL) *Buceros bicornis* 95–105cm FIELD NOTES: Generally seen in pairs or small groups; may gather in larger flocks at fruiting trees or at communal roosts. Mainly arboreal, although may descend to the ground to pick up fallen fruit. In flight shows white tips to flight feathers, buff-white wing-bar and white tail with a black subterminal band. Juveniles lack the casque. VOICE: A loud, reverberating *tok…tok…tok*, also various hoarse grunts, barks and roars; in flight utters a loud *ger-onk*. HABITAT: Broadleaved evergreen and mixed deciduous forests. DISTRIBUTION: Resident in SW China and throughout the south, except C Thailand and Singapore.

5 HELMETED HORNBILL *Rhinoplax vigil* 110–120cm FIELD NOTES: Usually seen singly or in pairs. Forages in the canopy of tall trees, searching for fruit, small animals, snakes and birds. VOICE: A series of loud *hoop* notes that quicken to *ke-hoop* notes before ending in a manic laugh; in flight utters a loud, clanking *ka-hank*. HABITAT: Broadleaved evergreen forest. DISTRIBUTION: Resident in S Myanmar (Tenasserim), S Thailand and Peninsular Malaysia.

6 BROWN HORNBILL (AUSTEN'S BROWN HORNBILL) *Anorrhinus austeni* 60–65cm FIELD NOTES: Mainly arboreal, often encountered in small noisy, restless flocks, often accompanied by other fruit-eating birds. In flight, males show white tips to primary feathers and outer-tail feathers. Juvenile similar to male, but with pale fringes to wing-coverts and pink orbital skin. VOICE: A loud, yelping *klee-ah*; also various croaks, chuckles and screams. HABITAT: Evergreen and deciduous forests. DISTRIBUTION: Resident in SW China, W, N, E Myanmar, C, N Thailand, Laos, W Cambodia and N, C Vietnam.

7 TICKELL'S BROWN HORNBILL *Anorrhinus tickelli* 60–65cm FIELD NOTES: Actions and habits similar to Brown Hornbill. Often considered conspecific with Brown Hornbill. VOICE: Similar to Brown Hornbill. HABITAT: Broadleaved evergreen forest, occasionally in nearby mixed deciduous. DISTRIBUTION: Resident in S Myanmar (S Tenasserim) and SE Thailand.

156

dark form

1 ♀ ♂

2 ♀ ♂ ♂

3 ♀ ♂

4 ♀ ♂

10] 凡
♂
Thailand
Ko Samui

5 ♂ ♀

6 ♂ ♀

7 ♂ ♀

74 HORNBILLS

1 BUSHY-CRESTED HORNBILL *Anorrhinus galeritus* 65–70cm FIELD NOTES: Usually found in flocks of 5–15 birds; forages in or just below the canopy. VOICE: A loud, excited *klia-klia-klia kliu-kliu* that rises and falls, often uttered by all members of a group and builds into a crescendo. When alarmed utters a loud *aak aak aak*. HABITAT: Broadleaved evergreen forest. DISTRIBUTION: Resident in S Myanmar (S Tenasserim), S Thailand and Peninsular Malaysia.

2 WHITE-CROWNED HORNBILL *Berenicornis comatus* 75–85cm FIELD NOTES: Forages in dense tangled growth in lower storeys or on the ground, spends much time digging in bark and debris searching for food. VOICE: A deep *hoo hu-hu-hu-hu-hu-hu* or *kuk kuk kuk kuk kuk* that often fades away. HABITAT: Broadleaved evergreen forest. DISTRIBUTION: Resident in S Myanmar (S Tenasserim), S Thailand and Peninsular Malaysia.

3 RUFOUS-NECKED HORNBILL *Aceros nipalensis* 90–100cm FIELD NOTES: Usually seen in pairs or small groups feeding in the top of trees, or flying across forested valleys. Generally arboreal, although may descend to the ground to pick up fallen fruit. In flight shows white tips to outer primaries and white-tipped tail. Juvenile has greyish bill with faint or no markings. VOICE: A short, repeated bark, said to resemble the noise made by an axe striking a sapling; also various loud roars, croaks or cackles. HABITAT: Broadleaved evergreen forest. DISTRIBUTION: Resident in SW China, Myanmar (except SW, S), W, NW Thailand, N, C Laos and N Vietnam (W Tonkin and N Annam).

4 WREATHED HORNBILL *Rhyticeros undulatus* 75–85cm FIELD NOTES: Generally in pairs or small parties and in larger groups where food is plentiful or at communal roosts. Forages mainly in the canopy, although will descend to the ground to pick up fallen fruit or take small animals. Juveniles lack the wreathed casque and bill markings, both develop in the first year, gaining a new wreath each subsequent year. VOICE: A very loud, breathless *kuk-KWEHK*. HABITAT: Broadleaved evergreen, mixed deciduous and island forests. DISTRIBUTION: Resident in SW China and throughout the south, except C Myanmar, C Thailand, N Vietnam and Singapore.

5 PLAIN-POUCHED HORNBILL *Rhyticeros subruficollis* 65–70cm FIELD NOTES: Generally found in pairs, occasionally in small groups. Forages mainly in the treetops, although will descend to the ground to collect fallen fruit or to capture small animals. VOICE: A loud *keh-kek-kehk*. HABITAT: Broadleaved evergreen and mixed deciduous forest. DISTRIBUTION: Resident in S Myanmar, W, S Thailand and N Peninsular Malaysia.

6 WRINKLED HORNBILL *Rhabdotorrhinus corrugatus* 75cm FIELD NOTES: Usually encountered in pairs or small flocks. Forages in the canopy of large emergent trees. VOICE: A sharp barking *kak kak-kak* or an echoing *wakowwakowkow* or *rowwrow*. HABITAT: Broadleaved evergreen forest and freshwater swamp forest. DISTRIBUTION: Resident in S Thailand and Peninsular Malaysia.

75 BARBETS

1 SOOTY BARBET *Calorhamphus fuliginosus* 17–20cm FIELD NOTES: Regularly forages in small groups, from the understorey to the canopy. Often feeds acrobatically, like a tit. VOICE: A sibilant series of *pseeee* calls; also a thin *pseeoo*. HABITAT: Broadleaved evergreen forest, secondary growth and open areas with scattered trees. DISTRIBUTION: Resident in S Myanmar (S Tenasserim), S Thailand and Peninsular Malaysia.

2 FIRE-TUFTED BARBET *Psilopogon pyrolophus* 29cm FIELD NOTES: Forages in pairs or small groups, acrobatic when attempting to reach fruit. VOICE: A cicada-like *dddzza-ddzza* that increases to a *zz-zz-zz-zz*; also utters a whistled note and a squeak. HABITAT: High-level broadleaved evergreen forest. DISTRIBUTION: Resident in extreme S Thailand and Peninsular Malaysia.

3 GREAT BARBET (GIANT BARBET) *Psilopogon virens* 32–35cm FIELD NOTES: Usually seen singly or in small parties, with bigger groups where trees are in fruit. When not feeding, sits motionless in the topmost branches. VOICE: A mournful *piho piho piho*, a rapid *tuk tuk tuk* and a harsh *karr-r*. HABITAT: Broadleaved evergreen, occasionally deciduous forests and gardens with fruiting trees. DISTRIBUTION: Resident in China, Myanmar (except S Tenasserim), north-western Thailand, N, C Laos and N Vietnam.

4 RED-VENTED BARBET *Psilopogon lagrandieri* 29cm FIELD NOTES: Arboreal; little recorded, probably forms groups at fruiting trees. VOICE: Male call is a throaty, strident *choa* or *chorwa*; female utters a descending *uk uk uk-ukukukukukuk...* when alarmed gives a harsh, high-pitched *grrric...grrric* or *brrret...brrret*. HABITAT: Broadleaved evergreen and semi-evergreen forest. DISTRIBUTION: Resident in N, E Cambodia, C, S Laos and Vietnam.

5 GREEN-EARED BARBET *Psilopogon faiostrictus* 24cm FIELD NOTES: Forages in the canopy, feeding on fruits such as figs and berries. VOICE: A loud, rapidly repeated, throaty *took-a-prruk*; also a mellow, rising *pooouk*. HABITAT: Broadleaved evergreen, semi-evergreen and mixed deciduous forest, also open areas with scattered trees. DISTRIBUTION: Resident in SE China, Thailand (except C, S), Cambodia, Laos and Vietnam.

6 LINEATED BARBET (GREY-HEADED BARBET) *Psilopogon lineatus* 25–30cm FIELD NOTES: Variable, dark and light form shown. Usually seen singly or in small groups; larger groups occur at trees laden with fruit. Juvenile has less prominent streaking on breast. VOICE: A monotonous *kotur kotur kotur...* or a trill followed by a long series of *poo-tok* notes. HABITAT: Deciduous forests, open areas with scattered trees, coastal scrub and plantations. DISTRIBUTION: Resident from SW China southwards, except N Vietnam and C Thailand.

7 GOLD-WHISKERED BARBET *Psilopogon chrysopogon* 30cm FIELD NOTES: Forages mainly in the canopy, feeding on fruits. VOICE: A loud, rapid *too-tuk too-tuk too-tuk...* or *tehoop-tehoop-tehoop...* also utters a repeated, low-pitched trill. HABITAT: Broadleaved evergreen forest. DISTRIBUTION: Resident in S Thailand and Peninsular Malaysia.

8 RED-CROWNED BARBET *Psilopogon rafflesii* 25–27cm FIELD NOTES: Forages in the canopy, feeding on fruits and insects. VOICE: A loud *took* followed by a rapid, repeated series of *tuk* notes. HABITAT: Broadleaved evergreen forests. DISTRIBUTION: Resident in S Myanmar (S Tenasserim), S Thailand, Peninsular Malaysia and Singapore.

9 RED-THROATED BARBET *Psilopogon mystacophanos* 23cm FIELD NOTES: Forages mainly in the canopy, descends to the understorey to rummage in deep cover. VOICE: A slow, uneven series of deep notes, *chok...chok-chok...chok...chok-chok...chok...*; also a repeated high-pitched trill, which gradually gets shorter. HABITAT: Broadleaved evergreen forest. DISTRIBUTION: Resident in S Myanmar (S Tenasserim), S Thailand and Peninsular Malaysia.

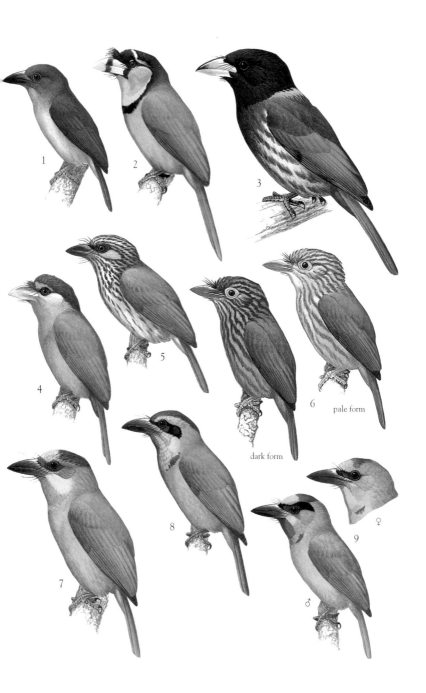

pale form

dark form

♀

♂

76 BARBETS

1 BLACK-BROWED BARBET *Psilopogon oorti* 21–24cm FIELD NOTES: Active forager in canopy and sub-canopy. VOICE: A loud, throaty *too-tuk-trrrrrk*, repeated about once a second. HABITAT: Broadleaved evergreen forest. DISTRIBUTION: Resident in S Thailand and Peninsular Malaysia.

2 INDOCHINESE BARBET *Psilopogon annamensis* 21–24cm FIELD NOTES: Actions as Black-browed Barbet; this and the following two species were often regarded as conspecific with Black-browed Barbet. VOICE: Probably similar to Black-browed Barbet. HABITAT: Broadleaved evergreen forest. DISTRIBUTION: Resident in S Laos, S, C Vietnam and E Cambodia.

3 TAIWAN BARBET *Psilopogon nuchalis* 21–24cm FIELD NOTES: Active forager in upper and middle storey. VOICE: Probably similar to Black-browed Barbet. HABITAT: Subtropical forests. DISTRIBUTION: Resident in Taiwan.

4 CHINESE BARBET *Psilopogon faber* 21–24cm FIELD NOTES: Frequents the middle and upper storey. Race *P. f. sini* (4b) occurs in S China. VOICE: A hollow *tok-tr-trrrrrt*, repeated about 20 times a minute. HABITAT: Subtropical and tropical forests. DISTRIBUTION: Resident in Hainan and S China (Yaoshan in Guangxi).

5 GOLDEN-THROATED BARBET *Psilopogon franklinii* 23cm FIELD NOTES: Unobtrusive, forages in middle storey and canopy, sometimes descends to understorey. Large groups may gather in fruiting trees. Race *P. f. auricularis* (5b) occurs in S Laos and Vietnam (S Annam); *P. f. ramsayi* (5c) occurs in C Myanmar, NW, W, S Thailand and Peninsular Malaysia. VOICE: A monotonous, ringing *ki-ti-yook* or *pukwowk*; also a wailing *peeyu peeyu*. HABITAT: Broadleaved evergreen forest. DISTRIBUTION: Resident from S China southwards, except C, SE Thailand, Cambodia, S Vietnam and Singapore.

6 BLUE-THROATED BARBET *Psilopogon asiaticus* 23cm FIELD NOTES: Usually encountered in pairs or small parties; also occurs in mixed-species flocks. Forages in the canopy, descends to understorey for fruits. Race *P. a. chersonesus* (6b) occurs in S Thailand; *P. a. davisoni* (6c) occurs in SE Myanmar east to SW China, N, C Vietnam and N Laos. VOICE: A rapid, harsh *took-a-rook took-a-rook*. HABITAT: Broadleaved evergreen forest and secondary growth. DISTRIBUTION: Resident in SW China, Myanmar, Thailand (except C, SE) N Laos and N Vietnam.

7 MOUSTACHED BARBET *Psilopogon incognitus* 22–23cm FIELD NOTES: Tends to stay in forest cover. VOICE: Variable, including a repeated *u ik-a-ruk u ik-a-ruk…* a *tuk-uk* or *tuk-a-tuk* and a *tuk-tuk-trrrr*. HABITAT: Broadleaved woodland. DISTRIBUTION: Resident in S Myanmar (N Tenasserim), W, NW, NE, SE Thailand, Cambodia, Laos and Vietnam (except Cochinchina).

8 YELLOW-CROWNED BARBET *Psilopogon henricii* 21–23cm FIELD NOTES: Spends much time foraging in tree canopy feeding on figs and fruits. VOICE: A short trilled *trrok* followed by a loud *tok-tok-tok-tok-tok…* HABITAT: Broadleaved evergreen forest. DISTRIBUTION: Resident in S Thailand and Peninsular Thailand.

9 BLUE-EARED BARBET *Psilopogon duvaucelli* 17cm FIELD NOTES: Occurs in pairs or small parties, with larger groups in fruiting trees. *P. d. cyanotis* (9b) occurs in S China and N Thailand; *P. d. orientalis* (9c) in E Thailand, Cambodia, Laos and Vietnam. VOICE: An endlessly repeated *tk-trrt tk-trrt*, *koo-turr koo-turr* or *too-rook too-rook*; also a whistled *teeow-teeow…* HABITAT: Dense broadleaved evergreen forest, semi-evergreen forest, mixed deciduous forest and secondary growth. DISTRIBUTION: Resident southwards from SW China, except N, E Myanmar and C Thailand.

10 COPPERSMITH BARBET *Psilopogon haemacephalus* 17cm FIELD NOTES: Generally in pairs or small parties, with larger groups occurring in fruiting trees. Juveniles lack the red markings. VOICE: A monotonous, metallic *tuk tuk tuk tuk tuk tuk tuk…* HABITAT: Deciduous forest, forest edge, lightly wooded areas, mangroves, parks and gardens. DISTRIBUTION: Resident south from SW China, except N Vietnam.

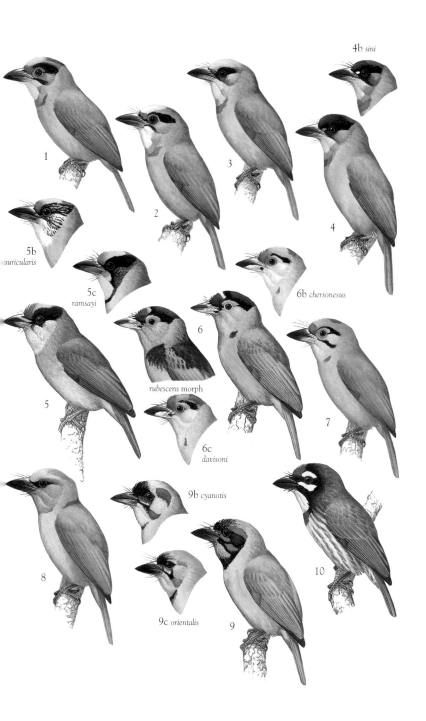

4b *sini*

5b
auricularis

5c
ramsayi

6b *chersonesus*

rubescens morph

6
6c
davisoni

9b *cyanotis*

9c *orientalis*

9

10

77 HONEYGUIDES; WRYNECK; PICULETS; WOODPECKERS

1 MALAYSIAN HONEYGUIDE *Indicator archipelagicus* 16–18cm FIELD NOTES: May sit motionless for long periods. Frequently seen in the vicinity of bee's nests. Females lack the small yellow shoulder patch. VOICE: A mewing, followed by an ascending rattle. HABITAT: Broadleaved evergreen forests; occasionally in plantations and gardens. DISTRIBUTION: Resident in W, S Thailand and Peninsular Malaysia.

2 YELLOW-RUMPED HONEYGUIDE *Indicator xanthonotus* 15cm FIELD NOTES: Regularly sits motionless on topmost branches of trees before making clumsy flycatcher-like sallies after insects. VOICE: Calls include a quiet *weet*, a chipping *tzt* and a *chaenp-chaenp*; mostly recorded from flying birds. HABITAT: Mixed forests and wooded gorges near cliffs with Giant Rock Bee colonies. DISTRIBUTION: Rare resident in N Myanmar.

3 WRYNECK (EURASIAN WRYNECK) *Jynx torquilla* 16–17cm FIELD NOTES: Generally shy. Feeds mainly on the ground. VOICE: A plaintive *quee-quee-quee-quee*. HABITAT: Open scrub, cultivations and secondary growth. DISTRIBUTION: Winter visitor to much of China, Hainan, Myanmar (except Tenasserim), Thailand (except S), N, C Laos and N, S Vietnam.

4 SPECKLED PICULET *Picumnus innominatus malayorum* 10cm FIELD NOTES: Agile forager, also makes aerial sallies after insects. Presence usually revealed by persistent tapping while searching for food. *P. i. chinensis* (4b) occurs in C, E, S, SE China and N Vietnam. VOICE: A high-pitched *ti-ti-ti-ti-ti* and a squeaky *sik-sik-sik*. Drums on bamboo or dead branch with a persistent *brr-r-r brr-r-r...* HABITAT: Bamboo, broadleaved evergreen forest, mixed deciduous forest and secondary growth. DISTRIBUTION: Resident throughout, except SW Myanmar, C, SE, S Thailand and Singapore.

5 WHITE-BROWED PICULET *Picumnus ochracea* 9–10cm FIELD NOTES: Agile and restless forager. Persistent tapping helps to locate feeding birds. *S. o. reichenowi* (5b) occurs in S Myanmar (Tenasserim) and W Thailand. VOICE: A short, sharp *chi*, also a fast, high-pitched trill. Drumming is loud and tinny. HABITAT: Bamboo, broadleaved evergreen forest, mixed deciduous forest, secondary growth with bushes. DISTRIBUTION: Resident south from S China, except C, SE, S Thailand, Cambodia, Peninsular Malaysia and Singapore.

6 RUFOUS PICULET *Picumnus abnormis* 8–10cm FIELD NOTES: Active forager, singly or in small parties. Persistent tapping helps to locate feeding birds. VOICE: A high-pitched *kik-ik-ik-ik-ik-ik*; also a sharp *tic* or *tsit*. Drumming consists of a fast rattle slowing to paired beats. HABITAT: Bamboo, broadleaved evergreen forest and secondary growth. DISTRIBUTION: Resident in S Myanmar (S Tenasserim), S Thailand and Peninsular Malaysia.

7 YELLOW-CROWNED WOODPECKER *Leiopicus mahrattensis* 17–18cm FIELD NOTES: Forages singly or in pairs mainly in the crown of trees or on trunks. VOICE: A feeble *peek*, a sharp *click-click* and a rapid, repeated *kik-kik-kik-r-r-r-h*. HABITAT: Deciduous woodland, open areas with scattered trees and scrub. DISTRIBUTION: Resident in SW, W, C, S Myanmar, E Cambodia, S Laos and S Vietnam (S Annam).

8 SUNDA WOODPECKER (SUNDA PYGMY WOODPECKER) *Yungipicus moluccensis* 12–13cm FIELD NOTES: Works slowly over branches, favouring the smaller twigs of trees and shrubs. VOICE: A sharp, wheezy, trilled *kikikikikiki* or a whirring *trrrrr-i-i*. HABITAT: Mangroves, coastal scrub and occasionally parks and gardens. DISTRIBUTION: Mainly coastal resident in Peninsular Malaysia and Singapore.

9 GREY-CAPPED WOODPECKER (GREY-CAPPED PYGMY WOODPECKER) *Yungipicus canicapillus* 14–16cm FIELD NOTES: Forages in the tops of trees, bushes and saplings, favouring outer branches and twigs. Agile, often hanging upside-down in search of food. Race *Y. c. kaleensis* (9b) occurs in Taiwan, China, N Myanmar and N Vietnam. VOICE: A rattling *tit-tit-erh-r-r-r-r-h*; also utters a squeaky *kweek-kweek-kweek*. Call is a *kik* or *pit*, which often precedes the rattling song. HABITAT: Broadleaved evergreen forest, deciduous forest, secondary growth and coastal scrub. DISTRIBUTION: Resident throughout, except Singapore.

1

2

3

4

4b *chinensis*

♂

♀ ♂

5b *reichenowi*
♂

5
♀ ♂

6
♂ ♀

♂

♂

9
♂ ♀

7
♀

8
♀

9b *kaleensis*
♂

78 WOODPECKERS

1 FULVOUS-BREASTED WOODPECKER *Dendrocopos macei* 18–19cm FIELD NOTES: Favours tall trees. Usually encountered singly, in pairs or small parties, foraging on trunks and branches; also descends to the ground to feed on ants. VOICE: A rapid *pik pipipipipipipipipi*, a loud, sharp *tchick* and a soft *chik-a-chik-a-chit*. HABITAT: Open deciduous forests, open areas with scattered trees, plantations and gardens. DISTRIBUTION: Resident in N Myanmar.

2 FRECKLE-BREASTED WOODPECKER *Dendrocopos analis* 18–19cm FIELD NOTES: A recent split from Fulvous-breasted Woodpecker; actions and habits therefore probably similar. VOICE: Similar to Fulvous-breasted Woodpecker. HABITAT: Open deciduous forest, secondary forest and open areas with scattered trees. DISTRIBUTION: Resident in S Myanmar, NW, W, C, Thailand, Cambodia, C, S Laos and S Vietnam.

3 STRIPE-BREASTED WOODPECKER *Dendrocopos atratus* 21–22cm FIELD NOTES: Red on nape and more boldly streaked underparts separate this from the similar Fulvous-breasted Woodpecker. VOICE: An explosive *tchick* and a whinnying rattle. HABITAT: Open oak and pine woodland in evergreen forest, edges of open broadleaved forest and cultivations. DISTRIBUTION: Resident in SW China, W, S, E Myanmar, W, NW, NE Thailand, Laos and C Vietnam (C Annam).

4 RUFOUS-BELLIED WOODPECKER *Dendrocopos hyperythrus* 20–25cm FIELD NOTES: Usually seen singly or in pairs, occasionally joins mixed-species feeding flocks. VOICE: A reeling *chit-chit-chit-r-r-r-r-h* and a fast *ptikitititititit* when alarmed. Drums in short fading rolls. HABITAT: Open oak forests, pine forest, mixed broadleaved evergreen and coniferous forest; locally in deciduous forests. DISTRIBUTION: Resident in SW China, W, N, C, E Myanmar, NW, NE Thailand, Cambodia and S Vietnam (S Annam). Winter visitor in SE China and N Vietnam; passage migrant in China.

5 CRIMSON-BREASTED WOODPECKER *Dendrocopos cathpharius* 17–19cm FIELD NOTES: Usually forages low down in trees and bushes, favours dead trees. Race *D. c. pyrrhothorax* (5b) occurs in W Myanmar, it has whole nape red. VOICE: A loud, repetitive *chip* or *tchick*; also a short, rapid descending rattle. HABITAT: Broadleaved evergreen forests. DISTRIBUTION: Resident in SW, C China, W, C, N, E Myanmar, N, W Thailand, N Laos and N Vietnam (W Tonkin).

6 DARJEELING WOODPECKER *Dendrocopos darjellensis* 25cm FIELD NOTES: Forages from the ground to the tree canopy, sometimes in mixed-species feeding flocks. Juveniles lack the ochre sides of neck. VOICE: A rattling *di-di-di-d-ddddddt*, a low *puk puk* and a *tsik tsik tsik* when alarmed. HABITAT: Broadleaved evergreen forest. DISTRIBUTION: Resident in SW China, W, N Myanmar and N Vietnam (W Tonkin); winter visitor to E Tonkin.

7 GREAT SPOTTED WOODPECKER *Dendrocopos major* 24cm FIELD NOTES: Forages mainly in the upper branches of trees. Agile, often clinging tit-like to extricate prey. Juvenile duller with red crown and pinkish ventral area. VOICE: A high-pitched *kik* or a soft *chik*. Drumming loud and far-carrying. HABITAT: Temperate woodlands, broadleaved evergreen forest; also in alder and rhododendron in Myanmar. DISTRIBUTION: Resident in China, W, N, E Myanmar, N Laos and N Vietnam.

8 WHITE-BACKED WOODPECKER *Dendrocopos leucotos* 23–28cm FIELD NOTES: In flight shows white lower back and rump. Actions similar to Great-spotted Woodpecker. VOICE: A soft, sharp *kiuk*, *kok* or *gig*; when alarmed gives a series of *kyig gyig* notes. Drumming loud, long and accelerating. HABITAT: Deciduous and mixed mountain forests. DISTRIBUTION: Resident in Taiwan and C China.

9 THREE-TOED WOODPECKER (EURASIAN THREE-TOED WOODPECKER) *Picoides tridactylus* 21–24cm FIELD NOTES: Forages low down, tends to favour dead trees and stumps. VOICE: A short, soft *kip* or *kyuk* and a *kip-kip-kip-kip* when alarmed. Drumming bursts are loud and slightly accelerating. HABITAT: Mountain forests. DISTRIBUTION: Resident in SW China.

5b *pyrrhothorax*

79 WOODPECKERS

1 WHITE-BELLIED WOODPECKER *Dryocopus javensis* 40–48cm FIELD NOTES: Usually encountered singly, in pairs or small groups of 4–6 birds. Forages in tall trees, on or near the ground; has a liking for dead trees, stumps, fallen logs and leaf litter. Flight crow-like, with leisurely, deliberate wing-beats, when white rump and underwing-coverts are prominent. VOICE: A laughing *kek-kek-kek-kek-kek…* or *kiau-kiau-kiau-kiau…* also a single, loud, sharp *kiyow, kyah* or *keer.* Drumming is loud and accelerating, lasting about 3 seconds, sometimes longer. HABITAT: Deciduous and broadleaved evergreen forests, occasionally coniferous forests and plantations. DISTRIBUTION: Resident south from SW China, except C Thailand, N Laos and N Vietnam (E Tonkin and N Annam).

2 BLACK WOODPECKER *Dryocopus martius* 45–55cm FIELD NOTES: Forages on the lower parts of trunks, at base of trees and on the ground. Flight slow and loose, slightly undulating. VOICE: A loud *kwee kwee-kwee-kwee-kwee…* also a clear *bleep* or *ke-yaa*; in flight utters a far-carrying *krry-krry-krry* or a softer *kruek-kruek-kruek.* Drumming loud, recalling a machine-gun. HABITAT: Subalpine conifer forests. DISTRIBUTION: Possibly occurs in the mountainous areas in the NW of the region.

3 RUFOUS WOODPECKER *Micropternus brachyurus* 25cm FIELD NOTES: Usually seen in pairs, digging at tree-ant nests or foraging on fallen branches and termite nests; also recorded feeding on fruit. Race *M. b. fokiensis* (3b) occurs in S China and N Vietnam; *M. b. holroydi* (3c) occurs in Hainan. VOICE: A high-pitched *kenk kenk kenk.* Drumming said to sound like a stalling motorcycle engine: *bdddd-d-d-d-dt.* HABITAT: Broadleaved evergreen forest, deciduous forest, forest edge and secondary growth. DISTRIBUTION: Resident in C, S China, Hainan and throughout the south of the region.

4 BANDED WOODPECKER *Chrysophlegma miniaceum* 25–27cm FIELD NOTES: Unobtrusive, usually encountered singly or in pairs foraging among vines and dense branches in the lower storey, although will use all levels. VOICE: A screaming *kwee* or *chewerk-chewerk-chewerk-chewerk*; also utters a *keek* call note. HABITAT: Broadleaved evergreen forest, secondary growth, plantations and occasionally mangroves. DISTRIBUTION: Resident in S Myanmar (S Tenasserim), S Thailand and Peninsular Malaysia.

5 CHECKER-THROATED WOODPECKER *Chrysophlegma mentale* 26–30cm FIELD NOTES: Usually found singly or in pairs, sometimes forms part of mixed-species flocks. Lively forager in lower and middle storey and higher parts of understorey. VOICE: A long series of *wi* notes; call includes a *kyick* and a *kiyee…kiyee…kiyee…* HABITAT: Broadleaved evergreen forest and occasionally mangroves. DISTRIBUTION: Resident in S Myanmar (S Tenasserim), S Thailand and Peninsular Malaysia.

6 GREATER YELLOWNAPE *Chrysophlegma flavinucha* 33–34cm FIELD NOTES: Often encountered in small loose groups foraging on trunks and branches; also rummages on the ground searching for ants, termites and grubs. Race *C. n. wrayi* (6b) occurs in Peninsular Malaysia. VOICE: Calls include a long, accelerating *kwee-kwee-kwee-kwee-kwee-kwee-kwee-kwee-kwi-kwi-kwi-kwi-wi-wi-wi-wik,* a loud, plaintive *pee-u…pee-u…* and a metallic *chenk.* When disturbed utters a rich, laughing *kwek-kwek-kwek-kwek…* HABITAT: Broadleaved evergreen, deciduous and native pine forest. DISTRIBUTION: Resident south from southern China and Hainan, except C, S Thailand and Singapore.

7 LESSER YELLOWNAPE *Picus chlorolophus* 25–28cm FIELD NOTES: Usually found in pairs, regularly forms part of mixed-species feeding flocks. Often ventures onto the ground to search for ants and termites. *P. c. rodgeri* (6b) occurs in Peninsular Malaysia; *P. c. citrinocristatus* (6c) occurs in N Vietnam. VOICE: A loud, mournful *peee-ui, pee-a* or *pee-oow*; also a descending *kwee-kwee-kwee-kwee-kwee-kwee-kwee…* HABITAT: Broadleaved evergreen and deciduous forest. DISTRIBUTION: Resident south from S, E China and Hainan, except C, S Thailand and Singapore.

3b *fokiensis*

3c *holroydi*

7b
rodgeri

7c *citrinocristatus*

6b *wrayi*

80 WOODPECKERS

1 CRIMSON-WINGED WOODPECKER *Picus puniceus* 24–28cm FIELD NOTES:
Generally found singly or in loose pairs, often forms part of mixed-species feeding flocks.
Favours tall trees; forages in the canopy on trunks and large branches. VOICE: A distinctive
pee-bee or an extended *pee-dee-dee-dee*; also utters a short *peep* and a *wee-eek*, the latter used
when two birds are in close proximity. HABITAT: Broadleaved evergreen, secondary growth
and plantations. DISTRIBUTION: Resident in S Myanmar (S Tenasserim), S Thailand and
Peninsular Malaysia.

2 LACED WOODPECKER *Picus vittatus* 30–33cm FIELD NOTES: Usually encountered
in pairs. Forages low in trees, on fallen trees and on the ground. In flight shows a yellowish
rump. VOICE: A fast, low-pitched *pew-pew-pew…* also a keep or *kee-ip.* HABITAT: Broadleaved
evergreen and deciduous forest, secondary growth, bamboo, plantations, coastal scrub,
mangroves and gardens. DISTRIBUTION: Resident in E, S Myanmar, Thailand (except S),
Cambodia, Laos, C, S Vietnam, S Peninsular Malaysia and Singapore.

3 STREAK-BREASTED WOODPECKER *Picus viridanus* 30cm FIELD NOTES:
Regularly forages on the ground, on moss-covered logs and boulders, in search of ants. In
flight shows a dull yellow-green rump. VOICE: A *tcheu-tcheu-tcheu-tcheu…* also an explosive
kirr and a squirrel-like *kyup.* HABITAT: Broadleaved evergreen forest, coastal scrub and
mangroves. DISTRIBUTION: Resident in E, S, SW, C Myanmar, W, S Thailand and NW
Peninsular Malaysia.

**4 STREAK-THROATED WOODPECKER (LITTLE SCALY-BELLIED
WOODPECKER)** *Picus xanthopygaeus* 30cm FIELD NOTES: Generally solitary. Spends a
great deal of time foraging on the ground. In flight shows a yellow rump. VOICE: A sharp
queemp, otherwise rather silent. HABITAT: Deciduous forests and open areas with scattered
trees. DISTRIBUTION: Resident in SW China, W, C, S Myanmar, W, NW, NE Thailand,
Cambodia, S Laos and S Vietnam.

5 RED-COLLARED WOODPECKER *Picus rabieri* 30cm FIELD NOTES: Usually
found singly, in pairs or as a member of a mixed-species feeding flock. Generally forages
low down on trunks or on the ground. VOICE: Not recorded. Drums in fast irregular rolls.
HABITAT: Primary and secondary semi-evergreen forest. DISTRIBUTION: Resident in SW
China, Laos and C, N Vietnam.

6 BLACK-HEADED WOODPECKER *Picus erythropygius* 31–35cm FIELD NOTES:
Active, generally encountered in small, noisy groups. Forages in the canopy, understorey,
on stumps and on the ground. Black-billed race *P. e. nigrigenis* (6b) occurs in Myanmar
and W Thailand. VOICE: A yelping *ka-tek-a-tek-a-tek-a-tek…* or *cha-cha-cha…cha-cha-
cha…* also gives a low double note. HABITAT: Deciduous dry forest and open scrub country.
DISTRIBUTION: Resident in C, S, E Myanmar, W, NW, NE Thailand, Cambodia, C, S Laos
and S Vietnam.

**7 GREY-HEADED WOODPECKER (GREY-FACED or BLACK-NAPED
WOODPECKER)** *Picus canus* 25–26cm FIELD NOTES: Regularly forages on the ground
in search of ants, termites and grubs. In flight shows a yellowish rump. VOICE: A mournful
kiu kiu kiu kiu kiu… or *pew pew pew pew pew…* also gives a *keek…kak kak ka* and a short
kik. HABITAT: Various open forests, including deciduous, moist tropical and native pine.
DISTRIBUTION: Resident throughout, except C, S Thailand, C Vietnam (N Annam) and
Singapore.

6b *nigrigenis*

81 WOODPECKERS

1 OLIVE-BACKED WOODPECKER *Dinopium rafflesii* 28cm FIELD NOTES: Forages from low to middle levels, usually singly or in pairs. Moves slowly, with only brief pauses to look for food. VOICE: A slow *ckakchakchakchakchak...* a similar but faster call, longer with 10–50 notes; also a single *chak*. HABITAT: Dense, wet evergreen forests and mangroves. DISTRIBUTION: Resident in S Myanmar (S Tenasserim), W, S Thailand and Peninsular Malaysia.

2 HIMALAYAN FLAMEBACK (HIMALAYAN GOLDENBACK) *Dinopium shorii* 30–32cm FIELD NOTES: Forages on trunks, branches and the ground. Often forms part of mixed-species feeding parties. VOICE: A rapid, tinny *klak-klak-klak-klak-klak-klak*. HABITAT: Deciduous and semi-evergreen forests. DISTRIBUTION: Resident in western Myanmar.

3 COMMON FLAMEBACK (COMMON GOLDENBACK) *Dinopium javanense* 28–30cm FIELD NOTES: Found at all forest levels, although prefers lower parts. Climbing is rapid and erratic. VOICE: A long, trilled *ka-di-di-di-di-di-di...* a *kow* or *kow kow* and a *kowp-owp-owp-owp* uttered in flight. HABITAT: Open deciduous forest, scrub, gardens and occasionally mangroves. DISTRIBUTION: Resident southwards from SW China, except N Myanmar.

4 BLACK-RUMPED FLAMEBACK (LESSER FLAMEBACK or LESSER GOLDENBACK) *Dinopium benghalense* 26–29cm FIELD NOTES: Usually seen in pairs or family parties, also forms part of mixed-species feeding flocks. VOICE: A laughing *kyi-kyi-kyi-kyi* and a strident *kierk*. HABITAT: Light and open deciduous woodland, plantations and trees near villages. DISTRIBUTION: Resident in SW Myanmar.

5 GREATER FLAMEBACK (GREATER GOLDENBACK) *Chrysocolaptes guttacristatus* 33cm FIELD NOTES: Tends to prefer large trees, working up from lower trunk in jerky spurts and spirals. Often seen in mixed-species feeding flocks. VOICE: A single *kik* and a monotone *di-di-di-di-di-di* or similar. HABITAT: Deciduous and broadleaved evergreen forests, forest edge, old plantations and mangroves. DISTRIBUTION: Resident southward from SW China, except C Thailand.

6 PALE-HEADED WOODPECKER *Gecinulus grantia* 25–27cm FIELD NOTES: Noisy. Forages on bamboo, trees, fallen logs and occasionally the ground. Green-headed race G. g viridadanus (6b) occurs in SE China. VOICE: An accelerating, nasal *chaik-chaik-chaik-chaik* or *kweek kwek-kwek* that is repeated four or five times. Drums with fast steady rolls. HABITAT: Bamboo, broadleaved and semi-deciduous forests. DISTRIBUTION: Resident in S, E China, western Myanmar, NW Thailand, Laos and Vietnam.

7 BAMBOO WOODPECKER *Gecinulus viridis* 25–26cm FIELD NOTES: Best located by pecking when foraging, usually alone or in pairs. VOICE: Utters an undulating, dry rattle and a loud, clear *keep-kee-kee-kee-kee-kee*. Also gives a *kweek-week-week-week-week* or similar during encounters with rivals. HABITAT: Bamboo, broadleaved and deciduous forests. DISTRIBUTION: Resident in S, E Myanmar, Thailand (except C), N Laos and Peninsular Malaysia.

8 MAROON WOODPECKER *Blythipicus rubiginosus* 23cm FIELD NOTES: Usually forages low down, on the base of trunks, fallen logs or on the ground. VOICE: A wavering, high-pitched *kik-kik-kik-kik-kik-kik-kik-kik....*that slows at the end, also a descending *chai-chai-chai-chai* or *keek-eek-eek-eek-eek-eek*. Other calls include a *pit, pyick* or *kyak* and a *kik-ik*. HABITAT: Broadleaved evergreen forest, bamboo and secondary growth. DISTRIBUTION: Resident in S Myanmar (S Tenasserim), W, S Thailand and Peninsular Malaysia.

9 BAY WOODPECKER (RED-EARED BAY WOODPECKER) *Blythipicus pyrrhotis* 27–30cm FIELD NOTES: Tends to forage low down on trunks, stumps and fallen logs; generally seen in pairs. B. p. cameroni (9b) occurs in Peninsular Malaysia. VOICE: An undulating, laughing *dit-d-d-di-di-di-di-dit-d-d-di-di-di...* or a *chake chake chake chake* that increases in tempo while dropping in pitch. Various other calls include an accelerating *pee-pee-pee-pee-pee-pee-pee-pee-pee-a* and a series of *kwaa* notes. When disturbed, utters a harsh *kecker-rak kecker-rak*. HABITAT: Broadleaved evergreen, occasionally semi-evergreen forest and mixed deciduous forest, nearby secondary growth and bamboo. DISTRIBUTION: Resident over most of the region, except the far north, C Myanmar, C, SE, S Thailand and Singapore.

172

6b *viridadanus*

9

9b *cameroni*

82 WOODPECKERS

1 ORANGE-BACKED WOODPECKER *Reinwardtipicus validus* 30cm FIELD NOTES:
Usually seen in pairs or small parties foraging on rotten logs, dead tree stumps, main
trunks and branches. Easily detected by loud pecking and hammering. VOICE: A rapid,
trilled *ki-i-i-i-i-i-ik*; also a squeaky *kit kit kit kit kit-it*. HABITAT: Broadleaved evergreen forest.
DISTRIBUTION: Resident in S Thailand and Peninsular Malaysia.

2 BUFF-RUMPED WOODPECKER *Meiglyptes tristis* 17–18cm FIELD NOTES: Active
forager from the canopy of tall trees down to smaller trees and saplings; generally
encountered in pairs. May be found in mixed-species feeding flocks. VOICE: A soft, rattled
drrrrrr… also utters a *pit, chit or pit-pit* and a *peee* when alarmed. HABITAT: Broadleaved
evergreen forest, forest edge and secondary growth. DISTRIBUTION: Resident in S Myanmar
(S Tenasserim), S Thailand and Peninsular Malaysia.

3 BLACK-AND-BUFF WOODPECKER *Meiglyptes jugularis* 22cm FIELD NOTES:
Actions much as Buff-rumped Woodpecker, although not noted as being a member of
mixed-species flocks. VOICE: A nasal *ki-yew* and a rattling *tititit-week week week* or *titititit
weerk weerk weerk…* interspersed with a *ki-yew*. HABITAT: Bamboo, open broadleaved
evergreen and semi-evergreen forest. DISTRIBUTION: Resident in SW, S, E Myanmar, W,
NW, NE, SE Thailand, Cambodia, Laos and C, S Vietnam.

4 BUFF-NECKED WOODPECKER *Meiglyptes tukki* 21cm FIELD NOTES: Forages in the
lower and middle storey, singly, in pairs or as part of a mixed-species feeding group. VOICE: A
high, trilled *kirr-r-r*; also a high-pitched *ti-ti-ti-ti-ti* and a single *pee*. HABITAT: Broadleaved
evergreen forest. DISTRIBUTION: Resident in S Myanmar (S Tenasserim), S Thailand and
Peninsular Malaysia.

5 GREY-AND-BUFF WOODPECKER *Hemicircus concretus* 13–14cm FIELD NOTES:
Forages in the canopy; best located by calls. Moves rapidly between twigs, branches and
leaf clusters. VOICE: A high-pitched, drawn-out *kiyow* or *kee-yew*, a vibrating *chitter* and a
sharp *pit*. HABITAT: Broadleaved evergreen forests. DISTRIBUTION: Resident in S Myanmar (S
Tenasserim), S Thailand and Peninsular Malaysia.

6 HEART-SPOTTED WOODPECKER *Hemicircus canente* 16cm FIELD NOTES:
Squeaky calls often give away the bird's presence. Generally encountered singly or in pairs
searching among the thin branches at the top of tall trees; regular member of mixed-species
feeding parties. VOICE: A squeaky nasal *ki-yew, ch-yew* or *chirrick*; also a high-pitched
kee-kee-kee-kee. Drumming is weak and infrequent. HABITAT: Broadleaved evergreen and
semi-evergreen forest, forest edge and bamboo. DISTRIBUTION: Resident in Myanmar (except
W, N, C), Thailand (except C, S), Cambodia, Laos and S Vietnam.

7 GREAT SLATY WOODPECKER *Mulleripicus pulverulentus* 45–51cm FIELD NOTES:
Regularly encountered in small parties, flying from one forest patch to another, in a loose
follow-my-leader fashion. Climbs trunks and branches of tall trees, although also noted
on small trees and saplings. VOICE: A soft *whu-ick* and a single loud *dwot*, said to sound
somewhere between the bleating of a goat and the barking of a dog. Also utters a whinnying
woi-kwoi-kwoi-kwoi… often in flight. HABITAT: Deciduous, broadleaved evergreen and semi-
evergreen forest, forest edge and mangroves. DISTRIBUTION: Resident south from SW China,
except C Thailand and N Vietnam.

83 PITTAS

1 EARED PITTA (PHAYRE'S PITTA) *Hydrornis phayrei* 22cm FIELD NOTES: Forages on the ground in leaf litter and among rotting logs; progresses in short hops, although said to be more static than others of the family. VOICE: A whistled *whee-ow-whit*, when alarmed utters a dog-like whine or yelp. HABITAT: Broadleaved evergreen and mixed deciduous forest and bamboo. DISTRIBUTION: Resident in S China, C, E, S Myanmar, Thailand (except S, C), Cambodia, Laos and C, N Vietnam.

2 BLUE-NAPED PITTA (NEPAL PITTA) *Hydrornis nipalensis* 22–25cm FIELD NOTES: Feeds on the ground, moving in short hops, stopping to turn over leaves or dig for food. Juvenile generally dark brown with dark buff spots above and below; belly and vent white. VOICE: A sharp *chow-whit, uk-wuip* or *ip-wuiip*; feeding couples utter soft chuckles. HABITAT: Usually near water, in tropical and subtropical secondary forest, bamboo and clearings with dense vegetation. DISTRIBUTION: Resident in S China, W, N, S Myanmar, N, C Laos and N Vietnam.

3 BLUE-RUMPED PITTA *Hydrornis soror* 22–24cm FIELD NOTES: Forages on the ground on snails, insects and earthworms; uses rocks and stones for cracking snail shells. Female slightly browner on mantle. Green-headed race *P. s. douglasi* (3b) occurs in Hainan. VOICE: A full, repeated *weaoe* or *weeya*, also a frog-like *ppew* or *eau*; when agitated may give a sharp *hwit* or *hwip*. HABITAT: Broadleaved evergreen, semi-evergreen and deciduous forest; also secondary forest. DISTRIBUTION: Resident in S China, SE Thailand, Cambodia, Laos (except N) and Vietnam.

4 RUSTY-NAPED PITTA *Hydrornis oatesi* 21–25cm FIELD NOTES: Forages on the ground among leaf litter. Brighter-crowned race *P. o. castaneiceps* (4b) occurs in SW China, C Laos and Vietnam (W Tonkin and N Annam). VOICE: Utters a sharp, repeated *chow-whit* and sometimes an explosive, descending *poouw;* when alarmed gives a *tchick* or *chek* that lengthens to a *chur-r-r-rt* or *wer-r-r-rt* when an intruder approaches the nest site. HABITAT: Broadleaved evergreen forest and bamboo. DISTRIBUTION: Resident in SW China, N, S, E Myanmar, W, NE, NW Thailand, Laos, C, N Vietnam and Peninsular Malaysia.

5 GIANT PITTA *Hydrornis caeruleus* 25–29cm FIELD NOTES: Forages on the ground among leaf litter. Feeds on snails, earthworms, frogs, small snakes and large insects; uses rocks and stones to smash snail shells. VOICE: A slow, mournful *hwoo-er*, a soft, repeated *wheer* and a falling *pheeeeeeoou.* HABITAT: Bamboo and broadleaved evergreen forest. DISTRIBUTION: Resident in S Myanmar (S Tenasserim), S Thailand and Peninsular Malaysia.

6 BLUE PITTA *Hydrornis cyaneus* 22–24cm FIELD NOTES: Forages on the ground, digging with bill in a thrush-like manner. Juvenile like a very dull female; mantle, crown and wings brown, underparts blotched and streaked brown; dull buff supercillium and dark eye-stripe. VOICE: A liquid *pleoow-whit.* HABITAT: Broadleaved evergreen forest and moist areas in mixed deciduous forest. DISTRIBUTION: Resident in SW, S, E Myanmar, Thailand (except C), Cambodia, Laos and Vietnam (except W Tonkin and Cochinchina).

7 MALAYAN BANDED PITTA *Hydrornis irena* 21–24cm FIELD NOTES: Forages on the ground, recorded scratching at the ground, much like a chicken, when searching for food. VOICE: A short, repeated *pouw* or *poww*; a whirring *kirr* or *pprrr* also a hollow *whup* and a moaning *who-oo.* HABITAT: Broadleaved evergreen and secondary forest. DISTRIBUTION: Resident in S Thailand and Peninsular Malaysia.

84 PITTAS

1 GURNEY'S PITTA *Hydrornis gurneyi* 18–21cm FIELD NOTES: Forages on the ground among leaf litter, tosses leaves aside with lateral flicks of bill. VOICE: A short, explosive *lilip*, repeated every 2–6 seconds. Utters a squeaky, falling *skyeew* when alarmed. HABITAT: Broadleaved evergreen forest, secondary forest and old rubber plantations near forests. DISTRIBUTION: Resident in S Myanmar (S Tenasserim) and S Thailand.

2 BAR-BELLIED PITTA (ELLIOT'S PITTA) *Hydrornis elliotii* 19–21cm FIELD NOTES: Forages by pecking at the ground or turns over leaves with bill in search of food. VOICE: A loud, repeated *chawee-wu, tu-wi-whil* or *per-ur-wu*; sometimes a mellow *hhwee-hwha*. When alarmed utters a harsh, shrill *jeeow* or *jow*. HABITAT: Bamboo, broadleaved evergreen, semi-evergreen and mixed deciduous forest; appears to prefer moist areas. DISTRIBUTION: Resident in NE, SE Thailand, Cambodia, Laos and Vietnam.

3 GARNET PITTA *Erythropitta granatina* 15–16cm FIELD NOTES: Forages on the ground, among leaf litter and around fallen branches and logs. Juvenile generally dull brown with dull blue on wings and tail; reddish nape. VOICE: A drawn-out monotone whistle that increases in volume; when agitated utters a purring *prrr prrr prrr*. HABITAT: Broadleaved evergreen forest. DISTRIBUTION: Resident in S Myanmar (S Tenasserim), S Thailand and Peninsular Malaysia.

4 HOODED PITTA *Pitta sordida* 19cm FIELD NOTES: Feeds on the ground; often perches on vines or branches while singing. Juvenile duller, underparts dirty buff, and lacks red vent. VOICE: A loud *whew-whew*. HABITAT: Broadleaved evergreen forest, secondary forest, mixed deciduous forest and old rubber plantations adjacent to forests. DISTRIBUTION: Summer visitor to SW China, Myanmar, W, NE, SE, Thailand, Cambodia, N, S Laos and N Vietnam (W Tonkin); resident in S Thailand and Peninsular Malaysia.

5 MANGROVE PITTA *Pitta megarhyncha* 20cm FIELD NOTES: Forages on muddy areas around mangrove roots and on nearby dryer ground. Juvenile duller; crown barred blackish. VOICE: A loud *tae-laew* or *wieuw-wieuw*. HABITAT: Mangroves. DISTRIBUTION: Mainly coastal resident in Myanmar, S Thailand, Peninsular Malaysia and Singapore.

6 BLUE-WINGED PITTA *Pitta moluccensis* 18–21cm FIELD NOTES: Forages on the ground, hops like a thrush. Juvenile duller and lacks the red belly and vent. VOICE: A loud, clear *taew-laew taew-laew*, repeated every few seconds; when alarmed utters a harsh *skyeew*. HABITAT: Open broadleaved evergreen and mixed deciduous forest, secondary growth, bamboo, mangroves, parks and gardens. DISTRIBUTION: Breeding visitor to SW China, S, SW, E Myanmar, Thailand (except C), Cambodia, Laos, C, S Vietnam and N Peninsular Malaysia; winter visitor in Peninsular Malaysia and Singapore.

7 FAIRY PITTA *Pitta nympha* 19cm FIELD NOTES: Forages on the ground among leaf litter. VOICE: A clear whistled *kwah-he-kwa-wu* also a *kriaih* or *kahei-kahei* given when alarmed. HABITAT: Broadleaved evergreen forest. DISTRIBUTION: Summer visitor in China and Taiwan; passage migrant in Vietnam.

85 BROADBILLS; GERYGONE; WHISTLER

1 DUSKY BROADBILL *Corydon sumatranus* 25–29cm FIELD NOTES: Small, noisy flocks occur in the upper storey; sitting quietly before making short sallies to pick insects off foliage. VOICE: Shrill, upward inflected whistles, also a shrill, falling *pseeoo.* HABITAT: Broadleaved evergreen, semi-evergreen and wet areas in mixed deciduous forest. DISTRIBUTION: Resident in S Myanmar, Thailand (except C), Cambodia, Laos, C, S Vietnam and Peninsular Malaysia.

2 BLACK-AND-RED BROADBILL *Cymbirhynchus macrorhynchos* 20–24cm FIELD NOTES: Unobtrusive; sits motionless for long periods. VOICE: An accelerating series of *parnk* notes and grating cicada-like notes; also various churrings, melodious whistles and a monotonous, repeated *tyook.* When alarmed, utters a rapid *pip-pip-pip-pip…* HABITAT: Broadleaved evergreen and semi-evergreen forests, forest edge near water, freshwater swamp forest and mangroves. DISTRIBUTION: Resident in SW, S Myanmar, W, SE, S Thailand, Cambodia, S Laos, S Vietnam (Cochinchina) and Peninsular Malaysia.

3 BANDED BROADBILL *Eurylaimus javanicus* 21–23cm FIELD NOTES: Often encountered in small, slow-moving parties in the middle storey. VOICE: A sharp *wheeoo* followed by a frantic, rising series of notes; also a nasal *whee-u,* a falling *kyeeow,* a rolling *keowrr* and a yelping *keek-eek-eek.* HABITAT: Broadleaved evergreen, semi-evergreen and wet areas in mixed deciduous forest. DISTRIBUTION: Resident in S Myanmar, Thailand (except C), Cambodia, Laos, S Vietnam and Peninsular Malaysia.

4 BLACK-AND-YELLOW BROADBILL *Eurylaimus ochromalus* 13–15cm FIELD NOTES: Small groups forage in the middle to upper storey. Generally sits quietly before making short sallies to capture insects from foliage. VOICE: A rapid, frantic series of notes, starting slowly then gradually gaining speed. HABITAT: Broadleaved evergreen forest. DISTRIBUTION: Resident in S Myanmar (Tenasserim), W, S Thailand and Peninsular Malaysia.

5 SILVER-BREASTED BROADBILL *Serilophus lunatus* 18cm FIELD NOTES: Forages in pairs or small groups, gleaning prey from branches or foliage; also makes short aerial sallies after flying insects. Grey-faced race *S. l. rubropygius* (5b) occurs in SW, W, N Myanmar. VOICE: A soft, musical *chir-r-r-r;* also a squeaky *ki-uu.* HABITAT: Broadleaved evergreen, bamboo and mixed deciduous forest. DISTRIBUTION: Resident southward from SW China, except C Thailand, S Vietnam and Singapore.

6 LONG-TAILED BROADBILL *Psarisomus dalhousiae* 28cm FIELD NOTES: Encountered in small, loose parties; forages by gleaning or making short sallies after flying insects. VOICE: A loud, sharp *tseeay-tseeay-tseeay-tseeay…* or *pseew-pseew-pseew-pseew…* HABITAT: Broadleaved evergreen and semi-evergreen forest. DISTRIBUTION: Resident south from SW China, except C Thailand, S Vietnam and Singapore.

7 GREEN BROADBILL *Calyptomena viridis* 15–17cm FIELD NOTES: Quiet; forages mainly in the lower levels and understorey. Has a preference for fruiting figs. VOICE: A soft, bubbling *toi toi-oi-oi-oi-oick* that starts quietly and then increases in tempo; also utters a *goik-goik, goik-goik-doyik,* a loud *oik,* a frog-like *oo-turr* and various wheezes, whines and cackles. HABITAT: Broadleaved evergreen forest. DISTRIBUTION: Resident in S Myanmar (Tenasserim), W, S Thailand and Peninsular Malaysia.

8 GOLDEN-BELLIED GERYGONE *Gerygone sulphurea* 10–11cm FIELD NOTES: Often gleans insects from the underside of leaves in the tree crown. VOICE: Various high-pitched whistles, also a rising *chu-whee.* HABITAT: Mangroves and coastal scrub, inland freshwater swamp forests, plantations, parks and gardens. DISTRIBUTION: Resident in coastal and inland S Thailand, S Vietnam, Peninsular Malaysia and Singapore.

9 MANGROVE WHISTLER *Pachycephala cinerea* 17cm FIELD NOTES: Unobtrusive and sluggish, gleans insects from trunks and branches. Juvenile has rusty edges to wing coverts and secondaries. VOICE: A rising, clear whistle, repeated 3 or 4 times. HABITAT: Mangroves and nearby vegetation, plantations and wooded gardens. DISTRIBUTION: Resident, mainly coastal, south of China, except N Vietnam (E Tonkin and N, C Annam).

86 JAYS; MAGPIES

1 CRESTED JAY *Platylophus galericulatus* 31–33cm FIELD NOTES: Generally encountered in pairs or small parties, foraging in the low to middle canopy. VOICE: An excited, stacatto, chattering rattle; also a single *chik* usually delivered while foraging in foliage. HABITAT: Broadleaved evergreen forest. DISTRIBUTION: Resident in S Myanmar (S Tenasserim), S, W Thailand and Peninsular Malaysia.

2 BLACK MAGPIE *Platysmurus leucopterus* 39–41cm FIELD NOTES: Usually found in pairs or small parties. Forages in trees from lower to upper canopy. When perched repeatedly bobs and bows head. VOICE: Noisy, varied vocabulary, including a loud, discordant *keh-eh-eh-eh-eh*, a bell-like *tel-ope* and *kontingka-longk*. Also utters a xylophone-like *tok-tok terklingk-klingk-klingk…* HABITAT: Broadleaved evergreen forest, forest edge and, occasionally, mangroves. DISTRIBUTION: Resident in S Myanmar (S Tenasserim), S Thailand, Peninsular Malaysia and Singapore.

3 SICHUAN JAY *Perisoreus internigrans* 30cm FIELD NOTES: Can be quite inquisitive, but usually unobtrusive; forages in the dense foliage of conifers at mid-storey level. Best located by mewing calls. VOICE: A high *kyip-kyip*, sometimes repeated to make a longer series; also a buzzard-like mewing note. HABITAT: Steep mountainside spruce and pine forest. DISTRIBUTION: Possibly occurs in the mountainous forests in the north-central parts of the region.

4 BLUE MAGPIE (RED-BILLED BLUE MAGPIE) *Urocissa erythrorhyncha* 66cm FIELD NOTES: Social. Mainly arboreal, often feeding in the canopy of fruiting trees. VOICE: A sharp, strident *chweh-chweh-chweh-chweh…* or *chwit-wit-wit…* Also gives a shrill *shrii* and a quieter *kluk*. HABITAT: Deciduous forest, secondary growth, bamboo and, occasionally, open broadleaved evergreen forest. DISTRIBUTION: Resident in China, Hainan, Myanmar (except Tenasserim), Thailand (except S), Cambodia, Laos and Vietnam.

5 GOLD-BILLED MAGPIE (YELLOW-BILLED BLUE MAGPIE) *Urocissa flavirostris* 63cm FIELD NOTES: Usually in pairs or small parties; forages both in trees and on the ground. VOICE: Various loud, harsh creaking and grating calls; also squealing whistles and mimicry. Transcribed as *bu-zeep-peck-peck-peck*, *pop-unclear*, *pu-pu-weer* and a high *clear-clear*. HABITAT: Broadleaved evergreen and open pine forest. DISTRIBUTION: Resident in SW, S China, W, N Myanmar and N Vietnam (W Tonkin).

6 TAIWAN BLUE MAGPIE *Urocissa caerulea* 69cm FIELD NOTES: Shy and wary; usually encountered in small parties foraging in the canopy. VOICE: A soft *kwee-eep* or *swee-eee*, usually uttered when relaxed; when alarmed gives a cackling *kyak-kyak-kyak-kyak*. HABITAT: Deciduous hill forests, lower forests in winter. DISTRIBUTION: Resident in Taiwan.

7 WHITE-WINGED MAGPIE *Urocissa whiteheadi* 45–46cm FIELD NOTES: Very social, forages in parties of 20–25 birds. Black-tailed race *U. w. xanthomelana* (7b) occurs in S China, Laos and Vietnam. VOICE: A harsh, rising *errreep errreep*, a hoarse, rising *shureek*, a low hoarse *churrreee* and a liquid, rippling *brrriii brrriii…* HABITAT: Broadleaved evergreen forest, forest edge and secondary forest. DISTRIBUTION: Resident in Hainan, S China, Laos and C, N Vietnam.

7b
xanthomelana

87 TREEPIES

1 HOODED TREEPIE (HOODED RACKET-TAILED TREEPIE) *Crypsirina cucullata* 29–31cm FIELD NOTES: Usually encountered in pairs or small parties.VOICE: A quiet purring *drrrriii-k;* also various discordant, harsh call notes. HABITAT: Open deciduous woodland, thorn-scrub jungle, bamboo and cultivation borders. DISTRIBUTION: Resident in W, N, C, S Myanmar.

2 RACKET-TAILED TREEPIE (BLACK RACKET-TAILED TREEPIE) *Crypsirina temia* 30–33cm FIELD NOTES: Generally found singly, in pairs or in small parties. Agile; forages in shrubbery. VOICE: A rasping *churg-churg, grasp-grasp, chrrrk-chrrrk* or *chrrrk-churrrk.* HABITAT: Various open lowland forests, including mixed deciduous woodland, bamboo and mangroves. DISTRIBUTION: Resident in SW China, E, S Myanmar, Thailand, Cambodia, Laos and Vietnam.

3 RATCHET-TAILED TREEPIE (NOTCH-TAILED TREEPIE) *Temnurus temnurus* 32cm FIELD NOTES: Unobtrusive, usually seen singly or in pairs; sluggish. Best located by persistent calls. VOICE: Calls include a ringing *clee-clee-clee,* a harsh *graak-graak* and a squeaky, rising *eeup-eeup-eeup.* Also utters a ringing *clipeeee,* a hollow *pupueeee* and a rasping, rippling *rrrrrrr.* HABITAT: Broadleaved evergreen forest, forest edge, bamboo and secondary growth. DISTRIBUTION: Resident in Hainan, Vietnam, C Laos, W Thailand and S Myanmar (S Tenasserim).

4 RUFOUS TREEPIE (INDIAN TREEPIE) *Dendrocitta vagabunda* 46–50cm FIELD NOTES: Usually encountered in pairs or small parties, with much larger groups where food is plentiful; also joins mixed feeding flocks to feed in fruiting trees. Juvenile has head and upper breast brown. VOICE: A flute-like *ko-ki-la,* often mixed with a harsh rattle. Also utters a variety of harsh metallic and mewing notes. HABITAT: Open wooded areas, cultivations parks and gardens. DISTRIBUTION: Resident in SW China, Myanmar, Thailand (except C, S), Cambodia, C, S Laos and S Vietnam.

5 GREY TREEPIE (HIMALAYAN TREEPIE) *Dendrocitta formosae* 36–40cm FIELD NOTES: Regularly found in small parties. Forages mainly in trees but will descend to feed on the ground; often forms part of mixed-species feeding flocks. Juvenile duller, with less black on chin and forehead. VOICE: A loud, rapid *klok-kli-klok-kli-kli;* also a variety of short harsh and musical calls. When alarmed, gives a Magpie-like chatter. HABITAT: Deciduous montane woodland, included tropical evergreen forest, scrubby hillsides with scattered trees, forest edge and clearings. DISTRIBUTION: Resident in Taiwan, Hainan, China, Myanmar, W, NW, NE Thailand, N, C Laos and N Vietnam.

6 COLLARED TREEPIE (BLACK-FACED or BLACK-BROWED TREEPIE) *Dendrocitta frontalis* 38cm FIELD NOTES: Arboreal, forages in small parties in dense forest; noted making flycatching sorties, much like a drongo. VOICE: Little recorded, said to have typical harsh, musical or grating treepie calls. HABITAT: Humid evergreen foothill forest with bamboo. DISTRIBUTION: Resident in SW China, N Myanmar and N Vietnam.

88 JAYS; MAGPIES; NUTCRAKER; CHOUGHS

1 JAY (EURASIAN JAY) *Garrulus glandarius* 34cm FIELD NOTES: Harsh alarm call can be the first sign of bird's presence. In flight shows a prominent white rump. Various races in the region including G. *g. leucotis* (main illustration), which occurs in S China, C, E Myanmar, Thailand, Cambodia, C, S Laos and S Vietnam; G. *g. oatesi* (1b) in W, C Myanmar; G. *g. sinensis* (1c) in C, E, S China and N Myanmar and G. *g. taivanus* (1d) in Taiwan. VOICE: A harsh *skaaaak-skaaaak* and a weak *piyeh*. HABITAT: Open broadleaved evergreen, pine, mixed evergreen and pine and deciduous forests; also forest edge. DISTRIBUTION: Resident in Taiwan, Hainan, China, Myanmar, W, NW, NE Thailand, Cambodia, C, S Laos and S Vietnam.

2 GREEN MAGPIE (COMMON GREEN MAGPIE) *Cissa chinensis* 37–39cm FIELD NOTES: Inconspicuous; presence is usually given away by whistled calls. Generally forages low down in shrubbery or in forest understorey. Post breeding forms small flocks, which are often part of mixed-species feeding parties. Golden-crowned race *C. c. margaritae* (2b) occurs in S Vietnam (S Annam). VOICE: Loud and variable shrieks, whistles and chattering. Calls include a *peep-peep*, *kik-wee*, a soft, chattering *churrk chak-chak-chak* and a short *chuurk-chak*. HABITAT: Broadleaved evergreen and mixed deciduous forest. DISTRIBUTION: Resident southwards from S China, except C, SE, S Thailand, Cambodia, S Vietnam (Cochinchina) and Singapore.

3 INDOCHINESE GREEN MAGPIE (EASTERN or YELLOW-BREASTED GREEN MAGPIE) *Cissa hypoleuca* 31–35cm FIELD NOTES: Actions similar to Green Magpie. Hainan race *C. h. katsumatae* (not illustrated) is more greenish below; yellower tail has a blue-grey tip. VOICE: Variable, including a loud, shrill *peeeoo-peeeoo-peeeoo-peeeoo…* a clipped, shrill *peu-peu-peu*, an abrupt *weep* and a long piercing *peeeeooo*. HABITAT: Broadleaved evergreen forest, semi-evergreen forest and bamboo. DISTRIBUTION: Resident in S China, Hainan, S, E Thailand, Cambodia, Laos (except N) and Vietnam (except W Tonkin).

4 AZURE-WINGED MAGPIE *Cyanopica cyanus* 34cm FIELD NOTES: Sociable, forms small family parties in breeding season, and larger parties post breeding. VOICE: A shivering *screep*, uttered by roving parties. Also a harsh chatter, a sharp *wee-wee-wee-u* and a harsh *karrah* alarm call. HABITAT: Mixed and deciduous woodland, forest edge, parks and well-wooded gardens. DISTRIBUTION: Resident in the NE of the region (NE, E China).

5 NUTCRACKER (SPOTTED NUTCRACKER) *Nucifraga caryocatactes* 32cm FIELD NOTES: Generally in pairs or small parties. Mainly arboreal, although will descend to feed on nuts dropped on the forest floor. First sightings are often of birds flying lazily from one treetop to another. VOICE: Quiet, musical, piping, whistling, clicking, squeaking and whining notes interspersed with some mimicry. Also utters a dry *kraaaak* call, often repeated to form a discordant rattle and a weak *zhree*. HABITAT: Conifer or conifer-dominated mixed forest. DISTRIBUTION: Resident in W China, Taiwan and N Myanmar.

6 MAGPIE (EURASIAN or BLACK-BILLED MAGPIE) *Pica pica* 45cm FIELD NOTES: Usually in pairs or small parties. VOICE: A chattering *chack-chack-chack-chack-chack…* also an enquiring *ch-chack* and a squealing *keee-uck*. HABITAT: Very varied, including open woodland, lightly wooded open country, cultivations, parks, gardens, towns and cities. DISTRIBUTION: Resident in Taiwan, Hainan, China, N, C, E Myanmar, N Laos and Vietnam; vagrant in Thailand.

7 ALPINE CHOUGH (YELLOW-BILLED CHOUGH) *Pyrrhocorax graculus* 38cm FIELD NOTES: Encountered in flocks, usually at higher elevations than Chough. VOICE: A descending, thin *sweeeoo*, a rippling *preep* and a rolling *churr*. HABITAT: High mountains, mountain pastures and cultivations. DISTRIBUTION: Possibly occurs in the mountainous areas of W China.

8 CHOUGH (RED-BILLED CHOUGH) *Pyrrhocorax pyrrhocorax* 38cm FIELD NOTES: Sociable, often in large flocks post breeding. VOICE: A far-carrying *chee-aw*, *chaow*, *chi-ah* or similar. HABITAT: Mountains, alpine pastures and cultivations. DISTRIBUTION: Possibly occurs in mountain areas of SW China.

2b *margaritae*

1

2

3

1b
oatesi

1c
sinensis

1d *taivanus*

4

5

6

7

8

89 CROWS

1 DAURIAN JACKDAW *Corvus dauuricus* 32cm FIELD NOTES: Sociable, usually in small flocks. Often feeds among grazing cattle and regularly associates with other crows. VOICE: In flight utters a short *chak*. HABITAT: Open meadowland with stands of trees, riverine plains and foothills and near human habitations. DISTRIBUTION: Resident in W China; winter visitor in C, E China.

2 HOUSE CROW (INDIAN HOUSE CROW) *Corvus splendens* 40cm FIELD NOTES: Bold, very sociable. VOICE: A flat, dry *kaaa-kaaa*. HABITAT: Villages, towns and cities, often common around ports; also in cultivated areas. DISTRIBUTION: Resident in SW China, Myanmar, Peninsular Malaysia and Singapore.

3 COLLARED CROW *Corvus torquatus* 54cm FIELD NOTES: Generally found in pairs or small parties. Sometimes forms mixed flocks with Large-billed Crow. VOICE: A loud, often repeated *kaaarr*, a *kaar-kaar* and various cawing, creaking and clicking notes. HABITAT: Open lowland cultivation with scattered trees, parks and gardens. DISTRIBUTION: Resident in C, E, S China, Hainan and N Vietnam (E Tonkin).

4 ROOK *Corvus frugilegus* 47cm FIELD NOTES: Baggy thighs compared to other crows. Juveniles have face feathered. Usually in flocks accompanied by other crows. VOICE: A dry *kraah* and a higher-pitched *kraa-a*. HABITAT: Mainly agricultural land with stands of trees. DISTRIBUTION: Resident in the north of the region; winter visitor in E China; vagrant in Hainan and Taiwan.

5 SLENDER-BILLED CROW *Corvus enca* 43–47cm FIELD NOTES: Regularly encountered in small flocks foraging in the forest canopy. VOICE: A high-pitched, nasal *ka ka ka-a-a*, a dry *ahk-ahk-ahk* and an explosive, croaking *krok kok-kok*. When excited utters a *caaaw* or *aaaaw* interspersed with a nasal, twanging *pe-yong* or *ne-awh*. HABITAT: Broadleaved evergreen forest and occasionally mangroves. DISTRIBUTION: Resident in Peninsular Malaysia.

6 LARGE-BILLED CROW *Corvus macrorhynchos* 41–49cm FIELD NOTES: Usually seen singly or in pairs; roosts colonially. Longer-billed race *C. m. levaillantii* (6b) occurs in Myanmar and northern Thailand and is sometimes considered a separate species (Eastern Jungle Crow). VOICE: A hoarse *kyarrh kyarrh* or *kyearh kyearh;* eastern birds utter a distinctive *nyark nyark*. HABITAT: Open forest and woodland, mangroves, open country and near habitations. DISTRIBUTION: Resident throughout the region.

7 CARRION CROW *Corvus corone* 52–56cm FIELD NOTES: Usually in pairs or small groups. Mainly a terrestrial feeder, often seen scavenging on carcases. VOICE: A vibrant *kraaa*, often repeated; sometimes utters a hollow *konk-konk*. HABITAT: Open country, cultivations and near habitations. DISTRIBUTION: Winter visitor to SW, SE, E China; vagrant in N Vietnam.

8 RAVEN (COMMON or NORTHERN RAVEN) *Corvus corax* 66cm FIELD NOTES: Wary, usually seen singly or in pairs; may be in larger groups at a rich food source or roosts. In flight shows a distinctive wedge-shaped tail. VOICE: A deep, hollow *pruk-pruk-pruk;* also various other croaks and a guttural rattle. HABITAT: Mountains, mountain plateau and rugged open country. DISTRIBUTION: Possibly occurs in the mountainous areas of SW China.

6b *levaillantii*

90 ORIOLES

1 SLENDER-BILLED ORIOLE *Oriolus tenuirostris* 23–26cm FIELD NOTES: Arboreal, usually stays hidden in foliage; attracted to fruit-bearing trees. Juvenile has a diffuse black line through eye; throat, breast and flanks streaked black. VOICE: A drawn-out *wheeow* or a liquid *chuck-tarry-you;* also a high-pitched *kich* and a cat-like *miaow.* HABITAT: Pine forests, open woods, plantations and open country with scattered trees. DISTRIBUTION: Resident in SW China, Myanmar (except N), N, S Laos and S Vietnam (S Annam). Winter visitor to W, NW, NE Thailand, may breed.

2 BLACK-NAPED ORIOLE *Oriolus chinensis* 27cm FIELD NOTES: Actions and habits similar to Slender-billed Oriole. Juvenile very similar to Slender-billed Oriole. VOICE: A liquid, fluty *luwee – wee – wee-leeow* or similar; also a harsh scolding *kyerrr,* which is often repeated. HABITAT: Open woodland, plantations, mangroves, parks and gardens. DISTRIBUTION: Summer visitor over most of China and N Laos; resident in SW China, Taiwan, Hainan, SW Myanmar, S Thailand, Peninsular Malaysia and Singapore. Winter visitor in the south, except SW, W, N Myanmar and N Vietnam.

3 BLACK-HOODED ORIOLE *Oriolus xanthornus* 25cm FIELD NOTES: Mainly arboreal, usually singly or in pairs, sometimes in small parties post breeding. Attracted to fruiting trees. Juvenile has the head duller with forehead and eye-ring yellow; throat and upper breast whitish streaked black. VOICE: A melodious, fluty *why-you* or *why-you-you* often interspersed with harsh *cheeahs* and *kwaaks.* HABITAT: Open broadleaved forest, well-wooded areas, cultivations, parks and wooded gardens. DISTRIBUTION: Breeds in SW China; resident in Myanmar, Thailand, Laos, Cambodia, C, S Vietnam and NW Peninsular Malaysia.

4 DARK-THROATED ORIOLE *Oriolus xanthonotus* 20–21cm FIELD NOTES: Usually forages from the middle storey to the forest canopy; sometimes part of mixed-species feeding flocks. VOICE: A melodious, fluty *tu-u-liu* or *peu-peu-peu-poh,* the last note a descending rasp. Call is a high-pitched, piping *kyew, pheeu* or *ti-u.* HABITAT: Broadleaved evergreen forest, forest edge and secondary growth. DISTRIBUTION: Resident in S Myanmar (S Tenasserim), S Thailand, Peninsular Malaysia and Singapore.

5 SILVER ORIOLE *Oriolus mellianus* 28cm FIELD NOTES: Usually forages in the canopy, singly or in pairs; forms part of mixed-species feeding flocks. VOICE: Fluty whistles and a cat-like call. HABITAT: Broadleaved evergreen and semi-evergreen forests. DISTRIBUTION: Breeds in S China; winter visitor in W, NE, SE Thailand and Cambodia; vagrant in NW Thailand.

6 MAROON ORIOLE *Oriolus traillii* 24–28cm FIELD NOTES: Arboreal, tends to keep to the tops of trees, singly or in a pair; often part of mixed-species flocks. Redder race *O. t. ardens* (6b) is resident in Taiwan. VOICE: A harsh *kee-ah* followed by a rich, fluty *pi-lo-lo.* HABITAT: Broadleaved evergreen forest, forest edge and, occasionally, deciduous forest. DISTRIBUTION: Breeding visitor to SW China; resident in Taiwan, Hainan, Myanmar (except Tenasserim), W, NW, NE Thailand, Cambodia, Laos and Vietnam (except Cochinchina). Winter visitor in W, NE, SE Thailand, N Laos and N Vietnam.

7 BLACK-AND-CRIMSON ORIOLE *Oriolus cruentus* 23–25cm FIELD NOTES: Forages singly or in pairs, from the understorey to the canopy; regularly joins mixed-species feeding flocks. VOICE: A short, melodious call and a hard *kek kreo;* also a shrill cat-like *keeeeu* or *squee-ee* and a strained *hhsssu* or *hsiiiu.* HABITAT: Broadleaved evergreen forest. DISTRIBUTION: Resident in Peninsular Malaysia.

91 CUCKOOSHRIKES; TRILLER

1 LARGE CUCKOOSHRIKE *Coracina macei* 30cm FIELD NOTES: On landing, flicks wings alternately. Usually forages in the tops of trees, in pairs or loose parties. Darker race *C. m. rexpineti* (1b) occurs in SE China, Taiwan, N Laos and N Vietnam. Race *C. m. larutensis* (1c), resident in Peninsular Malaysia, is sometimes considered a race of Javan Cuckooshrike. VOICE: A loud, whistled *tee-treee, ti-eee or pee-eeo-pee-eeo*, often uttered while flying from tree to tree. HABITAT: Open broadleaved evergreen forest and mixed deciduous forest, pine forest and open wooded country. DISTRIBUTION: Resident in SW, SE, E China, Hainan, Taiwan and throughout the south, except S Thailand, Peninsular Malaysia and Singapore.

2 BAR-BELLIED CUCKOOSHRIKE (BARRED CUCKOOSHRIKE) *Coracina striata* 27–30cm FIELD NOTES: Tends to keep to the top of trees; often part of mixed-species feeding parties. VOICE: A clear whinnying *kliu-kliu-kliu-kliu* and a shrill *kriiu-kriiu*. HABITAT: Broadleaved evergreen forest, freshwater swamp forest, forest edge and occasionally mangroves and plantations. DISTRIBUTION: Resident in S Thailand and Peninsular Malaysia.

3 BLACK-WINGED CUCKOOSHRIKE *Coracina melaschistos* 24cm FIELD NOTES: Arboreal. Active and conspicuous, forages singly or in pairs; regularly joins mixed-species feeding flocks. Very dark race *C. m. saturata* (3b) is resident in Hainan and N Vietnam and winters in NW Thailand, Cambodia and S Laos; *C. m. intermedia* (3c) breeds in China and winters in S China, Taiwan, S Myanmar, S Thailand and S Vietnam. VOICE: A slow, descending *twii-twii-weeo-weeow* or similar. HABITAT: Broadleaved evergreen forest; wintering birds occasionally in deciduous forests, open woods and gardens. DISTRIBUTION: Summer visitor in China; resident in Hainan, W, N, E Myanmar, W, NW, NE Thailand, N Laos, C, N Vietnam; winter visitor in Taiwan, C, S Myanmar, Thailand (except S), Cambodia, Laos and Vietnam.

4 INDOCHINESE CUCKOOSHRIKE *Coracina polioptera* 21–22cm FIELD NOTES: Slow, deliberate forager in the middle to upper storey; sometimes joins mixed-species feeding parties. Darker race *C. p. jabouillei* (4b) is resident in Vietnam (N, C Annam). VOICE: A high-pitched, descending *wi-wi-wi-wi-wu* or similar; also a nasal *uh uh uh uh-ik*. HABITAT: Deciduous, semi-deciduous and pine forests, locally also in peatswamp forest. DISTRIBUTION: Resident in W, C, E, S Myanmar, W, NW, NE Thailand, Laos, Cambodia and Vietnam (except W, E Tonkin).

5 LESSER CUCKOOSHRIKE *Coracina fimbriata* 19–21cm FIELD NOTES: Forages in the canopy and is frequently part of mixed-species feeding flocks. VOICE: A loud, clear *whit-it-it-chui-choi*; also a rapid *whit-whit-whit-whit-whit-whit*. When alarmed utters a squeaky, nasal *wherrrh-wherrrh-wherrrh…* and a high *whit-weei*. HABITAT: Broadleaved evergreen forest, secondary growth and plantations. DISTRIBUTION: Resident in S Myanmar (S Tenasserim), S Thailand, Peninsular Malaysia and Singapore.

6 BLACK-HEADED CUCKOOSHRIKE *Coracina melanoptera* 19–20cm FIELD NOTES: Forages in tall trees, usually singly, in pairs or in small parties. Also a regular member of mixed-species feeding flocks. VOICE: A mellow whistle followed by a rapid, repeated *pit-pit-pit*. HABITAT: Open deciduous and semi-deciduous forest, secondary growth, plantations and wooded gardens. DISTRIBUTION: Scarce winter visitor in SW, W Myanmar.

7 PIED TRILLER *Lalage nigra* 18cm FIELD NOTES: Usually occurs singly, in pairs or small groups, foraging at all levels; occasionally hunts on the ground in short grass. VOICE: A nasal *chaka-chevu*; also a rattling *wheek chechechecheche-chuk*. HABITAT: Coastal scrub, plantations and gardens. DISTRIBUTION: Resident in S Thailand, Peninsular Malaysia and Singapore.

1c *larutensis*

1b
rexpineti

1

3b
saturata

4b

jabouillei

3

4

3c
intermedia

5

6

7

92 MINIVETS

1 ROSY MINIVET *Pericrocotus roseus* 20cm FIELD NOTES: More sluggish than other minivets; often sits quietly at the top of trees. May occur in large flocks post breeding. VOICE: A whirring trill. HABITAT: Deciduous and semi-deciduous forest; occasionally open broadleaved evergreen forest. DISTRIBUTION: Summer visitor or resident in S China, Myanmar and N Vietnam (E Tonkin); winter visitor to Thailand, N, S Laos and S Vietnam.

2 SWINHOE'S MINIVET *Pericrocotus cantonensis* 20cm FIELD NOTES: Forages in the canopy, often part of mixed-species feeding flocks. VOICE: A metallic trill. HABITAT: Broadleaved evergreen forest, semi-evergreen forest, deciduous forest and forest edge. DISTRIBUTION: Breeds in China; winter visitor to S Myanmar, Thailand, Cambodia, Laos and S, C Vietnam.

3 ASHY MINIVET *Pericrocotus divaricatus* 18cm FIELD NOTES: Often in large flocks, forages in the outer branches of tree canopy. Regularly joins mixed-species flocks. VOICE: A jangling metallic trill, usually uttered in flight. HABITAT: Various woodlands, open areas with scattered trees, plantations and mangroves. DISTRIBUTION: Winter visitor south of China, except SW, N, E Myanmar and N Vietnam; passage migrant in China.

4 SMALL MINIVET *Pericrocotus cinnamomeus* 16cm FIELD NOTES: Flits about among foliage in search of insects, also makes short flycatching sallies. Often part of mixed-species feeding flocks. Dark race *P. c. sacerdos* (4b) occurs in Cambodia and S Vietnam. VOICE: A constantly repeated *tswee-swee*. HABITAT: Deciduous forest, forest edge, open areas with trees and gardens. DISTRIBUTION: Resident south of China, except N Myanmar, S Thailand, N Vietnam, Peninsular Malaysia and Singapore.

5 FIERY MINIVET *Pericrocotus igneus* 15–16cm FIELD NOTES: Often occurs in groups, foraging in the tree canopy. VOICE: A thin *swee-eet*. HABITAT: Broadleaved evergreen forest and forest edge. DISTRIBUTION: Resident in S Myanmar (S Tenasserim), S Thailand and Peninsular Malaysia.

6 JERDON'S MINIVET *Pericrocotus albifrons* 15–17cm FIELD NOTES: Usually in pairs or small parties. Regularly perches on bushes or long grass from where it drops to the ground to pick up prey; also hovers over grassland before dropping onto prey. VOICE: Various sweet, high-pitched notes, such as *thi, tuee* and *tchu-it*; also a soft *tchip* or *tsip-i-sip*. HABITAT: Open, dry scrub with scattered trees and dry cultivation. DISTRIBUTION: Resident in C, S Myanmar.

7 SHORT-BILLED MINIVET *Pericrocotus brevirostris* 19cm FIELD NOTES: Forages among foliage, in pairs or as part of mixed-species feeding flocks. VOICE: A thin, repeated *tsuuuit*; also a dry *tup*. HABITAT: Broadleaved evergreen forest, forest edge; sometimes pine forest. DISTRIBUTION: Summer visitor in southern China; resident in W, N, E, S Myanmar, NW Thailand, Laos and N Vietnam.

8 SCARLET MINIVET *Pericrocotus speciosus* 20–22cm FIELD NOTES: Gleans insects from foliage, also hovers or makes short sallies to capture flying insects. VOICE: A piercing *sweep-sweep-sweep-sweep* or similar. HABITAT: Forests and wooded areas. DISTRIBUTION: Resident south from C China, except C Thailand.

9 LONG-TAILED MINIVET *Pericrocotus ethologus* 20cm FIELD NOTES: Forages mainly in the canopy, actions much like Scarlet Minivet. VOICE: A sweet, rolling *prrr-wi prrr-wi* or *prrr-i prrr-i*; also a sibilant *swii-swii swii-swii-swii…* HABITAT: Broadleaved evergreen forest, pine forest and forest edge. DISTRIBUTION: Summer visitor in SW, W China; resident in W, N, E Myanmar, NE, NW Thailand and S Vietnam (S Annam). Winter visitor in C, E, S Myanmar, Laos and N Vietnam.

10 GREY-CHINNED MINIVET *Pericrocotus solaris* 17–19cm FIELD NOTES: Actions and habits similar to Scarlet Minivet. Dark-chinned race *P. s. montanus* (10b) occurs in Peninsular Malaysia. VOICE: A repeated *tzee-zip*, a slurred *swirrririit*; also a soft *trip* or stronger *trii-ti*. HABITAT: Broadleaved evergreen forest, forest edge and occasionally pine forests. DISTRIBUTION: Resident throughout, except the far north (China), SW Myanmar, C, SE, S Thailand, S Vietnam and Singapore.

93 MONARCH; PARADISE FLYCATCHERS; FANTAILS

1 BLACK-NAPED MONARCH *Hypothymis azurea* 16cm FIELD NOTES: Active; gleans insects from foliage. Also hovers or makes aerial sallies to capture flying insects. VOICE: A ringing *wii-wii-wii-wii-wii-wii*; also a high-pitched, rasping *sweech-which* or *che-chwe*. HABITAT: Broadleaved evergreen, semi-evergreen, deciduous and peatswamp forest, secondary growth, island forest and overgrown plantations. DISTRIBUTION: Summer visitor in Taiwan; resident in Hainan, S China and throughout the south, except C Thailand and N Vietnam (E Tonkin). Winter visitor to E China and C Thailand.

2 ASIAN PARADISE FLYCATCHER *Terpsiphone paradisi* 20cm; male with tail 45cm FIELD NOTES: Generally hunts from a perch in the lower part of tree canopy; usually in pairs. *T. p. incei* (2b) occurs in China; moves south post breeding. VOICE: A clear rolling *chu-wu-wu-wu-wu-wu...* also a loud *chee-tew* and a harsh *tst*. When mobbing utters a *weep-poor-willie weep-poor-willie*. HABITAT: Broadleaved evergreen forest, secondary growth, mangroves, parks and gardens. DISTRIBUTION: Summer visitor in central and northern parts of China; resident in SE China, most of the south, except N Myanmar, C Thailand, N Laos and N Vietnam. Northern birds migrate through or winter in the south.

3 JAPANESE PARADISE FLYCATCHER *Terpsiphone atrocaudata* 18cm FIELD NOTES: Actions similar to Asian Paradise Flycatcher. Dark race *T. a. periophthalmica* (3b) breeds on Lanyu Islet off SE Taiwan. VOICE: A whistled *tsuki-hi-hoshi-hoi-hoi-hoi*; call is a querulous *jouey*. HABITAT: Forest and forest edge; on migration found in mangroves, parks and wooded gardens. DISTRIBUTION: Resident in Taiwan; scarce winter visitor in S Thailand and Peninsular Malaysia; passage migrant in Thailand, Laos, Vietnam and Singapore.

4 YELLOW-BELLIED FANTAIL *Chelidorhynx hypoxantha* 13–14cm FIELD NOTES: Restless, tail often raised and fanned. Regular member of mixed-species feeding flocks. VOICE: A thin, high-pitched *sip-sip* followed by a feeble trill. HABITAT: Broadleaved evergreen forests. DISTRIBUTION: Resident in SW China, W, N, E Myanmar, NW Thailand, N Laos and N Vietnam (W Tonkin and N Annam).

5 WHITE-THROATED FANTAIL *Rhipidura albicollis* 17cm FIELD NOTES: Restless forager, often working up and down main tree trunk or nearby branches; also makes flycatching sallies. Tail often fanned and held erect. VOICE: A descending *tut-tut-tut-sit-sit-sit-sit* or *tsu sit tsu sit sit sit-tsu*; call is a sharp *cheep*, *jick* or chuck. HABITAT: Broadleaved evergreen forest, cultivations, parks and wooded gardens. DISTRIBUTION: Resident in western half of China, Hainan, Myanmar, Thailand (except C), Cambodia, Laos, Vietnam (except Cochinchina) and Peninsular Malaysia.

6 WHITE-BROWED FANTAIL *Rhipidura aureola* 17cm FIELD NOTES: Active forager, constantly flicking wings and fanning tail; gleans prey from foliage or makes sallies to capture flying insects. Often part of mixed-species feeding flocks. VOICE: A rising then descending series of tinkling notes, transcribed as *chee-chee-cheweechee-vi*; also utters a harsh *chuck-chuck*. HABITAT: Mixed deciduous forests and dry dipterocarp forest. DISTRIBUTION: Resident in SW China, Myanmar (except SW), W, NW Thailand, Cambodia, C, S Laos and C Vietnam.

7 PIED FANTAIL (MALAYSIAN PIED FANTAIL) *Rhipidura javanica* 17–20cm FIELD NOTES: Active, constantly on the move in vegetation interspersed with flycatching sallies. Regularly joins mixed-species feeding flocks. VOICE: A squeaky *chew-weet chew-weet chew-weet-chew* and various chattering and squawking calls. HABITAT: Mangroves, peatswamp forest, secondary growth, scrub, plantations, parks and gardens. DISTRIBUTION: Resident, mainly coastal, in S Myanmar (Tenasserim), Thailand (except NW), Cambodia, Laos (along the Mekong River), S Vietnam, Peninsular Malaysia and Singapore.

8 SPOTTED FANTAIL *Rhipidura perlata* 17–18cm FIELD NOTES: Active forager in the middle and upper storey; makes regular sallies after flying insects. Prominent member of mixed-species feeding flocks. VOICE: A melodious *chilip pechilip-chi*. HABITAT: Broadleaved evergreen forest. DISTRIBUTION: Resident in S Thailand and Peninsular Malaysia.

1

♀

♂

2

white
phase

♂

2b

♂ *incei*

rufous
phase

♀

3b

periophthalmica

♂

4

5

3

♀

♂

6

7

8

♂

94 DRONGOS

1 BLACK DRONGO *Dicrurus macrocercus* 30cm FIELD NOTES: Uses a prominent perch from where it makes flycatching sallies. Captures prey in the air or pounces on insects on the ground; attracted to areas where grazing animals disturb insects. VOICE: A harsh *ti-tui*, rasping *jeez, cheece* or *cheece-cheece-chichuk*. HABITAT: Open country, cultivations, scrub and roadsides. DISTRIBUTION: Mainly summer visitor in China; resident in Hainan, Taiwan and throughout the south, except S Thailand, Peninsular Malaysia and Singapore. Northern birds winter throughout the south.

2 ASHY DRONGO *Dicrurus leucophaeus* 30cm FIELD NOTES: Makes flycatching sorties from the tops of trees. The grey race *D. l. salangensis* (2b) is a winter visitor in S Myanmar (Tenasserim), C, SE, S Thailand, Cambodia, N, S Vietnam and Peninsular Malaysia. VOICE: Varied and complex; includes a harsh *cheece-cheece-chichuck* followed by a querulous *kil-kil-kil-kil* or *tililili*, a loud *tchik wu-wit tchik wu-wit* and a wheezy *phuuuu* or *hieeeeer*. HABITAT: Forest clearings, forest edge, secondary growth, mangroves and coastal scrub. DISTRIBUTION: Summer visitor to China; resident in Hainan and throughout the south, except Singapore. Northern birds winter in the south.

3 CROW-BILLED DRONGO *Dicrurus annectans* 28cm FIELD NOTES: Keeps to tall undergrowth and lower tree branches, making flycatching sallies from a hidden perch. VOICE: Loud, musical whistles, chatterings and churrs. HABITAT: Broadleaved evergreen forest, mixed deciduous forest, mangroves, coastal scrub, secondary growth and plantations. DISTRIBUTION: Summer visitor to China, Hainan, C, W, NW Thailand, C, S Laos and N Vietnam; winter visitor in S Myanmar (S Tenasserim), SE, S Thailand, Peninsular Malaysia and Singapore.

4 BRONZED DRONGO *Dicrurus aeneus* 24cm FIELD NOTES: Arboreal, mainly in treetops; makes flycatching sallies after flying insects. A regular member of mixed-species feeding parties. VOICE: Loud, clear musical whistles. HABITAT: Broadleaved evergreen, semi-evergreen and deciduous forest, forest edge and secondary growth. DISTRIBUTION: Resident in Taiwan, Hainan, S China and throughout the south, except C Thailand and Singapore.

5 HAIR-CRESTED DRONGO *Dicrurus hottentottus* 32cm FIELD NOTES: Arboreal, attracted to flowering trees; feeds mainly on nectar. VOICE: A loud *chit-wiii*, also single *wiii* calls. HABITAT: Broadleaved evergreen, semi-evergreen and deciduous forests, secondary growth, parks and gardens. DISTRIBUTION: Summer visitor to China; resident in Myanmar, W, NW, NE, SE Thailand, Cambodia, Laos and Vietnam. Northern birds move south after breeding.

6 LESSER RACKET-TAILED DRONGO *Dicrurus remifer* 25cm, with tail up to 40cm FIELD NOTES: Arboreal; makes bold, dashing pursuits after flying insects, mainly in the canopy. Races *D. r. peracensis* and *D. r. lefoli* (not illustrated), south and east from S Myanmar (Tenasserim), have the tail spatulas thinner and longer. VOICE: A range of loud, metallic, musical whistles; also mimics the calls of other bird species. HABITAT: Broadleaved evergreen and semi-evergreen forests. DISTRIBUTION: Summer visitor in southern China; resident throughout the south, except C Thailand and Singapore.

7 GREATER RACKET-TAILED DRONGO *Dicrurus paradiseus* 30cm, with tail up to 65cm FIELD NOTES: Gleans insects from foliage or flowers; also makes flycatching sallies. Regular member of mixed-species parties. Race *D. p. grandis* (7b) occurs in SW China, N, E Myanmar, N Laos and N Vietnam. VOICE: A monotonous *kit-kit-kit-kit-kit…* HABITAT: Broadleaved evergreen, semi-evergreen, deciduous and peatswamp forests, secondary growth and plantations. DISTRIBUTION: Summer visitor in SW China; resident in Hainan and throughout the south.

8 ANDAMAN DRONGO *Dicrurus andamanensis* 32cm FIELD NOTES: Arboreal; gregarious, often in flocks of 12–20 birds. Regularly clings to tree trunks, woodpecker-like, when searching for insects; also makes flycatching sallies. VOICE: A variety of sharp metallic notes. HABITAT: Forests. DISTRIBUTION: Resident in the Coco Islands.

95 FAIRY BLUEBIRD; LEAFBIRDS; IORAS

1 ASIAN FAIRY-BLUEBIRD *Irena puella* 25cm FIELD NOTES: Forages in the tops of trees, especially those in fruit. Keeps on the move, hopping from branch to branch and flying from tree to tree. VOICE: A percussive, liquid *weet-weet be-quick peepit whats-it*, usually repeated every few seconds. In flight utters a sharp *chichichichik*. HABITAT: Broadleaved evergreen forest and, occasionally, in mixed deciduous forest. DISTRIBUTION: Resident southwards from SW China, except C Thailand.

2 GREATER GREEN LEAFBIRD *Chloropsis sonnerati* 20–23cm FIELD NOTES: Frequents the middle to upper storey, singly or in pairs; sometimes part of mixed-species feeding parties. VOICE: Musical whistles interspersed with brief chattering notes; also indulges in mimicry. HABITAT: Broadleaved evergreen forest and occasionally mangroves. DISTRIBUTION: Resident in S Myanmar (S Tenasserim), W, S Thailand, Peninsular Malaysia and Singapore.

3 LESSER GREEN LEAFBIRD *Chloropsis cyanopogon* 16–19cm FIELD NOTES: Forages in the canopy, singly or in pairs; often a member of mixed-species feeding flocks. Race *C. c. septentrionalis* (3b) occurs in S Myanmar (S Tenasserim), SW Thailand and N Malaysia Peninsular. VOICE: A loud, varied, sequence of rich warbling phases, including deep mellow notes. HABITAT: Broadleaved evergreen forest, open forest and forest edge. DISTRIBUTION: Resident in S Myanmar (S Tenasserim), Peninsular Malaysia and Singapore.

4 BLUE-WINGED LEAFBIRD *Chloropsis cochinchinensis* 20cm FIELD NOTES: Acrobatic searcher of insects, fruit and nectar; often part of mixed-species flocks. Yellow-headed race *C. c. moluccensis* (4b) occurs in S Thailand, Peninsular Malaysia and Singapore. VOICE: Various sweet musical notes; also mimics other species. HABITAT: Deciduous and broadleaved evergreen forests, forest edge and secondary growth. DISTRIBUTION: Resident southwards from SW China.

5 GOLDEN-FRONTED LEAFBIRD *Chloropsis aurifrons* 19cm FIELD NOTES: Acrobatic forager in the thick foliage of trees, singly in pairs or in small parties. VOICE: A musical *swich-chich-chich-weee*; also a repeated *tzik* and a *chup-chaw*. Mimics the calls of other species. HABITAT: Mixed deciduous, dry dipterocarp, broadleaved and semi-broadleaved evergreen forest and secondary growth. DISTRIBUTION: Resident in SW China and throughout the south, except S Thailand, N Vietnam, Peninsular Malaysia and Singapore.

6 ORANGE-BELLIED LEAFBIRD *Chloropsis hardwickii* 20cm FIELD NOTES: Forages in tree foliage, acrobatically probing flowers for nectar and leaves for insects. Race *C. h. lazulina* (6b) is resident in Hainan. VOICE: Various ringing and melodious calls. Said to have the sweetest song of all leafbirds. HABITAT: Broadleaved evergreen forest and forest edge. DISTRIBUTION: Resident in S, E China, Hainan, Myanmar, W, NW, NE Thailand, N, C Laos, Vietnam (except Cochinchina) and Peninsular Malaysia.

7 COMMON IORA *Aegithina tiphia* 14cm FIELD NOTES: Acrobatic forager in the canopy. *A. t. horizoptera* (7b) occurs in S Myanmar (Tenasserim), W, S Thailand, Peninsular Malaysia and Singapore; *A. t. deignani* (7c) is resident in W, N, C, S Myanmar. VOICE: Various strident, unmusical, whistling and whining songs. HABITAT: Open forests, mangroves, freshwater and peatswamp forest, secondary growth, plantations, parks and gardens. DISTRIBUTION: Resident in SW China and throughout the south.

8 GREEN IORA *Aegithina viridissima* 12–15cm FIELD NOTES: Forages in tree foliage, in pairs or small parties; regularly forms part of mixed-species feeding flocks. VOICE: A thin, high-pitched *itsu tsi-tu tsi-tu*; also a chattering *tit-teeer* and a subdued *chititititit*. HABITAT: Broadleaved evergreen forest, mangroves and forest edge. DISTRIBUTION: Resident in SW China, S Myanmar (S Tenasserim), S Thailand and Peninsular Malaysia.

9 GREAT IORA *Aegithina lafresnayei* 15–18cm FIELD NOTES: Regular member of mixed-species feeding flocks. Yellow-faced race *A. l. xanthotis* (9b) occurs in Cambodia and S Vietnam. VOICE: A clear *chew-chew-chew…* HABITAT: Broadleaved evergreen, semi-evergreen and mixed deciduous forest; also forest edge. DISTRIBUTION: Resident in SW China, SW, S Myanmar, Thailand, Cambodia, Laos, Vietnam and Peninsular Malaysia.

3b *septentrionalis*

2 ♀

3b ♂

1 ♀

1 ♂

3 ♀

3 ♂

4b ♂

4 ♀

4 ♂

moluccensis

5

6

6b *lazulina*

6 ♀

6 ♂

7 ♀

7 ♂

dark morph

7b *horizoptera*

7c *deignani* ♂

9 ♂

9b *xanthotis*

8 ♀

8 ♂

9 ♀

9 ♂

96 SHRIKES; WOODSHRIKES

1 TIGER SHRIKE (THICK-BILLED SHRIKE) *Lanius tigrinus* 17cm FIELD NOTES: Perches in cover more than most *Lanius* species; captures insect prey from leaves and branches. VOICE: Song is quiet and musical; calls are a repeated *tcha* and a sharp *tchik*. HABITAT: Open forest, forest edge and clearings. DISTRIBUTION: Breeds in the north of the region; winter resident in S, E China, Peninsular Malaysia and Singapore. Passage migrant over much of the south.

2 BULL-HEADED SHRIKE *Lanius bucephalus* 19cm FIELD NOTES: Behaves like a typical shrike: uses a prominent perch to launch flights to capture prey from on or near the ground. In flight shows white flashes at base of primaries. VOICE: A noisy, chattering *ju-ju-ju.* HABITAT: Light hill forest, tree-lined agricultural land and light riverine forest. DISTRIBUTION: Winter visitor in C, E China; vagrant in C Vietnam.

3 BROWN SHRIKE *Lanius cristatus* 18cm FIELD NOTES: Actions as Bull-headed Shrike. Grey-headed race *L. c. lucionensis* (3b) is a winter visitor throughout the south. VOICE: A subdued jerky warble that includes mimicry; also a harsh *chr-r-r-ri.* HABITAT: Forest edge, scrub and open cultivations. DISTRIBUTION: Summer visitor to the east and north of the region; resident in E China. Winter visitor in Taiwan, S, E China, Hainan and throughout the south.

4 BURMESE SHRIKE *Lanius collurioides* 20cm FIELD NOTES: Confiding; feeding actions similar to Bull-headed Shrike. VOICE: Sweet, with musical and grating notes; when alarmed utters a rapid, harsh *chikachikachitchit* or similar. HABITAT: Open woodland, forest edge, clearings, secondary growth and cultivations. DISTRIBUTION: Resident in S China, Myanmar (except NW, S, SW), W, NW Thailand, Cambodia, Laos, C, S Vietnam. Winter visitor in SW Myanmar and N Vietnam.

5 LONG-TAILED SHRIKE *Lanius schach* 24cm FIELD NOTES: Noisy, restless and aggressive; otherwise actions typical of most *Lanius* shrikes. Race *L. s. tricolor* (5b) occurs in SW China, N Myanmar, N Laos and N Thailand; '*fuscatus*' morph (5c) occurs in Hainan, SE China and N Vietnam (E Tonkin). VOICE: A metallic warble that often contains mimicry; also utters a harsh *tchick* and a scolding *chaak-chaak* when alarmed. HABITAT: Open wooded country, cultivations and gardens. DISTRIBUTION: Resident throughout, except SW, S Myanmar, Cambodia and S Vietnam.

6 GREY-BACKED SHRIKE (TIBETAN SHRIKE) *Lanius tephronotus* 22cm FIELD NOTES: Feeding actions as Bull-headed Shrike. In flight shows a rufous rump. VOICE: A prolonged, subdued, melodious warble interspersed with mimicry; also harsh grating calls. HABITAT: Forest clearings, high-altitude scrub; winters in open country, scrub and cultivations. DISTRIBUTION: Breeds in W China; resident in SW China. Winter visitor to northern Myanmar and northern Thailand, Cambodia, Laos and N Vietnam.

7 CHINESE GREY SHRIKE (LONG-TAILED SHRIKE) *Lanius sphenocercus* 29cm FIELD NOTES: Uses a prominent perch as a lookout, usually hovers for 10–30 seconds before dropping on prey. VOICE: A nasal *tsceee*, usually given when alarmed. HABITAT: Open country with scattered trees and bushes. DISTRIBUTION: Winter visitor to E China.

8 LARGE WOODSHRIKE *Tephrodornis virgatus* 23cm FIELD NOTES: Usually in small parties in treetops; occasionally makes aerial sallies after flying insects. *T. v. hainanus* (8b) is resident in Hainan, N Laos and N Vietnam. VOICE: A ringing *kew-kew-kew-kew*; also a harsh *chreek-chreek-chreek…* HABITAT: Broadleaved evergreen forests, mixed deciduous forest, forest edge and secondary growth. DISTRIBUTION: Resident in Hainan, S, E China and throughout the south, except C Thailand and Singapore.

9 COMMON WOODSHRIKE *Tephrodornis pondicerianus* 18cm FIELD NOTES: Forages among foliage, in pairs or small parties. VOICE: A plaintive *weet-weet* followed by a quick *whi-whi-whi-whee*; also soft trills when breeding. HABITAT: Dry dipterocarp and mixed deciduous forest; also open country with scattered trees. DISTRIBUTION: Resident in Myanmar, W, NW, NE, C Thailand, Cambodia, C, S Laos and S Vietnam.

3b *lucionensis*

♀

♂ n-br

♀

3

1

2

♂ br

4

5b
tricolor

5

6

7

♂

5c '*fuscatus*'

♀

8

8b *hainanus*

♀

♂

♂

9

97 PHILENTOMAS; FLYCATCHER-SHRIKES; WOODSWALLOWS; WAXWINGS

1 RUFOUS-WINGED PHILENTOMA *Philentoma pyrhoptera* 16–17cm FIELD NOTES: Sluggish. Frequents the lower to middle storey, also in low undergrowth and on the ground. VOICE: A mellow, piping *tu-tuuuuu,* also harsh scolding notes. HABITAT: Broadleaved evergreen forest. DISTRIBUTION: Resident in S Myanmar (S Tenasserim), S Thailand and Peninsular Malaysia.

2 MAROON-BREASTED PHILENTOMA *Philentoma velata* 19–21cm FIELD NOTES: Often sits motionless for long periods. Movements generally sluggish but will make sallies after flying insects; frequents middle to upper storey. VOICE: A clear, bell-like *phu phu phu phu phu…* also a strong, *clear chut-ut chut-ut chut-ut…* and a grating, metallic *churr.* HABITAT: Broadleaved evergreen forest. DISTRIBUTION: Resident in S Myanmar (Tenasserim), W, S Thailand and Peninsular Malaysia.

3 BLACK-WINGED FLYCATCHER-SHRIKE *Hemipus hirundinaceus* 13–15cm FIELD NOTES: Hovers to snatch insects from terminal foliage and makes short sallies to capture flying insects. Often part of mixed-species feeding flocks. VOICE: A course *tu-tu-tu-tu hee-tee-tee-teet* and a *hee-too-weet* interspersed with a high *cheet-weet-weet-weet.* HABITAT: Broadleaved evergreen forest, freshwater swamp forest and forest edge, occasionally plantations and mangroves. DISTRIBUTION: Resident in S Myanmar (S Tenasserim), S Thailand and Peninsular Malaysia.

4 BAR-WINGED FLYCATCHER-SHRIKE *Hemipus picatus* 15cm FIELD NOTES: Makes flycatching sallies from regularly used perches. Brown-backed race *H. p. capitalis* (4b) occurs in SW China, N, C, E Myanmar, NW Thailand, N Laos and N Vietnam. VOICE: A sharp *chisik* or *chir-up*; also a high-pitched trilling. HABITAT: Open forests, plantations, mangroves and coastal vegetation. DISTRIBUTION: Resident in SW, S China and throughout the south, except C Thailand and Singapore.

5 ASHY WOODSWALLOW *Artamus fuscus* 19cm FIELD NOTES: Gregarious, groups often perch together on bare treetop branches or wires from where aerial sallies are made after flying insects. VOICE: A harsh *chek-chek-chek* or *chake-chake-chake*; the latter sets off and finishes a pleasant twittering song. HABITAT: Open areas with scattered trees. DISTRIBUTION: Resident in S China, Hainan and throughout the south, except S Myanmar (S Tenasserim), S Thailand, Peninsular Malaysia and Singapore.

6 WHITE-BREASTED WOODSWALLOW *Artamus leucorynchus* 19cm FIELD NOTES: Actions similar to Ashy Woodswallow. VOICE: A chattering that includes mimicry; calls include a rasping *wek-wek-wek* and sharp *pirt pirt.* HABITAT: Open areas with scattered trees. DISTRIBUTION: Resident in coastal W Peninsular Malaysia and the Coco Islands.

7 WAXWING (BOHEMIAN WAXWING) *Bombycilla garrulus* 18cm FIELD NOTES: Gregarious, occurring in small to large parties; can be quite confiding. Flight Starling-like. Juvenile duller with shorter crest; lacks the black throat. VOICE: A shivering, trilled *sirrrr*; feeding flocks utter a low twittering. HABITAT: Open areas with fruiting trees and bushes. DISTRIBUTION: Winter visitor to the NE corner of the region; vagrant elsewhere in China and Taiwan.

8 JAPANESE WAXWING *Bombycilla japonica* 16cm FIELD NOTES: Gregarious. Crest held erect more often than Waxwing. VOICE: A high-pitched, lisping *hee-hee-hee.* HABITAT: Various areas with fruiting bushes and trees. DISTRIBUTION: Winter visitor to the NE of the region; vagrant elsewhere in China and Taiwan.

blue morph

♂

♀

1

♂

2

♀

♂

3

♀

♂

4b *capitalis*

4

♂

♀

♂

5

7

♀

6

♂

8

98 ROCK THRUSHES; WHISTLING THRUSHES

1 BLUE-CAPPED ROCK THRUSH *Monticola cinclorhynchus* 17cm FIELD NOTES:
Mainly arboreal, picks insects off trunks and branches; also feeds on the ground among leaf
litter. VOICE: A fluty *tew-li-di – tew-li-di – tew-li-di* or *tra-trr-treee-tree-treea...* HABITAT: Open
pine and oak forests, also rocky grass-covered slopes with scattered trees; winters in moist
forest and well-wooded areas. DISTRIBUTION: Recorded in SW Myanmar.

2 BLUE ROCK THRUSH *Monticola solitarius* 20cm FIELD NOTES: Forages on
the ground or drops onto prey from a low perch; sometimes makes aerial sorties after
flying insects. Rufous-bellied race M. *s. philippensis* (2b) breeds in China and winters
throughout the south. VOICE: A loud, fluty, melodic *chu sree chur tee tee wuchi-trr-trrt-
tri* that may include some mimicry. Also utters a deep *chak-chak*, a plaintive *see* and a
wit-wit. HABITAT: Open rocky areas, cliffs, cultivations, roadsides and urban buildings.
DISTRIBUTION: Resident in China, N Myanmar, S Thailand, N Laos, N Vietnam (W
Tonkin) and Peninsular Malaysia; winter visitor throughout the south.

3 CHESTNUT-BELLIED ROCK THRUSH *Monticola rufiventris* 23cm FIELD NOTES:
Forages mainly on the ground, occasionally makes flycatching sorties from high trees.
VOICE: A pleasant warble and a sharp whistle followed by an upslurred *fweeeur-fweet* that
is usually delivered from a treetop. Also utters a *quock*, a course *quach* and a shrill *tick*.
HABITAT: Open broadleaved evergreen and coniferous forests on rocky hillsides, forest
edge, scrub and rocky outcrops. DISTRIBUTION: Resident in China, W, N, E Myanmar, NW
Thailand, N Laos and N Vietnam.

4 WHITE-THROATED ROCK THRUSH *Monticola gularis* 18cm FIELD NOTES:
Forages on the ground or in small trees. VOICE: Melancholic, flute-like, rising whistles
combined with a *chat-at-at* call. Calls include a sharp *tack-tack*, a soft *queck-queck* and a
thin *tsip*, the latter given in flight. HABITAT: Open deciduous and broadleaved evergreen
forest, plantations and secondary growth. DISTRIBUTION: Winter visitor to SW, E China
and throughout the south, except SW, N, S Myanmar, C Thailand, N Vietnam, Peninsular
Malaysia and Singapore. Passage migrant or vagrant in N Vietnam, Peninsular Malaysia
and Singapore.

5 MALAYAN WHISTLING THRUSH *Myophonus robinsoni* 25–26cm FIELD NOTES:
Very shy. Forages on the ground and in the lower storey of trees; occasionally seen on
mountain roadsides at dawn or dusk. VOICE: A soft mix of fluty and scratchy notes, similar to
that of Blue Whistling Thrush; also a high-pitched *tsee*. HABITAT: Broadleaved evergreen
forest, usually near streams. DISTRIBUTION: Resident in Peninsular Malaysia.

6 TAIWAN WHISTLING THRUSH *Myophonus insularis* 28cm FIELD NOTES: Forages
on the ground, usually close to rivers or streams. Wary; when disturbed flees into cover
with shrieking alarm calls. VOICE: A screeching *zi* or *sui yi*. HABITAT: Dense broadleaved
evergreen forest with bamboo, near rivers or streams. DISTRIBUTION: Resident in Taiwan.

7 BLUE WHISTLING THRUSH *Myophonus caeruleus* 33cm FIELD NOTES: Generally
seen feeding from rocks in strong flowing streams, dipping to collect food from the water's
surface. Yellow-billed race M. *c. temminckii* (7b) occurs in much of Myanmar and NW
Thailand. VOICE: A disjointed string of melodious, high-pitched, human-like whistles;
sometimes includes mimicry. Calls include a far-carrying *tzeet-tze-tze-tzeet* or *tzeet-tzuit-
tzuit-zuit* and a shrill *skreee*. HABITAT: Broadleaved evergreen and mixed deciduous
forests, usually with rocky rivers or streams, waterfalls and occasionally mangroves.
DISTRIBUTION: Summer visitor to C, E China; resident in SW China and throughout the
south, except C Thailand and S Vietnam (Cochinchina).

1

♀

♂

2b *philippensis*

♂

2

♀

♂

♀

3

♂

♀

4

♂

6

5

7

7b *temminckii*

99 THRUSHES

1 CHESTNUT-CAPPED THRUSH *Geokichla interpres* 17–19cm FIELD NOTES: Shy, usually singly or in pairs; forages from the ground to mid storey. VOICE: Flute-like, rising whistles, interspersed with chirrups, transcribed as *see it-tu-tu tyuu…* Calls include a harsh *tac* and a high-pitched, falling *tsi-i-i-i.* HABITAT: Broadleaved evergreen forest. DISTRIBUTION: Resident in S Thailand and Peninsular Malaysia.

2 ORANGE-HEADED THRUSH *Geokichla citrina* 20–23cm FIELD NOTES: Shy, forages on the ground in thick vegetation and forest undergrowth, also feeds in fruiting trees and bushes. May form into small flocks post breeding. G. c. innotata (2b) occurs in SW China, E Myanmar, N, NE Thailand, Laos, Cambodia and S Vietnam; moves south in winter. G. c. melli (2c) is resident in E China. VOICE: A loud, clear series of lilting phrases; calls include a soft *chuk* and a screeching *kreeee* or *teer-teer-teer.* HABITAT: Broadleaved evergreen forest, forest edge, secondary growth and thickets. DISTRIBUTION: Summer visitor in N Myanmar, NW, NE Thailand; resident in S, E China, Hainan, SW, W, S Myanmar, W Thailand, Cambodia and C Vietnam. Winter visitor in S Thailand, S Vietnam and Peninsular Malaysia. Passage migrant or vagrant elsewhere.

3 SIBERIAN THRUSH *Geokichla sibirica* 22cm FIELD NOTES: Secretive; feeds on the ground or in trees when in fruit. VOICE: A weak *tseee*, a soft *zit* and a gruff squawk when alarmed. HABITAT: Broadleaved evergreen forests. DISTRIBUTION: Winter visitor in Vietnam (W Tonkin and S, C Annam), Laos, Peninsular Malaysia and Singapore; passage migrant over much of the region.

4 SICHUAN THRUSH *Zoothera griseiceps* 26cm FIELD NOTES: Generally shy and unapproachable; feeds mainly on the ground. Very similar, newly described Himalayan Thrush Z. salimalii may occur in extreme SW of China. VOICE: Variable, rich musical phrases such as *plee-too ti-ti-ti* or *plee-too ch-up-ple-ooop*; calls include a thin *chuck* and a rattling alarm. HABITAT: Rhododendron and coniferous forest, low vegetation and rocky areas above the tree line. DISTRIBUTION: Resident in SW, W China and N Myanmar; winters in N Vietnam (W Tonkin) and S China.

5 LONG-TAILED THRUSH *Zoothera dixoni* 27–28cm FIELD NOTES: Secretive; feeds on the ground in thick vegetation. VOICE: Often starts with a *w-t-it* followed by a slow, slurred *wu-ut – cheet-sher – wut-chet-shuur*, interspersed with twitters and *too-ee* phrases. HABITAT: Broadleaved evergreen forest, coniferous and rhododendron forests. DISTRIBUTION: Resident in SW, W China, N Myanmar; winter visitor in E Myanmar, NW Thailand, N Laos and possibly W Myanmar and N Vietnam (W Tonkin).

6 SCALY THRUSH *Zoothera dauma* 27cm FIELD NOTES: Forages on the ground in thick cover; moves with a nervous jerky gait. VOICE: Repeated slow phrases, sometimes interspersed with squeaks and twitters. Calls include a soft *tsi* and a drawn-out *tzeep*; when alarmed utters a *chuck-chuck.* HABITAT: Mainly broadleaved evergreen forest. DISTRIBUTION: Summer visitor in SC China; resident in SW China, Taiwan, W, N, Myanmar, W, NW, NE Thailand, N Laos and N, S Vietnam (W, E Tonkin and S Annam). Winter visitor in W China and throughout the south, except SE, S Thailand, Cambodia, S Vietnam, Peninsular Malaysia and Singapore.

7 LONG-BILLED THRUSH *Zoothera monticola* 28cm FIELD NOTES: Forages on the ground in thick cover. VOICE: A melancholic series of plaintive whistles; *te-e-uw* or *sew-a-tew-tew*; when alarmed utters a loud *zaaaaaaa.* HABITAT: Fir forests, broadleaved evergreen forest, forest edge and bamboo, usually with nearby rocky streams. DISTRIBUTION: Resident in W, N Myanmar and N Vietnam (W Tonkin).

8 DARK-SIDED THRUSH *Zoothera marginata* 25cm FIELD NOTES: Very shy; often seen feeding in moist stream beds. VOICE: A thin whistle; calls include a low *chuck* and, when alarmed, a high-pitched *pit-pit-pit.* HABITAT: Dense broadleaved evergreen forest with nearby streams or moist areas. DISTRIBUTION: Resident in SW China, Myanmar (except N, C), Thailand (except C, S), Laos and Vietnam (W, E Tonkin and N, S Annam).

2b *innotata*

♂

♀

2c *melli*

♂

1

2

♂

♀

3

♂

4

5

6

7

8

100 THRUSHES

1 GREY-BACKED THRUSH *Turdus hortulorum* 24cm FIELD NOTES: Very shy; spends long periods in tree foliage. Feeds on the ground amongst leaf litter. In winter may be in loose flocks. VOICE: A series of loud fluty whistles; calls include a harsh *chack-chack*, a low chuckle and a shrill *chee* when alarmed. HABITAT: Broadleaved evergreen forest, open forests and secondary growth. DISTRIBUTION: Winter visitor in W, C, S China and N Vietnam (E Tonkin and N Annam).

2 BLACK-BREASTED THRUSH *Turdus dissimilis* 23cm FIELD NOTES: Forages on the ground and also in fruiting trees and bushes. VOICE: A sweet lilting series of short-spaced notes; calls include a thin *seeee* and a resounding *tuc tuc tuc*. HABITAT: Breeds in oak and coniferous forest, broadleaved evergreen forest and secondary growth; post breeding also occurs in scrub jungle and mangroves. DISTRIBUTION: Resident in SW China and W, N, E Myanmar; winter visitor in NW Thailand, C Laos and N Vietnam (E, W Tonkin).

3 JAPANESE THRUSH *Turdus cardis* 22cm FIELD NOTES: Usually shy, feeds on the ground or in fruiting trees; post breeding may associate with flocks of Siberian Thrushes or Grey-backed Thrushes. VOICE: Song consists of a series of fluty trills and whistles; calls is a thin *tsweee* or *tsuuu*. HABITAT: Broadleaved evergreen forest and secondary growth. DISTRIBUTION: Breeds in C China; winter visitor in S, SE China, Hainan, N, C Laos and N, C Vietnam.

4 WHITE-COLLARED BLACKBIRD *Turdus albocinctus* 28cm FIELD NOTES: Generally wary, more sociable post breeding. Forages on the ground or in fruiting bushes and trees. VOICE: A series of mellow, descending whistles, *tew-i-tew-u-tew-o* or similar. Call is a throaty *tuck-tuck-tuck*. HABITAT: Various forests with good ground cover. DISTRIBUTION: Winter visitor and possible breeder in N Myanmar.

5 GREY-WINGED BLACKBIRD *Turdus boulboul* 29cm FIELD NOTES: Generally shy. Forages mainly on the ground or in moss covered or fruiting trees. VOICE: Rich and melodious, consisting of a soft opening note followed by four high notes descending in tone; calls include a *chuck-chuck* and a *churi* contact note. HABITAT: Moist broadleaf forest of oak and rhododendron, conifer forest clearings and dry hillside scrub. DISTRIBUTION: Summer visitor in S China; resident in N Laos and N Vietnam (W Tonkin); winter visitor in S Myanmar and NW Thailand; vagrant elsewhere.

6 BLACKBIRD (EURASIAN BLACKBIRD) *Turdus merula* 27cm FIELD NOTES: Forages on the ground and in fruiting trees. VOICE: Rich, clear fluty notes that merge into short, continuous phrases. Calls include a drawn-out *see* and a low *chuck-chuck-chuck*. HABITAT: Open forest, secondary growth, cultivations, parks and gardens. DISTRIBUTION: Resident in China; winter visitor in E Myanmar, Hainan, Laos and N Vietnam; vagrant elsewhere.

7 ISLAND THRUSH *Turdus poliocephalus niveiceps* 21cm FIELD NOTES: Generally shy, forages mostly on the ground amongst leaf litter in dense cover. VOICE: A subdued melody of flute-like whistles; calls include a short *tchook, tchooo, tchack* or *chook-chook* and various high-pitched chattering. HABITAT: Mountain forests. DISTRIBUTION: Resident in Taiwan.

8 CHESTNUT THRUSH *Turdus rubrocanus* 24–28cm FIELD NOTES: Generally perches on the tops of trees. Feeds on the ground and in trees and bushes. Black-headed race *T. r. gouldi* (8b) is resident in SW China; winter visitor in N, E Myanmar, NW Thailand, N Laos and N Vietnam (W Tonkin). VOICE: Short warbled phrases repeated up to eight times. Call is a *chuck-chuck* and when alarmed a rapid *kwik-kwik kwik-kwik*. HABITAT: Broadleaved evergreen forest. DISTRIBUTION: Resident in SW China; winter visitor in W, N, E Myanmar, NW Thailand, N Laos and N Vietnam (W Tonkin).

101 THRUSHES

1 KESSLER'S THRUSH (WHITE-BACKED THRUSH) *Turdus kessleri* 28cm FIELD NOTES: Gregarious. Feeds on the ground and in fruiting bushes. VOICE: A leisurely series of mewing and squawking phrases; calls include a soft *squack*, a low *dug-dug*, a high *swi-swi-swi-swi* and harsh chuckles. HABITAT: High-altitude rocky scrub and dwarf bushes. DISTRIBUTION: Possibly resident in montane areas of SW China.

2 RED-THROATED THRUSH (RUFOUS-THROATED THRUSH) *Turdus ruficollis* 25cm FIELD NOTES: Forages on the ground and in low bushes. Often associates with other thrushes. VOICE: Calls include a hoarse, high *kwee-kweek*, a conversational *skrie-kri-kriek kukukukuk sweeseek* and a thin *tseep*, the latter given in flight. HABITAT: Forest, forest edge, cultivations and open land with scattered trees. DISTRIBUTION: Winter visitor in SW China and N, C, W Myanmar.

3 BLACK-THROATED THRUSH *Turdus atrogularis* 26cm FIELD NOTES: Gregarious; forages on the ground and in bushes. VOICE: Calls include a thin *seet*, a squeaky *qui-kwea* and a throaty chuckling when alarmed. HABITAT: Grassy scrubby hillsides, forest edge and cultivations. DISTRIBUTION: Winter visitor to W Myanmar.

4 BROWN-HEADED THRUSH *Turdus chrysolaus* 23cm FIELD NOTES: Feeds low down in or near the cover of bushes, or at all levels in fruiting trees. Often in large flocks. VOICE: A repeated *krurr krurr krr-zeee* or *kiron kiron tsee*; calls include a *chuck-chuck-chuck* and, when alarmed or in flight a thin *zeeee*. HABITAT: Broadleaved forests, secondary growth, clearings near cover, cultivations, well wooded parks and gardens. DISTRIBUTION: Winter visitor or passage migrant in Taiwan, Hainan and E China.

5 PALE THRUSH *Turdus pallidus* 22–23cm FIELD NOTES: Shy and wary, forages mainly on the ground or in fruiting bushes and trees. VOICE: Various double or triple whistles; calls include a *chook*, a *tuck-tuck*, a thin *tsee* or *tsee-ip* and a *think-think* when alarmed. HABITAT: Open areas, copses, scrub, cultivations and gardens. DISTRIBUTION: Winter visitor in Taiwan and N, W, SE, SW China.

6 GREY-SIDED THRUSH *Turdus feae* 23cm FIELD NOTES: Shy, mainly a ground feeder. In winter sometimes associates with Eyebrowed Thrush. VOICE: A thin *zeeee*. HABITAT: Broadleaved evergreen forest. DISTRIBUTION: Winter visitor in W Myanmar and NW Thailand. Scarce winter visitor to E, S Myanmar and C Laos.

7 EYEBROWED THRUSH *Turdus obscurus* 22cm FIELD NOTES: Forages on the ground and in fruiting trees and bushes. Often associates with other thrushes. VOICE: A soft *chuk*, a hard *tack-tack*, a *shree* and a *dzee* flight call. HABITAT: Open forests, mangroves and gardens. DISTRIBUTION: Winter visitor in Taiwan, S China and throughout the south, except SW Myanmar, SE Thailand, N Vietnam (N Annam) and Singapore.

8 DUSKY THRUSH *Turdus eunomus* 23cm FIELD NOTES: Forages on the ground and in fruiting bushes and trees. VOICE: Calls include a low stacatto *chuck* and a rhythmic *chek-chek-chek*. HABITAT: Open broadleaved evergreen forest, forest edge, open areas with scattered trees, scrubby hillsides, winter stubble fields, parks and gardens. DISTRIBUTION: Winter visitor in China (except C), Taiwan, N, C, S Myanmar, NW Thailand and N Vietnam (E Tonkin).

9 CHINESE THRUSH *Turdus mupinensis* 23cm FIELD NOTES: Usually in undergrowth; shy. VOICE: A pleasant *drip-dii-du dudu-du-twi dju-wi-wi chu-wii-wr up chu-wi i-wu-wrrh dju-dju-wiii u...* and shorter twitterings and *se-wee* phrases. HABITAT: Mixed or deciduous montane forest, plantations and woodlands with rich undergrowth. DISTRIBUTION: Resident in W, SW China; vagrant, recorded from N Vietnam.

102 SHORTWINGS; ROBINS

1 GOULD'S SHORTWING *Heteroxenicus stellatus* 13cm FIELD NOTES: Mouse-like forager among tangled roots and fallen branches. VOICE: A high-pitched *tssiu – tssiu – tssiu – tssiu – tsitsitsiutssiutssiutssisitsitsiu…* utters a *tik-tik* when alarmed. HABITAT: Boulder strewn areas in rhododendron, bamboo and conifer forests; also broadleaved evergreen forest with nearby streams. DISTRIBUTION: Resident in SW China, N Myanmar and N Vietnam (W Tonkin).

2 LESSER SHORTWING *Brachypteryx leucophris* 13cm FIELD NOTES: Very skulking; often holds tail erect while foraging among dead leaves on the forest floor. Rufous race *B. l. carolinae* (2b) is resident in S, SE China, E Myanmar, NW Thailand, N Laos, N Cambodia and N Vietnam. VOICE: A single note followed by a melodious, sibilant warble with a jumbled finish of buzzy and rich musical notes; calls include a thin whistle and a harsh *tack*. HABITAT: Dense undergrowth in broadleaved evergreen forest. DISTRIBUTION: Resident in southern China, W, N, E, S Myanmar, W, NW, SE, S Thailand, Cambodia, Laos, N Vietnam (W, E Tonkin and N, S Annam) and Peninsular Malaysia.

3 WHITE-BROWED SHORTWING *Brachypteryx montana* 14cm FIELD NOTES: Skulking; forages on the ground, actions much like a Robin. Brown race *B. m. goodfellowi* (3b) occurs in Taiwan. VOICE: Song starts slowly with a few single notes, then speeds to a plaintive babble then ends abruptly. Call is a hard *tack*. HABITAT: Broadleaved evergreen forest. DISTRIBUTION: Resident in China (except NE), Taiwan, W, N, E Myanmar, NW Thailand, N Laos and N, C Vietnam.

4 RUSTY-BELLIED SHORTWING *Brachypteryx hyperythra* 13cm FIELD NOTES: Skulking; forages on the ground in thick undergrowth. VOICE: A *tu-tiu* that leads into a fast warble of slurred notes; calls include a *chack* and a *gueh*. HABITAT: Dense bamboo, thickets and undergrowth in broadleaved evergreen forest. DISTRIBUTION: Possibly resident in SW China.

5 SIBERIAN BLUE ROBIN *Larvivora cyane* 14cm FIELD NOTES: Shivers tail while foraging on the ground or in low cover; said to run and hop like a small crake. VOICE: Calls include a subdued *tak*, a louder *se-ic* and when alarmed a *chuck-chuck-chuck*. HABITAT: Broadleaved evergreen and mixed deciduous forest, bamboo, secondary growth, mangroves, parks and gardens. DISTRIBUTION: Winter visitor in SW, E China and throughout the south, except N Myanmar and parts of Thailand and Cambodia.

6 JAPANESE ROBIN *Larvivora akahige* 14cm FIELD NOTES: Skulks on or near the ground, tends to keep to dense undergrowth. VOICE: Song is a repeated *tsee – chararararararararar* or similar; calls include a thin *tsip*. HABITAT: Broadleaved evergreen forest, parks and gardens. DISTRIBUTION: Winter visitor in E China, Taiwan, C, SE Thailand, C Laos and Vietnam (E Tonkin and C Annam).

7 INDIAN BLUE ROBIN *Larvivora brunnea* 14cm FIELD NOTES: Forages on the ground or in low growth; runs rapidly and flicks wings and tail. VOICE: Song starts with a few introductory whistles followed with a short, sweet jumble of hurried phrases; calls include a high-pitched *tsee* and a hard *tuk-tuk* when alarmed. HABITAT: Dense undergrowth in forests. DISTRIBUTION: Resident in W Myanmar.

8 RUFOUS-TAILED ROBIN *Larvivora sibilans* 13cm FIELD NOTES: Skulks on or near the ground, shivers tail. VOICE: A repeated accelerating trill, falling in pitch towards the end; calls include a *chirp* or *chirrup*. HABITAT: Broadleaved and semi-evergreen forest. DISTRIBUTION: Winter visitor in S, SE, SW China, Hainan, NW, NE Thailand, Laos and Vietnam.

9 RYUKYU ROBIN *Larvivora komadori* 14cm FIELD NOTES: Forages on the ground or in low bushes. VOICE: Song similar to that of Japanese Robin but weaker with more variation; calls include a penetrating *tsiiii* and a *kirrick* when alarmed. HABITAT: Dense undergrowth in broadleaved evergreen forest, often near small streams. DISTRIBUTION: Vagrant, recorded in Taiwan.

2b *carolinae*

1

2

♂

♀

3

♀

3b *goodfellowi*

4

♂

♀

5

♀

6

♀

♂

♂

7

♀

♂

8

9

♀

♂

103 ROBINS; RUBYTHROATS; BUSH ROBINS

1 RUFOUS-HEADED ROBIN *Larvivora ruficeps* 15cm FIELD NOTES: Skulks, usually on the ground in thick cover, often cocks tail. VOICE: Rich, powerful, melodious phrases preceded by a single note, transcribed as *ti-chulululu – ti-chewtchwetchew – tititichewtchewtchew...* calls include a deep *tuc* or *toc* and a thin *si*. HABITAT: Dense scrubby subalpine forest. DISTRIBUTION: Vagrant, recorded in Peninsular Malaysia.

2 BLACK-THROATED ROBIN (BLACKTHROAT) *Calliope obscura* 14cm FIELD NOTES: Skulks in thickets; flicks tail. VOICE: Shrill, cheerful phrases alternating with purring trills; contact call is a subdued *tup*. HABITAT: Bamboo thickets, scrub and secondary growth. DISTRIBUTION: Vagrant, recorded from NW Thailand.

3 FIRETHROAT *Calliope pectardens* 14cm FIELD NOTES: Flicks tail; skulks in thick cover. VOICE: Song is loud, long, sweet and varied; each note repeated several times. Also includes some mimicry, transcribed as *wiu-wihui wi – wi chu-wi chu – whi-iiii – wi-chudu chudu – t sii-sii – wi chu-wi chu-wi chu – chu tsri sri...* call is a hard *tok*. HABITAT: Broadleaved evergreen forest, bamboo and dense scrub. DISTRIBUTION: Possibly resident in SW China and N Myanmar.

4 SIBERIAN RUBYTHROAT *Calliope calliope* 15cm FIELD NOTES: Shy, skulks in dense vegetation, more exposed when singing; cocks tail. VOICE: A loud, varied, sustained warbling interspersed with harsh notes; calls include a *chak-chak* and a falling, whistled *ee-uk*. HABITAT: Scrub thickets, forest edge, grassy areas with bushes and occasionally gardens. DISTRIBUTION: Winter visitor in Taiwan, Hainan, S China and throughout the south, except S Myanmar, S Thailand, Peninsular Malaysia and Singapore.

5 WHITE-TAILED RUBYTHROAT (HIMALAYAN RUBYTHROAT) *Calliope pectoralis tschebaiewi* 15cm FIELD NOTES: Secretive, although often more exposed when singing. Regularly cocks tail while foraging on the ground. VOICE: Song is a complex series of shrill, undulating, warbling trills and twitters; calls include a *tchuk* and a *siiii-siiii* when alarmed. HABITAT: Dwarf rhododendron, juniper and scrub above the tree line; post breeding also in marshy grassland and scrub. DISTRIBUTION: Resident in N Myanmar and possibly SW China; vagrant, recorded in Thailand.

6 RED-FLANKED BLUETAIL (ORANGE-FLANKED BUSH ROBIN or HIMALAYAN BLUETAIL) *Tarsiger cyanurus* 14cm FIELD NOTES: Forages on the ground and in low cover. Flicks tail downwards. Race *T. c. rufilatus* (Himalayan Bluetail), which may breed in N Myanmar, is sometimes considered a full species by some authorities; it is very similar to nominate. VOICE: A rolling *tree trr-tretritt*; calls include a deep croaking *tok-tok-tok* and a mournful *pheeou*. HABITAT: Summers in oak, coniferous and rhododendron forest; winters in broadleaved evergreen forest. DISTRIBUTION: Resident in SW China and N Myanmar; winter visitor in China, Hainan, Taiwan, W, C, E Myanmar, NW, NE Thailand, Laos and N, C Vietnam.

7 WHITE-BROWED BUSH ROBIN *Tarsiger indicus* 15cm FIELD NOTES: Forages on or near the ground in thick cover, sings from small trees. VOICE: A rapidly repeated, sharp, bubbling *shri-de-de-dew...shri-de-de-dew* or *whi-wi'which'u-wi'rr*; calls include a sweet *heed* or *tuit-tuit*, a croaking *churr* and a clucking *tukukukukukukuk*. HABITAT: Bamboo, conifer and rhododendron forest. DISTRIBUTION: Resident in SW China, Taiwan, N Myanmar and N Vietnam (W Tonkin).

8 RUFOUS-BREASTED BUSH ROBIN *Tarsiger hyperythrus* 13cm FIELD NOTES: Forages on or near the ground, often adopts an upright stance. VOICE: A lisping, warbled *zeew-zeew-zeew...* calls include a low *duk* or *duk-duk-duk-tseak*. HABITAT: Mixed conifer and rhododendron forests, winters in broadleaved evergreen forests and forest edge along streams. DISTRIBUTION: Resident in SW China and N Myanmar.

104 BUSH ROBINS; BLUETHROAT; SHAMAS

1 GOLDEN BUSH ROBIN *Tarsiger chrysaeus* 15cm FIELD NOTES: Forages on the ground or in low cover; often holds tail cocked. VOICE: A wispy *tse-tse-tse-tse-tse-chu-r-r* or similar; calls include a croaky *trrr* and a scolding *chirik-chirik*. HABITAT: Rhododendron and conifer forest, forest edge, clearings and scrub; winters in thickets and broadleaved evergreen forest. DISTRIBUTION: Resident in SW China and W, N Myanmar; winter visitor in E Myanmar and NW Thailand.

2 COLLARED BUSH ROBIN *Tarsiger johnstoniae* 12cm FIELD NOTES: Forages in shade, on the ground and in lower storey. VOICE: A short, jolly *wiwi s-wizuwu wiwi s-wu-wi wiwi s-wu-srr;* calls include a piping *pi-pi-pi…* and a grating *sipsipsip grrgrrgrr sipsip grrgrr*. HABITAT: Mountain forest and forest edge. DISTRIBUTION: Resident in Taiwan.

3 BLUETHROAT (RED-SPOTTED BLUETHROAT) *Luscinia svecica* 14cm FIELD NOTES: Forages on the ground or in low cover. Chestnut tail bases often 'flash' as birds flit into cover. VOICE: Vigorous, bell-like *ting-ting* and a throaty *torr-torr-torr-torr*. Often mimics other birds or insects; calls include a *tucc-tucc*, a croaky *turrc-turrc* and a plaintive *hweet*. HABITAT: Winters in scrub and tall grass, usually near water. DISTRIBUTION: Winter visitor in SW, E China, Myanmar, NW, NE, C Thailand, Cambodia, Laos and Vietnam (except W Tonkin and N, S Annam).

4 WHITE-BELLIED REDSTART *Luscinia phaenicuroides* 19cm FIELD NOTES: Retiring; forages mainly on the ground. Tail often held vertically and spread. VOICE: Whistled song, transcribed as *he-did-so;* calls are a *chack* and when alarmed a *tsiep-tsiep-tk-tk* or *tck-tck-sie*. HABITAT: Rhododendron and coniferous forest and dense low scrub above the tree line; winters at lower levels in dense low scrub or undergrowth. DISTRIBUTION: Resident in SW, W China, W, N Myanmar, N Laos and N Vietnam (W Tonkin); winter visitor in E Myanmar and NW Thailand.

5 RUFOUS-TAILED SHAMA *Copsychus pyrropygus* 21–23cm FIELD NOTES: Regularly sits still for prolonged periods; often cocks tail. VOICE: Song is a loud, whistled *whi-iii whi-iii whi-uuu;* call is a scolding *tchurr*. HABITAT: Broadleaved evergreen and freshwater swamp forests. DISTRIBUTION: Resident in S Thailand and Peninsular Malaysia.

6 WHITE-RUMPED SHAMA *Copsychus malabaricus* 25cm FIELD NOTES: Usually forages on the ground or in low cover; wings make a clicking sound when flying over open ground. VOICE: Rich melodious phrases including mimicry. Aarm call is a harsh *tshak*. HABITAT: Forest undergrowth, bamboo and secondary growth. DISTRIBUTION: Resident in SW China, Hainan and throughout the south.

7 ORIENTAL MAGPIE-ROBIN *Copsychus saularis* 20cm FIELD NOTES: Confiding; usually conspicuous but can become more secretive post breeding. VOICE: Varied musical warbling, alternating with churrs and sliding whistles; calls include a clear rising whistle and a harsh *che-e-e-e-h* when alarmed. HABITAT: Open forests, secondary growth, mangroves, cultivations, parks and gardens. DISTRIBUTION: Resident throughout the region.

8 WHITE-TAILED ROBIN *Myiomela leucura* 18cm FIELD NOTES: Shy, forages in dark thickets. Often spreads tail, revealing white bases. There is a white neck spot that is usually concealed. VOICE: Song consists of clear, liquid, separated phrases, transcribed as *tey-tlee-i-ta-wey-*i; calls are a low *tuc* and a thin whistle. HABITAT: Dense undergrowth in montane broadleaved evergreen forest, lower-level forest in winter. DISTRIBUTION: Resident in western China, Hainan, Taiwan, Myanmar (except SW, C), Thailand (except C), Cambodia, Laos, N, C Vietnam and Peninsular Malaysia.

9 BLUE-FRONTED ROBIN *Cinclidium frontale* 19cm FIELD NOTES: Forages by clambering among bamboo and probably on the ground. VOICE: A series of short melodious phrases, transcribed as *tuee-be-tue* and *tuu-buudy-doo*. Calls include a shrill *shraak,* a faint *tch-tch-tch-tch-tch* and a harsh buzzy *zschwick* when alarmed. HABITAT: Broadleaved evergreen forest and bamboo. DISTRIBUTION: Resident in SW China and probably NW Thailand, Laos and N Vietnam (W Tonkin).

105 REDSTARTS

1 PRZEVALSKI'S REDSTART (ALASHAN REDSTART) *Phoenicurus alaschanicus*
15cm FIELD NOTES: Drops from a twig or rock to pick up insects; flicks tail up and down.
VOICE: A whistled *few-eet* and a croaking *gre-er*. HABITAT: Montane coniferous forest, dense
bushes and rocky slopes. DISTRIBUTION: Possibly winters in the mountain areas in northern
part of the region.

2 BLACK REDSTART *Phoenicurus ochruros rufiventris* 15cm FIELD NOTES: Flits from
a low perch to catch insects from the ground, or by making short flycatching aerial sallies.
VOICE: A rapid warble, interspersed with a rattle, ending with a rushed burst of ringing
notes; calls include a *tsip*, a *tucc-tucc* and a *tititicc* when alarmed. HABITAT: Open country;
winters in plantations and cultivations. DISTRIBUTION: Resident in SW China; winters in
W, N, C, E Myanmar; vagrant, N Vietnam.

3 DAURIAN REDSTART *Phoenicurus auroreus* 15cm FIELD NOTES: Forages in trees
and bushes, often in the manner of a flycatcher. Shivers tail. VOICE: A series of cheerful,
whistled, descending phrases, opening with 1–2 short clear notes; calls include a *tsip*, a rapid
titititik and a *teck-teck*. HABITAT: Subalpine forest, clearings and scrub; winters in bushy
areas and cultivations. DISTRIBUTION: Breeds in SW, NC China; winters in China (except
C), Myanmar (except SW, S), NW Thailand, Laos and N Vietnam.

4 HODGSON'S REDSTART *Phoenicurus hodgsoni* 15cm FIELD NOTES: Makes
short flycatching sallies from a branch or rock. VOICE: Short phases of tinny, tinkly
notes; calls include a *prit* and a *trr* or *tschrrr* when alarmed. HABITAT: Trees, bushes
and scrub on mountain-sides; winters in open areas, dry riverbeds and cultivations.
DISTRIBUTION: Probable resident in SW China; winters in W China and N Myanmar.

5 WHITE-THROATED REDSTART *Phoenicurus schisticeps* 15cm FIELD NOTES:
Restless, often feeds in a flycatcher-like manner. VOICE: A series of dry trilled phrases,
usually accelerating towards the end; call is a drawn-out *zieh* followed by a rattle.
HABITAT: Scrub in subalpine conifer forest. DISTRIBUTION: Resident in SW China and
possibly N Myanmar.

6 BLUE-FRONTED REDSTART *Phoenicurus frontalis* 15cm FIELD NOTES: Flicks
tail up and down. Descends from rock or branch to capture insects. VOICE: Song like
Black Redstarts, but less wheezy. Calls include a *tic* and a repeated *ee-tit – ti-tit* when
alarmed. HABITAT: Subalpine scrub; winters in open forests and open areas with bushes.
DISTRIBUTION: Resident in SW China and possibly N Myanmar; winter visitor in E
Myanmar, possibly W Myanmar, N Laos and N Vietnam.

7 GÜLDENSTÄDT'S REDSTART (WHITE-WINGED REDSTART) *Phoenicurus
erythrogastrus* 18cm FIELD NOTES: Makes short flights to capture insects, constantly moves
from perch to perch. VOICE: A series of clear notes followed by a burst of short, wheezy
notes; calls include a weak *lik* and a hard *tek*. HABITAT: High altitude boulder-strewn slopes,
rocky meadows and scrubby hillsides often near water. DISTRIBUTION: Winters in the
mountains of SW China.

8 PLUMBEOUS REDSTART (PLUMBEOUS WATER REDSTART) *Phoenicurus
fuliginosus* 14cm FIELD NOTES: Continuously opens and shuts tail; also wags tail up and
down. Makes sallies from rocks or low branches. VOICE: A rapid *streee-treee-tree-treeeh;* calls
include a sharp *ziet-ziet* or a threatening *kree*. HABITAT: Fast flowing streams and rivers.
DISTRIBUTION: Resident in Taiwan, Hainan, China, W, N Myanmar, NW Thailand, Laos
and N, C Vietnam; winters in SW, C, E Myanmar.

9 WHITE-CAPPED REDSTART (WHITE-CAPPED WATER REDSTART)
Phoenicurus leucocephalus 19cm FIELD NOTES: Continuously flicks tail; sits on rocks
in or close to water. VOICE: A weak undulating whistle, call is a plaintive *tseeit-tseeit*.
HABITAT: Mountain streams and rivers. DISTRIBUTION: Summers in NE China; resident in
W, C China, N Myanmar, N, C Laos and N Vietnam; winter status is uncertain.

106 FORKTAILS; GRANDALA; WHEATEAR

1 LITTLE FORKTAIL *Enicurus scouleri* 12–14cm FIELD NOTES: Constantly wags tail up and down, also rapidly opens and closes tail in a scissor-like movement. Juvenile browner and lacks white forehead. VOICE: A loud, thin *ts-youeee*, also a soft, clear *tji-u tji-u tji-u…* HABITAT: Mountain streams, rivers and waterfalls. DISTRIBUTION: Resident in China, Taiwan, W, N Myanmar and N Vietnam (W Tonkin).

2 CHESTNUT-NAPED FORKTAIL *Enicurus ruficapillus* 18–20cm FIELD NOTES: Wary, searches for food along stream edges and on rocks in water. Flicks tail on landing. VOICE: Utters a series of thin, shrill whistles and a high *dir-tee*. HABITAT: Rivers, streams and waterfalls. DISTRIBUTION: Resident in S Myanmar (Tenasserim), W, S Thailand and Peninsular Malaysia.

3 BLACK-BACKED FORKTAIL *Enicurus immaculatus* 20–25cm FIELD NOTES: Forages among rocks or along the water's edge, constantly wags tail. Juvenile browner and lacks white forehead. VOICE: A hollow *huu* often followed by a shrill *zeee*; also a squeaky *weeng*. HABITAT: Fast-flowing waters with uncovered rocks and waterfalls in dense forests. DISTRIBUTION: Resident in Myanmar (except Tenasserim) and NW Thailand.

4 SLATY-BACKED FORKTAIL *Enicurus schistaceus* 22–25cm FIELD NOTES: Hops or flits from rock to rock in search of food; flight undulating, much like a wagtail. Sways tail, slowly up and down. Juvenile browner above, lacks white forehead; underparts dirty-white, breast streaked brown. VOICE: A mellow *cheet* and a metallic *teenk*. HABITAT: Fast-flowing rocky rivers. DISTRIBUTION: Resident throughout the region, except northern China, SW Myanmar, C Thailand, Cambodia, S Vietnam and Singapore.

5 WHITE-CROWNED FORKTAIL *Enicurus leschenaulti* 25–28cm FIELD NOTES: Forages on rocks or along the water's edge; when disturbed often disappears into nearby forest cover. Juvenile browner and lacks white on head. VOICE: An elaborate series of sweet high-pitched whistles; calls include a harsh *tssee* or *tssee-chit-chit-chit*. HABITAT: Fast-flowing rivers and streams in dense evergreen forest. DISTRIBUTION: Resident throughout the region, except SW Myanmar, C, SE Thailand, Cambodia, S Vietnam and Singapore.

6 SPOTTED FORKTAIL *Enicurus maculatus* 26–27cm FIELD NOTES: Actions and habits much as Slaty-backed Forktail. Juvenile browner and lacks the white forehead. VOICE: A sharp, creaky *cheek-chik-chik-chik-chik*, a rasping *kreee*, *tseek* or *tsueee* and a rapid cracking *zhih-zhih-zhih…* HABITAT: Rocky streams in dense mountain forests; winters at lower elevations and often on wider watercourses. DISTRIBUTION: Resident in SW, S, E China, SW, W, N, E Myanmar and Vietnam (W Tonkin and S Annam).

7 GRANDALA *Grandala coelicolor* 19–23cm FIELD NOTES: Forages mainly on the ground; posture much like a rock thrush. Winter flocks act starling- or wader-like, wheeling and circling around before dropping onto the top branches of trees or on cliffs. VOICE: Song is a subdued *tju-u tiu-u ti-tu tji-u*; call is ringing *tji-u* or *djew*. HABITAT: Alpine meadows, bare rocky areas above the treeline and open forests. DISTRIBUTION: Resident in SW China; winter visitor in N Myanmar.

8 ISABELLINE WHEATEAR *Oenanthe isabellina* 17cm FIELD NOTES: Often has a very upright stance and jerky emphatic tail-wagging. In flight shows a white rump and outer-tail bases. VOICE: A piped *weep* or *dweet*, a high-pitched *wheet-whit* and a quiet *cheep*. HABITAT: Plains and plateaux with sparse vegetation; winters in sandy semi-desert. DISTRIBUTION: Vagrant, recorded in C Myanmar.

107 COCHOAS; BUSHCHATS; STONECHATS

1 GREEN COCHOA *Cochoa viridis* 25–28cm FIELD NOTES: Lethargic forager in trees, undergrowth and the ground; frequently in pairs or small groups. Juvenile has similar wing pattern to adult but body is generally dark brown with ochre spotting; crown whitish with dark barring. VOICE: A pure, thin monotonous whistle; calls include a harsh note and a high, thin *pok*. HABITAT: Dense, moist broadleaved evergreen forest, often near streams, locally in dry evergreen forest and tall forests in limestone valleys. DISTRIBUTION: Resident in SW, SE China, S, E Myanmar, W, NW, SE Thailand, Laos, Cambodia and N, C Vietnam.

2 PURPLE COCHOA *Cochoa purpurea* 25–28cm FIELD NOTES: Secretive; generally arboreal, feeds in fruiting trees, but will also forage on the ground. Juvenile has same wing pattern as adult female; body generally dark brown with ochre scaling below and ochre spotting above. VOICE: Song is a pure whistled *fwhiiiiiiiit, peeeee* or *peee-you-peeee*; calls are a thin *sit* or *tssri*, a chuckling *nyerr* and a soft, high *pink-pink-trrrrrew*. HABITAT: Dense broadleaved evergreen forest. DISTRIBUTION: Resident in SW China, E, S Myanmar, NW Thailand, N Laos and N Vietnam.

3 GREY BUSHCHAT *Saxicola ferreus* 15cm FIELD NOTES: Sits on a prominent perch in order to make frequent sallies to capture insects from on or near the ground, occasionally makes aerial flycatching sorties. VOICE: Song is a short, feeble trill ending with a rolling whistle; calls include a soft *zizz*, a clear *hew* and a sharp *tak-tak-tak-tak*. HABITAT: Open woodland, open scrubby and bushcovered hillsides, cultivations, parks and gardens. DISTRIBUTION: Resident in China, Myanmar (except C Tenasserim), NW Thailand and Vietnam (W Tonkin and S Annam); winter visitor in C Myanmar, Thailand (except SE, S), Laos and N Vietnam (E Tonkin).

4 SIBERIAN STONECHAT *Saxicola maurus* 13cm FIELD NOTES: Actions similar to Grey Bushchat. VOICE: A variable, scratchy series of twittering and warbling notes; calls include a hard *chack* and a thin *hweet*. HABITAT: Open areas with scrub and cultivations. DISTRIBUTION: Breeds in SW China, winters throughout the south.

5 WHITE-TAILED STONECHAT (WHITE-TAILED BUSHCHAT) *Saxicola leucurus* 12–14cm FIELD NOTES: Actions similar to other *Saxicola* species. VOICE: Song is lark-like, consisting of rapid, scratchy, squeaky notes ending with a high slurred note; calls include a short *peep-cha*, a hard dry *kek-kek-kek* and a warning *pseep*. HABITAT: Tall grassland, reeds and nearby scrub. DISTRIBUTION: Resident in N, E, S Myanmar.

6 STEJNEGER'S STONECHAT *Saxicola stejnegeri* 14cm FIELD NOTES: Actions similar to Grey Bushchat. VOICE: At the time of writing no difference known from calls of Siberian Stonechat. HABITAT: Moist meadows with rich grass, shrubby marshes and dry pinewoods. DISTRIBUTION: Winter visitor south from the Changjiang River in E China.

7 PIED BUSHCHAT (PIED STONECHAT) *Saxicola caprata* 13–14cm FIELD NOTES: Feeding action similar to Grey Bushchat. VOICE: Song is a brisk, whistled *chip-chepee-chewee-chu* or similar; calls include a plaintive *chep-chep-hee* and a scolding *chuh*. HABITAT: Open areas with scrub or scattered trees, grasslands and cultivations. DISTRIBUTION: Resident in SW China and throughout the south, except SE, S Thailand, N Vietnam, Peninsular Malaysia and Singapore.

8 JERDON'S BUSHCHAT *Saxicola jerdoni* 15cm FIELD NOTES: Actions and habits typical of the genus. VOICE: Song comprises of a series of sweet, clear, mellow warbled phrases, often ending with a trilled flourish; calls include a high, nasal, down-slurred *heeew*, a plaintive, high-pitched *chirr* or *chir-churr* and a dry rapid ticking when alarmed. HABITAT: Tall grass, scrub particularly by watercourses. DISTRIBUTION: Resident in SW China, N, W, C, E, S Myanmar, NW Thailand, N Laos and N Vietnam (E Tonkin).

108 FLYCATCHERS

1 GREY-HEADED FLYCATCHER *Culicicapa ceylonensis* 12–13cm FIELD NOTES: Frequents the middle to upper storey, making aerial sallies to capture flying insects. VOICE: A sweet, clear whistle; calls include a soft *pit – pit – pit* and a rattling *churrru*. HABITAT: Forests, mangroves, parks and wooded gardens. DISTRIBUTION: Summers in western half of China; resident in S China, Myanmar, Thailand (except SE, C), Cambodia, Laos, Vietnam (except Cochinchina), and Peninsular Malaysia. Winters in SE, C Thailand.

2 BROWN-CHESTED JUNGLE FLYCATCHER *Cyornis brunneatus* 15cm FIELD NOTES: Frequents the lower canopy and bushes; captures insects in flight but also forages among leaf litter on the forest floor. VOICE: A series of loud descending whistles; calls include harsh *churrs*. HABITAT: Broadleaved leaved evergreen forest, bamboo thickets. Frequents semi-evergreen and mixed deciduous forest, mangroves and scrub post breeding. DISTRIBUTION: Breeds in E China; winters in S Thailand, Peninsular Malaysia and Singapore.

3 FULVOUS-CHESTED JUNGLE FLYCATCHER *Cyornis olivaceus* 15cm FIELD NOTES: Usually in the lower and middle storey. Makes sallies after flying insects; occasionally cocks and fans tail. VOICE: A rapid series of short phrases, alternating in pitch, consisting of musical, scratchy, tinkling and churring notes. Calls include a low *tchuck-tchuck*, a *trrt* and a harsh *tac*. HABITAT: Broadleaved evergreen forest. DISTRIBUTION: Resident in S Myanmar (S Tenasserim) and S Thailand.

4 GREY-CHESTED JUNGLE FLYCATCHER *Cyornis umbratilis* 15cm FIELD NOTES: Forages from the undergrowth to the middle canopy, occasionally makes aerial sallies after insects. Cocks and spreads tail. VOICE: A thin, sweet, descending *si ti-tu-ti tlooeeu*. Calls include a scolding *churr-churr-churr*, a *trrrt it it it* and a clicking *tchk-tchk*. HABITAT: Broadleaved evergreen forest. DISTRIBUTION: Resident in S Thailand and Peninsular Malaysia.

5 GREY-STREAKED FLYCATCHER (GREY-SPOTTED FLYCATCHER) *Muscicapa griseisticta* 14cm FIELD NOTES: Usually solitary; makes rapid dashes after flying insects, often returning to the same treetop perch. VOICE: Call is a loud *chipee, tee-tee* or *zeet zeet zeet*. HABITAT: Open woodland, forest edge and clearings; also grassy areas with trees. DISTRIBUTION: Winter visitor in Taiwan; vagrant, recorded in Vietnam and Singapore.

6 DARK-SIDED FLYCATCHER (SIBERIAN or SOOTY FLYCATCHER) *Muscicapa sibirica* 13cm FIELD NOTES: Makes darting aerial sallies after flying insects from a prominent perch. VOICE: A series of repetitive thin notes with trills and whistles; call is tinkling *chi-up-chi-up-chi-up*. HABITAT: Open broadleaved, coniferous, mixed-deciduous and rhododendron forests and secondary growth. DISTRIBUTION: Breeds in SW China, W, N, E Myanmar and N Vietnam. Winters in Taiwan, Hainan, S China and throughout the south, except S, W, N Myanmar, N, C Laos and N Vietnam. Passage migrant elsewhere.

7 BROWN FLYCATCHER (ASIAN BROWN FLYCATCHER) *Muscicapa dauurica* 13cm FIELD NOTES: Actions similar to Dark-sided Flycatcher. VOICE: A faint, squeaky, melodious whistle; calls include a soft rattling, a short *tzi* and a soft *churr*. HABITAT: Open forests, secondary growth, mangroves, parks and gardens. DISTRIBUTION: Resident in S Myanmar (N Tenasserim), NW Thailand and S Vietnam (S Annam). Winter visitor in S, SE China, Hainan and throughout the south, except N, E Myanmar; passage migrant elsewhere.

8 BROWN-STREAKED FLYCATCHER *Muscicapa williamsoni* 14cm FIELD NOTES: Actions as Dark-sided Flycatcher. VOICE: Similar to Brown Flycatcher, calls include a thin *tzi* and a harsh, slurred *cheititit*. HABITAT: Open broadleaved evergreen and semi-evergreen forests, parks and gardens. DISTRIBUTION: Resident in S Myanmar, S Thailand, S Vietnam and NW Peninsular Malaysia; winter visitor in Singapore.

9 BROWN-BREASTED FLYCATCHER *Muscicapa muttui* 14cm FIELD NOTES: Secretive; frequents low vegetation from where it makes short sallies to catch flying insects. VOICE: Pleasant, feeble song; calls include a thin *sit* and a rapid *chi-chi-chi-chi*. HABITAT: Broadleaved evergreen forests. DISTRIBUTION: Breeds in W, SW China, N, E Myanmar, NW Thailand and N Vietnam (N Tonkin); passage migrant in W, C Myanmar.

109 FLYCATCHERS

1 FERRUGINOUS FLYCATCHER *Muscicapa ferruginea* 12–13cm FIELD NOTES: Flycatches in sweeping aerial pursuits; returns to a favourite, or nearby prominent perch. VOICE: A shrill *tsit-tittu-titt* and a soft, trilling *si-si-si*. HABITAT: Broadleaved evergreen and forest edge. DISTRIBUTION: Summers in SW China and N Vietnam (W Tonkin); resident in Taiwan. Winters in Hainan, S Vietnam, S Thailand and Peninsular Malaysia.

2 RUFOUS-BROWED FLYCATCHER *Anthipes solitaris* 12–13cm FIELD NOTES: Spends long periods in the lower storey, resting on a shady perch. Makes short aerial flycatching forays; also collects insects from the ground. VOICE: A thin, tremulous '*three-blind-mice*'. Calls include a thin *tseep*, a sharp *tchik* and a harsh churring. HABITAT: Broadleaved evergreen forest and bamboo. DISTRIBUTION: Resident in S Myanmar (Tenasserim), W, S Thailand, S Laos, S Vietnam and Peninsular Malaysia.

3 WHITE-GORGETED FLYCATCHER *Anthipes moniliger* 11–13cm FIELD NOTES: Forages in dense undergrowth or lower levels of trees, occasionally makes flycatching sorties. Flicks and spreads tail. Race *A. m. leucops* (3b) occurs in all areas mentioned in distribution, except SW China and SW Myanmar. VOICE: High-pitched whistles alternating with wispy, scratchy and musical notes. Calls include a buzzing *grzzt-grzzt-grzzt*, a rapid *djuh* and a scolding rattle. HABITAT: Broadleaved evergreen forest and bamboo. DISTRIBUTION: Resident in SW China, Myanmar (except NW, C), W, NE, NW Thailand, Laos and N, C Vietnam.

4 TAIGA FLYCATCHER (RED-THROATED FLYCATCHER) *Ficedula albicilla* 11–12cm FIELD NOTES: Forages among foliage with occasional sallies after flying insects, when white outer-tail bases are prominent. VOICE: A buzzing *drrrrt* and a harsh *zree*. HABITAT: Open forests, forest edge, plantations, parks and gardens. DISTRIBUTION: Winters in E China, Hainan and throughout the south, except Peninsular Malaysia.

5 RUFOUS-GORGETED FLYCATCHER *Ficedula strophiata* 14cm FIELD NOTES: Forages in undergrowth or low down in trees; flits and spreads tail when white tail sides show. VOICE: A spirited *tin-ti-ti*. Calls include a low *tchuk-tchuk* and a metallic *pink*. HABITAT: Broadleaved evergreen forest. DISTRIBUTION: Resident in SW, W China, N, W Myanmar, E Laos and C Vietnam; winters in C, S Myanmar and NW, W Thailand.

6 YELLOW-RUMPED FLYCATCHER *Ficedula zanthopygia* 13cm FIELD NOTES: Forages in tree foliages or undergrowth; often makes sallies after flying insects. VOICE: A dry rattling *tr-r-r-rt*. HABITAT: Forest, forest edge, coastal scrub, mangroves, parks and gardens. DISTRIBUTION: Breeds in the north; winters in S Thailand, Peninsular Malaysia and Singapore.

7 NARCISSUS FLYCATCHER *Ficedula narcissina* 13–14cm FIELD NOTES: Makes sallies from middle storey or canopy or forages in bushy undergrowth and low vegetation. VOICE: Calls include a soft *tink-tink*. HABITAT: Open woodland, cultivation with scattered trees, scrub, parks and gardens. DISTRIBUTION: Winter visitor in Hainan.

8 GREEN-BACKED FLYCATCHER *Ficedula elisae* 13–14cm FIELD NOTES: Recently split from Narcissus Flycatcher: actions and habits similar. VOICE: Calls include a low *tok tok tok*, a sharp *tek tek* and a high-pitched *pee*. HABITAT: Forest, plantations, parks and gardens. DISTRIBUTION: Winter visitor in S Thailand and Peninsular Malaysia.

9 SLATY-BACKED FLYCATCHER (RUSTY-BREASTED FLYCATCHER) *Ficedula hodgsonii* 13cm FIELD NOTES: Makes flycatching sallies from tree-canopy perch; occasionally takes insects from the ground. VOICE: A constant ripple of descending, whistling notes; calls include a hard *tchat* and a rattled *terrht*. HABITAT: Forest, forest edge and secondary growth. DISTRIBUTION: Breeds in SW China; resident in W, N, E Myanmar; winters in C, S Myanmar, W, NW, NE Thailand and N, C Laos.

10 MUGIMAKI FLYCATCHER *Ficedula mugimaki* 13cm FIELD NOTES: Unobtrusive forager in the middle and upper canopy. Often flicks and spreads tail. VOICE: Calls include a soft rattled *trrrr*. HABITAT: Forests, plantations, parks and gardens. DISTRIBUTION: Winters in SE China, Hainan, NE, SE, S Thailand, Cambodia, Laos, C Vietnam and Peninsular Malaysia.

3b *leucops*

110 FLYCATCHERS

1 SNOWY-BROWED FLYCATCHER *Ficedula hyperythra* 11–13cm FIELD NOTES: Forages low down in scrub and thickets or runs about on the ground much like a shortwing. VOICE: A thin *sip* and an upslurred *seep*; song is a wheezy, shrill *tsit-sit-si-sii tsi-sii-swrri* or *tsi-sit-i*. HABITAT: Broadleaved evergreen forest; favours damp areas. DISTRIBUTION: Resident in S China, Taiwan, Myanmar (except S, SW), NW, NE, Thailand, Laos, Vietnam (W, E Tonkin, S Annam) and Peninsular Malaysia.

2 LITTLE PIED FLYCATCHER *Ficedula westermanni* 11–12cm FIELD NOTES: Forages in treetops, constantly on the move, also makes short sallies after flying insects. VOICE: A mellow *tweet*; song is a thin, high *pi-pi-pi* followed by a rattling *churr-r-r-r*. HABITAT: Broadleaved evergreen and pine forests. May winter in more open woodland and plantations. DISTRIBUTION: Resident in S, SW China and in south, except C, SE Thailand, Cambodia, Vietnam (E Tonkin, C Annam, Cochinchina) and Singapore.

3 SLATY-BLUE FLYCATCHER *Ficedula tricolor* 12–13cm FIELD NOTES: Secretive; forages in undergrowth and lower branches of trees. Often cocks tail. Race *F. t. cerviniventris* (3b) occurs in W Myanmar. VOICE: A three-note whistled *zieth-ti-zietz*; calls include an *ee-tik* and a rapid *ee-tick-tick-tick-tick*. HABITAT: Secondary growth, scrub, tall grass and bamboo. DISTRIBUTION: Resident in SW China, W, N, E Myanmar and N Vietnam (W Tonkin); winter visitor in NW Thailand, N Laos and N Vietnam (E Tonkin).

4 SAPPHIRE FLYCATCHER *Ficedula sapphira* 11cm FIELD NOTES: Forages in undergrowth and trees, occasionally picks food from the ground or makes aerial sallies after flying insects. VOICE: A low, rattled *tit-tit-ti*; song consists of several high-pitched notes followed by a series of short rattles. HABITAT: Open broadleaved evergreen forest. DISTRIBUTION: Resident in SW China, N, E Myanmar, N, C, Laos and N Vietnam (W Tonkin); winter visitor in NW Thailand.

5 RUFOUS-CHESTED FLYCATCHER *Ficedula dumetoria* 11–12cm FIELD NOTES: Forages low down in dense vegetation, often near streams; regularly catches insects in flight. VOICE: Song is a distinctive high-pitched, rising and falling *sii wi-sii si-wi-si-ii* and *si-wi-oo*; calls include a soft *sst-sst*. HABITAT: Broadleaved evergreen forest. DISTRIBUTION: Resident in S Thailand and Peninsular Malaysia.

6 ULTRAMARINE FLYCATCHER *Ficedula superciliaris* 12cm FIELD NOTES: Forages in the foliage of low trees and bushes; occasionally descends to feed on the ground. VOICE: A high-pitched, disjointed *tseep-te-e-te-e-te-e-tih…tseep…tse-e-eep* or a repeated *chee-tr-r-r*; calls include a soft *tick* and a low rattling *trrrt*. HABITAT: Open mixed forests. DISTRIBUTION: Breeds in SW China and possibly C, E Myanmar; winter visitor in NW Thailand.

7 VERDITER FLYCATCHER *Eumyias thalassinus* 15–17cm FIELD NOTES: Makes aerial sallies after flying insects from an exposed perch on trees, wires and buildings. VOICE: A pleasant, trilled *p-p-pwe…p-p-pwe…pe-tititi-wu-pitititi-weu*; calls include a short, plaintive *pseeut* and a dry *tze-ju-jui*. HABITAT: Broadleaved evergreen forest, forest clearings, wooded gardens and mangroves. DISTRIBUTION: Breeds in W, C, S China; resident throughout the south, except C, S Myanmar and C Thailand. Winters in the latter.

8 BLUE-AND-WHITE FLYCATCHER *Cyanoptila cyanomelana* 17cm FIELD NOTES: Forages mainly within the tree canopy but also gleans insects from low branches and the understorey. Makes flycatching sorties from a prominent perch, but rarely returns to the same perch. VOICE: Calls include a harsh *tchk-tchk* and a soft *tic* or *tac*. HABITAT: Open broadleaved evergreen forest, island forest, plantations, parks and wooded gardens. DISTRIBUTION: Winter visitor in Hainan, Taiwan and Peninsular Malaysia; otherwise a passage migrant throughout the region.

3b
cerviniventris

111 FLYCATCHERS

1 LARGE NILTAVA *Niltava grandis* 21cm FIELD NOTES: Skulks and flits about in low bushes; occasionally feeds on the ground. Less agile than most flycatchers. Females of the SC Vietnam race *N. g. decorata* (1b) have the crown and nape blue. VOICE: A whistled, ascending *whee-whee-wip tee-ti-tree* or *uu-uu-du-di*; calls include a nasal *dju-ee* a loud *trr-k trr-k* and a harsh rattle. HABITAT: Broadleaved evergreen forest. DISTRIBUTION: Resident in SW China and throughout the south, except SW, C, S Myanmar, C Thailand, C, S Vietnam and Singapore.

2 SMALL NILTAVA *Niltava macgrigoriae* 13–14cm FIELD NOTES: Forages in shady undergrowth and bushes; regularly makes sallies after flying insects. VOICE: A high-pitched, rising and falling *twee-twee-ee-twee*. Calls include a high-pitched *see-see* and metallic scolding and churring notes. HABITAT: Clearings and edges in broadleaved evergreen forest; also winters in dense reeds and tall grassy areas with scattered trees. DISTRIBUTION: Resident in S China, N, E Myanmar, W, NW Thailand, Laos and N Vietnam; winters in SE China.

3 FUJIAN NILTAVA *Niltava davidi* 18cm FIELD NOTES: Forages mainly in dense undergrowth, sits quietly before pouncing on prey. VOICE: A repeated, high-pitched *sssew* or *ssiiiii*; calls include a sharp, metallic *tit-tit-tit* and a harsh *trrt-trrt-trrt-tit-tit-trrt-trrt*. HABITAT: Broadleaved evergreen woodland; on migration also in scrub, parks and gardens. DISTRIBUTION: Resident in W, SW, C China, Hainan and N Vietnam; winters in SE China, N, C Vietnam and Laos.

4 RUFOUS-VENTED NILTAVA (SUMATRAN NILTAVA) *Niltava sumatrana* 15cm FIELD NOTES: Forages on the ground, in dense undergrowth and in the lower to middle storeys of forest trees. VOICE: A monotonous series of undulating clear whistles, also a series of rapid, scratchy, slurred notes. Calls include a hard *chik*. HABITAT: Broadleaved evergreen forest. DISTRIBUTION: Resident in central Peninsular Malaysia.

5 VIVID NILTAVA *Niltava vivida* 18–19cm FIELD NOTES: Sallies after flying insects in the middle and upper storey, said to run along tree branches. VOICE: A series of slow mellow whistles interspersed with scratchier notes; calls include a clear, whistled *yiyou-yiyou*. HABITAT: Broadleaved evergreen forest. DISTRIBUTION: Resident in SW China, Taiwan and possibly N Myanmar; winter visitor in W, C, E, S Myanmar, NW, C Thailand.

6 RUFOUS-BELLIED NILTAVA *Niltava sundara* 15–18cm FIELD NOTES: Regularly flicks and spreads tail. Sits unobtrusively on a low perch, makes flycatching sallies or drops to ground to capture insects. VOICE: A *sweeee-eh tri-tri-tr-tih*, a soft *cha cha* or a high *tsi-tsi-tsi-tsi*. Calls include a thin *seee*, a hard *tic* and a sharp *trrt*. HABITAT: Broadleaved evergreen forest. DISTRIBUTION: Resident in SW, W China and W, N, E Myanmar; winter visitor in C, S Myanmar, NW Thailand and N, C Laos.

7 HAINAN BLUE FLYCATCHER *Cyornis hainanus* 13–14cm FIELD NOTES: Forages in the middle level of forest trees. VOICE: Often transcribed as *hello mummy*; calls include a series of soft *tic* notes. HABITAT: Broadleaved evergreen, semi-evergreen and mixed deciduous forests, bamboo forest and mangroves. DISTRIBUTION: Resident in S, E China, Hainan, C, S, E Myanmar, Thailand (except C, S), Laos, Cambodia and Vietnam (except S Annam).

8 WHITE-TAILED FLYCATCHER *Cyornis concretus* 18cm FIELD NOTES: Forages low down in undergrowth or lower branches of forest trees; often spreads tail to reveal white panels. VOICE: A variable series of penetrating, sibilant whistles; calls include a soft *pweee* and a harsh *scree*. HABITAT: Broadleaved evergreen forest. DISTRIBUTION: Resident in SW China, N, S Myanmar, W, S Thailand, Laos, N, C Vietnam and Peninsular Malaysia.

9 PALE-CHINNED FLYCATCHER *Cyornis poliogenys* 14cm FIELD NOTES: Forages from undergrowth to the canopy. VOICE: A series of loud, rising and falling high-pitched notes, often interspersed chuckling and harsh notes. Calls include a grating rattle and a repeated *tic*. HABITAT: Broadleaved evergreen forest. DISTRIBUTION: Resident in SW China and N, W, SW, S Myanmar.

1b *decorata*

112 FLYCATCHERS

1 PALE BLUE FLYCATCHER *Cyornis unicolor* 18cm FIELD NOTES: Makes aerial sorties after flying insects, also forages in the middle and upper storeys of trees. VOICE: Song is rich and melodious, very thrush-like; gives a soft *tr-r-r-r* when alarmed. HABITAT: Broadleaved evergreen forest. DISTRIBUTION: Summers in China; resident in Hainan, Myanmar (except SW, S), Thailand (except C, SE), Cambodia, Laos, N Vietnam (N Annam) and Peninsular Malaysia.

2 CHINESE BLUE FLYCATCHER *Cyornis glaucicomans* 14–15cm FIELD NOTES: Forages low down in undergrowth, also makes sallies after flying insects. Recent split from Blue-throated Flycatcher. VOICE: Song rich with varied warbling notes; calls include a soft *tac* and a harsh *trrt* or *trrt-trt*. HABITAT: As Blue-throated Flycatcher. DISTRIBUTION: Breeds in W China; winters in C, S Thailand and Peninsular Malaysia.

3 BLUE-THROATED FLYCATCHER (BLUE-THROATED BLUE FLYCATCHER) *Cyornis rubeculoides* 14cm FIELD NOTES: Forages low down, frequently chases insects in flight. Flicks wings and tail while calling. VOICE: Song consists of sweet trilling and slurred tinkling notes mixed with sharp *tit-it trt-rrt* notes and warbling whistles. Calls include hard *tac* and *trrt* notes. HABITAT: Broadleaved evergreen, semi-evergreen and mixed deciduous forests, secondary growth and bamboo. Also frequents gardens and mangroves during migration. DISTRIBUTION: Resident in Myanmar, N, W, E Thailand, S Laos and S Vietnam.

4 HILL BLUE FLYCATCHER *Cyornis banyumas* 15cm FIELD NOTES: Unobtrusive; hawks insects from a low perch. VOICE: Song similar to Tickell's Blue Flycatcher, but descends overall; calls include a harsh *tac* and a scolding *trrt-trrt-trrt*. HABITAT: Dense humid forest with abundant undergrowth. DISTRIBUTION: Resident in SW China, N, E Myanmar, N, SE, S Thailand, N, C Laos, N Vietnam (W Tonkin, N Annam) and C Peninsular Malaysia.

5 LARGE BLUE FLYCATCHER *Cyornis magnirostris* 15cm FIELD NOTES: Actions probably similar to Hill Blue Flycatcher, which some authorities consider conspecific. VOICE: Unrecorded, possibly similar to Hill Blue Flycatcher. HABITAT: Broadleaved evergreen forest. DISTRIBUTION: Winter visitor in C, S Myanmar, S Thailand and Peninsular Malaysia.

6 MALAYSIAN BLUE FLYCATCHER *Cyornis turcosus* 13–14cm FIELD NOTES: Makes aerial pursuits of insects from a low perch. VOICE: A soft, whistled *diddle diddle dee diddle dee*. Calls include a hard *tik-tk-tk* when alarmed, and a harsh *chrrk*. HABITAT: Broadleaved evergreen forest, often near rivers or streams. DISTRIBUTION: Resident in S Thailand and Peninsular Malaysia.

7 TICKELL'S BLUE FLYCATCHER *Cyornis tickelliae* 14cm FIELD NOTES: Forages from undergrowth up to forest middle levels, regularly makes sallies to capture flying insects. VOICE: Song consists of a short metallic trill of 6–10 notes, firstly descending and then ascending. Calls are a harsh *tac* or *kak*, a *tik-tik* and a sharp, churring *trrt-trrt*. HABITAT: Broadleaved evergreen, semi-evergreen and deciduous forest and bamboo. DISTRIBUTION: Resident south from China, except SW Myanmar, C Thailand, N Laos, N Vietnam and Singapore.

8 MANGROVE BLUE FLYCATCHER *Cyornis rufigastra* 14–15cm FIELD NOTES: Forages low down, frequently sallying out from a secluded perch to capture passing insects. VOICE: Similar to Tickell's Blue Flycatcher but slower and deeper; calls include a repeated dry *psst* and a sharp, staccato *chi-chik-chik-chik*. HABITAT: Mangroves. DISTRIBUTION: Resident in S Thailand, Peninsular Malaysia and Singapore.

9 PYGMY BLUE FLYCATCHER *Muscicapella hodgsoni* 10cm FIELD NOTES: Active, leaf warbler-like, forager in the foliage of trees; often flicks wings and tail. VOICE: A high-pitched *tzit-che-che-che-ckeeee;* calls include a feeble *tsip* and a low *churr*. HABITAT: Broadleaved evergreen forest. DISTRIBUTION: Resident in SW China, W, N, Myanmar, Laos, Vietnam (N Annam) and Peninsular Malaysia; winters in E Myanmar and W, NW Thailand.

113 STARLINGS

1 ASIAN GLOSSY STARLING *Aplonis panayensis* 20cm FIELD NOTES: Mainly arboreal. Gregarious. Juvenile dark above, grey-white below with dark streaking. VOICE: A series of metallic squeaks. HABITAT: Coastal scrub, secondary growth, plantations, cultivations and urban areas. DISTRIBUTION: Mainly coastal resident in SW, S Myanmar, S Thailand, Peninsular Malaysia and Singapore.

2 SPOT-WINGED STARLING *Saroglossa spiloptera* 19cm FIELD NOTES: Usually encountered in the canopy of trees, feeding on insects, fruit and nectar. Often forms large flocks alongside other starling species. VOICE: Noisy chattering, an aggressive *chek-chek-chek* and a soft *chik-chik*; song consists of a musical warbling and dry discordant notes. HABITAT: Open deciduous woodland, open areas with scattered trees and cultivations. DISTRIBUTION: Rare winter visitor in N, E, C, S Myanmar and W, NW Thailand.

3 CHESTNUT-CHEEKED STARLING *Agropsar philippensis* 16–18cm FIELD NOTES: Mainly arboreal.Gregarious, often occurs with other starling species. VOICE: When excited utters an *airr* or *tshairr*, when alarmed gives a penetrating *tshick*. Flight call is a melodious *chrueruchu*. HABITAT: Secondary growth, open areas and cultivations. DISTRIBUTION: Winter visitor in Taiwan; passage migrant in E China; vagrants recorded from Peninsular Malaysia and Singapore.

4 DAURIAN STARLING (PURPLE-BACKED STARLING) *Agropsar sturninus* 17cm FIELD NOTES: Gregarious, often associates with Asian Glossy Starlings. VOICE: Calls include loud crackling sounds and a soft *prrp* given in flight. HABITAT: Forest edge, secondary growth, open areas and cultivations. DISTRIBUTION: Winter visitor C, S Thailand, Peninsular Malaysia and Singapore; passage migrant elsewhere.

5 WHITE-SHOULDERED STARLING *Sturnia sinensis* 17cm FIELD NOTES: Usually gregarious, forages in trees and on the ground. VOICE: A harsh *kaar* and a soft *preep* given in flight. HABITAT: Open areas with scattered trees, scrub, cultivations and urban areas. DISTRIBUTION: Breeds in southern China; possible resident in N Vietnam; winter visitor in Taiwan and in the south, except Myanmar, most of Laos, Peninsular Malaysia and Singapore.

6 BRAHMINY STARLING *Sturnia pagodarum* 21cm FIELD NOTES: Forages mainly on the ground, often in the company of cattle; also feeds in fruiting and flowering trees. VOICE: Various croaking and chattering notes and short grating *churrs* when alarmed. HABITAT: Open deciduous forest, scrub, cultivations and around human habitations. DISTRIBUTION: Vagrant, recorded in S Thailand and SW China.

7 CHESTNUT-TAILED STARLING *Sturnia malabarica* 20cm FIELD NOTES: Gregarious; forages mainly in trees. Grey race *S. m. nemoricla* (7b) occurs over most of the area, the nominate (main illustration) is found in the north of W Myanmar. VOICE: Song is a series of short hard notes and low squeaky churrs, the same notes are given in rapid subdued outbursts. Calls include short buzzes and whistles. HABITAT: Open woodland and open country with scattered trees. DISTRIBUTION: Resident in SW China, Myanmar, W, NW Thailand, Laos and Vietnam (except W Tonkin); winter visitor in Thailand (except S where recorded as a vagrant) and Cambodia.

8 ROSE-COLOURED STARLING (ROSY PASTOR or STARLING) *Pastor roseus* 21cm FIELD NOTES: Usually gregarious. Juvenile grey-brown above, slightly paler below; bill dark. VOICE: In flight utters a short *ki-ki-ki*. Flocks emit a constant chatter. HABITAT: Open country, wooded areas including cultivations. DISTRIBUTION: Vagrant, recorded in W, S Thailand, N Vietnam (E Tonkin) and Singapore.

114 STARLINGS

1 STARLING (COMMON or EUROPEAN STARLING) *Sturnus vulgaris* 22cm FIELD NOTES: Gregarious. Mainly a ground forager. Juveniles are grey-brown above, slightly paler below, especially on throat; bill dark. VOICE: Calls include a harsh *tcherrr*, a hard *kyik* and a grating *schaahr*. HABITAT: Open country, cultivations and around urban habitations. DISTRIBUTION: Vagrant, recorded in E, S China, N Myanmar, NW, NE Thailand and N, C Vietnam.

2 WHITE-CHEEKED STARLING *Spodiopsar cineraceus* 22cm FIELD NOTES: Gregarious. Mainly forages on the ground. VOICE: A monotonous, creaking *chir-chir-chay-cheet-cheet...* HABITAT: Open country, cultivations and open woodland. DISTRIBUTION: Winter visitor in S, E China, Hainan, Taiwan and N Vietnam (E Tonkin); vagrants recorded in N Myanmar and NW, C Thailand.

3 RED-BILLED STARLING (SILKY STARLING) *Spodiopsar sericeus* 22cm FIELD NOTES: Gregarious, with winter flocks numbering 100 plus. Forages on the ground and in trees. VOICE: Song is sweet and melodious; calls similar to those of Starling. HABITAT: Cultivated areas with scattered trees, scrub groves and gardens. DISTRIBUTION: Resident in China and Hainan; winter visitor in N Vietnam and Taiwan.

4 ASIAN PIED STARLING (PIED MYNA) *Gracupica contra* 22–25cm FIELD NOTES: Forages on the ground, usually in pairs or small parties with larger flocks post breeding. Race *G. c. supercilliaris* (4b) occurs in Myanmar. VOICE: A prolonged series of shrill churrs with a few croaking and buzzing notes; sometimes includes mimicry of other birds. Calls include a loud *staar-staar,* a shrill *shree-shree* also various chuckles, warbles and whistles. HABITAT: Open, usually moist areas with scattered trees, cultivations and urban areas. DISTRIBUTION: Resident in SW China, Myanmar, most of Thailand, Cambodia and N Laos; winter visitor to S Thailand and W Peninsular Malaysia.

5 BLACK-COLLARED STARLING *Gracupica nigricollis* 26–30cm FIELD NOTES: Forages on the ground, occasionally among grazing cattle. VOICE: A mixture of dry rattles and melodic notes, also a harsh *kraak-kraak*. HABITAT: Open grasslands, scrub, cultivations and urban areas. DISTRIBUTION: Resident in S, E China and throughout the south, except SW, S Myanmar and Singapore.

6 VINOUS-BREASTED STARLING *Acridotheres burmannicus* 21–24ccm FIELD NOTES: Mainly a ground forager, favours short, well-watered grassland. Race *A. b. leucocephalus* (6b) occurs in Thailand (except NW, S), Cambodia, C, S Laos and C, S Vietnam. VOICE: A harsh *tchew-it, tchew-tchieuw* or *tchew iri-tchew iri-tchieuw...* HABITAT: Semi-desert, dry open country, scrub, cultivation and forest clearings. DISTRIBUTION: Resident in Myanmar, W, C, NE, SE, S Thailand, Cambodia, C, S Laos and C, S Vietnam. Recorded as a vagrant in Peninsular Malaysia and Singapore.

7 BLACK-WINGED STARLING *Acridotheres melanopterus* 22–24cm FIELD NOTES: Usually encountered in pairs or small parties foraging on the ground or in trees and bushes. Breeds and roosts colonially. VOICE: A throaty *chok*, a harsh *kaar* and a drawn-out *keeer*; in flight gives a high, whistled *tsoowit* or *tsoowee*. HABITAT: Open areas with scrub. DISTRIBUTION: Introduced resident in Singapore.

1

br

n-br

2

3

♀

♂

4

4b *superciliaris*

5

6b *leucocephalus*

6

7

115 MYNAS

1 COMMON MYNA *Acridotheres tristis* 23cm FIELD NOTES: Very tame. In flight shows bold white primary patches. VOICE: A querulous *kwerrh* and many gurgling and chattering notes; when alarmed utters a harsh *chake-chake*. Song is a tuneless mixture of gurgling and whistled phrases. HABITAT: Around human habitations, open areas and cultivations. DISTRIBUTION: Resident in SW China, Hainan, Taiwan and throughout the south.

2 JUNGLE MYNA *Acridotheres fuscus* 23cm FIELD NOTES: Gregarious; forms large flocks at roosts. Forages mainly on the ground. In flight shows white primary patches. VOICE: A repeated *tiuck-tiuck-tiuck*; other calls and song similar to Common Myna. HABITAT: Open dry and grassy areas, often near water, cultivations and near human habitations. DISTRIBUTION: Resident in Myanmar (except N), C, W, S Thailand and Peninsular Malaysia.

3 JAVAN MYNA *Acridotheres javanicus* 24–25cm FIELD NOTES: Forages mainly on the ground in pairs or small groups, with larger flocks where food is plentiful. In flight shows white patch at base of primaries. VOICE: Very similar to that of Common Myna. HABITAT: Open country, cultivations and urban areas. DISTRIBUTION: Introduced resident in S Peninsular Malaysia and Singapore.

4 COLLARED MYNA *Acridotheres albocinctus* 23cm FIELD NOTES: Forages mainly on the ground. In flight shows white primary patches. VOICE: At the time of writing undescribed. HABITAT: Tall grassland and cultivated areas. DISTRIBUTION: Resident in SW China and W, N, C, E Myanmar.

5 GREAT MYNA *Acridotheres grandis* 25cm FIELD NOTES: Forages mostly on the ground. In flight shows white primary patches. VOICE: Song and calls similar to Common Myna. HABITAT: Open country, cultivations and urban areas. DISTRIBUTION: Resident in SW China and throughout the south, except SW Myanmar and Singapore.

6 CRESTED MYNA *Acridotheres cristatellus* 25cm FIELD NOTES: Usually occurs in flocks foraging on the ground. Sometimes forms large post-breeding flocks that roost colonially. In flight shows white flashes at base of primaries. VOICE: Similar to Common Myna, but song is more whistled, less fluty. HABITAT: Open areas, scrub, cultivations and urban areas. DISTRIBUTION: Resident in China, Hainan, Taiwan, C, S, Laos and Vietnam (except Cochinchina); feral resident in Peninsular Malaysia and Singapore.

7 GOLDEN-CRESTED MYNA *Ampeliceps coronatus* 19–21cm FIELD NOTES: Arboreal, regularly perches in exposed tops of tall trees. In flight shows yellow primary patches. VOICE: Calls include a metallic bell-like note, otherwise all calls similar to Hill Myna, but higher-pitched. HABITAT: Broadleaved evergreen and deciduous forest, forest edge and clearings. DISTRIBUTION: Resident in SW China, C, S Myanmar, Thailand (except C), Cambodia, Laos, Vietnam (except W Tonkin) and perhaps NW Peninsular Malaysia.

8 HILL MYNA (COMMON HILL MYNA) *Gracula religiosa* 25–29cm FIELD NOTES: Arboreal, generally encountered in pairs or small groups in the exposed tops of tall trees. In flight shows white patches at the base of primaries. VOICE: Various chip notes, soft um-sounds, whisper-whistles and many types of whistles, croaks and wails. HABITAT: Broadleaved evergreen and deciduous forest, forest edge and clearings. DISTRIBUTION: Resident in S China, Hainan and throughout the south (except C Thailand).

10/18
Taiwan
Thailand

1

2

10/22/18
Singapore

3

4

5

6

7

10/18 Cambodia

♀

♂

8

116 NUTHATCHES

1 NUTHATCH (EURASIAN NUTHATCH) *Sitta europaea sinensis* 14cm FIELD NOTES: Typical nuthatch actions: climbs up, down and along trunks or branches foraging for prey. Occasionally feeds on the ground. VOICE: Variable, including a slowish *pee-pee-pee…* and a long, rapid trill. Calls include a liquid *dwip* or *dwip-dwip*, a shrill *sirrr*, a harsh *trah* and a thin *tsee-tsee-tsee*. HABITAT: Deciduous and mixed forests. DISTRIBUTION: Resident over much of China and Taiwan.

2 CHESTNUT-VENTED NUTHATCH *Sitta nagaensis* 12–14cm FIELD NOTES: Actions similar to Nuthatch, although possibly feeds more often on the ground and on rocks. VOICE: Song is a fast, flat, monotonous trill; calls include a squeaky *sit* or *sit-sit*, a trilling *chit-it-it-it* and a whining *quir, kner* or *mew*. HABITAT: Evergreen hill forests, pine forest, open oak and deciduous forests. DISTRIBUTION: Resident in SW China, W, N, E, SW Myanmar, S Laos and Vietnam (S Annam).

3 NEGLECTED NUTHATCH (BURMESE NUTHATCH) *Sitta neglecta* 13cm FIELD NOTES: Usually forages on the upper trunk or upper branches. Recently split from Chestnut-bellied Nuthatch. VOICE: Song is a mellow, wavering trill; calls include a screechy *chreet-chreet* and a hard explosive rattle. HABITAT: Dry dipterocarp and pine forest. DISTRIBUTION: Resident in W, E Myanmar, N, W Thailand, C, S Laos, Cambodia and C Vietnam.

4 CHESTNUT-BELLIED NUTHATCH *Sitta cinnamoventris* 14cm FIELD NOTES: Actions similar to Nuthatch. VOICE: Song is a fast, repeated trill; calls include a mellow *tsup*, a thin *sit* or *sit-sit* and a clipped *chreet chreet chreet…* HABITAT: Deciduous forests. DISTRIBUTION: Resident in SW China, N Myanmar, NW Thailand, N Laos and NW Vietnam.

5 WHITE-TAILED NUTHATCH *Sitta himalayensis* 12cm FIELD NOTES: Forages mostly on mossy branches in upper parts of trees. VOICE: Calls include a *nit, shree*, a *tschak*, a *chak-chak* and a monotonous rattle. Trilling song consists of a rapid repetition of a single *pee* note. HABITAT: Broadleaved evergreen and mixed broadleaved and coniferous forests. DISTRIBUTION: Resident in SW China, W, N, E Myanmar, N Laos and N Vietnam (W Tonkin).

6 WHITE-BROWED NUTHATCH *Sitta victoriae* 11–12cm FIELD NOTES: Forages on the smaller, outer branches of trees. VOICE: A 9–12 note crescendo, *whi-whi-whi-whi-whi-whi…* calls include a soft, liquid *pit* or *plit* and an insistent *pee-pee-pee…* HABITAT: Oak and mixed oak and rhododendron forests. DISTRIBUTION: Resident in W Myanmar (South China Hills).

7 PRZEWALSKI'S NUTHATCH *Sitta przewalskii* 12–13cm FIELD NOTES: Forages mainly in the tops of trees. Recently split from White-cheeked Nuthatch. VOICE: Calls include a muffled *chip*, a whistled *dweep* or *dweep-eep* and a thin *pee-pee-pee-pee*;. Possible song is a clear *ti-tui ti-tui ti-tui…* HABITAT: Spruce and fir forests. DISTRIBUTION: Possibly occurs in SW China.

8 CHINESE NUTHATCH *Sitta villosa* 11–12cm FIELD NOTES: Forages among small twigs and branches at the top of trees; occasionally makes flycatching sorties. VOICE: Song consists of a series of upward-inflected whistles, *tsi-pui-pui-pui-pui*; calls include a harsh *schraa-schraa*, a *wip-wip-wip* and a repeated *quir-quir*. HABITAT: Coniferous forests. DISTRIBUTION: Possibly occurs in the mountainous areas of the extreme NW of the region.

9 YUNNAN NUTHATCH *Sitta yunnanensis* 12cm FIELD NOTES: Forages, tit-like, among needle clusters of pine trees. VOICE: Calls include a nasal *nit*, an abrupt *chit-chit*, a piping *pi-pi-pi-pi…* and a scolding *schri-schri-schri…* HABITAT: Open mature pine forests. DISTRIBUTION: Resident in SW Yunnan.

10 GIANT NUTHATCH *Sitta magna* 20cm FIELD NOTES: Actions much as other nuthatches, but less restless. Occasionally cocks tail; in flight wings give out a whirring sound. VOICE: Calls include a chattering *gd-da-da*, *dig-er-up* or *get-it-up*, also a *ge-de-ku* that sometimes becomes a gamebird-like *gu-drr gu-drr gu-drr*. HABITAT: Open mature pine and mixed oak and pine forest. DISTRIBUTION: Resident in SW China, C, E Myanmar and NW Thailand.

117 NUTHATCHES; WALLCREEPER; TREECREEPERS

1 VELVET-FRONTED NUTHATCH *Sitta frontalis* 12–13cm FIELD NOTES: Forages from undergrowth to the canopy; often part of mixed-species flocks. VOICE: Song is a rattling *sit-sit-sit-sit...* Calls include a hard *chat, chip* or *chlit* and a thin *sip*. HABITAT: Broadleaved evergreen, semi-evergreen and mixed deciduous forest, also mixed oak and pine forest. DISTRIBUTION: Resident southwards from SW China and Hainan.

2 BLUE NUTHATCH *Sitta azurea* 13–14cm FIELD NOTES: Forages mainly in the upper storey, on trunks and main branches. Often occurs in small parties and in mixed species flocks. VOICE: A short *chit*, which when excited lengthens into a *chi-chit*, a *chit-chit-chit*, a *chir-ri-rit* or a trilling *tititititititik*. Also utters a mellow *tup*, a squeaky *zhe* or *zhe-zhe* and a nasal *kneu*. HABITAT: Broadleaved evergreen forests. DISTRIBUTION: Resident in Peninsular Malaysia.

3 YELLOW-BILLED NUTHATCH *Sitta solangiae* 12–14cm FIELD NOTES: Found singly or in small parties, often part of mixed-species flocks, foraging from undergrowth to the trunks and main branches in the upper storey. VOICE: A stony *chit* that often lengthens into a *chit-it-it-it-it-it...* Song is a fast *sit-ti-ti-ti-ti-ti...* HABITAT: Broadleaved evergreen forest. DISTRIBUTION: Resident in Hainan, S Laos and N, C Vietnam.

4 BEAUTIFUL NUTHATCH *Sitta formosa* 16–17cm FIELD NOTES: Forages up, down and along branches; usually high up in tall trees covered with epiphytes; more sluggish than other nuthatches. VOICE: A soft, liquid *plit* and an explosive *chit* that sometimes lengthens to a *chit-it chit-it chit-it* or *chit-it-it chirririt*. Song is a *chi it it it it it it it...* HABITAT: Broadleaved evergreen and semi-evergreen forests. DISTRIBUTION: Resident in SW China, N, E Myanmar, N, C Laos and N Vietnam (W Tonkin); possibly resident in NW Thailand.

5 WALLCREEPER *Tichodroma muraria* 16–17cm FIELD NOTES: Forages on cliff faces and in crevices; regularly flicks wings open to reveal red and white markings. VOICE: A drawn-out, piping *tu-tuee-zreeeeeu* or *chewee-cheweeooo*. Calls are a whistled *tseeoo*, a rapid twitter, a buzzing *zree* and a *chup*. HABITAT: High-altitude cliffs and rock faces, in winter often forced to lower altitudes when may occur on old buildings. DISTRIBUTION: Winter visitor to E, C and W China.

6 BAR-TAILED TREECREEPER *Certhia himalayana* 14cm FIELD NOTES: Forages by climbing up tree trunks and along branches; sometimes flycatches or feeds on the ground. VOICE: A lilting *tsee tsu-tsu tsut tut tut li tee* or *ti ti tu-du-du-du-du*. Calls include a thin *tsui*, a *tsee* and a rising *tseet*. HABITAT: Coniferous, mixed broadleaved-coniferous and broadleaved evergreen forest. DISTRIBUTION: Resident in SW China and N, W Myanmar.

7 RUSTY-FLANKED TREECREEPER *Certhia nipalensis* 14cm FIELD NOTES: Forages among mosses and plants on trunks and branches. VOICE: A high-pitched, accelerating trill; calls with a thin *sit*. HABITAT: Broadleaved evergreen and mixed broadleaved and coniferous forests. DISTRIBUTION: Resident in SW China and W Myanmar.

8 SIKKIM TREECREEPER *Certhia discolor* 14cm FIELD NOTES: Creeps up mossy trunks and branches. VOICE: A monotonous *chit-it-it-it-it-it-it-it...* calls include a *tchip*, a *tsit* and a rattling *chi-r-r-it*. HABITAT: Broadleaved evergreen and mixed broadleaved and pine forest. DISTRIBUTION: Resident in SW China.

9 HUME'S TREECREEPER *Certhia manipurensis* 14cm FIELD NOTES: Actions similar to Brown-throated Treecreeper. VOICE: An explosive *tchit*, which may lengthen into a rattle; song is a monotonous slow rattle. HABITAT: Moist evergreen hill forest. DISTRIBUTION: Resident in SW China, N, S, E Myanmar, N, NW Thailand, N Laos and Vietnam (W Tonkin, S Annam).

10 HODGSON'S TREECREEPER *Certhia hodgsoni* 11–12cm FIELD NOTES: Creeps up and around trees in jerky movements. VOICE: A high-pitched *tzee-tzee-tzizizi*; calls include a *tsree* or *tsree-tsree*. HABITAT: Mixed conifer and birch forest. DISTRIBUTION: Resident in SW China and N Myanmar.

118 PENDULINE TIT; TITS

1 CHINESE PENDULINE TIT *Remiz consobrinus* 10–11cm FIELD NOTES: Agile, active forager on reed heads and scrub foliage; sometimes in small to large flocks. VOICE: A repeated, see-sawing *si si tiu si si tiu*; calls include a thin *tseee* or *pseee*, a *piu* and a series of *siu* notes. HABITAT: Reedbeds, scrub and rank vegetation. DISTRIBUTION: Winter visitor to SW, SE and N China; vagrant, recorded in N Vietnam.

2 FIRE-CAPPED TIT *Cephalopyrus flammiceps* 10cm FIELD NOTES: Active and agile forager in tall trees and occasionally in bushes; often in small groups. VOICE: Song variable with many phrases, including a high-pitched *tink-tink-tink-tink* a slow *pitsu-pitsu* a quicker *pissu-pissu-pissu* and a vibrant *psing-psing-psing*; call is a constantly, repeated *tsit*. HABITAT: Broadleaved evergreen and semi-evergreen forest. DISTRIBUTION: Breeds in SW China; winter visitor in E Myanmar, NW Thailand and N Laos.

3 BLACK-BIBBED TIT *Poecile hypermelaenus* 11–12cm FIELD NOTES: Forages from low down in scrub to the mid storey and canopy; occurs singly or in small flocks of 3–5 birds. VOICE: Calls include a high thin *stip*, a thin *si-si* and an explosive *psiup*, also utters a chattering *chrrrrr* and a scolding *chay*. HABITAT: Open broadleaved evergreen and pine forest, forest edge and scrub. DISTRIBUTION: Resident in SW, N, NE China and W Myanmar (Mount Victoria).

4 WILLOW TIT *Poecile montanus songarus* 13cm FIELD NOTES: Often occurs in small parties, regularly feeds on catkins in spring. This race is sometimes split as Songar Tit. VOICE: Calls include a nasal, scolding *dzee*, a thin *psit* or *psit-dzee* and a *chick-a-dee*. HABITAT: Coniferous and mixed forests. DISTRIBUTION: Possibly resident in SW China.

5 PÈRE DAVID'S TIT (RED or RUSTY-BELLIED TIT) *Poecile davidi* 12–13cm FIELD NOTES: Acrobatic feeder, mainly in the canopy of tall trees. Often occurs in small flocks post breeding. VOICE: Calls include *tsip*, *psit* and a drawn-out *chi-it-it*; in song utters a *tsip zee zee*. HABITAT: Mature mixed forest. DISTRIBUTION: Resident in NW of the region.

6 WHITE-BROWED TIT *Poecile superciliosus* 13–15cm FIELD NOTES: Feeds low down, typical active tit habits. VOICE: Variable, complex song, *tsee-tsee-tsee-pwi-pee*, *tchip-tchip-pwi-pee*, *tsir'r'r'r'r'r-pee-pee-pee*, *peta-peta-peta-peta-peta* etc.; calls include a thin *si-si,* an insect-like *trrrrrr* and a *tsi-sit-sit-sit-sit-sit-sit-sip*. HABITAT: Dwarf alpine shrubs, scrub and bushes, usually near watercourses; post breeding occurs in taller vegetation and open areas of spruce forests. DISTRIBUTION: May occur in the mountainous areas of W China.

7 CHESTNUT-BELLIED TIT *Sittiparus castaneoventris* 12–14cm FIELD NOTES: Forages mostly in the upper storeys, collecting food from foliage and trunks, occasionally catches insects in flight. VOICE: Calls include a weak *tsuu tsuu tsuu*, a drawn-out, high *spit-see-see-see* and a scolding *chi-chi-chi*; song variable, monotone whistles usually combined with a ringing *peee*. HABITAT: Open deciduous and mixed forest. DISTRIBUTION: Resident in Taiwan.

8 RUFOUS-VENTED TIT *Periparus rubidiventris* 12–13cm FIELD NOTES: Forages mostly in the canopy but will also descend to lower levels and undergrowth; often forms part of mixed-species feeding flocks. VOICE: A rattling *chi-chi-chi-chi…* or *chip-chip-chip-chip-chip* etc; calls include a thin *seet* or *psset*, a clear *pee* a clicking *chip* and a scolding *chit-it-it-it*. HABITAT: Broadleaved evergreen and coniferous forest. DISTRIBUTION: Resident in SW China and N Myanmar.

119 TITS

1 COAL TIT *Periparus ater* 11cm FIELD NOTES: Agile active forager; forms part of mixed-species feeding flocks post breeding. VOICE: Song variable, includes a thin *chip-pe chip-pe…* a *peechoo-peechoo-peechoo* and a *wee-tsee wee-tsee wee-tsee.* Calls include a cheeping *tsi-tsi* and a hoarse *szee.* HABITAT: Coniferous and mixed coniferous and broadleaved forest. DISTRIBUTION: Resident in SW, W, NE China, Taiwan and N Myanmar.

2 GREY CRESTED TIT *Lophophanes dichrous* 12cm FIELD NOTES: Shy; usually in pairs or small parties. VOICE: In song utters a *whee-whee-tz-tz-tz;* calls include a high *zai* and a rapid *ti-ti-ti-ti-ti.* HABITAT: Mainly in oak or other broadleaved forests, also occurs in mixed and conifer forests. DISTRIBUTION: Resident in SW China and N Myanmar.

3 YELLOW-BELLIED TIT *Pardaliparus venustulus* 10cm FIELD NOTES: Forages in middle to low levels in trees and in undergrowth; usually in pairs or small parties. VOICE: Song consists of a series of metallic phrases, *swi-swi-swi, suwi-suwi-suwi, sipu-sipu-sipu* occasionally interspersed with more complex phrases. Calls include a *dzee-dzee-dzee*, a rapid *si-si-si-si* and a soft *sit-too.* HABITAT: Open broadleaved deciduous and evergreen forests, bamboo and plantations. DISTRIBUTION: Resident in China (except S).

4 GREEN-BACKED TIT *Parus monticolus* 12–13cm FIELD NOTES: Forages from the ground up to the canopy, post breeding may occur in small flocks of up to 20 birds. VOICE: Variable song includes a *seta-seta-seta*, a *tu-weeh-tu-weeh* and a *whit-ee whit-ee.* Calls include a rapid *si-si-si-si*, a harsh *shick-shick-shick* a clear *te-te-whee* and a musical *pling-pling-pling-tee-eurr.* HABITAT: Evergreen, deciduous and mixed forests. DISTRIBUTION: Resident in W China, Taiwan, W, N Myanmar, C Laos and N, S Vietnam (E Tonkin, S Annam).

5 CINEREOUS TIT *Parus cinereus* 13–14cm FIELD NOTES: Bold, less agile than many of the smaller tits. Recently split from Great Tit (*Parus major*). VOICE: Song is a rapidly, repeated *chew-a-ti chew-a-ti chew-a-ti* or similar. Calls include a harsh *tcha-tcha-tcha* and a ringing *pink-pink-pink.* HABITAT: Deciduous forest mixed with pines, dry teak forests, bamboo and mangroves. DISTRIBUTION: Resident in Hainan and throughout the south, except S Myanmar (Tenasserim), W, C, SE Thailand and Singapore.

6 JAPANESE TIT *Parus minor* 13–14cm FIELD NOTES: Bold and less agile than many of the smaller tits. Recently split from Great Tit (*Parus major*). VOICE: Song is a shrill *shi-ju shi-ju shi-ju;* calls similar to Cinerous Tit. HABITAT: Open woodland, stands of pines in hill evergreen forest (Thailand), light forest, wooded cultivations and gardens. DISTRIBUTION: Resident in China, N, E Myanmar, N Thailand, N, Laos and N Vietnam.

7 YELLOW TIT *Machlolophus holsti* 13cm FIELD NOTES: Usually encountered in the canopy or upper storey, singly or in pairs. May also join mixed-species foraging flocks. VOICE: Song consists of a variety of trisyllabic ringing notes, *tu-wich-ch…* or similar; calls include a thin *si-si-si*, a sibilant *tzee-tzee-tzee* and a scolding *dz-za-za-za-za.* HABITAT: Broadleaved and occasionally primary mixed forest and open secondary growth. DISTRIBUTION: Resident in Taiwan.

8 YELLOW-CHEEKED TIT *Machlolophus spilonotus* 14cm FIELD NOTES: Actions similar to Cinerous Tit. Race *P. s. rex* (8b) occurs in S China, N Vietnam and NE Laos. VOICE: Song is a ringing, rapidly repeated *chee-chee-piu chee-chee-piu chee-piu…* or *dzi-dzi-pu dzi-dzi-pu…* Calls include a *sit*, a *si-si-si* a lisping *tsee-tsee-tsee* and a *witch-a-witch-a-witch* that is often combined with a harsh *churr-r-r-r-r.* HABITAT: Broadleaved evergreen forest, light oak or pine forests. Also rhododendrons and secondary growth with scattered trees. DISTRIBUTION: Resident in S China, Myanmar (except SW, C), W, NE, NE Thailand, Laos and N, C Vietnam.

120 TITS; LONG-TAILED TITS

1 YELLOW-BROWED TIT *Sylviparus modestus* 10cm FIELD NOTES: Active and acrobatic forager in tree foliage, often part of mixed-species feeding flocks. VOICE: Probable song is a shrill *zee-zi-zee-zi-zee-zi...* calls include a *tsip* a *tchup* a rapid, trilling *tszizizizizizizizi...* and a metallic *pli-pli-pli-pli.* HABITAT: Broadleaved evergreen forest. DISTRIBUTION: Resident in SW, W, EC China, W, N, NE Myanmar, NW Thailand, N, S Laos and N, S Vietnam (W Tonkin, S Annam).

2 SULTAN TIT *Melanochlora sultanea* 20–21cm FIELD NOTES: Acrobatic forager in foliage of trees and bushes; crest is raised when excited. Black-crested race M. *s. gayeti* (2b) occurs in S Laos and C Vietnam. VOICE: Song consists of a mellow, whistled *piu-piu-piu-piu-piu* or similar; calls include a rattling *chi-dip tri-trip* and a fast, squeaky *tria-tria-tria, tcheery-tcheery-tcheery* or *squear-squear-squear.* HABITAT: Broadleaved evergreen, semi-evergreen and mixed deciduous forests. DISTRIBUTION: Resident in SW, S, SE China, Hainan and in south except C Thailand, Cambodia, S Vietnam and Singapore.

3 SILVER-THROATED BUSHTIT *Aegithalos glaucogularis* 13–16cm FIELD NOTES: Always on the move, sometimes in flocks. Often treated as conspecific with Long-tailed Tit (*Aegithalos caudatus*). VOICE: Calls include a high-pitched *see-see-see* or *see-see-see-sit* and a louder *tsirrrup.* HABITAT: Forest edge and scrub. DISTRIBUTION: Resident in N China.

4 BLACK-THROATED BUSHTIT *Aegithalos concinnus* 10–11cm FIELD NOTES: Gregarious, often in quite large flocks. Active and acrobatic. Juveniles lack the black throat. Race A. *c. pulchellus* (4b) is found in E Myanmar, NW Thailand; A. *c. annamensis* (4c) occurs in S Laos and C Vietnam. VOICE: Calls include a *si-si-si-si* and a rattling *churr-trrrt-trrrt*; song is a repeated twittering combined with the odd single chirp. HABITAT: Broadleaved evergreen and mixed broadleaved and pine forest, forest edge and secondary growth. DISTRIBUTION: Resident in China, Taiwan, W, N, E Myanmar, NW Thailand, E Cambodia, Laos and Vietnam.

5 BLACK-BROWED BUSHTIT *Aegithalos iouschistos* 11cm FIELD NOTES: Active and agile forager. VOICE: A constant *see-see-see see*, a *tup* or *trrup* and, when alarmed, a shrill *zeet* and *trr-trr-trr.* Song is a jumbled twittering. HABITAT: Open broadleaved evergreen and mixed broadleaved and coniferous forest, pine forest, forest edge and secondary growth. DISTRIBUTION: Resident in SW China and N Myanmar.

6 BURMESE BUSHTIT (MYANMAR TIT) *Aegithalos sharpei* 11cm FIELD NOTES: Typically agile and active. Often considered conspecific with Black-browed Bushtit. VOICE: Calls include a high-pitched *tsi-si-si-si*, a rolling *tseep*, a soft *tsup* and a slurred, rattling *tsirrup.* HABITAT: Open pine forest, occasionally high-altitude oak and rhododendron forest. DISTRIBUTION: Resident in W Myanmar (Mt Victoria).

7 SOOTY BUSHTIT *Aegithalos fuliginosus* 11–12cm FIELD NOTES: Agile forager in the shrub layer. Post breeding forms fast-moving flocks of up to 40 individuals. VOICE: 'Song' is a quiet jumble of twittering and trilling; calls include a high-pitched *see-see-see*, a clipped *tup* and a rattling *tchrrrp.* HABITAT: Mixed forests with scrub of willow, birch, rhododendron or bamboo. DISTRIBUTION: Possibly occurs in the mountainous areas of W China.

1

2

♀

2b *gayeti*

3

♂

4c *annamensis*

4b *pulchellus*

4

5

7

6

121 MARTINS

1 WHITE-EYED RIVER MARTIN *Pseudochelidon sirintarae* 15cm (with tail 24cm) FIELD NOTES: Little known, may be extinct; said to have a buoyant, graceful flight. The juvenile is browner with a pale throat, lacks tail streamers. VOICE: Not recorded. HABITAT: Roosts in reeds of marshy reservoirs. DISTRIBUTION: May possibly breed in Myanmar or Thailand; winters in central Thailand.

2 SAND MARTIN (COLLARED SAND MARTIN) *Riparia riparia* 12cm FIELD NOTES: Gregarious, regularly associates with other swallows. Rapid, light flight, usually low over water or ground. VOICE: A harsh *tschr* and a *schrrp* uttered when excited. HABITAT: Lakes, rivers and marshes; also over open country on migration. DISTRIBUTION: Winter visitor in SW China, SW, W, C, S Myanmar, NW, W Thailand, N, C Laos, Cambodia and C, S Vietnam.

3 PALE MARTIN (PALE SAND MARTIN) *Riparia diluta* 13cm FIELD NOTES: Very similar to Sand Martin but with a less well-defined breast-band. Fast fluttery flight, often in the company of other swallows. VOICE: Calls include a short *ret* or *brrit*. HABITAT: Open country, usually near water; regularly roosts in reedbeds. DISTRIBUTION: Winter visitor in S China and N Vietnam (E Tonkin).

4 PLAIN MARTIN (PLAIN SAND MARTIN or BROWN-THROATED MARTIN) *Riparia paludicola* 12cm FIELD NOTES: Gregarious. Weak fluttering flight that can recall a small bat. Occasionally some birds show a paler throat. VOICE: A soft twittering, often uttered in flight. Calls include a low *chrrr* or *skrr*, and a harsh *svee-svee*. HABITAT: Rivers, streams and lakes; also forages over grasslands. DISTRIBUTION: Resident in Taiwan, SW China, Myanmar, NW, NE Thailand, Cambodia, Laos and N Vietnam.

5 CRAG MARTIN (EURASIAN CRAG MARTIN) *Ptyonoprogne rupestris* 15cm FIELD NOTES: Powerful, slow but agile flight, with much gliding. Shows pale spots when tail is spread. Usually encountered in small parties; larger parties post breeding. VOICE: A quiet, throaty, rapid twitter; calls include a *prrit,* a warning *zrrr* and a plaintive *whee*. HABITAT: Cliffs, gorges and old buildings. DISTRIBUTION: Resident in SW China.

6 DUSKY CRAG MARTIN *Ptyonoprogne concolor* 13cm FIELD NOTES: Usually in pairs or small groups with larger parties post breeding. Flight slow with frequent periods of gliding. Shows pale spots when tail is spread. VOICE: A twittering song and a soft *chit-chit* contact call. HABITAT: Mountainous and hilly areas with cliffs, caves and gorges, also around buildings. DISTRIBUTION: Resident in SW China, C, E, S Myanmar, Thailand (except SE), Laos, N, C Vietnam and Peninsular Malaysia.

122 SWALLOWS; HOUSE MARTINS

1 SWALLOW (BARN SWALLOW) *Hirundo rustica* 18cm FIELD NOTES: Flies with twists and turns to capture flying insects. Rusty race *H. r. tytleri* (1b) recorded in Myanmar, Thailand, C Vietnam and Peninsular Malaysia. VOICE: A melodious twittering interspersed with a grating rattle; calls include a *vit-vit* and a *chir-chir* when agitated. HABITAT: Open country, usually not far from water and habitations. DISTRIBUTION: Breeds in China, Taiwan, Hainan, NW, NE Thailand, N Laos and N Vietnam; winters throughout the south.

2 PACIFIC SWALLOW *Hirundo tahitica* 13cm FIELD NOTES: Flight fast with frequent swerving, gliding and banking. VOICE: A twittering *twsit-twsit-twsit*; calls include a *titswee* and a low *swoo.* HABITAT: Coastal areas, often near habitations; above forests, forest clearings and open country. DISTRIBUTION: Resident in Taiwan and in coastal areas in the south, except C Thailand and C, N Vietnam.

3 WIRE-TAILED SWALLOW *Hirundo smithii* 14–21cm FIELD NOTES: Flight fast, often low over water. Juvenile has brown crown and lacks the long outer-tail filaments. VOICE: A twittering *chirrickweet-chirrickweet*; calls include a *chit-chit* and a *chichip-chichip* given when alarmed. HABITAT: Grasslands, cultivations and urban areas, usually near water. DISTRIBUTION: Resident in Myanmar, NW, NE Thailand, Cambodia, Laos and S Vietnam (S Annam).

4 STRIATED SWALLOW *Cecropis striolata* 19cm FIELD NOTES: Flight slow and buoyant, usually low over the ground or around cliffs. VOICE: A soft twittering; calls include a drawn-out *quitsch*, a *pin* and a repeated *chi-chi-chi.* HABITAT: Open areas, often near water, cliffs and river gorges. DISTRIBUTION: Resident in Taiwan, S China, N, C, E, S Myanmar, W, NW, NE, S Thailand, Cambodia, Laos, S Vietnam, Peninsular Malaysia and Singapore.

5 RED-RUMPED SWALLOW *Cecropis daurica* 16–17cm FIELD NOTES: Flight slow and graceful with much gliding and soaring. Race *H. d. japonica* (5b) breeds in E China and winters in the south. VOICE: A quiet twittering; calls include a mewing, an aggressive *krr* and a *djuit* contact note. HABITAT: Open country, lightly wooded areas, rocky gorges and cliffs, also open scrub and cultivations. DISTRIBUTION: Summers in China, winters throughout the south.

6 RUFOUS-BELLIED SWALLOW *Cecropis badia* 19–20cm FIELD NOTES: Actions similar to Striated Swallow, which is often considered conspecific. VOICE: A twittering a warble; calls include a *tweep*, a trembling *schwirrr* and a *chi-chi-chi.* HABITAT: Open hilly country, rocky outcrops, over open country and forest and, occasionally, around habitations. DISTRIBUTION: Resident in S Thailand, Peninsular Malaysia and Singapore.

7 HOUSE MARTIN (EUROPEAN or NORTHERN HOUSE MARTIN) *Delichon urbicum* 13cm FIELD NOTES: Flies with much gliding and soaring, often at a great height. Regularly in the company of other swallows. VOICE: Calls include an abrupt *prrt* a *pri-pit* and a *za-za-za.* HABITAT: Open areas, over forests and cultivations. DISTRIBUTION: Winter visitor in N, C, E, S Myanmar, NW, NE Thailand, Laos and C, S Vietnam.

8 ASIAN HOUSE MARTIN *Delichon dasypus* 12cm FIELD NOTES: Square-ended tail. Flight contains frequent gliding, swooping and banking, often at a great height. Regularly accompanied by swifts and swallow species. VOICE: Shrill flight call and a soft trilling song. HABITAT: Gorges, valleys and around villages in hilly or mountain areas. DISTRIBUTION: Breeds in W, C China; resident in E China and Taiwan; winter visitor in W, N, S Myanmar, Thailand, Cambodia, Laos, S Vietnam and Peninsular Malaysia.

9 NEPAL HOUSE MARTIN *Delichon nipalense* 13cm FIELD NOTES: Rump and underparts greyer and tail shallower forked than House Martin. Flight actions as Asian House Martin. VOICE: In flight utters a high-pitched *chi-i.* HABITAT: Wooded mountain ridges with cliffs and river valleys. DISTRIBUTION: Resident in SW China, SW, W, N Myanmar, NE Thailand, Laos and N Vietnam (W Tonkin).

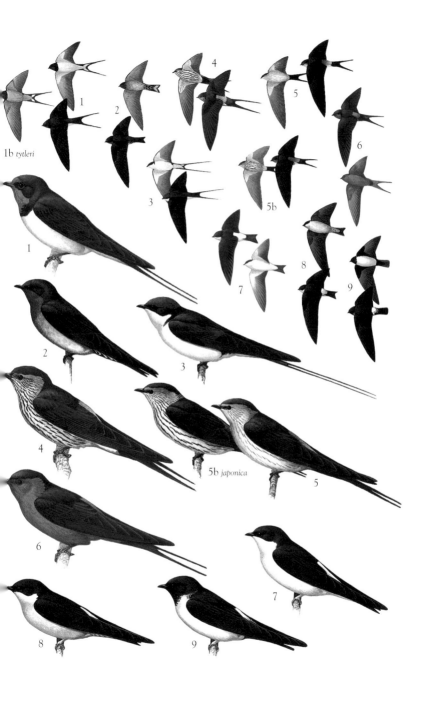

1b *tytleri*

1

1b *tytleri*

2

3

4

5

5b

6

7

8

9

1

2

3

4

5b *japonica*

5

6

7

8

9

123 BULBULS

1 CRESTED FINCHBILL *Spizixos canifrons* 22cm FIELD NOTES: Often found in small groups. VOICE: A bubbling *purr-purr-prruit-pruit-prruit*; calls include a buzzy *grz-grz-grz*. HABITAT: Open woodland, secondary growth, overgrown forest clearings and scrub. DISTRIBUTION: Resident in SW China, W, N, C, E Myanmar, NW Thailand, N Laos and N Vietnam (W Tonkin).

2 COLLARED FINCHBILL *Spizixos semitorques* 22cm FIELD NOTES: Often uses prominent perches that protrude from shrubbery. Regularly occurs in large post-breeding flocks. VOICE: A quick, steady-paced *chuwichu-chuwichu-cguwichu-chuwi*; calls include an upslurred *wirrrrp* that may merge into the song. HABITAT: Open woods, second growth and scrub. DISTRIBUTION: Resident in China, Taiwan and N Vietnam.

3 STRAW-HEADED BULBUL *Pycnonotus zeylanicus* 29cm FIELD NOTES: Usually encountered in small family groups foraging from the ground up to the canopy. VOICE: A melodious, rich warbling; utters a weak chattering and gurgling while foraging. HABITAT: Broadleaved evergreen forest, secondary growth, scrub, plantations and occasionally mangroves. DISTRIBUTION: Resident in S Myanmar (S Tenasserim), S Thailand, Peninsular Malaysia and Singapore.

4 STRIATED BULBUL *Pycnonotus striatus* 23cm FIELD NOTES: Most often occurs in the top of trees, generally hidden in dense foliage. VOICE: A series of pleasant warbling notes; call include a hard *pyik…pyik*, and a harsh *djrrri*. HABITAT: Broadleaved evergreen forest, forest edge and secondary growth. DISTRIBUTION: Resident in SW China, Myanmar (except C), W, NE, NW Thailand, N, C Laos and N Vietnams (W Tonkin).

5 BLACK-AND-WHITE BULBUL *Pycnonotus melanoleucos* 18cm FIELD NOTES: Most often encountered in the forest canopy, although also ventures to forage in low shrubs. VOICE: Generally quiet; occasionally utters a tuneless *pet-it* or *tee-too* and a longer *cherlee-chlee-chlee-chee-chee*. HABITAT: Broadleaved evergreen forest and forest edge. DISTRIBUTION: Resident in S Thailand, Peninsular Malaysia and Singapore.

6 BLACK-HEADED BULBUL *Pycnonotus atriceps* 18cm FIELD NOTES: Usually found in pairs or small parties foraging in trees or bushes. Grey form is rare, there is also a greener form occurring in Thailand. VOICE: Song is a disjointed series of rising and falling *tink* notes; calls include an emphatic *chew* or *chewp*. HABITAT: Broadleaved evergreen forest, forest edge and secondary growth. DISTRIBUTION: Resident in SW China and throughout the south, except N Myanmar and N Vietnam.

7 BLACK-CRESTED BULBUL *Pycnonotus flaviventris* 22cm FIELD NOTES: Arboreal, generally seen singly or in pairs. Red-throated race *P. f. johnsoni* (7b) occurs in C, NE, SE Thailand, Cambodia, Laos and Vietnam. VOICE: A sweet *weet-tre-trippy-weet, whik-whik whirru weet* or similar. HABITAT: Open forests, mixed deciduous forest, abandoned clearings, tall hedgerows, plantations and gardens. DISTRIBUTION: Resident in S China and throughout the south.

8 GREY-BELLIED BULBUL *Pycnonotus cyaniventris* 16–17cm FIELD NOTES: Usually keeps to the canopy, in pairs or small parties. Agile, often hanging tit-like to gather berries. VOICE: A sweet *pi-pi-pwi…pi-pi-pwi-pwi…* also a trilled, bubbling *pi-pi-pi-pi-pi-pi-pi* and a subdued *wit-wit-wit*. HABITAT: Broadleaved evergreen forest and forest edge. DISTRIBUTION: Resident in S Myanmar (S Tenasserim), S Thailand and Peninsular Malaysia.

9 SCALY-BREASTED BULBUL *Pycnonotus squamatus* 14–16cm FIELD NOTES: Usually seen in the canopy, singly or in small groups; a regular member of mixed-species foraging flocks. VOICE: Calls include high-pitched *wit* or *tit* notes. HABITAT: Broadleaved evergreen forest. DISTRIBUTION: Resident in S Myanmar (S Tenasserim), S Thailand and Peninsular Malaysia.

124 BULBULS

1 RED-WHISKERED BULBUL *Pycnonotus jocosus* 20cm FIELD NOTES: Usually found singly, in pairs or small parties. Juveniles lack the red cheek patch. VOICE: Variable musical phrases; calls include a rolling *prroop* and a harsh, raspy *bzeep*. HABITAT: Open forest, scrub, cultivations, parks and gardens. DISTRIBUTION: Resident in S China, Hainan and throughout the south.

2 BROWN-BREASTED BULBUL *Pycnonotus xanthorrhous* 20cm FIELD NOTES: Often occurs in groups, picking fruit from various trees and plants. VOICE: A simple, repeated *chirriwu-i-whi-chu whirri*-ui; calls include a harsh *chi* or *brzzp* and a thin *ti-whi*. HABITAT: Secondary growth, scrub, tall grass, thickets, clearings, streamside vegetation, cultivations and gardens. DISTRIBUTION: Resident in China, N, E, S Myanmar, NW Thailand, N Laos and N Vietnam (W Tonkin).

3 LIGHT-VENTED BULBUL (CHINESE BULBUL) *Pycnonotus sinensis* 19cm FIELD NOTES: Regularly perches prominently on bush-tops. Often occurs in large flocks post breeding. Race *P. s. formosae* (3b) is found in Taiwan; *P. s. hainanus* (3c) is resident in SE China, Hainan and N Vietnam; winter visitor in Vietnam. VOICE: A range of cheerful phrases and peculiar notes; calls with a loud *tocc-tocc-tocc*. HABITAT: Open woodland, cultivations and scrub. DISTRIBUTION: Resident in China (except SW), Taiwan and N Vietnam; winter visitor in Hainan and N Vietnam. Vagrants recorded in Thailand and Laos.

4 STYAN'S BULBUL *Pycnonotus taivanus* 19cm FIELD NOTES: Usually seen singly or in pairs, forms large flocks post breeding. VOICE: A loud, variable *qiao-keli qiao-keli*. HABITAT: Secondary growth, farms and developed areas in coastal lowlands. DISTRIBUTION: Resident in S Taiwan.

5 SOOTY-HEADED BULBUL *Pycnonotus aurigaster* 19–21cm FIELD NOTES: Often occurs in large flocks post breeding. Various races occur in the region. Those depicted are *P. a resurrectus* (main illustration), which is found in SE China and N Vietnam; yellow-vented race *P. a. germani* (5b) from NE Thailand, Cambodia, S Laos and S Vietnam and orange-vented race *P. a. schauenseei* (5c), which occurs in S Myanmar (S Tenasserim) and W Thailand. VOICE: A chatty *whi-wi-wiwi-wiwi, u whi hi hu* or *wh-i-i-wi*. HABITAT: Forest clearings, secondary growth, scrub and cultivations. DISTRIBUTION: Resident in southern China, E, S Myanmar, Thailand (except S), Cambodia, Laos and Vietnam.

6 RED-VENTED BULBUL *Pycnonotus cafer* 20cm FIELD NOTES: Usually in pairs or small parties, arboreal but may make flycatching sallies from a perch. VOICE: A cheery *be-care-ful*; calls include a chattering *peep-a-peep-a-lo*, a slow *peet-wit-wit-wit-wit* and a rapid *pitititit*. HABITAT: Open deciduous forest, scrub and gardens. DISTRIBUTION: Resident in SW China and Myanmar (except Tenasserim).

7 PUFF-BACKED BULBUL *Pycnonotus eutilotus* 20–22cm FIELD NOTES: Forages in trees after fruit and insects, usually singly or in pairs; sometimes joins mixed-species feeding flocks. VOICE: A loud, high-pitched, quavering warble, sometimes transcribed as *cheeu cheeu eeraloo eeraloo* or *chiaee-ruraleeoo*. HABITAT: Broadleaved evergreen forest and forest edge. DISTRIBUTION: Resident in S Myanmar (S Tenasserim), S Thailand and Peninsular Malaysia.

8 BARE-FACED BULBUL *Pycnonotus hualon* 19cm FIELD NOTES: Generally encountered singly, in pairs or small groups; predominantly arboreal although frequently seen on limestone cliff edges or jagged crags on steep hillsides. (Recent [Woxvold *et al.* 2009] described species). VOICE: A rising, bubbling trill, short dry bubbling notes and a harsh churring. HABITAT: Sparse open deciduous forest and shrubs on limestone substrate. DISTRIBUTION: Resident in central Laos (Pha Lom in Savannakhet province) and possibly adjacent parts of central Vietnam.

3b *formosae*

3c *hainanus*

5b *germani*

5c
schauenseei

resurrectus

125 BULBULS

1 STRIPE-THROATED BULBUL *Pycnonotus finlaysoni* 19–20cm FIELD NOTES: Usually seen singly or in pairs. Grey-headed race *P. f. davisoni* (1b) is found in S, E Myanmar VOICE: A throaty *whit-chu whic-i, whit-tu-iwhit-whitu-tu* or similar. HABITAT: Forest clearings, forest edge and secondary growth. DISTRIBUTION: Resident in SW China and throughout the south, except W, N, C Myanmar, C Thailand and Singapore.

2 FLAVESCENT BULBUL *Pycnonotus flavescens* 22cm FIELD NOTES: Shy, forages mainly in undergrowth, higher if trees are in fruit. Yellow-bellied race *P. f. vividus* (2b) occurs in SW China, N, E Myanmar, NW Thailand, N, C Laos and N, C Vietnam. VOICE: A rising and falling, chuckling *brzk bzeek zink-zenk-zink* and a tumbling *johi bwiki-bwiki-bwik;* both song types sometimes combined. Calls include a rasping *brzzk brzzk.* HABITAT: Open forest, forest edge, secondary growth and scrub. DISTRIBUTION: Resident in SW China, Myanmar (except C), W, NW, NE Thailand, N, S Laos and N, S Vietnam.

3 YELLOW-VENTED BULBUL *Pycnonotus goiavier* 20–21cm FIELD NOTES: Forages singly, in pairs or small parties. Sometimes makes flycatching sallies from an exposed perch. VOICE: Calls include a rapid, babbling *chic-chic-chic…* a sharp *chwich-chwich* and a bubbling *tiddloo-tiddloo-tiddloo* or *tud-liu tud-liu tud-liu.* HABITAT: Coastal scrub, mangroves, secondary growth and cultivations. DISTRIBUTION: Resident in S Myanmar (S Tenasserim), W, C, SE, S Thailand, Cambodia, C, S Laos, S Vietnam, Peninsular Malaysia and Singapore.

4 STREAK-EARED BULBUL *Pycnonotus blanfordi* 17–20cm FIELD NOTES: Generally found singly, in pairs or small groups foraging in trees, also makes flycatching sallies. Browner race *P. b. conradi* (4b) occurs in Thailand, S Laos, Cambodia, C, S Vietnam and Peninsular Malaysia. VOICE: Calls include a rasping *which-which-which*, a piping *brink-brink-brink* and a harsh *chu-chu-chu.* HABITAT: Open mixed deciduous forest, scrub, cultivations and gardens. DISTRIBUTION: Resident in Myanmar (except SW, N), Thailand, Cambodia, Laos, C, S Vietnam and N Peninsular Malaysia.

5 OLIVE-WINGED BULBUL *Pycnonotus plumosus* 20–21cm FIELD NOTES: Usually seen low down, singly or in pairs. Joins other bulbuls in fruiting trees. VOICE: A variable, soft, liquid chirping, transcribed as *quick-doc-tor-quick;* calls include a throaty *whip-whip* and a purring *wrrh-wrrh-wrrh.* HABITAT: Secondary growth, coastal scrub and mangroves. DISTRIBUTION: Resident in S Myanmar (S Tenasserim), S Thailand, Peninsular Malaysia and Singapore.

6 CREAM-VENTED BULBUL *Pycnonotus simplex* 18cm FIELD NOTES: Seen singly or in pairs; often joins other bulbuls in fruiting trees. VOICE: A quavering, subdued *whi-whi-whi-whi-whi…* interspersed with a low *pru-pru, prr* or *prr-pru.* HABITAT: Broadleaved evergreen forest, forest edge and secondary growth. DISTRIBUTION: Resident in S Thailand, Peninsular Malaysia and Singapore.

7 RED-EYED BULBUL (ASIAN RED-EYED BULBUL) *Pycnonotus brunneus* 19cm FIELD NOTES: Arboreal, usually occurs singly or in pairs, occasionally joins mixed-species feeding flocks. VOICE: A high-pitched, bubbling, rising *pri-pri-pri-pri-pri-pit-pit*, also brief trills and a strident *chirrup* or *whit-it.* HABITAT: Broadleaved evergreen forest, forest edge and secondary growth. DISTRIBUTION: Resident in S Myanmar (S Tenasserim), S Thailand, Peninsular Malaysia and Singapore.

8 SPECTACLED BULBUL *Pycnonotus erythrophthalmos* 16–18cm FIELD NOTES: Usually encountered singly or in pairs; often found in fruiting trees with other bulbuls. VOICE: A high-pitched mechanical *pip-pippidi or wip-wip-wi i i i i.* HABITAT: Broadleaved evergreen forest, forest edge and secondary growth. DISTRIBUTION: Resident in S Myanmar (S Tenasserim), S Thailand and Peninsular Malaysia.

9 FINSCH'S BULBUL *Alophoixus finschii* 16–17cm FIELD NOTES: Forages mainly in the middle storey, comes lower to feed on fruit at lower tree levels and shrubs;. Occasionally makes short sallies after flying insects. VOICE: Calls include a subdued *wek* or *twut*, a loud nasal *hwuiikt* and a grating *scree.* HABITAT: Broadleaved evergreen forest. DISTRIBUTION: Resident in S Thailand and Peninsular Malaysia.

1b
davisoni

2b
vividus

2

4b
conradi

1

3

4

5

7

6

8

9

126 BULBULS

1 WHITE-THROATED BULBUL *Alophoixus flaveolus* 22cm FIELD NOTES: Creeps and clambers about undergrowth in chattering parties. VOICE: A strident, nasal *nyak nyark nyark* or *nyeek*, a higher-pitched *yap* and a shrill *shree-shree-shree*. HABITAT: Undergrowth in broadleaved evergreen forest. Sometimes found in scrub and bushes in winter. DISTRIBUTION: Resident in SW China, Myanmar and W, NW Thailand.

2 PUFF-THROATED BULBUL *Alophoixus pallidus* 23cm FIELD NOTES: Occurs in small active parties, regularly forms part of mixed-species feeding flocks. Brighter race *A. p. griseiceps* (2b) occurs in S Myanmar. VOICE: Calls include a harsh, abrupt *churt churt churt…chutt-chutt-chutt…* or *chutt-chutt chik-it chik-it*, also a weak *twee twee twee*. HABITAT: Broadleaved evergreen forest and open woodland in lowlands and foothills. DISTRIBUTION: Resident in S, SW China, S, E Myanmar, NW, NE Thailand, Cambodia (except SW) Laos and Vietnam (except Cochinchina).

3 OCHRACEOUS BULBUL *Alophoixus ochraceus* 19–22cm FIELD NOTES: Usually encountered in loose, noisy parties feeding on fruit in trees and shrubs. VOICE: Calls include a harsh *chrrt-chrrt-chrrt-chrrt… chik-chik-chik-chik* or *chi-it-chit-it-chit-chit-it*, all often preceded by a fluty, nasal *eeyi* or *iiwu*. HABITAT: Broadleaved evergreen forest. DISTRIBUTION: Resident in S Myanmar (S Tenasserim), W, SE, S Thailand, SW Cambodia, S Vietnam and Peninsular Malaysia.

4 GREY-CHEEKED BULBUL *Alophoixus bres* 21–22cm FIELD NOTES: Noisy; usually seen singly, in pairs or small groups foraging in fruiting trees and shrubs. VOICE: Variable; song consists of a mournful *whi-u wiu iwi* followed by a high-pitched *ii-wi-tchiu-tchiu* or similar. Also gives a clear *prii chiu chew chew* and a longer *uu-ii-chewi-chew-chew* interspersed with short rattling notes. HABITAT: Broadleaved evergreen forest. DISTRIBUTION: Resident in S Myanmar (S Tenasserim), S Thailand and Peninsular Malaysia.

5 YELLOW-BELLIED BULBUL *Alophoixus phaeocephalus* 20–21cm FIELD NOTES: Generally seen singly, in pairs or in small parties. Frequents lower storey; regularly descends to feed on the ground, although quickly returns to lower branches. VOICE: A subdued, buzzy *whi-ee whi-ee whi-ee* or a rasping *cherrit-berrit*; also a variety of grating notes. HABITAT: Broadleaved evergreen forest. DISTRIBUTION: Resident in S Myanmar (S Tenasserim), S Thailand and Peninsular Malaysia.

6 HAIRY-BACKED BULBUL *Tricholestes criniger* 16–17cm FIELD NOTES: Usually encountered in pairs in the lower or middle storey. Unassuming but can also be inquisitive, often approaching human observers. VOICE: A scratchy, chattering warble interspersed with a quavering *whirrrh*; calls include a high-pitched, rising *whiiii*. HABITAT: Broadleaved evergreen forest. DISTRIBUTION: Resident in S Myanmar (S Tenasserim), S Thailand and Peninsular Malaysia.

7 OLIVE BULBUL *Iole virescens* 19cm FIELD NOTES: Shy and unobtrusive; forages in high bushes and in the middle and top storeys of trees. VOICE: An upslurred, strident, mewing *whee-ik*. HABITAT: Broadleaved evergreen forest, semi-evergreen forest and tall secondary growth. DISTRIBUTION: Resident in Myanmar and N, NW Thailand.

8 BUFF-VENTED BULBUL *Iole olivacea* 20–21cm FIELD NOTES: Forages in the canopy and middle storey, sometimes descends to lower levels to feed on fruiting shrubs. VOICE: Calls include a musical *cherrit*, a *whe-ic* and a flatter *whirr*. HABITAT: Broadleaved evergreen forest and secondary growth. DISTRIBUTION: Resident in S Myanmar (S Myanmar), W, S Thailand, Peninsular Malaysia and Singapore.

9 GREY-EYED BULBUL *Iole propinqua* 17–19cm FIELD NOTES: Generally unobtrusive, seen singly or in pairs with larger parties at fruiting trees or shrubs. Race *I. p. cinnamomeoventris* (9b) occurs in S Myanmar (S Tenasserim) and S Thailand. VOICE: Calls include a nasal, loud *uuu-wit*, *beret* or *prrrit*, also a *whi-it* and a flatter *wowh* or *weeao*. HABITAT: Broadleaved evergreen forest, forest edge and secondary growth. DISTRIBUTION: Resident in S, SW China, E, S Myanmar, Thailand (except C), Cambodia, Laos and Vietnam.

2b
griseiceps

9b
cinnamomeoventris

127 BULBULS

1 ASHY BULBUL *Hemixos flavala* 20–21cm FIELD NOTES: Forages in the middle to upper storey; sociable, especially post breeding. *H. f. bourdellei* (1b) occurs in S China, E Myanmar, NE Thailand and N, C Laos; *H. f. remotus* (1c) in S Laos, S Vietnam (S Annam) and SE Cambodia. VOICE: A metallic, perky *skrink-er rink-er-rink*; calls include twangy buzzes and musical chatters. HABITAT: Broadleaved evergreen forest. DISTRIBUTION: Resident in SW China, NW, E, S Myanmar, NE, SW, W Thailand, SE Cambodia, Laos and N, C Vietnam.

2 CINEREOUS BULBUL *Hemixos cinereus* 20–21cm FIELD NOTES: Forages mainly in the middle storey and canopy; often gregarious. VOICE: A brief, sweet *beelee-bear beelee burlee*; calls include a loud, ringing *tree-tree-tree*, a whining *whear*, a sharp *chiap* and a whistled *wheesh-wheesh*. HABITAT: Broadleaved evergreen forest and secondary growth. DISTRIBUTION: Resident in S Thailand and Peninsular Malaysia.

3 CHESTNUT BULBUL *Hemixos castanonotus* 21–22cm FIELD NOTES: Noisy and conspicuous, often in large post-breeding flocks. Race *H. c. canipennis* (3b) occurs in SE, E China and NE Vietnam. VOICE: A clear, simple *whi-wi-wu* or *to-to te-wee*, usually interspersed with churring notes. HABITAT: Broadleaved evergreen forest, forest edge and secondary growth. DISTRIBUTION: Resident in SE, E China, Hainan and N Vietnam.

4 WHITE-HEADED BULBUL *Cerasophila thompsoni* 20cm FIELD NOTES: Arboreal, forages in loose flocks of up to 20 individuals. VOICE: A rhythmic *chit-chirui chit-chiriu…* HABITAT: Secondary forest, scrub, forest edge and grassy areas with scattered trees. DISTRIBUTION: Resident in N, C, E, S Myanmar and W, NW Thailand.

5 STREAKED BULBUL *Ixos malaccensis* 23cm FIELD NOTES: Forages mainly in the canopy, singly or in pairs; occasionally makes sorties after flying insects. VOICE: A high-pitched, descending *chiri-chiri-chu* or similar; calls include a harsh, loud rattle. HABITAT: Broadleaved evergreen forest. DISTRIBUTION: Resident in S Myanmar (S Tenasserim), S Thailand and Peninsular Malaysia.

6 MOUNTAIN BULBUL *Ixos mcclellandii* 21–24cm FIELD NOTES: Pairs or small parties forage in the tops of trees, although descend to feed on fruiting bushes. *I. m. similis* (6b) is found in SW China, NE Myanmar, N Cambodia, N Laos and N Vietnam; *I. m. tickelli* (6c) from E Myanmar and N Thailand; *I. m. peracensis* (6d) from S Thailand and N Peninsular Malaysia. VOICE: A screechy *chirrut chewt chirrut chewt*; calls include a downward inflected *tsiuc*. HABITAT: Broadleaved evergreen forest and secondary growth. DISTRIBUTION: Resident in China (except NE), Hainan, Myanmar, Thailand (except C, SE), Laos, N, C Vietnam and Peninsular Malaysia.

7 BROWN-EARED BULBUL *Hypsipetes amaurotis* 28cm FIELD NOTES: Sociable and noisy, post breeding often occurs in quite large flocks. Flight strong and undulating. VOICE: A loud, fluty *peet-peet-pii-yieyo* or similar. HABITAT: Deciduous woodland, plantations, parks and gardens. DISTRIBUTION: Resident in Taiwan; winter visitor in NE China.

8 BLACK BULBUL *Hypsipetes leucocephalus* 23–27cm FIELD NOTES: Forages mainly in the topmost branches; often launches sorties after flying insects. Forms large post-breeding flocks. Various races occur nominate (main illustration) breeds in SE China and Hainan; winters in E Myanmar, N Laos, N, Cambodia and N, Vietnam; *H. l. ambiens* (8b) occurs in SW China and N Myanmar; *H. l. nigerrimus* (8c) in Taiwan; *H. l. psaroides* (8d) in NW Myanmar. VOICE: Song is a series of discordant and high notes; calls include a mewing *hwiiii* and an abrupt, nasal *ber-ber-bic-ber – ber*. HABITAT: Broadleaved evergreen and mixed deciduous forest. DISTRIBUTION: Breeds in northern China (moves south post breeding). Resident in S China, Hainan, Taiwan, Myanmar, NW, W, NE Thailand, Cambodia, Laos and Vietnam (except Cochinchina). Winter visitor in W, N, C, E Myanmar, NW, NE Thailand, Cambodia, C, S Laos and N, C Vietnam.

1b *bourdellei*

1c *remotus*

1

3b *canipennis*

2

3

4

5

6c *tickelli*

6d *peracensis*

8d *psaroides*

8c *nigerrimus*

8b *ambiens*

6b *similis*

6

7

8

128 WHITE-EYES; CRESTS; TESIAS

1 CHESTNUT-FLANKED WHITE-EYE *Zosterops erythropleurus* 11–12cm FIELD NOTES: Gregarious, often in mixed-species feeding flocks along with Japanese White-eye. VOICE: A twittering *dze-dze*. HABITAT: Broadleaved evergreen forest and secondary forest. DISTRIBUTION: Winter visitor in SW China, W, C, S, E Myanmar, W, NW, NE Thailand, Cambodia, N, C Laos and N Vietnam.

2 EVERETT'S WHITE-EYE *Zosterops everetti* 11–12cm FIELD NOTES: Gregarious, usually in flocks of 5–20 individuals, although can be many more, foraging in treetops. VOICE: A series of sweet, weak twittering notes; calls include a *tsee-tsee*, a metallic *spreet* or *peeet* and a buzzing *dzee* or *dzee-ap*. HABITAT: Broadleaved evergreen forest. DISTRIBUTION: Resident in SE, W, S Thailand and Peninsular Malaysia.

3 JAPANESE WHITE-EYE *Zosterops japonicus* 10–12cm FIELD NOTES: Gregarious, restless forager in treetop foliage; often part of mixed-species feeding flocks. VOICE: Calls include a staccato *tsip-tsip-tsip*, a *chi-i chi-i*, a *jeet-jeet* and a cicada-like trill. HABITAT: Forest, secondary growth, cultivations, parks and gardens. DISTRIBUTION: Breeds in N China (moves south post breeding); resident in S, E China, Hainan, Taiwan and N Vietnam (E Tonkin); winter visitor in C, S, E Myanmar, NW, NE Thailand, Laos and N, C Vietnam.

4 ORIENTAL WHITE-EYE *Zosterops palpebrosus* 9–11cm FIELD NOTES: Restless, agile forager among tree foliage and blossoms. Variable race *Z. p. siamensis* (4b) occurs in S Myanmar, N, E, SW Thailand, N, Laos, N Vietnam (W Tonkin). VOICE: Wispy, made up of slurred call notes; calls include a twittering *dzi-da-da* and a raspy, down-slurred *djeeeer*. HABITAT: Broadleaved evergreen, deciduous and swamp forest, secondary growth, mangroves, cultivations, parks and gardens. DISTRIBUTION: Resident in SW China and throughout the south, except N Vietnam (E Tonkin and N Annam) and Singapore.

5 GOLDCREST *Regulus regulus* 9cm FIELD NOTES: An agile forager; often hovers to capture insects. A regular member of mixed-species feeding flocks. VOICE: A jingling, high-pitched *ze-zezeezee-ze-zezeezee-ze-zezeezee...* calls include a high-pitched *zee-zee-zee* or *zit-zit-zit* usually given on the move. HABITAT: Coniferous and broadleaved evergreen forest. DISTRIBUTION: Resident in SW, W China and N, E Myanmar; winter visitor in E China and Taiwan.

6 FLAMECREST *Regulus goodfellowi* 9cm FIELD NOTES: Agile, active forager in tree foliage; regular member of mixed-species feeding flocks. VOICE: A high-pitched *seeh-seeh-seeh*; call is a quiet *seeeh*. HABITAT: Coniferous and montane forest. DISTRIBUTION: Resident in Taiwan.

7 SLATY-BELLIED TESIA *Tesia olivea* 9–10cm FIELD NOTES: Forages on or close to the ground, often tossing leaf litter into the air while foraging. Has a bouncing gait when excited or alarmed. VOICE: Starts with 4–11 single whistled notes, followed by an explosive jumble of tuneless notes; calls include a sharp *tchirik* and a spluttering *trrrrt trrrrt trrrrt...* HABITAT: Dense undergrowth in broadleaved evergreen forest, often near watercourses. DISTRIBUTION: Resident in SW China, W, N, E, S Myanmar, W, NW Thailand, N, C Laos and N Vietnam.

8 GREY-BELLIED TESIA *Tesia cyaniventer* 9–10cm FIELD NOTES: Restless forager, on or near the ground. VOICE: A few high-pitched notes followed by a series of loud slurred phrases; call is a loud, rattling *trrrrrrk*. HABITAT: Dense tangled undergrowth in thick forest, usually near water. DISTRIBUTION: Resident in S, SW China, W, N, E, S Myanmar, NW Thailand, N Laos and N Vietnam.

9 CHESTNUT-HEADED TESIA *Oligura (Cettia) castaneocoronata* 8–10cm FIELD NOTES: Forages, wren-like, in and around dense undergrowth or moss-covered logs or rocks. Included in the bush warblers (*Cettia*) by some authorities. VOICE: A loud, explosive *cheep-cheeu-che-wit* or rapid *ti-tisu eei* followed by a slower *tis-tit-ti-wu*; calls include a sharp *whit* or *tit* and a high-pitched *pseet*. HABITAT: Undergrowth in broadleaved evergreen forest and secondary growth, often near water. DISTRIBUTION: Resident in SW China, W, N, E Myanmar, NW Thailand, N Laos and N Vietnam.

4b *siamensis*
(yellow morph)

129 BUSH WARBLERS

1 ASIAN STUBTAIL (ASIAN STUBTAIL WARBLER) *Urosphena squameiceps* 10–12cm FIELD NOTES: Skulking; forages accentor-like among forest undergrowth. VOICE: Calls include a soft *sit, zik* or *chip-chip-chip.* HABITAT: Swampy areas in dense broadleaved evergreen forest and open scrub jungle. DISTRIBUTION: Winter visitor in SE China, Hainan, Taiwan, S, E, C, W Myanmar, Thailand (except NE), Laos and Vietnam (except Cochinchina).

2 PALE-FOOTED BUSH WARBLER *Urosphena pallidipes* 11–13cm FIELD NOTES: Skulking, flits through bushes or grasses; best located by voice. VOICE: An explosive jumble of chattering notes; calls include a short *chik-chik.* HABITAT: Grassy areas, scrub, bracken-covered slopes and, occasionally, in open broadleaved evergreen and pine forests. DISTRIBUTION: Resident in SW China, C, E, S Myanmar, NW Thailand, N, C Laos and Vietnam (E Tonkin and S Annam).

3 BROWNISH-FLANKED BUSH WARBLER (BROWN-FLANKED BUSH WARBLER) *Horornis fortipes* 12cm FIELD NOTES: Skulks in thick cover; more often heard than seen. VOICE: A sustained, rising *weeeee* followed by an explosive *chiwiyou;* calls include a harsh *chuk* or *tchuk tchuk.* HABITAT: Undergrowth and bamboo clumps in broadleaved evergreen forest, overgrown clearings and forest edge. DISTRIBUTION: Resident in China, Taiwan, W, N Myanmar, N Laos and N Vietnam.

4 ORIENTAL BUSH WARBLER (MANCHURIAN BUSH WARBLER) *Horornis canturians* 18cm FIELD NOTES: Often remains immobile in thick foliage. VOICE: A loud, fluty *wrrrrr-whuciuchi;* calls include a dry *tchet-tchet-tchet* and rattling *trrt.* HABITAT: Dense thickets, scrub and secondary forest. DISTRIBUTION: Breeds in N China; winter visitor in W, E China, Hainan, Taiwan, NW Thailand, N, C Laos and Vietnam (except Cochinchina).

5 YELLOWISH-BELLIED BUSH WARBLER *Horornis acanthizoides* 11–12cm FIELD NOTES: Skulks in thick cover, best located by voice. VOICE: 3 or 4 thin drawn-out whistles, followed by a short series of fast see-sawing notes; calls include a rasping *brrr* and a sharp *tik-tik-tik.* HABITAT: Bamboo and undergrowth in broadleaved and mixed evergreen and coniferous forest. DISTRIBUTION: Resident in China (except SE, E), Taiwan and N Myanmar.

6 ABERRANT BUSH WARBLER *Horornis flavolivaceus* 12–14cm FIELD NOTES: Skulking, sometimes inquisitive; constantly flicks wings and tail. VOICE: A series of thin rising notes followed by a long whistle; calls include a soft *brrt-brrrt* and a sharp *chick.* HABITAT: Thickets and tall grass clumps at forest edge or in clearings; also bamboo and undergrowth in forests. DISTRIBUTION: Resident in SW China, W, N, E Myanmar, N Laos and N Vietnam (W Tonkin); winter visitor in NW Thailand.

7 GREY-SIDED BUSH WARBLER *Cettia brunnifrons* 10–11cm FIELD NOTES: Skulking, occasionally ventures to the edge of cover or sings from a bush top. VOICE: A high-pitched *dzit-su-ze-sizu* followed by a nasal *bzeeuu.* Calls include a metallic *tiss* or *tiss-ui.* HABITAT: Scrub and grassy areas near forests. DISTRIBUTION: Resident in SW, W China and NW Thailand.

8 CHESTNUT-CROWNED BUSH WARBLER *Cettia major* 13cm FIELD NOTES: Shy and skulking; creeps, mouse-like on the ground. VOICE: Short whistle followed by a rapid shrill warble; calls with a sharp *tzip* or *pseet.* HABITAT: Scrub and forest undergrowth. DISTRIBUTION: Resident in SW China; vagrant in NW Thailand.

9 TAIWAN BUSH WARBLER *Locustella alishanensis* 13cm FIELD NOTES: Skulking, forages low down. VOICE: Loud, clear monotonous notes ending with 2 or 3 clicks; calls with a scratchy *ksh ksh ksh.* HABITAT: Open grassy slopes, thickets, forest clearings and undergrowth in cultivations. DISTRIBUTION: Resident in Taiwan.

10 BROWN BUSH WARBLER *Locustella luteoventris* 13–14cm FIELD NOTES: Skulking, although occasionally sings from a prominent perch. VOICE: A dry reeling; calls include a hard *tack* and a higher *tink-tink-tink.* HABITAT: Dense grass, weedy areas or scrub near forest edge or clearings. DISTRIBUTION: Resident in China, W, N Myanmar and N Vietnam (W Tonkin); winters in S Myanmar and NW, NE Thailand.

130 BUSH WARBLERS; GRASSHOPPER WARBLERS

1 SPOTTED BUSH WARBLER *Locustella thoracica* 11–13cm FIELD NOTES: Secretive, especially post breeding; generally keeps to thick cover. VOICE: A series of clicks and buzzing sounds; calls include a harsh *shtak* and a low *tuk*. HABITAT: Scrubby thickets near forests and in high level meadows; winters in rank vegetation by watercourses. DISTRIBUTION: Breeds in W, SW China and possibly N Myanmar; winters in C, E Myanmar, W, NW, NE, C Thailand and Laos.

2 RUSSET BUSH WARBLER *Locustella mandelli* 13–13cm FIELD NOTES: Skulking, very little else recorded. The warmer-flanked race *L. m. idonea* in S Annam may prove to be a full species. VOICE: A rapid *cre-ut cre-ut cre-ut cre-ut…* calls include a short *shtuk*. HABITAT: Low vegetation in forest clearings and edge, also in grass and scrub. DISTRIBUTION: Resident in SW, C, E China, W, N Myanmar, NW Thailand, N Laos and N, S Vietnam.

3 CHINESE BUSH WARBLER *Locustella tacsanowskia* 13–14cm FIELD NOTES: Keeps well hidden, creeps about in tangled vegetation. VOICE: A rasping, insect-like *raaasp… raaasp…raaaaasp…raaaaaaasp…raaasp…* call is a *chirr-chirr*. HABITAT: Grassy upland meadows with shrubby thickets and tall grasses. Winters in lowland grasslands, reeds and scrubby edges of cultivation. DISTRIBUTION: Breeds in SW, W China; winters in S Myanmar, NW Thailand, N Laos and C Vietnam (S Annam).

4 PALLAS'S GRASSHOPPER WARBLER (RUSTY-RUMPED WARBLER) *Locustella certhiola* 13–14cm FIELD NOTES: Skulks and creeps mouse-like among tall grasses and reeds. VOICE: A high-pitched twittering that leads into a ringing *che-che-che-che-che;* calls include a repeated *pwit* and a rapid *tiktiktiktiktik*. HABITAT: Tall grasses, reeds and tangled vegetation in marshes or other wetlands. DISTRIBUTION: Winter visitor throughout from S China; except western Myanmar, C Laos and N, C Vietnam.

5 LANCEOLATED WARBLER *Locustella lanceolata* 12cm FIELD NOTES: Very secretive, tends to run through vegetation or along ground through roots; reluctant to fly. VOICE: Calls include a loud, urgent *chirr-chirr*, an explosive *tzht-tzht-tzht* and a repeated *pit*. HABITAT: Scrub, grass and weedy vegetation often in marshy areas. DISTRIBUTION: Winter visitor in the south, except SW, W, N, C Myanmar and N Vietnam (W Tonkin).

6 JAPANESE SWAMP WARBLER (MARSH GRASSBIRD) *Locustella pryeri* 12–13cm FIELD NOTES: Skulking; clambers nimbly among grass or reed stems. Sings from prominent reed perch or in flight, although unlikely to be heard in winter. VOICE: A low-pitched *djuk-djuk-djuk*; call is a low *chuk*. HABITAT: Dense grass or reedbeds by rivers or lakes. DISTRIBUTION: Winter visitor in C China.

7 STYAN'S GRASSHOPPER WARBLER *Locustella pleskei* 15–16cm FIELD NOTES: Skulking, but often ventures into the open to forage. VOICE: A *chip-chit-chip-chir-chit-chi-schwee-schee*; call is a short *chit*. HABITAT: Coastal mangroves, water vegetation, reedbeds and nearby scrub, also among seashore rocks. DISTRIBUTION: Winter visitor in coastal C China around Hong Kong.

8 GRAY'S GRASSHOPPER WARBLER *Locustella fasciolata* 16–18cm FIELD NOTES: Very secretive, forages in deep cover. Darker race *L. f. amnicola* (8b) possibly migrates alongside nominate. VOICE: Contact call is trilling *cherr-cherr*. HABITAT: Thickets, forest edge and tall grass. DISTRIBUTION: Passage migrant in E China.

9 MIDDENDORFF'S GRASSHOPPER WARBLER *Locustella ochotensis* 13–15cm FIELD NOTES: Skulking, forages in or under low cover. VOICE: Call is a quiet *chit*. HABITAT: Damp scrub, grasslands and marshes with emergent vegetation. DISTRIBUTION: Passage migrant in E China.

131 CISTICOLAS; PRINIAS

1 ZITTING CISTICOLA *Cisticola juncidis* 10–12cm FIELD NOTES: Best located while singing from an exposed perch or during song-flight. Forages mainly on the ground among grass and other vegetation. VOICE: A simple *zit-zit-zit-zit-zit…* calls include a *tew* and a *tsipp-tsipp-tsipp.* HABITAT: Grasslands, marshes and rice paddies. DISTRIBUTION: Resident throughout the region.

2 BRIGHT-HEADED CISTICOLA *Cisticola exilis* 10cm FIELD NOTES: Sings from an exposed perch or in flight; forages mainly on the ground in tangled vegetation. VOICE: Buzzing notes followed by a liquid *scrrrrr plook*; call is a scolding *squee.* HABITAT: Tall marshland vegetation, grassland with scattered bushes. DISTRIBUTION: Resident over much of China, Taiwan, W, N, S Myanmar, Thailand (except S), Cambodia, N, C, S Laos and C, S Vietnam.

3 STRIATED PRINIA *Prinia crinigera* 16cm FIELD NOTES: Usually skulking; during breeding sings from a prominent perch on bushes or trees. VOICE: A jaunty, wheezy *chitzereet-chitzereet-chitzereet-chitzereet-chitzereet,* the last few notes speeding to a slight climax. HABITAT: Open grassy mountainsides or hillsides with scattered shrubs, also rank herbage in cultivations. DISTRIBUTION: Resident in China, Taiwan and W, N Myanmar.

4 BROWN PRINIA *Prinia polychroa* 16cm FIELD NOTES: Keeps to thick cover; if disturbed tends to creep through vegetation rather than fly. VOICE: A wheezy *chirt-chirt-chirt* or *chook-chook-chook*; call is a loud *twee-ee-ee-eet.* HABITAT: Grassland with low scrub, cultivations and open deciduous forest with low shrubby growth. DISTRIBUTION: Residents in SW China, S, C, E Myanmar, NW, NE, E, C Thailand, Cambodia, C, S Laos and C Vietnam.

5 BLACK-THROATED PRINIA *Prinia atrogularis* 17cm FIELD NOTES: Skulking but active forager in thick cover; regularly flicks tail. VOICE: Repeated scraping, buzzy notes; calls include a dry buzz and a soft, scolding *chrr-chrr-chrr.* HABITAT: Open grassy mountainsides or hillsides with scattered shrubs, and scrub in forest clearings. DISTRIBUTION: Resident in W Myanmar and possibly SW China.

6 HILL PRINIA *Prinia superciliaris* 17cm FIELD NOTES: Noisy and active in grass and low vegetation. VOICE: A loud, piercing *cho-ee cho-ee cho-ee.* HABITAT: Bracken covered slopes, grass, scrub and overgrown clearings. DISTRIBUTION: Resident in southern China, E, NE Myanmar, W, NW, NE Thailand, Laos and Vietnam.

7 RUFESCENT PRINIA *Prinia rufescens* 11cm FIELD NOTES: Very secretive, occasionally in small parties. Tail is regularly waved up, down or sideways. VOICE: A rhythmic *chewp-chewp-chewp-chewp*; calls include a *chip chip chip* and a buzzy *peez-peez-peez.* HABITAT: Grassy areas in open forests, grasslands with scattered trees. DISTRIBUTION: Resident in SW China and throughout the south, except C Thailand and Singapore.

8 YELLOW-BELLIED PRINIA *Prinia flaviventris* 13cm FIELD NOTES: Restless forager among grasses; sings from a prominent perch or during song-flight. Russet/buff-vented race *P. f. sonitans* (8b) occurs in N Vietnam (E Tonkin). VOICE: Flute-like, starting with a *chirp* followed by a descending trill. Calls include a *chink-chink* and a plaintive *twee-twee.* HABITAT: Waterside vegetation, coastal scrub and mangroves. DISTRIBUTION: Resident in S, E China, Hainan, Taiwan and throughout the south.

9 GREY-BREASTED PRINIA *Prinia hodgsonii* 11cm FIELD NOTES: Active, moves quickly through bushes or undergrowth; often forms parties post breeding. VOICE: A squeaky, warbling *chiwee-chiwee-chewi-chip-chip-chip.* Calls include a tinkling *zeee-zeee-zeee* and a thin *chew-chew-chew.* HABITAT: Dry grassland, scrub and secondary growth. DISTRIBUTION: Resident in SW China and throughout the south, except S Myanmar (S Tenasserim), S Thailand, Peninsular Malaysia and Singapore.

10 PLAIN PRINIA *Prinia inornata* 10cm FIELD NOTES: Keeps low in vegetation; VOICE: An insect-like *jirt-jirt-jirt-jirt…* Calls include a buzzy *bzzp* and a clear *clact.* HABITAT: Scrubby grassland, reedbeds and mangroves. DISTRIBUTION: Breeds in China, Hainan, Taiwan and throughout the region, except S Thailand, Peninsular Malaysia and Singapore.

1

2

fresh

fresh

worn

worn

3

fresh

worn

4

fresh

worn

5

fresh

worn

6

fresh

worn

7

fresh

worn

8

8b *sonitans*

9

fresh

worn

10

fresh

worn

132 REED WARBLERS

1 SPECKLED REED WARBLER *Acrocephalus sorghophilus* 13cm FIELD NOTES: Forages low down in vegetation, climbs reed stems and sings from a prominent perch. VOICE: A series of rasping churring notes. HABITAT: Reedbeds, boggy grassland, rice and millet fields. DISTRIBUTION: Possible winter visitor to extreme E China.

2 BLACK-BROWED REED WARBLER *Acrocephalus bistrigiceps* 12cm FIELD NOTES: Shy and skulking, forages in thick cover, sings from exposed perches during breeding season. VOICE: Short phrases interspersed with rasping and churring notes; calls include a soft *dzak* and a harsh *chur*. HABITAT: Emergent vegetation near marshes or watery areas. DISTRIBUTION: Breeds in NE China; winter visitor in SE China and throughout the south, except SW, W, N, C Myanmar and Vietnam (W Tonkin and N, S Annam).

3 PADDYFIELD WARBLER *Acrocephalus agricola* 13cm FIELD NOTES: Constantly cocks and flicks tail; forages low in cover and sometimes on the ground. VOICE: A hurried series of melodious, chortled notes interspersed with mimicry. Calls include a sharp *chik-chik*, a harsh *chr-chuck* and a slurred *zack-zack*. HABITAT: Waterside vegetation and paddyfields. DISTRIBUTION: Winter visitor or vagrant in N Myanmar, NW Thailand and N Laos.

4 MANCHURIAN REED WARBLER *Acrocephalus tangorum* 13–15cm FIELD NOTES: Actions incompletely known; noted climbing to reed tops with tail cocked. VOICE: A series of warbled phrases interspersed with squeaky notes. Calls include a sharp *chi-chi*, a harsh *chr-chuck* and a slurred *zack-zack*. HABITAT: Reedbeds and emergent vegetation in marsh and lake borders. DISTRIBUTION: Winter visitor in S Myanmar, SE, C, W Thailand, Cambodia and S Laos.

5 BLYTH'S REED WARBLER *Acrocephalus dumetorum* 13cm FIELD NOTES: Mainly arboreal, often fans and flicks tail. Note short primary projection. VOICE: Calls include a clicking *thik*, a harsh *tchirr* and a hard *chack*. HABITAT: Scrub, rank vegetation in dry or wet locations, cultivation and forest borders. DISTRIBUTION: Winter visitor in SW, C, S, E Myanmar.

6 BLUNT-WINGED WARBLER *Acrocephalus concinens* 13cm FIELD NOTES: Skulking, although regularly calls while foraging in cover. VOICE: Repeated slurred whistles, clear and buzzing notes; calls include a quiet *tcheck* and a soft *churr*. HABITAT: Reedbeds, rank vegetation and scrub in swamps and marshes; also dryer areas in mountain valleys. DISTRIBUTION: Breeds in N, C China; winters in S China, S, E Myanmar, NW, NE, C Thailand and N, C Laos.

7 ORIENTAL REED WARBLER *Acrocephalus orientalis* 18cm FIELD NOTES: Clambers clumsily among reed stems. VOICE: Deep guttural churring and croaking notes interspersed with warbling phrases. HABITAT: Reedbeds and emergent vegetation alongside marshes. DISTRIBUTION: Breeds in China; winters in S China and throughout the south, except SW, W, N, E Myanmar and Vietnam (W Tonkin and N Annam).

8 REED WARBLER (EUROPEAN or EURASIAN REED WARBLER) *Acrocephalus scirpaceus* 13cm FIELD NOTES: Often calls while moving, furtively, in reeds or bushes. VOICE: Calls include a *churr* and a harsh *tcharr*. HABITAT: Reedbeds and bushes, the latter not always near water. DISTRIBUTION: Vagrant, recorded in NE China.

9 CLAMOROUS REED WARBLER *Acrocephalus stentoreus* 18cm FIELD NOTES: Clambers clumsily low down among reed stems or in bushes. VOICE: Variable; generally a loud combination of grating, chattering, squeaky and sweet notes, transcribed as *karra-karra-kareet-kareet-kareet*, *skareet-skareet-skareet*. Calls include a harsh *chack* and a low *churr*. HABITAT: Reedbeds, waterside vegetation and scrub. DISTRIBUTION: Resident in SW China, SW, C, E Myanmar, N Laos and C Vietnam.

10 THICK-BILLED WARBLER *Iduna aedon* 18–19cm FIELD NOTES: Elusive, clumsy forager in vegetation and bushes. VOICE: Calls include a *chack chack* and a harsh chatter. HABITAT: Thickets, tall grass, marshy places with reeds and bushes. DISTRIBUTION: Winter visitor south from China, except S Thailand, N Vietnam (W Tonkin), Peninsular Malaysia and Singapore.

133 TAILORBIRDS; TIT-WARBLERS; LESSER WHITETHROAT

1 MOUNTAIN TAILORBIRD *Phyllergates cucullatus* 11–12cm FIELD NOTES: Elusive, forages in low thickets; also makes aerial sorties after flying insects. Juvenile has forehead, crown and nape grey. VOICE: A thin high-pitched 4–6 note whistle, *pee-pee-peeeeeeeeee-pee-pee* or similar. Calls include a dry descending trill, a low buzzy *kiz-ki*, a repeated, thin *trit* and a long nasal chatter. HABITAT: Bushy thickets and undergrowth in broadleaved evergreen forest. DISTRIBUTION: Resident in S, SW China, Myanmar (except C, SW), W, NW, NE Thailand, Cambodia, Laos, N, C Vietnam and Peninsular Malaysia.

2 RUFOUS-TAILED TAILORBIRD *Orthotomus sericeus* 12–14cm FIELD NOTES: Shy and skulking, keeps to dense foliage; usually seen singly or in pairs. VOICE: A variety of rapid, loud disyllabic notes; calls include a harsh *terr-terr* and a *chi-chi*. HABITAT: Forest edge, overgrown clearings, cultivation and mangrove edges, also dense gardens. DISTRIBUTION: Resident in S Myanmar (Tenasserim), S Thailand, Peninsular Malaysia and Singapore.

3 DARK-NECKED TAILORBIRD *Orthotomus atrogularis* 11–12cm FIELD NOTES: Restless forager in undergrowth; more often heard than seen. VOICE: A high, shivery *pirra pirra* … and a trilled *kri-kri-kri*; partners duet with a *titrrrrrt-churrit*. HABITAT: Heavy scrub and edges of broadleaved evergreen forest, secondary growth, scrub and mangroves. DISTRIBUTION: Resident in SW China and throughout the south (except SW, W Myanmar).

4 COMMON TAILORBIRD *Orthotomus sutorius* 10–14cm FIELD NOTES: Forages in cover or on the ground under cover, often seen in pairs. Breeding males develop long central tail feathers. Darker-faced race *O. s. maculicollis* (4b) occurs in S Thailand, Peninsular Malaysia and Singapore. VOICE: A rapid, repetitive, loud *pitchik-pitchik-pitchik* or *cheeyup-cheeyup-cheeyup*; calls include a sharp, repeated *cheep...* and a quicker *pit-pit-pit...* HABITAT: Woodlands, scrub, bamboo thickets, cultivation edge, mangroves and gardens. DISTRIBUTION: Resident in S China, Hainan and throughout the south.

5 CAMBODIAN TAILORBIRD *Orthotomus chaktomuk* 10–11cm FIELD NOTES: Very elusive, generally in pairs foraging in dense vegetation. VOICE: Multiple repeated trilled phrases, some rising, some falling and some slurred (rising and falling). Calls include a nasal squeak, occasionally repeated in quick succession. HABITAT: Dense, humid evergreen scrub, sometimes mixed with tall grasses or trees. DISTRIBUTION: Resident in Cambodia in the floodplain of the Mekong, Tonle Sap and Bassac Rivers.

6 ASHY TAILORBIRD *Orthotomus ruficeps* 11–12cm FIELD NOTES: Retiring, although less so in urban areas; keeps to undergrowth, singly or in pairs. VOICE: A repeated *tirrree-yip* or *chip-wii-chip chip-wii-chip*; call is a repeated *chu-iip chu-iip*. HABITAT: Coastal scrub, mangroves, peatswamp forest and occasionally inland forests. DISTRIBUTION: Resident in S Myanmar (Tenasserim), S Thailand, S Vietnam, Peninsular Malaysia and Singapore.

7 WHITE-BROWED TIT WARBLER (SEVERTZOV'S TIT WARBLER) *Leptopoecile sophiae* 10cm FIELD NOTES: Acrobatic forager in thick undergrowth; often forms part of mixed-species feeding flocks. VOICE: A sweet, loud, chirping cry; calls include a constant, high-pitched *tzret*. HABITAT: Montane scrub and thickets; winters at lower elevations in valley-bottom thickets. DISTRIBUTION: Possibly breeds in the mountainous areas of SW China.

8 CRESTED TIT-WARBLER *Leptopoecile elegans* 11cm FIELD NOTES: Usually forages high in tree canopy; very active, actions much like a Goldcrest. VOICE: A thin *pseee* and a shrill wren-like chatter. HABITAT: Coniferous forest, dwarf alpine juniper and birch scrub above the tree line. DISTRIBUTION: Possibly resident in SW China.

9 LESSER WHITETHROAT *Sylvia curruca* 13cm FIELD NOTES: Very skulking; often sings or calls from within cover. VOICE: A quiet warble followed by a dry rattle; calls include a hard *tac-tac* and a scolding *churr*. HABITAT: Deciduous woods, secondary growth and scrub. DISTRIBUTION: Vagrant, recorded in Thailand.

276

1

2

♀
3

♂

♂
4b
maculicollis

♀

♂
4

♀
5
♂

♀
6

♂

♀
7
♂

♀
8
♂

9

1 DUSKY WARBLER *Phylloscopus fuscatus* 12–13cm FIELD NOTES: Skulking. Active forager, in thick vegetation or on the ground. VOICE: Clear whistled phrases and trills; calls include a sharp *chac*. HABITAT: Bushes and tall grass, often near water; winters in foothills and open plains with low bushes, often near water. DISTRIBUTION: Breeds in SW China; winter visitor in S, SW, C, E China, Hainan, Taiwan and the south, except S Thailand, C Vietnam (S Annam), Peninsular Malaysia and Singapore.

2 IJIMA'S LEAF WARBLER *Phylloscopus ijimae* 12cm FIELD NOTES: Often makes flycatching sorties, otherwise typical active forager. VOICE: Calls include a loud *twee* and a thin *phi-phi-phi*. HABITAT: Deciduous and mixed subtropical evergreen forest, forest edge, bamboo and tangled scrub. DISTRIBUTION: Vagrant or passage migrant in Taiwan.

3 TICKELL'S LEAF WARBLER *Phylloscopus affinis* 11–12cm FIELD NOTES: Active, acrobatic forager low down in thick vegetation; occasionally makes sallies after flying insects. VOICE: A *tchip-chi-chi-chi-chi-chi*; calls include a sharp *chep* and a rapid *tak-tak*. HABITAT: Open bushy alpine scrub; winters in bushes and scrub. DISTRIBUTION: Breeds in W China; winters in SW, C China and Myanmar, except S Myanmar (Tenasserim).

4 ALPINE LEAF WARBLER *Phylloscopus occisinensis* 10–11cm FIELD NOTES: Usually seen singly or in pairs, with small parties post breeding; often thought conspecific with Tickell's Leaf Warbler. VOICE: A fast *chip-chi-chi-chi-chi-chi*. HABITAT: Among rocks and bushes on dry barren mountains. DISTRIBUTION: Possibly breeds in extreme W China, winters in SW China and possibly N Myanmar.

5 BUFF-THROATED WARBLER *Phylloscopus subaffinis* 11–12cm FIELD NOTES: Active, nervous forager, low down in thick vegetation or on the ground. VOICE: A soft *tuee-tuee-tuee-tuee*; calls include a weak *trrup* or trip. HABITAT: Montane forest, open hillsides with scrub; winters in grassland and bushes in foothills. DISTRIBUTION: Breeds in China and N Vietnam (W Tonkin); winters in SW China, N, E Myanmar, NW Thailand, N Laos and N Vietnam (W, E. Tonkin).

6 YELLOW-STREAKED WARBLER *Phylloscopus armandii* 13–14cm FIELD NOTES: Slow, deliberate forager in bushes, lower tree branches and on the ground. VOICE: A series of rapid, husky, slurred undulating phrases, sometimes introduced by a few *zick* notes. Call is a sharp *zick*. HABITAT: Low bushes, thickets and subalpine spruce forest; winters in low bushes in plains and hills and forest edge. DISTRIBUTION: Breeds in W China. Winters in SW China, W, C, S, E Myanmar, NW, NE, SE Thailand, N Laos and N Vietnam (E Tonkin).

7 RADDE'S WARBLER *Phylloscopus schwarzi* 13–14cm FIELD NOTES: Skulking, movements quite slow; frequently flicks wings and tail. VOICE: A clear trill, followed by 1–2 quiet notes; calls include a *chek* and *pwit*. HABITAT: Low vegetation in open forest, forest clearings and forest edge; also scrub and grass in open areas. DISTRIBUTION: Winters in SE China and the south, except SW, N Myanmar, S Thailand, N Vietnam (E Tonkin), Peninsular Malaysia and Singapore.

8 BUFF-BARRED WARBLER *Phylloscopus pulcher* 11–12cm FIELD NOTES: Forages mainly in the tree canopy. VOICE: One or more call notes followed by a trill; call is a repeated *tsip*. HABITAT: Broadleaved evergreen forests. DISTRIBUTION: Resident in N, W Myanmar; breeds in SW China and N Myanmar; winters in E, S Myanmar, N Laos and NW Thailand.

9 ASHY-THROATED WARBLER *Phylloscopus maculipennis* 9–10cm FIELD NOTES: Forages in the tree canopy; flicks wings and tail, which shows off white tail sides. VOICE: A thin sweet *wee-ty-wee-ty-weet* or a slower *whee-teew whee-teew*; call is a repeated *zip*. HABITAT: Broadleaved evergreen forest with thick undergrowth. DISTRIBUTION: Resident in SW China, W, N, E Myanmar, NW Thailand, N, S Laos and Vietnam (W Tonkin and S Annam).

135 LEAF WARBLERS

1 PALLAS'S WARBLER (PALLAS'S LEAF WARBLER) *Phylloscopus proregulus* 10cm
FIELD NOTES: Often hovers to glean insects from foliage; frequently flicks wings and tail.
VOICE: Calls include a soft nasal *duee* and a soft *wseep*. HABITAT: Broadleaved evergreen and
semi-evergreen forest and secondary growth. DISTRIBUTION: Winter visitor in China (except
C), Hainan, NW Thailand, N, S Laos and N Vietnam.

2 LEMON-RUMPED WARBLER *Phylloscopus chloronotus* 10cm FIELD NOTES: Actions
similar to Pallas's Warbler. VOICE: A thin, drawn-out rattle, followed by a longer, lower, series
of evenly pitched notes. Also a long series of stuttering notes on an alternating pitch. Call
is a high *psit*. HABITAT: Broadleaved evergreen forest, semi-evergreen forest and secondary
growth. DISTRIBUTION: Breeds in W China; winter visitor in SW China, scarce in W, N, E
Myanmar (may be resident in W, N), NW Thailand and N Vietnam (W Tonkin).

3 YELLOW-BROWED WARBLER *Phylloscopus inornatus* 11–12cm FIELD NOTES: Active
forager at all levels: hovers or makes flycatching sallies to catch insects. VOICE: Calls include
a high *tswe-eeet* or *tsweet*. HABITAT: Woodlands, secondary growth, parks and gardens.
DISTRIBUTION: Winter visitor in S China, Hainan, Taiwan and throughout the south.

4 CHINESE LEAF WARBLER *Phylloscopus yunaanensis* 10cm FIELD NOTES: Forages
mainly in the canopy, hovers and makes sallies after insects. VOICE: A mechanical,
monotonous *tsiridi-tsiridi-tsridi…* Calls include a scolding *tueet-tueet-tueet…* or similar,
and a single *tueet* or *swit*. HABITAT: Broadleaved evergreen forest and secondary growth.
DISTRIBUTION: Breeds in NW China; winter visitor in SE China, C Myanmar, NW, NE
Thailand, N Laos and N Vietnam (E Tonkin).

5 HUME'S LEAF WARBLER *Phylloscopus humei* 11–12cm FIELD NOTES: Forages at all
levels. VOICE: An excited, repeated *wesoo* often followed by a drawn-out, nasal *zweeeeeeeeee*
or *eeeeeeeeezzzzzzz*; call is a *wesoo* or *dsweet*. HABITAT: Hillside and mountain forest; winters
in wooded areas and secondary growth. DISTRIBUTION: Breeds in W China; winters in SW
China, W, S Myanmar, NW Thailand, N Laos and N Vietnam (W Tonkin).

6 ARCTIC WARBLER *Phylloscopus borealis* 12–13cm FIELD NOTES: Active, agile mainly
arboreal forager; frequently flicks wings and tail. VOICE: Calls include a husky *dzit*, *dz-dzit* or
chizzick. HABITAT: Broadleaved evergreen and mixed deciduous forest, secondary growth,
mangroves and gardens. DISTRIBUTION: Winter visitor in SE China, E, S Myanmar, W, C,
SE, S Thailand, S Laos, S Vietnam, Peninsular Malaysia and Singapore.

7 JAPANESE LEAF WARBLER *Phylloscopus xanthodryas* 12–13cm FIELD NOTES:
Recent split from Arctic Warbler, actions similar. VOICE: Calls as Arctic Warbler. HABITAT:
Woodlands, secondary forest and mangroves. DISTRIBUTION: Winter visitor in Taiwan.

8 GREENISH WARBLER *Phylloscopus trochiloides* 12cm FIELD NOTES: Mainly arboreal;
highly mobile, flitting among foliage or hovering to capture insects. VOICE: Variable,
high-pitched accelerating phrases that culminates in an abrupt ending trill; calls include a
che-wee, *chirree* and a *chis-weet*. HABITAT: Deciduous, mixed and coniferous woodlands with
rich undergrowth. DISTRIBUTION: Breeds in W, SW China; winters in SW China, Myanmar
(possibly resident in N), W, NW, NE Thailand, N Laos and N Vietnam.

9 PALE-LEGGED LEAF WARBLER *Phylloscopus tenellipes* 12–13cm FIELD NOTES:
Forages in undergrowth and lower tree branches. VOICE: Calls with a metallic *tik-tik*
or loud *peet*. HABITAT: Various forests, secondary growth, mangroves and gardens.
DISTRIBUTION: Winter visitor S Myanmar, Thailand, Cambodia, Laos, S Vietnam and
Peninsular Malaysia; passage migrant in China and N, C Vietnam.

10 TWO-BARRED GREENISH WARBLER (TWO-BARRED WARBLER)
Phylloscopus plumbeitarsus 12cm FIELD NOTES: Arboreal, forages mainly in middle
levels. VOICE: Call is a *tissheep* or *chi-ree-wee*. HABITAT: Forests, parks and gardens.
DISTRIBUTION: Winters in Hainan, Myanmar, Thailand, Cambodia, S Laos and C, S
Vietnam; passage migrant in China.

136 LEAF WARBLERS

1 LARGE-BILLED LEAF WARBLER *Phylloscopus magnirostris* 10–11cm FIELD NOTES: Shy; forages in the upper canopy along boughs rather than among foliage. VOICE: A penetrating, descending *tee-ti-tii-tu-tu* or *si si-si su-su*; calls include a *dir-tee* and an ascending *yaw-wee-wee*. HABITAT: Broadleaved evergreen forests usually near water, also in coniferous forest post breeding. DISTRIBUTION: Breeds in W China and N Myanmar; winters in C, S Myanmar.

2 EMEI LEAF WARBLER *Phylloscopus emeiensis* 11–12cm FIELD NOTES: Forages at all levels. Often gives quick wing flicks. VOICE: A clear, slightly quivering trill; call is a soft *tu-du-du* or *tu-du-du-di*. HABITAT: Subtropical broadleaf forest. DISTRIBUTION: Breeds locally in W China; probably winters in S Myanmar.

3 EASTERN CROWNED WARBLER *Phylloscopus coronatus* 12–13cm FIELD NOTES: Active forager at all levels. VOICE: A tit-like *sweetoo-sweetoo-sweetoo-swe-swe-zueee* or similar; call is a soft *phit phit* or a harsh *dwee*. HABITAT: Mixed and evergreen forests, low trees and bushes. DISTRIBUTION: Breeds in NW China; winters in S Myanmar, S Thailand, S Laos, Peninsular Malaysia and Singapore.

4 BLYTH'S LEAF WARBLER *Phylloscopus reguloides* 10–12cm FIELD NOTES: Acrobatic forager, often clinging upside down like a nuthatch. When agitated slowly flicks one wing at a time. VOICE: Call is a *pit-chew*; song is a trilling extension of the call. HABITAT: Broadleaved, conifer and mixed forests; winters in open forest and forest edge. DISTRIBUTION: Breeds in China; resident in W, N, E Myanmar, NW Thailand, S Laos and Vietnam (W Tonkin, S Annam). Winters in C, S Myanmar, Thailand, Laos and N, C Vietnam.

5 HARTERT'S LEAF WARBLER *Phylloscopus goodsoni* 11–12cm FIELD NOTES: Actions similar to Blyth's Leaf Warbler, which is often considered conspecific. VOICE: Presumed similar to Blyth's Leaf Warbler. HABITAT: Broadleaved evergreen forests. DISTRIBUTION: Resident in SE China and Hainan.

6 CLAUDIA'S LEAF WARBLER *Phylloscopus claudiae* 11–12cm FIELD NOTES: Actions similar to Blyth's Leaf Warbler, best separated by voice. VOICE: Begins with 1–2 notes followed by a single-note rapid trill. HABITAT: Forests. DISTRIBUTION: Possibly breeds in W China; winter visitor in SW China, N Myanmar and N Vietnam (W Tonkin).

7 DAVISON'S LEAF WARBLER *Phylloscopus davisoni* 11–12cm FIELD NOTES: Generally forages in the canopy. When agitated, flicks both wings simultaneously. VOICE: A single, high call note followed by a *tit-sui-titsui-titsui* or *see-chee-wee see-chee-wee see-chee-wee*. Calls include a *pitsiu*, *wit-see* or *pitsitsui*. HABITAT: Deciduous woodland or mixed conifer woodland and bamboo. DISTRIBUTION: Resident and summer visitor in SW China, resident in N, E, C Myanmar, NW Thailand, N, C Laos and N, C Vietnam.

8 KLOSS'S LEAF WARBLER *Phylloscopus ogilviegranti* 10–11cm FIELD NOTES: Actions similar to Davison's Leaf Warbler, which is often considered conspecific. VOICE: Presumed similar to White-tailed Leaf Warbler. HABITAT: Deciduous woodland or mixed conifer woodland and bamboo. DISTRIBUTION: Resident in SE China, SE Thailand, SW Cambodia, S Laos and C Vietnam.

9 HAINAN LEAF WARBLER *Phylloscopus hainanus* 10–11cm FIELD NOTES: Active forager in the middle and upper canopy. VOICE: High-pitched, variable phrases, *tsitsitsui-tsitsui…titsu-titsui-titsui…titsu-titsui-titsui* etc.; call is a *pitsitsui*, *pitsiu* or *pitsi-pitsu*. HABITAT: Mountain secondary forest and forest edge scrub. DISTRIBUTION: Resident in Hainan.

10 MOUNTAIN LEAF WARBLER *Phylloscopus trivirgatus* 11–12cm FIELD NOTES: Forages mainly in the upper canopy, singly, in pairs or in mixed-species feeding flocks. VOICE: Slurred, high-pitched, rapid phrases, *tisiwi-tsuwiri-swit*; call is a jangling *tersiwit* and *cheecheechee*. HABITAT: Broadleaved evergreen forest and secondary growth. DISTRIBUTION: Resident in Peninsular Malaysia.

137 LEAF WARBLERS; *SEICERCUS* WARBLERS

1 LIMESTONE LEAF WARBLER *Phylloscopus calciatilis* 11cm FIELD NOTES: Actions probably similar to Sulphur-breasted Warbler. VOICE: A short series of 7–9 soft whistled notes of varying pitch, length and structure on a slightly falling scale. Calls include a short, soft *pi-tsiu, pi-tsu* or similar, often repeated when agitated. HABITAT: Broadleaved evergreen and semi-evergreen forests on limestone karst. DISTRIBUTION: Resident in C, N Vietnam, C, N Laos and, possibly, S China.

2 SULPHUR-BREASTED WARBLER *Phylloscopus ricketti* 11cm FIELD NOTES: Active forager in the canopy, often making aerial flycatching sallies. VOICE: A high-pitched series of short notes that speeds up towards the end; call is a subdued *wi-chu, pi-chu* or *pit-choo.* HABITAT: Mainly broadleaved evergreen and mixed deciduous forests. DISTRIBUTION: Breeds across C China; resident in C Laos and C Vietnam. Winter visitor Thailand (except C, S), S Laos and N Vietnam.

3 YELLOW-VENTED WARBLER *Phylloscopus cantator* 10cm FIELD NOTES: Active forager in bushes or the low to middle level of trees. When calling, spreads tail and flicks it upwards. VOICE: A high *sit weet weet seep seep seep si-chu-chu to-you.* Calls include a soft *see-chew* and occasionally a *see-chew-chew.* HABITAT: Broadleaved evergreen and semi-evergreen forests. DISTRIBUTION: Possibly breeds in N Myanmar and N, C Laos; winters in Myanmar (except Tenasserim), W, NW Thailand and N Laos.

4 GREY-HOODED WARBLER *Phylloscopus xanthoschistos* 10cm FIELD NOTES: Agile forager in trees and shrubs; fans and cocks tail. VOICE: A repeated *tsi-tsi-tsi-weetee*; call is a high *psit-psit* or a plaintive *tyee-tyee.* HABITAT: Forests and secondary growth. DISTRIBUTION: Resident in W, N S Myanmar.

5 GREY-CHEEKED WARBLER *Seicercus poliogenys* 10cm FIELD NOTES: Very active forager in the understorey; flicks wings, cocks and fans tail. VOICE: Various whistled phrases, often fast and trilling. Calls include a thin *tsew tsew tsew* and an explosive *twit twit.* HABITAT: Broadleaved evergreen forest and secondary growth. DISTRIBUTION: Resident in SW China, N Myanmar, Laos and N, C Vietnam.

6 WHISTLER'S WARBLER *Seicercus whistleri* 11–12cm FIELD NOTES: Forages in the understorey and canopy of low trees. VOICE: A simple, whistled *chu chu-weet-tu-chuwee… chu chu-weet-tu-chu-wee…* Call is a soft *chip* or *tiu-du.* HABITAT: High-level broadleaved evergreen forest with rich undergrowth and secondary growth. DISTRIBUTION: Resident in W Myanmar.

7 GREY-CROWNED WARBLER *Seicercus tephrocephalus* 11–12cm FIELD NOTES: Agile forager in foliage or undergrowth. Post breeding often forms small parties or joins mixed-species feeding flocks. Flicks wings and cocks and fans tail. VOICE: A few single notes followed by a trill; call is a soft *trrup* or *turup.* HABITAT: Broadleaved evergreen forest with lush undergrowth and secondary growth; in winter also in forest edge, bamboo and scrub. DISTRIBUTION: Breeds locally in W, SW China; resident in W, N Myanmar and N Vietnam (W Tonkin). Winter visitor in S Myanmar, NW, NE Thailand, N Laos and Vietnam (E Tonkin and Cochinchina).

8 MARTENS'S WARBLER *Seicercus omeiensis* 11–12cm FIELD NOTES: Forages mainly in the understorey, makes short sallies to capture insects. VOICE: Various short, abrupt phrases, some ending in trills, *chu-si-tsu-chu-si-tsu…pi tsu-pi-tsu-hueetse…huee-huee-tse-tse-tse-tse…chu-wee-chu-tsiu-tsiu-wis* etc. Calls include a faint *chup* a *chu-du* and a *chu-du tsip.* HABITAT: Understorey of broadleaved evergreen forest. DISTRIBUTION: Breeds in C, SW China; winter visitor in C, E Myanmar, Thailand, N Laos, N Vietnam and Cambodia.

9 BIANCHI'S WARBLER *Seicercus valentini* 11–12cm FIELD NOTES: Forages in the understorey and the canopy of low trees, often makes short flycatching sallies. VOICE: Similar to Whistler's Warbler but lower pitched; calls include a soft *tiu* or *tiu tiu.* HABITAT: Broadleaved evergreen forest with lush undergrowth and secondary growth. DISTRIBUTION: Breeds locally in C, NE, SE, SW China; resident in N Vietnam (W Tonkin); winters in S China, NW Thailand and N Laos.

1 PLAIN-TAILED WARBLER (ALSTRÖM'S WARBLER) *Seicercus soror* 11–12cm FIELD NOTES: Forages mainly in the understorey, often making flights to capture insects. VOICE: A simple *chip chu-se-sis-chu-se-sis…* or similar. Calls include a high-pitched *tsrit*. HABITAT: Broadleaved evergreen forest with lush undergrowth. DISTRIBUTION: Breeds locally in NE, SE China; winters in S Myanmar, W SE Thailand, Cambodia and Vietnam (S Annam).

2 WHITE-SPECTACLED WARBLER *Seicercus affinis* 11–12cm FIELD NOTES: Forages mainly in the understorey; often makes flycatching sallies. Flicks wings, cocks and fans tail. VOICE: Song starts hesitantly then accelerates, *uee-tiu uee-tiu-chu-weet-chu-chu-weet-chu-weet…* Calls include a quick, rising *u-di-si* and a rolling, *churrrruwedichi*. HABITAT: Broadleaved evergreen forest with lush undergrowth. DISTRIBUTION: Local resident in W, C, NE, SE China, N Myanmar and S Vietnam; winter visitor in SE China, N Vietnam and Laos.

3 CHESTNUT-CROWNED WARBLER *Seicercus castaniceps* 9–10cm FIELD NOTES: Forages in the upper canopy. Flicks wings and tail. VOICE: A thin, upward-inflected *see see see-see-see-see-see*; calls include a quiet *chik* and a *chee-chee*. HABITAT: Broadleaved evergreen forest. DISTRIBUTION: Breeds in southern China; resident in W, N, E Myanmar, NW, W, S Thailand, Laos, N, C Vietnam and Peninsular Malaysia. Winters in SE China.

4 YELLOW-BREASTED WARBLER *Seicercus montis* 9–10cm FIELD NOTES: Forages mainly in foliage of the middle canopy, often hovers or makes flycatching sallies. VOICE: A high-pitched, rising then fading *ziziziziziz-azuuuu* interspersed with *chit chit* notes. HABITAT: Broadleaved evergreen forest. DISTRIBUTION: Resident in Peninsular Malaysia.

5 BROAD-BILLED WARBLER *Tickellia hodgsoni* 10cm FIELD NOTES: Very active; hovers and makes flycatching sallies. VOICE: A long series of high-pitched notes, also a rapid, metallic *witiwiwitiwi-chu-witiwiwitiwit* or similar. HABITAT: Undergrowth and bamboo thickets. DISTRIBUTION: Resident in SW China, W Myanmar, NE Laos and N Vietnam.

6 BLACK-FACED WARBLER *Abroscopus schisticeps* 9cm FIELD NOTES: Highly active, frequently flicks wings and tail. *A. s flavimentalis* (6b) occurs in W Myanmar. VOICE: A thin, high-pitched tinkling; calls include a subdued *tit* and high-pitched *tz-tz-tz-tz-tz*. HABITAT: Broadleaved evergreen forest. DISTRIBUTION: Resident in SW China, W, N, E Myanmar and N Vietnam (W Tonkin).

7 RUFOUS-FACED WARBLER *Abroscopus albogularis* 8cm FIELD NOTES: Forages in the understorey; flicks wings and occasionally fans tail. VOICE: A repetitive, high-pitched, drawn-out whistle and a shrill twittering. HABITAT: Undergrowth and bamboo in broadleaved evergreen forest. DISTRIBUTION: Resident in southern China, Hainan, Taiwan, W, N Myanmar, NW Thailand, N, C Laos and C, N Vietnam.

8 YELLOW-BELLIED WARBLER *Abroscopus superciliaris* 9–11cm FIELD NOTES: Forages mainly in the understorey; frequently flicks wings. VOICE: A halting, tinkling, high-pitched whistle that rises at the end, repeated 2–3 times. HABITAT: Undergrowth in or near broadleaved evergreen forest. DISTRIBUTION: Resident in SW China and the south, except C, SE Thailand, S Cambodia and Singapore.

9 STRIATED GRASSBIRD *Megalurus palustris* 22–24cm FIELD NOTES: Forages in reeds and bushes and occasionally on the ground. VOICE: A strong, rich warble, also a subdued whistle followed by a loud *wheeechoo*. Calls include an explosive *pwit* and a harsh *chat*. HABITAT: Tall damp grasslands, reedbeds and scrub. DISTRIBUTION: Resident in S, SW China, Myanmar, C, NW, NE Thailand, Cambodia, N Laos and Vietnam (except S Annam).

10 CHINESE GRASSBIRD *Graminicola striatus* 18cm FIELD NOTES: Forages low-down in thick vegetation; best located while singing. VOICE: A high-pitched piping, ending with a rattle, also a soft ringing *tseenk-tseenk*. Calls include a repeated *jur-jur-jur* and a harsh *chick*. HABITAT: Vegetation bordering water or marsh. DISTRIBUTION: Resident in E Myanmar, C, S China and Cambodia.

139 LAUGHINGTHRUSHES

1 BLACK LAUGHINGTHRUSH *Garrulax lugubris* 25–27cm FIELD NOTES: Forages in pairs or small flocks, usually close to the ground. VOICE: A hollow whooping *huup-huup-huup* and a rapid *okh-ohk-okh-okh-okh-okh* accompanied by harsh *awk* or *aak* notes. HABITAT: Broadleaved evergreen forest, forest edge and secondary growth. DISTRIBUTION: Resident in extreme S Thailand and Peninsular Malaysia.

2 STRIATED LAUGHINGTHRUSH *Grammatoptila striata* 29–34cm FIELD NOTES: Arboreal, favours fruiting trees. Forages from undergrowth to the canopy. *G. s. brahmaputra* (2b) occurs in N Myanmar. VOICE: A repeated, vibrant *prrrit-you prrrit-pri-prii-u* or *krrrrwhit kwit-kwitwheeuuw*. Calls include a high, soft *wer-wer-wer-wewr-wer*, a rising *wu-wiw* and a grumbling *greip-greip-greip*. HABITAT: Broadleaved evergreen forest, bamboo and secondary growth. DISTRIBUTION: Resident in SW China and W, N Myanmar.

3 MASKED LAUGHINGTHRUSH *Garrulax perspicillatus* 28–32cm FIELD NOTES: Forages mainly on the ground and under thick undergrowth, usually in small parties. VOICE: A set of grunting, chuckling and babbling notes; calls include a loud *jhew* or *jhow*. HABITAT: Scrub, woodland, thickets, reeds, bamboo, hedges and cultivations. DISTRIBUTION: Resident C, S China and N, C Vietnam.

4 WHITE-THROATED LAUGHINGTHRUSH *Garrulax albogularis* 28–31cm FIELD NOTES: Gregarious, often in large flocks. Regularly forages on the ground or up to middle storey. VOICE: A thin wheezy, whistled *tsu'ueeee, hiuuuu, huiiii* and *hsiii*; calls include a gentle *chrrr*, a soft *teh* and a subdued chattering. HABITAT: Broadleaved evergreen, deciduous and coniferous forest, secondary growth, scrub and light jungle. DISTRIBUTION: Resident in W, SW China and N Vietnam (W Tonkin).

5 RUFOUS-CROWNED LAUGHINGTHRUSH *Garrulax ruficeps* 27–29cm FIELD NOTES: Forages in middle strata, usually in pairs or flocks of 15–20 individuals. Often considered conspecific with White-throated Laughingthrush. VOICE: Song similar to White-throated Laughingthrush. Calls include a thin, shrill *tswiiiii* or *dziiiii*. HABITAT: Primary forest of oak, fir and cedar; secondary growth and scrub. DISTRIBUTION: Resident in Taiwan.

6 WHITE-CRESTED LAUGHINGTHRUSH *Garrulax leucolophus* 26–31cm FIELD NOTES: Noisy, constantly uttering contact chuckles; gregarious at all times, often in the company of other species. White-bellied race *G. l. diardi* (6b) occurs in SW China, SE Myanmar, NW, NE, SE Thailand, Cambodia, Laos and Vietnam. VOICE: A rapid, laughing, chattering cackle; also a subdued, staccato *ker-wick-erwick* HABITAT: Broadleaved evergreen, semi-evergreen and dry deciduous forests, secondary growth and bamboo. DISTRIBUTION: Resident in SW China and the south, except C, S Thailand and Peninsular Malaysia.

7 LESSER NECKLACED LAUGHINGTHRUSH *Garrulax monileger* 27cm FIELD NOTES: Forages mainly on the ground. *G. m. pasquieri* (7b) occurs in C, S Laos and Vietnam (C Annam). VOICE: A mellow, repeated *u-wi-uu*, a more subdued *ui-ee-ee-wu, wiu-wiu-wiu* or *ui-ui-ui* and a downslurred *tieew ti-tiew…* HABITAT: Broadleaved evergreen forest, deciduous forest and secondary growth. DISTRIBUTION: Resident in NE, E, SW China and the south, except C, S Thailand, Peninsular Malaysia and Singapore.

8 GREATER NECKLACED LAUGHINGTHRUSH *Garrulax pectoralis* 29cm FIELD NOTES: Forages mainly on the forest floor, often with other laughingthrush species. *G. p. picticollis* (8b) occurs in C, NE China. VOICE: A repeated, clear, ringing *kleer-eer-eer-eer…* or an upslurred, mellow *tu-tweetu-tweetu-twee…* also a clear, rapid *chit-it* or *chit-it-it-it*. HABITAT: Broadleaved evergreen forest, deciduous forest and secondary growth. DISTRIBUTION: Resident in C, NE, S China, Myanmar, W, NW Thailand, N, C Laos and N Vietnam.

9 WHITE-NECKED LAUGHINGTHRUSH *Garrulax strepitans* 28–32cm FIELD NOTES: Forages mainly among leaf litter. Often found in large parties. VOICE: Cackling laughter combined with rapid chattering, interspersed or preceded with clicking *tick* or *tekh* notes, the latter also used as contact calls. HABITAT: Broadleaved evergreen forest. DISTRIBUTION: Resident E, S Myanmar, W, NE, NW Thailand and N Laos.

2b *brahmaputra*

6b *diardi*

7b *pasquieri*

8b *picticollis*

1 CAMBODIAN LAUGHINGTHRUSH *Garrulax ferrarius* 28–30cm FIELD NOTES: Forages mainly on the ground in dense undergrowth, often in flocks of up to ten individuals. Occasionally consorts with other species. Frequently considered conspecific with White-necked Laughingthrush. VOICE: A rapid cackling laughter. HABITAT: Broadleaved evergreen forest. DISTRIBUTION: Resident in SW Cambodia.

2 BLACK-HOODED LAUGHINGTHRUSH *Garrulax milleti* 28–30cm FIELD NOTES: Forages from the ground up to the lower canopy, usually in flocks of 3–10 individuals. Occasionally found with other laughingthrushes. VOICE: Loud outbursts of extended, rapid, cackling laughter interspersed with rattling and tinkling notes. HABITAT: Broadleaved evergreen forests. DISTRIBUTION: Resident in S Laos and C Vietnam.

3 GREY LAUGHINGTHRUSH *Garrulax maesi* 28–31cm FIELD NOTES: Forages mainly on the ground in leaf litter. Gregarious; usually in flocks of ten or more, and sometimes mixes with other laughingthrushes. VOICE: Sudden outbursts of loud cackling laughter combining rapid chattering and repeated double-note phrases preceded by a few subdued *ow* notes. HABITAT: Broadleaved evergreen forest. DISTRIBUTION: Resident in W, S China and N Vietnam.

4 RUFOUS-CHEEKED LAUGHINGTHRUSH *Garrulax castanotis* 28–31cm FIELD NOTES: Habits and actions similar to Grey Laughingthrush, which is sometimes regarded as conspecific. *G. c. varennei* (4b) occurs in N, C Vietnam and E Laos. VOICE: Outbursts of extending cackling, combining rapid chattering and repetitive double-note phrases. HABITAT: Submontane broadleaved evergreen forest. DISTRIBUTION: Resident in Hainan, N, C Vietnam (Mt Ba Vi in E Tonkin and N, C Annam) and E Laos.

5 RUFOUS-NECKED LAUGHINGTHRUSH *Garrulax ruficollis* 22–27cm FIELD NOTES: Forages on the ground and in low bushes; forms large parties post breeding. VOICE: Quickly repeated, jolly whistled phrases, more prolonged scratchy phrases and a slightly shrill *krkrkrkeeeerkookeeeerkoo*, which begins with a few short notes that rises and falls before ending with a louder crescendo. Calls include a shrill *ch'yaa* or *cher*, a harsh *whit-it* and slow short rattles. HABITAT: Broadleaved evergreen forest, forest edge, secondary growth, scrub, bamboo jungle, tall grass and reeds. DISTRIBUTION: Resident in SW China and W, E, N Myanmar.

6 CHESTNUT-BACKED LAUGHINGTHRUSH *Garrulax nuchalis* 23–26cm FIELD NOTES: Forages mainly on or near the ground, often mixes with other laughingthrush species. VOICE: Similar to Black-throated Laughingthrush. Includes mellow whistles mixed with higher and lower slurred notes, also a slightly different type with hardly a pause, transcribed as *whit-oo-whit-oo-whit, wheeoo-wheeoo-wheeoo, tiu-whit-tiu tiu-whit-tiu tiu-whit-tiu, whit-oo-whit-oo*. HABITAT: Secondary growth, thickets, scrub jungle, rocky ravines with scrub, overgrown cultivations and forest edge. DISTRIBUTION: Resident in N Myanmar.

7 BLACK-THROATED LAUGHINGTHRUSH *Garrulax chinensis* 23–30cm FIELD NOTES: Generally in pairs or small parties; skulking forager in trees and bushes. *G. c. monachus* (7b) occurs in Hainan; *G. c. germaini* (7c) is found in S Vietnam and E Cambodia. VOICE: A repetitive, rich fluty song mixed with course *wraah* notes and squeaky whistles; calls include a repeated, low *how*. HABITAT: Broadleaved evergreen and mixed deciduous forest, secondary growth, scrub and grass. DISTRIBUTION: Resident in S China, Hainan, C, E, S Myanmar, W, NW, NE Thailand, E Cambodia, NE, C Laos and Vietnam.

8 WHITE-CHEEKED LAUGHINGTHRUSH *Garrulax vassali* 26–29cm FIELD NOTES: Gregarious, often in large parties of over 20 individuals; forages mainly on or near the ground. VOICE: A simple, repeated *whii-u*, foraging flocks utter quick *whi* notes and harsh rattles. HABITAT: Broadleaved evergreen forest, secondary growth, scrub and grass. DISTRIBUTION: Resident W, E Cambodia, S Laos and C Vietnam.

4b *varennei*

7b
monachus

7c
germaini

141 LAUGHINGTHRUSHES

1 YELLOW-THROATED LAUGHINGTHRUSH *Garrulax galbanus* 23–25cm FIELD NOTES: Forages on or near the ground, usually in pairs or small parties. VOICE: A feeble chirping. HABITAT: Tall grass mixed with shrubs and trees, open areas and edge of broadleaved evergreen forest. DISTRIBUTION: Resident in W Myanmar.

2 BLUE-CROWNED LAUGHINGTHRUSH *Garrulax courtoisi* 24–25cm FIELD NOTES: Forages on the ground, in bushes and trees. VOICE: A continuous, tittering, also pleasant *piiuu, djew* or *djoh* notes and, occasionally, a louder *dju-dju-dju-dju…* HABITAT: Mixed evergreen and deciduous forest, forest patches and nearby bushy areas. DISTRIBUTION: Resident in China (border of Anhui and Jiangxi provinces).

3 RUFOUS-VENTED LAUGHINGTHRUSH *Garrulax gularis* 23–26cm FIELD NOTES: Gregarious, forages mainly on the ground. VOICE: Sweet, chiming whistles, upslurred then downslurred; calls include harsh rattling *churrs* interspersed with high-pitched whistled phrases. HABITAT: Broadleaved evergreen forest, secondary growth and scrub. DISTRIBUTION: Resident in N Myanmar, N, C Laos, and C Vietnam.

4 GREY-SIDED LAUGHINGTHRUSH *Garrulax caerulatus* 27–29cm FIELD NOTES: Forages on the ground, in bushes and sometimes in taller trees; post breeding occurs in small flocks. VOICE: Clear, loud, spaced whistled phrases; calls include a harsh grating *grrrh, grriiih* or *grrititit*. HABITAT: Broadleaved evergreen forest, secondary growth and bamboo. DISTRIBUTION: Resident in SW China and N Myanmar.

5 RUSTY LAUGHINGTHRUSH *Garrulax poecilorhynchus* 27–29cm FIELD NOTES: Forages in small groups in undergrowth and lower parts of trees. VOICE: A slow, melodic whistling; calls include various chirring notes and low cat-like contact notes. HABITAT: Broadleaved evergreen or deciduous forest; also mixed broadleaf deciduous and coniferous forest; often along watercourses. DISTRIBUTION: Resident in Taiwan.

6 CHESTNUT-WINGED LAUGHINGTHRUSH *Garrulax berthemyi* 27–29cm FIELD NOTES: Forages mainly on the ground and in undergrowth, occasionally venturing to middle storey. VOICE: Loud, melodious and variable whistles; calls include mewing notes and odd loud whistles. HABITAT: Broadleaved evergreen forest, bamboo and low ground cover in conifer plantations. DISTRIBUTION: Resident across central China.

7 MOUSTACHED LAUGHINGTHRUSH *Garrulax cineraceus* 21–24cm FIELD NOTES: Forages mostly on the ground. Generally in pairs or small parties. Rusty race *G. c. cinereiceps* (7b) occurs in China. VOICE: A repeated high-pitched, upslurred *pr'r'r'r'ip* that is sometimes interspersed with hard, chuckling, staccato notes. HABITAT: Thickets at the edge of forests, secondary growth, abandoned cultivations, scrub, bamboo and grass. DISTRIBUTION: Resident in SW, C, E China and W, E Myanmar.

8 CHESTNUT-EARED LAUGHINGTHRUSH *Garrulax konkakinhensis* 24cm FIELD NOTES: Skulking; forages in the understorey, singly, in pairs or in small parties. VOICE: A rambling series of well-spaced and stressed notes and mimicry; calls include a low grumbling *rrreeek rrreeek rrreeek*. HABITAT: Broadleaved forest, forest edge and secondary growth. DISTRIBUTION: Resident in central highlands of Vietnam and adjacent S Laos.

9 RUFOUS-CHINNED LAUGHINGTHRUSH *Garrulax rufogularis* 23–26cm FIELD NOTES: Skulking; forages on the ground or in low bushes. Race *G. r. intensior* (9b) occurs in N Vietnam (W Tonkin). VOICE: A repeated, clear, husky *whi-whi-whu-whi* or *whi-whi-whi-whi*. Also utters short grating rattles, a low buzzing *jzzzzz* and a twangy *gshwee*. HABITAT: Dense undergrowth in broadleaved evergreen forest. DISTRIBUTION: Resident in SW China, N Myanmar, N Vietnam and possibly S Laos and C Vietnam.

10 BARRED LAUGHINGTHRUSH *Garrulax lunalatus* 24–25cm FIELD NOTES: Forages in groups, mainly on the ground. VOICE: A loud and fluty *chu-whi-u—wu-whu'u*, repeated every 3–7 seconds. HABITAT: Open broadleaved and mixed broadleaf conifer forests and bamboo thickets. DISTRIBUTION: Resident in NW China.

7b *cinereiceps*

9b
intensior

142 LAUGHINGTHRUSHES

1 WHITE-SPECKLED LAUGHINGTHRUSH *Garrulax bieti* 25–26cm FIELD NOTES: Forages mainly on the ground. VOICE: A clear descending *wi wi-wi-wuu*, a less descending *wi chi'wi wi chiu-wu* and a *wi chiu-wu wu-wu-wi* that rises at the end. HABITAT: Forests, bamboo and thickets in open mixed forests. DISTRIBUTION: Resident in SW China.

2 GIANT LAUGHINGTHRUSH *Garrulax maximus* 30–35cm FIELD NOTES: Secretive; forages mainly on the ground, often in the company of other laughingthrushes. VOICE: A repeated, rich, melodious *chwi-chwi-chwi-chwi-wuu* or similar, also a brief *fuwit* or *fuweeo* or a rhythmic *fuwit-fwit-fweet-fweet-fuwit-fwit-fweet-fweet…* HABITAT: Dry subalpine forests with understorey and bamboo scrub. DISTRIBUTION: Resident in SW, W China.

3 SPOTTED LAUGHINGTHRUSH *Garrulax ocellatus* 30–33cm FIELD NOTES: Forages in pairs or family parties on the ground or in bushes. Dark-faced race *G. o. artemisiae* (3b) occurs in W China. VOICE: A repeated rich and fluty *wu-it wu-u wu-u wi-u wi'you uu-i w'you uu-i* or similar; calls include a screechy *cacree-cree-cree-cree-rrr-cacree-cree*. HABITAT: Light open mixed forest with undergrowth, rhododendron scrub and bushes. DISTRIBUTION: Resident SW, W China and N Myanmar.

4 CHESTNUT-CAPPED LAUGHINGTHRUSH (SPECTACLED LAUGHINGTHRUSH) *Garrulax mitratus* 22–24cm FIELD NOTES: Forages in pairs or small parties among creepers and thick foliage in the lower and middle storey. VOICE: A subdued, shrill *wi wu-wi-wu-wi, wi wu-wi, wi-wu-wiu-wu-wi* or *wiu-wu-wui-wi* etc. Calls include a sibilant *ju-ju-ju-ju-ju* or *wi-jujujujujuju* and a cackling *wikakakaka*. HABITAT: Broadleaved evergreen forest and forest edge. DISTRIBUTION: Resident in Peninsular Malaysia.

5 SPOT-BREASTED LAUGHINGTHRUSH *Garrulax merulinus* 25–26cm FIELD NOTES: Unobtrusive; forages on or near the ground, singly, in pairs or family groups. VOICE: A rambling mix of rich, loud musical phrases and mimicry. HABITAT: Understorey, shrubbery, broadleaved evergreen forest edge, dense secondary growth and scrub. DISTRIBUTION: Resident in SW China, W, N Myanmar, NW Thailand, N Laos and N Vietnam (W Tonkin; rare in N Annam).

6 ORANGE-BREASTED LAUGHINGTHRUSH *Garrulax annamensis* 24–25cm FIELD NOTES: Forages on or near the ground. VOICE: Loud, rich, musical, rambling phrases and mimicry. HABITAT: Broadleaved evergreen forest, forest edge, overgrown clearings and secondary growth. DISTRIBUTION: Resident in C Vietnam (S Annam).

7 HWAMEI (CHINESE HWAMEI) *Leucodioptron canorum* 21–24cm FIELD NOTES: Forages mainly on the ground, singly, in pairs or in small parties. VOICE: Rich, varied and high-pitched with regular repetition and some mimicry; starts slowly then increases in volume and pitch. HABITAT: Shrubland, thickets, open woodland, scrub and overgrown plots in urban areas. DISTRIBUTION: Resident in China, Hainan, Laos and N Vietnam.

8 TAIWAN HWAMEI *Leucodioptron taewanum* 21–24cm FIELD NOTES: Forages on the ground, singly, in pairs or small parties. VOICE: Similar to Hwamei but less complex, containing fewer syllables but more repeated phrases. HABITAT: Secondary growth and lower tree strata. DISTRIBUTION: Resident in Taiwan.

9 WHITE-BROWED LAUGHINGTHRUSH *Pterorhinus sannio* 22–24cm FIELD NOTES: Forages on the ground or in low bushes, singly or in pairs. VOICE: A harsh, shrill *tcheu… tcheu…tcheu*, also a harsh *tcheurr* and harsh, buzzy *dzwee* notes. HABITAT: Scrub, grass, secondary growth, bamboo thickets, open hillsides with scrub patches, parks and gardens. DISTRIBUTION: Resident in China, N, C, E Myanmar, NW Thailand, N Laos and N Vietnam.

10 STRIPED LAUGHINGTHRUSH *Trochalopteron virgatum* 23cm FIELD NOTES: Skulking; generally occurs singly or in pairs. VOICE: A clear, hurried *chwi-pieu* and a loud, staccato, rattling trill often preceded by a *cho-prrrrrt* or *chrrru-prrrrrt*. Calls include a harsh *chit* and a *chrrrrrr*. HABITAT: Thick scrub and ground cover near broadleaved evergreen forest, forest edge, and secondary growth. DISTRIBUTION: Resident in W Myanmar.

2

3

3b
artemisiae

1

4

5

6

7

8

9

10

143 LAUGHINGTHRUSHES

1 BROWN-CAPPED LAUGHINGTHRUSH *Trochalopteron austeni* 24cm FIELD NOTES: Skulking, usually in pairs or small parties; forages on the ground or in low vegetation. VOICE: A repeated, clear, jolly *whit-wee-wi-weeoo*; calls include a harsh *grrrret-grrrret-grrrret* given when alarmed. HABITAT: Oak and rhododendron forest, secondary forest, forest edge, bamboo thickets and bushes in ravines and clearings. DISTRIBUTION: Resident in W Myanmar.

2 BLUE-WINGED LAUGHINGTHRUSH *Trochalopteron squamatum* 22–25cm FIELD NOTES: Skulking; forages close to the ground, usually in pairs or small groups. VOICE: A rich *cur-white-to-go, free-for-you or wheeooowheee*; calls include a buzzy *jrrrrr-rrr-rrr,* a harsh *cher-cherrrru* and a thrush-like *chuk*. HABITAT: Dense undergrowth in open broadleaved evergreen forest, secondary growth, bamboo, scrub and bushes near forests. DISTRIBUTION: Resident in SW China, W, N, E Myanmar and N Vietnam (W Tonkin).

3 SCALY LAUGHINGTHRUSH *Trochalopteron subunicolor* 23–26cm FIELD NOTES: Forages on the ground or in tangled vegetation; forms post breeding flocks of 10–20 individuals. VOICE: A clear 'wolf-whistle', *whiu-whiiiu or whi'ii'i whi'ii'i*; calls include a squeaky chatter and a shrill alarm note. HABITAT: Broadleaved evergreen forest with thick undergrowth, secondary growth, bramble thickets, rhododendron shrubberies and bamboo. DISTRIBUTION: Resident in SW China, N Myanmar and N Vietnam (W Tonkin).

4 ELLIOT'S LAUGHINGTHRUSH *Trochalopteron elliotii* 23–26cm FIELD NOTES: Forages mainly on the ground, in pairs or small parties. VOICE: A wavering *whi-pi-piu*; calls include a subdued, high-pitched chattering. HABITAT: Thickets, undergrowth and bamboo, at or above the treeline; also in open broadleaf forest, mixed and juniper forests, sometimes close to human habitations. DISTRIBUTION: Resident in W, SW China.

5 BLACK-FACED LAUGHINGTHRUSH *Trochalopteron affine* 24–26cm FIELD NOTES: Forages on or near the ground and occasionally in trees, usually in pairs, with larger parties post breeding. VOICE: A repeated, shrill *wiee-chiweeoo, wiee-chweeiu or wiee-weeoo-wi*; calls include a high-pitched rattle, a low chuckle and wheezy purrs and whines. HABITAT: Forest undergrowth, thickets, bamboo, rhododendrons and shrubberies above the treeline. DISTRIBUTION: Resident in W, SW China, N Myanmar and N Vietnam (W Tonkin).

6 WHITE-WHISKERED LAUGHINGTHRUSH *Trochalopteron morrisonianum* 25–28cm FIELD NOTES: Forages on the ground and up to middle tree levels. VOICE: A rich, clear, whistled *wit-chi'wi or wip chi'rri*, a repeated, laughing *hee-hee-hee-hee hee-hee* and a bell-like *di di di…* also various quiet whistles and churrs. HABITAT: Undergrowth and low trees in coniferous and mixed deciduous forests. Also open forest with clearings, coniferous scrub, bamboo, juniper, trackside shrubbery and brush above the treeline. DISTRIBUTION: Resident in Taiwan.

7 COLLARED LAUGHINGTHRUSH *Trochalopteron yersini* 26–28cm FIELD NOTES: Forages on the ground or low down in dense vegetation, in pairs or small parties. VOICE: A loud, high-pitched rising *wueeeeoo, u-weeeeoo, uuu-weeoo* etc. Whistles are sometimes answered (presumably by females) with harsh mewing calls, but these are sometimes given on their own. HABITAT: Understorey of primary broadleaf evergreen forest, thick regrowth and scrub bordering forests. DISTRIBUTION: Resident in Vietnam (S Annam).

8 RED-WINGED LAUGHINGTHRUSH *Trochalopteron formosum* 27–28cm FIELD NOTES: Skulking; forages in pairs or small parties, on or close to the ground. VOICE: Thin, clear, whistled *chu-weevu* or a rising *chiu-wee*; also a *chiu-wee – u-weeoo*, which may be dueting. HABITAT: Broadleaved evergreen forest, secondary growth and scrub near forests. DISTRIBUTION: Resident in W, SW China and N Vietnam (W Tonkin).

9 RED-TAILED LAUGHINGTHRUSH *Trochalopteron milnei* 26–28cm FIELD NOTES: Forages in pairs or small parties in dense vegetation. *T. m vitryi* (9b) occurs in S Laos (Bolovens Plateau). VOICE: A clear, whistled *uuu-weeoo, eeoo-wee, uuuwi or uuu-hiu hiu*, the latter with slight rising introduction and faster, soft laughter at the end. HABITAT: Understorey of broadleaf evergreen forest, dense secondary growth, bamboo, scrub and grass near forest. DISTRIBUTION: Resident in S, W, E China, N, E Myanmar, NW Thailand, Laos and N, C Vietnam.

144 LAUGHINGTHRUSHES; LIOCICHLAS; RAIL-BABBLER

1 CHESTNUT-CROWNED LAUGHINGTHRUSH *Trochalopteron erythrocephalum* 25–26cm FIELD NOTES: Forages mainly on the ground or in low cover. VOICE: Various repeated short phrases, transcribed as *pearl-lee to-reaper to-real-year you-reap*. Calls include a loud *wee-ou-wee-whip* and a grating *mu-r-r-r*. HABITAT: Dense undergrowth, forest edge, bamboo thickets and scrub. DISTRIBUTION: Possibly occurs in extreme SW China.

2 ASSAM LAUGHINGTHRUSH *Trochalopteron chrysopterum* 23–25cm FIELD NOTES: Forages mainly on or close to the ground, singly, in pairs or small groups. *T. c. woodi* (2b) occurs in SW China and N Myanmar. VOICE: Variable downslurred then upslurred phrases; calls include a low purring *squar-squar-squar*. HABITAT: Understorey and bamboo in broadleaved evergreen, pine and mixed forests, stunted oaks and dwarf rhododendron scrub. DISTRIBUTION: Resident in SW China, W, SW, N Myanmar.

3 SILVER-EARED LAUGHINGTHRUSH *Trochalopteron melanostigma* 26cm FIELD NOTES: Forages mainly on or near the ground, singly, in pairs or small groups. VOICE: A loud, liquid *wi-wiwioo*, *wu-weeeoo* or *tu-tweeoo*, sometimes a fast *wiu-wip*; also utters clear mewing notes. HABITAT: Broadleaved evergreen, pine and mixed broadleaf-pine forests, secondary growth, bamboo and scrub. DISTRIBUTION: Resident in SW China, SE, NE, S, E Myanmar, NW, N, W, S Thailand, Laos and N Vietnam.

4 MALAYAN LAUGHINGTHRUSH *Trochalopteron peninsulae* 25–27cm FIELD NOTES: Forages on or near the ground. VOICE: A clear *wip-weeoo*, *wiw-weeoo* or a quicker *wip-wi-eeoo*. HABITAT: Understorey and bamboo in broadleaved evergreen forest, secondary growth, scrub and grass. DISTRIBUTION: Resident in S Thailand and Peninsular Malaysia.

5 GOLDEN-WINGED LAUGHINGTHRUSH *Trochalopteron ngoclinhense* 27cm FIELD NOTES: Forages singly or in pairs; sometimes associates with Red-tailed Laughingthrush. VOICE: A double-noted cat-like mewing. HABITAT: Understorey and bamboo in montane broadleaf evergreen forest. DISTRIBUTION: Resident in the central highlands of C Annam in Vietnam.

6 CRIMSON-FACED LIOCICHLA *Liocichla phoenicea* 21–23cm FIELD NOTES: Very skulking, forages on the ground, in undergrowth and occasionally in trees. *L. p. bakeri* (6b) occurs in SW China (W Yunnan) and Myanmar. VOICE: Various clear, beautiful, repeated phrases; calls include a rasping *chrrt-chrrt* and an upslurred, buzzy *grssh grssh*. HABITAT: Dense undergrowth in broadleaved evergreen forest, dense thickets and scrub. DISTRIBUTION: Resident in SW China (W, NW Yunnan) and N Myanmar.

7 SCARLET-FACED LIOCICHLA *Liocichla ripponi* 21–23cm FIELD NOTES: Unobtrusive; forages in undergrowth or on the ground. VOICE: A clear, repeated *chu'u-wiu-wwuu* or similar; calls include a mewing and a falling, mellow *tyuuuuu*. HABITAT: Ravines, open forest and bamboo jungle near swamps. DISTRIBUTION: Resident in SW, SE China, SE, E Myanmar, NW Thailand, N Laos and N Vietnam.

8 EMEI SHAN LIOCICHLA *Liocichla omeiensis* 19–21cm FIELD NOTES: Skulking; forages in thick vegetation. VOICE: Weak, shrill whistled phrases of long slurred notes, e.g. *chwi-weeiee-eeoo* or *chui-weeiee-ieeoo-ueeoo*. HABITAT: Undergrowth in secondary broadleaved evergreen forest, dense secondary growth, bamboo thickets and scrub. DISTRIBUTION: Resident in China (NE Yunnan and S Sichuan).

9 TAIWAN LIOCICHLA *Liocichla steeri* 17–19cm FIELD NOTES: Forages in low vegetation. VOICE: Calls include a rasping *djr* or *djr drrrrrr*. Variable song consists of high-pitched, quavering and buzzy notes. HABITAT: Forests, forest edge, tangled shrubbery and orchards. DISTRIBUTION: Resident in Taiwan.

10 RAIL-BABBLER *Eupetes macrocerus* 29cm FIELD NOTES: Forages on forest floor. Walks with a nodding head, much like a chicken; also dashes over ground and fallen branches in pursuit of insects or spiders. VOICE: A long, drawn-out, monotonous whistle. HABITAT: Broadleaved evergreen forest. DISTRIBUTION: Resident in S Thailand and Peninsular Malaysia.

298

2b *woodi*

6b *bakeri*

145 WREN; WREN-BABBLERS

1 WREN *Troglodytes troglodytes* 10cm FIELD NOTES: Restless, forages mouse-like in low vegetation or over rocks, showing only in fleeting glimpses. More prominent when singing. VOICE: A very loud mixture of trills and rattling warbles ending with a long, dry rattling trill. Calls include a repeated *tek* and a rapid chittering. HABITAT: Very varied, including woodland, scrub, rocky areas and cultivations. DISTRIBUTION: Resident in SW, W, NW China, Taiwan and N Myanmar; winters in coastal NE, E, SE China.

2 INDOCHINESE WREN-BABBLER *Rimator danjoui* 18–19cm FIELD NOTES: Forages on or close to the ground. VOICE: A series of short, monotone, clear, high-pitched whistles; calls include a scolding *chrrr-chrrr-chrrr…* HABITAT: Broadleaved evergreen forest, secondary forest and bamboo. DISTRIBUTION: Resident in C Laos and N, C Vietnam.

3 NAUNG MUNG WREN-BABBLER *Rimator naungmungensis* 18–19cm FIELD NOTES: Actions and habits similar to Indochinese Wren-babbler. VOICE: Probably much like Indochinese Wren-babbler. HABITAT: Primary and secondary broadleaved evergreen forest and rocky areas. DISTRIBUTION: Resident in N Myanmar (Naung Mung).

4 LONG-BILLED WREN-BABBLER *Rimator malacoptilus* 11–12cm FIELD NOTES: Skulking, forages on the ground and in undergrowth, usually in pairs. VOICE: A short, clear, whistled *chiiuuh* or *fueeer* that falls in pitch but rises in volume, given every few seconds. HABITAT: Broadleaved evergreen forest, forest edge, secondary growth and bamboo. DISTRIBUTION: Resident in SW China and N Myanmar.

5 WHITE-THROATED WREN-BABBLER *Rimator pasquieri* 11–12cm FIELD NOTES: Skulks in undergrowth, rummages among fallen leaves. VOICE: A whistled *chiiii'uh* or *tiiiii'u*, often interspersed with short *pit'wip* or *pi-wip* notes; call is a low *prrp* or *prrt*. HABITAT: Broadleaved evergreen forest, secondary growth and bamboo. DISTRIBUTION: Resident in N Vietnam (Fan Si Pan Mts – W Tonkin).

6 STRIPED WREN-BABBLER *Kenopia striata* 14–15cm FIELD NOTES: Forages on or close to the ground, among fallen logs and leaf litter. VOICE: A clear, monotone, whistled *chuuii, chiuuu* or *chi-uuu* repeated every few seconds. Calls include a soft *pee-pee-pee* and a soft, frog-like *churrh-churrh-churrh*. HABITAT: Broadleaved evergreen forest. DISTRIBUTION: Resident in S Thailand and Peninsular Malaysia.

7 LARGE WREN-BABBLER *Turdinus macrodactylus* 19cm FIELD NOTES: Forages on or close to the ground; sings from higher perches. VOICE: Variable; consists of short, loud clear whistled phrases, repeated every few seconds. HABITAT: Broadleaved evergreen forest. DISTRIBUTION: Resident in S Thailand and Peninsular Malaysia.

8 MARBLED WREN-BABBLER *Turdinus marmoratus* 21–22cm FIELD NOTES: Shy and secretive, forages on or near the ground, in undergrowth; often in damp areas. VOICE: A clear double or single whistle e.g. *puuu-chiiii, pyuuu-jhiiii* or *puuui-jhiiii.* HABITAT: Broadleaved evergreen forest. DISTRIBUTION: Resident in Peninsular Malaysia.

9 LIMESTONE WREN-BABBLER *Napothera crispifrons* 15–16cm FIELD NOTES: Forages among tangled vegetation and rocks. *N. c. annamensis* (9b) occurs in SW China, N Laos and N Vietnam; *N. c. calcicola* (9c) is found in NE Thailand (Saraburi Province); the white-throated morph occurs in S Myanmar. VOICE: A rapid series of uneven, harsh slurred notes; calls with harsh scolding rattles. HABITAT: Evergreen and mixed deciduous forest and scrub on limestone hill country. DISTRIBUTION: Resident in SW China, S Myanmar (Tenasserim), W, NW, NE Thailand, N Laos and N Vietnam.

10 STREAKED WREN-BABBLER *Napothera brevicaudata* 14cm FIELD NOTES: Forages among rocks and tangled vegetation. *N. b. leucosticta* (10b) occurs in S Thailand and Peninsular Malaysia. VOICE: Various loud, clear, melancholy, ringing whistles; calls include a hard *churk-urt-churk-urt* and a buzzy *trrreeettt*. HABITAT: Broadleaved evergreen forest on limestone, often in the vicinity of rocky outcrops. DISTRIBUTION: Resident in S China and the south, except SW, C Myanmar, C Thailand, S Vietnam and Singapore.

9c *calcicola*

9b *annamensis*

10b
leucosticta

9

9
white-throated morph

10

146 WREN-BABBLERS

1 EYEBROWED WREN-BABBLER *Napothera epilepidota roberti* 10cm FIELD NOTES: Forages in low vegetation and on mossy boulders. *N. e. granti* (1b) occurs in S Myanmar (S Tenasserim), S Thailand and Peninsular Malaysia; *N. e. davisoni* (1c) in N, W Thailand and S Myanmar (N Tenasserim); *N. e. amyae* (1d) in SW China and N, C Vietnam; *N. e. hainana* (1e) in Hainan. VOICE: A thin, falling *cheeeoo, cheeeeeu* or *piiiiiu*, repeated every few seconds. Calls include a loud, *chyurk*, a low *pit pit pit* and a rattling *prrrt-prrrt-prrrt*. HABITAT: Broadleaved evergreen forests. DISTRIBUTION: Resident in S China, Hainan, N, C, E, S Myanmar, Thailand (except C, SE), Laos, Vietnam (except Cochinchina) and Peninsular Malaysia.

2 PYGMY WREN-BABBLER *Pnoepyga pusilla* 9cm FIELD NOTES: Forages on or near the ground, in leaf litter, tangled vegetation and on mossy logs and branches. Often stands upright. VOICE: A slow, drawn-out *ti – ti – tu*, each syllable lasting a second, with a two-second interval; call is a repeated *tchit*. HABITAT: Broadleaved evergreen forest and secondary growth. DISTRIBUTION: Resident in China, Hainan, Myanmar (except SW, C, S), NW, S Thailand, Laos, N, C Vietnam and Peninsular Malaysia.

3 SCALY-BREASTED WREN-BABBLER *Pnoepyga albiventer* 9–10cm FIELD NOTES: Nervously flicks wings. Forages in tangled undergrowth and among mossy logs. VOICE: A rapid, high-pitched, jumbled warble; call is an explosive *tschik*. HABITAT: Undergrowth in damp, shady forests and forest edge; usually with water nearby. DISTRIBUTION: Resident in SW China, W, N Myanmar and N Vietnam (W Tonkin).

4 TAIWAN WREN-BABBLER *Pnoepyga formosana* 8–9cm FIELD NOTES: Foraging actions similar to Scaly-breasted Wren Babbler. VOICE: A group of very high-pitched whistles; calls with a wheezy, querulous *pwshhhhht*. HABITAT: Dense tangled undergrowth and bamboo in montane broadleaved evergreen and mixed broadleaf-conifer forests. DISTRIBUTION: Resident in Taiwan.

5 SPOTTED WREN-BABBLER *Elachura formosa* 10cm FIELD NOTES: Actions presumably similar to other wren babblers. VOICE: A high, drawn-out tinkling; call is a spluttering trill. HABITAT: Broadleaved evergreen forest, scrub and weeds in steep-sided gulleys. DISTRIBUTION: Resident in SW, C China, W, N Myanmar, N, C Laos and N Vietnam (W Tonkin, N Annam).

6 BAR-WINGED WREN-BABBLER *Spelaeornis troglodytoides* 10cm FIELD NOTES: Clambers on bamboo stems and mossy tree trunks. VOICE: A 5–8 note, husky, rapid rolling warble. HABITAT: Dense undergrowth and bamboo in moist forests. DISTRIBUTION: Resident in W, SW China and N Myanmar.

7 GREY-BELLIED WREN-BABBLER *Spelaeornis reptatus* 11cm FIELD NOTES: Forages in low, thick vegetation. VOICE: A loud, strident accelerating trill that changes into a descending warble; contact call is a soft, repeated *pt…pt…* HABITAT: Broadleaved evergreen forest, forest edge, secondary growth, scrub and grass near forest. DISTRIBUTION: Resident in SW China, W, N, E Myanmar and W Thailand.

8 CHIN HILLS WREN-BABBLER *Spelaeornis oatesi* 10cm FIELD NOTES: Forages in low vegetation. VOICE: A repeated, loud, undulating, warble; calls include a soft *tuc-tuc tuc* and a *chit-chit-chit*. HABITAT: Broadleaved evergreen forest, forest edge, secondary growth, bamboo scrub and tangled grass. DISTRIBUTION: Resident in W Myanmar.

9 PALE-THROATED WREN-BABBLER *Spelaeornis kinneari* 11–12cm FIELD NOTES: Forages close to the ground. VOICE: Trills that either slow towards the end or are stressed at the end with a stuttering middle. HABITAT: Broadleaved evergreen forest. DISTRIBUTION: Resident in S China (SE Yunnan, NW Guangxi) and N Vietnam (W Tonkin).

10 CHEVRON-BREASTED WREN-BABBLER *Sphenocichla roberti* 18cm FIELD NOTES: Clambers on tree trunks and in thick undergrowth. VOICE: A melodious, fluty *uu-wii-wuu-yu*; calls include strident whistles and a low *hrrrh hrrrh hrrrh hrrr'it hrrrh hrrrh…* HABITAT: Broadleaved evergreen forest, secondary growth and bamboo. DISTRIBUTION: Resident in SW China and N Myanmar.

1b *granti*

1d *amyae*

1e
hainana

1c *davisoni*

1

rufous
morph

2

pale
morph

3

pale
morph

rufous
morph

rufous
morph

4

pale
morph

5

6

♀

7

8

♂

♀

9

♂

10

147 BABBLERS

1 BUFF-BREASTED BABBLER *Pellorneum tickelli* 13–16cm FIELD NOTES: Skulking; forages close to the ground. *P. t. assamense* (1b) occurs in N, W Myanmar. VOICE: A loud, quickly repeated *wi-twee* or *wi-choo*; calls include a rattling *prree* and an explosive *whit*. HABITAT: Broadleaved evergreen forest, secondary growth, bamboo and occasionally mixed deciduous forest. DISTRIBUTION: Resident in SW China and the south, except W, C Myanmar, C, SE Thailand and Singapore.

2 SPOT-THROATED BABBLER *Pellorneum albiventre* 14–15cm FIELD NOTES: Very skulking, forages near the ground. *P. a. pusillum* (2b) occurs in SE China and N Vietnam (W Tonkin). VOICE: A rich mix of short whistles and hard ringing notes; calls include a buzzing *chrrr-chrrr-chrrr-chrrrit…* and a quickly repeated *tip* or *tchip*. HABITAT: Undergrowth in pine forest, overgrown clearings, scrub, bamboo and secondary growth. DISTRIBUTION: Resident in SW, SE China, W, N, E, S Myanmar, NW Thailand, Laos, N, C Vietnam.

3 PUFF-THROATED BABBLER *Pellorneum ruficeps* 15–17cm FIELD NOTES: Forages on or near the ground. Various races occur; depicted are *P. r. minus* (main illustration) from S Myanmar; *P. r. chthonium* (3b) occurs in N Vietnam and *P. r. stageri* (3c) in southern N Myanmar. VOICE: Variable; includes a repeated, shrill *wi-chu* and a descending *tuituititi-twititi-tititi…* Calls include a nasal *chi* and a rasping *rrrrit*. HABITAT: Mixed deciduous and evergreen forest, secondary growth, bamboo and scrub. DISTRIBUTION: Resident in SW China and the south, except S Peninsular Malaysia and Singapore.

4 BLACK-CAPPED BABBLER *Pellorneum capistratum* 16–17cm FIELD NOTES: Forages among leaf litter. VOICE: A loud, high-pitched *teeu*, repeated every few seconds; calls include a subdued *hekhekhekhek* and a nasal *nwit-nwit-nwit*. HABITAT: Broadleaved evergreen forest. DISTRIBUTION: Resident in S Myanmar (S Tenasserim), S Thailand and Peninsular Malaysia.

5 WHITE-CHESTED BABBLER *Trichastoma rostratum* 15–17cm FIELD NOTES: Forages on or near the ground on roots, rocks or branches at water's edge. VOICE: A repeated, high-pitched *wi-ti-tiu*, *chui-chiwi-chew* or *chwi-chi-cheei*, occasionally introduced with a short trill. HABITAT: Riverine broadleaved evergreen, secondary and freshwater peatswamp forest and mangroves. DISTRIBUTION: Resident in S Myanmar (S Tenasserim), S Thailand, Peninsular Malaysia and Singapore.

6 FERRUGINOUS BABBLER *Trichastoma bicolor* 16–18cm FIELD NOTES: Forages mainly in the lower to middle storey, in pairs or loose parties. VOICE: A repeated, loud, sharp *u-wit* also variable jolly phrases, e.g. *wit wi-ti-tu-tu*. Calls include explosive *wit* notes and dry rasping sounds. HABITAT: Broadleaved evergreen forest and secondary forest. DISTRIBUTION: Resident in S Myanmar (S Tenasserim), S Thailand and Peninsular Malaysia.

7 HORSFIELD'S BABBLER *Malacocincla sepiaria* 15–17cm FIELD NOTES: Forages on the ground, in low vegetation and, occasionally, in the middle storey. VOICE: A strident *wi-cho-teuu* or *tip top tiu*, first note high, second low and the last high and shrill. Variations occur when excited. HABITAT: Broadleaved evergreen forest usually near water. DISTRIBUTION: Resident in S Thailand and Peninsular Malaysia.

8 SHORT-TAILED BABBLER *Malacocincla malaccensis* 13–15cm FIELD NOTES: Forages on or just above the ground, usually in pairs. VOICE: A series of 6–7 loud, rich, descending, whistled notes, introduced by a dry trill; calls include a harsh, mechanical *chututututututut…* interspersed with soft *yer* notes. HABITAT: Broadleaved evergreen forest and secondary growth. DISTRIBUTION: Resident in S Myanmar (S Tenasserim), S Thailand, Peninsular Malaysia and Singapore.

9 ABBOTT'S BABBLER *Malacocincla abbotti* 15–17cm FIELD NOTES: Forages on the ground, alone or in pairs. VOICE: A series of 3–4 rich, fluty whistled phrases, e.g. *chiu-woo-wooi*, *wiu-wuoo-wiu* or *wi-wu-yu-wi*. Calls include a mewing, a purring trill and an explosive *cheu*. HABITAT: Broadleaved evergreen, semi-evergreen and riverine forest, forest edge, secondary growth and scrub. DISTRIBUTION: Resident in SW, S Myanmar, W, NE, SE, S Thailand, Cambodia, Laos, C, S Vietnam, Peninsular Malaysia and Singapore.

1b *assamense*

2b *pusillum*

2

3 *minus*

3b *chthonium*

3c *stageri*

1

4

5

6

7

8

9

1 RUFOUS-CROWNED BABBLER *Malacopteron magnum* 18–20cm FIELD NOTES: Forages mainly in the middle storey and undergrowth. VOICE: Song in three parts, transcribed as *phu-phu-phi-phi-chuwee-chuwee-chuwee-chuwu-chuwu-chut-chut-chut-chut-chut-chut-chut*. HABITAT: Broadleaved evergreen forest. DISTRIBUTION: Resident in S Myanmar (S Tenasserim), S Thailand and Peninsular Malaysia.

2 SCALY-CROWNED BABBLER *Malacopteron cinereum* 14–16cm FIELD NOTES: Forages in the middle storey, occasionally in large parties. M. c. indochinense (2b) occurs in E Thailand, Cambodia, C, S Laos and S Vietnam. VOICE: Variable, transcribed as *dit-dit-dit-dit-dit-dit-du-du-du-du-du-du-phu-phu-phu-phu-wiwiwiwiwi-wi-wi-wi-wu* or similar; calls include a subdued *chit-chit* and shrill *chit* or *tcheu* notes. HABITAT: Broadleaved evergreen forest. DISTRIBUTION: Resident in NE, SE, S Thailand, Cambodia, C, S Laos, Vietnam and Peninsular Malaysia.

3 MOUSTACHED BABBLER *Malacopteron magnirostre* 18cm FIELD NOTES: Forages mainly in the middle storey. VOICE: A clear, sweet *tii-tu-ti-tu* or *ti-tiee-ti-ti-tu*; calls include a buzzy *bzzii* and an explosive *whit*. HABITAT: Broadleaved evergreen forest. DISTRIBUTION: Resident in S Myanmar (S Tenasserim), S Thailand, Peninsular Malaysia and Singapore.

4 SOOTY-CAPPED BABBLER *Malacopteron affine* 15–17cm FIELD NOTES: Forages in small trees and bushes. VOICE: A series of 6–9 rising and falling whistles; calls include sharp *which-it* or *pit-wit*. HABITAT: Broadleaved evergreen, swamp forest and forest edge, often with nearby water. DISTRIBUTION: Resident in S Thailand and Peninsular Malaysia.

5 GREY-BREASTED BABBLER *Malacopteron albogulare* 14–16cm FIELD NOTES: Usually forages in the understorey. VOICE: Long, subdued, discordant *whu-whi*, *whit-whu* and *uu-whi-u* phrases, with variants; calls include a *trr* and persistent *churring*. HABITAT: Broadleaved evergreen and freshwater swamp forests. DISTRIBUTION: Resident in Peninsular Malaysia.

6 SLENDER-BILLED SCIMITAR BABBLER *Pomatorhinus superciliaris* 20cm FIELD NOTES: Shy, restless and noisy; forages on or near the ground, in pairs or small parties. VOICE: A rapid, hollow piping, which may be accompanied with a high-pitched *u-wi* or *ti-wee*. HABITAT: Broadleaved evergreen forest with thick undergrowth, bamboo and thick secondary growth. DISTRIBUTION: Resident in SW China, W, N Myanmar and N Vietnam (W Tonkin).

7 GREY-SIDED SCIMITAR BABBLER *Pomatorhinus swinhoei* 22–24cm FIELD NOTES: Forages on the ground often amongst dead leaves. VOICE: A whip-like *whi'ru-chi-whi'ru* or *whi'wu-pi-whi'wu*; call is a harsh *chut'ut'ut'ut'ut'ut'ut...* HABITAT: Dense cover in deciduous forest, damp summit forest, brush-covered hillsides, thickets near woods. DISTRIBUTION: Resident in E China.

8 SPOT-BREASTED SCIMITAR BABBLER *Pomatorhinus mcclellandi* 22–23cm FIELD NOTES: Forages on or near the ground, often rummaging among leaf litter. VOICE: A quick, far-carrying, fluty *wi-wru-pi...* the last sharp note is an answer from female; calls include a harsh rattle preceded by a *whoip-tutututututut*. HABITAT: Forest undergrowth, scrub-jungle and thickets in forest clearings. DISTRIBUTION: Resident in W Myanmar.

9 BLACK-STREAKED SCIMITAR BABBLER *Pomatorhinus gravivox* 21–25cm FIELD NOTES: Forages on or near the ground, usually among leaf litter. VOICE: A quick, husky *whi-wip*, a rapid *whi-chu* or *whi-tu*; calls include a *whup-which'ch'ch'ch'ch'ch*, *whoip-tut'ut'ut'ut'ut'ut* or *whoi-t't't't't'*. HABITAT: Open forest, forest edge, scrub-jungle, bamboo, secondary growth, thickets, scrub, grass and abandoned cultivations. DISTRIBUTION: Resident in W, SW China, NE, E Myanmar, N Laos and N Vietnam.

10 BLACK-NECKLACED SCIMITAR BABBLER *Pomatorhinus erythrocnemis* 23–25cm FIELD NOTES: Forages mainly on the ground, rummaging amongst leaf litter. VOICE: Male gives a hurried *wiu'wi* or *whiu'whi* quickly answered by a female with a *wuu* or *woh*; also recorded is a hoarse, whistled *wrih wrii-wrii-wrii-wrii-wrii* given by an individual responding to a dueting pair. HABITAT: Upper undergrowth and lower storey in foothill, sub-montane and montane forests. DISTRIBUTION: Resident in Taiwan.

2b *indochinense*

149 SCIMITAR BABBLERS

1 LARGE SCIMITAR BABBLER *Pomatorhinus hypoleucos* 26–28cm FIELD NOTES:
Skulking; forages on or near the ground, in an ungainly manner. *P. h. tickelli* (1b) occurs in
S China, S Myanmar (S Tenasserim), Thailand, SW Cambodia, Laos and N Vietnam; *P. h.
wrayi* (1c) in S Thailand and Peninsular Malaysia. VOICE: Three short, hollow notes, often
from dueting pairs e.g. *wiu-pu-pu – wup-up-piu*. Calls include a grating rattle and a hard *puh*.
HABITAT: Broadleaved evergreen forest, mixed deciduous forest, bamboo, scrub-jungle, reeds
and elephant grass. DISTRIBUTION: Resident in S China, Hainan and throughout the south,
except C, E Myanmar, C, S Thailand and Singapore.

2 RUSTY-CHEEKED SCIMITAR BABBLER *Pomatorhinus erythrogenys* 22–27cm
FIELD NOTES: Forages on the ground and occasionally in trees. VOICE: A dueted *whi-u-ju-
whi-u...iu-chu-ip-iu-chu...*or *yu-u-yi-yu-u...*, etc. Also utters a high *pu* or *ju* repeated, rolling
jrr-jrr-jrr and, when alarmed, a rattling *whih-whihihihihi*, a harsh *whit-it* or a *whoi-whititititititit*.
HABITAT: Thick scrub and dense undergrowth at forest edge, scrub in open pine forest and
secondary growth. DISTRIBUTION: Resident in C, E, S Myanmar and NW Thailand.

3 STREAK-BREASTED SCIMITAR BABBLER *Pomatorhinus ruficollis* 16–19cm
FIELD NOTES: Forages in pairs or small groups, on the ground, in bushes or in trees. *P. r. bakeri*
(3b) occurs in W Myanmar. VOICE: A high piping *u-hu-hu* or similar; calls include a raspy
wreep or *wreep-wreep* and a scolding rattle. HABITAT: Thick forest, open forest with thick
undergrowth and hillside scrub. DISTRIBUTION: Resident in China, Hainan, W, N Myanmar,
C Laos and N Vietnam.

4 TAIWAN SCIMITAR BABBLER *Pomatorhinus musicus* 19–21cm FIELD NOTES:
Usually in pairs or small parties foraging on or near the ground, often around tree
trunks. VOICE: A husky *wuh-wuh-wuh-wree* answered with a jolly *wu-wii*, also a piping
uh-pu-pu-pu answered with a harsh *wheer-wu'wu*; calls include a rich, musical *tui-tui* and
a burry *jrrr-jeee*. HABITAT: Undergrowth in foothill, sub-montane and montane forest.
DISTRIBUTION: Resident in Taiwan.

5 WHITE-BROWED SCIMITAR BABBLER *Pomatorhinus schisticeps* 19–23cm FIELD
NOTES: Forages on the ground or in thick cover. VOICE: A series of 3–7 quick, hollow, piping
notes; calls include a raspy *wheesh-whurweeweesh* and a jumbled chattering mixed with
high *who* notes. HABITAT: Broadleaved evergreen and deciduous forest, secondary growth,
bamboo, scrub and grass. DISTRIBUTION: Resident in Myanmar, Thailand (except C, SE),
Cambodia, N, C, S Laos C, S Vietnam.

6 CHESTNUT-BACKED SCIMITAR BABBLER *Pomatorhinus montanus* 19–21cm
FIELD NOTES: Usually forages in undergrowth and lower middle storey, singly in pairs or small
parties, also joins mixed-species feeding groups. VOICE: A clear resonant *whu-whoi, woi-woip*
or *yu-bu-bu* etc., second bird responds with a *wu-pu'pu'pu'pu'pu'pu* or a husky *whor-wup*.
HABITAT: Broadleaved evergreen forest. DISTRIBUTION: Resident in Peninsular Malaysia.

7 RED-BILLED SCIMITAR BABBLER (SCARLET-BILLED SCIMITAR BABBLER)
Pomatorhinus ochraceiceps 22–24cm FIELD NOTES: Forages in trees, bushes and the ground. *P.
o. stenorhynchus* (7b) occurs in N Myanmar. VOICE: Groups utter a variety of mellow and harsh
notes; song is a hurried, staccato, piping *wu-wu-wu* or similar, sometimes answered with thin
wyee. HABITAT: Broadleaved evergreen forest and bamboo. DISTRIBUTION: Resident in SW
China, Myanmar (except SW, W), W, NW, NE Thailand, Cambodia, Laos, N, C Vietnam.

8 CORAL-BILLED SCIMITAR BABBLER *Pomatorhinus ferruginosus* 24cm FIELD
NOTES: Elusive; forages on the ground. *P. f. phayrei* (8b) occurs in SW Myanmar.
VOICE: Many birds congregate to produce a variety of sounds, including soft *whu, whiuv*
and *whoiee* notes, meowing notes, yelping notes, short squeaky notes and a typical, harsh,
scolding *whit whittchrrrrt*; calls include a harsh *krrrrrt* or *krrrirrrurut*. HABITAT: Broadleaved
evergreen forest, bamboo and secondary growth. DISTRIBUTION: Resident in SW China,
Myanmar (except C), W, NW Thailand, Laos and C, N Vietnam.

1b *tickelli*

1c *wrayi*

1

2

3b *bakeri*

4

5

3

7b
stenorhynchus

6

8b *phayrei*

7

8

150 BABBLERS

1 RUFOUS-FRONTED BABBLER *Stachyridopsis rufifrons* 12cm FIELD NOTES: Lively forager in undergrowth and bamboo, usually in pairs, small groups, or as part of mixed-species groups. VOICE: A monotonous, piping *tuh tuh-tuh-tuh-tuh-tuh* or *pe pe-pe-pe-pe-pe*. Calls include a short, rolling *wirrri*, a fast *wu-yu-yu-yu-yu-tu-yi* and a soft *wit* or *wi* contact note. HABITAT: Dense undergrowth and bamboo clumps in open forest and clearings, broadleaved evergreen and secondary growth. DISTRIBUTION: Resident in SW China, Myanmar, Thailand (except C, SE), Laos, N Vietnam and Peninsular Malaysia.

2 RUFOUS-CAPPED BABBLER *Stachyridopsis ruficeps* 12cm FIELD NOTES: Actions tit-like; forages low in undergrowth. May join other small babblers post breeding. VOICE: Like Rufous-fronted Babbler but lower in tone and with no gap between the first and second note; utters a harsh *trrrrt-trrrrt-trrrrt* in alarm. HABITAT: Broadleaved evergreen forest, dense bushes in forest clearings and bamboo stands. DISTRIBUTION: Resident in China, Hainan, Taiwan, N, E Myanmar, N, S Laos and Vietnam (except Cochinchina).

3 GOLDEN BABBLER *Stachyridopsis chrysaea* 10cm FIELD NOTES: Active, agile forager in tangled undergrowth and tree foliage. *S. c. binghami* (3b) occurs in W Myanmar. VOICE: A level-toned *tu tu-tu-tu-tu-tu-tu, chink chink-chink-chink-chink-chink* or similar. Calls include a soft twittering, a *chirik-chirik* and a scolding *chrrrrr*. HABITAT: Broadleaved evergreen forest, bamboo, secondary growth and dense bushes. DISTRIBUTION: Resident in SW China and the south, except SW, C Myanmar, C, SE Thailand, Cambodia, S Vietnam and Singapore.

4 SOOTY BABBLER *Stachyris herberti* 16–18cm FIELD NOTES: Forages on rocks, in undergrowth and in the canopy. Runs rapidly along vines with tail fanned. VOICE: Calls include a soft, repeated *tip* or *tu-ip* and subdued, metallic *cheet cheet cheet* contact notes. HABITAT: Broadleaved evergreen forest on limestone, near cliffs and outcrops. DISTRIBUTION: Resident in C Laos and C Vietnam.

5 NONGGANG BABBLER *Stachyris nonggangensis* 16–18cm FIELD NOTES: Forages on the ground, on rocks or low branches. VOICE: Unrecorded. HABITAT: Seasonal rainforest on limestone karst. DISTRIBUTION: Resident in SE China (SW Guangxi).

6 GREY-THROATED BABBLER *Stachyris nigriceps* 12cm FIELD NOTES: Constantly on the move, foraging in small parties in low growth. *S. n. coltarti* (6b) occurs in SW China and N, NE Myanmar; *S. n. rileyi* (6c) is found in S Laos and C, S Vietnam. VOICE: A high-pitched, quavering, rising *ti tsuuuuuuuueee* or similar. Calls include a constant *chi chi chi* and a scolding *chrrrt* or *chrrrrrr-rrr-rrt*. HABITAT: Broadleaved evergreen forest, secondary growth and bamboo. DISTRIBUTION: Resident in SW China and in the south, except C, E Thailand, Cambodia, S Vietnam and Singapore.

7 GREY-HEADED BABBLER *Stachyris poliocephala* 13–15cm FIELD NOTES: Forages in undergrowth and in trees. VOICE: Clear high-pitched, repeated phrases, e.g. *chit-tiwi-wioo-iwee* or *yit-uip-ui-wiee* and a higher *chu-chi-chiee* or similar. Calls include a descending *dji-dji-dji-du*, a scolding *chrrrttutut* and soft *tip-tip-tip* contact calls. HABITAT: Broadleaved evergreen forest and secondary growth. DISTRIBUTION: Resident in S Thailand and Peninsular Malaysia.

8 SNOWY-THROATED BABBLER *Stachyris oglei* 15cm FIELD NOTES: Forages in fast-moving flocks, in thick cover. VOICE: A thin high-pitched rattle. HABITAT: Broadleaved evergreen forest, secondary growth, bamboo and scrub in ravines. DISTRIBUTION: Resident in N Myanmar.

9 SPOT-NECKED BABBLER *Stachyris strialata* 15–17cm FIELD NOTES: Shy and skulking. Forages in undergrowth, on the ground, in pairs or small parties. VOICE: A high-pitched, whistled *tuh tih tih, tuh tih tuh* or *tuh-tih* sometimes accompanied by a rattling *whiiii-titititititi*. Calls include a scolding *tirrrirrirr* or *tchrrrt-tchrrrt* and high-pitched *tip* notes. HABITAT: Broadleaved evergreen forest, secondary growth, scrub and grass. DISTRIBUTION: Resident in S China, Hainan, N, S Myanmar, W, NW, S Thailand, N, C Laos and N, C Vietnam.

3b *binghami*

6c *rileyi*

6b *coltarti*

151 BABBLERS

1 WHITE-NECKED BABBLER *Stachyris leucotis* 14–15cm FIELD NOTES: Forages on or near the ground, singly, in pairs or small groups, occasionally in the company of other small babblers. VOICE: A simple, whistled *uu-wi-u-wi*, *uu-wi-u-wi-u* or *uui-wi-oi-wi*; the second note lower pitched. HABITAT: Broadleaved evergreen forest. DISTRIBUTION: Resident in S Thailand and Peninsular Malaysia.

2 BLACK-THROATED BABBLER *Stachyris nigricollis* 15–16cm FIELD NOTES: Generally forages in low vegetation, sometimes in the company of other small babblers. VOICE: A well-spaced, monotonous, piping *pu-pu-pu-pu-pu-pu* or a faster *pupupupupupupupupu*, frequently followed by a low churring from a mate. Also utters a hollower *chu-chuwu-chu-chu-chu-chu*. Calls include a slow, rattled *tchrrr-rrt* or *tchrrrt-trrerrt-trrerrt*, a harsh, descending *chi-chi-chew-chew* or *ti-tu-chu-chu* and a high *tchi-tchu*. HABITAT: Broadleaved evergreen forest and freshwater swamp forest. DISTRIBUTION: Resident in S Thailand and Peninsular Malaysia.

3 CHESTNUT-RUMPED BABBLER *Stachyris maculata* 17–19cm FIELD NOTES: Forages in the lower and middle storey in noisy, busy groups of up to eighteen or more individuals. VOICE: Variable; several birds call together with loud, full, quavering or tremulous phrases mixed with females' harsh, jumbled trills and quiet conversational notes. HABITAT: Broadleaved evergreen forest. DISTRIBUTION: Resident in S Thailand and Peninsular Malaysia.

4 CHESTNUT-WINGED BABBLER *Stachyris erythroptera* 12–14cm FIELD NOTES: Forages in the middle storey in small parties, gleaning from foliage and twigs. VOICE: A mellow, quite quick, variable piping whistle of 7–10 notes, e.g. *hu-hu-hu-hu-hu-hu-hu*, a slower *chu hu-hu-hu-hu* or a faster *hu hu'u'u'u'u'u'u*. May be accompanied by low churrs, presumably given by the female. Calls include a scolding *trrrrrt-trrrrrt* and a soft wip or *wit*. HABITAT: Broadleaved evergreen forest and secondary growth. DISTRIBUTION: Resident in S Myanmar (S Tenasserim), S Thailand, Peninsular Malaysia and Singapore.

5 STRIPED TIT-BABBLER (PIN-STRIPED TIT-BABBLER) *Macronus gularis* 11cm FIELD NOTES: Noisy, forages in bushes or trees; feeding actions tit-like. Post breeding gathers in parties of twelve or more. VOICE: Variable; includes a well-spaced *chut-chut-chut-chut-chut* or *ti-chut-chutut-chut…* calls include a harsh *chrrt-chrr* and a scolding *tseep*. HABITAT: Light and dense forest with bushes and undergrowth, bamboo and tall grass. DISTRIBUTION: Resident in SW China and throughout the south, except C Thailand.

6 GREY-FACED TIT-BABBLER *Macronus kellyi* 14cm FIELD NOTES: Forages mainly in trees singly or in pairs; post breeding in small parties, which may include other species. VOICE: A soft, even, well-spaced *tuh-tuh-tuh-tuh-tuh-tuh-tuh-tuh…* calls include a harsh *chrrrrii-chrrruu-chrrrii-chru*, *chrrree-chrrrer* or *chit-chrrerr*, a course *wi-ti-tichu* and a harsh, squeaky *trrrrrrt-trrrrrt…* HABITAT: Broadleaved evergreen and secondary forest. DISTRIBUTION: Resident in E Cambodia, C, S Laos and C, S Vietnam.

7 FLUFFY-BACKED TIT-BABBLER *Macronus ptilosus* 16–17cm FIELD NOTES: Forages in foliage, usually pairs. VOICE: A repeated, low, long, liquid *puh-puh-puh-puh*, a slower *wuh wu-hu wu-hu*, *wuh-wuh hu-wu hu-wu* or a *poop-poop…poop-poop*, often accompanied by husky churring, presumably by a female. Calls include a *gertcha* or a harsh *ker*. HABITAT: Broadleaved evergreen forest edge, freshwater swamp forest, secondary forest and bamboo. DISTRIBUTION: Resident in S Thailand and Peninsular Malaysia.

8 CHESTNUT-CAPPED BABBLER *Timalia pileata* 15–17cm FIELD NOTES: Elusive, threads through tangles of tall grass and bushes. Usually in pairs or after breeding in groups of 6–8 birds. VOICE: Husky phrases ending with thin, metallic notes, e.g. *wher-wher witch-it-it* or similar, also a *tseeen-weer-skrich-richrichit* or a *whinnying tweer'r'r'r'r'r'r'r'r'r'r*, fading at the end. Calls include a short *tzit*, a harsh *chrrt* and various chuntering notes. HABITAT: Tall grass, reeds, scrub and secondary growth. DISTRIBUTION: Resident in S China and in the south, except S Thailand, Peninsular Malaysia, Singapore and N Vietnam (W Tonkin).

1 YELLOW-EYED BABBLER *Chrysomma sinense* 18cm FIELD NOTES: Elusive, clambers in reeds in a tit-like manner. Climbs to exposed perches to call, but quickly dives back into cover. VOICE: Variable clear, high phrases, e.g. *wi-wu-chiu, wi-wu'chrieu, wi-wu-wi'tchu-it, wi-wi-chu* and *tchwi-wi-tchiwi*, often mixed with nasal calls and rising trills. Calls include a dry, trilling and a falling, nasal *sttyeww*. HABITAT: Scrub, grassland and secondary growth. DISTRIBUTION: Resident in S China, Myanmar, Thailand (except S), Laos and Vietnam (W Tonkin, C Annam).

2 JERDON'S BABBLER *Chrysomma altirostre* 17cm FIELD NOTES: Highly skulking; best located while singing from the top of a reed stem. Grey-throated race *C. a. griseigulare* (2b) occurs in N Myanmar. VOICE: A repeated weak *chi-chi-chi-chew-chew-chew* or *ih-ih-ih-h chew chitit chew i'wwiuu* etc. Calls include a thin, high-pitched *tic, tsik* or *ts-ts-tsik*. HABITAT: Tall grassland and reedbeds. DISTRIBUTION: Resident in N, S Myanmar.

3 RUFOUS-TAILED BABBLER *Moupinia poecilotis* 15cm FIELD NOTES: Rather sluggish forager in very dense undergrowth. VOICE: A clear, quickly delivered *phu pwii*, occasionally introduced by a short *chit* or similar. When agitated utters various combinations of short stuttering notes, which may also be given before the song. HABITAT: Grass, scrubby hillsides and thickets near streams. DISTRIBUTION: Resident in SW China.

4 SLENDER-BILLED BABBLER *Turdoides longirostris* 23cm FIELD NOTES: Skulking, gregarious and noisy; forages on the ground and on reed or grass stems. VOICE: Variable; includes a high-pitched series of shrill notes; also gives a strident *chiu-chiu-chiu-chiu*, a discordant *tiu-tiu-tit-tit-tu-tu* and a buzzy call that leads into an irregular rattle. HABITAT: Tall grass and reeds, usually near water. DISTRIBUTION: Resident in SW Myanmar.

5 STRIATED BABBLER *Turdoides earlei* 21cm FIELD NOTES: Gregarious, usually in small parties. Clambers in reeds and tall grass. VOICE: A repeated *tiew-tiew-tiew-tiew*, interspersed with *quip-quip-quip* calls from other flock members. Calls include a descending *chsweerp* answered by a short *tsee*; presumably given by the female. HABITAT: Grass, reeds and scrub, usually near water. DISTRIBUTION: Resident in SW, N, C, S Myanmar.

6 WHITE-THROATED BABBLER *Turdoides gularis* 25–27cm FIELD NOTES: Forages on the ground, under scrub and in small trees. VOICE: Flocks utter a sibilant, low *trrrr trrrr trrrr* and a louder, constantly repeated *chr'r'r'r'r'r'r* or *whir'r'r'r'r'r'r*. HABITAT: Scrub and bushes in semi-desert, cultivation edge, thickets, thorn hedges and patches of bamboo. DISTRIBUTION: Resident in SW, C, S Myanmar.

7 TIBETAN BABAX (KOSLOV'S BABAX) *Babax koslowi* 28cm FIELD NOTES: Wary, forages on the ground or in low vegetation, in pairs or small parties; often cocks tail. VOICE: A dry, scolding rattle. HABITAT: Juniper forest and scrub. DISTRIBUTION: Possibly occurs in SW China.

8 CHINESE BABAX *Babax lanceolatus* 22–30cm FIELD NOTES: Forages on the ground or in low scrub. Occasionally ascends trees to feed in the topmost branches, especially in mornings and evenings. VOICE: A full, clear, whistled *pu-i, tchu-wi, pu-i pu-i pu-i pu-i pu-i pu-i…* or a more hurried *pui-pui-pui-pui…* Calls include a chuntering *witchawithcha*, a grouchy *jhu-wit* and various chattering rattles. HABITAT: Open broadleaved evergreen forest, forest edge and secondary growth. DISTRIBUTION: Resident in E, SE, W, SW China and W, N, C, E Myanmar.

2b
griseigulare

153 MESIA; LEIOTHRIX; CUTIAS; SHRIKE-BABBLERS

1 SILVER-EARED MESIA *Leiothrix argentauris* 15–17cm FIELD NOTES: Forages in bushes and trees; post breeding forms parties of 5–30 individuals. *M. a. cunhaci* (1b) occurs in S Laos, E Cambodia and C Vietnam; *M. a. ricketti* (1c) in SW China, N, C Laos and N Vietnam. VOICE: A cheerful, descending *che tchu-tchu cher-it* or *che-chu chiwi chwu*; calls include a flat, piping *pe-pe-pe-pe-pe* and a harsh chattering. HABITAT: Bushes and undergrowth in forests, forest edge, secondary growth and scrub. DISTRIBUTION: Resident in SW China, Myanmar (except SW, C), W, NW, NE, S Thailand, E Cambodia, Laos, N, C Vietnam and Peninsular Malaysia.

2 RED-BILLED LEIOTHRIX (PEKING ROBIN) *Leiothrix lutea* 14–15cm FIELD NOTES: Forages on the ground or in undergrowth; post breeding forms small, noisy parties. VOICE: A fluty warble of up to fifteen notes; calls include a nasal *zhirk*, a *shreep*, a rattling *zhri-zhri-zhri...* and a when alarmed a buzzy *zhriti-zhriti-zhriti...* HABITAT: Undergrowth in forests, forest edge, secondary growth and scrub. DISTRIBUTION: Resident in much of China, W, N Myanmar and N Vietnam.

3 CUTIA (HIMALAYAN CUTIA) *Cutia nipalensis* 20cm FIELD NOTES: Creeps along branches and on trunks; post breeding forms small parties. VOICE: Variable, generally a long series of ringing notes sometimes interspersed with high *jiw* notes; calls include a light *chick-chick-chick...* a loud *chip* and a low *jert*. HABITAT: Broadleaved evergreen forest. DISTRIBUTION: Resident in SW China, NW, N, E, SE Myanmar, NW Thailand, N, C Laos, N Vietnam (W Tonkin) and Peninsular Malaysia.

4 VIETNAMESE CUTIA *Cutia legalleni* 17–20cm FIELD NOTES: Actions and habits similar to Cutia. VOICE: Variable, including a distinctive *wuyeet wu wi wi wi wi woo*, a *wipwi-weei-weei-weei* and a fast, loud, high-pitched *wei-wuu-wei-wuu*. HABITAT: Broadleaved evergreen and mixed broadleaf-pine forest. DISTRIBUTION: Resident in S Laos and C Vietnam (C, S Annam).

5 BLACK-HEADED SHRIKE-BABBLER *Pteruthius rufiventer* 18–20cm FIELD NOTES: Lethargic, forages from undergrowth to the canopy. VOICE: A mellow *wip-wu-yu*, repeated every few seconds; calls include a scolding *rrrrt-rrrrt-rrrrt...* and a quick *ukuk-wrrrrrii-yiwu*. HABITAT: Broadleaved evergreen forest. DISTRIBUTION: Resident in SW China, W, N Myanmar and N Vietnam (W Tonkin).

6 BLYTH'S SHRIKE-BABBLER *Pteruthius aeralatus* 16cm FIELD NOTES: Shuffles sideways along branches, searching mosses and lichens. *P. a. ricketti* (6b) occurs in SW, SE China, Hainan, NW Myanmar, NW Thailand, N Laos and N Vietnam. VOICE: A variable, repeated, strident series, e.g. *ip ch-chu ch-chu, ip chip chip chip ch-chip* or *ip chu ch-chu*; calls include a harsh grating and a short *pink*. HABITAT: Broadleaved evergreen forest and mixed evergreen-coniferous forest. DISTRIBUTION: Resident in W, S, E China, Hainan and throughout the south, except SW Myanmar, C Thailand, S Vietnam and Singapore.

7 GREEN SHRIKE-BABBLER *Pteruthius xanthochlorus* 13cm FIELD NOTES: Acts like a sluggish leaf warbler. VOICE: A rapid, monotonous repeated series, eg *wheet-wheet-wheet* or *chiwichiwichiwhichiwi...*, etc.; calls include a nasal *nyeep*, a *jerr* and a higher *jerri*. HABITAT: Broadleaved evergreen forest. DISTRIBUTION: Resident in SW, NE China and W, N Myanmar.

8 BLACK-EARED SHRIKE-BABBLER *Pteruthius melanotis* 11cm FIELD NOTES: Arboreal, sluggish; regular part of mixed-species flocks. VOICE: A monotonous *twi-twi-twi-twi-twi...* slow or fast versions; calls include a short *chid-it* and a high, nasal *nyeep nyeep*. HABITAT: Broadleaved evergreen forest. DISTRIBUTION: Resident in SW China, W, N, E Myanmar, NW Thailand, Laos, N, C Vietnam and Peninsular Malaysia.

9 CHESTNUT-FRONTED SHRIKE-BABBLER (TRILLING SHRIKE-BABBLER) *Pteruthius aenobarbus* 11–12cm FIELD NOTES: Actions similar to Black-eared Shrike-Babbler. VOICE: A monotonous *chip-chip-chip* or similar calls; include a buzzy *jer-jer-jer* and a sharp *pwit*. HABITAT: Broadleaved evergreen forest. DISTRIBUTION: Resident in SW, SE China, Hainan, Myanmar (except SW), W, NW, NE Thailand, Laos and N, C Vietnam.

2

4

1

1b
cunhaci

1c ricketti

3

♀

♂

♂

5

6

♀

♂

6b
ricketti

♂

♀

9

8

♀

7

♂

♂

♀

154 BABBLERS; BARWINGS; CROCIAS; MYZORNIS

1 WHITE-HOODED BABBLER *Gampsorhynchus rufulus* 23–24cm FIELD NOTES: Forages in middle storey or bamboo canopy, often in parties. Juvenile has crown and ear-coverts rufous. VOICE: A soft, mellow series of low whistles; typical call is a hollow, rapid, nervous cackling. HABITAT: Bamboo in or near broadleaved evergreen forest, secondary growth and scrub, bushes and grass at forest edge. DISTRIBUTION: Resident in SW China and N, W, C Myanmar.

2 COLLARED BABBLER *Gampsorhynchus torquatus* 23–24cm FIELD NOTES: Actions and habits as White-hooded Babbler. *G. t. luciae* (2b) occurs in SW China (SE Yunnan), NE, C Laos and N Vietnam. VOICE: Calls include a harsh, stuttering rattle, e.g. *rrrrtchu-rrrrtchu-rrrrtchu*. HABITAT: Bamboo, broadleaved evergreen forest and secondary growth. DISTRIBUTION: Resident in SW China, SE, S Myanmar, W, N, S Thailand, Laos and Vietnam.

3 RUSTY-FRONTED BARWING *Actinodura egertoni* 23cm FIELD NOTES: Forages from the undergrowth to the canopy, often among epiphytic growth; regular member of mixed-species flocks. VOICE: A warbled *ti-wi-wi-wu-ti-wi-wi-wu* or *titu-titu tiyu-titu-titu-tiyu*. Calls include a high-pitched rattle and a harsh, buzzy *gursh-gursh…* HABITAT: Undergrowth in broadleaved evergreen forest, forest edge and secondary growth. DISTRIBUTION: Resident in SW China and Myanmar (except C and Tenasserim).

4 STREAK-THROATED BARWING *Actinodura waldeni* 20–22cm FIELD NOTES: Clambers among mossy branches and tree trunks. *A. w. poliotis* (4b) occurs in W Myanmar. VOICE: A strident, rising *tchrrr-jo-jwiee*, *dddrt-juee-iwee* or a shorter *jorr-dwidu*. Calls include a nasal, grumbling *grrr-ut grrr-ut* and a *grr-grr-grr-grr-grr*. HABITAT: Broadleaved evergreen forest and mixed forest. DISTRIBUTION: Resident in SW China and W, N Myanmar.

5 BLACK-CROWNED BARWING *Actinodura sodangorum* 24cm FIELD NOTES: Forages in the canopy and on mossy trunks and branches, singly or in pairs. VOICE: Starts quickly, more paced at end, e.g. *tutututu'tu'tudi-duuu* or *tutututu'tu'tee-tuuu*, occasionally followed by a grumbling *hwerr'rr'rr*, presumably given by the female. HABITAT: Broadleaved evergreen forest, forest edge, secondary growth and tall grass and scrub near forests. DISTRIBUTION: Resident in S Laos and C Vietnam.

6 SPECTACLED BARWING *Actinodura ramsayi* 23–25cm FIELD NOTES: Forages in pairs or groups. *A. r. yunnanensis* (6b) occurs in S China and N Vietnam. VOICE: A repeated, high-pitched, descending *iee-iee-iee-iuu*, sometimes followed by a high-pitched *ewh ewh ewh*, presumably uttered by a female. Calls include a low, harsh *baoh*. HABITAT: Broadleaved evergreen forest, bamboo, forest edge, scrub and grass. DISTRIBUTION: Resident in S China, C, E, S Myanmar, NW Thailand, N, C Laos and N Vietnam.

7 STREAKED BARWING *Actinodura souliei* 21–23cm FIELD NOTES: Often in small, slow-moving parties. VOICE: Calls include soft contact notes and harsh churrs. HABITAT: Broadleaved evergreen and semi-evergreen forest and open fir forest with bamboo. DISTRIBUTION: Resident in SW China and N Vietnam (W Tonkin).

8 TAIWAN BARWING *Actinodura morrisoniana* 18–19cm FIELD NOTES: Forages in the canopy and middle storey. VOICE: A loud, clear *whit chiwewii*, a quavering *chiriririrt* and a short *hiu* or *huu*. HABITAT: Broadleaf evergreen, broadleaf deciduous and mixed broadleaf-coniferous forest. DISTRIBUTION: Resident in Taiwan.

9 GREY-CROWNED CROCIAS *Crocias langbianis* 22cm FIELD NOTES: Arboreal, forages from the canopy down to undergrowth. VOICE: A loud, repeated *wip'ip'ip-wiu-wiu-wiu-wiu-wiu-wiu-wiu*; call is a buzzing *pzah-pzah-pzah-pzah*. HABITAT: Broadleaved evergreen forest. DISTRIBUTION: Resident in C Vietnam (S Annam).

10 FIRE-TAILED MYZORNIS *Myzornis pyrrhoura* 13cm FIELD NOTES: Regularly visits rhododendron flowers in search of nectar, also climbs mossy trunks like a treecreeper. VOICE: High-pitched, quickly repeated *si* notes, sometimes forming into a twittering *si-si-si-si-si*. HABITAT: Montane forests, juniper and rhododendron scrub and bamboo. DISTRIBUTION: Resident in SW China and N Myanmar.

1

2

2b *luciae*

4b *poliotis*

4

3

6b
yunnanensis

5

6

7

8

9

♀

10

♂

155 MINLAS; SIBIAS

1 BLUE-WINGED MINLA *Minla cyanouroptera* 14–16 FIELD NOTES: Forages in the tops of bushes and trees. *S. c. sordida* (1b) occurs in S Thailand and Peninsular Malaysia. VOICE: A repeated, high-pitched *psii sii suuu*; calls include a short *whit* or *bwik* and dry staccato buzzes. HABITAT: Broadleaved evergreen forest and secondary growth. DISTRIBUTION: Resident locally in S China, Hainan and throughout the south, except SW, C, S Myanmar, C, SE Thailand, S Vietnam and Singapore.

2 CHESTNUT-TAILED MINLA (BAR-THROATED MINLA) *Minla strigula* 16cm FIELD NOTES: Forages in high bushes and medium-height trees. *M. s. malayana* (2b) occurs in Peninsular Malaysia, *M. s. traii* (2c) in C Vietnam. VOICE: A high-pitched, quavering *tui-twi ti-tu, twi ti-u* or *twi-twi-twi-twi*. Calls include a sharp *kip*, a soft *yeep* and a trilling buzz. HABITAT: Broadleaved evergreen and mixed broadleaf-conifer forest. DISTRIBUTION: Resident in SW China, W, N, E, S Myanmar, NW Thailand, N, C Laos N, C Vietnam and Peninsular Malaysia.

3 RED-TAILED MINLA *Minla ignotincta* 14cm FIELD NOTES: Forages in treetop mossy branches and trunks. VOICE: A high-pitched, repeated *wi ti wi-wu* or a slurred, falling *si-swee-sweeeuuuu*. Calls include a harsh *wih-wih-wih-wih*, short *wit* and a fast *witty-wi-wrrh*. HABITAT: Broadleaved evergreen forest and secondary growth. DISTRIBUTION: Resident in S, W, C China, W, N, S, E Myanmar, N, C, S Laos and N, C Vietnam.

4 RUFOUS-BACKED SIBIA *Heterophasia annectens* 18cm FIELD NOTES: Forages in the canopy, searching mosses and lichens. *L. a. saturata* (4b) occurs in E Myanmar and W, NW Thailand, *L. a. davisoni* (4c) in S Myanmar and W Thailand. VOICE: A pretty, descending warble; calls include a harsh chattering and a buzzy chortling. HABITAT: Broadleaved evergreen forest. DISTRIBUTION: Resident in SW China, Myanmar (except C, S), W, NW Thailand, N, S Laos and C, N Vietnam.

5 GREY SIBIA *Heterophasia gracilis* 23–25cm FIELD NOTES: Forages among epiphytes and on mossy trunks. VOICE: A repeated, descending *tu-tu-ti-ti-ti-tu* or similar. Calls include a soft *ti-tew*, a squeaky *witwit-witarit* and a grating *trrit-trrit*. HABITAT: Broadleaved evergreen forest. DISTRIBUTION: Resident in SW China and W, N Myanmar.

6 BLACK-HEADED SIBIA *Heterophasia desgodinsi* 21–25cm FIELD NOTES: Forages among mossy epiphytes. *M. d. engelbachi* (6b) occurs in S Laos, M, *d. robinsoni* (6c) in Vietnam (S Annam). VOICE: A slightly descending *hi wi-wi wi wi*; contact calls consist of thin *tsrrri* notes. HABITAT: Broadleaved evergreen forest. DISTRIBUTION: Resident in SW, W China, N Myanmar, S Laos and N, C, S Vietnam.

7 DARK-BACKED SIBIA *Heterophasia melanoleuca* 21–23cm FIELD NOTES: Forages mainly in the treetops. *M. m. castanopterus* (7b) occurs in SE Myanmar. VOICE: A high-pitched wavering whistle with a drop in pitch at the end; calls include a harsh *trr-trr-trr*. HABITAT: Broadleaved evergreen forest. DISTRIBUTION: Resident in SE, E, S Myanmar, W, NW Thailand and N Laos.

8 BEAUTIFUL SIBIA *Heterophasia pulchella* 23cm FIELD NOTES: Forages in the canopy, on mossy branches and trunks. VOICE: A strident, repeated *ti-ti-titi-tu-ti*; calls include a rattling and a high trill. HABITAT: Broadleaved evergreen forest. DISTRIBUTION: Resident in SW China and N Myanmar.

9 WHITE-EARED SIBIA *Heterophasia auricularis* 22–24cm FIELD NOTES: Forages mainly in the middle to upper storey. VOICE: A resonant *weep-weeo-weep-weeeooo* or similar; calls include a tailing-off *sirrrrrrrr*. HABITAT: Broadleaf evergreen forest. DISTRIBUTION: Resident in Taiwan.

10 LONG-TAILED SIBIA *Heterophasia picaoides* 28–35cm FIELD NOTES: Forages mainly in the canopy. VOICE: A rich, six-note whistled phrase; calls include a *tsip-tsip-tsip-tsip*, sometimes interspersed with a rattle or a trilling. HABITAT: Broadleaved evergreen forest, forest edge and secondary growth. DISTRIBUTION: Resident in SW China, W, N, E, S Myanmar, W, NW Thailand, Laos, N Vietnam and Peninsular Malaysia.

2b *malayana*

2c *traii*

1

1b *sordida*

2

3

♂

♀

4b *saturata*

4c *davisoni*

4

5

6b
engelbachi

6c *robinsoni*

6

10

7b
castanopterus

7

8

9

1 GOLDEN-BREASTED FULVETTA *Lioparus chrysotis* 10–12cm FIELD NOTES: Forages low in undergrowth. *L. c. amoenus* (1b) occurs in SW China and N Vietnam. VOICE: A thin *si-si-si-si-suu*; call is a staccato *witrrrit* or *wit* given in short bursts. HABITAT: Undergrowth in broadleaved evergreen forest and secondary growth. DISTRIBUTION: Resident in WC, SW China, N Myanmar and N, C Vietnam.

2 GOLDEN-FRONTED FULVETTA *Alcippe variegaticeps* 10–12cm FIELD NOTES: Forages in undergrowth and bamboo. VOICE: A chattering alarm call. HABITAT: Broadleaved evergreen, mixed deciduous and pine forest, with bamboo cover. DISTRIBUTION: Resident in W, C China.

3 YELLOW-THROATED FULVETTA *Alcippe cinerea* 10–11cm FIELD NOTES: Frequents dense undergrowth and understorey, often in small flocks. VOICE: A series of thin notes that end in a complex, rapid jumble. Also utters a thin *si-si-si-si-si-si-si'si'si* interspersed with *tit* notes. HABITAT: Broadleaved evergreen forest. DISTRIBUTION: Resident in SW China, N Myanmar, N Laos and C Vietnam.

4 RUFOUS-WINGED FULVETTA *Alcippe castaneceps* 10–13cm FIELD NOTES: Forages about moss and lichen-covered trunks. VOICE: A high-pitched, tinkling *si tju-tji-tju-tji-tju*; calls include a harsh *tcht*, a *tchrr* and dry rattles. HABITAT: Broadleaved evergreen forest and secondary growth. DISTRIBUTION: Resident in SW China, Myanmar (except SW, C), W, NW, NE Thailand, Laos, C, N Vietnam and Peninsular Malaysia.

5 BLACK-CROWNED FULVETTA *Alcippe klossi* 12–13cm FIELD NOTES: Forages on mossy trunks in the under storey. VOICE: A long series of thin, shrill notes, trailing at the end, also a grating *hht't't't't't'it'it…* mixed with hard *tid* and *tid-rr* notes. HABITAT: Broadleaved evergreen forest and secondary growth. DISTRIBUTION: Resident in Vietnam (S Annam).

6 TAIWAN FULVETTA *Fulvetta formosana* 12cm FIELD NOTES: Forages, mouse-like on or near the ground. VOICE: A repeated *ti tuuu*. HABITAT: Undergrowth and bamboo in coniferous and deciduous forest. DISTRIBUTION: Resident in Taiwan.

7 WHITE-BROWED FULVETTA *Fulvetta vinipectus valentinae* 10–12cm FIELD NOTES: Forages in low trees, bushes and undergrowth. *F. v. perstriata* (7b) occurs in SW China, N Myanmar. VOICE: A thin *si-si-swi'i'i'i'i'i* or similar; calls include a low *trr*, *trr-trr*, a high jeering *stu-tu-tu-tu-tu-tu* and a descending rattling trill. HABITAT: High-level scrub, bamboo, open broadleaved forest and forest edge. DISTRIBUTION: Resident in W, SW China, W, N Myanmar and N Vietnam.

8 CHINESE FULVETTA *Fulvetta striaticollis* 11–12cm FIELD NOTES: Forages low down in vegetation. VOICE: A simple *ti tsew* or *ti chuu*; calls include a low rattle. HABITAT: High-level, scrub, rhododendron and prickly oak. DISTRIBUTION: Resident in SW, W China.

9 SPECTACLED FULVETTA *Fulvetta ruficapilla* 10–11cm FIELD NOTES: Forages low down or in the canopy of small trees. VOICE: Unrecorded. HABITAT: Broadleaved evergreen oak forest and secondary growth. DISTRIBUTION: Resident in SW, W China.

10 INDOCHINESE FULVETTA *Fulvetta danisi* 11–12cm FIELD NOTES: Forages singly, in pairs or in small parties of up to eight individuals. VOICE: Calls with a quickly repeated, rapid *chrrrit* or *chrrt-chrrt-chrrt…* HABITAT: Broadleaved evergreen forest, bamboo and scrub. DISTRIBUTION: Resident in Laos and C Vietnam.

11 GREY-HOODED FULVETTA *Fulvetta cinereiceps* 12cm FIELD NOTES: Actions tit-like. VOICE: A high, thin *ti wuu wiiuu*; call is a thin, churring rattle. HABITAT: Undergrowth and bamboo in forests, secondary growth. DISTRIBUTION: Resident in W, C, E China.

12 MANIPUR (STREAK-THROATED) FULVETTA *Fulvetta manipurensis* 11–13cm FIELD NOTES: Forages mainly close to or on the ground. VOICE: A high-pitched *ti ti si-su*, *si-swu* or *si-si-suu-swee*. Calls include a low *tirrru*, a high, sibilant *swi-swi-swi-swi…* and a dry metallic *twit'it'it'it-it it it it'it'it…* HABITAT: Broadleaved evergreen forest, forest edge, bamboo and scrub. DISTRIBUTION: Resident in SW China, W, N Myanmar and N Vietnam.

1b *amoena*

7b *perstriata*

157 FULVETTAS

1 BROWN FULVETTA *Alcippe brunneicauda* 14–15cm FIELD NOTES: Forages in the lower middle storey and in low vegetation, in pairs or small parties. VOICE: A slow, high-pitched *hi-tu-tu ti –tu ti ti-tu* or similar. Calls include a stressed *whit* and short harsh rattles. HABITAT: Broadleaved evergreen forest, often near streams. DISTRIBUTION: Resident in S Thailand and Peninsular Malaysia.

2 BROWN-CHEEKED FULVETTA *Alcippe poioicephala* 16–17cm FIELD NOTES: Forages from undergrowth up to the canopy, sometimes in parties of up to 20 individuals. *A. p. phayrei* (5b) occurs in SW Myanmar. VOICE: A pleasant *chu uwi-uwi-uwee* or similar; calls include harsh, buzzy, spluttering rattles. HABITAT: Undergrowth in forests, secondary growth, bamboo and scrub. DISTRIBUTION: Resident in SW China, Myanmar, W, NW, NE, S Thailand, N, C Laos and N Vietnam.

3 MOUNTAIN FULVETTA *Alcippe peracensis* 14–16cm FIELD NOTES: Forages in pairs or small parties, often in the company of other species. VOICE: A pleasant *iti-iwu uwi-i wheer wheer* or similar; calls include a harsh *chrr'rr'r*. HABITAT: Montane broadleaf forest. DISTRIBUTION: Resident in C, S Laos, C Vietnam, S Thailand and Peninsular Malaysia.

4 BLACK-BROWED FULVETTA *Alcippe grotei* 15–17cm FIELD NOTES: Forages in the middle storey and undergrowth, in parties and as part of mixed-species flocks. VOICE: A pleasant *yu-chi-chiwi-chu-woo* or similar; calls include a rasping, spluttering *wit-it-itrrrt, witchititit* or *err-rittirrirrrt* etc. HABITAT: Broadleaved evergreen forest, forest edge, secondary growth, bamboo and scrub. DISTRIBUTION: Resident in SE Thailand, E Cambodia, C, S Laos and Vietnam.

5 GREY-CHEEKED FULVETTA *Alcippe morrisonia* 12–14cm FIELD NOTES: Forages in the middle storey and low undergrowth, in parties and mixed-species flocks. *A. m. davidii* (8b) occurs in W China, *A. m. yunnanensis* (8c) in SW China and N Myanmar. VOICE: A repeated, high-pitched it *chi wi-wi, yu yu wi wi-you* or similar; calls include a *chr'rr'r* and a harsh *chitititit*. HABITAT: Montane broadleaf evergreen forest, secondary forest, bamboo and scrub. DISTRIBUTION: Resident in W, C, SW, NE China, Hainan, Taiwan, N, E, C, S Myanmar, W, NW, NE Thailand, N, C Laos and N Vietnam.

6 NEPAL FULVETTA *Alcippe nipalensis* 12cm FIELD NOTES: Agile forager in undergrowth and the tops of low trees. Post breeding often in flocks of up to 20 individuals, also joins mixed-species feeding flocks. VOICE: A simple *chu-chui-chiwi*; calls include a *chr'rr'r* or similar. HABITAT: Broadleaved evergreen forest, forest edge, secondary growth, bamboo and scrub. DISTRIBUTION: Resident in N, SW, W, S Myanmar.

7 RUFOUS-THROATED FULVETTA *Schoeniparus rufogularis* 12–13cm FIELD NOTES: Forages in dense cover on or near the ground, singly, in pairs or in small parties post breeding. VOICE: A shrill, repeated *wi-chuw-i-chewi-cheeu* or similar. Calls include a *whit-whit-whit*, a whining *whiri-whiri-whiri...* and a *wrrreet wrrreet*. HABITAT: Broadleaved evergreen forest. DISTRIBUTION: Resident in SW China, N Myanmar, NW, NE, SE Thailand, N, C Laos and N Vietnam.

8 DUSKY FULVETTA *Schoeniparus brunneus* 13–14cm FIELD NOTES: Skulking, forages on or near the ground, in small parties. VOICE: A hurried, shrill *whi wi-wi wich'uu, uu wi-witchi-chuu* or similar; foraging birds utter a low *jurt*. HABITAT: Broadleaved evergreen forest and grass-jungle. DISTRIBUTION: Resident in W, C, NE China, Hainan and Taiwan.

9 RUSTY-CAPPED FULVETTA *Schoeniparus dubius* 14–15cm FIELD NOTES: Forages in dense undergrowth, close to or on the ground. *S. d. mandellii* (3b) occurs in W Myanmar. VOICE: A sweet fluty warble, e.g. *chu-chi-chu, chu-witee-wee* or similar. Calls include a low rattle, buzzy trills and a quiet *peet-seet-seet*. HABITAT: Broadleaved forest edge, secondary growth, bamboo and scrub. DISTRIBUTION: Resident in SW China, W, N, C, E, S Myanmar, Laos and N, C Vietnam.

2b *phayrei*

5c *yunnanensis*

5b *davidii*

9b *mandellii*

158 YUHINAS; ERPORNIS

1 STRIATED YUHINA *Yuhina castaniceps* 13–14cm FIELD NOTES: Forages in bushes and low trees. *S. c. plumbeiceps* (1b) occurs in SW China, N Myanmar, *S. c. striata* (1c) in E, S Myanmar, W, NW Thailand. VOICE: High-pitched, shrill *tchu, tchi* or *tchi-chi* notes. Flocks utter an incessant chattering interspersed with squeaky notes. HABITAT: Undergrowth and scrub in broadleaf evergreen forest. DISTRIBUTION: Resident in SW China, Myanmar and W, NE Thailand.

2 INDOCHINESE YUHINA *Yuhina torqueola* 14–15cm FIELD NOTES: Forages in high bushes and low trees, often in parties of 20–30. VOICE: A loud *tu'whi*; calls include a continuous chattering, high squeaks and dry trills. HABITAT: Scrub and undergrowth in broadleaf forest. DISTRIBUTION: Resident in China, N Thailand, Laos and N Vietnam.

3 WHISKERED YUHINA *Yuhina flavicollis* 12–13cm FIELD NOTES: Forages in the lower branches of trees and bushes, actions tit-like. VOICE: A repeated high-pitched *tzii-jhu ziddi* or *twe-tyurwi-tyawi-tyawa*; calls include a thin squeaky *swii-swii-swii*, and buzzy notes. HABITAT: Broadleaved evergreen forest, forest edge and secondary growth. DISTRIBUTION: Resident in SW China, W, N, E Myanmar, NW Thailand, N, C Laos and N Vietnam.

4 WHITE-NAPED YUHINA *Yuhina bakeri* 12–14cm FIELD NOTES: Forages in bushes and treetops, usually in small parties. VOICE: Thin high notes, repeated every few seconds; calls include a short metallic *tsit*, a falling *seep* and a *seet-chuut*. HABITAT: Broadleaved evergreen forest and secondary growth. DISTRIBUTION: Resident in SW China and N Myanmar.

5 BURMESE YUHINA *Yuhina humilis* 12–13cm FIELD NOTES: Forages in pairs or small groups, often in flowering trees. VOICE: Flocks utter a low *chuck-chuck* or *chir-chir-chir-chir*. HABITAT: Broadleaved evergreen forest, forest edge and secondary growth. DISTRIBUTION: Resident in E, S Myanmar and W, NW Thailand.

6 STRIPE-THROATED YUHINA *Yuhina gularis* 12–16cm FIELD NOTES: Forages in tall bushes and lower branches of trees. VOICE: Descending nasal, mewing, sometimes followed by a hurried *whu-whu-whu-whi-whi-whi*; also a short *wiht* and an abrupt *squip*. HABITAT: Broadleaved evergreen and mixed broadleaved-conifer forest, forest edge. DISTRIBUTION: Resident in SW, W China, W, N, E Myanmar, N Laos and N, C Vietnam.

7 WHITE-COLLARED YUHINA *Yuhina diademata* 14–18cm FIELD NOTES: Forages in bushes and treetops, usually in parties, with larger parties post breeding. VOICE: A hurried, high *tsu'tsu'tsu, tsu'tst* or *tsu'tsu'tsut*; calls include a *seep* and a *seet-chuut*. HABITAT: Primary and secondary broadleaf evergreen forest. DISTRIBUTION: Resident in W, SW China, N Myanmar and N Vietnam.

8 RUFOUS-VENTED YUHINA *Yuhina occipitalis* 12–14cm FIELD NOTES: Forages in the canopy on mossy branches and trunks; also in bushes. VOICE: A weak, high-pitched *swi'si'si su'su'su swi'si'si si'si'si su'su'su…* HABITAT: Broadleaved evergreen forest, forest edge and secondary growth. DISTRIBUTION: Resident in SW China and N Myanmar.

9 BLACK-CHINNED YUHINA *Yuhina nigrimenta* 9–10cm FIELD NOTES: Forages in tall trees and low shrubs. VOICE: A sequence of thin, ringing whistles; calls include a chattering and a *pik pik pik*. HABITAT: Broadleaved evergreen forest, forest edge, overgrown clearings and secondary growth. DISTRIBUTION: Resident in W, SW, NE, SE China, N Myanmar, E Cambodia, N, C Laos and N Vietnam.

10 TAIWAN YUHINA *Yuhina brunneiceps* 11–12cm FIELD NOTES: Forages from low strata to canopy. VOICE: A jaunty '*to-meet-you*' or '*so-pleased-to-meet-you*'. HABITAT: Forests, forest edge and clearings. DISTRIBUTION: Resident in Taiwan.

11 WHITE-BELLIED ERPORNIS *Erpornis zantholeuca* 11–13cm FIELD NOTES: Forages in high bushes or the lower canopy. VOICE: A high-pitched trilling or a *ss-ss-ss-se-se-se*; calls include a nasal *jeer-jeer-jeer* mixed with trills and chitterings. HABITAT: Broadleaved evergreen and mixed deciduous forests. DISTRIBUTION: Resident southern China, Hainan and in the south, except C Thailand.

1b *plumbeiceps*

1c *striata*

159 PARROTBILLS

1 GREAT PARROTBILL *Conostoma aemodium* 28cm FIELD NOTES: Forages on or near the ground on green bamboo shoots and fruit. VOICE: A loud, repeated *whip whi-uu* or similar; calls include a nasal wheezes, squeals, cackling and churring. HABITAT: Open evergreen forest, bamboo and rhododendron thickets. DISTRIBUTION: Resident in SW China and N Myanmar.

2 BROWN PARROTBILL *Cholornis unicolor* 21cm FIELD NOTES: Skulking; acrobatic, often hangs upside-down when foraging. VOICE: A loud *ii-wuu-iiew* or *it ik ik – ii-wuu-iiew.* Calls include a shrill *whi-whi-whi*, a low *brrh* and a cackling *churrrh*. HABITAT: Bamboo in open broadleaved evergreen forest. DISTRIBUTION: Resident W, SW China and N Myanmar.

3 SPOT-BREASTED PARROTBILL *Paradoxornis guttaticollis* 18–22cm FIELD NOTES: Noisy, usually in small parties, which may incude other species. VOICE: A staccato *whit-whit-whit-whit…* or similar. Calls include a low *ruk-ruk, ruk-uk-uk* or *rut-rut-rut-rut*. HABITAT: Secondary growth, scrub and tall grass. DISTRIBUTION: Resident in S, E China, W, N, E Myanmar, NW Thailand, N Laos and N Vietnam.

4 BLACK-BREASTED PARROTBILL *Paradoxornis flavirostris* 19–21cm FIELD NOTES: Forages low down, but regularly sings from the top of reed or grass stems, usually in small parties. VOICE: A clear, high *woi-woi-woi-woi-woi-woi, whii-whii-whii-whii* or a huskier *jhor-jhor-jhor-jhor-jhor-jhor*; calls include a wu-wi-wi and a nasal *uh-uh-uh-uh-uh-uh.* HABITAT: Reeds and tall grass. DISTRIBUTION: Disputed records from W Myanmar (Mt Victoria).

5 REED PARROTBILL *Paradoxornis heudei* 18–20cm FIELD NOTES: Forages in reedbeds in small or large flocks. VOICE: A long series of *chut, chu, hui* or *tui* notes, delivered at varying rates. Calls or secondary song is a gentle, low *u uui-uui-uui-uui* or similar, also a rapid thin chirping and a subdued *jhew-jhew* or *jhjo-jhjo*. HABITAT: Reedbeds by rivers or estuaries. DISTRIBUTION: Resident in NE China.

6 GREY-HEADED PARROTBILL *Psittiparus gularis* 21cm FIELD NOTES: Forages from the treetops down to the undergrowth and, sometimes, on the ground. VOICE: A shrill *eu-chu-chu* or *eu-chu-chu-chu* and a high *wi-wuu* or *wi-wuu-wuu-wuu*. Calls include a harsh, slurred *jiew* and a scolding *chit-it-it-it-it-it*. HABITAT: Broadleaf evergreen forest, secondary growth, bamboo and scrub. DISTRIBUTION: Resident in NE, W, C, S China, W, N, E Myanmar, NW Thailand, Laos and C, N Vietnam.

7 BLACK-HEADED PARROTBILL *Psittiparus margaritae* 15–16cm FIELD NOTES: Forages from shrub level up to the canopy. VOICE: A husky *jhu'jhu'jhu* or *eu'ju'jhu'jhu*; calls similar to Grey-headed Parrotbill. HABITAT: Broadleaved evergreen forest, secondary growth and scrub. DISTRIBUTION: Resident in E Cambodia and C Vietnam (S Annam).

8 RUFOUS-HEADED PARROTBILL *Psittiparus bakeri* 18cm FIELD NOTES: Clambers acrobatically among small twigs and branches, usually in pairs or small parties and sometimes in the company of other species. VOICE: A repeated, breathless *wi-wi-wi-wu* interspersed with *jhaowh* call notes. Calls include a rattling *trrrrt trrrrrrrrrrt trrrrrrrrrrt* and a twangy *jhew*. HABITAT: Bamboo in or near broadleaved evergreen forest and forest edge. DISTRIBUTION: Resident in SW China, N, E, S Myanmar, N Laos and N Vietnam.

160 PARROTBILLS

1 GREY-HOODED PARROTBILL Sinosuthora zappeyi 12–13cm FIELD NOTES: Forages in low vegetation; usually found in small parties. VOICE: A high, piercing ss-ss-su-si; calls include rasping trr'ik and trrrh notes. HABITAT: Bamboo and bushes in open mountain-top conifer forest and mixed fir-rhododendron forest. DISTRIBUTION: Resident in W China (SC Sichuan and NW Guizhou).

2 VINOUS-THROATED PARROTBILL Sinosuthora webbiana 11–13cm FIELD NOTES: Forages in fast-moving flocks, in the understorey or the tops of small flowering trees. VOICE: Quick introductory notes are followed by rapid notes, ending with high, thin notes, e.g. ri riti ri ri chididi wii-ssi-tssu. Flocks call with a rapid, subdued chattering interspersed with thin, high notes and chuntering chur'ir'ir or chrr'rr'rr notes. HABITAT: Scrub, thickets, bamboo, secondary growth, reeds and plantations. DISTRIBUTION: Resident in China, Taiwan and N Vietnam.

3 ASHY-THROATED PARROTBILL Sinosuthora alphonsiana 12–13cm FIELD NOTES: Forages in fast-moving flocks of 10–40 individuals. VOICE: A loud, high-pitched tssu-tssu-tssu-tssu, tsser-tsser-tsser-tsser or similar. Calls include a harsh chuntering twer-trr'ir'ir'irrit, twi'it'ti, trr'it'it'it tcher'der'der, chip-ip-ip-ip or similar, also light tu, twi or du contact notes. HABITAT: Scrub, grass thickets and plantations. DISTRIBUTION: Resident in W, SW China and N Vietnam.

4 BROWN-WINGED PARROTBILL Sinosuthora brunnea 12–13cm FIELD NOTES: Usually occurs in fast-moving flocks. VOICE: A continuous twittering while feeding; no other information. HABITAT: Montane scrub and grass thickets, sometimes in open forest or forest edge. DISTRIBUTION: Resident in SW China and N, C Myanmar.

5 GOLDEN PARROTBILL Suthora verreauxi 11–12cm FIELD NOTES: Forages in pairs or small parties, also found in mixed-species flocks. VOICE: A weak chuur-dii and a high-pitched, wispy hsu-ssu-ssu-ssi. Calls include a low, spluttering trr'it or trr'eet. Foraging flocks utter a jumble of it, twit and tip notes. HABITAT: Broadleaved evergreen forest edge and bamboo. DISTRIBUTION: Resident in SW, W, C China, Taiwan, E Myanmar, Laos and N Vietnam.

6 FULVOUS PARROTBILL Suthora fulvifrons 12–13cm FIELD NOTES: Post breeding forages in fast-moving flocks of 20–30, occasionally more. VOICE: A high-pitched si-tsiiii chuu, si-si juu or si-ti ti tituuuu-jhiiu; calls include a husky chew-chew-chew, a cher-cher-cher and a spluttering trrrip. HABITAT: Bamboo thickets, in or near forests. DISTRIBUTION: Resident in SW, W China and N Myanmar.

7 BLACK-THROATED PARROTBILL Suthora nipalensis 11–12cm FIELD NOTES: Acrobatic forager in small to large flocks. Various races occur, those depicted are: S. n. poliotis (main portrait) from SW China and N Myanmar; S. n. beauliei (7b) in N, C Laos, NE Thailand and N Vietnam (N Annam); S. n. ripponi (7c) in W Myanmar. VOICE: A wheezy, nasal chu-irrr-diii-dirrr or similar. Contact calls are a soft tu, ti, tit or tip, which when given by flocks makes a constant twittering. HABITAT: Bamboo and undergrowth in forests, secondary growth and forest edge. DISTRIBUTION: Resident in SW China, W, N, E, S Myanmar, W, NE, NW Thailand, Laos and C Vietnam.

8 SHORT-TAILED PARROTBILL Neosuthora davidiana 10cm FIELD NOTES: Forages in bamboo or occasionally trees. VOICE: A thin, high-pitched, rapid ascending ih'ih'ih'ih'ih'ih'ih or zu'zu'zu'zu'zu'zu'... also a tit tiwit tit tit-tew hiuuuu-ti-di'di'di. Flocks call with tip or tut notes that can run into a twittering. HABITAT: Bamboo, grass and edge of broadleaved evergreen forest. DISTRIBUTION: Resident in SE, E China, E Myanmar, NW, NE Thailand, N Laos and N Vietnam.

9 PALE-BILLED PARROTBILL (LESSER RUFOUS-HEADED PARROTBILL) Chleuasicus atrosuperciliaris 15cm FIELD NOTES: Acrobatic forager, often in small parties of 6–12. VOICE: A chirping tik-tik-tik-tik-tik-tik or similar. Flocks utter a chattering, interspersed with harsh metallic notes. HABITAT: Bamboo in or near broadleaf evergreen forest, forest edges and tall grass. DISTRIBUTION: Resident in SW China, N, S Myanmar, NW Thailand, N, C Laos and N Vietnam.

7c *ripponi*

7b
beauliei

7
poliotis

161 LARKS

1 AUSTRALASIAN BUSH LARK *Mirafra javanica* 13–15cm FIELD NOTES: Forages on the ground, singly, in pairs or small loose groups. Sings from a perch or in towering song-flight. VOICE: Repeated short varied phrases, often including mimicry. Calls include an explosive *pitsi pitsi pitsipipipipi* or *tsitsitsitsi*. HABITAT: Short grassland with bushes, dry marshland edge and paddyfield stubble. DISTRIBUTION: Resident in SE China, C, E Myanmar, W, NW, NE, C Thailand, Cambodia, N, C Laos and C, S Vietnam.

2 BENGAL BUSH LARK *Mirafra assamica* 16cm FIELD NOTES: Forages on the ground. VOICE: A monotonous repeated, squeaky disyllabic note, usually given in flight. Also utters a jingle of short varied notes, with some mimicry, generally given from a low perch or the ground. Calls include an explosive series of high-pitched notes. HABITAT: Open grassy areas on plains and plateaux, also edge of open forest. DISTRIBUTION: Resident in SW Myanmar.

3 INDOCHINESE BUSH LARK *Mirafra erythrocephala* 15cm FIELD NOTES: Mainly terrestrial, also perches on trees and overhead wires. VOICE: Quick series of thin, clear, mainly drawn-out notes, given in 2–8 second strophes, from an elevated perch or the ground. Calls include a high, metallic rattle and variable high-pitched whistles. HABITAT: Open dry areas with scattered trees and bushes, cultivation and forest edge with scrub, bamboo and trees. DISTRIBUTION: Resident in E, S Myanmar, Thailand (except S), Cambodia, Laos and C, S Vietnam.

4 BURMESE BUSH LARK *Mirafra microptera* 13–15cm FIELD NOTES: Mainly terrestrial, also perches on trees or overhead wires. VOICE: Short hurried jingle of varied high-pitched whistles, given from an elevated perch; a similar song is given in a high song-flight. Also utters a series of high-pitched drawn-out whistles, given in a low song flight or from the ground. Calls include a short-pitched *heep*. HABITAT: Semi-desert scrub with scattered trees and cultivation. DISTRIBUTION: Resident in C, S Myanmar.

5 SHORT-TOED LARK (GREATER SHORT-TOED LARK) *Calandrella brachydactyla* 14–15cm FIELD NOTES: Forages on the ground, runs around in typical zigzag jerky spurts. VOICE: Calls include a dry *chirrup* or *dreet* and a *trlip*. HABITAT: Dry open areas. DISTRIBUTION: Rare winter visitor N, S Myanmar.

6 ASIAN SHORT-TOED LARK *Calandrella cheleensis* 13–14cm FIELD NOTES: Forages on the ground; note long primary projection. VOICE: Dry buzzing *pritt* or *chirrick*. HABITAT: Dry open areas. DISTRIBUTION: Winter visitor in NE China; vagrant in N Myanmar.

7 SAND LARK *Alaudala raytal* 12cm FIELD NOTES: Forages on the ground; sings in flight or on the ground. During song-flight soars high, flying aimlessly around with an intermittent series of rapid wing-flaps before parachuting to the ground in a series of steps. VOICE: Short, with disjointed, dry rattling phrases; calls include a low *chirr, cherr* or *chirr-de*. HABITAT: Sandy banks and islets in rivers or lakes. DISTRIBUTION: Resident in C, S Myanmar.

8 SKYLARK (EURASIAN or COMMON SKYLARK) *Alauda arvensis* 16–19cm FIELD NOTES: Forages on the ground, walks and runs; longer primary projection than Oriental Skylark. VOICE: A liquid *chirrup* and a shorter *prryih*. HABITAT: Grassland, cultivated areas, coastal areas including beaches. DISTRIBUTION: Winter visitor to NE, E China.

9 ORIENTAL SKYLARK *Alauda gulgula* 15–18cm FIELD NOTES: Forages on the ground; shorter primary projection than Skylark. Sings from a low perch or in a very high display-flight, where on quivering wings delivers a beautiful song before dropping, in steps, to the ground. VOICE: A prolonged mix of warbling, twittering and short whistles. Calls include a buzzy *baz-baz* or *baz-terr* and a *twip*. HABITAT: Grasslands, crop fields, coastal mudflats, dry edges of lakes, rivers and paddyfields. DISTRIBUTION: Resident in China, Hainan, Taiwan, Myanmar (except Tenasserim), Thailand (except S), Cambodia, N Laos and Vietnam (except W Tonkin).

162 SUNBIRDS

1 PURPLE-NAPED SUNBIRD *Hypogramma hypogrammicum* 14–15cm FIELD NOTES: Forages mainly in the understorey, often in cover; flicks and fans tail. This species may prove to be a spiderhunter. VOICE: A high, strong *sweet sweet sweet sweet*; calls include a strident *schewp, tsit-tsit, tchu* or *chip.* HABITAT: Broadleaved evergreen forest, freshwater swamp forest and secondary growth. DISTRIBUTION: Resident in SW China and throughout the south, except SW, W, S, E Myanmar, C, NE, SE Thailand, Cambodia and Singapore.

2 PLAIN SUNBIRD *Anthreptes simplex* 13cm FIELD NOTES: Forages much like a leaf warbler, gleans from leaves. VOICE: Metallic chips and trills and a high-pitched *seep.* HABITAT: Various forests, forest edge, secondary forests and scrub, including coastal scrub and mangroves. DISTRIBUTION: Resident in S Myanmar, S Thailand, Peninsular Malaysia and Singapore.

3 BROWN-THROATED SUNBIRD *Anthreptes malacensis* 14cm FIELD NOTES: Forages singly or in pairs, mainly in the canopy, but also at all other levels; gleans from leaves and twigs. VOICE: A *sweet-sweet, swit-swit-sweet* or *wee-chew-chew-wee.* Calls include a much-repeated *kelichap,* a hard *chip,* a drawn-out, high-pitched *siiewei* and a shrill *whiiu.* HABITAT: Forest edge, mangroves, freshwater swamp forest, secondary growth, coastal scrub, plantations and gardens. DISTRIBUTION: Resident, mainly coastal in SW, S Myanmar, Thailand (except NW, NE), Cambodia, N, S Laos, C, S Vietnam, Peninsular Malaysia and Singapore.

4 RED-THROATED SUNBIRD *Anthreptes rhodolaemus* 12–13cm FIELD NOTES: Gleans from foliage, usually in the canopy but also at lower levels. VOICE: A high-pitched *sit-sit-sit-see* or a slurred *sit-sit-sit-swe-er.* Calls include various chirps and trills. HABITAT: Broadleaved evergreen forest and forest edge. DISTRIBUTION: Resident in S Myanmar (S Tenasserim), S Thailand and Peninsular Malaysia.

5 RUBY-CHEEKED SUNBIRD *Chalcoparia singalensis* 10–11cm FIELD NOTES: Forages mainly in the upper storey, probes flowers for nectar and gleans from leaves. VOICE: A shrill trill, e.g. *tirr-titi trirr tir tir,* also a rapid, high *switi-ti-chi-chu, tusi-tit swit-swit...* Calls include a shrill *seet-seet,* a *tweest-wit* and a soft *chi-wip.* HABITAT: Forests, secondary growth, coastal scrub and mangroves. DISTRIBUTION: Resident in SW China and throughout the south, except N, E Myanmar, C Thailand and Singapore.

6 VAN HASSELT'S SUNBIRD (MAROON-BELLIED SUNBIRD) *Leptocoma brasiliana* 10cm FIELD NOTES: Usually forages in the treetops, hovers to take insects or water from foliage and nectar from flowers. VOICE: A series of discordant *psweet* notes. Calls include a weak *chip chip,* a sharp *si-si-si,* an upslurred *psweet,* a *fut-chit* and short, high trills. HABITAT: Various forests, forest edge, secondary growth, coastal scrub, cultivations and gardens. DISTRIBUTION: Resident in SW, S Myanmar, C, NE, SE, S Thailand, Cambodia, S Laos, C, S Vietnam, Peninsular Malaysia and Singapore.

7 PURPLE-RUMPED SUNBIRD *Leptocoma zeylonica* 11–12cm FIELD NOTES: Forages among flowers and foliage, singly or in pairs. VOICE: A sharp, twittering *tityou tityou tityou trr-r-r-tit tityou...* a weak *sisisiwee-sisisiwee...* or a *sit-sit tseet-tseet-tseet tsut-tsut-tsut-tsut.* Calls include a constant *sweety-swee sweety-sweety-swee* and a high, metallic *tzip.* HABITAT: Various forests and jungle, forest edge, cultivations and gardens. DISTRIBUTION: Resident in SW Myanmar.

8 COPPER-THROATED SUNBIRD *Leptocoma calcostetha* 14cm FIELD NOTES: Forages in mangroves, feeding on nectar and small arthropods. VOICE: A high trill and a deep melodious trill. HABITAT: Mangroves, coastal scrub, secondary growth and cultivations. DISTRIBUTION: Mainly coastal resident in S Myanmar (S Tenasserim), SE, S Thailand, Cambodia, S Vietnam, Peninsular Malaysia and Singapore.

163 SUNBIRDS

1 OLIVE-BACKED SUNBIRD *Cinnyris jugularis* 11–12cm FIELD NOTES: Feeds on insects, spiders, nectar and small fruits. *C. j. rhizohorae* (1b) occurs in SE China, Hainan and N Vietnam. VOICE: A feeble twittering. Calls include a *chip* and a nasal *sweei*; female utters a persistent *sweep*. DISTRIBUTION: Resident in SE China, Hainan and throughout the south, except N Myanmar.

2 PURPLE SUNBIRD *Cinnyris asiaticus* 10–12cm FIELD NOTES: Attracted to flowering trees and shrubs. Sings from a high, exposed perch. VOICE: An excited, repeated *cheewit-cheewit*. Calls include a *chip*, a *chweet* and a hard *zik*. HABITAT: Deciduous forests, thorn scrub, coastal scrub, cultivations and gardens. DISTRIBUTION: Resident in SW China, Myanmar, Thailand (except SE, S), Cambodia, N, C, S Laos and C, S Vietnam.

3 MRS GOULD'S SUNBIRD *Aethopyga gouldiae* 10cm (male with tail 14–15cm) FIELD NOTES: Attracted to flowers of rhododendrons and loranthus. *A. g. dabryii* (3b) occurs in C, S China, Myanmar, N Laos and N Vietnam. VOICE: A powerful seesawing sound. Calls include a *tzit-tzit*, a *squeeeee* and a *tshi-stshi-ti-ti-ti* alarm. HABITAT: Forests, forest edge, scrub-jungle and secondary growth. DISTRIBUTION: Resident in W, C, S China, W, N, C, E, S Myanmar, Laos and C, N Vietnam; winter visitor NW, NE Thailand.

4 GREEN-TAILED SUNBIRD *Aethopyga nipalensis koelzi* 10cm (male with tail 14–15cm) FIELD NOTES: Attracted to flowering trees and shrubs. *A. n. ezrai* (4b) occurs in C Vietnam (C, S Annam); *A. n. angkanensis* (4c) in NW Thailand. VOICE: A lively, twittering, mixed with high notes and a dry metallic trill. Calls include a sharp *dzii*, a repeated *tee-tzree-tzweeeet* and staccato *stip* notes. HABITAT: Broadleaved evergreen forest, forest edge and secondary growth. DISTRIBUTION: Resident SW China, W, N, E Myanmar, NW, S Thailand, N, C, S Laos and C, N Vietnam.

5 BLACK-THROATED SUNBIRD *Aethopyga saturata* 10cm (male with tail 14–15cm) FIELD NOTES: Forages from undergrowth to treetops, attracted to flowering trees and shrubs. *A. s. petersi* (5b) occurs in S China, E Myanmar, N Thailand, N Laos and N Vietnam, *A. s. johnsi* (5c) in C Vietnam (S Annam). VOICE: A series of high-pitched notes and rapid trills. Calls include a high *titi-tit-tit* and a *tu-ti-tee-tee*. HABITAT: Primary forests, secondary growth, scrub and gardens. DISTRIBUTION: Resident in S China, W, N, C, E, S Myanmar, Thailand (except C), Cambodia, Laos, C, N Vietnam and Peninsular Malaysia.

6 FORK-TAILED SUNBIRD *Aethopyga christinae* 10cm FIELD NOTES: Attracted to flowering trees and shrubs. *A. c. latouchii* (6b) occurs in SE China, C Laos and N Vietnam. VOICE: An accelerating *pe-et pe-et pit pit*. Calls include a *twisk* and a *chip-chip* that develops into trill. HABITAT: Forest, forest edge. DISTRIBUTION: Resident in China, Hainan, C, S Laos and Vietnam.

7 CRIMSON SUNBIRD *Aethopyga siparaja* 10cm (male with tail 12–14cm) FIELD NOTES: Forages among blossoms of trees and shrubs. VOICE: A loud chirping trill; calls include a *zit-zit* and a soft *siesiep-siepsiep*. HABITAT: Forests, secondary growth, cultivations, scrub and gardens. DISTRIBUTION: Resident south from southern China, except C Thailand.

8 TEMMINCK'S SUNBIRD *Aethopyga temminckii* 10cm (male with tail 13cm) FIELD NOTES: Forages mainly in the canopy, singly or in pairs and, occasionally, in mixed-species flocks. VOICE: A soft *cheet-cheet* and a rhythmic *tit-ti tit-it tit-it tit-it…* HABITAT: Dipterocarp forest, lower montane forest and peatswamp forest. DISTRIBUTION: Resident in S Thailand and Peninsular Malaysia.

9 FIRE-TAILED SUNBIRD *Aethopyga ignicauda* 10cm (male with tail 15–20cm) FIELD NOTES: Very active around flowering bushes. VOICE: A series of descending high-pitched notes. Calls include a repeated, high-pitched *dzdzi-dzidzidzidzi* and a rapid twittering. HABITAT: Conifer and oak forest with rhododendron understorey. DISTRIBUTION: Resident in SW China and W, N Myanmar.

♂ n-br

1

1b *rhizohorae*

♂

2

♂

3b *dabryii*

♀

♂

♀

3

♂

♀

5

♂

4

♂

4b *ezrai*

♂

4c *angkanensis*

♂

6b *latouchii*

♂

5b *petersi*

5c *johnsi*

♂

♂

♀

6

♂

♀

7

♀

♂

8

♂ n-br

♀

♂

9

164 FLOWERPECKERS

1 YELLOW-BREASTED FLOWERPECKER *Prionochilus maculatus* 10cm FIELD
NOTES: Forages in the middle to upper storey. VOICE: High-pitched *tswik*, a hoarse *tsweet-tsweet* and harsh metallic chittering calls. HABITAT: Lowland and hill dipterocarp, alluvial,
peatswamp and secondary forest, forest edge and scrub. DISTRIBUTION: Resident in S
Myanmar (S Tenasserim), S Thailand and Peninsular Malaysia.

2 CRIMSON-BREASTED FLOWERPECKER *Prionochilus percussus* 10cm FIELD
NOTES: Forages mainly in middle and lower storeys. VOICE: A *see-sik* and a fast *weg.*
HABITAT: Dipterocarp, alluvial, peatswamp, lower montane, mangroves and secondary forest.
DISTRIBUTION: Resident in S Myanmar (S Tenasserim), S Thailand and Peninsular Malaysia.

3 SCARLET-BREASTED FLOWERPECKER *Prionochilus thoracicus* 9–10cm FIELD
NOTES: Forages at all levels; sometimes climbs tree trunks, like a nuthatch. VOICE: A
metallic, clicking twitter and a harsh *chink.* HABITAT: Forests, forest edge, secondary growth
and coastal vegetation. DISTRIBUTION: Resident in S Thailand and Peninsular Malaysia.

4 THICK-BILLED FLOWERPECKER *Dicaeum agile* 9–11cm FIELD NOTES: Restless,
habitually twitches tail from side to side; attracted to flowering or fruiting trees and shrubs,
especially if infested with mistletoes. VOICE: 6–8 notes of differing pitches mixed with dry
trills. Calls include a sharp *chik-chik-chik-chik* and a rattling *tititititili.* HABITAT: Forests and
secondary growth. DISTRIBUTION: Resident south of China, except SW, W, N Myanmar, N
Vietnam and Singapore; rare non-breeding visitor to Singapore.

5 BROWN-BACKED FLOWERPECKER *Dicaeum everetti* 10cm FIELD NOTES: Forages
at low levels, feeding on spiders, insects and flowers, possibly also nectar and mistletoe
fruits. VOICE: A sharp, metallic *chip-chip.* HABITAT: Edge of lowland broadleaved evergreen
and swamp forest. DISTRIBUTION: Resident in Peninsular Malaysia.

6 YELLOW-VENTED FLOWERPECKER *Dicaeum chrysorrheum* 10cm FIELD NOTES:
Active forager at all levels; attracted to mistletoes and small figs. VOICE: Calls include a
zeet, a repeated *chip-a-chip-tree*, a *zit-zit-zit* and various soft squeaks. HABITAT: Broadleaved
evergreen, semi-evergreen and mixed deciduous forest, forest edge, secondary growth and
gardens. DISTRIBUTION: Resident in SW China and throughout the south.

7 YELLOW-BELLIED FLOWERPECKER *Dicaeum melanoxanthum* 11–13cm FIELD
NOTES: Elusive; noted making flycatching sallies from dead branches; often sits upright.
VOICE: A harsh, agitated *zit-zit-zit-zit.* HABITAT: Pine forest, tall trees in open forests
clearings in dense forest and forest edge. DISTRIBUTION: Resident in SW China and W, E
Myanmar; winter visitor in S China, N Thailand, N Laos and N Vietnam.

8 SCARLET-BACKED FLOWERPECKER *Dicaeum cruetatum* 9cm FIELD NOTES:
Forages at all levels, although mostly in the canopy; often among clumps of mistletoe.
VOICE: A rising and falling *see-sip-see-sip-see-sip* and a ringing *chipi-chipi-chipi dzee-dzee-dzee*;
calls include various twitterings, a *chip-chip*, a clicking *tchik-tchik-tchik* and a high-pitched
chizee. HABITAT: Open forests, forest edge, secondary forest, mangroves, parks and gardens.
DISTRIBUTION: Resident in SE, E China, Hainan and throughout the south.

9 ORANGE-BELLIED FLOWERPECKER *Dicaeum trigonostigma* 9cm FIELD NOTES:
Forages mainly in the treetops, favours flowering or fruiting trees. VOICE: A high-pitched *psee-psee-psee-psee-psee ptit-ptit-ptit-ptit-ptit tsi-si-si-si-sew*; calls include a shrill and twittering
and wheezy notes. HABITAT: Glades and edges of forests, secondary growth and gardens.
DISTRIBUTION: Resident in SW, E, S Myanmar, S Thailand, Peninsular Malaysia and Singapore.

10 FIRE-BREASTED FLOWERPECKER *Dicaeum ignipectus* 9cm FIELD NOTES:
Restless, agile forager, attracted to mistletoes. *D. i. formosum* (10b) occurs in Taiwan; *D. i.
cambodianum* (10c) occurs in SE Thailand and Cambodia. VOICE: A high-pitched *titty-titty-titty* or similar. Calls include a metallic *chip* and a rattling trill. HABITAT: Broadleaved
evergreen forest. DISTRIBUTION: Resident in China (except NE), Hainan, Taiwan and
throughout the south (except SW Myanmar, C Thailand, C, S Vietnam.

1

2 ♂

♀ 2

3 ♀

4

5

6

7 ♀

♂ 7

8 ♂ ♀

9 ♂

10b *formosum* ♂

10 ♀

♀

♂

10c *cambodianum* ♂

165 FLOWERPECKERS; SPIDERHUNTERS

1 PALE-BILLED FLOWERPECKER *Dicaeum erythrorhynchos* 8cm FIELD NOTES:
Restless, usually forages in the tops of trees; attracted to mistletoe fruits. VOICE: A series of
twittering notes or a reel; calls include a repeated, high-pitched *pit* and a sharp *chik-chik-
chik*. HABITAT: Deciduous forest, plantations and gardens. DISTRIBUTION: Resident in SW,
W Myanmar.

2 PLAIN FLOWERPECKER *Dicaeum minullum* 7–9cm FIELD NOTES: Active, agile
forager at all levels; attracted to the flowers and fruits of mistletoes. VOICE: A high-
pitched trill; calls include twitterings, a sharp *chek*, a short, ticking *chrik* and a *tik-tik-tik*.
HABITAT: Open broadleaved evergreen, semi-evergreen and deciduous forest and secondary
growth. DISTRIBUTION: Resident in Taiwan, southern China, Hainan, and throughout the
south, except S Myanmar, S Thailand and tip of S Vietnam.

3 LITTLE SPIDERHUNTER *Arachnothera longirostra* 13–16cm FIELD NOTES:
Restless, acrobatic forager, mostly at lower levels; attracted to banana blossoms. VOICE: A
monotonous, metallic *which-which*. Calls include a harsh *cheep*, *chee-chee-chee* and a loud
sheep repeated up to 25 times. HABITAT: Broadleaved evergreen forest, forest edge, secondary
growth, cultivations and gardens. DISTRIBUTION: Resident from SW China southwards,
except C Thailand.

4 THICK-BILLED SPIDERHUNTER *Arachnothera crassirostris* 16–17cm FIELD NOTES:
Forages from canopy down to understorey, singly or in pairs. VOICE: A hard, nasal *chit-chit*
or *chissie-chissie*, also a *tch-tch* and a *chek-chek-chek* or similar. HABITAT: Forests, forest edge,
secondary growth, banana groves and gardens. DISTRIBUTION: Resident in S Thailand and
Peninsular Malaysia.

5 LONG-BILLED SPIDERHUNTER *Arachnothera robusta* 21–22cm FIELD NOTES:
Forages mainly in the canopy; solitary and aggressive. VOICE: A rising *choi choi choi
choi…* Calls include a harsh *chuu-luut chuut-luut*, given from a high perch, and a high-
pitched *chit-chit chit-chit* flight call. HABITAT: Broadleaved evergreen forest and forest edge.
DISTRIBUTION: Resident in S Thailand, Peninsular Malaysia and Singapore.

6 SPECTACLED SPIDERHUNTER *Arachnothera flavigaster* 21–22cm FIELD NOTES:
Forages in the middle and upper levels, singly or occasionally in pairs; small groups occur
at fruiting trees. VOICE: A high-pitched *chit-chit*, also an explosive *tak*, *cha-tak*, *cha-ta-tak*
or variants. HABITAT: Broadleaved evergreen forest, forest edge and secondary growth.
DISTRIBUTION: Resident in S Thailand and Peninsular Malaysia.

7 YELLOW-EARED SPIDERHUNTER *Arachnothera chrysogenys* 17–18cm FIELD
NOTES: Acrobatic; forages mainly in the canopy, searches bark and broken branches.
VOICE: A rough *chit* and a high-pitched *twit-twit-twit-twee-ee* flight call. HABITAT:
Broadleaved evergreen forest, forest edge, secondary growth and gardens. DISTRIBUTION:
Resident in S Myanmar (S Tenasserim), S Thailand, Peninsular Malaysia and Singapore.

8 GREY-BREASTED SPIDERHUNTER *Arachnothera modesta* 17–18cm FIELD NOTES:
Active, flies rapidly through foliage; forages in all forest levels. VOICE: A continuous *tee-
chu*, first note rising the second falling. HABITAT: Broadleaved evergreen forest, secondary
growth, cultivations and gardens. DISTRIBUTION: Resident in S Myanmar (Tenasserim), S
Thailand and Peninsular Malaysia.

9 STREAKED SPIDERHUNTER *Arachnothera magna* 17–21cm FIELD NOTES: Noisy
agile forager from treetops to low levels. VOICE: Begins with a soft *vijvitte vij* that accelerates
to become rapid and monotonous. Calls include a *chirruping chiriririk* or *chirik chirik*, in
flight utters a loud musical trill. HABITAT: Broadleaved evergreen and mixed deciduous
forest, secondary growth, scrub and gardens. DISTRIBUTION: Resident in SW, S China and
southwards, except C, SE, S Thailand, Cambodia and Singapore.

166 SPARROWS; WEAVERS

1 HOUSE SPARROW *Passer domesticus* 15cm FIELD NOTES: Generally in small parties, bigger groups occur post breeding. Forages on the ground and in vegetation. VOICE: An excited series of mostly call notes, e.g. *chirrup-chirrup-cheep-chirp-chirrup...*, etc. Calls include a *chirrup, chirp* and a *chissick*; also utters a soft *swee-swee* and a rolling *chur-r-r-it-it* when alarmed. HABITAT: Urban areas, including towns and cities, cultivations and scrub in dry areas. DISTRIBUTION: Resident in Myanmar, W, NW, NE, C Thailand and N, S Laos; feral resident in Singapore.

2 TREE SPARROW (EURASIAN TREE SPARROW) *Passer montanus* 14cm FIELD NOTES: Note black cheek spot. Usually in pairs with larger flocks post breeding; forages on the ground and in vegetation. VOICE: Song consists of a series of call notes interspersed with *tsooit, tsveet* or *tswee-ip* notes. Calls include a high *chip*, a sharp *tet* and a dry *tet-tet-tet* flight note. HABITAT: Around habitations, including towns and cities; also in lightly wooded areas and cultivations. DISTRIBUTION: Resident throughout the region.

3 RUSSET SPARROW (CINNAMON SPARROW) *Passer rutilans* 14–15cm FIELD NOTES: Forages mainly on the ground but also in vegetation, in pairs or small flocks with larger flocks post breeding. VOICE: A frequently repeated *cheep-chirrup-cheweep* or *chwe-cha-cha*. Calls include a *cheep* or *chilp*, also a *swee-swee* and a rapid *chit-chit-chit* uttered when alarmed. HABITAT: Mountain or upland open woodland, cultivations and occasionally villages and towns. DISTRIBUTION: Resident in China (except SE), Taiwan, W, N, E Myanmar, N Laos and N Vietnam; winters in S China and NW Thailand.

4 PLAIN-BACKED SPARROW (PEGU SPARROW) *Passer flaveolus* 13–15cm FIELD NOTES: Forages mainly on the ground, in loose groups with larger flocks post breeding. VOICE: Song and calls similar to those of House Sparrow, although slightly louder and harsher. HABITAT: Open woodland, coastal scrub, dry open areas, cultivations and near human habitations. DISTRIBUTION: Resident in SW, W, C, E, S Myanmar, Thailand, Cambodia, Laos, C, S Vietnam and Peninsular Malaysia.

5 ASIAN GOLDEN WEAVER *Ploceus hypoxanthus* 15cm FIELD NOTES: Gregarious, breeds in small colonies. VOICE: Chattering notes ending with a long rattle; calls with harsh *chit* notes. HABITAT: Usually near water, e.g. marshes, paddyfields and flooded grasslands. DISTRIBUTION: Resident in SW, C, S Myanmar, NW, NE, C Thailand, Cambodia, S Laos and C, S Vietnam.

6 BLACK-BREASTED WEAVER *Ploceus benghalensis* 14cm FIELD NOTES: Gregarious, often in the company of other weavers, waxbills and starlings. VOICE: A soft series of sibilant notes ending with a low buzzing; in flight utters a quiet *chit-chit*. HABITAT: Tall grass or reedy areas near water. DISTRIBUTION: Disputed record from S Myanmar.

7 STREAKED WEAVER *Ploceus manyar* 14cm FIELD NOTES: Gregarious, forages and roosts in flocks; breeds in small scattered colonies. VOICE: A trill of high-pitched whistles that ends with a wheezy note; calls include a *re tre cherrer cherrer* often uttered by displaying males and a *chirt-chirt* given in flight. HABITAT: Reedbeds, reed-swamps, tall grass and seasonally flooded areas. DISTRIBUTION: Resident in SW China, Myanmar (except Tenasserim), NW, C, W Thailand, Cambodia and C, S Vietnam; feral resident in Singapore.

8 BAYA WEAVER *Ploceus philippinus* 15cm FIELD NOTES: Gregarious: roosts and forages in flocks, often found in the company of other weavers, waxbills, sparrows and starlings. VOICE: A chittering followed by a wheezy whistle, a buzz and finally some chirps; calls with a harsh *chit*. HABITAT: Generally open areas with nearby water, including grassland, scrub with scattered trees, paddyfields, cultivations and secondary growth. DISTRIBUTION: Resident in SW China and throughout the south, except C Laos and C, N Vietnam.

167 WAGTAILS; DIPPERS

1 FOREST WAGTAIL *Dendronanthus indicus* 16–18cm FIELD NOTES: Runs or walks rapidly, swaying tail and rear of body from side to side. VOICE: A repeated, high-pitched, squeaky *zlic-zhee…* Calls with a hard, shrill *pick* or *pick-pick*. HABITAT: Forest tracks and trails, wooded cultivations, mangroves and gardens. DISTRIBUTION: Breeds in northern China; winters in southern China, Hainan and throughout the south (except N Myanmar, N, C Laos and N, C Vietnam).

2 WHITE WAGTAIL *Motacilla alba* 17–18cm FIELD NOTES: Walks, wagging tail up and down. Various races occur, depicted are; M. *a. alboides* (main portraits) resident in SW China, N Myanmar, N Laos and N Vietnam; M. *a. personata* (2b) winter visitor in N Myanmar; M. *a. ocularis* (2c) winters in Taiwan, S China, Hainan and the south; M. *a. baicalensis* (2d) winters in SE China, Hainan, Myanmar and Thailand; M. *a. leucopsis* (2e) breeds in China, winters Hainan, Taiwan and throughout the south. VOICE: A twittering interspersed with call notes; calls include a *ts-lee-wee, tslee-vit* or similar. HABITAT: Open habitats often near water. DISTRIBUTION: Breeds and resident in northern China, N Myanmar, N Laos and N Vietnam. Winter visitor in southern China, Hainan, Taiwan and throughout the south, except only a vagrant in S Thailand and Singapore.

3 MEKONG WAGTAIL *Motacilla samveasnae* 17–18cm FIELD NOTES: Regularly forages in bushes in water. Sings from a bush top or boulder. VOICE: A rapid series of thin, high-pitched harsh notes, interspersed with long pauses. In flight utters a harsh *dzeer*. HABITAT: Broad, lowland rivers with sandbars, emergent rocks and bushes. DISTRIBUTION: Lower Mekong River and tributaries in S Laos, NE Cambodia; marginally in adjacent parts of Thailand, Vietnam.

4 JAPANESE WAGTAIL *Motacilla grandis* 21–23cm FIELD NOTES: Actions as White Wagtail. VOICE: Calls include a harsh, shrill *bzzr, tzzr* or *tzreh*, uttered singly or repeated. HABITAT: Dry riverbeds, river shores and coastal areas. DISTRIBUTION: Winter visitor in Taiwan.

5 CITRINE WAGTAIL *Motacilla citreola* 16–20cm FIELD NOTES: Actions similar to White Wagtail, although tail wagging less pronounced. M. *c. calcarata* (5b) winters in SW, N, S Myanmar. VOICE: Calls include a *dzreeip* and a soft *tslee*. HABITAT: High-altitude wet grassland; winters in freshwater wetlands. DISTRIBUTION: Breeds in W China; resident in SW China. Winters in S, SE China, Myanmar, NW, NE, C Thailand and N Laos; vagrant elsewhere.

6 EASTERN YELLOW WAGTAIL *Motacilla tschutschensis* 16–18cm FIELD NOTES: Actions similar to Citrine Wagtail. Races include M. *t. taivana* (6b). VOICE: Similar to Western Yellow Wagtail. HABITAT: As for Western. DISTRIBUTION: Winters in Taiwan, S, E China and throughout the south, except W, S Myanmar.

7 WESTERN YELLOW WAGTAIL *Motacilla flava* 16–18cm FIELD NOTES: Actions similar to Citrine Wagtail. Races occurring are the widespread M. *f. macronyx* (main illustration) and M. *f. thunbergi* (7b). VOICE: Calls with a loud *pseeu* and a *tsreep*. HABITAT: Damp grasslands and pastures. DISTRIBUTION: Winters in Taiwan, S, E China and throughout the south, except W, S Myanmar.

8 GREY WAGTAIL *Motacilla cinerea* 17–20cm FIELD NOTES: Constantly pumps rear body and tail. VOICE: Calls with a high-pitched *zit-zit*. HABITAT: Mountain streams; winters by lowland waters. DISTRIBUTION: Resident in Taiwan; winters in S, W, E China, Hainan and throughout the south.

9 DIPPER (WHITE-THROATED DIPPER) *Cinclus cinclus* 18–20cm FIELD NOTES: Swims and walks underwater; bobs whole body while perched. VOICE: A rippling warble; calls with a rasping *zink* or *zzit zzit*. HABITAT: Fast-flowing mountain streams. DISTRIBUTION: Resident in SW China, scarce winter visitor in N Myanmar.

10 BROWN DIPPER *Cinclus pallasii* 20cm FIELD NOTES: Actions as Dipper. VOICE: A rich warbling, including buzzes, trills and rattles; calls with a buzzing *zzit-zzit*. HABITAT: Rivers and streams. DISTRIBUTION: Resident in China, Hainan, Taiwan, W, N, E Myanmar, N, C Laos and C, N Vietnam.

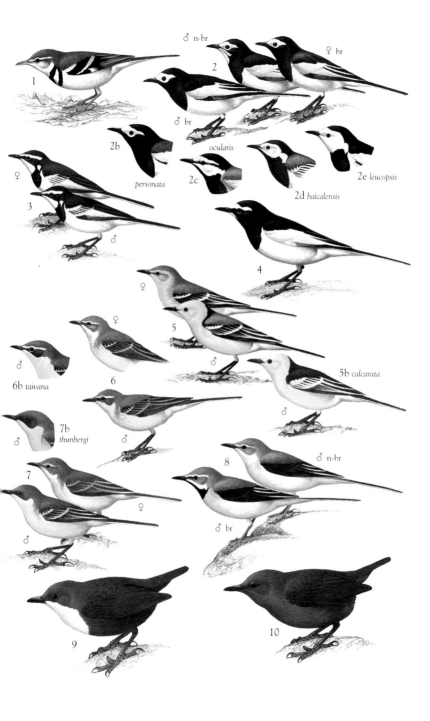

1

♂ n-br
2
♀ br

♂ br
ocularis

2b
personata

2c

2d baicalensis

2e leucopsis

♀
3
♂

4

♀
5
♂

5b calcarata
♂

6b taivana

6

♂
7b thunbergi

7
♂
♀

8
♂ n-br

♂ br

9

10

168 PIPITS

1 RICHARD'S PIPIT *Anthus richardi* 17–20cm FIELD NOTES: Forages on the ground; when agitated often stands very upright with neck stretched. Flight powerful and undulating, with long dips; regularly hovers above grass before landing. VOICE: A simple, grinding *tschivu-tschivu-tschivu-tschivu-tschivu…* given in flight. Calls include a harsh *schreep* or a longer *sherrreeep* given as bird takes flight; also a short *chup*, a subdued *chirp* and a *r-rump*. HABITAT: Open country, grassy areas and cultivations. DISTRIBUTION: Breeds in China (except SE); resident in E China. Winters in SE China, Hainan, Taiwan and throughout the south (except Peninsular Malaysia and Singapore).

2 PADDYFIELD PIPIT *Anthus rufulus* 15cm FIELD NOTES: Forages on the ground, call note is the best way to distinguish from the similar, but larger Richard's Pipit; often stands more upright than shown. VOICE: Similar to Richard's Pipit, but faster and higher-pitched. Calls include a hard *chep* or *chep-chep*, a thin *pipit* and harsh *chwist*. HABITAT: Open country, short grasslands, paddyfields, stubble fields and cultivations. DISTRIBUTION: Resident in SW China and throughout the south.

3 BLYTH'S PIPIT *Anthus godlewskii* 16cm FIELD NOTES: Actions similar to the slightly larger Richard's Pipit, best distinguished by voice. Generally has back more heavily streaked than Paddyfield Pipit. VOICE: Calls include a loud *chup, chep* or *chep-chep* and a longer *pshee* or *pshee-chep-chep*. HABITAT: Grasslands, dry paddyfields and edges of cultivations. DISTRIBUTION: Winter visitor in W, C, S Myanmar.

4 LONG-BILLED PIPIT *Anthus similis* 17–20cm FIELD NOTES: Forages on the ground. Tends to creep about; when flushed, regularly lands on rocks, bushes or trees. VOICE: A series of monotonous, unmusical, well-spaced phrases, such as *tjup-threee-tjup-tjup-threee* or *chreep-shreep-chew-ee*. Calls include a *klup* or *klup-klup* and a loud *che-vlee*. HABITAT: Rocky hillsides with sparse cover. Winters on grassy plains, sparsely scrubbed country and fields. DISTRIBUTION: Resident in W, C, E, S Myanmar.

5 TREE PIPIT *Anthus trivialis* 15cm FIELD NOTES: Pumps tail up and down while foraging on the ground; when disturbed usually flies to settle in a nearby tree. VOICE: Calls include a drawn-out *tseep* or *teez* and a high-pitched *seet-seet-seet*. HABITAT: Open forests, cultivations, open country with scattered trees and stubble fields. DISTRIBUTION: Vagrant, recorded in S Myanmar.

6 OLIVE-BACKED PIPIT *Anthus hodgsoni* 14–15cm FIELD NOTES: Pumps tail up and down while foraging on the ground; when disturbed flies to settle in a nearby tree. Sings from tree perch or in a song-flight that ascends then parachutes down with wings spread. Plainer-backed race *A. h. yunnanensis* (6b) winters southward from S China. VOICE: Repeated trilled phrases and dry rattles; calls include a loud *teaze*, and a thin *teez* or *tseep*. HABITAT: Open forests, forest clearings, forest edge, secondary growth and wooded cultivations. DISTRIBUTION: Breeds in W China; resident in SW China and N, W Myanmar. Winters in N, E, S China and throughout the south, except S Thailand and Singapore; passage migrant or vagrant elsewhere.

7 PECHORA PIPIT *Anthus gustavi* 15cm FIELD NOTES: Skulking; forages mainly on the ground. Tends to hover before landing, unlike other small pipits. VOICE: Calls with a sharp *tsip, tsip-tsip* or *tsi-tsi-tsi-tsip*. HABITAT: Wet grassy areas and open woodland. DISTRIBUTION: Passage migrant in E China.

8 RED-THROATED PIPIT *Anthus cervinus* 14–15cm FIELD NOTES: Forages on the ground, often in small flocks; regularly perches on rocks, bushes, wires or fences. VOICE: Calls include a short *tew* and a longer, high-pitched *pseeeu*. HABITAT: Grasslands, stubble fields and grassy edges of lakes and rivers. DISTRIBUTION: Winter visitor in China, Hainan, Taiwan and throughout the south, except W, N Myanmar, N Vietnam and Peninsular Malaysia; vagrant in Peninsular Malaysia.

6b *yunnanensis*

6

5

7

br

8

n-br

169 PIPITS; ACCENTORS

1 UPLAND PIPIT *Anthus sylvanus* 17cm FIELD NOTES: When agitated, stands upright, often on a rock, and flicks tail; otherwise creeps around in low vegetation. VOICE: A repeated *seettyu-seetyu* or *tyu-see-tyu-ee*. Also utters a more monotonous *weeeee-tch-weeeee-tch* or a drawn-out, whistled *wichee-wichee-wichee*, rendered from a prominent perch or, less often, in flight. Calls with a sparrow-like *chirp*. HABITAT: Steep rocky and grassy slopes with scattered bushes, and abandoned cultivations. DISTRIBUTION: Resident in W, SC, E China.

2 ROSY PIPIT *Anthus roseatus* 15–17cm FIELD NOTES: Forages on the ground, usually in pairs with small loose flocks post breeding. VOICE: Song-flight consists of a monotonous *tree-tree-tree* mixed with some drawn-out notes, given as the bird rises and a *tsuli-tsuli-tsuli…* uttered during descent. Calls include a *tzeep* or *tzeep-tzeep-tzeep*. HABITAT: Breeds on alpine meadows and boulder-strewn grassy slopes; winters on short grassland, marshy areas and paddyfields. DISTRIBUTION: Resident W, SW China; winters in S China, N, E Myanmar, NW Thailand and N Vietnam.

3 WATER PIPIT *Anthus spinoletta* 15–17cm FIELD NOTES: Wary; forages on the ground, usually singly, in pairs or in loose flocks. VOICE: Calls include a *pheet, tsip, wisst, tsi, tsiip, dzip, tsupi* or *chui*. HABITAT: Damp grassland, marshes, irrigated cultivations and grassy edges of watercourses. DISTRIBUTION: Winter visitor in W, C, E China.

4 BUFF-BELLIED PIPIT *Anthus rubescens* 15–17cm FIELD NOTES: Actions as Water Pipit, but gait tends to be quicker and lighter. Often gathers in flocks. VOICE: Calls include a high *sipit* or *sip*, a high *tsweep* and a *tsi-tsi-tsi-tsip* uttered when flushed. HABITAT: Marshes, damp grassland, irrigated cultivations and wetland edges. DISTRIBUTION: Winters in China, vagrant in Hainan, Taiwan, N Myanmar, NE Thailand and N Vietnam.

5 ALPINE ACCENTOR *Prunella collaris* 15–17cm FIELD NOTES: Forages on the ground, among rocks, stones and vegetation. Generally in pairs, post breeding occurs in small parties of up to 20. Song given from a rock or during a short display flight. Juvenile duller, grey areas browner and with dark streaking on underparts. VOICE: A variable warble consisting of low-pitched trills and ripples with fluty whistles, much like a Skylark. Calls include a rolling *chirrup* or *chirrirrip* and a low *chit-chittur*. HABITAT: Rocky mountain slopes with sparse vegetation, may descend in winter when regularly occurs around upland villages. DISTRIBUTION: Resident in Taiwan, SW, W China and N Myanmar.

6 RUFOUS-BREASTED ACCENTOR *Prunella strophiata* 15cm FIELD NOTES: Skulking; wing twitching gives the bird a nervous look while it forage, mouse-like, under bushes. Juvenile has buff-washed breastband and dark streaking on underparts. VOICE: A long, melodious, wren-like warbling and trilling; call is a fast *tr-r-r* or *trr-r-rit*. HABITAT: Forest and scrub near or above the treeline; in winter occupies scrub-jungle and pastures at lower altitudes. DISTRIBUTION: Resident in SW, W China and possibly N Myanmar.

7 MAROON-BACKED ACCENTOR *Prunella immaculata* 14–15cm FIELD NOTES: Secretive; forages on the ground under thick vegetation. Juvenile much duller with dark streaking above and below. VOICE: Call is a weak, high-pitched *zieh-dzit* or *tzip*. HABITAT: Undergrowth in humid conifer and rhododendron forests; winters in secondary forest and forest edge. DISTRIBUTION: Resident in SW China and possibly N Myanmar.

8 SIBERIAN ACCENTOR *Prunella montanella* 14–15cm FIELD NOTES: Forages mainly on the ground, but also in bushes and trees. Juvenile less rufous, head pattern duller, underparts with large brown spots on breast and chest. VOICE: Calls is a *tsee-ree-see* or *dididi*. HABITAT: Thickets and scrub usually along watercourses. DISTRIBUTION: Rare winter visitor in NE China (Jiangsu).

170 PARROTFINCHES; MUNIAS

1 TAWNY-BREASTED PARROTFINCH (GREEN-TAILED PARROTFINCH) *Erythrura hyperythra* 10–11cm FIELD NOTES: Forages on the ground on seeds and small fruits; usually in small parties. VOICE: A series of soft notes followed by four bell-like notes; calls include a high-pitched, hissing *tzit-tzit* contact note, given in flight. HABITAT: Bamboo, montane forest, forest edge, and scrub. DISTRIBUTION: Resident in Peninsular Malaysia.

2 PIN-TAILED PARROTFINCH *Erythrura prasina* male 15cm, female 11–12cm FIELD NOTES: Forages singly or in pairs; also in small parties, especially when bamboo is in seed. Yellow morph is rare. VOICE: A series of abrupt clinking or chirping notes. Calls include a sharp *teger-teter-terge* and a high-pitched *tseet-tseet*. HABITAT: Bamboo, open forest, forest edge and secondary growth. DISTRIBUTION: Resident in S Myanmar (Tenasserim), Thailand (except C), N, C Laos, C, S Vietnam and Peninsular Malaysia.

3 WHITE-RUMPED MUNIA *Lonchura striata* 11–12cm FIELD NOTES: Feeds on seeds. Gregarious, usually in small parties, with larger flocks in winter. VOICE: A series of rising and falling twittering notes. Calls include a plaintive *peep* and a twittering *tr-tr-tr*, *prrrit* or *brrt*. HABITAT: Forest clearings, secondary growth, scrub and grassy areas. DISTRIBUTION: Resident in S, E China, Hainan, Taiwan and throughout the south.

4 JAVAN MUNIA *Lonchura leucogastroides* 10–11cm FIELD NOTES: Forages on the ground and in vegetation, usually in small flocks. VOICE: A pleasant purring or series of *prreet* notes; calls include a short *tit*, also *p'tit* and *peteet* contact calls. HABITAT: Secondary growth, scrub and gardens. DISTRIBUTION: Introduced resident in Singapore.

5 CHESTNUT MUNIA (BLACK-HEADED MUNIA) *Lonchura atricapilla* 11–12cm FIELD NOTES: Forages on the ground, usually in pairs or small parties; bigger flocks occur post breeding. *L. a sinensis* (5b) occurs in Peninsular Malaysia; *L. a. formosana* (5c) in Taiwan. VOICE: Calls include a loud *pink pink* and a clear *pee* or *peet* contact note. HABITAT: Edge of marshes or swamps, reedbeds, grasslands and cultivation edges. DISTRIBUTION: Resident in S China, Taiwan, Myanmar, Thailand (except C, NE), Laos, Vietnam and Peninsular Malaysia.

6 WHITE-BELLIED MUNIA *Lonchura leucogastra* 11cm FIELD NOTES: Usually forages in pairs or small groups. VOICE: A rapidly repeated *di-di-ptchee-pti-pti-ti-pteep*. Calls include a strong *tik* or *tchek*, a *twyrt* and a *tee-tee-tee*. HABITAT: Open and secondary broadleaved evergreen forest, forest edge, scrub and cultivations. DISTRIBUTION: Resident in S Myanmar (S Tenasserim), S Thailand and Peninsular Malaysia.

7 SCALY-BREASTED MUNIA *Lonchura punctulata* 10–12cm FIELD NOTES: Forages on the ground or on grasses, usually in small groups with bigger flocks post breeding. *L. p. topela* (7b) occurs in SW China, Taiwan, S Myanmar, Thailand, Laos, Cambodia and Vietnam. VOICE: A series of quiet notes, followed by a short series of whistles and churrs, ending with a long slurred whistle. Contact calls are a repeated *tit-ti* and a *kit-teee kit-teee*. HABITAT: Open country with scrub and trees, bushy hillsides, secondary growth with grass patches, cultivations and gardens. DISTRIBUTION: Resident in Taiwan, and throughout south from central China.

8 WHITE-HEADED MUNIA *Lonchura maja* 11–12cm FIELD NOTES: Feeds on seeds taken on the ground or in vegetation, often occurs in large groups. VOICE: A series of clicks and then a drawn-out *weeeee-heeheeheeheehee*; calls include a soft *preet*. HABITAT: Grassland, paddyfields, cultivations and scrub. DISTRIBUTION: Resident in S Thailand, S Vietnam, Peninsular Malaysia and Singapore.

9 JAVA SPARROW *Lonchura oryzivora* 15cm FIELD NOTES: Feeds on seeds, from the ground or grass seedheads, usually in small flocks. Juvenile generally brownish with a pink-buff face and dark crown. VOICE: Bell-like trilling and clicking notes ending with a drawn-out whistle; call is a *tup* or *tack*. HABITAT: Grassland, cultivations and gardens. DISTRIBUTION: Introduced resident in Thailand, E China, C, S Thailand, Peninsular Malaysia and Singapore.

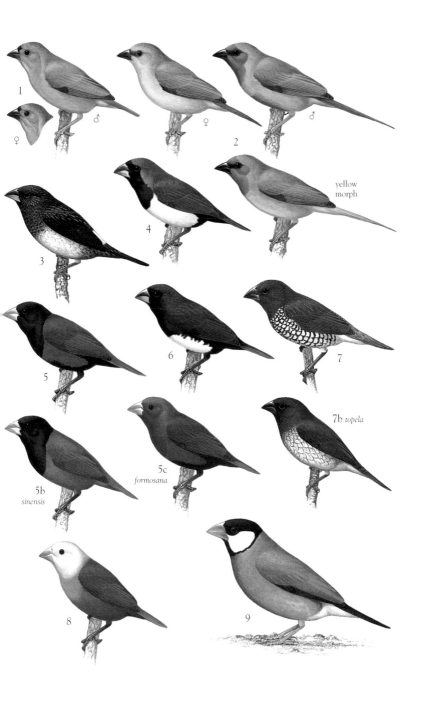

171 AVADAVAT; FINCHES; BULLFINCHES; CROSSBILL

1 RED AVADAVAT (RED MUNIA or STRAWBERRY FINCH) *Amandava amandava* 10cm FIELD NOTES: Forages on the ground and on grass heads, in small flocks; winter flocks may be bigger and include other species. VOICE: A weak, high-pitched warble combined with sweet twittering notes; calls include a thin *teei* or *tsi* and various chirps and squeaks. HABITAT: Swampy grasslands, reeds and tall grass near marshes and watercourses, grass, secondary growth and scrub. DISTRIBUTION: Resident in SW China, Myanmar (except Tenasserim), NW, C, SE Thailand, Cambodia and N, S Vietnam; scarce feral resident in Singapore.

2 GOLDEN-NAPED FINCH *Pyrrhoplectes epauletta* 15cm FIELD NOTES: Secretive, forages on the ground or in the interior of bushes and undergrowth; in winter occurs in small flocks often in the company of rosefinches. VOICE: A rapid, high-pitched *pi-pi-pi-pi-pi*, also a low piping. Calls include a thin, repeated *teeu, tseu* or *peeu*, a *pur-lee* and a *plee-e-e*. HABITAT: Undergrowth in high-altitude oak and rhododendron forests. DISTRIBUTION: Resident in SW China and N Myanmar.

3 CHAFFINCH *Fringilla coelebs* 15cm FIELD NOTES: Forages on the ground and in tree foliage. Usually encountered in flocks, often in the company of other finches and buntings. VOICE: Calls include a loud *pink* or *pink-pink*, a loud *whit*, a wheezy *eeese* and a *tsup* flight note. HABITAT: Fields with nearby bushes or trees. DISTRIBUTION: Vagrant, recorded from NW Thailand.

4 BRAMBLING *Fringilla montifringilla* 15cm FIELD NOTES: In flight shows a white rump. Non-breeding male similar to breeding female, but darker headed. Forages on the ground, usually in flocks that often include other finches and buntings. VOICE: Calls include a nasal *tsweek* or *zweee* and a *chuk-chuk* flight note. HABITAT: Open forests and cultivations. DISTRIBUTION: Winter visitor in Taiwan and China (except SE); vagrant in NW Thailand and N Vietnam.

5 SCARLET FINCH *Haematospiza (Carpodacus) sipahi* 18–19cm FIELD NOTES: Forages in trees, bushes and the ground, alone, in pairs or in scattered flocks. In winter often seen in single-sex flocks. VOICE: A clear, liquid *par-ree-reeeeee*; calls include a loud *too-eee* or *pleeau* and a *kwee-i-iu* or *chew-we-auh*. HABITAT: Edges and clearings in montane coniferous forest; in winter also in oak and bamboo forest. DISTRIBUTION: Resident in SW China and W, N Myanmar; winter visitor in NW Thailand, N Laos and N Vietnam (W Tonkin).

6 BROWN BULLFINCH *Pyrrhula nipalensis ricketti* 16–17cm FIELD NOTES: Often in pairs or small parties foraging in the tops of bushes or trees. White rump band shows during fast direct flight. *P. n. uchidai* (6b) occurs in Taiwan; white-cheeked *P. n. waterstradti* (6c) in Peninsular Malaysia. VOICE: A hastily repeated, mellow *her-dee-a duuee*; calls include a mellow *per-lee* and a soft whistling twitter. HABITAT: Undergrowth in broadleaved evergreen and coniferous forests, forest edge and secondary growth. DISTRIBUTION: Resident in Taiwan, S, E China, W, N Myanmar, N, C Vietnam (W Tonkin, S Annam) and Peninsular Malaysia.

7 GREY-HEADED BULLFINCH *Pyrrhula erythaca* 17cm FIELD NOTES: Forages low down in bushes or on the ground, in pairs or small parties. White rump shows well in flight. VOICE: A descending then rising mellow whistled warble mixed with long slurred and creaky notes. Call is a slow *soo-ee*. HABITAT: Conifer and rhododendron forests, also thickets. DISTRIBUTION: Resident in W, SW China, Taiwan and N Myanmar.

8 CROSSBILL (COMMON or RED CROSSBILL) *Loxia curvirostra* 16–17cm FIELD NOTES: Usually in small parties. Smaller *L. c. himalayensis* (8b) occurs in Myanmar. VOICE: A *cheeree-cheeree-choop-chip-chip-chip cheeree* mixed with various trills, twitters and call notes; call is *chip-chip* or *chuk-chuk*. HABITAT: Coniferous forests. DISTRIBUTION: Resident in SW China, N Myanmar and C Vietnam (S Annam); winter visitor in NE China and SW, C, S, N Myanmar.

1

♂

♀

2

♂

4

♀

♂

3

♂

5

♀

♂

6c
waterstradti

8b *himalayensis*

6b
:hidai

7

♀

8

♀

6

8

♂

7

♂

172 FINCHES

1 ORIENTAL GREENFINCH (GREY-CAPPED or CHINESE GREENFINCH)
Chloris sinica 14cm FIELD NOTES: Usually in pairs or small groups, forages in trees, shrubs and on the ground. Often sings in stiff-winged, slow display-flight. VOICE: A mixture of chattering and course notes interspersed with call notes; calls include a distinctive *dzi-dzi-dzi-i* and a nasal *dzwee*. HABITAT: Woodlands, hedgerows, cultivations, parks and gardens. DISTRIBUTION: Resident in China and locally in N, C Vietnam (E Tonkin, S Annam).

2 YELLOW-BREASTED GREENFNCH (HIMALAYAN GREENFINCH) *Chloris spinoides* 14cm FIELD NOTES: Forages in treetops, bushes or on the ground, usually in pairs or small family parties, with larger flocks post breeding. VOICE: A long series of rapid twitters interspersed with short *chip* and *tew* notes; calls include a distinct *swee-tu-tu* and a twittering followed a by a harsh *dzwee*. HABITAT: Open forest, forest edge, scrub and cultivations. DISTRIBUTION: Resident in W Myanmar.

3 VIETNAMESE GREENFINCH *Chloris monguilloti* 13–14cm FIELD NOTES: Forages in pairs or small flocks, in trees and bushes. VOICE: A slowly rising *seeuuu-seeuuu-seeuuu* or *teoo-teoo-teoo*, followed by a nasal *weeeee* or *chweee*; calls include a twittering *chi-chi-chi...* and a dry nasal *zwee*. HABITAT: Open pine forest, forest edge, cultivations and gardens. DISTRIBUTION: Resident in C Vietnam (S Annam).

4 BLACK-HEADED GREENFINCH (TIBETAN GREENFINCH) *Chloris ambigua* 14cm FIELD NOTES: Forages in bushes, low vegetation and on the ground; in winter often in large flocks. VOICE: A drawn-out, wheezy *wheeeeeeuu wheeeeeeuu* mixed with metallic notes, trills and a harsh *scree* or *treeee-tetrah*; calls include a wheezy *twzyee* and a twittering, often interspersed with harsh notes. HABITAT: Open conifer or deciduous forest, forest edge, forest clearings, scrub and cultivations. DISTRIBUTION: Resident in SW China, N, E Myanmar, N Laos and N Vietnam; winter visitor in NW Thailand.

5 SISKIN (EURASIAN SISKIN) *Serinus spinus* 12cm FIELD NOTES: Acrobatic forager, mainly in trees, usually encountered in small parties. VOICE: Calls include a plaintive *dlu-ee*, a dry *tet* or *tet-tet* and a *twilit, tirrillilit* or *titteree* uttered in flight. HABITAT: Open forests, forest edge and secondary growth. DISTRIBUTION: Winter visitor in N, S, E China and Taiwan; vagrant in N Vietnam.

6 TIBETAN SISKIN (TIBETAN SERIN) *Spinus thibetanus* 12cm FIELD NOTES: Usually in small flocks, forages in treetops or on the ground under bushes. VOICE: A nasal, buzzy twittering interspersed with trills and *ti-ti tweeoo* phrases; calls include a dry twittering, a wheezy twang; in flight utters short twitters, trills and a *chut-chut-chut*. HABITAT: Open forest and forest edge. DISTRIBUTION: Resident in SW China and N Myanmar.

7 REDPOLL (COMMON REDPOLL) *Acanthis flammea* 13cm FIELD NOTES: Forages on the ground or acrobatically in trees, in pairs or small parties. VOICE: Calls include a metallic, twittering *chuch-uch-uch-uch*, a plaintive *teu-teu-teu-teu* and a *tooee*. HABITAT: Coastal and lowland open woods. DISTRIBUTION: Winter visitor in extreme NE China.

8 PLAIN MOUNTAIN FINCH *Leucosticte nemoricola* 14–15cm FIELD NOTES: Forages on the ground, flying into nearby treetops when disturbed; gregarious, often flies in large wheeling, twisting flocks. VOICE: A sharp twittering *rick-pi-vitt* or *dui-dip-dip-dip* interspersed with twittering trills and sweet warbling notes; calls include a soft twittering *chi-chi-chi-chi* and a double-noted shrill whistle. HABITAT: Mountains, hillsides and alpine meadows; winters in open areas and cultivations. DISTRIBUTION: Resident in SW China; winter visitor in NE Myanmar.

9 BRANDT'S MOUNTAIN FINCH *Leucosticte brandti* 16–19cm FIELD NOTES: Forages on the ground, usually in pairs or small parties; large winter flocks wheel, circle, plunge and rise around cliffs. VOICE: A short trill; calls include a loud *twit-twitt, twee-ti-ti* or *peek-peek* and a harsh churr. HABITAT: High altitude cliffs and crags, barren, stony mountain tops. DISTRIBUTION: Resident in SW China.

173 ROSEFINCHES

1 LONG-TAILED ROSEFINCH *Carpodacus sibiricus* 16–17cm FIELD NOTES: Forages on the ground and in undergrowth, agile actions while picking at seedheads; usually singly, in pairs or small family parties. VOICE: Various pleasant rippling trills. Calls include a liquid *pee-you-een* or *su-we-su-wee-sweeeoo-cheweeoo*; also a rising *sit-it-it.* HABITAT: Dense willow and birch thickets, grasslands, reedbeds, riverine woods, tall vegetation in ditches and wet meadows. DISTRIBUTION: Resident in extreme W, SW China.

2 COMMON ROSEFINCH (SCARLET ROSEFINCH) *Carpodacus erythrinus* 15cm FIELD NOTES: Skulking; forages on the ground, in low vegetation or bushes and trees. In winter often in flocks mixed with other finches, sparrows or buntings. *C. e. roseatus* (2b) is found over much of the noted distribution; the nominate winters in N Myanmar and NW Thailand. VOICE: A cheery *twee-twee-tweeou, ti-dew-di-dew* or similar; calls include a rising *ooeet, ueet* or *too-ee* and a sharp *chay-eeee* when alarmed. HABITAT: Montane and sub-montane juniper, thornbush, scrub and cultivations. DISTRIBUTION: Breeds in W China; winters in N, E, S China, Myanmar, W, NE, NW Thailand, N Laos and N Vietnam.

3 BLANFORD'S ROSEFINCH *Agraphospiza rubescens* 15cm FIELD NOTES: Little known. Sings from the top of trees; forages on the ground, generally in pairs, with larger parties in winter. VOICE: A loud musical warble that rises and falls in pitch, with a down-slurred last note. Calls include a high, thin *sip* and a series of short rising and falling *pitch-ew, pitch-it, chit-it* or *chit-ew* notes. HABITAT: Open areas in coniferous or mixed conifer and birch forest. DISTRIBUTION: Resident in SW, W China.

4 DARK-BREASTED ROSEFINCH (DARK or NEPAL ROSEFINCH) *Procarduelis nipalensis* 15–16cm FIELD NOTES: Shy; feeds on the ground and in or under bushes, in pairs or small parties. Often occurs in large, single-sex flocks mixed with other rosefinches. VOICE: A monotonous chirping; calls include a plaintive, wailed double whistle, a twittering and a *cha-a-rr* given when alarmed. HABITAT: Mixed forests of oak, conifer and rhododendrons, low scrub and bushes; also weedy areas above the treeline. In winter also found in forest edge and clearings. DISTRIBUTION: Resident in SW, W China, N Myanmar and N Vietnam; winter visitor in E Myanmar and NW Thailand.

5 BEAUTIFUL ROSEFINCH *Carpodacus pulcherrimus* 15cm FIELD NOTES: In flight shows a pink rump. Forages on the ground or low down in bushes and scrub, in pairs or small flocks. VOICE: Calls include a subdued *trip, trilp* or *trillip*, a tit-like twitter and in flight utters a harsh *chaaannn.* HABITAT: Steep hillsides with rhododendron and other bushes near or above the treeline; winters on open scrub-covered hillsides and cultivation with nearby bushes. DISTRIBUTION: Resident in SW China.

6 PINK-RUMPED ROSEFINCH *Carpodacus waltoni* 15cm FIELD NOTES: Forages on the ground, often around the edges of trees or bushes, usually in pairs or small parties, bigger flocks occur post breeding, often mixed with other species. VOICE: Calls include a sharp *pink* or *tink*, a *tsip* or *tsick*, a thin rattle and a harsh *pip-rit.* HABITAT: Forest edge, secondary growth, scrub and cultivation borders. DISTRIBUTION: Winter visitor in SW China; vagrant in NW Thailand.

7 VINACEOUS ROSEFINCH *Carpodacus vinaceus* 13–16cm FIELD NOTES: Shows distinct whitish tips to tertials. Forages on the ground, in dense vegetation or in low bushes, usually in pairs or small parties. The slightly darker race *C. v. formosanus*, which is sometimes considered a full species, occurs in Taiwan. VOICE: A simple *pee-dee – be – do-do*; calls include a whiplash-like *pwit* or *zieh*, a high *tip* and a low *pink* or *zick.* HABITAT: Moist mixed or bamboo forests and scrubby open hillsides. DISTRIBUTION: Resident in Taiwan, W China and N, E Myanmar.

2b *roseatus*

174 ROSEFINCHES; CRIMSON-BROWED FINCH

1 DARK-RUMPED ROSEFINCH *Carpodacus edwardsii* 16–17cm FIELD NOTES: Skulking, forages on the ground under bushes. Usually alone or in small parties; post breeding may occur in larger flocks. Paler chinned than similar Vinaceous Rosefinch. VOICE: Calls include a metallic *twink* and a rasping *che-wee*. HABITAT: Undergrowth in montane and sub-montane juniper, rhododendron, birch and silver fir forests, bamboo clumps, secondary growth, scrub and thickets. DISTRIBUTION: Resident in SW, W China and N Myanmar.

2 SHARPE'S ROSEFINCH *Carpodacus verreauxii* 17–20cm FIELD NOTES: Generally shy and retiring, although regularly perches prominently on bush tops; forages on the ground. VOICE: Usually silent, but occasionally gives a *chirp* or an upslurred *churr-weee*. HABITAT: High elevation scrub and bushes, descends to bamboo thickets, bushes and mixed forests in winter. DISTRIBUTION: Resident in SW China and N, E Myanmar.

3 PALLAS'S ROSEFINCH *Carpodacus roseus* 16–18cm FIELD NOTES: Forages in trees, bushes or on the ground, usually in large flocks. VOICE: Calls include a short *fee*, a soft *tsiiin*, a *chee-chee*, a loud metallic *tsuiii* and a bunting-like *dzih* and *chek-chek*. HABITAT: Open deciduous woods, thickets with bushy undergrowth, dwarf pines and aspens along river valleys, cultivations and gardens. DISTRIBUTION: Winter visitor to NE China.

4 WHITE-BROWED ROSEFINCH *Carpodacus thura* 17–18cm FIELD NOTES: Forages on the ground, usually in pairs or small parties, occasionally mixes with other rosefinches or grosbeaks. Females of *C. t. femininus* lack the buff wash on breast. VOICE: A series of loud, short whistles followed by 3–4 short warbled notes ending with several longer whistles, transcribed as *drit-drit-drit-drit quip-quip-quip-quip dreep-dreep-dreep-dreep* or a shorter *pew-pew-pew chit-chit naaar naar nah nah nah*, the later song given by *C. t. femininus*. Calls include a buzzing *deep-deep deep-de-de-de-de*, a bleating *veh ve ve ve ve ve ve*, a rapid piping and a loud *pwit-pwit*. HABITAT: High-altitude open forest or forest edge, rhododendron, juniper and bamboo scrub above the treeline; winters on open hillsides with bushes and scrub. DISTRIBUTION: Resident in mountains of extreme SW China.

5 RED-BREASTED ROSEFINCH (RED-FRONTED ROSEFINCH) *Carpodacus puniceus* 20cm FIELD NOTES: Forages on the ground among boulders, bushes or by melting snow, alone, in pairs or small parties. VOICE: A short *twiddle-le-de* with various melodious down-slurred whistles; calls include a loud, cheery *are-you-quite-ready*, cat-like *maaau* and a *chirp* or *jeelp* uttered in flight. HABITAT: High-altitude boulderfields, rocky screes and slopes. DISTRIBUTION: Resident in SW, W China.

6 THREE-BANDED ROSEFINCH *Carpodacus trifasciatus* 17–20cm FIELD NOTES: Lethargic, often sits immobile for long periods hidden in bushes or trees; forages on the ground or in bushes, usually in pairs or small groups. VOICE: Generally silent. HABITAT: Undergrowth and thickets in conifer forest; in winter also in cultivation edge, orchards, hedges and open fields. DISTRIBUTION: Resident in SW China.

7 CRIMSON-BROWED FINCH (RED-HEADED FINCH) *Carpodacus subhimachalus* 19–20cm FIELD NOTES: Unobtrusive, forages on the ground or in bushes and low trees; usually in pairs or small parties. VOICE: A bright variable warble, which may include a *ter-ter-ter* or *terp terp tee* phrase; call is a sparrow-like *chirp*. HABITAT: Dense high-altitude scrub; winters in thick undergrowth in forests. DISTRIBUTION: Resident in SW, W China and N Myanmar.

175 HAWFINCH; GROSBEAKS

1 HAWFINCH *Coccothraustes coccothraustes* 16–18cm FIELD NOTES: Wary; forages in trees or on the ground below trees, often in very large flocks. Female slightly duller. VOICE: An abrupt *tick* or *tzik* and a thin *seep* or *sree*. HABITAT: Deciduous and mixed woodlands, orchards, parks and open areas with bushes. DISTRIBUTION: Winter visitor in N, E, SW China and Taiwan.

2 YELLOW-BILLED GROSBEAK (CHINESE GROSBEAK) *Eophona migratoria* 15–8cm FIELD NOTES: Forages in trees, bushes and on the ground; often remains concealed in foliage or in upper branches Generally in pairs with larger parties post breeding. VOICE: A loud series of whistles, transcribed as *chee chee choree kirichoo*. Call is a loud *tek-tek*. HABITAT: Edges and clearings in mixed or deciduous forests, wooded hills, river valleys, marsh edge, cultivations, orchards, parks and gardens. DISTRIBUTION: Breeds in C, N China; winters in S, E China, Taiwan; vagrant in N Myanmar, NE Thailand, N Laos and N Vietnam.

3 JAPANESE GROSBEAK *Eophona personata* 23cm FIELD NOTES: Best located by calls. Forages in the foliage of the canopy, occasionally lower down, in bushes. Usually seen in pairs or small flocks. VOICE: Calls include a short, hard *tak tak* and a high-pitched *kik* or *kick* uttered by foraging or flying birds. HABITAT: Mixed and deciduous forests and woodlands, well-wooded hills and river valleys, cultivation edge, parks and gardens. DISTRIBUTION: Winter visitor in S, E China.

4 SPOT-WINGED GROSBEAK *Mycerobas melanozanthos* 22–23cm FIELD NOTES: Shy, usually sits and forages in treetops, also feeds low down or on the ground. Generally in pairs or in sizable flocks post breeding. VOICE: A loud, melodious *tew-tew – teeeu*, also some mellow *tyop-tiu* or *tyu-tio* whistles. Call is a rattling *krrr* or *charrarauk*, said to sound like the shaking of a matchbox containing only a few matches; feeding flocks keep up a constant cackling. HABITAT: Broadleaved evergreen forest, mixed broadleaved and coniferous forest, forest edge and secondary growth. DISTRIBUTION: Resident in SW, W China, W, N, E Myanmar, NW Thailand, N Laos and N Vietnam.

5 COLLARED GROSBEAK *Mycerobas affinis* 22–24cm FIELD NOTES: Forages in tree canopy, in bushes or low vegetation and also on the ground. Usually in pairs or small loose parties, with larger flocks post breeding. VOICE: A loud, clear, piping *ti-di-li-ti-di-li-umm*, also a constantly repeated creaky phrase, interspersed with musical bulbul-like notes; calls include a rapid, mellow *pip-pip-pip-pip-pip-pip-ugh* and a sharp *kurr* given when alarmed. HABITAT: Broadleaved evergreen and mixed broadleaved and conifer forest, forest edge and secondary growth. DISTRIBUTION: Resident in SW China and N Myanmar; vagrant in NW Thailand.

6 WHITE-WINGED GROSBEAK *Mycerobas carnipes* 22–24cm FIELD NOTES: Forages mainly in the treetops, also in scrub and undergrowth. Generally in pairs or small groups with larger flocks post breeding. VOICE: A piping *add-a-dit – un-di-di-di-dit* or *dja-dji-dji-dju*. Calls include a nasal *shwenk* or *chwenk*, a strident *wit* or *wet*, a grating *goink* and a rapid, harsh *chet-et-et-et*. HABITAT: Dwarf juniper forest above the treeline, mixed juniper and fir near the treeline; at lower elevations mixed fir, juniper and rhododendron forest or fir forest with bamboo undergrowth. DISTRIBUTION: Resident in SW China and N Myanmar.

176 BUNTINGS

1 CRESTED BUNTING *Emberiza lathami* 16–17cm FIELD NOTES: Forages on the ground, regularly by roadsides, tracks and near cereal crops. Frequently perches on rocks or bushes. Sings from a prominent perch, such as a treetop, rock or overhead wire. In winter forms loose small flocks. VOICE: Begins with a few subdued notes followed by low, mellow notes and finishing with 2–3 descending notes, transcribed as *tzit dzit dzit see-see-suee* or similar. Call is a soft *tip* or *tup*, which is uttered more emphatically in flight. HABITAT: Dry rocky or grassy hillsides and terraced cultivation with rocky outcrops and scattered bushes. DISTRIBUTION: Resident in China, Myanmar, N, C Laos and N Vietnam; winter visitor in W, NW Thailand.

2 SLATY BUNTING *Emberiza siemsseni* 13cm FIELD NOTES: Forages on the ground, often keeping in cover; forms small parties post breeding. VOICE: Variable, including a high-pitched *zii-ziiiu-tzitzitzitzi hee, a ze-ze-ze-ze swee twiitwit* and a *tze-tze-tze teez teez teez.* Call is a sharp *zick,* often repeated. HABITAT: Breeds in subtropical valley forests in hills and mountains; favours bamboo thickets in secondary forest and scrubby cover of degraded forest. Descends to foothills in winter where often seen in parks and around villages. DISTRIBUTION: Breeds locally in W, NE China; winters in NW, SW, SE, NE China.

3 CHESTNUT-EARED BUNTING *Emberiza fucata* 16cm FIELD NOTES: Forages on the ground, usually in pairs or small parties; post breeding often roosts in marshy reedbeds. VOICE: A rapid, twittering *zwee-zwizewezwizizi-triip-triip* or similar. Calls include an explosive *pzick,* a high-pitched *zii* or *zii-zii* and a lower-pitched *chutt.* HABITAT: Hillsides with bushes and scrub, especially near rivers. In winter favours wet stubble, marshes, grassland and bushes. DISTRIBUTION: Resident in SW, NE China; winters in China, Myanmar, W, NE, NW Thailand, Laos, C, N Vietnam. Vagrant further south.

4 PINE BUNTING *Emberiza leucocephalos* 16–18cm FIELD NOTES: Forages on the ground, usually in small to large flocks, often in the company of other buntings and finches. Non-breeding males have head pattern and back obscured with pale fringes. VOICE: Calls include a metallic *tsit,* a thin *see* and a clicking *tit-tit-tit-tit.* HABITAT: Grassy slopes with bushes, fallow and stubble fields. DISTRIBUTION: Possibly winters in NW China; vagrant, recorded in NE, SE China.

5 TRISTRAM'S BUNTING *Emberiza tristrami* 15cm FIELD NOTES: Forages on the forest floor, usually in small flocks. VOICE: Calls with an explosive *tzick.* HABITAT: Undergrowth in forest, forest edge and secondary growth. DISTRIBUTION: Winter visitor in S China and NW Thailand, and rarely to N Laos and N Vietnam.

6 MEADOW BUNTING *Emberiza cioides* 16cm FIELD NOTES: Forages mainly on the ground, hopping with a hunched posture. Winter flocks may include other buntings and finches, often encountered at water-holes in the early morning or late afternoon. Sings from a bush top or other elevated perch. VOICE: A sort, simple *chi-hu chee-tsweet-tsweet-tuee;* calls with a thin, repeated *zit zit zit.* HABITAT: Lightly wooded rolling hills and mountain foothills; also shrub thickets. DISTRIBUTION: Resident in northern China; vagrant in SE China and Taiwan.

7 GODLEWSKI'S BUNTING *Emberiza godlewskii* 17cm FIELD NOTES: Forages mainly on the ground; small winter flocks are occasionally accompanied by rosefinches. Sings from the top of a rock or tree. VOICE: A monotonous series of high-pitched notes, e.g. *chit-chit-chu-chitu-tsi-chitu-chu-chitrru* or *chit-situ-chit-tsi-situ-chi…* Calls include a thin, drawn-out *tzii* and a hard *pett pett.* HABITAT: Bushy and rocky slopes in hills and mountains, often near forests, also in farmland and cultivated fields in winter. DISTRIBUTION: Resident in SW, W China; winters in W China and N, E Myanmar.

177 BUNTINGS

1 YELLOW-BREASTED BUNTING *Emberiza aureola* 15cm FIELD NOTES: Forages on the ground, when disturbed retreats to sit in nearby bushes or trees; usually in flocks, sometimes with 200 or so individuals. Non-breeding males have back and face pattern obscured by pale feather edges. Race *E. a. ornata* with a black forecrown winters in SE China. VOICE: A sweet, twittering; calls include a sharp *tsik* and an abrupt *chup* when flushed. HABITAT: Cultivations, farmland hedgerows, paddyfields, stubble fields, grasslands, reedbeds, scrub and gardens. DISTRIBUTION: Winter visitor in Taiwan, SE China, Hainan and throughout the south, except C Vietnam.

2 YELLOW-THROATED BUNTING *Emberiza elegans* 15cm FIELD NOTES: Forages on the ground; forms small winter flocks, usually of up to 25, larger parties occur on migration. VOICE: A long, monotonous twitter, e.g. *tswit tsu ri tu tswee witt tsuri weee dee tswit tsuri tu…* calls is a sharp *tzik*. HABITAT: Deciduous and mixed deciduous-conifer forest, forest edge and clearings, in winter also in orchards and riverside vegetation. DISTRIBUTION: Resident in SW, W China; winter visitor in Taiwan, SW, C, E China and possibly N Myanmar.

3 RED-HEADED BUNTING *Emberiza bruniceps* 16cm FIELD NOTES: Actions and habits similar to Black-headed Bunting. Male head pattern obscured by pale fringes in winter. VOICE: Song similar to that of Black-headed Bunting; calls include a *chip*, a *chuupp*, a *zrit*, a sharp *tsit* and a series of clicks; all calls very similar to those of Black-headed Bunting. HABITAT: Cereal cultivations. DISTRIBUTION: Possible vagrant, recorded from SE China (Hong Kong).

4 BLACK-HEADED BUNTING *Emberiza melanocephala* 16–18cm FIELD NOTES: Forages mainly on the ground, retreats into nearby bushes or trees when disturbed; often in large flocks in the company of Red-headed Buntings. In winter head and back colours of male are obscured by pale fringes. VOICE: A low-pitched *zrit zrit srutt-sruttsutteri-sutt sutterrih* or similar; calls include a *cheep* or *chlip*, a *dzuu* and a *chuhp* uttered in flight. HABITAT: Cereal cultivations, roosts in thickets. DISTRIBUTION: Vagrant recorded in E, SE, China, S Thailand, N Laos and Singapore.

5 CHESTNUT BUNTING *Emberiza rutila* 14cm FIELD NOTES: Forages on the ground, retreats into nearby bushes or trees when disturbed; usually in small flocks. Non breeding adults have chestnut areas obscured by variable amounts of pale scaling. VOICE: A high-pitched *wiie-wiie-wiie tzree-tzrree-tzrree zizizitt…* calls include a *zick* and a thin, high *teseep*. HABITAT: Open forest, woodland edge and clearings, cultivations and rice stubbles. DISTRIBUTION: Winter visitor in S, E China, Myanmar (except Tenasserim), W, NW, NE Thailand, N, C Laos and Vietnam.

6 LITTLE BUNTING *Emberiza pusilla* 12–14cm FIELD NOTES: Forages on the ground and low in bushes and trees, often in the company of other seed-eaters. VOICE: A metallic *zree zree zree tsutsutsutsutzriiitu, tzru tzru tzru zee-zee-zee-zee zriiiiiru* or similar; calls include a hard *tzik* or *pwick*. HABITAT: Open and semi-open areas, including forest edge, scrubby hillsides, crop, stubble and paddyfields, orchards and gardens. DISTRIBUTION: Winter visitor in China, Taiwan, Myanmar, NW, NE Thailand, N, C Laos and N Vietnam.

7 RUSTIC BUNTING *Emberiza rustica* 13–15cm FIELD NOTES: Forages on the ground and in low vegetation, often in very large flocks. VOICE: A hurried, melodious, mellow *dudeleu-dewee-deweea-weeu* or similar; calls include a sharp *tzik* and a high-pitched *tsiee* given in alarm. HABITAT: Dry forest and woodland, riverine scrub, reedbeds, rank field-side vegetation, open areas and urban parks. DISTRIBUTION: Winter visitor in C, NE China.

178 BUNTINGS

1 BLACK-FACED BUNTING *Emberiza spodocephala* 15cm FIELD NOTES: Forages mainly on the ground. Face pattern of non breeding males partly obscured by pale fringes. *E. s. personata* (1b) occasionally occurs on coasts of E, S China; *E. s. sordida* (1c) breeds in SW, W, NW China; winters N, W Myanmar, NW Thailand, N Laos and C, N Vietnam. VOICE: A variable series of ringing trills and chirps; calls include a sharp *tzit* or *tzii*. HABITAT: Breeds in shrubby and tall dense grass areas interspersed with trees along watercourses and floodplains, mixed and moist conifer forest, open areas in sparse woodland and forest edge; in winter also in scrub, grass and cultivations, often near water. DISTRIBUTION: Breeds in SW, W NW China; winters in much of China away from western breeding areas, Hainan, Taiwan, W, N Myanmar, NW Thailand, N Laos and C, N Vietnam.

2 JAPANESE YELLOW BUNTING (YELLOW BUNTING) *Emberiza sulphurata* 13–14cm FIELD NOTES: Forages on the ground, usually in small flocks. VOICE: Various alternating twittering phrases; call is a short metallic *tsip*. HABITAT: Grasslands, weedy and bushy areas. DISTRIBUTION: Winter visitor in SE China and Taiwan.

3 REED BUNTING (COMMON REED BUNTING) *Emberiza schoeniclus* 14–17cm FIELD NOTES: Forages on the ground and in low vegetation, regularly perches and feeds on reed stems; usually found in pairs or small parties. Non breeding male head pattern is browner with pale scaling. Large pale race *E. s. pyrrhuloides* (3b) is a possible vagrant in extreme W China. VOICE: A short, simple *zrit-zreet-zreet-zreet-zritt-zriuuu* or similar; calls include a plaintive *seeoo* and a harsh *brzee*. HABITAT: Reedbeds, scrub, bushes and fields. DISTRIBUTION: Winter visitor in E China; vagrant in Taiwan, SE China and possibly W China.

4 PALLAS'S REED BUNTING (PALLAS'S BUNTING) *Emberiza pallasi* 14cm FIELD NOTES: Forages on the ground, on grass-heads and in bushes, usually in large flocks mixed with other buntings and finches. VOICE: A simple, monotonous *chi chi chi chi chi chi, srri srri srri srri srri srri srri* or similar; calls include a sparrow-like *chleep* or *tsilip* and a slurred *dziu*. HABITAT: Reedbeds, grassy fields, paddyfields, arable land and shrubs near watercourses. DISTRIBUTION: Winter visitor in E, NE China; vagrant, recorded in SE china, Taiwan and C Myanmar.

5 JAPANESE REED BUNTING (OCHRE-RUMPED BUNTING) *Emberiza yessoensis* 14–15cm FIELD NOTES: Actions similar to Reed Bunting. VOICE: A brief twittering; calls include a short *tick* and a *bziu* given in flight. HABITAT: Coastal marshes, open cultivations and agricultural fields near water. DISTRIBUTION: Winter visitor in NE China; vagrant in SE China (Hong Kong).

6 GREY BUNTING *Emberiza variabilis* 14–17cm FIELD NOTES: Secretive, forages on the ground, alone or in pairs. VOICE: A simple, slow *swee swee chi chi chi, hsuuu twis-twis-twis* or *hsuuu tsisisisisis*; calls with a sharp *tzii*. HABITAT: Dense vegetation, usually in evergreen forest undergrowth, near streams; also in open cultivations, parks and gardens. DISTRIBUTION: Vagrant, recorded in NE China and Taiwan.

7 LAPLAND BUNTING (LAPLAND LONGSPUR) *Calcarius lapponicus* 15–17cm FIELD NOTES: Forages on or near the ground, usually in small to large flocks; often mixes with other buntings, finches and larks. Winter males much like breeding female. VOICE: A short, jangling warble; calls include a high-pitched *jeeb*, a short clear *chu* or *tew* and a dry rattled *prrt*. HABITAT: Pastures, stubble fields and coastal marshes. DISTRIBUTION: Winter visitor to northern China.

1b *personata*

1c *sordida*

FURTHER READING

Ali, S. & Ripley, S. D. (1987 2nd edn) *Compact Handbook of the Birds of India and Pakistan.* Oxford University Press.

Alström, P. & Mild, K. (2003) *Pipits and Wagtails of Europe, Asia and North America.* Helm.

Baker, K. (1997) *Warblers of Europe, Asia and North Africa.* Helm.

Beaman, M. & Madge, S. (1998) *The Handbook of Bird Identification for Europe and the Western Palearctic.* Helm.

Byers, C., Olsson, U. & Curson, J. (1995) *Buntings and Sparrows.* Helm.

Cheke, R. A., Mann, C. F. & Allen, R. (2001) *Sunbirds: A Guide to the Sunbirds, Flowerpeckers, Spiderhunters and Sugarbirds of the World.* Helm.

Clement, P., Harris, A. & Davis, J. (1993) *Finches and Sparrows.* Helm.

Clement, P. & Hathway, R. (2000) *Thrushes.* Helm.

Cramp, S., Simmons, K. E. L. & Perrins, C. M. (ed.) (1977–94) *The Birds of the Western Palearctic.* Vol. 1–9. Oxford University Press.

Dickinson, E. C. (ed.) (2003) *The Howard and Moore Complete Checklist of the Birds of the World.* Helm.

Feare, C. & Craig, A. (1998) *Starlings and Mynas.* Helm.

Fry, C. H., Fry, K. & Harris, A. (1992) *Kingfishers, Bee-eaters and Rollers.* Helm.

Grimmett, R., Inskipp, C. & Inskipp, T. (2011) *Birds of the Indian Subcontinent.* Helm.

Hancock, J. & Elliott, H. (1978) *Herons of the World.* London Editions.

Hancock, J., Kushlan, J. A. & Kahl, M. P. (1992) *Storks, Ibises and Spoonbills of the World.* Academic Press.

Harrison, P. (1983 & updates) *Seabirds; an Identification Guide.* Helm.

Harrop, S. & Quinn, D. (1996) *Tits, Nuthatches and Treecreepers.* Helm.

Hayman, P., Marchant, A. J. & Prater, A. H. (1986) *Shorebirds: An Identification Guide to the Waders of the World.* Helm.

del Hoyo, J., Elliott, A. & Sargatal, J. (eds) (1992–2011) *Handbook of the Birds of the World.* Vol. 1–16. Lynx.

Lefranc, N. & Worfolk, T. (1997) *Shrikes; A Guide to the Shrikes of the World.* Pica Press.

MacKinnon, J. & Phillipps, K. (2000) *A Field Guide to the Birds of China.* Oxford University Press.

Madge, S. & Burn, H. (1988) *Wildfowl: An Identification Guide to the Ducks, Geese and Swans of the World.* Helm.

Madge, S. & Burn, H. (1991) *Crows and Jays.* Helm.

Madge, S., McGowan, P. (2002) *Pheasants, Partridges and Grouse. Including Buttonquails, Sandgrouse and Allies.* Helm.

Mullarney, K., Svensson, L., Zetterström, D. & Grant, P. J. (1999) *Collins Bird Guide.* HarperCollins.

Olney D. & Scofield, P. (2007) *Albatrosses. Petrels and Shearwaters of the World.* Helm.

Olsen, K. M. & Larsson, H. (2004) *Gulls of Europe, Asia and North America.* Helm.

Olsen, K. M. & Larsson, H. (1997) *Skuas and Jaegers: A Guide to Skuas and Jaegers of the World.* Pica Press.

Olsen, K. M. & Larsson, H. (1995) *Terns of Europe and North America.* Helm.

Porter, R. F., Christensen, S. & Schiermacker-Hansen, P. (1996) *Birds of the Middle East.* Helm.

Porter, R. F., Willis, I., Christensen, S. & Neilsen, B. P. (1981 3rd edn) *Flight Identification of European Raptors.* Poyser.

Robson, C. (2000) *A Field Guide to the Birds of South-east Asia.* New Holland.

Robson, C. (2002) *A Field Guide to the Birds of Thailand.* New Holland

Taylor, B. & van Perlo, B. (1998) *Rails: A Guide to the Rails Crakes, Gallinules and Coots of the World.* Pica Press.

Turner, A. & Rose, C. (1989) *Swallows and Martins of the World.* Helm.

Vinicombe, K., Harris, A. & Tucker, L. (1989) *Bird Identification.* MacMillan.

Voous, K. H. (1988) *Owls of the Northern Hemisphere.* Collins.

Winkler, H., Christie, D. A. & Nurney, D. (1995) *Woodpeckers: A Guide to the Woodpeckers, Piculets and Wrynecks of the World.* Pica Press.

SPECIES DISTRIBUTION MAPS

Key to Maps

Breeding season

Non-breeding season

Resident season

Vagrants and most introduced species are not included in the distribution maps section. Species that spend most of their time at sea, occur only on islands, are very rare or have a very limited distribution are also not included in this section. Maps were compiled primarily using information from Robson (2002), Birdlife.org, and The Cornell Lab of Ornithology's ebird.org website that shows actual sightings of species across the region.

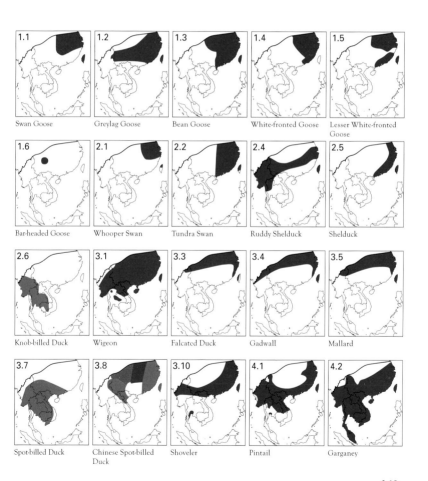

1.1 Swan Goose	1.2 Greylag Goose	1.3 Bean Goose	1.4 White-fronted Goose	1.5 Lesser White-fronted Goose
1.6 Bar-headed Goose	2.1 Whooper Swan	2.2 Tundra Swan	2.4 Ruddy Shelduck	2.5 Shelduck
2.6 Knob-billed Duck	3.1 Wigeon	3.3 Falcated Duck	3.4 Gadwall	3.5 Mallard
3.7 Spot-billed Duck	3.8 Chinese Spot-billed Duck	3.10 Shoveler	4.1 Pintail	4.2 Garganey

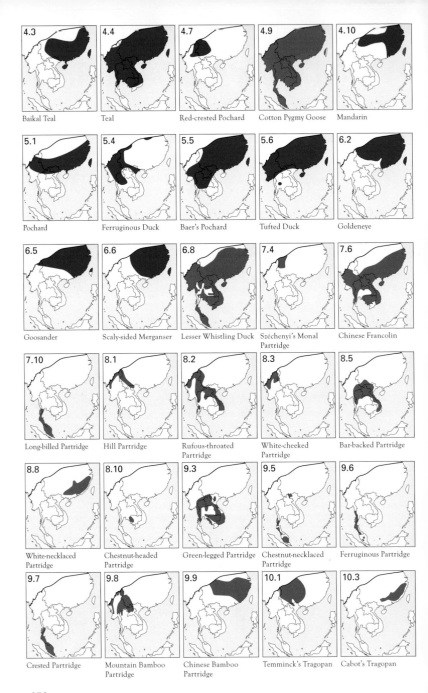

4.3 Baikal Teal	**4.4** Teal	**4.7** Red-crested Pochard	**4.9** Cotton Pygmy Goose	**4.10** Mandarin
5.1 Pochard	**5.4** Ferruginous Duck	**5.5** Baer's Pochard	**5.6** Tufted Duck	**6.2** Goldeneye
6.5 Goosander	**6.6** Scaly-sided Merganser	**6.8** Lesser Whistling Duck	**7.4** Széchenyi's Monal Partridge	**7.6** Chinese Francolin
7.10 Long-billed Partridge	**8.1** Hill Partridge	**8.2** Rufous-throated Partridge	**8.3** White-cheeked Partridge	**8.5** Bar-backed Partridge
8.8 White-necklaced Partridge	**8.10** Chestnut-headed Partridge	**9.3** Green-legged Partridge	**9.5** Chestnut-necklaced Partridge	**9.6** Ferruginous Partridge
9.7 Crested Partridge	**9.8** Mountain Bamboo Partridge	**9.9** Chinese Bamboo Partridge	**10.1** Temminck's Tragopan	**10.3** Cabot's Tragopan

370

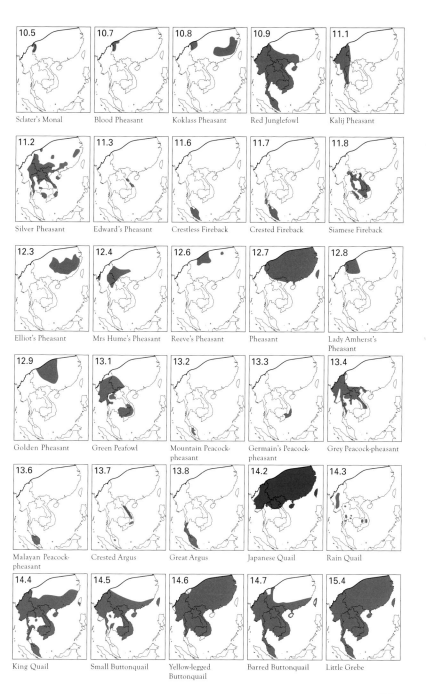

10.5 Sclater's Monal

10.7 Blood Pheasant

10.8 Koklass Pheasant

10.9 Red Junglefowl

11.1 Kalij Pheasant

11.2 Silver Pheasant

11.3 Edward's Pheasant

11.6 Crestless Fireback

11.7 Crested Fireback

11.8 Siamese Fireback

12.3 Elliot's Pheasant

12.4 Mrs Hume's Pheasant

12.6 Reeve's Pheasant

12.7 Pheasant

12.8 Lady Amherst's Pheasant

12.9 Golden Pheasant

13.1 Green Peafowl

13.2 Mountain Peacock-pheasant

13.3 Germain's Peacock-pheasant

13.4 Grey Peacock-pheasant

13.6 Malayan Peacock-pheasant

13.7 Crested Argus

13.8 Great Argus

14.2 Japanese Quail

14.3 Rain Quail

14.4 King Quail

14.5 Small Buttonquail

14.6 Yellow-legged Buttonquail

14.7 Barred Buttonquail

15.4 Little Grebe

371

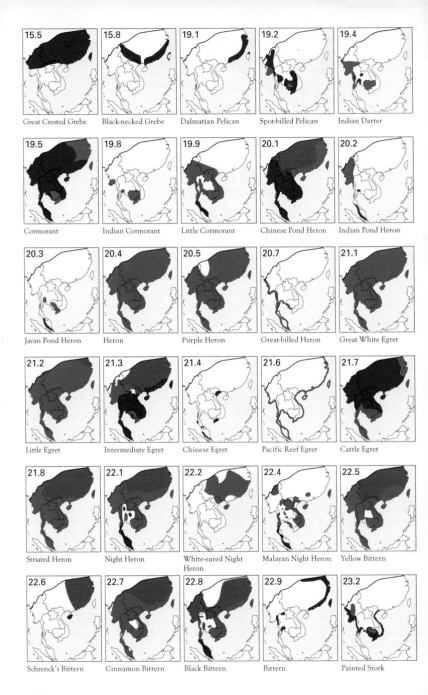

15.5 Great Crested Grebe	15.8 Black-necked Grebe	19.1 Dalmatian Pelican	19.2 Spot-billed Pelican	19.4 Indian Darter
19.5 Cormorant	19.8 Indian Cormorant	19.9 Little Cormorant	20.1 Chinese Pond Heron	20.2 Indian Pond Heron
20.3 Javan Pond Heron	20.4 Heron	20.5 Purple Heron	20.7 Great-billed Heron	21.1 Great White Egret
21.2 Little Egret	21.3 Intermediate Egret	21.4 Chinese Egret	21.6 Pacific Reef Egret	21.7 Cattle Egret
21.8 Striated Heron	22.1 Night Heron	22.2 White-eared Night Heron	22.4 Malayan Night Heron	22.5 Yellow Bittern
22.6 Schrenck's Bittern	22.7 Cinnamon Bittern	22.8 Black Bittern	22.9 Bittern	23.2 Painted Stork

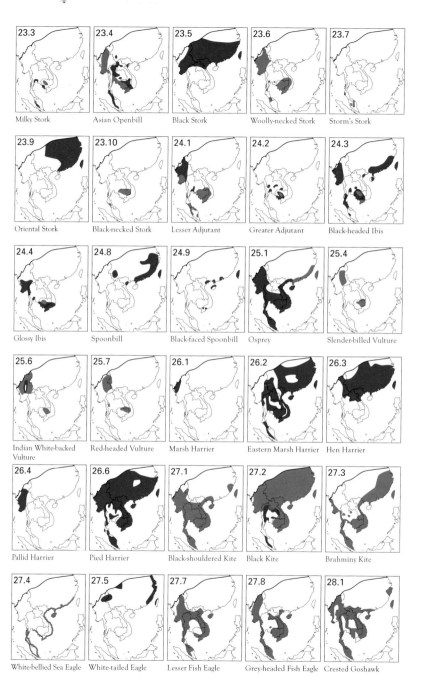

23.3 Milky Stork	23.4 Asian Openbill	23.5 Black Stork	23.6 Woolly-necked Stork	23.7 Storm's Stork
23.9 Oriental Stork	23.10 Black-necked Stork	24.1 Lesser Adjutant	24.2 Greater Adjutant	24.3 Black-headed Ibis
24.4 Glossy Ibis	24.8 Spoonbill	24.9 Black-faced Spoonbill	25.1 Osprey	25.4 Slender-billed Vulture
25.6 Indian White-backed Vulture	25.7 Red-headed Vulture	26.1 Marsh Harrier	26.2 Eastern Marsh Harrier	26.3 Hen Harrier
26.4 Pallid Harrier	26.6 Pied Harrier	27.1 Black-shouldered Kite	27.2 Black Kite	27.3 Brahminy Kite
27.4 White-bellied Sea Eagle	27.5 White-tailed Eagle	27.7 Lesser Fish Eagle	27.8 Grey-headed Fish Eagle	28.1 Crested Goshawk

373

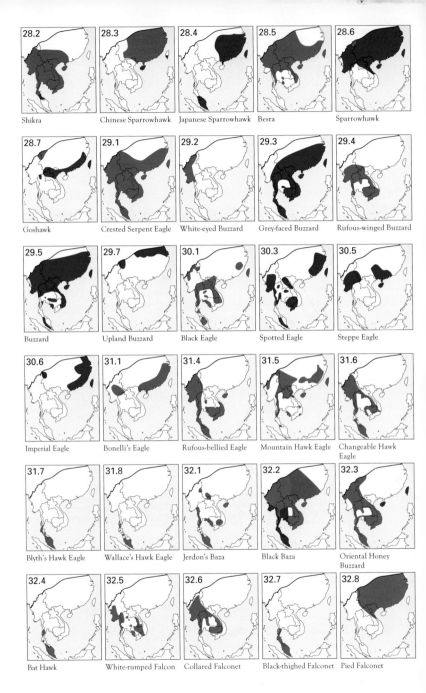

28.2 Shikra	28.3 Chinese Sparrowhawk	28.4 Japanese Sparrowhawk	28.5 Besra	28.6 Sparrowhawk
28.7 Goshawk	29.1 Crested Serpent Eagle	29.2 White-eyed Buzzard	29.3 Grey-faced Buzzard	29.4 Rufous-winged Buzzard
29.5 Buzzard	29.7 Upland Buzzard	30.1 Black Eagle	30.3 Spotted Eagle	30.5 Steppe Eagle
30.6 Imperial Eagle	31.1 Bonelli's Eagle	31.4 Rufous-bellied Eagle	31.5 Mountain Hawk Eagle	31.6 Changeable Hawk Eagle
31.7 Blyth's Hawk Eagle	31.8 Wallace's Hawk Eagle	32.1 Jerdon's Baza	32.2 Black Baza	32.3 Oriental Honey Buzzard
32.4 Bat Hawk	32.5 White-rumped Falcon	32.6 Collared Falconet	32.7 Black-thighed Falconet	32.8 Pied Falconet

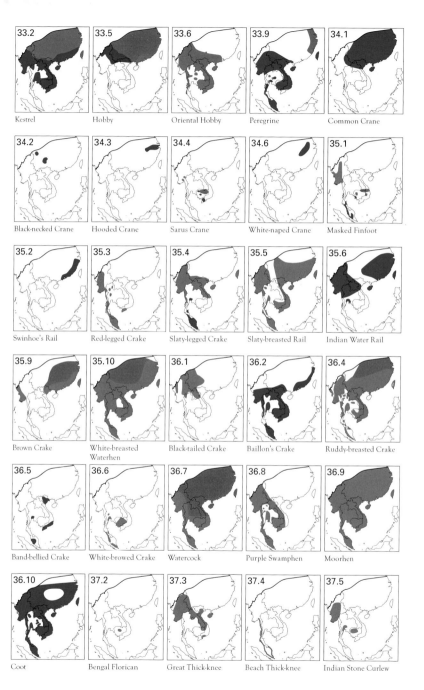

33.2 Kestrel	33.5 Hobby	33.6 Oriental Hobby	33.9 Peregrine	34.1 Common Crane
34.2 Black-necked Crane	34.3 Hooded Crane	34.4 Sarus Crane	34.6 White-naped Crane	35.1 Masked Finfoot
35.2 Swinhoe's Rail	35.3 Red-legged Crake	35.4 Slaty-legged Crake	35.5 Slaty-breasted Rail	35.6 Indian Water Rail
35.9 Brown Crake	35.10 White-breasted Waterhen	36.1 Black-tailed Crake	36.2 Baillon's Crake	36.4 Ruddy-breasted Crake
36.5 Band-bellied Crake	36.6 White-browed Crake	36.7 Watercock	36.8 Purple Swamphen	36.9 Moorhen
36.10 Coot	37.2 Bengal Florican	37.3 Great Thick-knee	37.4 Beach Thick-knee	37.5 Indian Stone Curlew

375

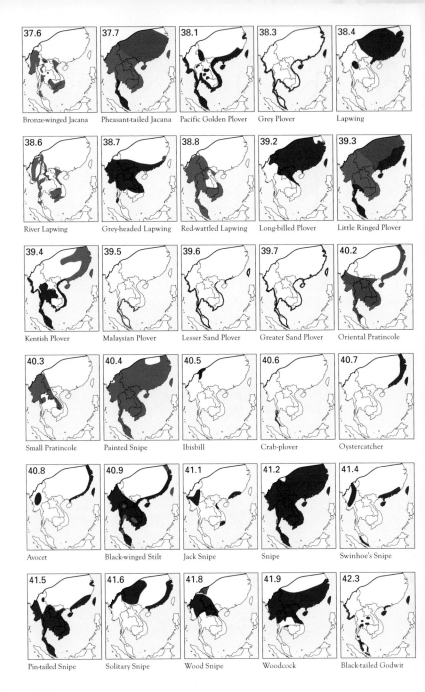

37.6 Bronze-winged Jacana	37.7 Pheasant-tailed Jacana	38.1 Pacific Golden Plover	38.3 Grey Plover	38.4 Lapwing
38.6 River Lapwing	38.7 Grey-headed Lapwing	38.8 Red-wattled Lapwing	39.2 Long-billed Plover	39.3 Little Ringed Plover
39.4 Kentish Plover	39.5 Malaysian Plover	39.6 Lesser Sand Plover	39.7 Greater Sand Plover	40.2 Oriental Pratincole
40.3 Small Pratincole	40.4 Painted Snipe	40.5 Ibisbill	40.6 Crab-plover	40.7 Oystercatcher
40.8 Avocet	40.9 Black-winged Stilt	41.1 Jack Snipe	41.2 Snipe	41.4 Swinhoe's Snipe
41.5 Pin-tailed Snipe	41.6 Solitary Snipe	41.8 Wood Snipe	41.9 Woodcock	42.3 Black-tailed Godwit

376

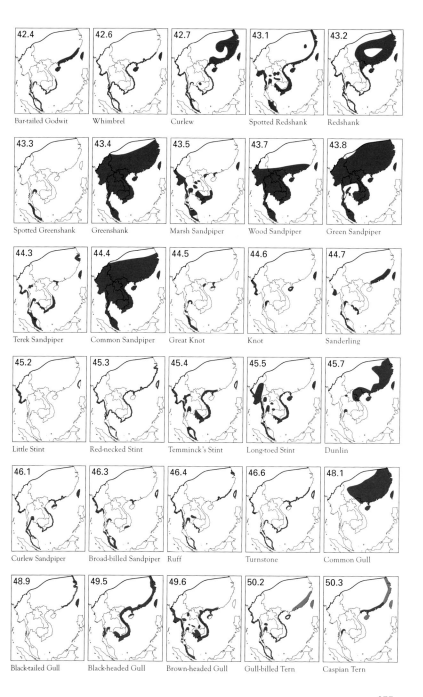

| 42.4 Bar-tailed Godwit | 42.6 Whimbrel | 42.7 Curlew | 43.1 Spotted Redshank | 43.2 Redshank |

| 43.3 Spotted Greenshank | 43.4 Greenshank | 43.5 Marsh Sandpiper | 43.7 Wood Sandpiper | 43.8 Green Sandpiper |

| 44.3 Terek Sandpiper | 44.4 Common Sandpiper | 44.5 Great Knot | 44.6 Knot | 44.7 Sanderling |

| 45.2 Little Stint | 45.3 Red-necked Stint | 45.4 Temminck's Stint | 45.5 Long-toed Stint | 45.7 Dunlin |

| 46.1 Curlew Sandpiper | 46.3 Broad-billed Sandpiper | 46.4 Ruff | 46.6 Turnstone | 48.1 Common Gull |

| 48.9 Black-tailed Gull | 49.5 Black-headed Gull | 49.6 Brown-headed Gull | 50.2 Gull-billed Tern | 50.3 Caspian Tern |

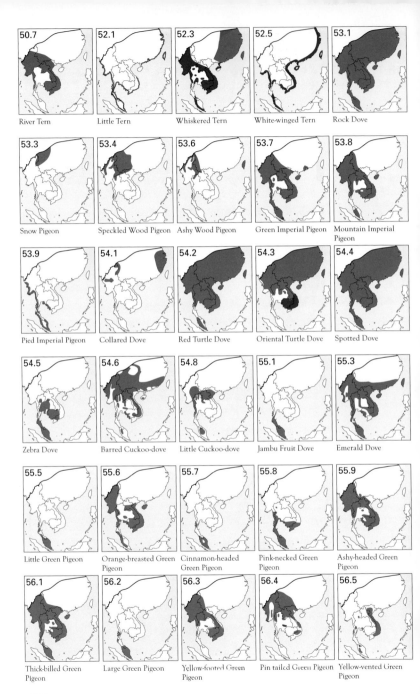

50.7 River Tern	52.1 Little Tern	52.3 Whiskered Tern	52.5 White-winged Tern	53.1 Rock Dove
53.3 Snow Pigeon	53.4 Speckled Wood Pigeon	53.6 Ashy Wood Pigeon	53.7 Green Imperial Pigeon	53.8 Mountain Imperial Pigeon
53.9 Pied Imperial Pigeon	54.1 Collared Dove	54.2 Red Turtle Dove	54.3 Oriental Turtle Dove	54.4 Spotted Dove
54.5 Zebra Dove	54.6 Barred Cuckoo-dove	54.8 Little Cuckoo-dove	55.1 Jambu Fruit Dove	55.3 Emerald Dove
55.5 Little Green Pigeon	55.6 Orange-breasted Green Pigeon	55.7 Cinnamon-headed Green Pigeon	55.8 Pink-necked Green Pigeon	55.9 Ashy-headed Green Pigeon
56.1 Thick-billed Green Pigeon	56.2 Large Green Pigeon	56.3 Yellow-footed Green Pigeon	56.4 Pin-tailed Green Pigeon	56.5 Yellow-vented Green Pigeon

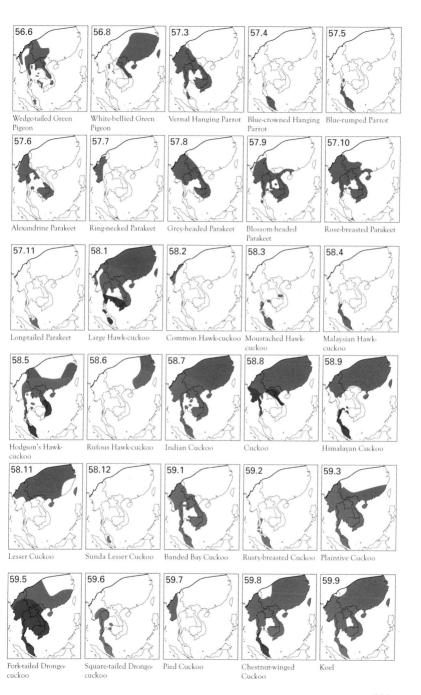

56.6 Wedge-tailed Green Pigeon

56.8 White-bellied Green Pigeon

57.3 Vernal Hanging Parrot

57.4 Blue-crowned Hanging Parrot

57.5 Blue-rumped Parrot

57.6 Alexandrine Parakeet

57.7 Ring-necked Parakeet

57.8 Grey-headed Parakeet

57.9 Blossom-headed Parakeet

57.10 Rose-breasted Parakeet

57.11 Long-tailed Parakeet

58.1 Large Hawk-cuckoo

58.2 Common Hawk-cuckoo

58.3 Moustached Hawk-cuckoo

58.4 Malaysian Hawk-cuckoo

58.5 Hodgson's Hawk-cuckoo

58.6 Rufous Hawk-cuckoo

58.7 Indian Cuckoo

58.8 Cuckoo

58.9 Himalayan Cuckoo

58.11 Lesser Cuckoo

58.12 Sunda Lesser Cuckoo

59.1 Banded Bay Cuckoo

59.2 Rusty-breasted Cuckoo

59.3 Plaintive Cuckoo

59.5 Fork-tailed Drongo-cuckoo

59.6 Square-tailed Drongo-cuckoo

59.7 Pied Cuckoo

59.8 Chestnut-winged Cuckoo

59.9 Koel

379

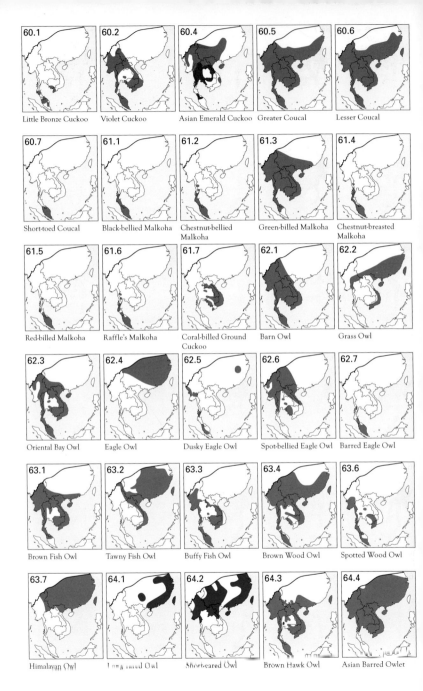

60.1 Little Bronze Cuckoo

60.2 Violet Cuckoo

60.4 Asian Emerald Cuckoo

60.5 Greater Coucal

60.6 Lesser Coucal

60.7 Short-toed Coucal

61.1 Black-bellied Malkoha

61.2 Chestnut-bellied Malkoha

61.3 Green-billed Malkoha

61.4 Chestnut-breasted Malkoha

61.5 Red-billed Malkoha

61.6 Raffle's Malkoha

61.7 Coral-billed Ground Cuckoo

62.1 Barn Owl

62.2 Grass Owl

62.3 Oriental Bay Owl

62.4 Eagle Owl

62.5 Dusky Eagle Owl

62.6 Spot-bellied Eagle Owl

62.7 Barred Eagle Owl

63.1 Brown Fish Owl

63.2 Tawny Fish Owl

63.3 Buffy Fish Owl

63.4 Brown Wood Owl

63.6 Spotted Wood Owl

63.7 Himalayan Owl

64.1 Long-eared Owl

64.2 Short-eared Owl

64.3 Brown Hawk Owl

64.4 Asian Barred Owlet

380

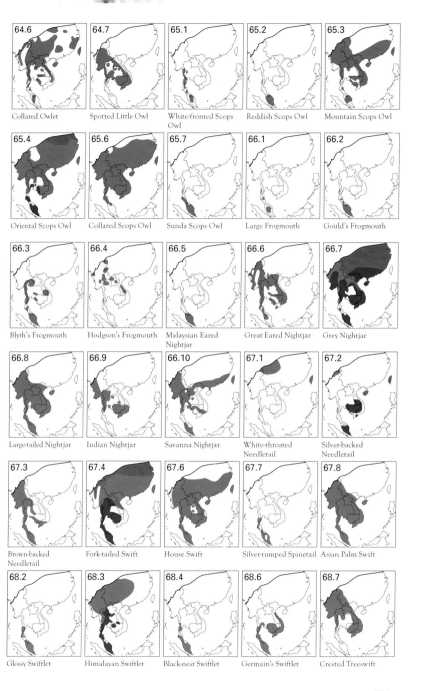

64.6 Collared Owlet

64.7 Spotted Little Owl

65.1 White-fronted Scops Owl

65.2 Reddish Scops Owl

65.3 Mountain Scops Owl

65.4 Oriental Scops Owl

65.6 Collared Scops Owl

65.7 Sunda Scops Owl

66.1 Large Frogmouth

66.2 Gould's Frogmouth

66.3 Blyth's Frogmouth

66.4 Hodgson's Frogmouth

66.5 Malaysian Eared Nightjar

66.6 Great Eared Nightjar

66.7 Grey Nightjar

66.8 Large-tailed Nightjar

66.9 Indian Nightjar

66.10 Savanna Nightjar

67.1 White-throated Needletail

67.2 Silver-backed Needletail

67.3 Brown-backed Needletail

67.4 Fork-tailed Swift

67.6 House Swift

67.7 Silver-rumped Spinetail

67.8 Asian Palm Swift

68.2 Glossy Swiftlet

68.3 Himalayan Swiftlet

68.4 Black-nest Swiftlet

68.6 Germain's Swiftlet

68.7 Crested Treeswift

381

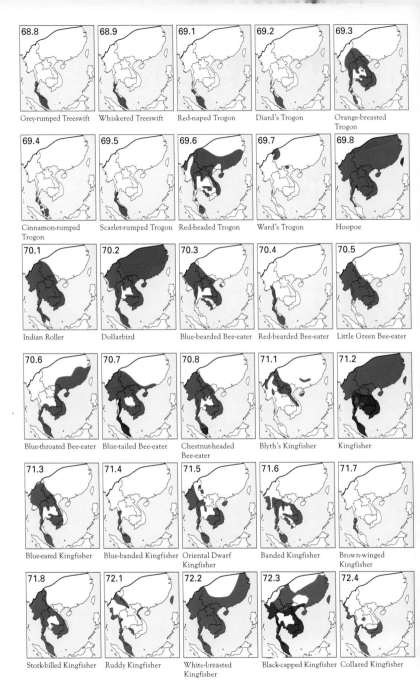

68.8 Grey-rumped Treeswift	68.9 Whiskered Treeswift	69.1 Red-naped Trogon	69.2 Diard's Trogon	69.3 Orange-breasted Trogon
69.4 Cinnamon-rumped Trogon	69.5 Scarlet-rumped Trogon	69.6 Red-headed Trogon	69.7 Ward's Trogon	69.8 Hoopoe
70.1 Indian Roller	70.2 Dollarbird	70.3 Blue-bearded Bee-eater	70.4 Red-bearded Bee-eater	70.5 Little Green Bee-eater
70.6 Blue-throated Bee-eater	70.7 Blue-tailed Bee-eater	70.8 Chestnut-headed Bee-eater	71.1 Blyth's Kingfisher	71.2 Kingfisher
71.3 Blue-eared Kingfisher	71.4 Blue-banded Kingfisher	71.5 Oriental Dwarf Kingfisher	71.6 Banded Kingfisher	71.7 Brown-winged Kingfisher
71.8 Stork-billed Kingfisher	72.1 Ruddy Kingfisher	72.2 White-breasted Kingfisher	72.3 Black-capped Kingfisher	72.4 Collared Kingfisher

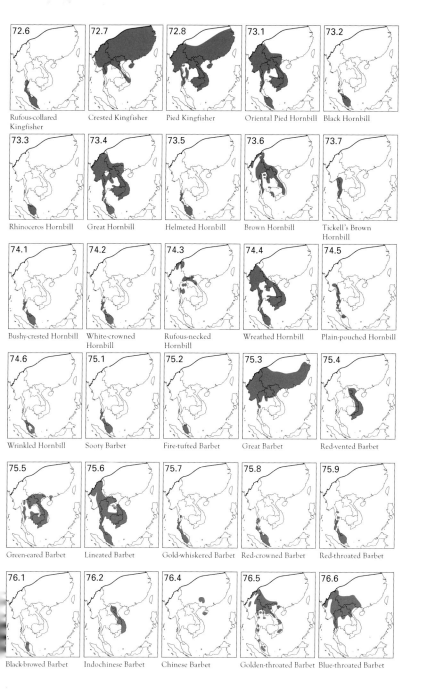

72.6	72.7	72.8	73.1	73.2
Rufous-collared Kingfisher	Crested Kingfisher	Pied Kingfisher	Oriental Pied Hornbill	Black Hornbill
73.3	73.4	73.5	73.6	73.7
Rhinoceros Hornbill	Great Hornbill	Helmeted Hornbill	Brown Hornbill	Tickell's Brown Hornbill
74.1	74.2	74.3	74.4	74.5
Bushy-crested Hornbill	White-crowned Hornbill	Rufous-necked Hornbill	Wreathed Hornbill	Plain-pouched Hornbill
74.6	75.1	75.2	75.3	75.4
Wrinkled Hornbill	Sooty Barbet	Fire-tufted Barbet	Great Barbet	Red-vented Barbet
75.5	75.6	75.7	75.8	75.9
Green-eared Barbet	Lineated Barbet	Gold-whiskered Barbet	Red-crowned Barbet	Red-throated Barbet
76.1	76.2	76.4	76.5	76.6
Black-browed Barbet	Indochinese Barbet	Chinese Barbet	Golden-throated Barbet	Blue-throated Barbet

383

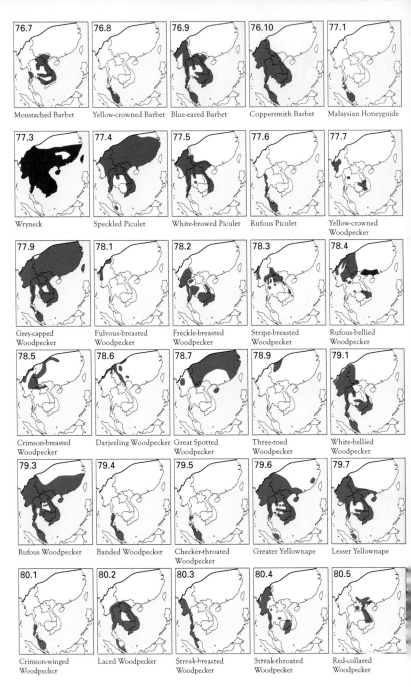

76.7	76.8	76.9	76.10	77.1
Moustached Barbet	Yellow-crowned Barbet	Blue-eared Barbet	Coppersmith Barbet	Malaysian Honeyguide
77.3	77.4	77.5	77.6	77.7
Wryneck	Speckled Piculet	White-browed Piculet	Rufous Piculet	Yellow-crowned Woodpecker
77.9	78.1	78.2	78.3	78.4
Grey-capped Woodpecker	Fulvous-breasted Woodpecker	Freckle-breasted Woodpecker	Stripe-breasted Woodpecker	Rufous-bellied Woodpecker
78.5	78.6	78.7	78.9	79.1
Crimson-breasted Woodpecker	Darjeeling Woodpecker	Great Spotted Woodpecker	Three-toed Woodpecker	White-bellied Woodpecker
79.3	79.4	79.5	79.6	79.7
Rufous Woodpecker	Banded Woodpecker	Checker-throated Woodpecker	Greater Yellownape	Lesser Yellownape
80.1	80.2	80.3	80.4	80.5
Crimson-winged Woodpecker	Laced Woodpecker	Streak-breasted Woodpecker	Streak-throated Woodpecker	Red-collared Woodpecker

384

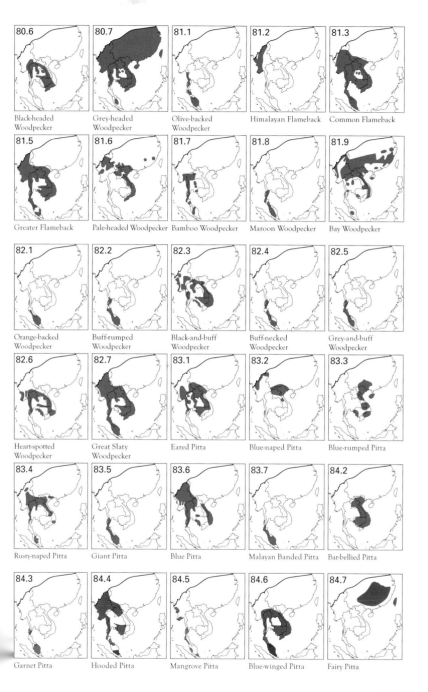

80.6 Black-headed Woodpecker	80.7 Grey-headed Woodpecker	81.1 Olive-backed Woodpecker	81.2 Himalayan Flameback	81.3 Common Flameback
81.5 Greater Flameback	81.6 Pale-headed Woodpecker	81.7 Bamboo Woodpecker	81.8 Maroon Woodpecker	81.9 Bay Woodpecker
82.1 Orange-backed Woodpecker	82.2 Buff-rumped Woodpecker	82.3 Black-and-buff Woodpecker	82.4 Buff-necked Woodpecker	82.5 Grey-and-buff Woodpecker
82.6 Heart-spotted Woodpecker	82.7 Great Slaty Woodpecker	83.1 Eared Pitta	83.2 Blue-naped Pitta	83.3 Blue-rumped Pitta
83.4 Rusty-naped Pitta	83.5 Giant Pitta	83.6 Blue Pitta	83.7 Malayan Banded Pitta	84.2 Bar-bellied Pitta
84.3 Garnet Pitta	84.4 Hooded Pitta	84.5 Mangrove Pitta	84.6 Blue-winged Pitta	84.7 Fairy Pitta

385

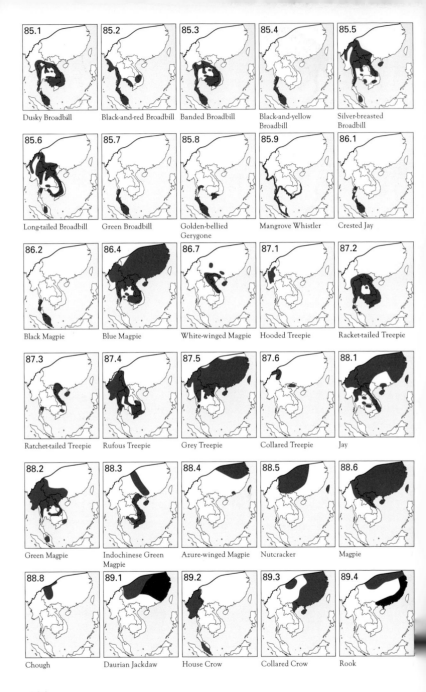

85.1 Dusky Broadbill

85.2 Black-and-red Broadbill

85.3 Banded Broadbill

85.4 Black-and-yellow Broadbill

85.5 Silver-breasted Broadbill

85.6 Long-tailed Broadbill

85.7 Green Broadbill

85.8 Golden-bellied Gerygone

85.9 Mangrove Whistler

86.1 Crested Jay

86.2 Black Magpie

86.4 Blue Magpie

86.7 White-winged Magpie

87.1 Hooded Treepie

87.2 Racket-tailed Treepie

87.3 Ratchet-tailed Treepie

87.4 Rufous Treepie

87.5 Grey Treepie

87.6 Collared Treepie

88.1 Jay

88.2 Green Magpie

88.3 Indochinese Green Magpie

88.4 Azure-winged Magpie

88.5 Nutcracker

88.6 Magpie

88.8 Chough

89.1 Daurian Jackdaw

89.2 House Crow

89.3 Collared Crow

89.4 Rook

386

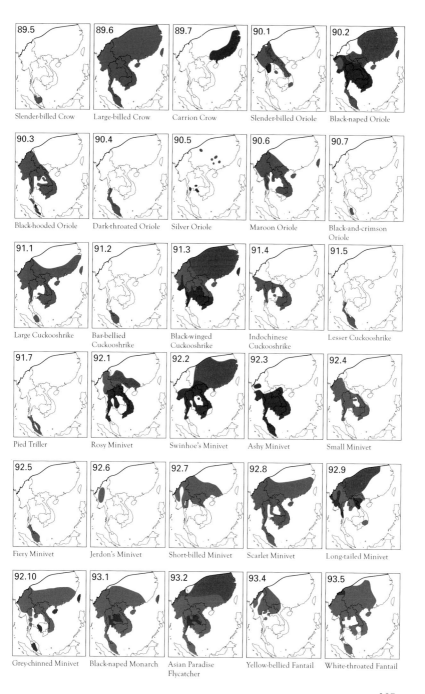

89.5 Slender-billed Crow	89.6 Large-billed Crow	89.7 Carrion Crow	90.1 Slender-billed Oriole	90.2 Black-naped Oriole
90.3 Black-hooded Oriole	90.4 Dark-throated Oriole	90.5 Silver Oriole	90.6 Maroon Oriole	90.7 Black-and-crimson Oriole
91.1 Large Cuckooshrike	91.2 Bar-bellied Cuckooshrike	91.3 Black-winged Cuckooshrike	91.4 Indochinese Cuckooshrike	91.5 Lesser Cuckooshrike
91.7 Pied Triller	92.1 Rosy Minivet	92.2 Swinhoe's Minivet	92.3 Ashy Minivet	92.4 Small Minivet
92.5 Fiery Minivet	92.6 Jerdon's Minivet	92.7 Short-billed Minivet	92.8 Scarlet Minivet	92.9 Long-tailed Minivet
92.10 Grey-chinned Minivet	93.1 Black-naped Monarch	93.2 Asian Paradise Flycatcher	93.4 Yellow-bellied Fantail	93.5 White-throated Fantail

387

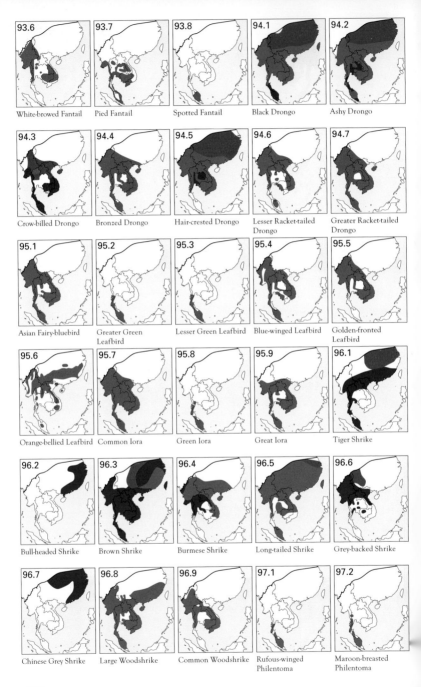

93.6 White-browed Fantail

93.7 Pied Fantail

93.8 Spotted Fantail

94.1 Black Drongo

94.2 Ashy Drongo

94.3 Crow-billed Drongo

94.4 Bronzed Drongo

94.5 Hair-crested Drongo

94.6 Lesser Racket-tailed Drongo

94.7 Greater Racket-tailed Drongo

95.1 Asian Fairy-bluebird

95.2 Greater Green Leafbird

95.3 Lesser Green Leafbird

95.4 Blue-winged Leafbird

95.5 Golden-fronted Leafbird

95.6 Orange-bellied Leafbird

95.7 Common Iora

95.8 Green Iora

95.9 Great Iora

96.1 Tiger Shrike

96.2 Bull-headed Shrike

96.3 Brown Shrike

96.4 Burmese Shrike

96.5 Long-tailed Shrike

96.6 Grey-backed Shrike

96.7 Chinese Grey Shrike

96.8 Large Woodshrike

96.9 Common Woodshrike

97.1 Rufous-winged Philentoma

97.2 Maroon-breasted Philentoma

388

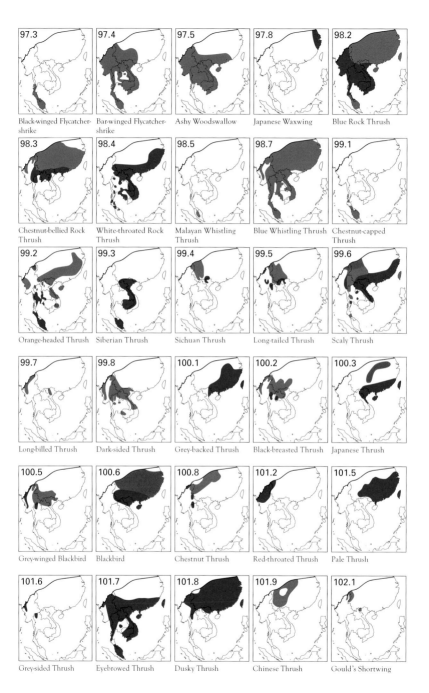

97.3 Black-winged Flycatcher-shrike

97.4 Bar-winged Flycatcher-shrike

97.5 Ashy Woodswallow

97.8 Japanese Waxwing

98.2 Blue Rock Thrush

98.3 Chestnut-bellied Rock Thrush

98.4 White-throated Rock Thrush

98.5 Malayan Whistling Thrush

98.7 Blue Whistling Thrush

99.1 Chestnut-capped Thrush

99.2 Orange-headed Thrush

99.3 Siberian Thrush

99.4 Sichuan Thrush

99.5 Long-tailed Thrush

99.6 Scaly Thrush

99.7 Long-billed Thrush

99.8 Dark-sided Thrush

100.1 Grey-backed Thrush

100.2 Black-breasted Thrush

100.3 Japanese Thrush

100.5 Grey-winged Blackbird

100.6 Blackbird

100.8 Chestnut Thrush

101.2 Red-throated Thrush

101.5 Pale Thrush

101.6 Grey-sided Thrush

101.7 Eyebrowed Thrush

101.8 Dusky Thrush

101.9 Chinese Thrush

102.1 Gould's Shortwing

389

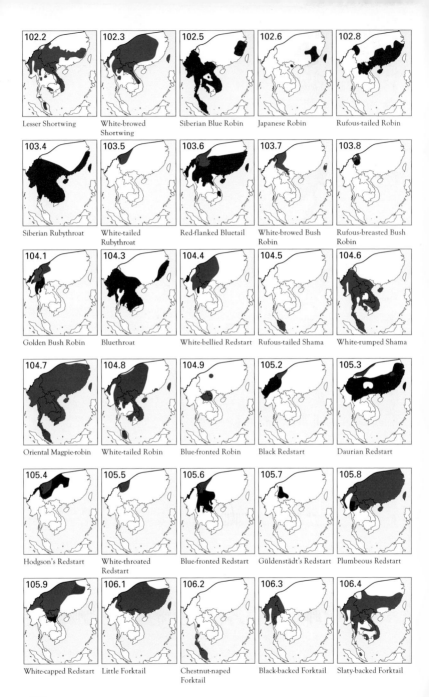

102.2 Lesser Shortwing	102.3 White-browed Shortwing	102.5 Siberian Blue Robin	102.6 Japanese Robin	102.8 Rufous-tailed Robin
103.4 Siberian Rubythroat	103.5 White-tailed Rubythroat	103.6 Red-flanked Bluetail	103.7 White-browed Bush Robin	103.8 Rufous-breasted Bush Robin
104.1 Golden Bush Robin	104.3 Bluethroat	104.4 White-bellied Redstart	104.5 Rufous-tailed Shama	104.6 White-rumped Shama
104.7 Oriental Magpie-robin	104.8 White-tailed Robin	104.9 Blue-fronted Robin	105.2 Black Redstart	105.3 Daurian Redstart
105.4 Hodgson's Redstart	105.5 White-throated Redstart	105.6 Blue-fronted Redstart	105.7 Güldenstädt's Redstart	105.8 Plumbeous Redstart
105.9 White-capped Redstart	106.1 Little Forktail	106.2 Chestnut-naped Forktail	106.3 Black-backed Forktail	106.4 Slaty-backed Forktail

390

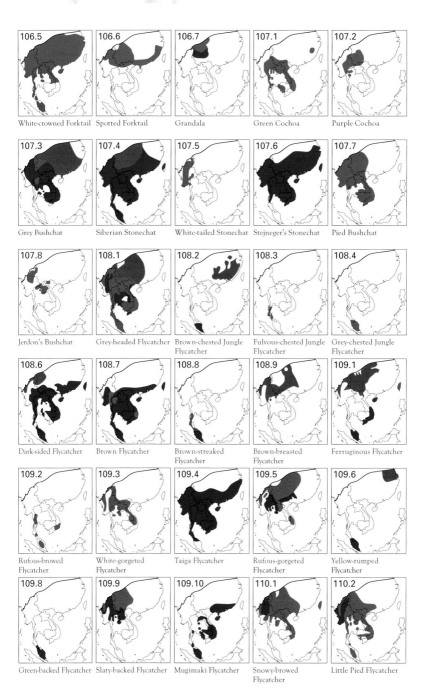

106.5 White-crowned Forktail
106.6 Spotted Forktail
106.7 Grandala
107.1 Green Cochoa
107.2 Purple Cochoa

107.3 Grey Bushchat
107.4 Siberian Stonechat
107.5 White-tailed Stonechat
107.6 Stejneger's Stonechat
107.7 Pied Bushchat

107.8 Jerdon's Bushchat
108.1 Grey-headed Flycatcher
108.2 Brown-chested Jungle Flycatcher
108.3 Fulvous-chested Jungle Flycatcher
108.4 Grey-chested Jungle Flycatcher

108.6 Dark-sided Flycatcher
108.7 Brown Flycatcher
108.8 Brown-streaked Flycatcher
108.9 Brown-breasted Flycatcher
109.1 Ferruginous Flycatcher

109.2 Rufous-browed Flycatcher
109.3 White-gorgeted Flycatcher
109.4 Taiga Flycatcher
109.5 Rufous-gorgeted Flycatcher
109.6 Yellow-rumped Flycatcher

109.8 Green-backed Flycatcher
109.9 Slaty-backed Flycatcher
109.10 Mugimaki Flycatcher
110.1 Snowy-browed Flycatcher
110.2 Little Pied Flycatcher

391

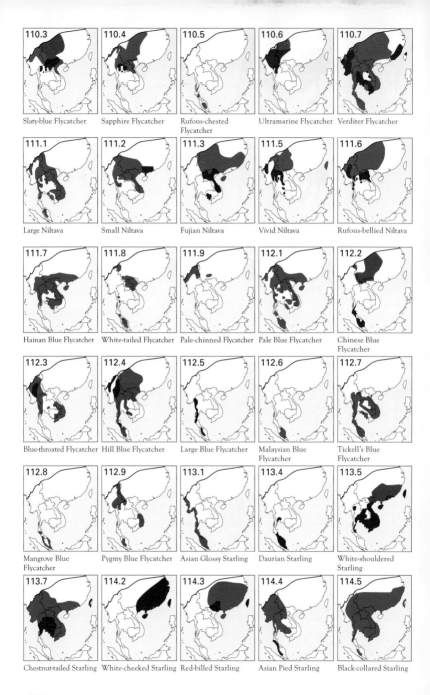

110.3	110.4	110.5	110.6	110.7
Slaty-blue Flycatcher	Sapphire Flycatcher	Rufous-chested Flycatcher	Ultramarine Flycatcher	Verditer Flycatcher
111.1	111.2	111.3	111.5	111.6
Large Niltava	Small Niltava	Fujian Niltava	Vivid Niltava	Rufous-bellied Niltava
111.7	111.8	111.9	112.1	112.2
Hainan Blue Flycatcher	White-tailed Flycatcher	Pale-chinned Flycatcher	Pale Blue Flycatcher	Chinese Blue Flycatcher
112.3	112.4	112.5	112.6	112.7
Blue-throated Flycatcher	Hill Blue Flycatcher	Large Blue Flycatcher	Malaysian Blue Flycatcher	Tickell's Blue Flycatcher
112.8	112.9	113.1	113.4	113.5
Mangrove Blue Flycatcher	Pygmy Blue Flycatcher	Asian Glossy Starling	Daurian Starling	White-shouldered Starling
113.7	114.2	114.3	114.4	114.5
Chestnut-tailed Starling	White-cheeked Starling	Red-billed Starling	Asian Pied Starling	Black-collared Starling

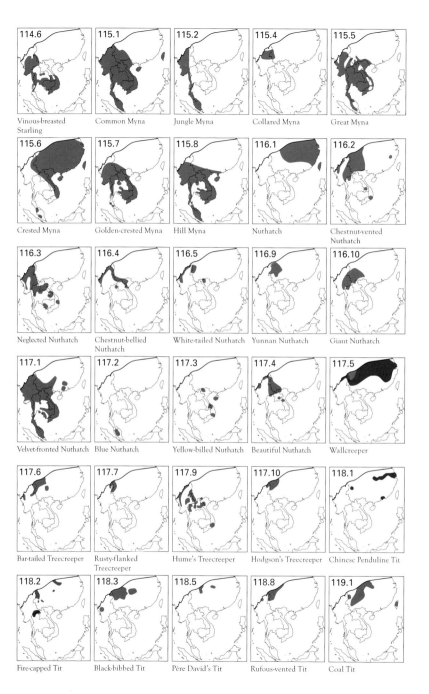

114.6	115.1	115.2	115.4	115.5
Vinous-breasted Starling	Common Myna	Jungle Myna	Collared Myna	Great Myna

115.6	115.7	115.8	116.1	116.2
Crested Myna	Golden-crested Myna	Hill Myna	Nuthatch	Chestnut-vented Nuthatch

116.3	116.4	116.5	116.9	116.10
Neglected Nuthatch	Chestnut-bellied Nuthatch	White-tailed Nuthatch	Yunnan Nuthatch	Giant Nuthatch

117.1	117.2	117.3	117.4	117.5
Velvet-fronted Nuthatch	Blue Nuthatch	Yellow-billed Nuthatch	Beautiful Nuthatch	Wallcreeper

117.6	117.7	117.9	117.10	118.1
Bar-tailed Treecreeper	Rusty-flanked Treecreeper	Hume's Treecreeper	Hodgson's Treecreeper	Chinese Penduline Tit

118.2	118.3	118.5	118.8	119.1
Fire-capped Tit	Black-bibbed Tit	Père David's Tit	Rufous-vented Tit	Coal Tit

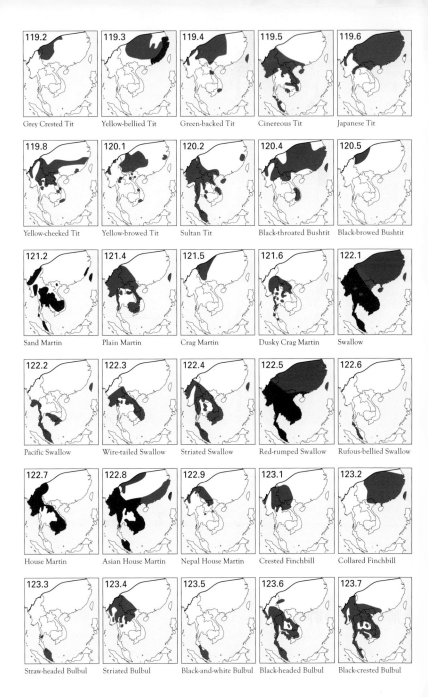

119.2 Grey Crested Tit	119.3 Yellow-bellied Tit	119.4 Green-backed Tit	119.5 Cinereous Tit	119.6 Japanese Tit
119.8 Yellow-cheeked Tit	120.1 Yellow-browed Tit	120.2 Sultan Tit	120.4 Black-throated Bushtit	120.5 Black-browed Bushtit
121.2 Sand Martin	121.4 Plain Martin	121.5 Crag Martin	121.6 Dusky Crag Martin	122.1 Swallow
122.2 Pacific Swallow	122.3 Wire-tailed Swallow	122.4 Striated Swallow	122.5 Red-rumped Swallow	122.6 Rufous-bellied Swallow
122.7 House Martin	122.8 Asian House Martin	122.9 Nepal House Martin	123.1 Crested Finchbill	123.2 Collared Finchbill
123.3 Straw-headed Bulbul	123.4 Striated Bulbul	123.5 Black-and-white Bulbul	123.6 Black-headed Bulbul	123.7 Black-crested Bulbul

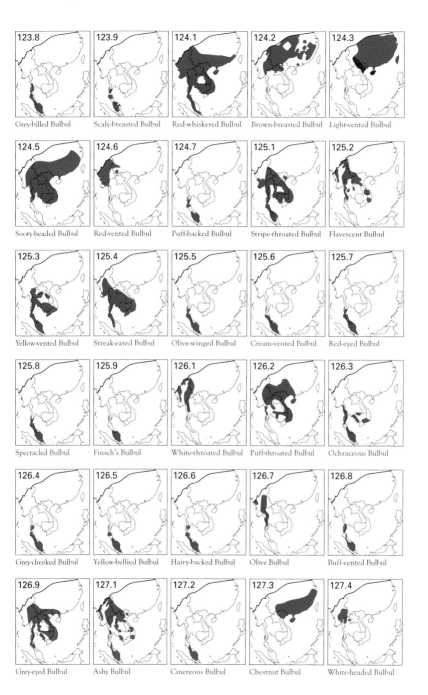

123.8 Grey-billed Bulbul	123.9 Scaly-breasted Bulbul	124.1 Red-whiskered Bulbul	124.2 Brown-breasted Bulbul	124.3 Light-vented Bulbul
124.5 Sooty-headed Bulbul	124.6 Red-vented Bulbul	124.7 Puff-backed Bulbul	125.1 Stripe-throated Bulbul	125.2 Flavescent Bulbul
125.3 Yellow-vented Bulbul	125.4 Streak-eared Bulbul	125.5 Olive-winged Bulbul	125.6 Cream-vented Bulbul	125.7 Red-eyed Bulbul
125.8 Spectacled Bulbul	125.9 Finsch's Bulbul	126.1 White-throated Bulbul	126.2 Puff-throated Bulbul	126.3 Ochraceous Bulbul
126.4 Grey-cheeked Bulbul	126.5 Yellow-bellied Bulbul	126.6 Hairy-backed Bulbul	126.7 Olive Bulbul	126.8 Buff-vented Bulbul
126.9 Grey-eyed Bulbul	127.1 Ashy Bulbul	127.2 Cinereous Bulbul	127.3 Chestnut Bulbul	127.4 White-headed Bulbul

395

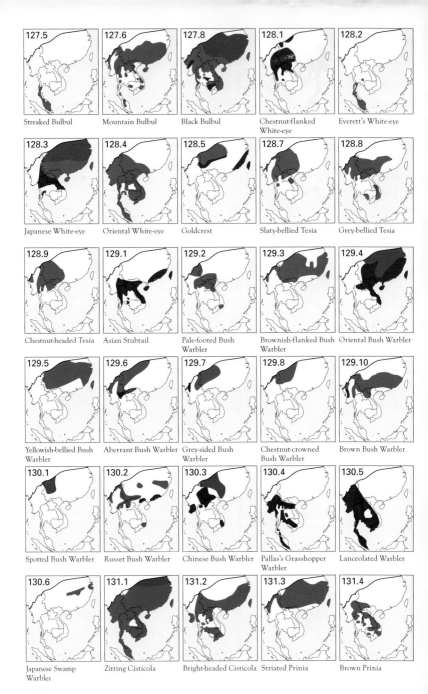

127.5	127.6	127.8	128.1	128.2
Streaked Bulbul	Mountain Bulbul	Black Bulbul	Chestnut-flanked White-eye	Everett's White-eye
128.3	128.4	128.5	128.7	128.8
Japanese White-eye	Oriental White-eye	Goldcrest	Slaty-bellied Tesia	Grey-bellied Tesia
128.9	129.1	129.2	129.3	129.4
Chestnut-headed Tesia	Asian Stubtail	Pale-footed Bush Warbler	Brownish-flanked Bush Warbler	Oriental Bush Warbler
129.5	129.6	129.7	129.8	129.10
Yellowish-bellied Bush Warbler	Aberrant Bush Warbler	Grey-sided Bush Warbler	Chestnut-crowned Bush Warbler	Brown Bush Warbler
130.1	130.2	130.3	130.4	130.5
Spotted Bush Warbler	Russet Bush Warbler	Chinese Bush Warbler	Pallas's Grasshopper Warbler	Lanceolated Warbler
130.6	131.1	131.2	131.3	131.4
Japanese Swamp Warbler	Zitting Cisticola	Bright-headed Cisticola	Striated Prinia	Brown Prinia

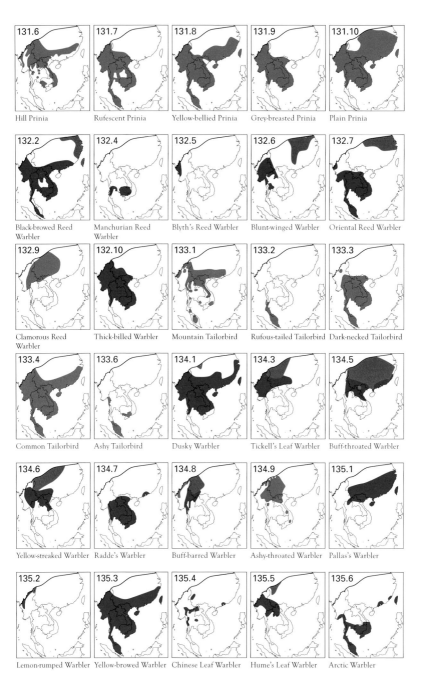

131.6 Hill Prinia

131.7 Rufescent Prinia

131.8 Yellow-bellied Prinia

131.9 Grey-breasted Prinia

131.10 Plain Prinia

132.2 Black-browed Reed Warbler

132.4 Manchurian Reed Warbler

132.5 Blyth's Reed Warbler

132.6 Blunt-winged Warbler

132.7 Oriental Reed Warbler

132.9 Clamorous Reed Warbler

132.10 Thick-billed Warbler

133.1 Mountain Tailorbird

133.2 Rufous-tailed Tailorbird

133.3 Dark-necked Tailorbird

133.4 Common Tailorbird

133.6 Ashy Tailorbird

134.1 Dusky Warbler

134.3 Tickell's Leaf Warbler

134.5 Buff-throated Warbler

134.6 Yellow-streaked Warbler

134.7 Radde's Warbler

134.8 Buff-barred Warbler

134.9 Ashy-throated Warbler

135.1 Pallas's Warbler

135.2 Lemon-rumped Warbler

135.3 Yellow-browed Warbler

135.4 Chinese Leaf Warbler

135.5 Hume's Leaf Warbler

135.6 Arctic Warbler

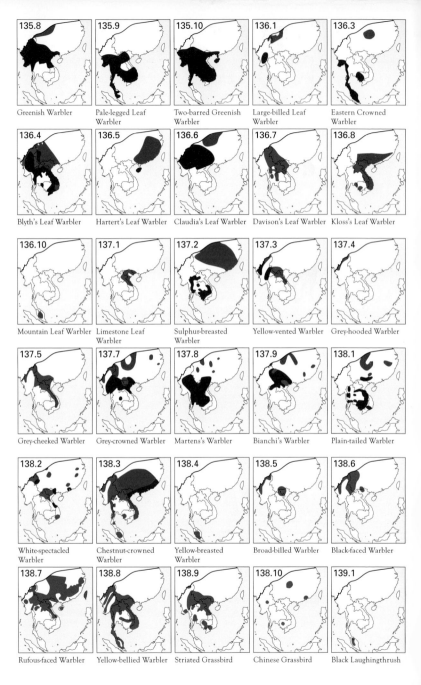

135.8 Greenish Warbler	135.9 Pale-legged Leaf Warbler	135.10 Two-barred Greenish Warbler	136.1 Large-billed Leaf Warbler	136.3 Eastern Crowned Warbler
136.4 Blyth's Leaf Warbler	136.5 Hartert's Leaf Warbler	136.6 Claudia's Leaf Warbler	136.7 Davison's Leaf Warbler	136.8 Kloss's Leaf Warbler
136.10 Mountain Leaf Warbler	137.1 Limestone Leaf Warbler	137.2 Sulphur-breasted Warbler	137.3 Yellow-vented Warbler	137.4 Grey-hooded Warbler
137.5 Grey-cheeked Warbler	137.7 Grey-crowned Warbler	137.8 Martens's Warbler	137.9 Bianchi's Warbler	138.1 Plain-tailed Warbler
138.2 White-spectacled Warbler	138.3 Chestnut-crowned Warbler	138.4 Yellow-breasted Warbler	138.5 Broad-billed Warbler	138.6 Black-faced Warbler
138.7 Rufous-faced Warbler	138.8 Yellow-bellied Warbler	138.9 Striated Grassbird	138.10 Chinese Grassbird	139.1 Black Laughingthrush

398

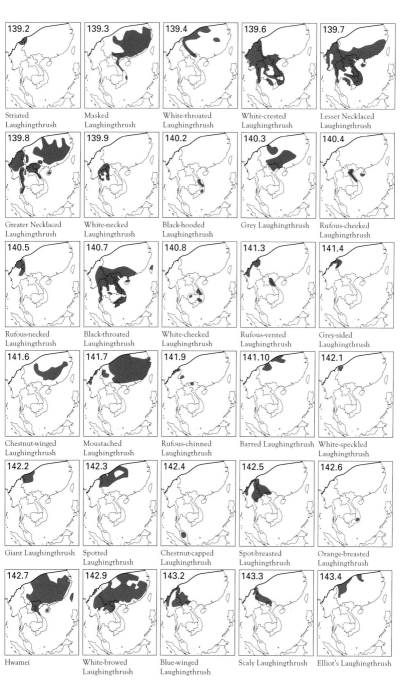

139.2 Striated Laughingthrush

139.3 Masked Laughingthrush

139.4 White-throated Laughingthrush

139.6 White-crested Laughingthrush

139.7 Lesser Necklaced Laughingthrush

139.8 Greater Necklaced Laughingthrush

139.9 White-necked Laughingthrush

140.2 Black-hooded Laughingthrush

140.3 Grey Laughingthrush

140.4 Rufous-cheeked Laughingthrush

140.5 Rufous-necked Laughingthrush

140.7 Black-throated Laughingthrush

140.8 White-cheeked Laughingthrush

141.3 Rufous-vented Laughingthrush

141.4 Grey-sided Laughingthrush

141.6 Chestnut-winged Laughingthrush

141.7 Moustached Laughingthrush

141.9 Rufous-chinned Laughingthrush

141.10 Barred Laughingthrush

142.1 White-speckled Laughingthrush

142.2 Giant Laughingthrush

142.3 Spotted Laughingthrush

142.4 Chestnut-capped Laughingthrush

142.5 Spot-breasted Laughingthrush

142.6 Orange-breasted Laughingthrush

142.7 Hwamei

142.9 White-browed Laughingthrush

143.2 Blue-winged Laughingthrush

143.3 Scaly Laughingthrush

143.4 Elliot's Laughingthrush

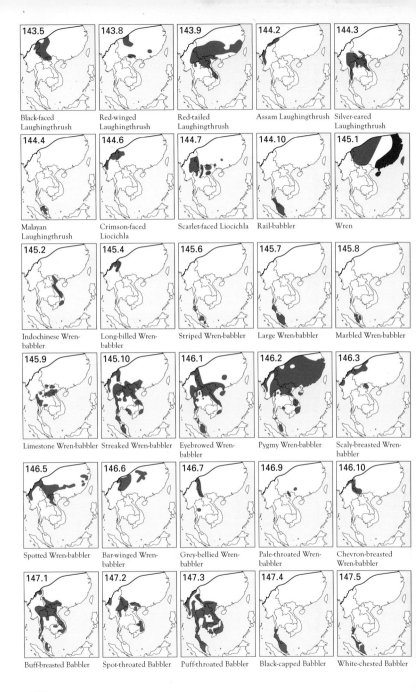

143.5 Black-faced Laughingthrush

143.8 Red-winged Laughingthrush

143.9 Red-tailed Laughingthrush

144.2 Assam Laughingthrush

144.3 Silver-eared Laughingthrush

144.4 Malayan Laughingthrush

144.6 Crimson-faced Liocichla

144.7 Scarlet-faced Liocichla

144.10 Rail-babbler

145.1 Wren

145.2 Indochinese Wren-babbler

145.4 Long-billed Wren-babbler

145.6 Striped Wren-babbler

145.7 Large Wren-babbler

145.8 Marbled Wren-babbler

145.9 Limestone Wren-babbler

145.10 Streaked Wren-babbler

146.1 Eyebrowed Wren-babbler

146.2 Pygmy Wren-babbler

146.3 Scaly-breasted Wren-babbler

146.5 Spotted Wren-babbler

146.6 Bar-winged Wren-babbler

146.7 Grey-bellied Wren-babbler

146.9 Pale-throated Wren-babbler

146.10 Chevron-breasted Wren-babbler

147.1 Buff-breasted Babbler

147.2 Spot-throated Babbler

147.3 Puff-throated Babbler

147.4 Black-capped Babbler

147.5 White-chested Babbler

400

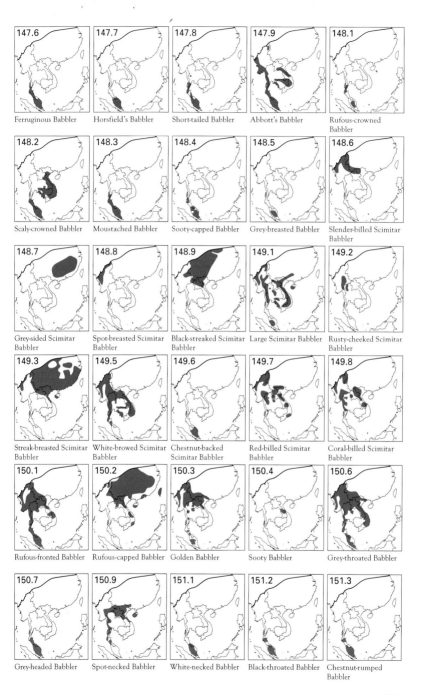

147.6	147.7	147.8	147.9	148.1
Ferruginous Babbler	Horsfield's Babbler	Short-tailed Babbler	Abbott's Babbler	Rufous-crowned Babbler
148.2	148.3	148.4	148.5	148.6
Scaly-crowned Babbler	Moustached Babbler	Sooty-capped Babbler	Grey-breasted Babbler	Slender-billed Scimitar Babbler
148.7	148.8	148.9	149.1	149.2
Grey-sided Scimitar Babbler	Spot-breasted Scimitar Babbler	Black-streaked Scimitar Babbler	Large Scimitar Babbler	Rusty-cheeked Scimitar Babbler
149.3	149.5	149.6	149.7	149.8
Streak-breasted Scimitar Babbler	White-browed Scimitar Babbler	Chestnut-backed Scimitar Babbler	Red-billed Scimitar Babbler	Coral-billed Scimitar Babbler
150.1	150.2	150.3	150.4	150.6
Rufous-fronted Babbler	Rufous-capped Babbler	Golden Babbler	Sooty Babbler	Grey-throated Babbler
150.7	150.9	151.1	151.2	151.3
Grey-headed Babbler	Spot-necked Babbler	White-necked Babbler	Black-throated Babbler	Chestnut-rumped Babbler

401

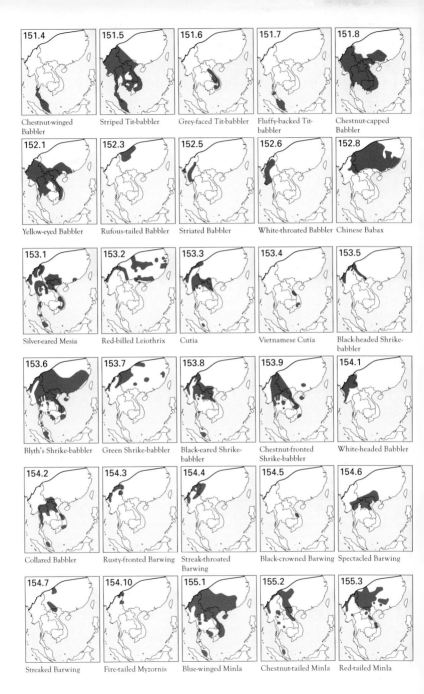

151.4 Chestnut-winged Babbler

151.5 Striped Tit-babbler

151.6 Grey-faced Tit-babbler

151.7 Fluffy-backed Tit-babbler

151.8 Chestnut-capped Babbler

152.1 Yellow-eyed Babbler

152.3 Rufous-tailed Babbler

152.5 Striated Babbler

152.6 White-throated Babbler

152.8 Chinese Babax

153.1 Silver-eared Mesia

153.2 Red-billed Leiothrix

153.3 Cutia

153.4 Vietnamese Cutia

153.5 Black-headed Shrike-babbler

153.6 Blyth's Shrike-babbler

153.7 Green Shrike-babbler

153.8 Black-eared Shrike-babbler

153.9 Chestnut-fronted Shrike-babbler

154.1 White-headed Babbler

154.2 Collared Babbler

154.3 Rusty-fronted Barwing

154.4 Streak-throated Barwing

154.5 Black-crowned Barwing

154.6 Spectacled Barwing

154.7 Streaked Barwing

154.10 Fire-tailed Myzornis

155.1 Blue-winged Minla

155.2 Chestnut-tailed Minla

155.3 Red-tailed Minla

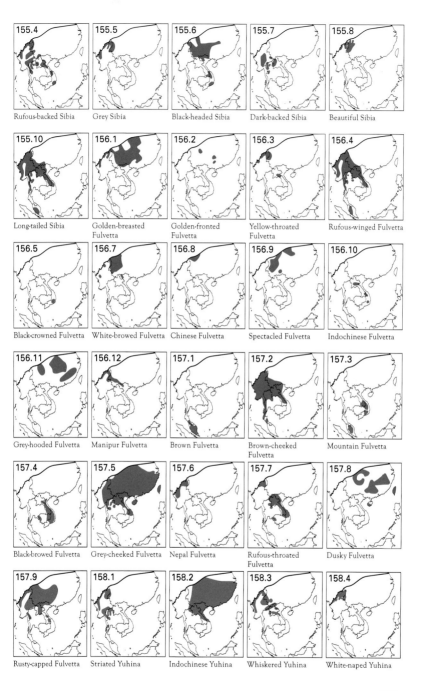

155.4 Rufous-backed Sibia	155.5 Grey Sibia	155.6 Black-headed Sibia	155.7 Dark-backed Sibia	155.8 Beautiful Sibia
155.10 Long-tailed Sibia	156.1 Golden-breasted Fulvetta	156.2 Golden-fronted Fulvetta	156.3 Yellow-throated Fulvetta	156.4 Rufous-winged Fulvetta
156.5 Black-crowned Fulvetta	156.7 White-browed Fulvetta	156.8 Chinese Fulvetta	156.9 Spectacled Fulvetta	156.10 Indochinese Fulvetta
156.11 Grey-hooded Fulvetta	156.12 Manipur Fulvetta	157.1 Brown Fulvetta	157.2 Brown-cheeked Fulvetta	157.3 Mountain Fulvetta
157.4 Black-browed Fulvetta	157.5 Grey-cheeked Fulvetta	157.6 Nepal Fulvetta	157.7 Rufous-throated Fulvetta	157.8 Dusky Fulvetta
157.9 Rusty-capped Fulvetta	158.1 Striated Yuhina	158.2 Indochinese Yuhina	158.3 Whiskered Yuhina	158.4 White-naped Yuhina

403

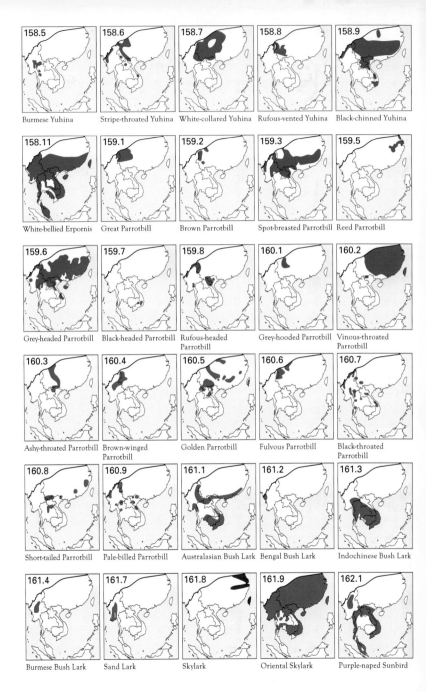

| 158.5 Burmese Yuhina | 158.6 Stripe-throated Yuhina | 158.7 White-collared Yuhina | 158.8 Rufous-vented Yuhina | 158.9 Black-chinned Yuhina |

| 158.11 White-bellied Erpornis | 159.1 Great Parrotbill | 159.2 Brown Parrotbill | 159.3 Spot-breasted Parrotbill | 159.5 Reed Parrotbill |

| 159.6 Grey-headed Parrotbill | 159.7 Black-headed Parrotbill | 159.8 Rufous-headed Parrotbill | 160.1 Grey-hooded Parrotbill | 160.2 Vinous-throated Parrotbill |

| 160.3 Ashy-throated Parrotbill | 160.4 Brown-winged Parrotbill | 160.5 Golden Parrotbill | 160.6 Fulvous Parrotbill | 160.7 Black-throated Parrotbill |

| 160.8 Short-tailed Parrotbill | 160.9 Pale-billed Parrotbill | 161.1 Australasian Bush Lark | 161.2 Bengal Bush Lark | 161.3 Indochinese Bush Lark |

| 161.4 Burmese Bush Lark | 161.7 Sand Lark | 161.8 Skylark | 161.9 Oriental Skylark | 162.1 Purple-naped Sunbird |

158.5 Burmese Yuhina
158.6 Stripe-throated Yuhina
158.7 White-collared Yuhina
158.8 Rufous-vented Yuhina
158.9 Black-chinned Yuhina
158.11 White-bellied Erpornis
159.1 Great Parrotbill
159.2 Brown Parrotbill
159.3 Spot-breasted Parrotbill
159.5 Reed Parrotbill
159.6 Grey-headed Parrotbill
159.7 Black-headed Parrotbill
159.8 Rufous-headed Parrotbill
160.1 Grey-hooded Parrotbill
160.2 Vinous-throated Parrotbill
160.3 Ashy-throated Parrotbill
160.4 Brown-winged Parrotbill
160.5 Golden Parrotbill
160.6 Fulvous Parrotbill
160.7 Black-throated Parrotbill
160.8 Short-tailed Parrotbill
160.9 Pale-billed Parrotbill
161.1 Australasian Bush Lark
161.2 Bengal Bush Lark
161.3 Indochinese Bush Lark
161.4 Burmese Bush Lark
161.7 Sand Lark
161.8 Skylark
161.9 Oriental Skylark
162.1 Purple-naped Sunbird

404

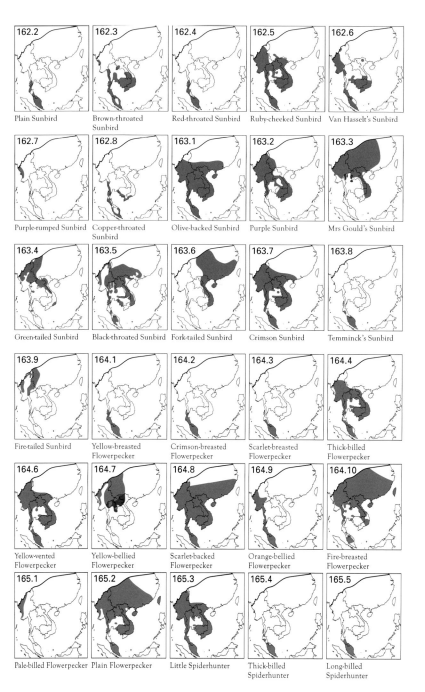

162.2 Plain Sunbird	162.3 Brown-throated Sunbird	162.4 Red-throated Sunbird	162.5 Ruby-cheeked Sunbird	162.6 Van Hasselt's Sunbird
162.7 Purple-rumped Sunbird	162.8 Copper-throated Sunbird	163.1 Olive-backed Sunbird	163.2 Purple Sunbird	163.3 Mrs Gould's Sunbird
163.4 Green-tailed Sunbird	163.5 Black-throated Sunbird	163.6 Fork-tailed Sunbird	163.7 Crimson Sunbird	163.8 Temminck's Sunbird
163.9 Fire-tailed Sunbird	164.1 Yellow-breasted Flowerpecker	164.2 Crimson-breasted Flowerpecker	164.3 Scarlet-breasted Flowerpecker	164.4 Thick-billed Flowerpecker
164.6 Yellow-vented Flowerpecker	164.7 Yellow-bellied Flowerpecker	164.8 Scarlet-backed Flowerpecker	164.9 Orange-bellied Flowerpecker	164.10 Fire-breasted Flowerpecker
165.1 Pale-billed Flowerpecker	165.2 Plain Flowerpecker	165.3 Little Spiderhunter	165.4 Thick-billed Spiderhunter	165.5 Long-billed Spiderhunter

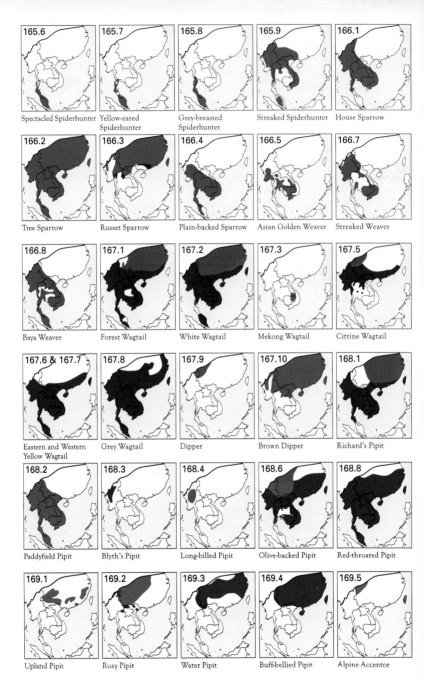

165.6	165.7	165.8	165.9	166.1
Spectacled Spiderhunter	Yellow-eared Spiderhunter	Grey-breasted Spiderhunter	Streaked Spiderhunter	House Sparrow
166.2	166.3	166.4	166.5	166.7
Tree Sparrow	Russet Sparrow	Plain-backed Sparrow	Asian Golden Weaver	Streaked Weaver
166.8	167.1	167.2	167.3	167.5
Baya Weaver	Forest Wagtail	White Wagtail	Mekong Wagtail	Citrine Wagtail
167.6 & 167.7	167.8	167.9	167.10	168.1
Eastern and Western Yellow Wagtail	Grey Wagtail	Dipper	Brown Dipper	Richard's Pipit
168.2	168.3	168.4	168.6	168.8
Paddyfield Pipit	Blyth's Pipit	Long-billed Pipit	Olive-backed Pipit	Red-throated Pipit
169.1	169.2	169.3	169.4	169.5
Upland Pipit	Rosy Pipit	Water Pipit	Buff-bellied Pipit	Alpine Accentor

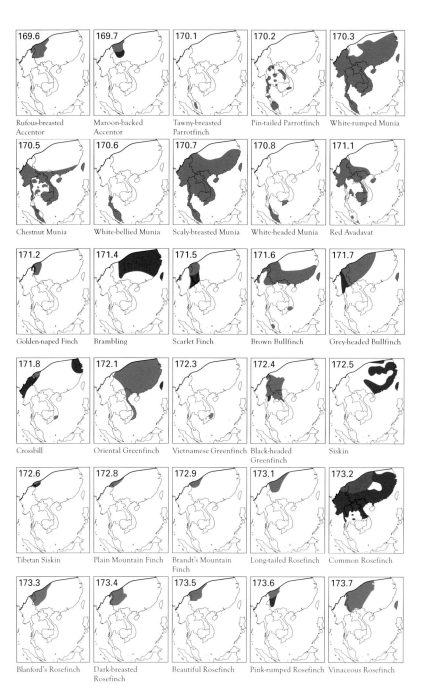

169.6 Rufous-breasted Accentor	169.7 Maroon-backed Accentor	170.1 Tawny-breasted Parrotfinch	170.2 Pin-tailed Parrotfinch	170.3 White-rumped Munia
170.5 Chestnut Munia	170.6 White-bellied Munia	170.7 Scaly-breasted Munia	170.8 White-headed Munia	171.1 Red Avadavat
171.2 Golden-naped Finch	171.4 Brambling	171.5 Scarlet Finch	171.6 Brown Bullfinch	171.7 Grey-headed Bullfinch
171.8 Crossbill	172.1 Oriental Greenfinch	172.3 Vietnamese Greenfinch	172.4 Black-headed Greenfinch	172.5 Siskin
172.6 Tibetan Siskin	172.8 Plain Mountain Finch	172.9 Brandt's Mountain Finch	173.1 Long-tailed Rosefinch	173.2 Common Rosefinch
173.3 Blanford's Rosefinch	173.4 Dark-breasted Rosefinch	173.5 Beautiful Rosefinch	173.6 Pink-rumped Rosefinch	173.7 Vinaceous Rosefinch

407

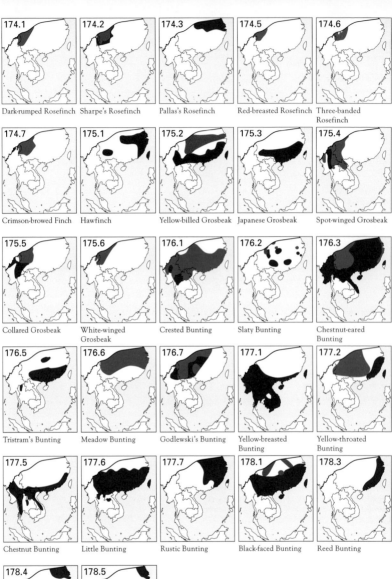

174.1 Dark-rumped Rosefinch

174.2 Sharpe's Rosefinch

174.3 Pallas's Rosefinch

174.5 Red-breasted Rosefinch

174.6 Three-banded Rosefinch

174.7 Crimson-browed Finch

175.1 Hawfinch

175.2 Yellow-billed Grosbeak

175.3 Japanese Grosbeak

175.4 Spot-winged Grosbeak

175.5 Collared Grosbeak

175.6 White-winged Grosbeak

176.1 Crested Bunting

176.2 Slaty Bunting

176.3 Chestnut-eared Bunting

176.5 Tristram's Bunting

176.6 Meadow Bunting

176.7 Godlewski's Bunting

177.1 Yellow-breasted Bunting

177.2 Yellow-throated Bunting

177.5 Chestnut Bunting

177.6 Little Bunting

177.7 Rustic Bunting

178.1 Black-faced Bunting

178.3 Reed Bunting

178.4 Pallas's Reed Bunting

178.5 Japanese Reed Bunting

INDEX

411

413

417

418

423